FAITH, FICTION & FORCE IN MEDIEVAL BAPTISMAL DEBATES

Marcia L. Colish

FAITH, FICTION & FORCE IN MEDIEVAL BAPTISMAL DEBATES

THE CATHOLIC UNIVERSITY OF AMERICA PRESS
Washington, D.C.

The paper used in this publication meets the minimum requirements of American National Standards for Information Science—Permanence of Paper for Printed Library Materials, ANSI Z39.48-1984.
∞

Library of Congress Cataloging-in-Publication Data
Colish, Marcia L.
Faith, fiction, and force in medieval baptismal debates / Marcia L. Colish.
pages cm
Includes bibliographical references and index.
ISBN 978-0-8132-2611-8 (cloth : alk. paper)
1. Baptism—History. I. Title.
BV803.C65 2014
234'.1610902—dc23 2013050343

FOR GARY MACY

CONTENTS

Preface ix

Abbreviations xi

INTRODUCTION 1

1. BAPTISM BY DESIRE 11

The Age of the Church Fathers 11

After the Fathers, before the Scholastics 25

The Twelfth Century: Canonists and Theologians to Mid-Century 27

The Twelfth Century: Peter Lombard and the Post-Lombardians 55

The Thirteenth Century 71

Conclusion 87

2. FICTIVE BAPTISM 91

The *Taufmime* 93

The Boys on the Beach 97

The Age of the Church Fathers 103

Anglo-Saxon and Carolingian Exegetes 119

The Norman Ruse 126

Publicists and Canonists 130

Reenter the *Taufmime* 146

The Twelfth Century: Theology to Mid-Century 152

The Later Twelfth Century: Peter Lombard and the Post-Lombardians 165

The Thirteenth Century: Theology to Mid-Century 180

The Mid-Thirteenth to the Early Fourteenth Century 188

Conclusion 217

3. FORCED BAPTISM 227

Late Antiquity 230

Medieval Jews 232

Preaching with an Iron Tongue: The Carolingians 250

Only the Saxons? 261

Preaching with an Iron Tongue: The Baltic Crusades 264

The View from the Ivory Tower: Canonists in the Twelfth and Thirteenth Centuries 279

The View from the Ivory Tower: Scholastic Theologians to the Early Fourteenth Century 292

Conclusion 311

AFTERWORD 319

Bibliography 327

Index 357

PREFACE

This book has been in the making for several years, on and off, in between other projects, and I have received encouragement, constructive criticism, and support from a variety of groups and colleagues as the research has proceeded and as my ideas have taken shape. The Medieval Studies community at Yale University has been my primary lifeline. But many others have pointed me toward valuable references, answered my questions, and suggested fruitful lines of research. In some cases, they have graciously shared their work with me and permitted me to cite it before its appearance in print. I want to offer a special vote of thanks for the extremely prompt and detailed comments and suggestions for correction and revision provided by the two anonymous readers of the manuscript as it was first submitted to the CUA Press. The book's final form owes much to their learning and to their eagle eyes. On a range of subjects on which they know more than I did before I received their help, I benefited richly from the advice of Mark Glen Bilby, George Hardin Brown, Mary Dzon, Cédric Giraud, Miriam Kartch Hughes, Ruth Mazo Karras, Timothy Le Croy, Ian Christopher Levy, Gary Macy, Constant Mews, Alastair Minnis, Joaquín Martínez Pizarro, Riccardo Quinto, Riccardo Saccenti, Bryan Spinks, Carol Symes, Denys Turner, and John Wei. All deserve my gratitude for their generous collegial assistance. In addition to sharing his expertise with me, in his work on his own chosen themes in the history of medieval Christian thought, Gary Macy has been an inspiring model. I respectfully dedicate this book to him.

Riccardo Quinto and Willemien Otten also deserve thanks for inviting me to contribute papers drawn from parts of the research that went into this book. I am also grateful to the copyright holders for permission to reuse material in these papers which first appeared in their publications:

"Fictive Baptism in the Early Middle Ages," *Archa Verbi* 6 (2009): 9–25, published by Aschendorff; and "*De obitu Valentiniani*: Abelard, Bernard of Clairvaux, and the Canonization of Ambrose of Milan on Baptism by Desire," in *How the West Was Won: Essays on Literary Imagination, the Canon, and the Christian Middle Ages for Burcht Pranger*, ed. Willemien Otten, Arjo Vanderjagt, and Hent De Vries, Brill's Studies in Intellectual History 188 (Leiden: Brill, 2010), 329–47.

A comment is in order about the coverage in this book. I have not attempted to treat every thinker who had something to say on the three debated baptismal questions across the time span which this book addresses. I have focused only on thinkers who add to these debates, omitting those who simply repeat what predecessors have said. Each section of the book begins at the historical point at which discussion of each topic began, and takes the account to the point at which medieval thinkers stopped considering it, or to the early fourteenth century. Research to date on some medieval thinkers who worked after, and in some cases within, my chosen time frame has not elicited their views, if any, on these baptismal issues. This topic is not what has drawn researchers to them. I have focused on figures whose works are available in print and acknowledge that this decision limits my findings. Yet, one has to make choices and to stop somewhere. While I mention some of the post-medieval fortunes of these baptismal questions in the afterword, the early fourteenth century is where my analysis ends. It will fall to other researchers to enlarge our fund of knowledge on this subject for the later medieval period and for figures whom I do not discuss.

I would like, as well, to note a few technical matters in this preface. Texts quoted are given in translation, with the originals in the notes. I have given my own translations except in cases where I refer specifically to other translators. As medievalists know, the Latin texts we use are sometimes published with classicizing spelling and sometimes not. For the sake of consistency, I have rendered the letter *u* throughout as *v*, although I have retained the letter *j* for *i* where it occurs in the publications cited. Latin grammar respects the same rule as English grammar in using "he" or "him" as a pronoun denoting a generic singular person. I have retained this usage in order to make grammatical sense of the passages quoted in translation. Readers will not find the substitution of "she" for "he" or the "he/she" formula in this book, or the solecism "they" and "them" used with a singular reference. Grammatical, not political, correctness is the flag under which I have sailed. Some names of authors and titles of works cited are given in their most common English forms, while others are left in Latin or other languages. These are inconsistencies with which medievalists have learned to live. I have given the known dates of the primary sources cited, or the dates of their authors if that is the best information we have, only on their first reference. Likewise, I note the authors' known professions, as pertinent, only on their first reference. I hope that these considerations will clarify the procedures I have followed in this book and will aid the reader in using it.

ABBREVIATIONS

AA SS	*Acta Sanctorum*
AHDLMA	*Archives d'histoire doctrinale et littéraire du moyen âge*
BGPMA	Beiträge zur Geschichte der Philosophie des Mittelalters
BGPTMA	Beiträge zur Geschichte der Philosophie und Theologie des Mittelalters
CCCM	Corpus christianorum continuatio medievalis
CCSL	Corpus christianorum series latina
CSEL	Corpus scriptorum ecclesiasticorum latinorum
DthC	*Dictionnaire de théologie catholique*
FC	Fathers of the Church
MGH	Monumenta Germaniae Historica
PG	*Patrologia graeca cursus completa*, ed. J. P. Migne
PL	*Patrologia latina cursus completa*, ed. J. P. Migne
RTAM	*Recherches de théologie ancienne et médiévale*
SC	Sources chrétiennes

FAITH, FICTION & FORCE IN MEDIEVAL BAPTISMAL DEBATES

INTRODUCTION

Contemporary catechisms of the Christian churches often present their teachings as unequivocal and universally held features of the orthodox consensus throughout the ages. Catechetical treatments of the three aspects of baptismal theology considered in this study are typical cases in point. Emblematic of this tendency is the statement on baptism by desire found in the most recent Roman Catholic catechism. While it affirms that the church "does not know any means other than baptism that assures entry into eternal beatitude,"[1] the text goes on to acknowledge that this spiritual benefit can be gained through baptism by desire, and not just through ritual ablution or through the martyr's baptism by blood: "For catechumens who die before their Baptism, their explicit desire to receive it together with repentance for their sins, and charity, assures them the salvation they were not able to receive through the sacrament."[2] "Sacrament" here means the liturgical rite. In support of this teaching, the catechism cites the decree *Lumen gentium* proclaimed at Vatican II on November 2, 1964. That document, without a backward look at the Christian tradition, simply supports baptism by desire in the following terms: "Catechumens who, moved by

1. *Catechism of the Catholic Church* 6.1257, 2nd ed., ed. Peter Cardinal Gasparri (Rome: Libreria Editrice Vaticana, 1994), 320.

2. Ibid., 6.1258–6.1260, 320–21; quotation at 6.1260, 321.

the Holy Spirit, seek with explicit intention to be incorporated into the Church are by that very intention joined to her. With love and solicitude Mother Church already embraces them as her own." But, in seconding *Lumen gentium*, the catechism goes well beyond its cited source. For it asserts that the doctrine in question is one on which "the church has always held a firm conviction."[3]

This catechetical claim is an illustration of church history as later invented and rewritten, rather than of church history as it actually occurred. Far from indicating how, and when, the church piloted baptism by desire into its present safe haven in the Catholic consensus, the catechism presents the voyage as never having taken place. If this retrojection of current theology into the earlier Christian tradition is not unique, and not the monopoly of any one Christian confession, it is nonetheless noteworthy. For, neither baptism by desire, the doctrine flagged by this example, nor fictive baptism, nor forced baptism—the three topics to be treated in this study—enjoyed a consensus reading in the western church during the Middle Ages. Understandings of these three themes varied, often quite sharply, and patristic and medieval authors at times gave them labels different from the terms adopted for convenience in this book. Centuries went by before thinkers first thought of addressing these matters, or of developing the evidence and arguments that could be brought to bear on them. When early Christian authors first took them up, they did not group them together but treated them as individual issues, at different times in the patristic period, in different historical contexts, and in different literary genres. Disagreements swiftly ensued, sometimes lodged in the writings of a single patristic figure. In all three cases, there was a time lag after the patristic period, of greater or lesser length, during which these questions did not surface in any known text. When they did reemerge, each at a different point in time, a specific range of local, circumstantial, methodological, and sometimes personal concerns animated and reanimated their ongoing discussion. Each took on a doctrinal life of its own, even as canonists and scholastics of the high Middle Ages inserted these topics into broad, inclusive, and elaborately organized treatises on baptism and on the sacraments in general. Between the twelfth century and the early fourteenth century, where this study ends, there were thinkers who chose not to treat one or more of these baptismal

3. Ibid., 6.1281, 325; cf. *Lumen gentium* 2.14–2.16, in *The Documents of Vatican II (1963–1965)*, ed. and trans. Joseph Gallagher (New York: Guild Press, 1966), 32–35; quotation at 2.14, 33. See also the post–Vatican II Dutch catechism, in *A New Catechism: Catholic Faith for Adults*, trans. Kevin Smyth (New York: Seabury Press, 1993), 290–91.

questions, despite an otherwise systematic bent. Some issues earlier associated with these aspects of baptism went into abeyance and were dropped. Others, even if obsolete, remained in play. New distinctions and formulae arose and were used to frame these debates, although they did not always yield the clarity desired or agreements either on the substance of doctrine or on the best strategies for defending the positions of particular masters. And so, across the patristic and medieval periods, baptism by desire, fictive baptism, and forced baptism remained in contestation, even as controversies on other features of baptismal thought and practice came and went, and as consensus positions emerged in the western church on other aspects of baptismal theology.

The debates considered in chapter 1 of this study focus on baptism by desire. Does a convert with sincere beliefs and moral commitments truly receive the baptism he desires if it is ritually unavailable? This question was first aired as a position to be articulated and defended in its own right in the year 392, placed on the patristic agenda by Ambrose of Milan. Other church fathers then took it up, although without citing Ambrose. Augustine became a key witness, contributing heavily, and variously, to later controversies because he expressed different views on baptism by desire in different works. He thus provided ample opportunities for citing Augustine against Augustine and for using a later master's chosen Augustinian opinion for or against Ambrose. This was a process, however, which had to wait virtually six hundred years before it began. With minor exceptions, baptism by desire lay fallow between the fifth century and the late eleventh century, receiving a notable revival of interest in the early twelfth century. That revival was conditioned in no small way by the friendship between Hugh of St. Victor and Bernard of Clairvaux and by the hostility of Bernard of Clairvaux toward Peter Abelard. Paradoxically, although it was Abelard who first put Ambrose's support of this doctrine back into circulation, a doctrine which he himself seconded, it was Abelard who was cast in the role of the contemporary theologian most in need of refutation by Bernard and other defenders of baptism by desire. There were, as well, other twelfth-century participants in this debate more adept than Abelard in applying his own stated norms for evaluating their biblical and patristic sources, whatever their conclusions on baptism by desire. Selectivity in handling their chosen authorities also characterized the thirteenth-century treatments of this doctrine, although scholastics in that century were far less interested than their twelfth-century predecessors in subjecting these sources to literary and historical criticism.

Quite different initial and subsequent circumstances undergirded the history of fictive baptism, to be treated in chapter 2 of this study. Could baptismal play, whether as a game or on stage by actors, be the occasion of a sincere baptismal intention held to validate it sacramentally? What of persons who gave or received the liturgical rite with a false intention or a lack of the requisite faith and moral attitude? The patristic period yielded diverse teachings and beliefs about these kinds of fictive baptism. Rather than being viewed as variations on a common theme, they arose and were discussed in different contexts and literary genres, with a nod to their respective conventions. The first version of fictive baptism emerged as an aspect of hagiography. The subgenre of the saint's life involved is the *vita* of a pagan actor, suddenly converted while performing a scenario mimicking Christian baptism. Typically, there is a pagan prince or magistrate in the audience who puts to death the convert whose fictive baptism has become fact. The former actor is thus venerated as an early Christian martyr. A second patristic view of fictive baptism accepted as fact occurs in the early fifth-century continuation of the *Ecclesiastical History* of Eusebius by Rufinus of Aquileia. In an age before infant baptism was the standard, the issue was the status of children playing at baptism, whose play sought to emulate, not to mock, the church's baptismal rites. Destined to receive considerable attention in the high Middle Ages, pro and con, Rufinus reports, and supports, a positive decision on this matter made by Alexander, predecessor of Athanasius as bishop of Alexandria, the latter prelate, and his see, being paradigmatic in Rufinus's story of the triumph of orthodox Christianity over paganism and heresy.

Other concerns informed two additional issues relating to fictive baptism faced by early Christian writers. One was the question of whether baptisms performed by heretics and schismatics were fictive or valid. Those deemed heterodox were held to believe sincerely, if erroneously, in the accuracy of their own faith and praxis and in many cases used the same ritual and baptismal formulae as the orthodox. Some sectarians thought it necessary to rebaptize converts to their congregations already baptized by orthodox clergy. Should the orthodox do likewise to those reclaimed from heresy or schism? A second issue was the status of persons who acceded to the font hypocritically, lacking true faith or a sincere commitment to a Christian way of life. Once Christianity became the official religion of Rome, converts of both types abounded. Bishops, the ordinary ministers of baptism, had to decide whether to admit them to the font. If they were admitted, did they receive the same spiritual benefits as correctly disposed neophytes?

Here, as with baptism by desire, Augustine bequeathed a substantial, and checkered, legacy to his successors, since he sometimes supported, and at other times opposed, fictive baptisms of both kinds. And it was not bishops alone who wrestled with the problem of hypocrisy at the font. For, in a much-cited commentary on Ezekiel, Jerome equated fraudulent or self-serving fictive baptism with the sin of Simon Magus. In Jerome's view, the ablutions of those who enter the font fictively have no more value or effect than the ablutions of Gentiles. Anglo-Saxon and Carolingian exegetes in the eighth and ninth centuries reflect a similar concern. They put their own contemporary twist on fictive baptizands who accede to the font for sub-sacramental reasons, and on those who confuse baptismal ablution with non-Christian rites.

A new and major pagan group whose fictive baptisms attracted attention starting in the tenth century was the Vikings. Already in the works of chroniclers such as Dudo of St. Quentin and Richer of Reims, the wily Norman became a standard *topos*, repeatedly characterizing these marauders as well as their later descendants. Before the Vikings' conversion to Christianity, fictive baptism was but one of a number of religiously tinctured modes of the fabled "Norman ruse." Both Dudo and Richer recount the schemes of Viking leaders who presented themselves as candidates for baptism as a deliberate ploy, designed to allay the fears and relax the vigilance of Christian enemies whom they then proceeded to ravage and slaughter. The Christian leaders and prelates who granted them the font did so in good faith, albeit one that was ill rewarded.

On another level, it was the status of the ministers of baptisms deemed fictive that bothered authors faced with the pastoral consequences of eleventh-century papal reform. They debated whether baptisms performed by some clerics were invalidated by flaws in their ministers' ordination. Disqualification could result from their own simony or that of the bishops who ordained them, or merely punish priests caught willy-nilly in the crossfire of the papal-imperial feud over control of ecclesiastical personnel. The validity of baptisms, and other sacraments, administered by clerics not in communion with the church, in the eyes of controversialists, generated bitter arguments, dividing writers otherwise united by their shared commitment to clerical reform.

At the turn of the twelfth century, interest revived in the fictive or valid status of baptisms enacted on the stage. This topic was reintroduced by Ivo of Chartres as he grappled with, amplified, or edited Augustine's diverse positions on fictive baptism. Ivo's initiative set the scene for contemporary and later scholastics, some of whom felt no need to accept uncritically the hostility of the early church to stage plays as *pompa diaboli*. An intriguing question is whether Ivo and the scholastics who shared his outlook reflect a revived appreciation of ancient texts or whether they were responding to the wider availability of stage plays themselves, survivals of the late-Roman tradition of mimes and jugglers or arrivals of liturgical drama, or both. Ivo could distinguish between theater as frivolous, fantastic, and morally corrupting and theater as truth-telling and morally improving, and between staged baptisms able to illustrate either approach. Hugh of St. Victor picked up the glove thrown down by Ivo, defending theater as a wholesome form of recreation and edification. Accordingly, a Christian rite such as baptism enacted on stage, while not a real sacrament, was not hypocrisy or fraud. Rather, like the enactment of scenes from the Christian story or the lives of the saints, it could be a real stimulus to piety.

Less hypothetical was the scholastics' recognition that Augustine's treatments of fictive baptism were inconsistent and that this subject stood in great need of review and principled clarification. The aspect of the doctrine to which they devoted most of their attention was the spiritual state of candidates who accede to the font without true faith and especially without true charity, deliberately retaining malice in their hearts toward their brethren. Whether their sins are removed in the instant of baptism, only to return in worse form later on; or whether, in their case, the baptismal rite is inefficacious altogether; or whether they receive baptismal grace at the font but it becomes operative only if they later repent; and whether they can activate such grace if it had not been granted to them initially were dimensions of the question that received extensive, and far from unanimous, treatment. Two notions taken up in the twelfth century helped to frame, without necessarily resolving, scholastic debates on fictive baptism, as was also the case with baptism by desire and forced baptism. One was the idea that the recipient of a non-repeatable sacrament such as baptism also receives an indelible sacramental character. But there was no agreement on what that character actually is and conveys, and whether it applies equally in all cases. The other notion was the distinction between the *sacramentum*, or the physical medium used in the liturgical rite, and the *res sacramenti*, or the spiritual grace conveyed by that medium. How baptismal character is similar to, or different from, these two aspects of the sacrament and the degree to which different kinds of baptizands receive any of these endowments remained contested. While helping to sharpen the debates, neither of these concepts produced or promoted doctrinal consensus on these matters.

Forced baptism, the topic treated in chapter 3 of this study, has a still different storyline, range of sources, itinerary, and set of road maps. Was the baptism of the unbelieving and the unwilling ever acceptable? If so, what conditions attached to the compulsion involved in enforcing such rites? What were their charismatic and institutional implications? In considering this part of the landscape, we need to distinguish between hostility toward groups living within western Christendom whose beliefs and practices did not square with Christian norms and hostility toward groups living on its borders who represented a political and military threat. Forced baptism also needs to be differentiated from other forms of discriminatory or punitive behavior. There is also the matter of the connection, or disconnection, between official statements and policy enactments on the books, as articulated by theologians, canonists, and lay and ecclesiastical authorities, and actual practice, whether stemming from policies implemented by rulers or from unlicensed mob action.

One dimension of this topic that has received so much scholarly attention that it will not need extended treatment in this study is the forced baptism of Jews. As is well known, during the Roman imperial era, public law guaranteed to the Jews the exercise of their religion. Early Christian and patristic writers, while concerned with doctrinal "Judaizing" within their own ranks, also established the theological principle that the Jews should be protected, pending their eventual conversion at the Apocalypse. Once Rome became officially Christian, the laws applying to the Jews remained in place. While there were indeed legal reprisals against pagans and heterodox Christians, however locally or currently defined, not to mention vigilante actions, there is little or no evidence that religious dissidents were forced into the font. But once the Roman Empire gave way to the Germanic successor states, there is evidence of the forced baptism of Jews in Merovingian Gaul and Visigothic Spain, reflected in reports from the field and the perceived need for repeated papal and conciliar condemnations of it. Visigothic Spain produced a conundrum at Toledo IV, presided over by Isidore of Seville in 633 and later cited as a precedent. This council ruled that Jews were not to be subjected to forced baptism. At the same time, it ruled that Jews who had been forced into the font were to be adjudged Christians. They should be held liable for derelictions from the duties and obligations of Christians, penalized by church and state if they failed to maintain the standards of their new religion or sought to pass on their old one to their children.

As has been richly documented, Christian attitudes toward the Jews later in the Middle Ages reveal additional paradoxes, whether in Iberia or elsewhere. In some settings, Jews and Christians lived amicably side by side, and Christians drew fruitfully on their Jewish neighbors' knowledge of the Hebrew Bible and on their expertise and skills in other fields. But forced baptism of Jews also occurred, provoked by unauthorized preaching of the Crusades. Those refusing were massacred. Pressure of this sort aimed at bringing Jews into the church, however brutally. Alternatively, in some jurisdictions the policy was to maintain Jews as Jews so that they could be exploited by the ruling authorities. If exploitation was deemed to have reached a terminal point, the Jews could be and were expelled. The high Middle Ages certainly witnessed antagonism toward actual Jewish beliefs and practices; attacks on Jews, their sacred books, and houses of worship; and staged interreligious debates whose outcomes were foregone conclusions. In addition, Jews were penalized for alleged perpetration of anti-Christian behaviors in which they did not engage. But the systematic and massive forced baptism of Jews in medieval Christian societies is belied by the continuing presence of vibrant Jewish communities in those same societies. It did not occur until this policy was activated in Iberia in the late fourteenth century, in a site-specific context and at a point in time that lies outside the temporal limits of this study.

In contrast with the Jews, the other religious communities victimized by forced baptism were groups whose existence posed a military and political threat to western Christendom. They were enemies to be subjugated, or at least neutralized, on the borders of Christian Europe. Better still, they and their lands provided opportunities to push back its frontiers. Typically, their forced baptism was the result of their losses to Christian armies. In this connection, it is striking that Muslims defeated in the Spanish Reconquest were not forced into the font, except in imaginative literature. The major groups involved were not Muslims but pagans. Their forcible Christianization entered a critical stage in the reign of Charlemagne. The Saxons constituted the hardest nut for him to crack. It took Charlemagne thirty years, repeated military campaigns, mass deportation, and much slaughter before the Saxons finally capitulated. Finally, since along the way they had been repeatedly forced into the font only to renounce Christian baptism in successive rebellions.

This Saxon behavior suggests an outlook that is better documented in the case of the pagans on the eastern fringes of Europe forcibly converted in the Baltic Crusades of the twelfth to fourteenth centuries. The pagans bested in these areas treated the font, or even the expression of willingness to consider accepting it, as one among the series of demands wrested from them by Christian victors. Like the other terms of capitulation, it was subject to renegotiation or abandonment if and when the political and military situation changed. It could be a preemptive concession forestalling what portended to be a crushing military defeat. It was a high card that a canny pagan leader played if need be with his Christian opponents in order to enlist them against internal rivals or other external enemies. It was to be kept in his hand, or up his sleeve, as long as possible. In addition, if possible, it could be played more than once. Baptism, for these pagans, was not a unique and life-changing event but a pragmatic, and temporary, transaction. As an alternative to the sword, it was sometimes accepted, and later rejected, in consultation with their own gods. From the conquerors' viewpoint, the pagans' repeated recidivism justified repeated punitive action. And, notwithstanding the longstanding objections to forced baptism in the Christian tradition, we find canonists and theologians from the thirteenth century onward developing extremely subtle analyses of what, exactly, constitute the types and degrees of compulsion required to validate, or invalidate, the baptism of the unwilling. By the end of the period covered by this study, forced baptism had acquired a new, and minutely graded, set of theological rationales, which narrowed to a vanishing point the gap between university intellectuals and the militant agents of forced Christianization in the Baltic.

The theological outcomes of these three distinct baptismal questions, the extent to which consensus on them replaced controversy by the end of our target period, and the circumstances affecting their histories thus diverge sharply. We might be inclined to regard forced baptism as a species of fictive baptism, for those compelled to enter the font without real Christian commitment, even leaving aside the issue of pagan survivals and religious syncretism. But it was largely the contrast rather than the overlap between fictive and forced baptism that was visible to medieval observers. We might, as well, be inclined to regard baptism in each of these cases as governed by the rule that an adult candidate's free will, true faith, and sincere intention are required for its efficacious reception. But while this principle received a notable hearing in discussions of baptism by desire and fictive baptism, it lost ground as the doctrine on forced baptism developed. Even as apposite knowledge and appropriate inner intention were seen as conditioning ethics and sacramental theology more generally, in some quarters a purely formulaic ritual of baptism was deemed sufficient, without clear proof of the candidate's understanding and acceptance of the Creed, and, indeed, without anything resembling meaningful catechesis before or after the fact. Broad areas of disagreement remained, not only within each of these three areas of doctrinal debate but also at times between theory and practice, underscoring the need to consider each of these aspects of baptismal thought in its own historical trajectory and in the light of the kinds of sources that yield information on it in each case. And it will be their patristic and medieval histories, and not the modern catechetical *imaginaire* of baptism by desire, fictive baptism, and forced baptism, that will be the subject of study in this book.

CHAPTER *One*

BAPTISM BY DESIRE

The Age of the Church Fathers

The doctrine of baptism by desire had a checkered career in the medieval west from the patristic period until its virtual disappearance from the scholastic agenda at the end of the thirteenth century. First proposed as a position defensible in its own right by Ambrose of Milan, it received fuller attention from early Christian thinkers who yoked it to a range of different, and often polemical, assignments. One concern was the relationship between Old Testament rites, and the salvation of Old Testament worthies, and the redemption available in the Christian dispensation. This issue drew attention from supersessionists and anti-supersessionists alike, in their debates on the authority of the Old Testament as such. Another issue was the felt need to associate, or contrast, baptism by desire with the martyr's baptism by blood, as well as with ritual ablution. That topic might also involve debate on the validity of the baptisms and martyrdoms of heretics and schismatics. The church fathers entering the lists on these matters often ignored Ambrose's contribution. The controversies that ensued are reflected much more broadly in the works of Augustine. When interest in this doctrine resurfaced in later centuries, the range of contrasting patristic opinions, including those that could be documented within the *oeuvre* of the bishop of Hippo alone, offered medieval thinkers numerous options as they drew on, added to, or dismissed the patristic legacy in developing their own positions on baptism by desire.

Since it was to loom large as a parallel or alternative to baptism by desire, baptism by blood requires attention as the first form of non-ritual baptism regarded by Christian writers as equal or even superior to the font. The first Latin Christian writer to provide a theological rationale for baptism by blood was Tertullian (d. ca. 220). Whether or not he was later cited by name, his explanation was widely accepted. Tertullian locates the salvific equivalence of the blood shed by martyrs with the baptismal font in the water and blood issuing from the side of the crucified Christ: "These two baptisms He sent forth from the wound in His pierced side, in order that those who believed in His blood might be washed with water, and those who had been washed with water might carry the stain of His blood."[1] Cyprian of Carthage (d. 256) agrees. But his overriding aim is to invalidate the baptisms and martyrdoms of heterodox Christians. It is catechumens of the true church alone, he insists, martyred before they can receive the rite, who "are not deprived of the pledge of baptism, on the grounds that they are baptized with the glorious and higher baptism of blood."[2] Another advantage of baptism by blood noted by Cyprian is that martyrs, since they proceed at once to heavenly bliss, do not run the risk of falling into post-baptismal sin. While Tertullian's lapse into the Montanist heresy in his later career may have had a chilling effect on his role as a named authority on baptism by blood, we will see references to the substance of

1. Tertullian, *De baptismo* 16.1–2, ed. J. G. P. Borleffs, CCSL 1 (Turnhout: Brepols, 1993), 290–91: "Proinde nos facere aqua vocatos sanguine electos duos baptismos de vulnere percussi lateris emisit, quia in sanguinem eius crederent aqua lavarentur, qui aqua lavissent et sanguine opporterent." Translation: Tertullian, *Concerning Baptism*, trans. Alexander Souter (London: SPCK, 1919), 66. Most useful on Tertullian's influence on this point in early and patristic theology is Franz Josef Dölger, "Tertullian über die Bluttaufe: Tertullian, *De baptismo* 16," in idem, *Antike und Christentum: Kultur- und religionsgeschichtliche Studien*, 2nd ed., 2 vols. (Münster: Aschendorff, 1974), 2:117–41. See also G. Barielle, "Baptême d'après les pères grecs et latins," *DthC* 2/1:208–11; Peter Cramer, *Baptism and Change in the Early Middle Ages, c. 200–c. 1150* (Cambridge: Cambridge University Press, 1993), 73–86; Everett Ferguson, *Baptism in the Early Church: History, Theology, and Liturgy in the First Five Centuries* (Grand Rapids, MI: William B. Eerdmans Publishing Company, 2009), 349–50, 360, 417–19, 487, 854.

2. Cyprian, *Epistulae* 73.22.2, ed. G. F. Diercks, CCSL 3C (Turnhout: Brepols, 1996), 556–57: "nec privari baptismi sacramento, utpote qui baptizentur gloriosissime et maximo sanguinis baptismo." Translation: Cyprian, *On the Church: Selected Letters*, trans. Allen Brent (Crestwood, NY: St. Vladimir's Seminary Press, 2006), 212. See, most recently, Attilio Carpin, *Battezati nell'unica vera chiesa? Cipriano di Cartagine e la controversia battesimale* (Bologna: Edizioni Studio Domenicano, 2007), 11–77, and for Cyprian's later influence, ibid.,78–251, with emphasis on the issue of local episcopal vs. Roman jurisdiction.

his teaching in the sequel, as well as the more frequent appeal to Cyprian.

Providing as it did the context for Cyprian's argument, heterodoxy remained an ongoing problem after the church gained legitimacy, and then official support, in the fourth century. An administrative issue which bishops now had to face was ensuring that converts embraced fully the beliefs and moral requirements of Christianity while also enjoining them not to delay baptism. At the same time, it was necessary to inoculate catechumens against the unacceptable sectarian interpretations of Christianity that competed for their attention. A good index of this multifaceted pastoral concern, and a close predecessor of Ambrose, is Gregory Nazianzus, preaching as bishop of Constantinople to his catechumens on Epiphany Sunday in 381. This text was among the works of Gregory translated into Latin by Rufinus of Aquileia (d. 410), thereby becoming part of the Latin theological tradition.[3] One flag that Gregory salutes is that of the anti-supersessionists.

3. Gregory of Nazianzus, *Oratio* 39.17–18, ed. Claudio Moreschini, trans. Paul Gallay, SC 358 (Paris: Les Éditions du Cerf, 1991), 186–93. See the translation by Rufinus of Aquileia, *Orationum Gregorii Nazianzeni novum interpretatio*, ed. Augustus Engelbrecht, CSEL 46 (Vienna: F. Tempsky, 1910), 129–31. On Rufinus as a translator of Gregory and the medieval availability of his work, see Claudio Moreschini, "Rufino traduttore di Gregorio Nazianzeno," in *Rufino di Concordia e il suo tempo*, 2 vols., Antichità altoadriatiche 31 (Udine: Arti Grafiche Friulane, 1987), 1:227–85 on pages 230 and 241. For background on the polemics involved in Gregory's argument, see idem, "Il battesimo come fondamento dell'istruzione del cristiano in Gregorio Nazianzeno," in *Sacerdozio battesimale e formazione teologica nella catechesi e nella testimonianza dei Padri*, ed. Sergio Felici (Rome: Libreria Ateneo Salesiano, 1992), 73–82; idem, *Introduzione a Gregorio Nazianzeno* (Brescia: Morcelliana, 2006), 51–52, 85, 88, 92, 100, 121; John A. McGuckin, *St. Gregory Nazianzus: An Intellectual Biography* (Crestwood, NY: St. Vladimir's Seminary Press, 2001), 337–48; Susanna Elm, "Inscriptions and Conversions: Gregory of Nazianzus on Baptism (*Or*. 38–40)," in *Conversion in Late Antiquity and the Early Middle Ages: Seeing and Believing*, ed. Kenneth Mills and Anthony Grafton (Rochester, NY: University of Rochester Press, 2003), 1–35; Brian E. Daley, *Gregory of Nazianzus* (London: Routledge, 2006), 127; Christopher A. Beeley, *Gregory of Nazianzus on the Trinity and Knowledge of God: In Your Light We See Light* (Oxford: Oxford University Press, 2008), 34–35, 43, 69, 71–72, 76–77, 102, 177. On page 43, Beeley claims that Epiphany Sunday was the date on which Gregory baptized catechumens. But in the fourth century, this was the normal date for enrolling those catechumens who wished to be baptized the following Easter, on which see Victor Saxer, *Les rites de l'initiation chrétienne du IIe au VIe siècles: Esquisse historique et signification d'après leur pricipaux témoins* (Spoleto: Centro Italiano di Studi sull'Alto Medioevo, 1988), 242–54, 263–64, 294–95, 303–14, 323–26, 329–32, 341–48, 350–57, 372. On baptism of tears in Gregory and his predecessors, see Ferguson, *Baptism*, 320 (with extensive literature cited in notes 74–76), 596. On general patristic objections to the delay of baptism, see Éric Rebillard, "La figure du catéchumène et le problème du delai du baptême dans la pastorale d'Augustin," in *Augustin prédicateur (395–411)*, Actes du Colloque international de Chantilly, 5–7 septembre 1996, ed. Goulven Madec (Paris: Institut d'Études Augustiniennes, 1998), 285–92, reprt. as "Catechumens and the Delay of Baptism in the Preaching of Augustine," trans. Aaron Pelttari in idem, *Transformations of Religious Practices in Late Antiquity* (Farnham, UK: Ashgate, 2013), no. IV.

He places Christian baptism in the context of its Old Testament forerunners. Gregory presents five modes of baptism. The first is the Israelites' baptism in the Red Sea, prefiguring the ablution of the Christian people of God to come. Next is the ablution administered by John the Baptist. This rite involved repentance for sin, and water alone. Third is the baptism of Christ. By this phrase, Gregory does not mean Christ's own baptism in the Jordan by John at the beginning of His public ministry, but rather the rite which Christ instituted. Gregory does not indicate when he thinks this institution took place, a debated topic not resolved until the thirteenth century. In any case, the baptism of Christ is perfect. It forgives all sins and involves both water and the Holy Spirit. Fourth is the martyr's baptism by blood, a theological given by Gregory's day needing no explanation or defense. Fifth and last is what Gregory calls the baptism of tears. His understanding of this notion is in tune with that of other early Christian writers, amplified by Gregory's attack on heterodox understandings of the sacrament. The baptism of tears is neither the same thing as ritual baptism nor a substitute for it. These two modes of baptism are not equivalent. In opposition to what some heretics teach, ritual baptism is not a free pass, rendering its recipients immune from post-baptismal sin. Nor, in contrast to what other heretics think, does the church lack a remedy for post-baptismal sin. It is sad but true that the baptized sometimes backslide. But post-baptismal sin can be forgiven by penance. Here, Gregory does not refer to the single, solemn, public penance available in the fourth-century church. Rather, what he wants to convey under the heading of the baptism of tears is a different and wider point. Just as candidates for baptism must renounce and repent their sins, pledging to live in accord with Christian ethics, so must they also recognize that sin, and repentance for sin, will be ongoing realities of the Christian life. The baptism of tears, then, is the repentance of Christians for post-baptismal sin, the sincere sorrow and mortification that this repentance involves.

With this background in mind, and given his sturdy defense of the importance of ritual baptism in other works directed to catechumens, Ambrose of Milan's originality on the subject of baptism by desire is striking indeed. Ambrose makes this case in his *De obitu Valentiniani*, a funeral oration on the emperor Valentinian II, who died in 392. This work was destined to make Ambrose one of the two most frequently cited authorities on this subject in the Middle Ages. Much of the scholarly attention lavished on this text has focused on Ambrose's Latin style and his use of biblical and classical rhetoric[4]

4. The best and most recent philological analysis is that of Martin Biermann, *Die Leichtenreden des Ambrosius von Mailand: Rhetorik, Predigt, Politik*, *Hermes* Einzelschriften 70, ed.

or on its political setting.[5] Its political setting is, to be sure, extremely important. The Roman Empire had been divided and ruled by eastern and western emperors for some time when Valentinian II succeeded his half-brother Gratian as emperor in the west. At that point, Valentinian was a minor dominated by his redoubtable mother Justina. Justina was a staunch opponent of Nicene Christianity. When Valentinian's court moved from Illyrium to Milan after the battle of Adrianople in 378, her hostility to Ambrose and to the orthodox faith was as blatant as it was toxic. It led to the famous basilica crisis of 386, one of the most dramatic confrontations between church and state in Ambrose's eventful episcopate. In 388 Justina died. Theodosius I, emperor in the east, decided that the imperial succession should go to his own sons, Arcadius in the east and Honorius in the west. He relegated Valentinian to Gaul under the tutelage of his chief general, the *magister militum* Arbogast. On May 15, 392, at the age of twenty-one, having asserted his independence by preparing to return to Italy in defiance of Arbogast, Valentinian was found strangled. Was this suicide? Was he assassinated by Arbogast? If so, did this occur at the behest of Theodosius or on Arbogast's own initiative? The last of these possibilities is suggested by the fact that, on August 22, 392, Arbogast named Eugenius, his own candidate, as emperor in the west. Warfare with Theodosius then ensued; Arbogast and Eugenius were defeated, and both were put to death.

The truth concerning the cause of Valentinian's death and the political fallout of these events were decidedly up in the air when the young emperor's body was returned to Milan for burial and Ambrose was charged

---

Jürgen Blänsdorf, Jochen Bleiken, and Wolfgang Kullmann (Stuttgart: Franz Steiner Verlag, 1995), 12, 21–24, 44–49, 51–57, 87–103, 121, 134–42, 151–78, 195. See also Franz Rozynski, *Die Leichtenreden des hl. Ambrosius inbesondere auf ihr Verhältnis zu der Redekunst und den antiken Trostschriften untersucht* (Breslau: Buchdruckerei der Schlesischen Volkszeitung, 1910), 71–94; Yves-Marie Duval, "Formes profanes et formes biblique dans les oraisons funèbres de saint Ambroise," in *Christianisme et formes littéraires de l'antiquité tardive en Occident*, ed. Alan Cameron et al., Entretiens sur l'Antiquité Classique 23 (Geneva: Fondation Hardt, 1977), 249, 254, 257, 258–74, 277, 286–93, 298–99.

5. For political background on Valentinian II's reign, see Neil B. McLynn, *Ambrose of Milan: Church and Court in a Christian Capital* (Berkeley: University of California Press, 1994), 84–91, 98–102, 105, 154–55, 160–61, 165–66, 170–208, 218, 279, 296–97, 337–41. On the basilica crisis of 386, see Marcia L. Colish, "Why the Portiana? Reflections on the Milanese Basilica Crisis of 386," *Journal of Early Christian Studies* 10 (2002): 361–72, reprt. in eadem, *The Fathers and Beyond: Church Fathers between Ancient and Medieval Thought* (Aldershot: Ashgate, 2008), no. VIII. For the debates of patristic authors on the suicide/assassination question (assassination being the more widespread view), see Thomas A. Kelly, intro. to his ed. and trans. of Ambrose, *De consolatione Valentiniani*, The Catholic University of America Patristic Studies 58 (Washington: The Catholic University of America Press, 1940), 38–41.

with presiding over his obsequies. That he was walking on eggs in this assignment, and knew it, is manifest in the rhetoric of his funeral oration.[6] In 387 Theodosius had married as his second wife, Galla, Valentinian's eldest sister. Neither member of the imperial couple was in Milan for the funeral, but they were certain to learn how Ambrose had officiated at it. At various stages of his argument, Ambrose aims his discourse at a host of different addressees: God; the Milanese Christian community; Justa and Gratia, Valentinian's remaining sisters and the chief mourners present; Gratian; and Valentinian, now at his brother's side in Heaven. Ambrose also tells his hearers that the sainted Gratian told him personally that Valentinian has been saved, which happy news the bishop conveys to his Milanese audience. Throughout this text, Ambrose skirts two ticklish questions: the anti-Nicene policy adopted by Valentinian under his mother's influence and the mode of his death. What he emphasizes, instead, are the virtues he imputes to Valentinian. His remarks about the emperor's earlier life are deliberately generic. When Valentinian saw the errors of his youthful ways, he corrected them, Ambrose claims. Once he was his own master, Valentinian committed himself to orthodox Christianity. He postponed his baptism because conflicts among the bishops of Gaul made it unclear to him whether any of them were acceptable, and largely because he wished to receive the rite from Ambrose's own hands: "He often intimated, when I was absent, that he wanted to be initiated into the sacred mysteries by me."[7] Far from being a nonbeliever receiving a posthumous surrogate baptism,[8] Ambrose's Valentinian was a fully instructed catechumen, hastening to the Milanese font when he was cut down by his sad and unexplained death.[9]

6. Ambrose, *De obitu Valentiniani*, ed. and trans. Gabriele Banterle in *Le orazioni funebri*, Sancti Ambrosii episcopi Mediolanensis opera 18 (Milan: Biblioteca Ambrosiana, 1985), 162–209. Good English translations include Ambrose, *Consolation on the Death of Valentinian*, trans. Roy J. Deferrari in *Funeral Orations by Saint Gregory Nazianzus and Saint Ambrose*, FC 22 (New York: Fathers of the Church, Inc., 1953) and Ambrose of Milan, *Political Speeches and Letters*, trans. J. H. W. Liebeschuetz and Carole Hill, Translated Texts for Historians 42 (Liverpool: Liverpool University Press, 2005). I have consulted these works with profit, but the translations given in the passages that follow are my own.

7. Ambrose, *De obitu Val.* c. 6, 9–21, 25, 34–38, 41, 54–57, 64–79b, 164–66, 168–76, 178, 182–86, 188, 198–208; quotation at c. 23, 176: "Illa privata, quod saepe me adpellabat absentem et a me initiandum se sacris mysteriis praeferabat."

8. Such is the opinion regarding Valentinian given by Jeffrey A. Trumbower, *Rescue from the Dead: The Posthumous Salvation of Non-Christians in Early Christianity* (New York: Oxford University Press, 2004), 4, 33–41, 104, 155. Cf. Marcia L. Colish, "The Virtuous Pagan: Dante and the Christian Tradition," in *The Fathers and Beyond* (as in note 5), no. XVII.

9. Ambrose, *De obitu Val.* c. 25–26, 178.

Ambrose thus urges his congregation, and especially Justa and Gratia, not to worry about Valentinian's lack of ritual baptism. For the beatified Gratian assured Ambrose and Valentinian alike that the highest possible authority has guaranteed the deceased emperor baptism by desire. As Gratian told his brother, "It was not just anyone, but Christ, who illuminated you with spiritual grace. He baptized you, since human rites were lacking in your case."[10] Given Valentinian's upright faith and morals, and his repeated requests and yearning for baptism, this validation by the Lord Himself leaves no room for doubt and should allay all anxiety. And so, Ambrose observes, "I hear your lament that he did not receive the rites of baptism.... But did he not have the grace he desired? Did he not have what he requested? And because he requested it, he received it."[11]

Having thus turned his rhetorical question into a declarative statement, Ambrose reformulates the same point as a syllogistic argument. Again, he addresses Valentinian's sisters in particular: "But if you are troubled by the fact that the mysteries were not solemnly celebrated, not even the martyrs are crowned if they are not catechumens. For, unless they are initiated, they are not crowned. But, even as they are washed by their blood, so he has been washed by his piety and desire."[12] With that assurance, Ambrose ends his discourse, presenting the validity of baptism by desire as an irrefutable logical conclusion which also makes baptism by desire as efficacious as baptism by blood.

The fact that this Ambrosian doctrine breaks fresh ground and that it was widely influential, if not in the immediate sequel, has received only fleeting scholarly attention.[13] Ambrose's editors have noted that this text was transmitted in a number of manuscripts written between the Caro-

10. Ibid., c. 75, 204: "Hoc est: non quicumque te, sed Christus inluminavit gratia spirituali. Ille te baptizavit, quia humana officia defuerunt."

11. Ibid., c. 51, 192–94: "Sed audio vos dolere, quod non acceperit sacramenta baptismatis.... Non habet ergo gratiam, quam desideravit, non habet, quod poposcit? Et quia poposcit, accepit." See also c. 30, 180: "Sed ille non amisit gratiam, quam poposcit?"

12. Ibid., c. 53, 194: "Aut si, quia sollemniter non sunt celebrate mysteria, hoc movet, ergo nec martyres, si catechumeni fuerint, coronatur; non enim coronatur, si non initiantur. Quodsi, suo abluuntur sanguine, et hunc sua pietas abluit et voluntas."

13. Noted by Banterle, intro. to his ed. and trans. of *De obitu Val.*, 15; Dorothea Sattler, "Begierdetaufe," in *Lexicon für Theologie und Kirche* (Freiburg: Herder, 1994), 2:143; Ernst Dassmann, *Ambrosius von Mailand: Leben und Werken* (Stuttgart: W. Kohlhammer, 2004), 178. Cf. Franca Ela Consolino, "L''optimus princeps' secondo S. Ambrogio: Virtù imperatorie e virtù cristiane nelle orazioni funebri per Valentiniano e Teodosio," *Rivista storica italiana* 96 (1984): 1025–45 on pages 1025–39, who argues that Ambrose is seeking to portray Valentinian as a martyr and as an exponent of clericalized virtues.

lingian era and the fourteenth century. These include S. Omer 72 (eighth through ninth century), Paris BN lat. 1913 (ninth century), Paris BN lat. 1719 (eleventh century), Durham Cath. Bib. B.II.6 (eleventh century), Milan Bib. Ambrosiana 317 Sup. (twelfth century), Heiligenkreutz 254 (twelfth century), and Paris BN lat. 1920 (fourteenth century).[14] Despite its post-patristic availability, the medieval fortunes of this text have not been investigated. But, as we will see in the following, although there are no known citations of or references to the *De obitu Valentiniani* between Ambrose's day and the early twelfth century, the latter period was to witness a remarkable revival of that work and its teaching, one that placed it front and center in discussions of baptism by desire. Until that revival, and side by side with Ambrose's funeral oration, the authority chiefly cited on this question was Augustine, who handled it with considerably less clarity and certitude.

The varied and sometimes conflicting positions taken by Augustine on baptism by desire across his career reflect both the development of doctrine on his part and the nature of the genres and contexts in which he writes. His first essay on this topic occurs in an early work, his *De diversis quaestionibus octoginta tribus* (389/96), in which Augustine addresses no particular agenda. Here, he foregrounds two biblical case studies, figures destined to reappear frequently in this story. They are Cornelius (Acts 10:1–44) and the good thief on the cross (Luke 23:40–43). Augustine agrees with the author of Acts that Cornelius was granted faith in Christ by the direct inspiration of the Holy Spirit. This fact was acknowledged by St. Peter. But, notwithstanding his recognition that Cornelius was already saved, Peter ruled that he should also receive ritual baptism. And so it was done. As for the good thief, Augustine observes here that "baptism was granted to the believing thief, considered as having received it in his free mind, since he could not receive it bodily on the cross."[15]

Augustine reiterates this conclusion concerning the thief in his anti-Donatist *De baptismo* (400/10), a work cited far more frequently by later

14. Banterle, intro. to his ed. and trans. of *De obitu Val.*, 22; and most recently Michaela Zelzer, "Quelques remarques sur la tradition des oeuvres d'Ambroise et sur leurs titres originaux," in *Lire et éditer aujourd'hui Ambroise de Milan*, ed. Gérard Nauroy (Bern: Peter Lang, 2007), 21–35 on pages 25–26, 31; see also eadem, "Zur Überlieferung und Rezeption der Kaiserreden des Ambrosius von Mailand im mailänder Raum," in *"Chartae caritatis": Études de patristique et d'antiquité tardive en hommage à Yves-Marie Duval*, ed. Benoît Gain, Pierre Jay, and Gérard Nauroy (Paris: Institut d'Études Augustiniennes, 2004), 113–25.

15. Augustine, *De diversis quaestionibue octoginta tribus* q. 62, ed. Almut Mutzenbecher, CCSL 44A (Turnhout: Brepols, 1975), 133: "etiam baptismum credente latrone, et pro accepto habitum in animo libero quod in corpore crucifixo accepi non poterat."

thinkers. Here he devotes a more elaborate analysis to the point. He appeals to earlier Christian writers. But, while familiar with Ambrose's sermons on the Gospel of Luke (collected 389/90), he does not advert to the bishop of Milan's treatment of that figure. Ambrose on Luke devotes attention to the good thief and, more importantly, to Christ's reaction to him, in order to emphasize considerations which Augustine evidently sees as marginal to anti-Donatist polemic. Ambrose emphasizes the swiftness with which Christ responded to the thief's appeal, and the generosity of His reply. From this event, we sinners can learn that whoever prays to the Lord will be heard and will receive even more than he requests or can imagine.[16] In this incident, Ambrose observes, Christ acted not in His divine nature but rather in His human nature. What He exercised was not His power to save, but rather His capacity to offer "a gift by priestly intercession," just as He interceded with the Father for the forgiveness of those responsible for His death.[17] Ethics and the role of Christ as an exemplar of the priesthood are what Ambrose accents in this exegesis, not baptism and the modes by which it may be obtained.

Another exegesis on the good thief which Augustine ignores is Jerome's. Jerome (c. 347–419) makes repeated references to the thief in other works but highlights his principal concern in his commentary on the Gospel of Matthew. The passage in question (Matthew 27:38–43) refers to the two thieves crucified along with the Lord, unbelievers who reject and mock Him. On the other hand, Luke reports the conversion of one of them, the good thief. How can these different accounts be reconciled? Jerome proposes the following solution: The good thief initially shared the hostile and dismissive views of the bad thief. This is the situation that Matthew recounts. But, at the last moment the good thief changed his mind, as Luke tells us: "At first, both had blasphemed, and then … one believed in Jesus and, in the sequel, amended his prior denial with confession."[18] These two

16. Ambrose, *Expositionis Evangelii secundum Lucam* 10.121, ed. Marcus Andriaen, trans. Giovanni Coppa, 2 vols., Sancti Ambrosii episcopi Mediolanensis opera 11–12 (Milan: Biblioteca Ambrosiana, 1978), 12:478.

17. Ibid., 10.129, 12:486: "sacerdotali intercessione donatum." For the composition and date of this work, its manuscript tradition, and later medieval knowledge and use of it, see Coppa's intro. in ibid. 11:11–16, 18–25, 60–63, 71.

18. Jerome, *Commentarium in Mattheum libri IV* 4.27.44, ed. David Hurst and Marcus Andriaen, CCSL 77 (Turnhout: Brepols, 1969), 272–73: "primum uterque blasphemaverint, dehinc … unus credederit in Iesum et priorem negationem sequenti confessione emendaverit." An outstanding discussion of Jerome on the various texts in which he treats the good thief, on which this paragraph depends, is Régis Courtray, "La figure des deux larrons chez Jérôme," in

thieves, Jerome continues, represent two peoples. The good thief stands for the Gentiles who have come to the faith; the bad thief stands for the unbelieving Jews who continue to blaspheme Christ to this day. Elsewhere Jerome adds two other points. The good thief enjoys a special privilege. He was the very first person to whom Christ opened the gates of Paradise, preceding even the Old Testament worthies, Christ's own apostles, and the later saints and martyrs: "The thief was the first admitted through that gate with the Lord."[19] While this distinction is unique, the good thief nonetheless remains an important example of virtue which Christians can imitate. The lesson he teaches is that it is never too late to repent. As Jerome enjoins his audience, "Have faith, and you can hope for the same thing."[20]

Edifying as these exegeses of the good thief by Ambrose and Jerome may be, neither author uses them as a platform on which to develop the theology of baptism. For this reason, and also because he wants to annex the legacy of Cyprian to his anti-Donatist cause, it is the bishop of Carthage to whom Augustine appeals in *De baptismo*. He agrees with Cyprian on the need to distinguish heterodox from orthodox baptisms and martyrdoms. He also agrees with Cyprian on the status of the good thief. Augustine now contrasts Cornelius more crisply with the good thief. While the good thief did receive the equivalent of baptism on the cross, we should not regard his sufferings on the cross as an act of Christian martyrdom. As Augustine explains,

> Again and again I find on consideration that, in addition to martyrdom for the name of Christ, faith and conversion of heart can supply what is lacking if the rite of baptism cannot be celebrated for lack of time. That thief was crucified not for the name of Christ but for his crimes. He suffered not because he believed, but believed while he was suffering. It is evident how powerful this is in the case of the thief … even without the visible sacrament, for baptism is accomplished invisibly when its administration is omitted by reason of necessity, not through contempt of religion.[21]

Jerome of Stridon: His Life and Legacy, ed. Andrew Cain and Josef Lössl (Aldershot: Ashgate, 2009), 105–16. For Jerome's predecessors on the good thief/bad thief as believing Gentiles/unbelieving Jews, see ibid., 107n6.

19. Jerome, *In die dominica Pascha II*, ed. D. Germanus Morin in Jerome, *Tractatus sive homeliae*, 2nd ed., CCSL 78 (Turnhout: Brepols, 1958), 549: "per hanc portam primus latro cum Domino ingressus est."

20. Ibid., 548: "Habetote fiduciam, et vos sperante similia."

21. Augustine, *De baptismo libri VII* 4.22.29, ed. M. Petchenig, CSEL 51 (Vienna: F. Tempsky, 1908), 257: "Quod etiam atque etiam considerans invenio non tantum passione pro nomine Christi id quod ex baptismo deerat posse supplere, sed etiam fidem conversionemque cordis, si forte ad celebrandum mysterium baptismi in angustiis temporum succurri non potuit

The anti-Donatist Augustine thus continues to be generous to the good thief and to accept without demur his baptism by desire on the cross. But he treats the thief's circumstances as exceptional. It is the scenario involving Cornelius that is the one to follow, unless urgent necessity, lack of time, the unavailability of the font, or imminent death—and not the contempt of religion—account for the omission of the rite.

In another work of his late career, the anti-Pelagian *De natura et origine animae* (419), Augustine returns to the good thief with a notable shift in strategy. He has a pressing reason for doing so. For the Pelagians invoked the example of the good thief in support of their own errant theology. According to the Pelagians, the thief believed in Christ; he had repented, and he was simply saved thereby. The conclusion to draw is that baptism is not a universal requirement. It is the ethical life of moral agents that counts. And moral agents cannot sin before they can exercise free will. Hence there is no need for infant baptism. As is well known, in opposition to this teaching Augustine heightened the importance of his doctrine of grace and predestination and his insistence on the irrefragable necessity of infant baptism. In his attack on the Pelagians' interpretation of the good thief, Augustine alludes to Tertullian: "It is not beyond belief," he states, "to say that the thief crucified next to the Lord then believed, and received a most holy baptism by the water flowing from His wounded side;" but, he adds, "none of us knows this for sure or can prove it."[22] Augustine proposes an alternate hypothesis, for which he offers no positive evidence and no sense of the need to reconcile the accounts of Matthew and Luke flagged by Jerome. For all we know, the good thief was ritually baptized before his crucifixion. Given the weakness of this claim, Augustine tries to bolster it with a flanking movement. He offers another, equally problematic, hypothesis. The good thief's case parallels that of Dinocrates, prayed out of Hell and into Heaven by his sainted sister, the early Christian martyr Perpetua. To be sure, her *vita* gives no information about the faith or religious status of Dinocrates, who died at the age of seven. But, although still a child, could Dinocrates not have converted and been baptized before he died?[23]

neque enim latro ille pro nomine Christi crucifixus est, sed pro meritis facinorum suum, nec quia credidit passus est, sed dum patitur credidit, quantum itaque valeat etiam sine visibili baptismi sacramento ... in illo latrone declaratum est, sed tunc impletur invisibiliter, cum ministerium baptismi non contemptus religionis, sed articulus necessitatis excludit."

22. Augustine, *De natura et origine animae* 1.9.11, ed. Carolus F. Urba and Josephus Zycha, CSEL 40 (Vienna: F. Tempsky, 1913), 311–12: "non incredibiliter dicitur latronem qui tunc credidit iuxta dominum crucifixum aqua illa, quae de vulnera lateris eius emicuit, tamquam sacratissimo baptismo fuisse perfusum; ... quoniam nemo nostrum novit, nemo convicit."

23. Ibid., 1.10.12, 3.9.12, 312, 369–70. It is in the latter passage that Augustine airs the un-

Then, there is the issue of Christ's own apostles. There existed among early Christians a debate on when the apostles were baptized, a question to which Augustine proposes no real solution. True, he observes, the New Testament is silent on when they were baptized. But would it not be shameful to think that their baptism had never taken place?[24] Here, the anti-Pelagian Augustine does not hesitate to venture onto argumentative and exegetical thin ice.

Yet another discussion of the good thief surfaces in Augustine's commentary on Leviticus (419). In this work, although his ostensible purpose is merely straightforward exegesis, he gives his own interpretation of the typology of the Red Sea event. As with the Epiphany sermon of Gregory Nazianzus, patristic writers typically view the passage as an ablution forecasting Christian baptism. Augustine's point is that this salvation of the Israelites was a non-ablution. Miraculously, the Red Sea was parted by God and they crossed it dry-shod. The meaning is clear, he continues. In Old Testament history, as in the Christian dispensation, the Holy Spirit sanctifies God's people invisibly, without the need for physical media, as well as visibly, by means of such media. A New Testament case in point is the good thief's invisible salvation and subsequent bliss. The thief was indeed redeemed and sanctified on the cross. But, Augustine stresses, he is a unique case. He is not a precedent for current practice. Even within the time span Augustine posits between the writing of Luke's Gospel and the Acts of the Apostles, Christian doctrine and practice had already changed. St. Peter's handling of the conversion of Cornelius reflects the new ground rules, which continue to apply to this day. For Cornelius, as for us, "visible sanctification is not judged superfluous even if invisible [sanctification] precedes it."[25] It is now necessary to proceed to the font.

In still another exegetical context, Augustine addresses the conversation between Christ and Nicodemus (John 3:3–5) in which the Lord states that one must be reborn by water and the Holy Spirit in order to enter the

provable possibility that the thief was already baptized. On Dinocrates, see *Passio S. Perpetuae* 3, 7–8, ed. J. Armitage Robinson (Cambridge: Cambridge University Press, 1891), 62, 72–74. See, more recently, *The Passion of Perpetua and Felicity*, ed. and trans. Thomas J. Heffernan (Oxford: Oxford University Press, 2012), 109–11 (Latin); 128–29 (translation). Heffernan, 229, notes that this text presents Dinocrates "as an unbaptized pagen." He cites Augustine's *De origine animae* on page 233 but not Augustine's claim that Dinocrates had been baptized before his death.

24. Augustine, *De natura et origine animae* 3.9.12, 369–70. A rich discussion on this debate is provided by Ernst Kantorowicz, "The Baptism of the Apostles," *Dumbarton Oaks Papers* 9/10 (1956): 203–51.

25. Augustine, *Quaestiones Levitici* 3.84, in *Quaestiones in Heptateuchum libri VII*, ed. Johannes Fraipont, CCSL 33 (Turnhout: Brepols, 1958), 228: "nec superflua iudicata est visibilis sanctificatio, quam invisibilis iam praecesserat."

kingdom of Heaven. John 3:3–5 is a biblical passage which we will encounter repeatedly in the history of baptism by desire. In understanding Augustine's emphasis here, we must note that his text is a sermon delivered to his congregation on Palm Sunday, March 30, 413. The catechumens among his hearers were entering the final week of their preparation for baptism, which they would receive at the end of the Easter vigil. Augustine aims his remarks at these catechumens specifically. He emphasizes their need for ritual baptism: "Now is the time to exhort you catechumens, who, although you believe in Christ, are still encumbered by your sins. No one will reign with Christ unless they are forgiven, and no one can be forgiven unless he is reborn of water and the Holy Spirit." Augustine adjures his catechumens, literally, to shed that encumbrance by taking the ritual plunge.[26] In the sermon he delivered the following day, he observes that, in the encounter with Christ reported by St. John, Nicodemus was in a state analogous to that of his catechumens. Nicodemus believed, but he had not yet been cleansed of his sins at the font. "This," Augustine states, "is the way it is with all catechumens."[27]

When Augustine set out to review his writings to date in the *Retractationes* (427), the only passages on the theme of baptism by desire that he thought needed correction were those in the *De diversis quaestionibus* and the *De baptismo*. In both cases, he wanted to revise what he had said about the good thief. As we have noted, his own later works offer a range of opinions, running the gamut from the thief's invisible sanctification, a perennial possibility; to his *sui generis* redemption on the cross as an option no longer available; to his possible pre-crucifixion ritual baptism. Augustine tells readers of the *Retractationes* that he has done further research on the last-named theory. He now concludes, "I do not know that this documentation can prove that the thief was not baptized,"[28] adding that "it is uncertain whether he was baptized or not."[29] In the first part of this statement, he tries to place the burden of proving the negative on the shoulders of those who reject his hypothesis regarding the pre-crucifixion baptism of the thief. But

26. Augustine, *In Ioannis Evangelium tractatus libri CXXIV* 11.1, ed. D. Radbodus Willems, CCSL 36 (Turnhout: Brepols, 1954), 109: "Tempus est enim ut vos exhortemur, qui adhuc estis catechumeni, qui, sic creditistis in Christum, ut adhuc vestra peccata portetis; quia nisi cui dimissa fuerint, non regnabit cum Christo; dimitti non possunt nisi ei renatus fuit ex aqua et Spiritu Sancto."

27. Ibid., 11.3–6, 12.1–6, 111–14, 120–24; quotation at 11.3, 111–12: "Tales sunt omnes catechumeni."

28. Augustine, *Retractationes* 1.26, ed. Almut Mutzenbecher, CCSL 57 (Turnhout: Brepols, 1984), 83: "sed quibus documentis satis possit ostendi, quod non fuerit ille latro baptizatus, ignoro."

29. Ibid., 2.18, 104: "quia utrum non fuerit baptizatus incertum est."

he then retreats to the default position of uncertainty. He refers readers to the arguments made in his anti-Pelagian works for a fuller elaboration of his views. In the *Retractationes*, Augustine concludes that he can no longer support the thief as an example or as a model for current practice. But he does not reject the idea that Christ did accept the thief's conversion on the cross, as the equivalent of ritual baptism, although as an unrepeatable event. As we will see, all the Augustinian perspectives on the good thief just discussed received attention, if not always support, from later thinkers. The same is true for many of the other opinions articulated by the end of the patristic period.

That this patristic legacy yielded a wide range of orthodox possibilities on baptism by desire by the end of Augustine's day can also be seen in a more abbreviated form in the contrasting views of two fifth-century figures, Theodore of Mopsuestia and Gennadius of Marseille. Theodore (d. 428) accents God's benevolence and not just the good thief's faith: "It is not by nature but by the acceptance of perfect faith through God's generosity that [He] is wont to receive [us] in baptism."[30] While not disparaging ritual baptism, Theodore regards the lack of the rite as no impediment. And, by accenting the divine side of the transaction, he implies that it is not the good thief alone who may benefit from God's infinite goodness. Theodore's work was not available in Latin during the Middle Ages, although, as we will see, there were later thinkers sensitive to the issue he raises whose views, if arrived at from other sources, accord with his.

On the opposite side of the spectrum is Gennadius (late fifth century), whose work was definitely known and cited later. Gennadius takes an unequivocal hard line on this question: "We believe that [ritual] baptism alone is the path to salvation. We believe that no catechumen, however abounding in good works, will gain eternal life, except by martyrdom." The martyr, he goes on, professes his faith before his persecutor; the baptismal candidate confesses his faith before the officiating priest. The candidate is then immersed in or sprinkled with water; the martyr is bathed by his own blood or is dipped in fire. The priest then lays his hands on the neophyte, conveys the Holy Spirit to him, and admits him to the Eucharist, which commemorates Christ's death. For his part, the martyr participates personally in Christ's death. The baptismal candidate renounces the things of this world;

30. Theodore of Mopsuestia, *In 1 Timotheum* 3:2, in *Theodori Episcopi Mopsuesteni in epistolas B. Pauli commentarii*, ed. and trans. Henry Barclay Swete, 2 vols. (Cambridge: Cambridge University Press, 1880–82), 2:107–8; quotation at 2:108: "Nec quae natura sed suscipientium fides perfectam Dei liberalitatem in baptisma adtrahere solet." Noted by Ferguson, *Baptism*, 532. This text, originally written in Greek, was preserved in Syriac.

the martyr renounces life in this world itself. By ritual baptism, all sins are remitted; by martyrdom all sins are extinguished.[31] In this passage, Gennadius alludes to the catechumen's faith only as a preface to his ritual ablution. It is his good works that are insufficient, absent the font. In no sense does Gennadius accept the omission of the rite by the non-martyr, whatever the extenuating circumstances. And he presents his position as that of the universal church, not just as one view, requiring a serious defense, among others.

After the Fathers, before the Scholastics

This array of opinions, ranging from the unqualified support of baptism by desire in Ambrose's *De obitu Valentiniani* to its unqualified dismissal by Gennadius, did not generate widespread attention until the turn of the twelfth century, with two exceptions. The first to reopen the discussion, focusing on the good thief, was Bede (d. 735) in his commentary on the Gospel of Luke. In this text, Bede reflects some awareness of his patristic predecessors but is more noteworthy for taking his own line, without explaining why he rejects opinions strongly held by some of his forebears. In addressing the case of the good thief, Bede attributes to him more than just faith. As Bede sees it, the thief possessed faith, hope, and charity. Although physically incapacitated on the cross, the thief retained the heart and voice with which he expressed these virtues. The good thief was granted divine inspiration, was absolved of his sins, and was accepted by Christ. Bede does not indicate whether these aspects of the thief's salvation occurred simultaneously or in the chronological sequence mentioned. If the latter, Christ's acceptance reads as an *ex post facto* ratification of a redemption that had already been granted. In any case, for Bede, "He who arrived on the cross because of guilt departed from it because of grace." As with Jerome, Bede contrasts that outcome with that of the bad thief, condemned for his blasphemy, although without Jerome's disquisitions on Gentiles and Jews or his concern with reconciling Matthew with Luke. But Bede swims against the patristic current by claiming that the good thief "was made a martyr by his confession."[32] Bede thereby dissociates himself from the careful distinction

31. Gennadius of Marseille, *Liber de ecclesiasticis dogmatibus* 74, *PL* (Paris, 1862), 58:997: "Baptizatis tantum iter esse salutis credimus. Nullum catechumenum, quamvis in bonis operibus, vitam aeternam habere credimus, excepto martyrio. . . ." Noted by Ferguson, *Baptism*, 770, although his concern with this passage is whether baptism is administered by immersion or aspersion.

32. Bede, *In Lucae Evangelium expositio* 23:40–43, ed. David Hurst, CCSL 120 (Turnhout:

between the thief's status and that of the martyr drawn by Cyprian and Augustine, without alerting his readers to his departure from tradition on that point. Bede's good-thief-as-martyr did not elicit much later support, although the idea did get a hearing in the thirteenth century.

A second post-patristic view which gained some scholastic traction was articulated by an anonymous ninth-century Carolingian writer. In 812 Charlemagne asked his archbishops for information on baptism. The answers varied, some focusing on patristic theology, some on early Christian liturgies, some on how the rite was performed locally, and some mixing these elements. Early responses were recycled later in the ninth century. The Carolingian anonymous reprises Gregory Nazianzus with his own salient modifications. Gregory mentions five forms of baptism. The anonymous agrees but handles the subdivisions somewhat differently. First is the typological baptism of the Israelites in the Red Sea. Next is John the Baptist's baptism of repentance, involving water but not the Holy Spirit. Third is the perfect baptism of Christ, involving water and the Holy Spirit.[33] Like Gregory, the author bypasses the debate on when Christ's institution of baptism occurred. But he then observes that the perfect baptism of Christ has its own three subdivisions:

> There are three kinds of baptism. The first is the baptism by which the stains of sin are washed away in the font of regeneration. The second is the baptism by which someone is baptized by his own blood in martyrdom.... And the third is the baptism of tears, achieved with much travail, as with the one who waters his couch with his tears the whole night long. [Psalms 6:77]

The anonymous cites not only the Psalmist but also a host of biblical figures, from the Old Testament and New Testament alike, who manifested this tearful repentance, "on account of which, mercy was the result."[34]

Two issues surface in this account. Without further discussion, the Carolingian anonymous gives Gregory's baptism of tears a creative misreading as a valid, non-ritual form of the perfect baptism instituted by

Brepols, 1960), 405–6: "Ille qui talis ad crucem venit ex culpa ecce qualis a cruce recedit ex gratia; ... est confessione martyr effectus."

33. Susan A. Keefe, ed., *Water and the Word: Baptism and the Education of the Clergy in the Carolingian Empire*, 2 vols. (Notre Dame: University of Notre Dame Press, 2002), text 8, c. 1–2, 2:226–27.

34. Ibid. c. 3, 2:227–28: "Tria sunt genera baptismi. Primum baptismum que sordes peccatorum per regenerationis lavacrum abluuntur. Secundum baptismum quoqui sanguine suo per martyrium baptizatur.... Est et tertium baptismum lacrimarum quod laboriosus transagitur, sicut ille qui per singulas noctes stratum suum lacrimis rigavit; ... per quam misericordiam consecuti sunt."

Christ, fully on a par with the font and the martyr's blood. And, despite his typological understanding of the Red Sea event, he draws no distinction between the Old Testament recipients of the baptism of tears, as he understands it, and those who benefited from it according to the New Testament. He withholds comment on whether this baptism of tears remains available in the post-biblical era. While sometimes inclined to reduce the nature and number of those baptized by their tears, and whether or not they were aware of his work, some later thinkers, as we will see, agree with the Carolingian anonymous that the baptism of tears so understood is an acceptable and efficacious form of baptism.

The Twelfth Century: Canonists and Theologians to Mid-Century

Bede and the Carolingian anonymous aside, the reemergence of widespread discussion of baptism by desire began at the turn of the twelfth century. The revival was launched by Bonizo of Sutri. Bonizo is known as a canonist and controversialist. He wrote, acted, and suffered in support of Matilda of Tuscany during the struggles in Italy unleashed by the Gregorian reform movement of the late eleventh century. He was forced out of the see of Sutri, and then out of the see of Piacenza, blinded and mutilated by his enemies. Most of the authorities on whom he draws in his *Liber de vita christiana* (1089/90) are earlier canonists. He typically cites their opinions and those of their ultimate patristic sources without naming names. This work addresses the problem of sacraments administered by contemporary clerics deemed by reformers to be heretics, schismatics, or excommunicates, a population enlarged and given a high profile by the investiture controversy. To that issue Bonizo adds his own theological and pastoral concerns. That his work manifests these concerns is no surprise. It has been recognized that canonical collections in this period, while they purport merely to anthologize earlier authorities, do not lack authorial agendas. Even if these works lack commentaries on the passages cited or prefaces explaining the authors' procedures and goals, their selectivity can express their opinions on disputed teachings in the received tradition. Collectors may suggest that there is more than one acceptable way of dealing with debated questions by citing authorities on various sides and leaving the matter open. But they sometimes take their own stands, if obliquely. They may omit authorities they oppose and confine their citations to authorities they support, presented as if they alone constitute the normative law of the church. They may edit or update the authorities they cite, recalling them so as to buttress the contemporary principles and practices which they themselves advocate.[35] Given the upheavals of the day, Bonizo thinks it important to spell out who may rightly administer the sacraments, including baptism, and not just who may receive them, and the correct procedures to be followed in each case.

Bonizo prefaces his instructions by citing, largely verbatim, Augustine's *De baptismo* treatment of the good thief. He underscores Augustine's agreement with Cyprian that the thief was no martyr. Bonizo concurs. The thief died for his crimes, not for the name of Christ: "Nor did he suffer because he believed, but believed while he was suffering."[36] Bonizo agrees that Christ granted the effects of baptism to the thief. At the same time, he shares the *De baptismo* comparison with, and assessment of, the case of Cornelius. Notwithstanding his prior illumination and salvation by the direct gift of the Holy Spirit, Cornelius did the right thing by presenting himself to St. Peter for ritual baptism, and Peter did the right thing by requiring it. It is Cornelius who supplies the suitable example, and the relevant precedent, in the present day.[37]

In addition to appropriating this aspect of the Augustinian legacy, Bonizo shares the misreading of Gregory of Nazianzus on the baptism of tears found in the Carolingian anonymous. For Bonizo, the baptism of tears redeemed the repentant in Old and New Testament history alike. He does not treat the baptism of tears merely as repentance for post-baptismal sin. He places all his biblical examples on a level charismatic playing field.[38] They also occupy an odd place in his argument. For Bonizo stresses the importance of ritual baptism in laying down the canonical and liturgical norms for its proper celebration. While he appeals to the unreconstructed Augustine on the good thief, he ends by rejecting baptism by desire as such, associating himself, virtually verbatim, with the lapidary judgment of Gen-

35. On this work, its place in Bonizo's career, and its sources, see Ludovico Gatto, *Bonizone di Sutri e il suo Libro ad Amicum: Ricerche sull'età gregoriana* (Pescara: Editrice Trimestre, 1968), 63–69; Bonizo of Sutri, *Liber de vita christiana*, 2nd ed., ed. Ernst Perels, Nachwort by Walter Berschin (Berlin: Weidemann, 1998), xvi–xxxiii, 405*. For fuller details, see Walter Berschin, *Bonizo von Sutri*, Beiträge zur Geschichte und Quellenkunde des Mittelalters 2 (Berlin: Walter De Gruyter, 1972), 3–21, 57–75, 95–101. For the characterization of pre-Gratian canonical collections in general, see James A. Brundage, *Medieval Canon Law* (London: Longman, 1995), 33–34, 37; Greta Austin, *Shaping Church Law around the Year 1000: The Decretum of Burchard of Worms* (Aldershot: Ashgate, 2009), 5, 9–12, 217, with Burchard as an exemplary case in point at 90–196.

36. Bonizo, *Liber*, praeambula 3, 2–3: "nec quia credidit passus est, set dum patitur credidit."

37. Ibid., 3–5.

38. Ibid., 1.3, 15.

nadius: "Strictly speaking, we do not believe that any catechumen, however much he dies with good works, has eternal life unless the sacrament [of ritual baptism] is fulfilled in him by martyrdom." Bonizo amplifies this assertion with the comparisons drawn by Gennadius between martyrs and baptismal candidates.[39]

Not all canonists in this period take such a dismissive line, even as they insist on the observance of the letter of the law in ritual practice. A sitting bishop as well as a canonist, Ivo of Chartres (1096–1116) warmly defends baptism by desire. The way he raises the question suggests that, by the time he writes, the investiture controversy, so problematic for Bonizo, had abated in France. The *Panormia* attributed to Ivo, if not by him, reflects his teachings. It launches its discussion with a critique of Augustine, one that makes highly selective use of the bishop of Hippo's authority, in support of a far more definite, and more liberal, policy than that found in the final stages of Augustine's *oeuvre*, or the *Liber* of Bonizo.

As we have seen, the anti-Donatist Augustine observes that it would be impious to think that Christ's apostles were never baptized, albeit we have no explicit evidence on when this event took place. He offers no opinion of his own on this debate. The *Panormia* resuscitates the question. Its opening salvo sides with those convinced that the foot-washing episode at the Last Supper (John 13:3–11) provides a clear answer. When Christ told St. Peter that, since he had already bathed, it was his feet alone that needed to be washed, the Lord was referring to Peter's prior baptism. And, in addressing Peter, Christ was referring to the apostles collectively, in the person of their leading member. Thus, all the apostles were baptized before the Last Supper. It would be calumny to say that we remain in ignorance on this subject.[40]

Given the next point, which the author addresses with no transitional

39. Ibid., 1.33, 28–29: "Catechumenum quamvis in bonis operibus defunctum est vitam eternam non credimus, excepto dumtaxat, nisi martyrii sacramentum in eo compleamur."

40. *Panormia* 1.105, ed. under the name of Ivo of Chartres by Bruce Brasington and Martin Brett, 64: "Si eos quibus scriptum non est utrum fuerint baptizati, sine baptismo de hac vita recessisse contendimus, ipsis calumpniamur apostolis qui preter apostolum Paulum, quando baptizati fuerint, ignoramus, sed ipsos baptizatos esse per hoc nobis innotescere potuit, quod beato Petro Dominus ait, Qui lotus est non indiget nisi ut pedes lavat." This text is drawn from the interim edition of Brasington and Brett, accessible at: http://wtfaculty.wtamu.edu/brasington/panormia.html, posted August 16, 2005. On the *Panormia* as a work not by Ivo but as abbreviating his *Decretum*, see Christof Rolker, "Ivo of Chartres and the *Panormia*: The Question of Authorship Revisited," *Bulletin of Medieval Canon Law*, n.s. 28 (2008): 39–53; idem, *Canon Law and the Letters of Ivo of Chartres* (Cambridge: Cambridge University Press, 2010).

remarks, we may wonder whether he thinks that the baptism of the apostles was a ritual baptism or a baptism by desire. For, having cited the consensus position on the martyrs who die for their faith in Christ and are redeemed without having passed through the font,[41] he moves on to catechumens as discussed by the anti-Donatist Augustine. Folding observations made elsewhere in Augustine's works on God's invisible grant of grace into his *De baptismo* defense of the salvation of the good thief, the *Panormia* author extracts several findings. First, beginning with the blunt assertion that the thief had not been previously baptized, he dismisses as beneath consideration Augustine's shaky anti-Pelagian hypothesis on that score. Second, he agrees that the thief was not a martyr. He was crucified for his crimes, not for the name of Christ. Third, God can and does convey His grace invisibly. No pride or contempt of religion was present in the thief. He was faced with imminent death and non-negotiable necessity. Since he manifested the faith and conversion of heart which validly substitute for the font if it is unavailable, he was granted salvation and the promise of heavenly bliss. Moreover, the author rejects the claim that this option was a one-off, applying to the good thief alone. He omits reference to Cornelius. In his concluding remarks, he maintains that the conditions applying to the thief continue to apply. True, these conditions would be obviated in the absence of sincere faith and conversion of heart or if a convert who could accede to the font chooses to spurn it. But, absent such defects, baptism by desire was, is, and remains valid. The *Panormia* offers a comparison with infant baptism. Just as God's power and beneficence supply what is lacking in the case of an infant who cannot have faith or exercise free will, so in the case of a believing and repentant adult convert, "the goodness of the Omnipotent supplies what is lacking," that is, the effects of the ritual made impossible by forces beyond his control.[42]

41. *Panormia* 1.106–108, 64–65.

42. Ibid. 1.109, pp. 65–66: "Augustinus de unico baptismo, libro IIII. Baptismi vicem aliquando implere passionem de latrone illo cui non baptizato dictum est, Hodie mecum in paradiso, beatus Ciprianus non leve documentum assumit, quod etiam atque etiam considerans invenio non tantum passionem pro nomine Christi is quod ex baptismo deerat posse supplere, sed etiam fidem conversionemque cordis, si forte ad celebrandum misterium baptismi in angustiis temporum succurri non potest. Neque enim latro ille pro nomine Christi crucifixus est, sed pro meritis facinorum suorum, neque quia credidit passus est, sed dum patitur credit. Quantum itaque valeat etiam sine visibili baptismi sacramento, quod ait apostolus, Corde creditur ad iustitiam, ore autem confessio fit ad salutem, in illo latrone declaratum est. Sed tunc impletur invisibiliter, cum misterium baptismi non contemptus religionis sed articulus necessitatis excludit, et sicut in illo latrone quod baptismi sacramento defuerit, complevit Omnipotentis benignitas, quod non superbia vel contemptu sed necessitate defuerat, sic infantibus qui baptizati

While Bonizo of Sutri and the author of the *Panormia* thus invoke their chosen sources to take sharply different tacks in treating baptism by desire, manipulating their authorities in their own ways, neither position is emphasized exclusively in Gratian's *Decretum*. Recent research indicates that this text underwent two recensions, the first by the author now called Gratian I (ca. 1140) and the second by the author now called Gratian II (ca. 1145). These two Gratians may be the same person, although there are cogent reasons for thinking that this is not the case.[43] In any event, baptism is treated in the third part of this text, the *De consecratione*, found only in the second recension. This part of the text does not contain authorial *dicta*, or the evaluations and judgments on conflicting authorities for which Gratian's work is so justly famous. The *De consecratione* cites at length and largely verbatim the passage also found in the *Panormia*, giving the anti-Donatist Augustine's defense of the good thief's conversion on the cross and its reception by Christ. Likewise referencing Augustine's *De baptismo* and Cyprian by way of Augustine, Gratian II agrees that the good thief was crucified for his crimes, not for the name of Christ. Headlining this passage with the notion that the martyr's shedding of blood can take the place of ritual baptism, he agrees that the thief was no martyr. What the thief did offer and what Christ accepted were his faith and conversion of heart. This mode of baptism is valid if the rite cannot be celebrated for lack

---

moriuntur eadem gratia omnipotentis explere credenda est, quod non ex impia voluntate sed ex etatis indigentia nec corde credere ad iustitiam possent, nec ore confiteri ad salutem. Baptismus quidem potest inesse ubi conversio cordis non defuerit. Conversio autem cordis potest quidem inesse non percepto baptismo, sed contempto baptismo non potest. Neque ullo modo dicenda est conversio cordis ad Deum cum Dei sacramentum contemnitur."

43. The leading proponent of the "two Gratians" thesis is Anders Winroth, *The Making of Gratian's Decretum* (Cambridge: Cambridge University Press, 2000), with conclusions on dating the two recensions on pages 140 and 142 and discussion of whether they were one or two distinct authors on pages 122, 175–95; see also Winroth's response to critics of this thesis in idem, "The Making of Gratian's *Decretum*," *Bulletin of Medieval Canon Law*, n.s. 26 (2004–06): 1–29; idem, "Marital Consent in Gratian," in *Readers, Texts, and Compilers in the Earlier Middle Ages: Studies in Medieval Canon Law in Honour of Linda Fowler-Magerl*, ed. Martin Brett and Kathleen G. Cushing (Aldershot: Ashgate, 2009), 111–21. Support for Winroth's thesis is indicated in Peter Landau, "Gratian and the *Decretum Gratiani*," in *The History of Medieval Canon Law in the Classical Period, 1140–1234: From Gratian to the Decretals of Gregory IX*, ed. Kenneth Pennington and Wilfried Hartmann (Washington: The Catholic University of America Press, 2008), 22–54 on pages 24–25, 37–40. Kenneth Pennington and Wolfgang Müller, "The Decretists: The Italian School," in ibid., 121–73 on page 129, note the argument that the *De consecratione* was written by an author different from Gratian II but do not either support or refute it. For more on the issue of dating the two recensions, see Atria A. Larson, "Early Stages of Gratian's *Decretum* and the Second Lateran Council," *Bulletin of Medieval Canon Law*, n.s. 27 (2007): 21–56.

of time, in an emergency situation. Gratian II agrees with the principle that this option is not applicable to converts able to receive ritual baptism who reject it out of contempt for the sacrament. When forces beyond their control supervene, God can, and does, make up the deficit, granting His grace without the visible sacrament. As with the *Panormia*, Gratian II omits Augustine's argument that the thief's acceptance was unique.[44]

But the *De consecratione* does not leave it at that. Gratian II also proposes that the model to be followed is that of Cornelius. Not confining himself to the *De baptismo* and other works where Augustine actually discusses Cornelius, he inserts the centurion's example into a text dealing with a rather different issue, fictive baptism. Gratian II cites Augustine's letter to the Donatist Vincentius Victor, adding quotations from John 3:3-5 and Matthew 5:20 and alluding to the case of Simon Magus in Acts 8:18–23. Even those saved invisibly by direct action of the Holy Spirit should proceed to the font, lest they tempt God and thereby nullify their own conversion. Unlike the hypocritical Simon, filled with an unclean spirit, Cornelius was filled with the Holy Spirit before the ritual baptism he fitly accepted. Entry into the kingdom of Heaven requires rebirth by both water and the Spirit, even if the candidate exceeds the righteousness of the Scribes and Pharisees. Weaving together this point about Cornelius with Augustine's plea to his addressee to give up his schism, the citation adds that when such catechumens receive the rite they should be sure to seek baptism in the Catholic church and not some heterodox sect. Otherwise, unlike Cornelius, they manifest a contempt for the sacrament that invalidates it in their case.[45] Still elsewhere, quoting in full the rigorous position of Gennadius

44. Gratian, *Decretum* D. 4 de cons. c. 34, ed. Aemilius Friedberg in *Corpus iuris canonici*, 2 vols. (Leipzig: Tauchnitz, 1879–80); reprt. Union, NJ: Lawbook Exchange, 2000), 1:1372–74. On Gratian's use of the *Panormia* as well as the authentic works of Ivo of Chartres, see Landau, "Gratian," 23–29, 31, 32, 38, 39.

45. Gratian, *Decretum* D. 4 de cons. c. 149, 1:1410: "Catecuminus catholicus heretico baptizato prefertur. Idem [i.e. Augustine, *Ad Vincentium Victorem* IV]. XXX. Pars. Non dubito, catecuminum catholicum divina karitate flagrantem heretico baptizato anteponere; sed etiam in ipsa intus ecclesia catecuminum malo baptizato anteponimus. Nec ideo tamen sacramento baptismi, quo iste nondum, ille iam inbutus est, facimus iniuriam. §. 1. Merito enim centurio nondum baptizatus Simoni baptizato anteponitur. Iste enim etiam ante baptismum S. Spiritu accepto repletus est: ille et post baptismum inflatus est inmundo spiritu. Verumtamen Cornelius, si Spiritu sancto iam accepto baptizari noluisset, contemptu tanti sacramenti reus fieret. §. 2. Sicut autem bono catecumino baptismus deest ad regnum celorum capessandum, sic malo baptizato vera conversio. Qui enim dixit; 'Nisi quis renatus fuerit ex aqua et Spiritu sancto, non potest intrare in regnum celorum,' ipse etiam dixit: 'Nisi habundaverit iustitia vestra plus quam scribarum et Phariseorum, non intrabis in regnum celorum'." The case of Simon Magus, minus

also cited by Bonizo but attributing it to Augustine's *Ad Fortunatum*, Gratian II asserts that a convert who has faith and good works but who dies before he can be ritually baptized is not to be regarded as saved, unless he is a martyr.[46] In sum, Gratian's *Decretum* gives with one hand and takes with the other. This classic text in the teaching of canon law supports Augustine on the efficacy of baptism by desire in the case of the good thief. But it also cites hard line authorities who would limit its sufficiency or even its availability altogether. While Gratian II devotes more space and more detailed attention to the passage defending the good thief's baptism by desire than he gives to the other two passages noted, beyond that it is hard to see in him a clear authorial position, aside from his decision to ignore Augustine's anti-Pelagian disquisitions on the thief. Nor does he raise the question of whether the good thief's salvation was unique or whether it reflects an ongoing possibility.

While the sources they include and conflate as well as those they dismiss by omission enable these canonists to focus the doctrine of baptism by desire in their own chosen way, when they have one, it is the theologians of the early twelfth century who grasp the torch, highlighting the patristic contradictions which they inherited and pitting the authorities who they think got it right against those with whom they disagree. They also go beyond the authors of late eleventh- and early twelfth-century canonical collections in several other respects. The theologians apply to baptism a distinction, one with a long future history, which had surfaced in the Eucharistic controversy sparked by Berengar of Tours in the late eleventh century. This is the distinction between the *sacramentum*, the physical medium of baptism, and the *res sacramenti*, the spiritual grace which this medium contains and effects. Key figures in both of these respects were Anselm of Laon (d. 1117) and the theologians associated with him.[47]

---

this comparison with Cornelius and not via Augustine as a source, will resurface in chapter 2 of this book.

46. Ibid., D. 4 de cons. c. 37, 1:1377.

47. A survey of the history of this distinction is given by Ronald F. King, "The Origin and Evolution of a Sacramental Formula: *Sacramentum tantum, res et sacramentum, res tantum*," *The Thomist* 31 (1967): 21–82, although King sees it as applied only to the Eucharist before Peter Lombard and as not systematically extended to baptism until the thirteenth century. He also sees this distinction as grasped imperfectly unless the tripartite form, as expressed in the title of his paper, is used. Earlier studies of baptism by desire starting with the Laon masters include Artur Michael Landgraf, "Das *sacramentum in voto*," in idem, *Dogmengeschichte der Frühscholastik*, 4 vols. in 8 (Regensburg: Friedrich Pustat, 1952–56), 3/1:210–53 on pages 218–20; Ludwig Ott, *Untersuchungen zur theologischen Briefliteratur der Frühscholastik unter besonderer*

Anselm of Laon and his followers certainly agree on the necessity of baptism, but they also offer strategies for circumventing the anti-Pelagian Augustine. One tactic is simply to remind readers that, although in the *Retractationes* Augustine reconsidered his *De baptismo* argument on the good thief and withdrew him as an example, he also confirmed the substance of his teaching on baptism by desire. Baptism by desire is, thus, efficacious, and Augustine supports that doctrine. A second gambit is to reinterpret both Augustine and the Acts of the Apostles in the light of the distinction between the *sacramentum* and *res sacramenti* of baptism. While infants require the *sacramentum*, the Laon masters observe that adult converts can sometimes receive the *res sacramenti* without it.[48]

The thinkers in this group do not speak with one voice on the good thief. Some regard him as saved and glorified but as a unique case and not as a precedent for current practice.[49] Others think that the thief's salvation and beatitude are by no means unique. Agreeing with Bede, they regard him as possessing the full complement of virtues: not just faith and conversion of heart but the faith, hope, and charity needed by all who attain the kingdom of Heaven.[50] The Laon masters are quite willing to turn Augustine's argument concerning Cornelius on its head. As they see it, Cornelius is a classic example of the availability of the *res sacramenti* before and apart from the *sacramentum*: "Before Peter arrived, Cornelius had the *res sacramenti*. Peter added the *sacramentum*."[51] And, far from modeling what some-

---

Beruchsichtigung des Viktorinerkreises, BGPTMA 34 (Münster: Aschendorff, 1937), 495–548; Marcia L. Colish, *Peter Lombard*, 2 vols. (Leiden: Brill, 1994), 2:232–39. The most recent treatment of Anselm of Laon and his followers on baptism is Cédric Giraud, *Per verba magistri: Anselme de Laon et son école au XII siècle* (Turnhout: Brepols, 2010), 272–85; Giraud notes their use of the *sacramentum/res sacramentum* distinction on pages 275–76.

48. On infants: *Sententie divine pagine* in *Anselms von Laon systematische Sentenzen*, ed. Franz Bliemetzrieder, BGPMA 18/2–3 (Münster: Aschendorff, 1919), 42–43, 46; *Liber Pancrisis* no. 46; Sentences of the School of Anselm of Laon no. 366, 369; *Antequam quicquam fieret* no. 7, ed. Odon Lottin, *Psychologie et morale aux XII et XIII siècle*, 6 vols. (Gembloux/Louvain: J. Duculot/Abbaye de Mont César, 1948–60), 5:42–43, 275, 337–38. On baptism by blood as the only alternative to the font: Sentences of the School of Laon no. 365 in Lottin, 5:273–74; *Dubitatur quibusdam* in *Das Schrifttum der Schule Anselms von Laon und Wilhelms von Champeaux in deutschen Bibliotheken*, ed. Heinrich Weisweiler, BGPTMA 33/1–2 (Münster: Aschendorff, 1936), 347. On these two issues, see Giraud, *Per verba magistri*, 275–80, 282–85.

49. Sentences of the School of Laon no. 367 in Lottin (as in note 48), 5:274.

50. *Deus hominem fecit perfectus* in Weisweiler (as in note 48), 297, repeated verbatim in *Dubitatur quibusdam*, ibid., 317: "Tribus de causis latro paradisum introivit: Fidem habuit, quando hominum secum morientem regnaturum credidit; spem, quando aditum celi ab eo petiit; caritatem, quando confratrem et conlatronem iniquitatis sue redarguit."

51. Sentences of the School of Laon no. 364 in Lottin (as in note 48), 5:273: "Cornelius

one already possessing the *res sacramenti* needs must do, Cornelius models, simply, those persons granted baptism by desire then and now: "For if, before they can be baptized, death prevents them, by reason of necessity and not out of any negligence on their part, good will alone suffices for their salvation and brings them into union with the church."[52]

Whether citing Augustine positively or citing Augustine against Augustine, these masters open the door to the efficacy of baptismal grace to those prevented from receiving the rite by extenuating circumstances and through no fault of their own. This is a position which the Laon masters apply to sacraments in general, and not just to baptism. In a statement which, as reformulated by Peter Lombard, had a long career ahead of it, the author of the *Liber Pancrisis* asserts, "God, who alone can do all things and who forgives the sins of whomever and howsoever He wills, in no way has to remit them with the help of the sacraments."[53]

Those familiar with Peter Abelard will not be surprised to learn that he does not credit Anselm of Laon or the Laon masters for their willingness to criticize authorities with whom they disagree, or for the deftness of their maneuvers in subverting or relativizing them. Yet, in the event, Abelard does not receive the credit he deserves for supporting baptism by desire either. Instead, he is cast by Bernard of Clairvaux in the role of the villain of the piece, the chief opponent of that doctrine who most needs to be refuted by its advocates. Not only does Abelard share that doctrine with him but, *pace* Bernard, he is also instrumental in bringing Ambrose's *De obitu Valentiniani* back into play, an authority to whom Bernard also appeals. However, Abelard yokes Ambrose, and baptism by desire, with some troublesome fellow travelers. How the more basic agreement of Bernard and Abelard on that doctrine was obscured and devolved into a theological stand-off is critical for understanding the status which Ambrose acquired as a key

---

antequam Petrus venisset, habuit rem sacramenti. Petrus addidit sacramentum." See also *Sententie Atrebatensis*; *Liber Pancrisis* no. 52 in ibid. 5:49, 428.

52. *Sententie Anselmi* in Bliemetzrieder (as in note 48), 84: "Sed tamen, antequam baptizari possint, si morte preventi fuerint, ita quod necessitas et nulla eorum negligentia impediveret, sola bona voluntas eos sufficit ad salvationem, et hec eos in ecclesie unitatem facit." See also *Liber Pancrisis* no. 59 in Lottin (as in note 48), 5:54: "salvi sunt et bene possunt dici baptizati"; *Sententie divine pagine* in Bliemetzrieder (as in note 48), 46: "non contemptus religionis sed articulus excludit necessitas."

53. *Liber Pancrisis* no. 57 in Lottin (as in note 48), 5:53: "Deus qui omnia solus potest et qui, cui vult et quomodo vult, peccata dimittit, nullius indiguit ad illa remittenda auxilio sacramenti." Cf. Peter Lombard, *Sententiae in IV libris distinctae* 4. d. 4. c. 4.10, 3rd rev. ed., ed. Ignatius C. Brady, 2 vols. (Grottaferrata: Collegium S. Bonaventurae, 1971–81), 2:258: "... Deus, qui suam potentiam sacramenti non alligavit."

authority on this subject and for the ways in which masters henceforth address it, whatever their conclusions.

Abelard places Ambrose's funeral oration front and center in his *Sic et non* and his *Theologia christiana.* In the earliest versions of the *Sic et non,* he treats only the doctrine of God, the Trinity, and Christology. It is not until the versions produced between 1121 and 1126 that he includes questions on the sacraments.[54] *Quaestio* 106 asks whether ritual baptism is always required for salvation. Choosing the most uncompromising authority on the affirmative side, who admits only the baptism by blood exception, he cites Gennadius. Moving to the debate's other side, he first brings forward two figures who, he claims, demonstrate the posthumous salvation of pagans. This topic, in addition to being abrasive, is actually off the subject. In raising it here, Abelard reflects his own failure to implement the sage counsels for validating the accuracy and relevance of authorities given in the preface of his *Sic et non.*[55] One of these pagan examples is the infant Dinocrates. Ignoring Augustine's hypothesis concerning his premortem state and attributing no particular virtues to him, Abelard simply notes that Perpetua prayed Dinocrates out of Hell, as related in her *vita.* Abelard's second example is an adult and a genuine virtuous pagan, the emperor Trajan. There already existed several versions of the *vita* of Gregory the Great, deemed to have prayed Trajan out of Hell. Abelard cites as his authority John the Deacon's tenth-century *vita* of Gregory. However, the version of the Trajan legend which Abelard presents is found neither in John the Deacon's text nor in any other known source, for that matter, prior to the *Sic et non* itself.[56] Abelard then moves on to cite authorities who support baptism by desire in adult Christian converts. After quoting 1 Corinthians on the point that the Holy Spirit bloweth where it listeth, he offers the two arguments that, in his estimation, really count: Augustine's *De baptismo* as modified by the *Retractationes* and Ambrose's *De obitu Valentiniani.* It is the latter text

54. Constant J. Mews, "On Dating the Works of Peter Abelard," *AHDMLA* 52 (1984): 73–134 at 121–23, 131; reprt. in idem, *Peter Abelard and His Legacy* (Aldershot: Ashgate, 2001), no. VII. For dates of other works of Abelard discussed here, see ibid., 110, 112–15, 129, 132.

55. Peter Abelard, *Sic et non* q. 106, ed. Blanche Boyer and Richard McKeon (Chicago: University of Chicago Press, 1976), 341–50. For the preface, see ibid., 89–104; trans. in *Medieval Literary Theory and Criticism,* ed. A. J. Minnis and A. B. Scott with the assistance of David Wallace (Oxford: Clarendon Press, 1988), 87–100.

56. Abelard, *Sic et non* q. 106, 348–49. Noted by Giraud, *Per verba magistri,* 279, 280–81, but without comment on Abelard's mangling of his sources or on the inappositeness of these examples. On these figures, see Colish, "The Virtuous Pagan" (as in note 8), no. XVII, on page 2 for Dinocrates and on pages 11, 20–22, for the Trajan legend and Abelard's treatment of it.

that Abelard uses to anchor this side of the debate.[57] If Abelard is listing these authorities in ascending order of importance, then he gives Ambrose's Valentinian top billing on the subject.

Quite possibly Abelard wanted his pupils to work their way through *quaestio* 106 of the *Sic et non* and to find the salvation of the virtuous pagan persuasive, and not just that of the believing convert deprived of the font. For, he reprises the theme of the virtuous pagan and presents it in passages where he also defends baptism by desire in other works. Abelard cites Cornelius as a virtuous pagan saved by faith prior to baptism in *Scito te ipsum* (1138/39).[58] In his commentary on Romans (1133/37), he makes the more general point that those predestined to salvation will be saved, whether they can be ritually baptized or not.[59] But it is in his *Theologia christiana* (by 1140) that he brings Ambrose's funeral oration most fully into play, in a discussion suggesting why this move led contemporary thinkers to regard Abelard as a flawed proponent of Ambrose and as unacceptable on baptism by desire itself.

In contrast to his methodology in the *Sic et non*, in the *Theologia christiana* Abelard only cites authorities who buttress his desired conclusions. He streamlines his defense of baptism by desire, confining himself to two citations.[60] One is a retread of his earlier garbled reference to the Gregory/Trajan story, which he again misattributes to John the Deacon.[61] The other is the *De obitu Valentiniani*. Dismissing John 3:3–5 and the martyr exception alone as irrelevant without further ado, Abelard offers the following assessment of the merits of Ambrose's Valentinian:

But evoking still greater admiration is what blessed Ambrose himself wrote to the emperor's sisters in the *Consolation on the Death of Valentinian*. There, the aforesaid saint indicated that everyone knew that he [Valentinian] had already been catechized by him, but not yet baptized. Before the act, on account of his life's good works, he was granted grace, and, without baptism, was numbered among the elect after his death.... Did he not receive what he requested?[62]

57. Abelard, *Sic et non* q. 106, 349–50.

58. Peter Abelard, *Scito te ipsum*, ed. Rainer M. Ilgner, CCCM 190 (Turnhout: Brepols, 2001), 42–43.

59. Peter Abelard, *Commentaria in Epistolam Pauli ad Romanos* 2, ed. Eligius M. Buytaert, CCCM 11 (Turnhout: Brepols, 1969), 119.

60. Peter Abelard, *Theologia christiana* 2.112–115, ed. Eligius M. Buytaert, CCCM 12 (Turnhout: Brepols, 1969), 182–84.

61. Ibid., 2.112, 182.

62. Ibid., 2.113–14, 182–84: "Sed fortasse illud maiori admiratione suscipitur quod *In consolationem super morte Valentiniani* imperatoris ad sorores ipsius beatus scripserit Ambrosius. Ubi

As with Ambrose, this last sentence is no rhetorical question but states a solid fact, although what Abelard accents is the doctrine of predestination and the emperor's virtues, omitting his orthodox faith and yearning for baptism. Then, after affirming Valentinian's baptism by desire, Abelard dragoons Ambrose's argument to the service of one of his most controversial positions. Both Trajan and Valentinian lived during the Christian era. But what of those upright pagan philosophers who lived before the gospel was preached? Should they not, as well, be included among the blessed, thanks to God's goodness and mercy?[63]

Prudently, Abelard's disciples do not go this last mile with him, although they second his stress on intentionality over ritual.[64] The Abelardian who offers the crispest defense of baptism by desire is the anonymous author of the *Ysagoge in theologiam* (1140s). He cites both the *De obitu Valentiniani* and Augustine's unmodified *De baptismo* in his clinching argument. Considering the fate of just persons who possess faith and love but who cannot receive the rite by reason of necessity, he concludes, "With respect to these good people, who are prevented, both authority and reason can confirm that they proceed to eternal rest; ... faith without the sacrament must be valid."[65]

Given this evidence, it is paradoxical indeed that, starting with Bernard of Clairvaux and Hugh of St. Victor, twelfth-century advocates of baptism by desire posit what they take to be Abelard's position as the one they need

---

quidem praedictus sanctus omnino adstruere intelligitur eum a se iam catechizatum sed nondum baptizatum, ex ante actae vitae bonis operibus veniam impetrasse post mortem et sortem electorum sine baptismi gratia percepisse; ... non habet quam poposcit?"

63. Ibid., 2.115, 184: "Quod si hi, post Evangelii traditionem, sine fide Iesu Christi, vel gratia baptismi, tanta apud Deum ex ante actae vitae meritis obtinuerant, quid de philosophis ante adventum Christi, tam fide quam vita clarissimis, diffidere cogamur ne indulgentiam sint assecuti, aut eorum vita et unius Dei cultus—quem ipsi tunc tempore praecipue habuerunt et scribendo praedicaverunt—magna eis a Deo dona tam in hac quam in futura vita non acquisierit et quae necessaria saluti essent ostenderit ... et tanta sit divinae gratia misericordiae, ut invitis quoque suae praestat beneficia?"

64. See, in general, Richard E. Weingart, "Peter Abailard's Contribution to Medieval Sacramentology," *RTAM* 34 (1967): 159–78 on pages 168–69, 177; idem, *The Logic of Divine Love: A Critical Analysis of the Soteriology of Peter Abailard* (Oxford: Clarendon Press, 1970), 186–92; Constant J. Mews, *Abelard and Heloise* (Oxford: Oxford University Press, 2005), 129–30, 190, 222; Mews extends this judgment to the *Sententie Hermannus*, which he reads, on pages 218 ff., as a *reportatio* of Abelard's teaching and not as the work of a disciple.

65. *Ysagoge in theologiam* 2, ed. Artur Michael Landgraf in *Écrits théologiques de l'école d'Abélard* (Louvain: Spicilegium Sacrum Lovaniense, 1934), 184–88; quotations on pages 184: "alii iusti dum in articulo necessitatis fides cum dilectio prevenitur"; and 187–88: "Nam de bonis, qui praeveniuntur, et auctoritas vel ratio afferri potest, quia ad requiem transeunt; ... fides sine sacramento debet valere."

to overturn.[66] A key text in promoting this outcome is Bernard's *Epistola* 77 (1125 or 1126/28). This letter responds to Hugh's request for clarification on a number of theological issues, among them the necessity of ritual baptism. Recent scholarship has made considerable headway in revising the earlier image of Bernard as a reactionary wet blanket determined to quash nascent scholasticism.[67] But it is above all to Hugh Feiss and his followers that we owe an appreciation of Bernard's role in placing baptism by desire at the center of scholastic debates, in stigmatizing Abelard as its most noxious opponent, and in bringing Ambrose's authority to bear on it, purged of the idiosyncratic baggage with which Abelard had saddled it.[68]

Hugh's original letter does not survive, but Bernard reprises its content before giving his reply. Hugh adverts to an unnamed current thinker whose insistence on the unqualified necessity of ritual baptism he finds problematic. Nor does Bernard mention this master's name, although he treats his identity and teaching as common knowledge. The consensus then, and now,

66. David E. Luscombe, *The School of Peter Abelard: The Influence of Abelard's Thought in the Early Scholastic Period* (Cambridge: Cambridge University Press, 1970), 210, 225, 246.

67. Jean Châtillon, "L'Influence de S. Bernard sur la pensée scolastique au XIIe et XIIIe siècle," in *Saint Bernard théologien*, Actes du Congrès de Dijon, 15–19 septembre 1953, Analecta Sacri Ordinis Cisterciensis 9 (Rome: Tipografia Pio X, 1953), 268–88; reprt. in idem, *D'Isidore de Séville à saint Thomas d'Aquin: Études d'histoire et de théologie* (London: Variorum Reprints, 1985), no. V, which notes Bernard's response to Hugh on pages 276–77, 279–80, 287, but without specifying its content; likewise, Artur Michael Landgraf, "Der hl. Bernhard in seinem Verhältnis zur Theologie des 12. Jahrhunderts," in *Bernhard von Clairvaux: Mönch und Mystiker*, ed. Joseph Lortz (Wiesbaden: Franz Steiner Verlag, 1955), 44–62 notes this correspondence on pages 44–45, 53 but without discussing its doctrinal content; that topic is not mentioned at all by John F. Sommerfeldt, "Bernard of Clairvaux and Scholasticism," *Papers of the Michigan Academy of Sciences, Arts, and Letters* 48 (1963): 265–77; William J. Courtenay, "Sacrament, Symbol, and Causality in Bernard of Clairvaux," in *Bernard of Clairvaux: Studies Presented to Jean Leclercq*, Cistercian Studies Series 23 (Kalamazoo: Cistercian Publications, 1973), 111–22; or Robert Baumkirschner, "Bernhard von Clairvaux als Kirchenlehrer in dogmengeschichtlicher Schau," *Cistercienser Chronik* 86, n.F. 145 (1979): 85–109. Matthew A. Doyle, *Bernard of Clairvaux and the Schools* (Spoleto: Centro Italiano di Studi sull'Alto Medioevo, 2005), reprises earlier literature on pages 8–9nn25–31; on pages 72–73 he simply notes Bernard's "dextrous use of the Fathers and the Bible" in this letter but does not discuss its teaching on baptism. Doyle's chief concern is Bernard's friendly relations with early scholastics, not doctrinal influences.

68. Hugh Feiss, "*Bernardus Scholasticus*: The Correspondence of Bernard of Clairvaux and Hugh of St. Victor on Baptism," in *Bernardus Magister*, ed. John R. Sommerfeldt, Cistercian Studies Series 135 (Kalamazoo: Cistercian Publications, 1992), 349–78; P. Marek Chojnacki, *Il Battesimo e l'Eucharistia: Fonti rituali della vita cristiana secondo San Bernardo di Chiaravalle* (Rome: Pontificia Università Gregoriana, 2002), 80, 96–97, 216; Emero Stiegman, intro. to Bernard of Clairvaux, *On Baptism and the Office of Bishop*, trans. Paulina Matarasso, Cistercian Fathers Series 67 (Kalamazoo: Cistercian Publications, 2004), 85–147.

is that he is Abelard, rather than some other contemporary supporter of the anti-Pelagian Augustine, or of Gennadius.[69] Bernard begins his defense of baptism by desire not by analyzing and refuting the unnamed opponent's argument but by citing the authorities who most strongly support his own case. These authorities are the same ones adduced by Abelard and by the later Abelardian author of the *Ysagoge in theologiam*, Augustine's *De baptismo* and Ambrose's *De obitu Valentiniani*. These patristic texts, says Bernard, are the foundations on which his teaching rests. And, he maintains, their doctrine is identical: "Both give the same opinion, which we also affirm."[70] Taking his cue from the Laon masters, Bernard argues that Augustine's *Retractationes* does not nullify the force of his *De baptismo* on the doctrinal essentials. The good thief was no martyr. But he underwent conversion of heart on the cross. He received the invisible grace of baptism without the rite, not out of contempt for religion but out of imminent necessity and lack of time. Even for martyrs, Bernard observes, it is not their suffering alone but also their faith and contrition that win them the crown. Bernard is well aware of Augustine's hypothesis concerning the thief's possible pre-crucifixion baptism. He dismisses it out of hand as the feeble argument it is. Bernard rejects Augustine's attempt to problematize the thief's earlier status as both unfounded and distasteful. It rests on no evidence whatsoever. It is a transparent debater's trick that tries to put Augustine's Pelagian opponents in the position of proving a negative. Bernard recognizes this move as a mere rhetorical ploy, one as unworthy as it is unavailing. Even more important, this shaky claim conflicts with Augustine's sounder and more basic teaching that some people receive grace and sanctification by invisible means.[71]

Having thus shown his grasp of rhetoric and his aptitude for playing the Augustine-versus-Augustine game, Bernard turns attention to Ambrose's text. His first move is to attack the unnamed opponent who, he claims, ignores or misunderstands Ambrose, with an *ad hominem* argument. The opponent is a negligent and misinformed scholar:

He really should read Ambrose's book *On the Death of Valentinian*, if he has not read it. If he has already read it, he should bring it to mind. If he recalls it, he

69. Stiegman, intro. to Bernard, *On Baptism* (as in note 68), 90–92, 94–97, 119–26, 145 gives full details on the adherents of this consensus identifying the unnamed master as Abelard.

70. Bernard of Clairvaux, *Epistola* 77.2.7 in *Opere di San Bernardo*, ed. Ferruccio Gastaldelli, trans. Ettore Paratore, 6 vols. (Milan: Scriptorium Claravallano, 1984–2000), 6/1:352: "uterque idem profecto sensit, quod fatemur et nos." Text also in *Sancti Bernardi opera*, 8 vols. in 9, ed. Jean Leclercq et al. (Rome: Editiones Cistercienses, 1955–77), 7:184–200.

71. Bernard, *Ep.* 77.2.7, ed. Gastaldelli, 6/1:352–54.

should not pretend otherwise, but should focus without uncertainty on the fact that the saint granted salvation to a man who died unbaptized, by faith alone, confidently conceding to good will what was lacking in opportunity.[72]

It is beyond belief, Bernard continues, that this unnamed opponent should fail to ground his opinion on "these two columns, I mean Augustine and Ambrose," on which correct doctrine is based, "with whom I also believe that a man can be saved by faith alone, through his desire to receive the sacrament, in the event that he is forestalled by imminent death or any other insuperable force."[73] The good thief shows that faith sufficed in biblical history. Valentinian shows that faith continues to suffice in the post-biblical age as well. Just as martyrdom can still replace ritual baptism in the here and now, so baptism by desire also remains an efficacious option. Now, as always, God scrutinizes the minds, hearts, and inner intentions of converts and accepts their faith and repentance without the shedding of blood or the pouring of water. Provided that such persons do not spurn the font if it is available, they are assured of salvation.[74] Thus Bernard concludes, having seized the flag of intentionalism from the Abelardian citadel by shifting the force of Ambrose's message from virtues and good works to faith and heartfelt desire.

Hugh of St. Victor takes Bernard's argument seriously and incorporates it into his *De sacramentis Christianae fidei* (1137), which in turn puts it into wide circulation in the twelfth century, along with the views of the Laon masters. As we would expect, Hugh's organization and presentation of his material are more scholastic than Bernard's. He starts by citing authorities who would exclude baptism by desire before wielding the weapons forged by Augustine's *De baptismo* and Ambrose's *De obitu Valentiniani* against them. Hugh offers two modest departures from Bernard. In Hugh's eyes, martyrdom, the most glorious form of baptism, may involve modes of death other than the shedding of blood, such as suffocation, strangling, or drowning.[75] This last point suggests that Hugh was aware that Valen-

72. Ibid., 6/1:352: "Librum certe Ambrosius *De morte Valentiniani* legat, si non legit; recolat si iam legit; non dissimulet, si recolit, et advertet sine dubio, sanctum homini non baptizato et morte fidenter de sola fide praesumere, et tribuere indubitanter bonae voluntati quod defuit facultati."

73. Ibid., 6/1:354: "Ab his ergo duabus columnis, Augustinum loquor et Ambrosium; … Cum his … credens et ipse sola fide hominem posse salvari, cum desiderio percipiendi sacramentum, mors anticipans seu alia quaecumque vis invincibilis obviaverit."

74. Ibid., 6/1:374–75.

75. Hugh of St. Victor, *De sacramentis Christianae fidei*, 2.6.7, ed. Rainer Berndt, Corpus Victorinum 1 (Münster: Aschendorff, 2008), 385–88.

tinian met his death by strangulation, whether by his own hand or not. Additionally, having added this new wrinkle to the understanding of martyrdom, Hugh, in agreement with the Laon masters, states that baptism by desire requires not faith alone or faith and repentance alone but a fuller complement of theological virtues: "Thanks to true faith and true charity it [baptism by desire] can be gained by one to whom the visible sacrament of water is not available." Along with the authorities already presented, Hugh adds in conclusion, "there are many others who could be adduced to support it."[76]

Scholastics in the next generation repeatedly cite the authorities presented by Hugh on baptism by desire in arguments that sometimes merely summarize his conclusions, whether to agree or disagree.[77] A rather straightforward reprise of Hugh's teaching, amplified by the inclusion of the *sacramentum/res sacramenti* distinction, is offered by the largely Victorine *Summa sententiarum* (1139/41). The anonymous author opens with the question of who can receive the *res* of baptism without the *sacramentum*. Along with the martyrs, he says, following Cyprian as cited in Augustine's *De baptismo* on the good thief and Ambrose on Valentinian, this condition applies to those who have faith in Christ but who cannot receive the rite by reason of imminent necessity. The author tackles head-on not only the contradictions he finds in Augustine but also the authority of St. John's Gospel. He agrees that the *Retractationes* does not trump Augustine's support of baptism by desire as such and that his anti-Pelagian disquisitions on the good thief do not offer a coherent or persuasive alternative. In addition, Augustine's acceptance of baptism by blood disproves his claim that the font is always required.

As for the conversation between Nicodemus and Christ in John 3:3–5, the author states that it is overturned by another New Testament text. In that connection, it is striking that neither he nor any other scholastic who later seeks to relativize or disqualify John 3:3–5 brings up what John himself goes on to say after this famous proof-text. For John 3:22 and John 4:1–2 report that Jesus and His disciples went into Judea, baptizing and making converts, although it was the disciples who did the baptizing; this behavior

76. Ibid., 387–88; quotation on page 388: "Nisi forte dicere velis neminem fidem veram et caritatem veram habere posse qui visibile sacramentum aque non sit habiturus; ... multa sunt alia que super hoc approbandum adduci potuissent."

77. On these debates, see Ott, *Untersuchungen*, 496–97, 499–526, 540; Landgraf, "Das *sacramentum in voto*," 210–37 with thirteenth-century figures treated on pages 237–53; Colish, *Peter Lombard*, 2:532–39.

aroused the anger of the Pharisees and led Jesus and the disciples to leave Judea, which they did via Samaria. The latter passage is the lead-in to the encounter between Christ and the Samaritan woman at the well recounted in John 4:7–30. Rather than taxing St. John with inconsistency, the author finds a pertinent countercitation in Matthew 10:39. As St. Matthew relates, in commissioning His apostles Christ says that he who loses his life for the Lord's sake will find it. We should understand Christ not only as referring to martyrs who give up their lives in the literal sense. The Lord is also referring to those who abandon a life of sin and false belief. They will find new life and eternal life in Christ. And they will find it by invisible grace. Matthew, the author notes, does not mention the need for any ritual in this passage. Accordingly, he concludes, "by these authorities it is evident that faith without the rite suffices, for those not having the time, which reason also proves."[78]

This was by no means the only strategy used to neutralize John 3:3–5 by the countercitation of the Gospel of Matthew. Roland of Bologna has another way of getting around that text. He opens the discussion of baptism in his *Sentences* (ca. 1150) by adverting to the debate on when Christ instituted ritual baptism.[79] One date cited was the moment when Christ received His own baptism in the Jordan. Another was at the point of his conversation with Nicodemus. The third was when Christ commissioned His apostles after His resurrection, charging them to baptize all nations in the name of the Trinity (Matthew 28:19). For Roland, this third view "seems the most

78. *Summa sententiarum* 5.6, *PL* (Paris, 1880), 176:131B–132C; the quotation is at 132A: "Istis auctoritatibus patet quod sufficit fides sine sacramento non habentis tempus, quod et ratio probat." At ibid. 132C, the author, in presenting the martyr exception alone for catechumens, cites one bishop Anselm as his source: "Item ex Anselmi episcopi: excepto duntaxat nisi sacramentum martyro compleat." This language comes closest to that of Bonizo of Sutri. The Anselm in question is neither Anselm of Canterbury nor Anselm of Lucca and has not been identified. The most recent scholarship has rejected the idea that the author of the *Summa sententiarum* was Otto bishop of Lucca (1138/46) or that theology was taught in Lucca at that time by him or anyone else. See Marcia L. Colish, "Otto of Lucca, Author of the *Summa sententiarum*?" in *Discovery and Distinction in the Early Middle Ages: Studies in Honor of John J. Contreni*, ed. Cullen J. Chandler and Steven A. Stofferahn (Kalamazoo: Medieval Institute Publications, 2013), 57–72; confirmed by Ronald G. Witt, *The Two Latin Cultures and the Foundation of Renaissance Humanism in Italy* (Cambridge: Cambridge University Press, 2012), 263–66.

79. Surveys of the range of twelfth-century opinions on this question are provided in the intro. to *Maître Simon et son groupe De sacramentis*, ed. Heinrich Weisweiler (Louvain: Spicilegium Sacrum Lovaniense, 1937), lxxx–lxxxix; Wendelin Knoch, *Die Einsetzung der Sakramente durch Christus: Eine Untersuchung zur Sakramententheologie der Frühscholastik von Anselm von Laon bis Wilhelm von Auxerre*, BGPTMA, n.F. 24 (Münster: Aschendorff, 1963), 92–94, 150; Colish, *Peter Lombard*, 2:524.

probable to us." From this perspective, Christ's message to Nicodemus was designed to inform him about a rite not currently offered but one that would soon be made available in the post-resurrection age.[80] Roland places this notion in a wider context. People, he observes, cannot be held responsible for failing to observe rules not yet legislated. His invocation of this principle may reflect the fact that Roland was a canonist, an early commentator on Gratian, as well as a theologian adept at the art of source criticism.

In rising to the defense of baptism by desire, this foundation laid, Roland draws primarily on the authority of Ambrose's *De obitu Valentiniani* and on Augustine to a far lesser extent. He recognizes the distinction between the external baptismal rite and its inner spiritual benefits, but he frames this distinction his own way. For Roland, baptism can be conveyed *in re et voluntate*, in fact and will, *in re tantum*, in fact alone, or *in voluntate tantum*, in will alone.[81] Roland sees the *res* as the physical medium of the sacrament used in the external rite, not as its inner spiritual content and effects. It is the *voluntas*, the candidate's inner intention and desire, that enables an adult convert to acquire its grace without the *res*. Despite his idiosyncratic vocabulary, Roland's affirmation of this possibility appeals directly to the example of Valentinian:

> By will alone, as in the situation of an adult and discerning person who hastens to the font in order to be baptized but is seized by death before he can receive it, he is advanced to salvation, as was the case with Valentinian, of whom St. Ambrose writes, ... "Did he not receive the grace he requested?"[82]

With Ambrose's language and his Valentinian in place, Roland also agrees with Hugh of St. Victor that such a candidate must have faith and charity. This finding settles the hash of authorities who argue that the rite is always required. Roland also refutes another claim hostile to Ambrose's position, one first arising in the twelfth century, of which we will hear more in the following. We cannot write off Ambrose's funeral oration merely as an effort to sanitize the posthumous image of Valentinian in order to console his sisters. Rather, Roland insists, Ambrose used this text and occasion

80. *Die Sentenzen Rolands nachmals Papstes Alexander III*, ed. Ambrosius M. Gietl (Freiburg: Herder, 1891), 198–99; quotation on page 199: "Que sentencia nobis probabiliter videtur."

81. Ibid., 209.

82. Ibid.: "Voluntate tantum, ut in adulto et discreto qui currit ad baptismo ut baptizetur, sed antequam accedat, morte in via preocupatur, qui profecto salvatur, ut habetur de Valentiniano, de quo scribit beatus Ambrosius ...'sed gratiam poposcit non amisit?'" On Roland's definitions of *res* and *voluntas*, see ibid., 209.

to proclaim a basic and universal principle: "Faith and conversion of heart toward God obtain the recompense of baptism; ... the will stands for the deed."[83]

Roland also brings in Augustine's *De baptismo* on the heels of his citation of Ambrose. He treats Augustine as useful primarily in reviewing the circumstances that may obviate but, more importantly, validate baptism by desire. Accenting those enabling conditions, Roland enlarges Augustine's list. In addition to sudden death enroute to the font, an adult with faith, charity, and the right intention may be saved if deprived of ritual baptism because he is incarcerated by an enemy before he can accede to it, or captured and held by barbarian infidels who know or care nothing about Christian baptismal rites.[84] The effect of Roland's entire analysis is to undermine opposition to baptism by desire and to offer some fresh reasons why its possibilities should be expanded.

While eclectic and independent, Roland of Bologna has sometimes been viewed as a follower of Abelard, if not on baptism by desire. Another mid-century scholastic who draws on Abelard as well as Hugh of St. Victor and who opposes the unnamed master stigmatized by Hugh and Bernard of Clairvaux is Robert of Melun.[85] Throughout his *oeuvre*, Robert treats baptism by desire as equivalent to baptism by blood, albeit their para-ritual modes differ. His exegesis dates to the 1140s. In his earliest work, the *Questiones de divina pagina*, he presents Augustine's conclusion in *De baptismo* as a sufficient refutation of John 3:3–5, although without expressly mentioning the good thief.[86] Next, in his *Questiones de Epistolis Pauli*, commenting on Romans 10:10, where the Apostle says that he who believes and confesses Christ and His resurrection from the dead will be justified and saved, Robert presents this statement as settling the matter by itself: "Thus, conver-

83. Ibid.: "fides et conversio cordis in Deum obtinet vicem baptismi; ... voluntas pro opera."

84. Ibid.

85. Raymond-M. Martin, "Les idées de Robert de Melun sur la péché originel," *Revue des sciences philosophiques et théologiques* 11 (1922): 390–415 on pages 404–6, citing many texts then unpublished. For Robert's *Questiones de divina pagina* and *Questiones de Epistolis Pauli* we will cite *Oeuvres de Robert de Melun*, ed. Raymond-M. Martin, 3 vols. in 4 (Louvain: Spicilegium Sacrum Lovaniense, 1932–52). Since the section of Robert's *Sentences* on the sacraments remains incomplete and unedited, we will rely, for that work, on the manuscript evidence supplied in Martin's paper. For the most recent treatment of Robert's life and works, see Constant J. Mews, "Between the Schools of Abelard and Saint-Victor in the Mid-Twelfth Century: The Witness of Robert of Melun," in *L'École de Saint-Victor de Paris: Influence et rayonnement du moyen âge à l'époque moderne*, ed. Dominique Poirel (Turnhout: Brepols, 2010), 121–38.

86. Robert of Melun, *Questiones de divina pagina* 93 in *Oeuvres* (as in note 85), 1:47–48.

sion of heart toward God justifies, before baptism is received."[87] Robert's last work is his *Sentences* (1150s), whose section on the sacraments was incomplete when he left the schools to accept ecclesiastical preferment in his native England. The manuscript evidence found by his editor shows the development of Robert's argument. He now cites the *De obitu Valentiniani* as well as Augustine's *De baptismo*. But his main addition to the debate is to propose another tactic for blunting the force of John 3:3–5. This passage, Robert observes, requires interpretation. It does not lay down a universal rule, as some would have it. Rather, it applies, and applies only, to converts desiring baptism who have the opportunity to receive the sacrament ritually but who fail to do so. It does not apply to those unable to receive the rite: "Indeed, to one who wills it but cannot accede to it in fact, [baptism] is accorded in the sight of God; the will is accepted for the deed, where the opportunity is lacking."[88]

Another English scholastic teaching in France in the second quarter of the twelfth century who supports baptism by desire is Robert Pullen. Many of the points he makes in his *Sentences* (ca. 1142) are found in other contemporary advocates of this doctrine. Robert Pullen's account is unusual in two respects. Unlike most commentators on this theme, he treats baptism by blood after, not before, baptism by desire. He also uses language in this context more typically applied to the sacrament of penance. Robert finds the idea that Christ instituted ritual baptism only after His resurrection quite helpful.[89] While nowadays the rite is generally available, Robert has no doubt that baptism by desire remains available as well. In his view, the reason for this judgment is unequivocal. It is God's grace that enables the saints in any age to acquire the faith, the good deeds, and the perseverance needed for their salvation, whatever the mode by which it is achieved.[90] Thus, to deny the continuing possibility of baptism by desire would be to place limits on the divine grace that was, is, and always will be granted. Robert Pullen buttresses this principle with a list of biblical worthies justified by their faith, before or apart from any ritual practices that may have obtained at the time. He begins with Abraham and ends with

87. Robert of Melun, *Questiones de Epistolis Pauli* in *Oeuvres* (as in note 85), 1:138: "Ecce quod conversio cordis a Deum iustificat antequam baptismus suscipiatur."

88. Robert of Melun, *Sententiae*, as quoted by Martin, "Les idées de Robert de Melun," 406n1: "Quod autem quis vult et non potest pro facto in conspectu dei habetur, qui voluntatem ubi facultas deest reputat pro opere."

89. Robert Pullen, *Sententiarum libri octo* 6.26, *PL* (Paris, 1854), 186:849A–B.

90. Ibid., 5.8, *PL* 186:835D–837A.

the good thief and Cornelius. Robert dismisses Augustine's disquisitions on the possible pre-crucifixion baptism of the thief, advising readers that ritual baptism had not yet been instituted. Augustine's hypothesis is thus based on an anachronism. The thief simply received salvation on the cross because of his faith. The same historical argument disposes of objections to baptism by desire based on John 3:3–5. Christ did not require Nicodemus to receive a rite not yet instituted. Robert shares this argument with Roland of Bologna although without specifically aligning himself with supporters of the post-resurrection thesis.[91] To be sure, once ritual baptism was established, one cannot be saved if he is able to receive it but rejects or abstains from it "against obedience." But, if "prevented by death, he cannot perish [eternally]."[92] Augustine on Leviticus is Robert's chosen authority for anchoring this assertion. Invisible grace also justified Cornelius. In his and in similar cases, if the baptismal rite is received it is merely an external *ex post facto* sign of that already existing condition.[93] For the truly repentant, "faith perfects the will and obtains salvation.... Faith thus saves even someone not washed by baptism.... For they [the aforementioned examples] were accepted by the Holy Spirit before baptism, that they might magnify God; and therefore, as believers, they were justified."[94] These opportunities continue to be granted by God before, during, and after baptism, then and now.[95] And the requisite repentance in one baptized by desire can be called both the "contrition of heart" and the "compunction" that make operative the works of love engendered by the faith that takes the place of the font.[96]

By the middle of the twelfth century, most of the masters entering the debate on baptism by desire had come to rely on Ambrose's *De obitu Valentiniani* and on Augustine's *De baptismo*, with or without reference to his *Retractationes*, and his Leviticus commentary. While they join contemporaries who defend this doctrine, two followers of Gilbert of Poitiers who left sentence collections in the 1140s presented as *reportationes* of their master's teaching take a different tack. Rather than seeing Ambrose and Augustine as supporting baptism by desire, if from different perspectives,

91. Ibid., 5.10, *PL* 186:838B–D.

92. Ibid., *PL* 186:838D: "contra obedientiam; ... morte praeventurus perire non potest."

93. Ibid., *PL* 186:838C.

94. Ibid., 5.11, *PL* 186:839B–C: "Fides ergo complet voluntatem, obtinet salutem.... Fides ergo salvat etiam quem baptismus non lavat.... Ergo ante baptismum spiritum sanctum acceperunt, ut magnificarent Deum, ac per hoc jam credentes, justi erant."

95. Ibid., 5.10, *PL* 186:839C.

96. Ibid., *PL* 186:838B–D; quotations at 838B: "corde contritro"; "compunctio."

they pit Ambrose, and especially Cyprian, against Augustine. One of these Porretans, after framing the question in terms of the *sacramentum/res sacramenti* distinction,[97] observes that "there are three things that give us certitude of eternal salvation: ritual baptism, martyrdom, and the testimony of Christ." Anyone baptized in any of these ways, if he dies suddenly, "is judged by Catholics to be saved." This condition applies as fully to the third condition as to the first two. Such is manifest in the case of "the thief, who is judged to be saved."[98]

The Porretans then turn to the controversies on the post-biblical availability of baptism by desire. They ignore the anti-Pelagian Augustine's hypothesis regarding the good thief's pre-crucifixion state and the question of when Christ instituted ritual baptism. As they present the debate, the battle lines are drawn between Cyprian and Ambrose, who got it right, and Augustine, who is the doctrine's chief enemy. The reason why Augustine got it wrong is that he garbled Cyprian's text. Rather than citing Cyprian correctly, Augustine distorted him to say that a catechumen, however rich in good works, cannot be saved without ritual baptism; indeed, he would be damned unless he received it. Here, they see Augustine's sloppy scholarship as the source of the position defended later in the fifth century by Gennadius, whom they do not name, making it even harsher. This sweeping claim, the Porretans note, has not gone unchallenged. Happily, defenders of the tradition of Cyprian and Ambrose have succeeded in correcting the teaching they ascribe to Augustine, showing that it does not apply globally: "Those maintaining Cyprian's opinion say that Augustine was referring to those holding [ritual] baptism in contempt."[99] Having thus disposed of Augustine as they choose to read him, the Porretans affirm that their position, illustrated by Cornelius as well as by the thief, applies to later ages as well. It receives unambiguous and authoritative backing from Cyprian, Ambrose, and their master Gilbert, and also the support of reason.[100]

97. Nikolaus M. Häring, ed., "Die Sententie magistri Gisleberti Pictavensis episcopi (I)," *AHDLMA* 45 (1978) 83–180 at 7.1, 146–47.

98. Ibid., 7.7, 148: "Tria enim sunt que dant nobis certum argumentum eterne salutis: baptismus scilicet, martirium, et testimonia Christi; ... iudicandus est a Catholicis esse salvatus ... ut de latrone, iudicandus est salvari." The same point is made, if less fully, in the second version of this text; see Nikolaus M. Häring, ed., "Die Sententie magistri Gisleberti Pictavensis episcopi (II): Die Version der florentiner Handschrift," *AHDLMA* 46 (1979): 45–105 at 7.9, 70.

99. "Sent. mag. Gisleberti (I)" 7.10–14, 148–49; quotation at 7.13–14, 149: "illi qui tenent Cypriani sententiam dicunt Augustinum dixisse de contemptoribus baptismi." See also "Sent. mag. Gisleberti (II)" 7.10–12, 70–71.

100. "Sent. mag. Gisleberti (I)" 7.11–12, 149; "Sent. mag. Gisleberti (II)" 7.11–12, 70–71.

While their defense of the continuing efficacy of baptism by desire and of unmediated salvation by the Holy Spirit coincides with the conclusion of some of their contemporaries, the Porretans's approach to this topic bears its own fingerprints. In this context, it is atypical to privilege Cyprian over Ambrose on the positive side of the argument. But their critique of Augustine as having misinterpreted Cyprian, and as an authority who can thus be dismissed as irrelevant as well as wrong, is distinctive. It is of a piece with the Porretans' handling of another baptismal issue, single versus triple immersion, on which they also stigmatize and discard Augustine for allegedly misquoting the correct, and currently useful, teaching of Cyprian.[101]

The Porretans, as noted, eschew the help that their argument might have received had they aligned themselves with masters who argue for Christ's institution of ritual baptism after His resurrection. At the same time, they testify to the vigor of the contemporary debate on baptism by desire and to the range and diversity of the source-critical analyses undergirding it from various directions. There are also influential masters who take issue with this doctrine, ranging from misgivings to the outright rejection of its current availability. One such figure is the master known only as Simon (ca. 1140/50). Master Simon capitalizes on the fact that the argument he defends is strengthened by the view that ritual baptism was already on the books when Christ spoke to Nicodemus.[102] He thinks that the church should be extremely wary of making exceptions to it. Simon accepts the martyr concession. He allows that the good thief and Cornelius, moved by faith and love, were most likely saved. While he cites Augustine, he argues that neither of these figures provides a model for post-biblical practice. Simon cites another authority, one not invoked elsewhere in this debate, Ezekiel 33:12. There, the prophet reports that the Lord has instructed him to inform the Israelites that the righteousness of the just will not deliver them when they sin. No one should trust in his own righteousness rather than in the law of the Lord. This text, for Simon, is a red flag. It advises circumspection. We cannot know the inner state of those apparently

101. For the Porretans on this question and their patristic source-criticism, see Marcia L. Colish, "Authority and Interpretation in Scholastic Theology," in *Religious Identity and the Problem of Historical Foundation: The Foundational Character of Authoritative Sources in the History of Christianity and Judaism*, ed. Judith Frishman et al. (Leiden: Brill, 2004), 369–86 on page 378; reprt. in eadem, *Studies in Scholasticism* (Aldershot: Ashgate, 2006), no. II, 1–16 on page 9. For the wider twelfth-century debate on that issue, see eadem, *Peter Lombard*, 2:541–43.

102. *Maître Simon et son groupe De sacramentis*, ed. Weisweiler (as in note 79), 9–10. See Weisweiler's discussion of Simon's position in his intro. on pages lxxxiii, xciii–xciv. His reading of that position as a defense of conditional baptism is an overinterpretation.

saved by God's direct response to their faith and charity. Prudence suggests that "judgment should be suspended on the aforesaid matters, since the unknown decision of God is hidden from us. For the church does not affirm that they are saved. Neither does she say that they are damned."[103] On the one hand, we should not think that God's power to save can be curtailed. On the other, if we allow that ritual baptism is optional, we contradict the Savior's express words in John 3:3–5. To the extent that Simon sees a way out of this dilemma, he offers the following proposal:

> God has the power to save them. But the church should not number them within the ranks of the faithful.... No one, unless [ritually] baptized, should be judged by the church to be among the faithful.... While it is found in Holy Scripture that such persons were saved, or might be saved, by the power of the omnipotent God to whom nothing is impossible, this condition does not apply to the church.[104]

Simon thus admits that persons may be saved by the grace of baptism before they arrive at the font or in its absence. Even if this is the case, however, they should not be buried in consecrated ground. Nor should special prayers be offered on their behalf, unless some definite information concerning their state is received by special divine command, as Augustine suggests. Absent such supernatural clarification, it is impossible to verify their inner condition. The church, therefore, should err on the side of caution. These reservations and institutional restrictions, Simon concludes, are the policies that the church should follow. Even if the status of those baptized by desire were to lack the incertitude with which he views it, their example would still fail to have normative value: "For the privileges of individuals do not make a general law."[105]

Simon attaches another condition to baptism, one which he does not explain with any clarity but one that was to receive later discussion. This is the notion of baptismal character. The church fathers had used this term without clearly defining it. Simon is also quite vague on what he means by it. He refers to it twice. "In baptism," he states, "the character of his king is signed upon the baptized."[106] In addition, Simon compares the character acquired in baptism with the character acquired in unction: "Baptism signs

103. Simon, *De sacramentis*, 9: "Sed de his dicitur, quod occulto nobis, quia incognito Dei iudicio, reservantur. Ecclesia enim eos salvatos esse non affirmat, quamvis nec dampnari dicat...."

104. Ibid., 9–10: "Potens est autem Deus salvare illos; sed eos Ecclesia in numero fidelium non computat.... Nemo nisi in baptismo consequitur, ut iudicio Ecclesie inter fideles reputetur. Si quando itaque in scripturis sanctis sic invenitur, quod salventur vel salvari possint, ad Dei omnipotentis, cui nihil impossibile est potentiam, non ad Ecclesie referendum est sententiam."

105. Ibid., 10: "Sed privilegia singulorum non faciunt legem communem."

106. Ibid.: "In baptismo quippe charactere sui regis baptizatus insignitur...."

with Christ's character those entering the world; that of unction designates those leaving it for the vision of God."[107] This observation makes an unhelpful comparison between what the consensus held to be a necessary and unrepeatable sacrament and what many twelfth-century masters regarded as an optional and repeatable one.[108]

Simon is judged by his editor to have been the first twelfth-century theologian to mention the concept of baptismal character, a view not universally shared.[109] Whether or not Simon was first out of the gate, his analogy compares baptismal character with the insignia worn by one enlisting in a ruler's service. Glosses on this theme later in the century attached to the writings of the canonist Huguccio compare this insignia to the belt worn by a military officer.[110] A real difficulty with these images is that military and political emblems of allegiance or office are external. They are put on when their wearer pledges his fealty or receives his commission. They can also be taken off when he is not on duty or when he retires or departs from active service or changes his political allegiance. Simon does not explain whether he regards baptismal character in this physical and temporal light, or whether he thinks it is a spiritual and durable acquisition. He does not explain

107. Ibid., 42–43: "sicut autem baptismus intrantium, sic est hec unctio exeuntium sacramentum. Baptismus hoc seculum ingredientes Christi caractere signat; unctio egredientes divine visione representat."

108. See Colish, *Peter Lombard*, 2:609–13.

109. Weisweiler, intro. to his ed., lxxxix–xci, xciii–xcvi. Previous scholarship has seen initial scholastic applications of this term mainly in the second half of the twelfth century, and in canonists not theologians. See F. Gillmann, "Der 'sakramentale Character' bei den Glossatoren Rufinus, Johannes Faventius, Sicard von Cremona, Huguccio und in der *Glossa ordinaria* des Dekrets," *Der Katholik* 90, ser. 4/5 (1910): 300–13; idem, "Zur Lehre vom 'sakramentalen Character,'" ibid., 90, ser. 4/6 (1910): 215–18. Gillmann deals with this notion as applied to all sacraments held to be unrepeatable. Landgraf, "Das *sacramentum in voto*," 146, 174, holds that Stephen Langton was the first thinker of the twelfth century to mention the idea, in the last quarter of the century. On the other hand, Nikolaus M. Häring, "Character, Signum und Signaculum: Die Einführung in die Sakramententheologie des 12. Jarhhunderts," *Scholastik* 32 (1956): 182–212, does not mention Master Simon and sees as the first theologian to apply this concept the anonymous author of the Pseudo-Peter of Poitiers gloss on Peter Lombard's *Sentences*, the first version of that text dating to 1160/70; he then tracks its use, as applied specifically to baptism, in theologians from the 1180s to the mid-thirteenth century. At the same time, in "St. Augustine's Use of the Word *Character*," *Mediaeval Studies* 14 (1952): 79–97, Häring shows that scholastics who credited Augustine with this coinage did so in error; the term existed in earlier Christian writers, without a clear definition, and we should not imitate the scholastics by retrojecting their later understandings of it back into the patristic period. The present study will omit scholastic discussions of baptismal character that were not specifically related by their authors to the themes of baptism by desire, fictive baptism, or forced baptism.

110. Gillmann, "Der 'sakramentale Character,'" 304n3, 306n1.

whether he thinks baptizands of all kinds receive it, or receive it equally. Nor does he indicate how baptismal character may be related either to the *sacramentum* or the *res sacramenti* of baptism itself. This topic will receive a good deal of future attention, not only in connection with baptism by desire but also in discussions of fictive and forced baptism, and not always with the cogency one might want. In his own day, and in this area, Simon's most important achievement was to articulate the disquiet of thinkers who were uncomfortable with the doctrine of baptism by desire and to suggest some of the arguments to which they might appeal.

One such master, known to have agreed with Simon on other aspects of baptismal theology as well, is the anonymous author of the largely Porretan *Sententiae divinitatis* (1138/41). This master's position is quite different from that of the contemporary Porretan sentence collectors discussed earlier. What he shares with them is a marked taste for source criticism. He invokes this methodology in taking a decidedly hard line in support of the necessity of ritual baptism. Nowadays, he asserts, no one can escape damnation without it. While the author is willing to concede that baptism by blood and baptism by desire may have saved some people in the past, he rules out both of these options in the present. To the extent that they were previously available, these alternatives must be viewed as unique personal exceptions from a rule that now universally applies. Two arguments support this contention. One weapon the author wields is that of historical criticism. The martyrs, he observes, lived in the *ecclesia primitiva* before the church was legitimate and before it received official support from the Roman state. But in the present age, Christians are no longer a persecuted minority. So, while baptism by blood may have been efficacious then, the church of the martyrs is not the church of today, and baptism by blood is now irrelevant. Baptism by desire, he admits, does describe the salvation of the good thief on the cross. But the promise of heavenly glory extended to him by Christ was unique. The thief's personal situation made his salvation *sui generis*. Agreeing here with Master Simon, the author of the *Sententiae divinitatis* concludes that the thief, like the ancient martyrs, does not represent a category of persons for whom the same possibilities exist today. The thief is neither a model nor a precedent for twelfth-century practice. Further, the author dismisses the claim that the elect will be saved, baptized or not. Even for the elect, he argues, salvation depends on their own behavior, in this case their willingness to accede to the font.[111]

111. *Die Sententiae divinitatis: Ein Sentenzenbuch der gilbertischen Schule* 5.1, ed. Bernhard Geyer, BGPMA 7/2–3 (Münster: Aschendorff, 1909), 115*–17*, 122*–24*; on the differential effects of baptism, see 122*–23*: "Quod omnibus dimittantur tam damnandis, quam salvandis, generaliter tenet ecclesia. Generale quidem beneficium est; omnibus prodesse debet. Econtra probatur, quod

The author's second line of attack on baptism by desire makes use of literary as well as historical criticism. His target here is a position noted and defended by Roland of Bologna. The *De obitu Valentiniani*, says the author, must be stricken from the list of authorities pertinent to this debate, given the circumstances in which it was written and its literary form. This speech was an occasion piece, he points out; *pace* Roland, it was not a treatise in which Ambrose aimed at presenting a global policy. He was eulogizing a figure whose life, as well as whose death, was problematic, putting the best construction on it that he could. In any case, the goal of a funeral oration is to praise the deceased, accenting his virtues. This is not a literary genre in which one speaks ill of the dead. The orator's task is to comfort the bereaved. Accordingly, Ambrose limited himself to laudatory remarks on Valentinian in addressing the emperor's sisters and chief mourners. Thus, the author concludes, Ambrose's protestations in this text were "words spoken in condolence: not as an assertion, but as a consolation."[112]

That the concerns articulated by Master Simon and the author of the *Sententiae divinitatis* struck a chord in a wider and less specialized segment of the twelfth-century audience can be well illustrated by Otto of Freising. Otto takes to heart the arguments of both of these masters in his *Chronica sive historia de duabus civitatibus*. Despite his pressing duties as a prelate and politician, Otto kept himself informed on the theological issues exciting attention in the schools since his own student days in Paris. Written in 1143/47 and revised with minor changes before 1157, Otto's history updates the two-cities theme of Augustine's *De civitate dei*. He summarizes the Roman past before addressing more recent events. Ancient Rome, he thinks, is of particular relevance to its current German imperial successors. Otto's

non valet nisi praedestinatis. Augustinus super locum ille [Tract. In Ioh. 5.7]: Ministerium baptizandi discipulis tradidit, potestatem vero sibi retinuit, quia sacramenta sunt id quod sunt, sed solis electis efficiunt id quod figurant.... Sacramenta sunt communia bonis et malis; virtus vero sacramentorum, id est peccatorum remissio, solis bonis.... His auctoritatibus probatur, quod solis electis peccata dimittuntur in baptismo. Si dicatur: Generale beneficium est baptismus; omnibus debet valere, subaudiendum est: praedestinatis. Generaliter omnibus praedestinatis omnia dimittuntur peccata. Si vero teneatur sententia illa, quod omnibus in baptismo scilicet salvandis et damnandis, peccata dimittuntur in baptismo, oportet determinari auctoritates illas. Sacramenta sunt id quod sunt, etc., ita debet intelligi: efficiunt, quod figurant, id est, sicut in praesenti coniungimur ecclesiae et efficimur membrum huius corporis, quod est ecclesia, ita in futuro Christo sociabimur, ut simus idem cum ipso, tunc scilicet cum tradetur regnum Deo Patri..." The passage goes on to argue that good baptizands are those who commit themselves to receive the sacrament of penance for their post-baptismal sins. The author does not indicate if this condition applies only to the baptized elect. As Geyer notes, at p. 123* n. 1, the attribution to the Augustinian work made by the author in the passsage quoted is incorrect, since it is not found in that text.

112. Ibid., 116*: "Consolatoria verba sunt; non assertio sed consolatio."

account of the last days of Valentinian II is not entirely accurate.[113] He sets the story of the young emperor's end and of Ambrose's eulogy on him in the year 388. Otto does not report Valentinian's move to Gaul, but he does record the disagreements of the sources on whether he was assassinated by Arbogast or took his own life. Otto then moves to Ambrose's funeral oration. He is forthright in stating that he finds its teaching on baptism by desire deeply problematic, in a passage that deserves to be quoted at length:

This is the Valentinian who, though he was made a catechumen by Ambrose, was prevented by a death of this sort from receiving the sacrament of baptism. The aforesaid bishop wrote a mournful letter with regard to this matter.... And therein we find written, by the same man: ... "He has not lost the grace which he asked for." With this utterance as authority certain theologians of our own time reason, even against the express statement of the Gospel [John 3:3–5] ... that one may be saved without the sacrament of baptism, whether by the pouring out of blood for a witness to Christ's passion, or, as it may be, the Lord's declaration. They argue this because ... they do not consider with proper care under what circumstances authors speak: what it is they say by way of opinion, what by way of consoling themselves in the extremity of their grief. But, although it is true that God's power is not restrained by ecclesiastical rules or by the sacraments, it will yet be necessary for me, who am bound by the Christian rule, to believe that no one can be saved except by such things. Wherefore, although it may be possible for God on His own express testimony ... to save the Jew or the Gentile or unbaptized person without the pouring of blood, yet it will be impossible for me to believe this. And so in such matters the divine power is limited, not for Him but for me.[114]

113. Otto of Freising, *Chronica sive historia de duobus civitatibus*, ed. Adolfus Hofmeister, MGH Scriptores rerum germanicorum in usum scolarum 46 (Hannover: Halm, 1912), 205–6; noted by Ott, *Untersuchungen*, 522–24.

114. Otto of Freising, *Chronica*, 205–6: "Hic est Valentinianus, qui ab Ambrosio catechuminus factus, antequam baptismi gratiam perceperit, morte huiusmodi preventus est. Qua de re predictus episcopus epistolam lugubrem dictavit, quae sic incipit: *Ventrem me doleo...* In qua ab eodem dictum invenitur: 'Quia, quem in Christo regeneraturus eram, amisi, ipse vero gratiam, quam poposcit, non amisit.' Ex qua auctoritate quidam nostri temporis theologi divinant post promulgatam Evangelii sententiam qua dicitur [John 3:3–5], ... aliquem sine sacramento baptismi vel effusione sanguinis ob testimonium passionis Christi vel attestione dominica salvari posse, sic ratiocinantes, quod 'non alligavit Deus sacramentis potentiam suam,' non bene considerantes, quia secundum quid loquantur auctores, quid opinando, quid asserendo, quid ex magnitudine doloris semet consolando. Quod tametsi verum sit, Dei potentiam regulis ecclesiasticis vel sacramentis non cohiberi, mihi tamen, qui Christiana regula stringor necessarium erit credere preter haec neminem salvari posse. Quare, quamvis Deo tanquam omnipotenti Iudeum vel gentilem vel non baptizatum sine effusione sanguinis, ut dictum est, vel attestatione propria possible sit salvare, mihi tamen hoc credere erit impossibile. Et ita divina potentia in talibus non sibi, sed mihi alligitur." Translation: Otto of Freising, *The Two Cities: A Chronicle of Universal History to the Year 1148*, ed. Austin P. Evans and Charles Knapp, trans. Charles Christopher Mierow, intro. by Karl F. Morrison (New York: Columbia University Press, 2002), 298–99.

With the author of the *Sententiae divinitatis*, Otto raises objections to the teaching of Ambrose's *De obitu Valentiniani* by applying literary criticism to that text. While he describes the work as a letter rather than as a funeral oration, and presents it as having been written to console Ambrose himself rather than Valentinian's sisters, he seizes on its perceived limitations as an occasion piece. And, speaking as a sitting bishop, while he admits the impropriety of placing limits on God's saving power, he shares with Master Simon a sense of the need of the Christian community, as well as his own professional need, to follow the ecclesiastical norms currently in force. Beyond that, Otto is less uncertain than Simon on what to believe. The doctrine of baptism by desire is one which he cannot bring himself personally to accept. Otto recognizes that this doctrine has its contemporary defenders. They are mistaken, in his view. Their error, as he presents it, stems from their inadequacy as literary critics. He declines to indicate any of their other positive arguments, contenting himself with John 3:3–5 as a sufficient refutation of them.

The Twelfth Century: Peter Lombard and the Post-Lombardians

One of the striking features of the debate on baptism by desire during the first half of the twelfth century is the number of masters who addressed this question and the range and ingenuity of the arguments which they offered for or against it, even when deploying the same catalogue of sources. This subject continued to attract notable attention in the second half of the century, if not from all masters active in that period. The most visible shift in the climate of opinion is the acceptance of a single text as the template for their discussion of this topic, the *Sentences* (1155/57) of Peter Lombard. The Lombard supports baptism by desire. Many masters in the second half of the twelfth century follow his lead. But unanimity is not the order of the day, be it in the conclusions they draw, the arguments they develop, or the issues with which they associate this doctrine. In particular, the resurgence of anti-sacramental heresy informed the need in some quarters to reassert the mandatory nature of ritual baptism.

Peter Lombard situates his discussion of baptism by desire in the tradition of Hugh of St. Victor and the *Summa sententiarum*, although on some points he sides with other recent and contemporary masters, or approaches his patristic authorities independently. The manner in which he formulates this question is distinctive.[115] The Lombard is well aware that the decision on

115. See, in general, Colish, *Peter Lombard*, 2:528–31, 533, 537–39; see also Philipp W. Rosemann, *Peter Lombard* (Oxford: Oxford University Press, 2004), 149, which states the Lom-

when Christ instituted ritual baptism could be quite useful in the contestations for or against baptism by desire. His handling of that question, however, does not maximize the help it could have given him. The Lombard acknowledges the appeal to St. Matthew by those opting for a post-resurrection dateline, as well as of the appeal to St. John by those arguing for Christ's conversation with Nicodemus. But the institution date which he himself favors is that of Christ's own baptism in the Jordan.[116] That said, he needs to finds a strategy for deactivating John 3:3–5 different from that of colleagues who rest their case on Matthew 28:19. On another front, the Lombard dissociates himself from the notion that baptism by desire was granted to a series of Old Testament examples, whether starting with the Red Sea event or as far back as Abraham. For the Lombard takes sharp exception to the idea that Old Testament rites or events had the same saving power as the New Testament rites or events to whose fulfillment they point.[117] Thus, for him, New Testament examples are the only ones that merit consideration.

The Lombard launches his discussion with a reprise of the *sacramentum/res sacramenti* distinction. With other supporters of baptism by desire, he agrees that adults who possess faith and repentance and who desire baptism of their own free will can, like the martyrs, receive the *res* without the *sacramentum*. As with baptizands who accede to the font, they put on Christ. Peter does not use the language of baptismal character in making this point. But he sees dying to the old man, conformity to Christ, and the sanctification attained thereby, as applying in all the modes of valid baptism.[118] Moving more specifically to baptism by desire, and with an unspoken nod to Bernard of Clairvaux, the Lombard states concisely the position on which he then elaborates: "It is not only suffering, but faith and contrition that take the place of [ritual] baptism."[119] The initial authority he cites in support of this assertion is Augustine's *De baptismo*, and Augustine's recycling of Cyprian on the salvation of the good thief, excused because he was prevented from receiving the rite by reason of necessity, owing to the pressure of time, and without contempt for the sacrament. A further authority not cited by either Augustine or Cyprian but brought forward by Robert of Melun is Romans 10:10, where St. Paul says that the believing heart and the oral confession of faith win jus-

bard's position accurately but which is not concerned with placing it in the context of contemporary debates or with its use of patristic sources.

116. Peter Lombard, *Sent.* 4. d. 4. c. 5, 2:247.

117. Ibid., *Sent.* 3. d. 40. c. 3.1; *Sent.* 4. d. 1. c. 1–2, 2:229, 231.

118. Ibid., *Sent.* 4. d. 4. c. 1.2–c. 4.1, 2:251–55.

119. Ibid., *Sent.* 4. d. 4. c. 4.3, 2:255: "Quod non modo passio, sed fides et contritio, implet vicem baptismi."

tification and salvation. As the Lombard organizes his argument, the Apostle controls the way in which Augustine's *De baptismo* should be read.

What, then, are we to make of Augustine's *Retractationes*? The Lombard presents three tactics for disarming that text, and, by extension, the anti-Pelagian Augustine whom he does not otherwise cite. First, those who claim that Augustine really changed his earlier position on the good thief misread him: "He [Augustine] withdrew the [thief's] example, not the opinion." Second, without mentioning Bernard of Clairvaux's critique of Augustine's attempt to throw the ball into the Pelagians' court by trying to make them prove a negative regarding the thief's putative pre-crucifixion state, Peter simply dismisses this late Augustinian maneuver as a lapse, not as an argument or even as a suggestion to be taken seriously. All that the *Retractationes* tells us for sure is that neither Augustine himself nor the additional research which he says he has done yields anything definite, "since whether he [the thief] was not baptized is uncertain."[120] The *Retractationes* can thus be eliminated as evidence since it sheds no helpful light on the question. That text certainly does not obviate the correct view of the thief stated in Augustine's *De baptismo*. Third, says Peter, Augustine's *Retractationes* position is overturned in any case by Ambrose's *De obitu Valentiniani*. The Lombard quotes the now-standard Ambrosian conclusion, rephrased as a declarative sentence: "For he [Valentinian] received the grace he requested."[121] Thus, while refuting the Augustine Peter rejects, Ambrose supports the Augustine he accepts.

It is only at this juncture, having cemented in place the part of his argument just noted, that Peter brings up John 3:3–5. He deals with it briskly, if laterally, since he holds that ritual baptism was available when Christ interviewed Nicodemus. To be sure, ritual baptism is one way to get to Heaven. But it is not the only way, "for that regeneration occurs not just by [ritual] baptism but also by repentance and blood." Citing St. Paul as well, that is, the Lombard's own exegesis of Hebrews which in turn makes use of the biblical *Glossa ordinaria*, the authorities, or, at least, those on whom Peter rests his case, confirm the sanctifying power of water, blood, and repentance alike. Furthermore, "reason also convinces" on this point.[122]

120. Ibid., *Sent.* 4. d. 4. c. 4.4, 2:256: "Retractavit quidem exemplum, sed non sententiam, … quia utrum non fuerit baptizatus incertum est."

121. Ibid., *Sent.* 4. d. 4. c. 4.5, 2:256: "ille tamen gratiam quam poposcit non amisit."

122. Ibid., *Sent.* 4. d. 4. c. 4.6–c. 4.8, 2:257–59; quotations at c. 4.7, 2:257: "Illa autem regeneratio fit non tantum per baptismum, sed etiam per poenitentiam et sanguinem"; at c. 4.8, 2:257: "Ratio enim suadet." For the citation of Peter's own Hebrews commentary and his use of the *Glossa ordinaria* on that text, see Ignatius C. Brady's annotation *ad loc.* 2:257n1.

The Lombard's technique is to nail down his positive argument before tackling the extreme view that no one except martyrs can be saved without ritual baptism. Here, his method is to cite again the Augustine with whom he agrees against the Augustine he opposes. The ultimate source of the Augustinian opinion which he thereby undermines is actually Gennadius. Having demolished it, he confirms that it is Augustine on Leviticus who gets it right: "Teaching openly on Leviticus, Augustine says that one can acquire and continue in invisible grace without visible sacraments." The function of the rite, if received, is merely to make visible that individual's preexisting possession of invisible baptismal grace. As with Cornelius, if the rite is available, and if time permits, and if necessity does not prevent it, such converts should accede to the font. But one who is prevented from doing so through no fault of his own receives invisible sanctification: "God does not hold it [the omission of the rite] against him, since His power is not bound by the sacraments."[123] This observation stands as Peter Lombard's final word on the modes of baptism now available to adult converts. As with the Laon masters, it is indeed striking that Peter affirms his most sweeping statement about the omnipotence of God's grace in application to baptism, notwithstanding the sacramental order divinely laid down for humankind.

On the whole, theologians writing during the second half of the twelfth century tend to agree with the master of the *Sentences* on baptism by desire. At the same time, they do not always use the same arguments. Less decisive than the Lombard, Bandinus is an interesting case in point. His *Sententiarum libri quatuor* (1170s) is basically an abbreviation of the Lombard's *Sentences*. The approach typical of the abbreviator is to cut to the chase, giving his master's solutions while gutting his text of the analysis and evaluation of sources on which they rest.[124] Bandinus presents a few pros and cons regarding persons who receive the *res sacramenti* without the *sacramentum*, although without citing either the Lombard's conclusions or advancing one

123. Ibid., *Sent.* 4. d. 4. c. 4.9–c. 4.11, 2:257–59; quotations at c. 4.11, 2:258: "aperte Augustinus super Leviticum tradit, dicens invisibilem sanctificationem quibusdam adfuisse et profuisse sine visibilis sacramentis"; at c. 4.10, 2:258: "non imputat ei Deus, qui suam potentiam sacramenti non alligavit." For Peter's confusion of Gennadius, via Fulgentius, with Augustine in this passage, see Brady, *ad loc.* 2:258n1.

124. On abbreviators of the Lombard, see Marcia L. Colish, "From the Sentence Collection to the *Sentence* Commentary to the *Summa*," in *Manuels, programmes de cours et techniques d'enseignement dans les universités médiévales*, ed. Jacqueline Hamesse (Louvain-la-Neuve: Institut d'Études Médiévales, 1994), 9–19 on pages 17–19; reprt. in eadem, *Studies in Scholasticism*, no. XIII.

of his own. Bandinus refers to the now-standard passages from Augustine's *De baptismo* and Ambrose's *De obitu Valentiniani* in support of the view that God saves those prevented from receiving ritual baptism by the pressure of time, provided that they have faith. He omits other virtues as required. He then cites the anti-Pelagian Augustine and John 3:3–5 without critiquing them, suggesting that there are also some catechumens who do not make the cut. Bandinus does not indicate whether, in his own opinion or that of contemporaries, either position carries the day. He then moves on to other aspects of baptism, leaving the question of baptism by desire unresolved.[125]

Another post-Lombardian master is Gandulph of Bologna, whose *Sentences* date most likely to 1170/85. Gandulph is sometimes regarded as an abbreviator and sometimes as a theologian or theologian/canonist in his own right. He concurs with the Lombard's conclusions and uses some of his authorities and strategies of argument. Gandulph agrees that it makes sense to preface this question by settling the matter of when Christ instituted ritual baptism. He also adopts the Lombard's date-line, opting for Christ's baptism in the Jordan. Gandulph brings forward only those authorities who support that view, ignoring the other alternatives.[126] He then continues with the distinction between the *sacramentum* and *res sacramenti*. Some people receive the *res tantum*, the spiritual benefits alone, without the sacrament's material medium.[127] That said, Gandulph cites the Lombard on Hebrews as the cornerstone of his structure, the notion that water, blood, and repentance are all valid forms of baptism. He has a particular interest in the Holy Innocents as martyrs. In addition to them, and to other martyrs, the Apostle's message, and his own conclusion, is that adult converts can gain spiritual ablution as well by repentance, without the font.[128]

Proceeding with his argument, Gandulph puts this position initially in the negative. This kind of baptism is invalid if religion has been scorned or if no pressing necessity obviates the font, or if the candidate lacks the requisite faith, contrition, and desire. But, absent these defects, Gandulph asserts, his earlier statement stands: The *res tantum* is granted to those "who have not received the baptismal rites."[129] As in his discussion of when ritual baptism was instituted, here Gandulph also cites only those authorities who

125. Bandinus, *Sententiarum libri quatuor*, In *Sent.* 4.4, *PL* (Paris, 1880), 192: 1093D–1094A.

126. Gandulph of Bologna, *Sententiarum libri quatuor* 4.35, ed. Johannes de Walter (Vienna: Aemilius Heim, 1924), 408.

127. Ibid., 4.41, 411.

128. Ibid., 4.48, 415.

129. Ibid., 4.49, 415–16; quotation on page 416: "qui sacramentum baptismi non susceperunt."

support his case, Augustine's unmodified doctrine in *De baptismo* and Ambrose's *De obitu Valentiniani.* While he also cites the Lombard on Hebrews, and makes passing reference to Jerome, he gives Ambrose the last word on the positive side of the question.[130]

Again following the sequence of the Lombard's argument, Gandulph next addresses the problem of John 3:3–5, although he departs from the strategy of counter-citing a different biblical authority. Gandulph, as noted, has asserted that ritual baptism was already available by the time of Christ's conversation with Nicodemus. In his own reading of John, he maintains that Christ's message in that text applies just to those able to receive the rite who spurn it out of contempt for religion. They, indeed, are denied the kingdom of Heaven. More to the point, and on this note he rests his case, the rebirth of which Christ speaks in John 3:3–5 extends not only to converts regenerated by both water and the Holy Spirit but also to those "who, we may know, are reborn by the Spirit through divine illumination alone, without the sacrament of [ritual] baptism."[131]

Another of the early pupils of the Lombard, who succeeded him in the chair of theology at Notre Dame in Paris and who comments and expands on his work, is Peter Comestor. In his *De sacramentis* (ca. 1165/70), Comestor addresses some but not all of the topics discussed in the fourth book of the master's *Sentences*, shortening the list of the Lombard's authorities and adding his own chosen sources to it. Beginning with the *sacramentum/res sacramenti* distinction, Comestor amplifies it. Those who receive the *res* without the *sacramentum* receive "internal justification and cleansing ... from all sin, both original and actual, and are released from all external satisfaction and punishment."[132] Persons in this category, who possess faith and contrition of heart but who, like the good thief, are prevented from receiving the rite by imminent necessity and without contempt of religion, are fully equal to the martyrs. While he reprises the language of Augustine's *De baptismo*, Comestor presents Cyprian as his sole authority. He omits all mention of Augustine's anti-Pelagian and *Retractationes* hypotheses. The sole objection to his own position which he presents as needing refutation is John 3:3–5.

130. Ibid., 4.48–4.50, 415–17.

131. Ibid., 4.51, 417: "regeneratos spiritu intelligamus divina tantum inspiratione sine sacramento baptismatis regeneratos." See also ibid., 4.52, 417–18, for more on this point as an exception to or qualification of the Johannine rule.

132. Peter Comestor, *De sacramentis* 8, ed. Raymond-M. Martin as appendix to *Maître Simon*, ed. Weisweiler (as in note 79), 17*: "interior mundicia et iustificatio ... ab omni peccatum originali quam actuali, et ab omni satisfactione exteriori et pena relaxamur." For the characterization and dating of this work, see Martin's intro. in ibid., xxiii–xvii.

He disposes of this text by arguing that it applies only to those lacking the time to get to the font. In his conclusion, he affirms forthrightly: "And so we hold that it is possible to have the *res* of baptism and sanctification, not only by water but also by faith and suffering and contrition," for God's power "is not bound by His sacraments."[133]

Another Paris master, Peter Comestor's successor for some three decades in the chair of theology at Notre Dame, is Peter of Poitiers. His goal, he tells the reader, is not to give a cursory commentary on the Lombard's *Sentences* or to expatiate on consensus positions. Rather, he will focus on *dubitabilia*, questions he regards as open on which he can offer his own ideas and insights. Peter of Poitiers wrote his own *Sentences* (1173) early in his career. Opening with the *sacramentum/res sacramenti* distinction, he presents, as an established view, the idea that some adults receive "the *res*, not the *sacramentum*, for instance, those who, prevented by death while hastening to the font out of charity, die before their ablution."[134] This accepted view, as he states it, gives charity as the sole qualification for baptism by desire, not faith and repentance, or all three of the theological virtues. In any case, he merely asserts this position, initially, and does not adduce any authorities or rational arguments in its defense. One might say that this sally is a rhetorical ploy rather than an accurate assessment of the contemporary state of play on this doctrine. Peter then amplifies the Lombard's dismissal of Old Testament rites and events as truly comparable to Christian baptism. They merely prefigure it, he agrees. He also agrees with the Lombard that we must draw a line in the sand here. For Christian baptism alone contains what it signifies and conveys salvific grace. However contrite and well-disposed the pre-Christian worthies may have been, the forgiveness they received did not remove the guilt (*culpa*) or the punishment (*poena*) for their sins, as baptism does. In the case of an adult with faith (which Peter now adds) and charity, ritual baptism purifies him thoroughly. It removes the satisfaction otherwise due for his pre-baptismal sins and not only his guilt for them. And, yes, given the time and opportunity, ritual baptism is not superfluous. But, absent the rite, if the convert is prevented from receiving it, his faith and contrition (now added) carry the day. So, having begun by stating that charity is the

133. Ibid., 9, 18*–19*: "Ecce habemus non solum per aquam posse habere rem baptismi, et sanctificationem, sed etiam per fidem et passionem et contricionem; ... [potentiam] suam sacramentis non alligavit."

134. Peter of Poitiers, *Sententiarum libri quinque* 5.6, *PL* (Paris, 1855), 211:1236D: "qui rem et non sacramentum, ut qui morte praeventi, et dum current ad baptismum ex charitate, decederunt ante intinctionem."

only requirement for baptism by desire, Peter of Poitiers concludes that a more typical range of virtues and inward dispositions is needed.[135]

Unlike Roland of Bologna, who widens the range of reasons why a convert desiring baptism may be unable to accede to the font, Peter of Poitiers limits the availability of baptism by desire to those impeded by sudden death. More notable as a course correction, which he offers to the Lombard, is the date of Christ's institution of the rite. Peter of Poitiers aligns himself with those opting for the post-resurrection date-line. He does not go as far as Robert Pullen, who uses this principle to impose historical criticism on the Augustine who claims that the rite was available before Christ's death. That same principle, as we have seen, could also be used to demolish the idea that ritual baptism was available to Nicodemus. Peter of Poitiers contents himself with observing that the non-ritual conferrals of baptismal grace made to persons not in danger of death before Christ's resurrection constitute an extremely small sample. His list of the biblical worthies included is, in some respects, peculiar, given his stated dismissal of Old Testament types as not equivalent to New Testament realities. Omitting Cornelius, useful as he might have been, Peter of Poitiers settles on three figures not previously named in this connection, who, he claims, were baptized non-ritually "thanks to a singular privilege"—the prophet Jeremiah, John the Baptist, and the Virgin Mary.[136] On when and how these personages were accorded baptism by desire, Peter of Poitiers remains silent.

As we move toward the last quarter of the twelfth century, other theologians with stronger or weaker connections to the Lombard emerge who agree with some features of the master's position and who make additional refinements to it. Wendelin Knoch cites an anonymous master whose unpublished collection of questions and glosses on the Lombard's *Sentences* dates to ca. 1200. This author frames the issue by distinguishing between water, as the material cause of the sacrament, and the word, the Trinitarian formula used by the baptismal minister, as its formal cause. He also regards Christ's statement to Nicodemus in John 3:3–5 as causal, although he does not explain if, or how, it fits into the Aristotelian scheme he puts forth. He agrees with Peter of Poitiers and with others who choose the post-resurrection date for Christ's institution of ritual baptism. The author's chief focus, in discussing baptism, is to give it pride of place in the list of sacraments of necessity, as contrasted with sacraments that are desirable but optional. Baptism, indeed, is required

135. Ibid., *PL* 211:1233B–1235A, 1236D.

136. Ibid., *PL* 211:1237A–B: "quia singulare privilegium obtinuit."

for salvation. But there are three valid forms of the sacrament: "What are the kinds of baptism? There are three, that is, in water, in blood, and in repentance."[137]

A far better known text from this period is the *Summa de sacramentis et animae consiliis* (1190s) of Peter the Chanter. Baptism by desire is far from the Chanter's primary interest in treating this sacrament. He is mainly concerned with infant baptism and its correct administration. He addresses such issues as whether a rite that does not invoke the Trinitarian formula is valid, or is a symptom of heresy; whether an infant who dies unbaptized should be prayed for or buried in consecrated ground; and the number and kinds of grammatical errors on the part of the minister that would impede the conferral of the sacrament, as well as whether that stricture applies to the use of vernacular languages, or Greek, at the font. The Chanter also touches on martyrdom as it may pertain to infants, and whether the situation of the Holy Innocents remains a precedent for current theory or practice.[138] By comparison, his interest in the baptism by desire of adults is marginal. Yet, the Chanter attaches some new considerations to this topic. Casting his eyes, if briefly, toward adults, he affirms that they need baptism even more than infants do, since they have actual sins on their conscience as well as original sin. Unlike infants, they can be saved by their repentance: "It is known to be the case, as it is said, that adults can be saved by contrition without [ritual] baptism, understood, that is, as the visible baptism made in water; for he who is truly contrite receives internal baptism."[139] The Chanter adds that such a convert who acknowledges and chastises himself for his sins does not need to confess them prior to baptism since the sacrament removes them, whether by ritual baptism or baptism by desire. He does not include the *culpa/poena* distinction mentioned by Peter Comestor and Peter of Poitiers. Nor does he discuss in any detail the conditions preventing access to the font on the part of repentant converts.

The Chanter certainly agrees that faith is a requirement for baptism by desire. Since faith is not more lacking in the current dispensation than it was in earlier times, the baptism by desire option remains on the books.

137. *Notule super IIII librum Sententiarum*, Vatican Reginensis lat. 411, fol. 64r–67v as cited by Knoch, *Die Einsetzung der Sakramente* (as in note 79), 255–56; quotation at fol. 67v, 256: "Quot sunt genera baptizandi? Tria scilicet in aqua, in sanguine, in penitentia."

138. Peter the Chanter, *Summa de sacramentis et animae consiliis* 25, 28–32, ed. Jean-Albert Dugauquier, 3 vols. in 5 (Louvain: Éditions Nauwelaerts, 1954–67), 1:82, 88–94.

139. Ibid., 18, 1:57: "Notandum vero quod cum dicitur sine baptismo per contritionem salvari adultus, intellige de isto baptismo visibile qui fit in aqua, interiori enim baptismum recepit qui conteritur."

Nonetheless, he finds it useful to make some distinctions among those who seek it.[140] Consider the following situation: There are two such adult converts. Both have the required virtues and the same desire for baptism. One has the opportunity to receive the rite but does not do so; the other "lacks the capacity to receive it." In this case, "the will of the one without the deed is sufficient for salvation; the will of the other is not. For the will of the former is more efficacious than that of the latter." Thus, while the ideal course of action is to proceed to the font when one can, the Chanter privileges the convert whose desire cannot be ritually fulfilled, while leaving in an ambiguous state the one who can accede to the font but has not done so. This latter convert is not saved; yet his desire, rather than being ineffectual, is merely less efficacious that that of the convert who is received without the rite. The Chanter does not indicate that the convert who has not acceded to the font is one whose baptism has been scheduled but has not yet taken place for some external reason. Rather, he seems to see this convert as someone who desires baptism, and who can receive it at any time, but who procrastinates. Peter the Chanter offers an analogy designed to clarify the comparison just made. The degrees of faith and repentance, and the degrees of will needed for baptism by desire, are stronger in some people and at some times than others. Likewise, clothing that is sufficient in summer is not sufficient in winter. Leaving aside whether this would-be clarification actually helps, what is most notable in the Chanter's support of baptism by desire is that he considers the question from the standpoint of the inner motivations and behavior of candidates desiring baptism, rather than from the standpoint of the divine concession which makes their inner dispositions possible and which also accepts them invisibly.

An argument quite similar to that of Peter the Chanter but one that reaches a somewhat different conclusion is found in the contemporary *Summa theologica* (1187/94) of Prepositinus of Cremona. Teaching in Paris when he wrote this work, Prepositinus also devotes most of his attention to other issues pertaining to baptism, emphasizing the correct requirements and procedures for its valid administration. When he turns attention to baptism by desire, he cites Cyprian and the unmodified *De baptismo* of Augustine on the good thief to support the view that a faith active in good works and conversion of heart make baptism by desire equivalent to baptism by blood. These inner dispositions are acceptable substitutes for the font so long as necessity presses and contempt for religion is not involved.

140. Ibid., 16, 1:53: "uni deest facultas; ... voluntas istius sine opere sufficit ad salutem, voluntas illius non. Ergo maioris efficatie est voluntas istius quam illius."

Following the Lombard and some of his successors, Prepositinus holds that John 3:3–5 applies only to persons with the requisite virtues who are not impeded by the aforementioned conditions.[141]

That foundation laid, Prepositinus raises his own question concerning two converts who both desire baptism. One of them hastens to the font but is prevented; the other hastens to the font and arrives. In his response, although he does not mention the *De obitu Valentiniani*, Prepositinus repeats Ambrose's conclusion, giving it his own slant: "We say that the will is accepted for the deed, and the former will counts as much as does the latter will combined with the deed. For baptism is not just the work of men, since God adds something else to it."[142] Placing both of these baptizands on the same plane, Prepositinus shifts his emphasis from their will and desire alone to God's gracious reception of it.

While the masters just discussed follow Lombardian doctrine in supporting baptism by desire, each adding his own teaching and accent to it, not all theologians in the second half of the twelfth century defend this notion so expressly. One scholastic in this period who leaves that issue unaddressed, so far as we know his teachings, is Peter of Capua. His *Summa theologiae* (late 1180s) is a collection of individual questions organized under Lombardian headings. Peter of Capua may have thought that the validity of baptism by desire was already so well established that it did not merit his attention or may have felt that he had nothing new to contribute on that topic. For he treats baptism mainly in relation to confirmation, a sacrament that inspired scant attention in this period. In effect, Peter's argument is designed to demolish a straw man, the idea that confirmation is superior to baptism, since it is received by persons who have reached the age of reason, who understand what it involves, and who freely will to accept it. Confirmation, in this view, is a greater sacrament than the baptism of infants unable to act for themselves. If there was no known master in the schools actively professing this position, we will see shortly why the matter could well be thought to have merited attention from so high-powered a scholastic as Peter of Capua. He firmly restates the consensus view. Baptism is a sacrament of necessity while confirmation is not: "One cannot be saved without

141. *Praepositini Cancellarii de Sacramentis et de Novissimis (Summa Theologica Pars Quarta)*, ed. Daniel Edward Pilarczyk, Collectio Urbanianae, ser. 3, Textus et Documenta 7 (Rome: Editiones Urbanianae, 1964), 24.

142. Ibid., 37: "Dicimus quod voluntas pro opere reputatur et tantum valet isti voluntas quantum illi voluntas et opus. Sed baptismum quod non est opus hominis sed Dei aliud illi addicit."

baptism. But one can be saved without confirmation."[143] Nonetheless, he takes a hard line on anyone able to receive confirmation who bypasses it even when faced by exigent obstructions. Such a person, he asserts, "sins mortally."[144] He lumps together the willful avoidance of confirmation with the rejection of baptism. Peter of Capua does not ask, or answer, the question of whether baptism as a sacrament of necessity can be received in any way other than ritual ablution. Unusual for his stress on confirmation, he simply omits discussion of baptism by desire and the conditions that would validate it and does not consider whether or not analogous conditions apply to confirmation as well.

In understanding what may have motivated Peter of Capua to take the aforementioned position, it is worth considering the treatment of both confirmation and baptism by desire found in the *Speculum universale* (1192/1200) of Radulphus Ardens.[145] Radulphus was well informed, wherever he may have been educated, but he was no master in the schools. He was a secular priest, a native of Poitou, who served there as court chaplain to Richard I of England between ca. 1190 and 1198. His work is basically a *summa* of Christian ethics designed for lay consumption. Its eighth book treats the sacraments received by all Christians; he omits marriage and holy orders since they are received only by some Christians. A sign of the burgeoning pastoral concerns of the later twelfth century is the extended attention he gives to penance, examined largely from the standpoint of the repentant sinner, with the goal of preparing him to receive the sacrament efficaciously and fruitfully. Radulphus's teachings in this work are derivative. For the sacraments discussed here, he basically relies on Peter Lombard and the authorities that master uses. Radulphus does not always recognize that the Lombard cites some sources only to disagree with them. This oversight leads him at times to present as conclusions views which the

143. On Peter of Capua, see Carlo Pioppi, "Teologia e politica in un cardinale del tempo d'Innocenzo III: L'opera di Pietro Capuano," *Annales theologici* 29 (2006): 127–47. The passage we discuss has not been edited. See Peter of Capua, *Summa theologiae* as found in Vatican lat. cod. 4296, fol. 66va–68rb, quoted by Knoch, *Die Einsetzung der Sakramente* (as in note 79), 288: "Sine baptismo non potest quis salvari. Sine confirmatione autem potest salvari."

144. Ibid., as quoted by Knoch, *Die Einsetzung der Sakramente*, 288: "peccat mortaliter." See Knoch's commentary on this point at ibid., 290.

145. Radulphus Ardens, *The Questions on the Sacraments: Speculum universale 8.31–92*, ed. and trans. Christopher P. Evans (Toronto: Pontifical Institute of Mediaeval Studies, 2010); see Evans's intro. at ibid., 1–10, 15, 20, for Radulphus's career, his works, their dates, and a general characterization of the *Speculum universale*. On page 20, Evans describes Radulphus as offering "precise and lucid solutions," a view that we find over-generous.

Lombard rejects. Radulphus sometimes adds considerations attached to his verbatim citations which the Lombard does not offer, or does not associate with the points in question. There are also some issues on which Radulphus waffles, contradicts himself, or leaves matters hanging.

On confirmation, for instance, he distinctly misses the Lombard's point. Radulphus lists four reasons why some regard confirmation as superior to baptism: The ordinary minister of confirmation is a bishop, of higher rank than the priest who ordinarily baptizes; the material medium used to anoint candidates for confirmation is applied only to the forehead, the worthiest part of the body; the seven-fold gifts of the Holy Spirit are granted in confirmation, not the lesser charismatic gifts presumed to be given in other sacramental rites; and, finally, many miracles are attested in the *ecclesia primitiva* on the occasion of confirmation.[146] These arguments, to be sure, are cited by the Lombard and those who follow him. And then, they are refuted. But Radulphus simply ends his discussion of confirmation there, as if these claims carry the day and represent what the church actually teaches. If he knew that lay people were being led astray in this way, *a fortiori* the influential people who frequent a royal court, a scholastic such as Peter of Capus might well have thought it important to keep the consensus position on the superiority of baptism to confirmation, and its easily grasped rationale, squarely before his students' eyes.

Similar methodological and substantive difficulties, and others, occur in Radulphus's handling of baptism, which occupies *quaestiones* 38–52 of Book 8 of the *Speculum universale*. In *quaestio* 40, he claims to be following the Lombard on when ritual baptism was instituted, but in fact tries to split the difference between the date the Lombard defends and the post-resurrection date accepted by other masters, including some Lombardians. As Radulphus would have it, when Christ Himself was baptized, "the form of baptism was then established, but it was not yet made public." The public announcement occurred only after Christ's resurrection.[147] What form this initial institution is deemed to have taken; why, if it was already instituted, Christ waited until after His resurrection to make baptism generally available; and who, if anyone, we can regard as having received baptism pararitually during His lifetime, are matters on which Radulphus declines to

146. Ibid., 8. q. 76, 130–32.

147. Ibid., 8. q. 40, 52: "Erat quidem formam baptizandi iam constituta, sed nondum erat divulgata." According to Evans's commentary, on pages 17, 228–29, Radulphus follows Hugh of St. Victor here, although the text of Hugh's *De sacramentis* cited places him more clearly in the post-resurrection camp.

comment at this point. It is only under a different rubric that he mentions any of the biblical figures whose names recur in the latter connection. And, when he does so, he raises more questions than he answers.

Radulphus notes in *quaestiones* 41–43 that baptism requires both a material and a spiritual element. The material element includes water, in virtue of the water and blood issuing from the side of the crucified Christ (at this juncture he ignores blood as the martyrs' baptismal medium), and the correct form of words used in the rite. The spiritual element, as some say, is correct intention on the part of both minister and recipient.[148] Radulphus then moves on to other issues. He takes up martyrs in *quaestio* 45, headed by the observation that some people receive the baptismal *res* without the *sacramentum*, others receive the *sacramentum* without the *res*, and still others receive both. In accord with the Lombard and most theologians of the second half of the twelfth century, he holds that martyrs receive the full baptismal *res*. So, too, do those who lack the rite but have faith and contrition. On the latter point, he cites, via the Lombard, Augustine's *De baptismo*, Romans 10:10, and Ambrose's *De obitu Valentiniani*.

Having thus defended the validity of non-ritual baptisms, Radulphus follows the sequence of the Lombard's account by turning to John 3:3-5. He offers two not entirely compatible readings of this text as if they were equally correct. In His remarks to Nicodemus, Christ was referring to those who can accede to the font but spurn it. At the same time, Christ was referring not merely to those who could be ritually baptized but also to those baptized by blood and repentance: "For that regeneration may be made not only by [ritual] baptism but also by blood and repentance." This conclusion is backed by the Lombard's gloss on Hebrews as well as by Augustine. But, was baptism in all three of these modes on offer when Christ spoke to Nicodemus? If the rite had been formally established at Christ's baptism, was the Lord adjuring him to go and receive it, posthaste? Or, if ritual baptism was not yet available, was Christ simply advising Nicodemus to plan to receive it in the future, when it became accessible? Given his ambiguous position on the baptismal institution date itself, it is perhaps no surprise to find that Radulphus does not resolve these questions. To confuse matters further, as his final authority he then cites Augustine, that is, Gennadius via the Lombard, on the point that catechumens, however rich in good works, martyrs excepted, will not gain eternal life unless they receive ritual baptism. On that note, Radulphus ends this *quaestio*. As he does so, he observes

148. Radulphus Ardens, *Speculum universale* 8. q. 41–q. 43, 56–66.

that the Gennnadian stricture undergirds the need for infant baptism.[149] Infant baptism, however, was not the topic under discussion in *quaestio* 45. Nor is it the topic to which the Lombardian citations given had been addressed. What options existed for Nicodemus in John 3:3–5 and what options exist for adult converts now are issues which Radulphus does not clarify. If his last-cited Gennadian reference is the one finally determinative for him, then it works at cross purposes with the defense of the parity of water, blood, and repentance which he maintains earlier in the same *quaestio*. Here, as with the superiority of confirmation to baptism, Radulphus seems unable to discriminate between positions which the Lombard cites in order to criticize and those he cites to support his own solutions. Nor does Radulphus seem aware of his own self-contradictions.

Still continuing with his discussion of infant baptism, Radulphus then turns to Cornelius, frequently encountered under the heading of baptism of desire in adults. As we have seen, Cornelius attracted a range of treatments from different authors. In *quaestio* 48, Radulphus asks what we should think about a person who approaches the font already justified, thanks to his possession of faith, love, and contrition: "As for one who accedes to [ritual] baptism already justified by faith, contrition, and charity, what is conferred?" Radulphus has an answer, which accords with that of some late-twelfth-century masters: "He is released from making exterior satisfaction for them [his sins]." But what if he has already been forgiven exterior punishments as well as interior sins when he comes to the font? "If they too are remitted, what is conferred?" His answer: "Grace and virtue are increased in him, and the inclination to sin is weakened."[150] This response has real substance. It is instructive that Radulphus views the matter from the perspective of the benefits received by the baptized. This teaching is also found in Peter Lombard. But it is not one that he offers in the context of baptism by desire.

To this, Radulphus adds a condition all his own, which he thinks was first exemplified by Cornelius. Sins are not remitted in para-ritual baptism on the basis of the adult convert's prior disposition (omitted here is the direct intervention of the Holy Spirit) unless he fully intends not only to proceed to the font but also to receive the sacrament of penance when he incurs post-baptismal sin. According to Radulphus, Cornelius was in-

149. Ibid., 8. q. 45, 66–68; quotation on page 66: "Illa autem regeneratio non tantum fit per baptismum, sed etiam per sanguinem et penitenciam."

150. Ibid., 8. q. 48, 72–74: "Sed ille, qui iam fides, contricione et caritas iustificatus, accedit ad baptismum, quid confertur? Exterior satisfactio ei dimittitur.... Sed si iam illa erat dimissa, quid confertur? Gracia et virtus ei augmentatur, fomesque peccati in eo debilitatur."

formed of this requirement before he presented himself to St. Peter: "Thus Cornelius, though already justified, was advised that he should approach Peter and be baptized by him."[151] The reason why this post-baptismal commitment to the sacrament of penance is a necessary part of the baptizand's intention is that, when we accept the Christian faith, we accept that the sacraments mutually entail each other. We do not get to pick and choose among them. Radulphus puts the point more strongly still: "If one [sacrament] is held in contempt, the others are not operative."[152] While this conclusion may well bespeak the desire to defend the ecclesiastical system against anti-sacramental heretics, it goes well beyond anything found in Radulphus's sources, ancient or modern, on the reception of the baptismal *res* before the *sacramentum* with which he characterizes Cornelius, or anyone else who may receive it. Altogether, if Radulphus Ardens represents the way in which lay people were being instructed, we can appreciate why masters in the schools may have seen the need to redouble their efforts in educating men for the priesthood, whether they placed themselves in the tradition of Peter Lombard on baptism by desire or not.

Much more sure-footed in addressing a broad audience on this subject is Alan of Lille, the final master writing in the last quarter of the twelfth century to be included here, final only in the light of what we currently know about the teachings of theologians in this period. Alan treats baptism by desire in his *De fide catholica contra haereticos libri quatuor*, written between 1180 and 1200 after he had left his lecture room in Paris to labor against the heretics and non-believers in the Midi.[153] Although not a Lombardian and a staunch defender of ritual baptism against the Cathars, Alan retains the principle, taught by many contemporaries who do follow the Lombard, that baptism can be acquired in three ways. His chosen formula for expressing this idea proved to be quite appealing to scholastics after his time. Baptism, Alan argues, is essential for all. Baptism alone remits all sins. The most important single authority needed here is John 3:3–5.

151. Ibid., 8. q. 48, 74: "Unde Cornelio, iam fide iustificato, precipitur ut accersiat Petrum et ab eo baptizetur."

152. Ibid., 74: "et uno contempto reliqua non possunt." Evans, on page 75, translates the end of this phrase as "are not efficacious," which would heighten its force still more, perhaps unduly.

153. On the dating and context of this work, see *Alain de Lille: Textes inédits avec une introduction sur sa vie et ses oeuvres*, ed. Marie-Thérèse d'Alverny (Paris: Vrin, 1965), 33–34, and more recently Joseph H. Pearson, "The Anti-Jewish Polemic of Alan of Lille," in *Alain de Lille, le docteur universel: Philosophie, théologie, et littérature au XIIe siècle*, ed. Jean-Luc Solère et al. (Turnhout: Brepols, 2005), 82–106.

And, Alan insists, we have to understand this biblical passage rightly. It embraces more than ritual baptism, also including baptism by blood and baptism by desire: "For baptism is indeed threefold: by water (*fluminis*), by the Holy Spirit (*flaminis*), and by blood (*sanguinis*)."[154] With the first of these terms, Alan invokes the flowing water of a river, but basically intends by this image ritual ablution at the font. With the second term, he invokes the image of the Pentecostal sending of the Holy Spirit as tongues of flame. The third term speaks for itself. Alan agrees that baptism *flaminis* resulting from the direct inspiration of the Holy Spirit can be equated with the baptism of repentance of the Hebrews gloss cited by Peter Lombard and his disciples. That said, Alan is more concerned with stating the general principle of the equality of the three modes of baptism than with considering whether baptism *flaminis* is of purely historical interest, having applied only to biblical persons, or whether and how it continues to work for adult converts up through the present age. Those larger questions are ones to which thirteenth-century scholastics will return.

The Thirteenth Century

Alan of Lille's *fluminis*, *flaminis*, *sanguinis* formula receives a wide hearing among the thirteenth-century scholastics who consider baptism by desire, as does the formula of water, blood, and repentance. The thirteenth-century masters known to have treated this topic do so primarily as commentators on the *Sentences*. Rarely if ever do they return to it in their later works, if there are later works. These scholastics sometimes reveal a closer dependence on the Lombard's teaching than that displayed by their twelfth-century predecessors. Even when such is the case, they add their own distinctions and terminology, or authorities not cited earlier in this connection. They attach this topic to other issues of interest to them, and offer fresh, and even idiosyncratic, perspectives on it. Sometimes these innovations have the effect of strengthening the doctrine of baptism by desire as they have inherited it, while at other times serve to limit its perceived value.

A notable change of pace from the theologians of the late twelfth century can be seen in William of Auxerre's *Summa aurea*. The first version of this work (1215/26) contains his teaching on baptism, which he does not revisit in its second recension (1225/29). His goal is clarification as well as

154. Alan of Lille, *De fide catholica contra haereticos libri quatuor* 1.42, *PL* (Paris, 1855), 210:348B: "Etenim triplex baptismus, fluminis, flaminis, sanguinis."

amplification. This trait is visible above all in the extended treatment he gives to the idea of baptismal character. As we have seen, while available in one sense or another since the age of the church fathers, this notion began to receive renewed attention in the twelfth century. It has to be said that the treatments of it by masters at that time left a good deal to be desired. William recognizes the problem. In particular, he holds, we need to understand the nature of baptismal character in relation to the *sacramentum* and *res sacramenti* of baptism. William begins by observing that baptismal character cannot be equated with the *sacramentum*, the water that is the material element of the rite. For unlike this water, which is physical and transient, the baptismal character is permanent, impressed on the soul of the baptized. It is a mistake to compare the character that distinguishes the baptized from the non-baptized with the circumcision which distinguishes Jewish males from Gentiles. William criticizes those who would defend this analogy. For circumcision, although permanent once administered, is visible and applies to the body, while the baptismal character is invisible and applies to the soul. William's first objective is to underscore the difference between baptismal character and the rite's external *sacramentum*: "But this character is not the visible form of invisible grace, since it is not visible and it is in the soul alone. Thus, it is not the *sacramentum*; thus, it is not baptism."[155]

Baptismal character is not to be confused with the external baptismal rite and its physical medium. But how can we distinguish it from the *res sacramenti*, baptismal grace, which is also spiritual and invisible? This is a trickier question altogether. William sets forth a series of possibilities. Is the baptismal character an accident, for instance, the accident of quality? Is it a *habitus*? Is it a disposition? Is it a passion of the soul such as anger, joy, or sorrow? Is it a natural potentiality? William rejects all of these options in turn. Citing John Damascene, he says that the baptismal character is a seal that guards the recipient's soul and sheds light on his regeneration. It disposes its recipient to faith and charity. So understood, William proposes, it is an integral aspect of baptism: "It seems to me that baptism is not just the water that washes or ablution by means of water, and not just the character, but both together are a single baptism." The baptismal character insures the

155. William of Auxerre, *Summa aurea* 4. tract. 5. c. 2. q. 1, ed. Jean Ribaillier, 5 vols., Spicilegium Bonaventurianum 16–20 (Paris/Grottaferrata: CNRS/Collegium S. Bonaventurae, 1980–87), 4:72: "Sed caracter ille non est invisibilis gratie visibilis forma, quia non est visibilis, cum sit tantum in anima; ergo non est sacramentum; ergo non est baptismus." On the dating of the two version of this text, see Ribaillier, 1:16.

continuation of the grace of baptism in the recipient's soul after the water departs. The character is the form, not the matter, of baptism.[156]

Despite this effort at clarification, William's account does not fully succeed in explaining how baptismal character differs from the spiritual grace of the *res sacramenti*. Both are spiritual and invisible. Both endure after the water of the external rite is gone. William grants to the baptismal character some charisms which other theologians see as aspects of baptismal grace itself. Further, baptized persons are capable of backsliding, losing or rejecting the grace of baptism, embracing sin or false belief, or rejecting God to the end. But they are deemed unable to efface the baptismal character they have received. William is adamant on the permanence of baptismal character regardless of a baptized person's subsequent disposition or behavior: "Baptismal character is perpetual. For it remains in heretics; it remains in the damned in Hell." It remains in sinners however horrendous their vices.[157] Baptismal grace, which is salvific, can be lost; baptismal character, which is not salvific, cannot be lost. William does not resolve this conundrum. While he makes this claim in defense of the unrepeatability of baptism, he leaves open the issue of how baptismal grace diverges from baptismal character, a character that is evidently more durable than divine grace.

Another question on which William's discussion is problematic is whether baptismal character is granted in the same way or in the same degree in all kinds of baptisms. He appeals the language of Alan of Lille's triad of baptismal forms. But William presents this doctrine as an objection which he plans to refute:

> Baptism is known to be threefold. For there is baptism *fluminis*, that is, achieved by water, and baptism *flaminis*, that is, achieved by a heart purified by faith, as when an adult condemns his sins, intends to be baptized, and then grace is infused in him, and his sins are forgiven with respect to their guilt (*culpa*), and this baptism is called baptism *flaminis*, that is, by the Holy Spirit.... Baptism *sanguinis* is that achieved in blood by martyrdom.... So, then, baptism is threefold. And, just as the character is impressed in baptism *fluminis*, so also by the same token the character is impressed in the other two baptisms.[158]

156. William of Auxerre, *Summa aurea* 4. tract. 5. c. 2. q. 1, 4:72–74; quotation at 4:74: "Ad hoc nobis videtur dicendum quod nec sola aqua abluens vel ablutio aqua est baptismus, nec solus caracter, sed illa duo, ita quod utroque sunt unus baptismus."

157. Ibid., 4. tract. 5. c. 6. q. 1, 4:125–26; quotation at 4:125: "Caracter enim baptismatis perpetuus est. Remanet enim in haereticis, remanet in dampnatis in inferno...."

158. Ibid., 4. tract. 5. c. 2. q. 1, 4:75: "Sciendum triplex est baptismus. Est enim baptismus

In presenting this objection, William adds that what baptism *flaminis* describes in the aforementioned passage is the situation of a candidate who, after receiving direct inspiration by the Holy Spirit, then proceeds to the font. This is the way in which John 3:3–5 should be read.

Before moving to William's argument against this objection, it is worth highlighting two features of baptism *flaminis* as he presents it in the passage quoted. First, this term denotes not baptism by desire pure and simple, but a condition that must be ratified. Unlike Radulphus, he does not consider what a person already justified by the direct action of the Holy Spirit receives at the font. Second, even though it removes the guilt (*culpa*) otherwise attaching to the sins of the adult convert, the punishment they deserve remains, unless and until he proceeds to the font. Thus, despite the ostensible parity of baptism *flaminis* with the other forms of baptism given in the objection, William does not present the three forms of baptism listed as charismatically equal.

In his response and counterargument, William retains this disparity between ritual baptism and baptism *flaminis* as reported in the objection, downgrading the latter still further. He even downgrades baptism *sanguinis* as well: "We say that only baptism *fluminis* is, simply and properly, baptism, and the other two are not baptism except metaphorically (*per similitudinem*)." He offers an analogy. As a cloth dipped in a precious dye retains its color, so the soul, in baptism *fluminis*, gains a still more precious character or grace. This happy outcome, however, does not fully occur except in baptism *fluminis*. The contrast continues: "Baptism *flaminis* is similar to baptism *fluminis*, to the extent that it removes sins with respect to their guilt, even though not with respect to their punishment. Thus, it is not a perfect baptism. Since baptism *flaminis* and *sanguinis* are baptism only metaphorically, they do not impress the [baptismal] character. For only baptism *fluminis* impresses the character."[159] This claim still leaves open the vexed ques-

fluminis, qui scilicet fit in aqua, et est baptismus flaminis, qui scilicet fit per fidem purificantem cor, quando aliquis adultus conteritur de peccatis suis et proponit suscipere baptismum, tunc infunditur ei gratia et dimittuntur ei peccata quantum ad culpa, et talis baptismus dicitur baptismus flaminis, Spiritus Sancto scilicet.... Baptismus sanguinis est qui fit in sanguine per martyrium.... Cum ergo triplex sit baptismus, et in baptismo fluminis imprimitur caracter, ergo eadem ratione alii duo baptismi imprimunt caracterem...."

159. Ibid., 4:76: "Dicimus quod solus baptismus fluminis est simpliciter et proprie baptismus, et alii duo non sunt baptismi nisi per similitudinem... Sicut enim pannus tinctus in aliquo precioso colore redditur quam prius esset, sic anima in baptismo fluminis tincta per caracterem vel gratiam preciosior fit quam prius esset ... Baptismus flaminis habet similitudinem cum baptismo fluminis quantum ad hoc, quod delet peccata quantum ad culpam, licet non quantum ad penam. Unde non est perfectus baptismus. Cum ergo baptismus flaminis et

tion of how baptismal character is to be defined and how it is related to the grace of the baptismal *res sacramenti*. The image of a cloth permanently dyed would appear to conflate the two, despite William's desire to distinguish them. William of Auxerre bequeathes that problem to thirteenth-century theology, along with the strategy of invoking a differential doctrine of baptismal character to undermine the value of baptism by desire, and still more surprisingly, the value of baptism by blood.

This teaching did not appeal to many of William's contemporaries and successors. A significant modification of his approach can be seen in the *Glossa* (1220/27) on the Lombard's *Sentences* by Alexander of Hales, although he was influenced by William of Auxerre in other areas.[160] Alexander's first move is to rise to the defense of baptism by blood, which William so atypically downgrades. Then, taking a leaf from the books of Bernard of Clairvaux and Peter Lombard, he aligns baptism by blood with baptism by desire, restoring both to parity with ritual baptism. Alexander begins by asserting that baptism by blood is even more meritorious than ritual baptism, a traditional position, which, he points out, William has chosen to ignore. As Alexander observes, echoing Cyprian, since the martyr dies immediately after confessing his faith he has no opportunity to commit any post-baptismal sins, unlike those regenerated at the font. To be sure, ritual baptism disposes its recipients to the reception of other graces, which can improve them morally. But martyrs, being perfect already, cannot get any better.[161]

Further, it is not suffering alone that wins the martyr's crown. Alexander proposes to defend this notion with a reinterpretation of the example of the good thief. He agrees that the thief was crucified and suffered, initially, as punishment for his crimes. But he was converted while on the cross. This conversion had two aspects. First, the thief underwent genuine compunction for the misdeeds that had brought him to this pass. He acknowledged his past sins and regretted the damage he had done to those he had robbed. This sorrow for his sins, according to Alexander, changed the import of the thief's suffering. It was no longer merely a sentence imposed on him, to be endured involuntarily. His suffering now became voluntary; he acquiesced

sanguinis non sint baptismus nisi per similitudinem, non imprimunt caracterem. Unde solus baptismus fluminis imprimit caracterem."

160. For the latest discussion of the date and character of this work, see Hubert Philipp Weber, "The *Glossa in IV Sententiarum* by Alexander of Hales," in *Mediaeval Commentaries on the Sentences of Peter Lombard*, ed. Philipp W. Rosemann (Leiden: Brill, 2010), 2:79–109.

161. Alexander of Hales, *Glossa in quattuor libros Sententiarum*, In *Sent.* 4.9, ed. Collegium S. Bonaventurae, 4 vols. (Quaracchi: Collegium S. Bonaventurae, 1951–57), 4:78–80.

in it as what he truly deserved. This shift from involuntary to voluntary suffering is crucial, for Alexander. But it is not the whole story. The thief's faith in Christ was also essential. Each of these two attitudinal changes contributed to the thief's salvation. For it was "on the basis of his formed faith (*fidei formatae*) that his guilt was remitted, and in virtue of his voluntary suffering that his punishment [was remitted]."[162] Alexander adopts the distinction between the guilt (*culpa*) and the punishment (*poena*) from which the thief, reclassified as a Christian martyr, was absolved. The thief's redefined suffering now becomes an act of will, an internal volitional state on a par with his newly acquired faith and conversion of heart. This faith, for Alexander, was not merely a vague or incipient condition, but a *fides formata*, a full and explicit confession. Bede had earlier held that the thief could be understood as a martyr, a decidedly minority opinion since the time of Cyprian. The effect of Alexander's account is to resurrect Bede's claim, albeit uncited, and to put flesh on its bare bones.

Whether or not Alexander actually had Bede in mind, the result of his treatment of the good thief is to reformulate baptism by blood as a species of baptism by desire. Alexander returns to the Lombard on baptism by desire, citing some of his authorities. He likewise argues that baptism by repentance, along with baptism by blood, is a valid substitute for ritual baptism, so long as the font is unavailable by reason of necessity and there is no contempt for religion. While he does not refer here either to Cyprian, to Augustine's *De baptismo*, or to Ambrose's *De obitu Valentiniani*, Alexander does cite Bernard of Clairvaux's *Epistola* 77 to Hugh of St. Victor. Alexander agrees with Bernard that the faith of the martyrs is as critical as their suffering. Yet and still, Alexander weakens this case by also agreeing with William of Auxerre that baptism by blood and by desire do not convey the indelible baptismal character imparted uniquely at the font.[163]

Alexander does seem to realize that the point he advances about differential baptismal character flies in the face of the argument for the parity of all three forms of baptism, which he also makes. Further along in his treatise on baptism, he tries to retrieve the high ground which he had seized and then so suddenly abandoned. He raises and answers positively the question of whether baptism by desire is salvific if access to the font is thwarted by death. Although he thinks that non-ritual baptisms do not convey an indelible character, Alexander allows that, since baptism is a sac-

162. Ibid., 4.10, 4:80: "virtute fidei formatae remittebatur culpa, et virtute passionis voluntarie poena."

163. Ibid., 4.12, 2:81–82.

rament of necessity, God in His mercy will make up the deficit and will grant salvation to those desiring baptism who are prevented by death from receiving it ritually. On this issue, he argues, we can distinguish between two aspects of the sacrament. There is "the effect of baptism," which differs from "the act of receiving it on the part of the baptized." One can acquire the former without the latter. This possibility exists, Alexander explains, because the effect of the sacrament depends not on the recipient but on the passion of Christ: "For it is not on the basis of his merit that this takes place but through the power of the sacrament, since the sacrament removes all satisfaction of punishment by virtue of the passion of Christ."[164] The wider concern informing Alexander's position on this issue is his wish to emphasize the objective power of baptism when administered to infants, who bring no intentions or beliefs to it. He is willing to include baptismal character in his account but makes no effort to address the problems connected with it raised and left open by William of Auxerre. Still, despite the differential limits which he places on the grant of baptismal character in different forms of baptism, his aims are twofold. Not only does he seek to restore the full validity of baptism by desire and by blood challenged by William, he also subordinates baptism by blood to the intentional norms defining baptism by desire, as seen in his reinterpretation of the good thief as a martyr rewarded for far more than his voluntary acceptance of suffering.

On the basis of what we now know about them, there is no evidence that theologians in the second quarter of the thirteenth century did much to advance any aspect of the debate on baptism by desire aired by William of Auxerre and Alexander of Hales. As we have seen, each of those masters offers fresh insights as well as doctrinal inconsistencies and unresolved problems. Starting in the mid-century, several major scholastics pick up the glove in this debate, with the mendicants mapping the terrain. The Franciscans largely return to the arguments of the Lombard, tipping their hat to Alexander while ignoring his martyrization of the good thief. Bonaventure's commentary on the Lombard's *Sentences* (1250/55) leads the way. His treatment of this topic is basic and straightforward. Bonaventure begins with the standard observation that some baptizands receive the *sacramentum* alone, some the *res sacramenti* alone, and some both the *sacramentum* and the *res*.[165]

164. Ibid., 4.14, 2:84–85, quotation at 2:85: "effectus baptismi … operationis suscipiendi baptismum.… Non enim per meritum evolat iste, sed per virtutem sacramenti, quod sacramentum ex virtute passionis Christi delet omnem poenam satisfactoriam."

165. Bonaventure, *In IV Sententiarum*, In *Sent.* 4. d. 4. pars 1. c. 1, in *Opera omnia*, ed. Collegium S. Bonaventurae, 10 vols. (Quaracchi: Collegium S. Bonaventurae, 1882–1902), 4:90.

Among those who receive the *res* alone, he lists the martyrs and those baptized by desire. His chosen authorities are the Augustine of the *De baptismo* and the Leviticus commentary. He agrees with the Lombard and with other predecessors that the Augustine of the *Retractationes* withdrew the example of the good thief but not his earlier support for the doctrine. He caps this list, again following the Lombard, with Ambrose's *De obitu Valentiniani*. Bonaventure also sees that the simplest way to deal with the objection to his desired solution raised by John 3:3–5 is to assert, without further ado, that what "baptism" means in that text includes baptism by blood and by repentance as well as by water. As Bonaventure concludes, because of the authority of these sources, read in these ways, and because "reason also convinces," he aligns himself expressly with Bernard of Clairvaux, with the Lombard, and with Alexander of Hales, in maintaining that "it is not [the martyrs'] suffering alone that takes the place of baptism, but also faith and contrition, where necessity obviates the [ritual] sacrament." While the case of Cornelius shows that one should not spurn the font if it is available, in the case of one who, "having faith and charity desires to be baptized, and cannot be, prevented by necessity, the goodness of the Omnipotent supplies what is lacking in the sacrament ... for His power is not bound by the sacraments."[166]

This largely Lombardian doctrine is not a topic to which Bonaventure returns in his later works. But it clearly influenced Franciscans later in the thirteenth century. A case in point is Richard of Mediavilla, writing his commentary on the *Sentences* soon after 1294. Richard addresses these issues in the preface to his treatise on baptism. Those receiving the *res sacramenti* without the *sacramentum*, he agrees, include recipients of baptism by blood and by desire. He recycles the citations of Cyprian, Augustine's *De baptismo*, Augustine on Leviticus, the re-imagined Augustine of the *Retractationes*, Ambrose's *De obitu Valentiniani*, and St. Paul on Romans. He repeats the point that, for martyrs, "it is not only suffering but also faith and contrition that confer remission" of sins and that persons who desire baptism but are prevented from receiving it may "be justified and saved without [ritual] baptism." As for John 3:3–5, it applies, in Richard's view, to those able to receive the rite but who reject it, not to the cases just mentioned. Richard concludes, with Bonaventure and the Lombard, that God makes up any

166. Ibid., d. 4. pars 2. c. 4, 4:91–92; quotations at 4:92: "Ratio etiam id suadet"; 4:91: "Nec tamen passio vicem baptismi implet, sed etiam fides et contritio, ubi necessitas excludit sacramentum"; 4:92: "Si enim aliquis habens fidem et caritatem voluerit baptizari et non potest, necessitate praeventus, supplet Omnipotentis benignitas quod sacramento defuerat, ... qui suam potentiam sacramentis non alligavit."

deficiency in the liturgical action, or non-action, of those receiving baptism by blood and by desire, since His power is not bound by His sacraments.[167]

To this consensus, Richard's contemporary, the Franciscan William of Ware, adds only one refinement. William was active in Paris ca. 1293, the likely date of his unpublished commentary on the *Sentences*. We are indebted to Willibrord Lampen for the passage that follows. William amplifies earlier relativizations of John 3:3–5 with a distinction of his own. When we consider the statement that baptism by water and the Holy Spirit is necessary, says William, there are two ways in which we can understand the meaning of "necessity." If we think of necessity "in absolute terms," then "the sacrament is not necessary for salvation, nor for the conferring of grace, nor for the remission of sins. For God can do all these things by Himself without any sacrament." But another way of understanding necessity is "conditionally, or by institution, and in this way the sacrament is necessary." William proposes that this latter sense is the way in which St. John intends Christ's remark to Nicodemus to be taken. From what we presently know about William of Ware on baptism, it is not clear that he is here taking a stand on the question of when Christ instituted ritual baptism. But the bottom line, for him, is that however one receives baptism, it is the power of God that grants its benefits, not any created elements or conditions, be they the material media of water or blood or the will and desire of those receiving the *res* without the *sacramentum*.[168] In this passage, William appears to be a good deal more comfortable with God's omnipotence than, say, Otto of Freising or Master Simon, and with God's willingness to exempt some people from ecclesiastical rules. But such an impression awaits confirmation, or not, by further research into William's commentary.

In the same generation as William of Ware, an index of waning Franciscan interest in baptism by desire is the Oxford *Ordinatio* (1297/1301) of John Duns Scotus, his first commentary on the *Sentences*. Scotus departs from both William and Richard of Mediavilla in insisting on the global ne-

167. Richard of Mediavilla, *In IV libros Sententiarum*, In *Sent.* 4. d. 4, prologus, ed. Ludovicus Silvestris à Sancto (Brescia: De Consensu Superiorum, 1591; reprt. Frankfurt: Minerva GMBH, 1963), 47–63; quotations on page 47: "non solus passionem, sed etiam fidem et contritionem conferre remissionem"; "sine baptismo aliquos iustificari et salvari."

168. William of Ware, *In IV Sententiarum* 1, cited from Bibl. Laurent. S. Crucis, Plut. 33, dext. 1, fol. 188v by Willibrord Lampen, *De causalitate sacramentorum iuxta scholam Franciscanam* (Bonn: Petrus Hanstein, 1931), 39: "uno modo absolute et sic sacramentum non est necessarium ad salutem, nec ad gratiam conferendam, nec ad peccatum dimittendum; posset enim Deus omnia ista facere per se sine aliquo sacramento. Alio modo dicitur aliquid necessarium ex conditione sive ex institutione, et hac modo sacramentum est necessarium ..."

cessity of ritual baptism. Christ's apostles probably received it at the Last Supper, prior to its institution for all mankind after His resurrection. He maintains that the Virgin Mary was also likely to have received some version of ritual baptism, despite her many privileges. True, God is all-powerful and can make exceptions to this law, but the only dispensation from baptism *fluminis* that Scotus is willing to mention is baptism *sanguinis*. He pointedly omits all reference to baptism *flaminis*.[169]

Dominican masters also made valuable contributions to the discussion of baptism by desire in the second half of the thirteenth century. Albert the Great's commentary on the *Sentences* (completed 1249) offers a number of fresh perspectives, while sharing many ideas with his Franciscan contemporaries. One of Albert's arguments helped to put paid to the debate on when Christ instituted ritual baptism. As we have seen, while a position on this question was of historical interest in its own right, it could also contribute significantly to a master's understanding of the conditions under which Christ redeemed those biblical persons held to have received baptism of one kind or another during His lifetime. The single most problematic text in this connection, as we have also seen, was John 3:3–5, which inspired a range of creative exegeses in the light of a master's desired conclusions. Albert states forthrightly that the institution of ritual baptism "did not occur until after the passion and resurrection of Christ." It was only at that time that the Lord established the rite "officially and causally," as related in Matthew 28:19. The key point, for Albert, is that when Christ commissioned His apostles to baptize all nations after His resurrection, He enjoined them to use both water and the full Trinitarian formula. These have been norms of orthodox baptism in the ecclesiastical dispensation ever since. As Albert observes, it was then settled, once and for all, that the rite was not sufficient if administered in the name of only one, or two, Persons of the Trinity. We may thus consider the earlier debate settled. We can also be assured that Christ's advice to Nicodemus did not impose on him a then-current requirement, but rather counseled him to receive the rite at a future time, when it would become available.[170] Albert deserves much of the credit for helping to close this long-standing controversy on the date of baptismal institution. In the sequel, as we will see shortly, it remained to add only one

169. John Duns Scotus, *Ordinatio* 4. pars 3. q. 1.1–2, ed. Josephus Rodríguez Carballo in *Opera omnia* (Vatican City: Typis Vaticanis, 2008), 11:262–65.

170. Albert the Great, *In IV Sententiarum*, In *Sent.* 4. d. 3D. a. 3, in *Opera omnia*, ed. Stephanus C. A. Borgnet, 38 vols. (Paris: Vivès, 1880–95), quotations at 29:69: "non fuit nisi passionem et resurrectionem Christi"; 29:69–70: "officialiter ... causaliter." On Christ's conversation with Nicodemus, ibid., d. 3D. a. 6, d. 4E praef., 29:76, 91–92.

salient embellishment to his argument on that theme for the matter to be successfully resolved and a new consensus launched.

Albert's position on the post-resurrection institution of baptism is by no means incidental to the stance he takes on baptism by desire. He opens his account with a reprise of points familiar to its defenders. There are three valid forms of baptism: by water, by blood, and by repentance. In the latter two cases, baptizands receive the *res sacramenti* without the *sacramentum*. And this condition is operative because they omit ritual baptism not out of contempt for religion but owing to forces beyond their control. Albert also cites the standard authorities, Augustine's *De baptismo*, his *Retractationes* rightly understood, and Ambrose's *De obitu Valentiniani*, adding Augustine's *De trinitate* to the mix. He agrees with contemporary Franciscans, and, through them, with Bernard of Clairvaux, that it is not just the suffering of martyrs but also their faith and contrition that win them the crown.[171] To these now-common teachings, Albert adds his own insights. What, he asks, might prevent a believer from acceding to the font? It could be his martyrdom. It could also be a natural death not in a martyrdom context. Returning to a condition not mentioned since the mid-twelfth century, particularly by Roland of Bologna, Albert also notes that the believer could be blocked by hostile human forces, "impeded by a tyrant."[172]

Another point made by Albert pertains to Cornelius. This figure, he thinks, inspires two considerations. First, dissociating himself from those who emphasize the importance of Cornelius's proceeding to the font, Albert stresses the sufficiency of divine inspiration. As a pendant to the Lombardian point that God's power is not bound by the sacraments, he observes, "This Cornelius and those who were with him were already baptized, sanctified by the Holy Spirit."[173] Here Albert includes the household of Cornelius along with Cornelius himself as receivers of direct divine inspiration. Albert then discusses the nature of the faith granted to Cornelius and to others redeemed by the Holy Spirit before, during, and apart from ritual baptism, from then until now. There are two possibilities. Cornelius's faith was implicit, faith *in habitu*. The faith of those baptized by desire may also be explicit, faith *in actu*, embracing a full knowledge and acceptance of the articles of the Creed.[174] While Albert would prefer adult converts

171. Ibid., d. 3A. a. 1. ad 2.1, d. 4D praef., d. 4D. a. 6, d. 4E praef., 29:57, 87–88, 91–93.

172. Ibid., d. 4D. a. 6. 29:86–90; quotation at 29:89: "impediente tyranno."

173. Ibid., d. 4E. praef., 29:93: "Hinc Cornelius et qui cum eo erant, iam Spiritu sanctificati baptizati sunt."

174. Ibid., d. 3A. a. 1. ad 3.1, 29:59: "illud tamen est in virtute baptismi in proposito existentis habitu, sicut in Cornelio: vel actu, sicut in aliis qui sciunt et credunt articulos explicite."

to possess an explicit faith, whether they receive baptism at the font or by desire, he also liberalizes the quality of the faith required for their valid reception of the sacrament. In either case, since faith is never perfect in this life, the grace they receive will enable them to progress in their understanding of it, even as they progress morally in the state which they now enter.

Writing his own commentary on the *Sentences* (1254/56) shortly after Albert's, Thomas Aquinas stands largely in agreement with his master, and in disagreement with some teachings of earlier thirteenth-century theologians, while handling baptism by desire in his own way. His innovations can be seen at the very beginning of his discussion of baptism in his treatment of the *sacramentum/res sacramenti* distinction. Aquinas considers it from the standpoint of causation. The *sacramentum tantum*, the water of the rite alone, is its material cause, what he also calls its remote natural cause. Spiritual ablution is the *res sacramenti*. The standard baptismal liturgy contains both the *res sacramenti* and the *sacramentum* which conveys it. What the rite imparts is the merits of the passion of Christ, which is the efficient cause of the benefits granted to the baptized. This causal analysis adds a potent theological rationale to the argument from church history used by Albert to establish the post-resurrection institution of ritual baptism. As Aquinas argues, baptism must have been instituted by Christ after His passion because it is from that very event that it gains its efficacy; and, the effect of a cause cannot precede the cause itself.[175]

Aquinas then takes issue with the idea that some forms of baptism are not as valid as ritual baptism. Here, his goal is to challenge the teachings of William of Auxerre and Alexander of Hales. He begins by affirming the consensus position that baptism is not repeatable. As he sees it, unrepeatability and the presence of an indelible baptismal character are mutually correlative. They must coexist as attributes of the same sacraments. Raising this question initially à propos of baptism by blood and then extending it to all forms of baptism, Aquinas gives this part of his answer without indicating the need to anchor it in an authority. Rather, he presents it as a rational conclusion. He then goes on to observe that what baptism effects is the conforming of the recipient to Christ. Without referring expressly to Tertullian, but instead to Cyprian via Augustine, he states that baptism by water and blood achieve this objective equally: "Baptism by water is efficacious thanks to the passion of Christ, which conforms us to Him. But baptism by

175. Thomas Aquinas, *Scriptum super libros Sententiarum magistri Petri Lombardi*, In *Sent.* 4. d. 3. q. 1. a. 19–a. 20, d. 4. q. 5. a. 2, ed. Pierre Mandonnet and Maria Fabianus Moos, 4 vols. (Paris: Lethielleux, 1929–47), 4:113, 136.

blood likewise conforms us to the passion of Christ. Thus, it takes the place of [ritual] baptism."[176] Citing an authority not heard from earlier in this discussion, the *Glossa ordinaria* on Judges, Aquinas next reinforces the traditional view that baptism by blood is still more excellent than ritual baptism. Baptism by blood conveys the *res* alone, and by it the martyr is freed from both the guilt (*culpa*) and the punishment (*poena*) attaching to his sins.

While Aquinas is eager to glorify the martyrs, he applies the same analysis to baptism by repentance. His comparison of these two states has the effect of turning Gennadius inside out. Just as martyrs are prevented from proceeding to the font by their persecutors, so non-martyrs desiring baptism may be prevented from doing so by human enemies and not just by natural impediments: "For it lies within the power of man to impede someone else, so that he cannot be baptized with the baptism of water. Thus, by faith and contrition alone he can be saved even without the baptism of water.… For he who has faith and contrition is saved, even without [ritual] baptism."[177] Aquinas certainly includes the usual disclaimers. These non-ritual modes of baptism are as efficacious as the font so long as the candidate faces a pressing necessity and does not spurn the rite out of contempt for religion. But his larger aim, in his commentary on the *Sentences*, handily achieved, is to align himself firmly and unequivocally with the defenders of baptism by desire and to equalize the nature and extent of its gifts with those of the other forms of baptism.

Unlike most scholastics in his century, Aquinas returns to the theme of baptism by desire in his later work. His treatment of it in his *Summa theologiae* (1266/73) is more streamlined than that in his *Sentences* commentary. Here, he lists only three objections to his planned acceptance of the equal validity of baptism *fluminis*, *flaminis*, and *sanguinis*. First, St. Paul in Ephesians 4:5 speaks of one faith, one baptism, not three. Second, many authorities agree that baptism requires water. And third, John Damascene lists a number of other forms of baptism beyond these three. Aquinas disposes of the first objection with the *Glossa ordinaria* passage on Hebrews cited by Peter Lombard and some of his disciples. There are, it follows, three baptisms—of water, blood, and repentance. Regarding the third objection,

176. Ibid., d. 4. q. 1. a. 1–a. 4, d. 4. q. 3. a. 3. c. 3, 4:161–64, 191; quotation at d. 4. q. 3. a. 3. c. 3, 4:191: "Baptismus aquae efficaciam habet ex passione Christi, cui nos conformat. Sed similiter baptismus sanguinis nos passioni Christi conformat. Ergo supplet vicem baptismi."

177. Ibid., d. 4. q. 3. a. 3. c. 2–c. 4, 4:190–94; quotation at d. 4. q. 3. a. 3. c. 2, 4:190: "Sed in potestate hominis est impedire alium ne baptizetur baptismo aquae. Ergo sine baptismo aquae per solam fidem et contritionem potest esse salus.… Ergo qui habet fidem et contritionem, etiam sine baptismo aquae esse salus."

Damascene was referring to a range of figurative events in Old Testament history, which do not count as baptism, properly speaking. But the main thrust of Aquinas's argument is directed against the second objection. It is based on an elaboration of the analysis of causation first given in his *Sentences* commentary.

Baptism, he begins, involves not just its material element, be it water or blood. It also requires the power of the Holy Spirit. The baptism of repentance is valid even without martyrdom. For the Holy Spirit is the first cause of baptism. Christ's passion is its efficient cause:

> Now while the effect depends on the first cause, the cause exceeds the effect; nor does it depend on the effect. And so, without the baptism of water, a person can acquire the effect of the sacrament by virtue of the passion of Christ, insofar as he is conformed to Christ by suffering for Him.... Likewise, a person can acquire the effect of baptism by virtue of the Holy Spirit, not only without the baptism of water but also without the baptism of blood. It follows that this takes place when his heart is moved by the Holy Spirit to believe in God and to love [Him], and to repent his sins. Hence it is called the baptism of repentance. So we therefore call these two other kinds of baptisms baptism, since they take the place of [ritual] baptism.[178]

Beyond the issue of causation, which applies to baptism by blood and by desire alike, Aquinas has more to say on baptism by desire alone. Not confining himself to the Hebrews gloss, he cites Augustine on Leviticus and Psalm 57:3 but assigns the heavy lifting to Ambrose's *De obitu Valentiniani*. One can lack baptism *re et voto*, either in fact or desire. But while one can lack it in fact, that is, without the rite, one cannot lack it in desire. Baptism by desire occurs when someone wants to be baptized but, by some chance, death prevents him before he can reach the font: "Such a one can gain salvation without actual baptism, on account of his desire for baptism, ... by which God, whose power is not bound by visible sacraments, sanctifies a person internally. Thus Ambrose says of Valentinian, ... 'truly, he did not fail to receive the grace he requested.'"[179] This desire, Aquinas affirms,

178. Thomas Aquinas, *Summa theologiae* IIIa. d. 66. a. 11, Blackfriars ed. and trans., 61 vols. (New York: McGraw-Hill, 1964–76), 57:48 "Licet autem effectus dependeat a prima causa, causa tamen superexcedit effectum, nec dependet ab effectu. Et ideo, praeter baptismae aquae, potest aliquis consequi sacramenti effectum ex passione Christi, inquantum quis ei conformatur pro Christi patiendo.... Eadem ratione aliquis per virtutem Spiritus Sancti consequitur effectum baptismi, non solum sine baptismo aquae, sed etiam sine baptismo sanguinis: inquantum scilicet alicujus cor per Spiritum Sanctum movetur ad credendum et diligendum Deum, et poenitendum de peccatis; unde etiam dicitur *baptismus poenitentiam*.... Sic igitur utrumque aliorum baptismatum nominatur baptismus, inquantum supplet vicem baptismi." The emphasis is given by the editors to indicate where Thomas cites the Hebrews gloss. See also ibid., IIIa. d. 66. a. 12, 57:52.

179. Ibid., IIIa. d. 68. a. 2, 57:84–86: "Talis autem sine baptismo actuali salutem consequi

"is accepted as fact before God."[180] Aquinas also returns in his *Summa theologiae* to the theme of the indelible baptismal character as part and parcel of the unrepeatability of the sacrament, by whichever of its three forms it is received. He dismisses without meriting comment the claim that they differ in their capacity to impart the same baptismal character to the baptized.[181]

Not all contemporary and later Dominicans commenting on the *Sentences* second Aquinas's arguments. Perhaps surprisingly, one who does is Durandus of St. Pourçain. Despite his vaunted anti-Thomism, the final version of his *Sentences* commentary (1317/27) takes issue with Duns Scotus and affirms, with Aquinas, that baptisms *fluminis*, *flaminis* and *sanguinis* are equally efficacious, although the latter is the most meritorious. They convey the same baptismal character.[182] A good example of a coeval of Aquinas who takes a somewhat different line is Peter of Tarentaise, later Pope Innocent V (1276), whose *Sentences* commentary dates to 1257/59. Peter's treatment of baptism by desire is both more traditional and less generous than that of Aquinas. Peter leads off in the preface to his treatise on baptism with the standard *sacramentum*/*res sacramenti* distinction. He agrees that those baptized by blood and repentance receive the *res* without the *sacramentum*. Among the standard authorities he cites are Cyprian via Augustine's *De baptismo* and the *Glossa ordinaria* on Hebrews via Peter Lombard. He concurs with his direct and indirect sources; the good thief was no martyr. In any case, he notes that martyrs are saved by their faith and contrition as well as their suffering. He joins those who dismiss the anti-Pelagian Augustine's beclouding of the issue of the pre-crucifixion status of the thief, using Ambrose's *De obitu Valentiniani* to refute him. He adds the usual disclaimers: Those receiving the *res* alone are saved only if ritual baptism is impossible for them but not if it is possible but they spurn it out of contempt for religion. All of the above, he observes, is proved by reason as well as authority. He ends these opening remarks by agreeing with the Lombard that God's power is not bound by the sacraments.[183]

---

potest, propter desiderium baptismi, ... per quam Deus interius hominem sanctificat, cujus potentia sacramentis visibilis non alligitur. Unde Ambrosius dicit de Valentiniano, ... *verumtamen ille gratiam quam poposcit, non amisit*."

180. Ibid., IIIa. d. 68. a. 2. ad 3, 57:86: "quae apud Deum reputatur pro facto."

181. Ibid., IIIa. d. 66. a. 9, 57:40.

182. Durandus of St. Pourçain, *In Petri Lombardi Sententias theologicas commentariorum libri IIII*, In *Sent.* 4. d. 4. q. 8.6–14, 2 vols. (Venice: Ex Typographia Guerraea, 1571; reprt. Ridgewood, NJ: Gregg Press Incorporated, 1964), 2:302r–302v.

183. Peter of Tarentaise, *In Sententiarum*, In *Sent.* 4. d. 4. q. 1. praef., ed. J.-B. de Marinis, 4 vols. (Toulouse: Arnaldus Colomerius, 1649–52; reprt. Ridgewood, NJ: Gregg Press, 1964), 4:40–41.

Moving to the body of his argument, Peter returns to Ambrose's text, having used it earlier to refute the unqualified necessity of water baptism. He now observes that "baptism can be spoken of in two ways: as baptism by water, in the proper sense of the word, in which case there is exterior and interior ablution, and metaphorically (*metaphorice*), as in baptism *flaminis* and *sanguinis*, in which case there is interior ablution. I say therefore that without baptism, either in the proper or metaphorical sense, an adult cannot be saved. But he is saved without baptism in the proper sense."[184] Ambrose's Valentinian is going to be the main evidence supporting this claim, against those who invoke metaphor to downgrade baptisms by blood and desire. In preparing to make use of him, Peter decides that he also needs to address another objection, found in the twelfth century in the *Sententiae divinitatis* and Otto of Freising and noted and shot down by Roland of Bologna. Ambrose, so this objection goes, was writing to console the chief mourners of the deceased emperor in the *De obitu Valentiniani*. This work was an occasion piece, a funeral oration, a genre whose task was to praise the departed's virtues. It was not a work in which Ambrose intended to announce a consensus position or a doctrine he regarded as globally applicable. Not so, says Peter of Tarentaise. Ambrose's position "was not, then, in opposition to ecclesiastical custom." The bishop of Milan's oration confirmed a basic principle.[185]

At the same time, despite what Peter has to say about the validity of baptism *flaminis*, he also thinks that the model of Cornelius should be followed if time permits, so as not to scorn religion. He offers the following rationale for this advice: "For baptism has been handed down not just for the private benefit of those who need it, but also for the public benefit of recognizing and conforming to the church." Peter accepts that a person baptized *flaminis* is truly baptized and has already been justified and saved. That individual's personal needs have thus been addressed. Nonetheless, if circumstances permit, he should see to it that the public needs just mentioned are also addressed. He should accept the obligation to hearken to the precepts of the church by acceding to the font.[186] This appeal to the legitimacy of the church's institutional needs recalls the position of Master

184. Ibid., d. 4. q. 2. a. 2–a. 3, 4:50–51; quotation at d. 4. q. 2. a. 2, 4:50: "Baptismus dupliciter dicitur: proprie de baptismo aquae, in quo est ablutio exterior et interior, et metaphorice de baptismo flaminis et sanguinis, in quibus est ablutio interior. Dico ergo quod sine baptismo proprie vel metaphorice dicto adultus non est salus. Sed sine baptismo dicto proprie esse salus."

185. Ibid., d. 4. q. 2. a. 3, 4:54: "non erat contra morem Ecclesiae."

186. Ibid., d. 4. q. 1. a. 3, 4:49: "Baptismus enim traditus est non solum propter utilitatem privatam personalis indigentiae, sed etiam propter utilitatem publicam distinctionis et conformitatis Ecclesiae."

Simon. But, like Radulphus Ardens, Peter makes it in the light of the duties of the baptizand. And, in contrast with Radulphus and Simon alike, he does not present it as a contingent condition. He does not call into question the redemption of those who receive the baptismal *res* invisibly or demand miraculous proof of it. Nor does he propose that they receive differential treatment by the Christian community.

Despite his recycling of many earlier positions and authorities, Peter of Tarentaise's treatment of several aspects of baptism by desire puts his personal stamp on this doctrine. While he uses the language of proper and metaphorical baptism to describe, respectively, baptism *fluminis*, and baptism *flaminis* and *sanguinis*, he rejects William of Auxerre's depreciation of the validity of the two latter forms of the sacrament. Peter neither complicates nor clarifies matters by folding the idea of baptismal character into his discussion. He is fully prepared to defend the principle that one can be saved by the invisible grace of baptism *flaminis*, even as he recognizes the importance, for the church, of identifying who the baptized are and of celebrating liturgically their entry into the fold. In addition, while he joins with contemporaries by invoking Ambrose's *De obitu Valentiniani*, relying on it as the industrial-strength solvent that best dispatches the opposition, Peter of Tarentaise reopens, and addresses, the issue of historical and literary criticism as it was applied to that text in the twelfth century. This interest is one atypical for a scholastic theologian of his own time.

Conclusion

After the end of the thirteenth century the theme of baptism by desire, having won a good deal of support except from Duns Scotus, tends to fall out of favor as a subject of scholastic disputation. As is well known, commentators on the *Sentences* in the fourteenth century feel no obligation to treat all the questions raised in Peter Lombard's work. Discussions of the sacraments in their commentaries and in any later works they produced are quite selective, with pride of place given to the Eucharist. To the extent that these later scholastics treat baptism, they repeat earlier views or direct attention to other aspects of the sacrament. Baptism by desire no longer functions as a hot topic on which an incipient theologian can cut his teeth, display his intellectual flair, and make his mark.

Some areas of agreement on substance, methodology, or strategy of argument had been reached by 1300. It is accepted that, in the game of citing Augustine against Augustine, it is the Augustine of the anti-Pelagian polemics and the Augustine of the *Retractationes* who has to be decommissioned. Starting with Ivo of Chartres and Bernard of Clairvaux, masters in the twelfth and thirteenth centuries do not hesitate to expose the weaknesses and contradictions of the late Augustine's lucubrations. Or, they express their judgment simply by ignoring them. The anti-Donatist Augustine, the Augustine of the Leviticus commentary, and Ambrose's *De obitu Valentiniani* remain the hardy patristic perennials used to ground refutations of authorities who make ritual baptism mandatory for adults, admitting only the martyr exception. More than any other source, Ambrose's work is subjected to historical and literary criticism, whether the goal is to dismiss its authority or to insist on it. While Gennadius, thought to be Augustine except by Peter Abelard, is actually the strongest patristic proponent of the necessity of the font, its most important foundation, and the chief authority to command attention, is seen to be John 3:3–5. A diverse number of ingenious readings of John's text are developed with the common goal of relativizing it. Some masters content themselves with the nude countercitation of other biblical texts, notably Matthew 28:19. But others offer their own imaginative exegeses of John himself, whether or not they read him in the light of when they think Christ instituted ritual baptism.

If notable points of concurrence emerge by 1300, not the monopoly of any one group of masters, there are some arguments associated with the debate on baptism by desire that fail to carry the day, or that lack a durable shelf-life across the twelfth and thirteenth centuries, or that are altered beyond recognition. With good reason, Abelard's revival of the Augustinian example of Dinocrates falls flat. Gregory of Nazianzus's baptism of tears understood as sorrow for post-baptismal sin appears to have morphed into the baptism by repentance seen as equivalent to ritual baptism or into the sacrament of penance. Whether or not he is consciously appealing to Bede, the attempt of Alexander of Hales to redefine the good thief as a Christian martyr goes down in flames. Peter of Poitiers's grant of pre-ritual baptism to Jeremiah, John the Baptist, and the Virgin Mary does not appeal; after him, Duns Scotus alone urges that the universal mandate of ritual baptism was not relaxed even for the Virgin. Other scholastics ignore that idea, and they do not ratify Scotus's decision to omit baptism by desire altogether. More generally, the Victorine inclination to place Old Testament worthies on a level playing field with their New Testament successors loses traction. Authorities cited only once or at most twice in connection with baptism by desire and then dropped include Ezekiel, John Damascene, Augustine's *De trinitate*, and the *Glossa ordinaria* on Judges.

Scholastics after Alan of Lille make use of his trio of baptism *fluminis*, *flaminis*, and *sanguinis* but without agreeing on the parity of their salvific efficacy or their equal capacity to impart the baptismal character. The question of what that character actually is and conveys, and how it differs from baptismal grace as the *res* of the sacrament, does not receive a generally accepted answer. Hugh of St. Victor expands the ways in which a martyr might meet his death, a topic in which thirteenth-century thinkers display no interest, although some second their predecessors' expansion of the kinds of man-made impediments that can block access to the font for one desiring baptism. Even while supporting that doctrine, thinkers in both centuries disagree on whether the dispositions brought to it that count the most are the candidate's desire, his will, his good deeds, his faith, his hope, his charity, his conversion of heart, or the master's personal selection and combination of these qualities. In some thirteenth-century quarters, the faith deemed satisfactory may be incipient; in others it has to be fully formed. Otto of Freising and Radulphus Ardens give us precious glimpses of how these debates trickle down, or not, from the theologians and canonists to the pulpits of pastoral ministers. Otto is an accurate index of the sharply divided positions taken in his day, on which he expresses a clear, if controversial, opinion. Despite the growing inclination of masters by the end of the twelfth century to support baptism by desire, Radulphus reflects a good deal of confusion on what to think about it and how to present it to a wider public.

In many of the areas where we can see significant agreement reached by 1300, Peter Lombard's *Sentences* act as a template, or at least a point of reference, owing as much to its growing role in theological education as to the acceptability of the master's views. Some of his opinions fail to carry the day, as with Christ's institution of ritual baptism with His own ablution in the Jordan. The rationales for the post-resurrection date-line given by Albert the Great and Thomas Aquinas prove more persuasive. In addition to simplifying the defense of baptism by desire, the Dominican solution, especially that of Aquinas, is deemed to carry more theological weight. While the Lombard's catalogue of sources and his particular arguments are used by masters who disagree as well as agree with him, his most frequently cited conclusion is that God's power is not bound by His sacraments. Several scholastics acknowledge that it is Bernard of Clairvaux and not just the Lombard who has played a seminal role in the twelfth-century debate, for the authorities he cites and for his nuancing of the understanding of martyrdom as well as for his defense of baptism by desire. Abelard never receives the credit he is due for reintroducing Ambrose's *De obitu Valen-*

tiniani into that debate. Altogether, side by side with the new or revived terminological refinements and modes of analysis added to the academic legacy, notable disagreements, problem areas, and soft spots remain, along with some arguments that prove to be dead ends. That said, and with all the qualifications we have noted, it remains the case that by 1300 baptism by desire as a real and continuing possibility has become the majority view. The same cannot be said for fictive baptism, to which this study now turns.

CHAPTER *Two*

FICTIVE BAPTISM

Fictive baptism, and the conditions thought to define, validate, or invalidate it, was a topic widely discussed by patristic and medieval thinkers. Beyond exegetes and theologians, it was addressed by authors of saints' lives and chronicles, and commentators on drama. Even leaving aside gaps between theory and practice, the theory itself drew diverse understandings. Few agreements had emerged by the end of our target period. Pastoral desiderata, polemical agendas, political objectives, legal considerations, and psychological presuppositions all informed participants in this debate. While some topics gained concurrence by the end of the twelfth century, and a handful of others in the thirteenth, most of the issues aired remained unresolved. Neither the arrival of new or revived formulae for framing ideas about fictive baptism or for distinguishing among its modes nor the establishment of administrative guidelines led to general agreement on those aspects of the doctrine that remained in contention. In some cases, these innovations led to the complication, not the clarification, of debated questions. While certain key authorities were cited repeatedly, some of them inspired rigorous criticism, and often outright manhandling, as well as different degrees of credence and different strategies for their defense or refutation. No less than the thinkers' conclusions, the headings under which they placed fictive baptism varied, as did the reasons why they considered it. The study of attitudes toward fictive baptism from the third to the early fourteenth century thus reflects discontinuities, fits, and starts. Many arguments, old and new, might gain passing support but then be abruptly dropped, while others were frequently repeated. The storyline in chapter 2 of this study will thus be less a tale of emerging consensus than one which opens windows onto the concerns and conceptual tools applied to this theme, and the differences of opinion that it elicited in its shifting historical settings.

While a number of scholars have treated the problem of hypocrisy and dissimulation in the Middle Ages, they have tended to give fictive baptism only cursory attention, or to ignore it entirely. Peter Godman's claim that "the *fictio* of faith is hardly mentioned in accounts of medieval theology, philosophy, and psychology"[1] in his study of false confessions in the twelfth century is not borne out by the evidence. Winrich Löhr and Karla Pollmann had already explored the theme of hypocrisy in early Christian and medieval hereseology,[2] while Fredric Amory had tracked its semantic history, in Greek and Latin, from the Bible through the twelfth century.[3] Irène Rosier-Catach comments briefly on fictive baptism in her studies of the semantic theory underlying the verbal formula used in the baptismal rite in thirteenth-century scholasticism.[4] For Rosier-Catach, the Eucharist is the paradigm case among the sacraments since the words of consecration are held to trigger a substantial change in the elements. In the case of baptism, she argues, while the physical medium is not transformed, the minister's words are thought to transfer its power; the verbal formula is regarded as the formal aspect of the sacramental sign. On this reading, the baptismal formula is what makes something happen at the font; the words spoken do not merely mean something. Rosier-Catach's interest in whether modern speech-act theory sheds light on this issue leads her to ascribe more una-

1. Peter Godman, *Paradoxes of Conscience in the High Middle Ages: Abelard, Heloise, and the Archpoet* (Cambridge: Cambridge University Press, 2009), 2; passim for the larger argument; on page 26, Godman sees Augustine as the first Christian thinker to raise this question.

2. Winrich Löhr, "Religious Truth, Dissimulation, and Deception in Late Antique Christianity," in *Double Standards in the Ancient and Medieval World*, ed. Karla Pollmann (Göttingen: Duehrkohp & Radicke, 2000), 287–304; Karla Pollmann, "The Splitting of Morality in Matthew 23 and Its Exegetical Consequences," in ibid., 263–86; eadem, "Hypocrisy and the History of Salvation: Medieval Interpretations of Matthew 23," *Wiener Studien* 114 (2001): 469–82.

3. Fredric Amory, "Whited Sepulchers: The Semantic History of Hypocrisy in the High Middle Ages," *RTAM* 53 (1986): 5–39.

4. Irène Rosier-Catach, *La parole efficace: Signe, rituel, sacré* (Paris: Éditions du Seuil, 2004), 191–261 on baptism; 290–92 on fictive baptism, especially in Albert the Great, Thomas Aquinas, Richard of Mediavilla, and John Duns Scotus; eadem, "Speech Acts and Intentional Meanings in the Medieval Philosophy of Language," *Bulletin de philosophie médiévale* 52 (2010): 55–80 on page 63.

nimity to scholastic accounts of fictive baptism than they in fact had. It also leads her to underrate the importance of ablution in making an act a baptismal rite. For, apart from their acceptance of baptism by blood and baptism by desire, theologians in the Christian tradition have agreed throughout the centuries that the rite of baptism requires water as much as the word.

To date, the only scholarly survey devoted to fictive baptism as such is the one published over half a century ago by Artur Michael Landgraf.[5] Tremendously useful in its own day for the wealth of unpublished manuscript material it contains, Landgraf's study does have its limits. His *optique* is a dated one. He focuses on texts and themes which will flower fully, and in his view more acceptably, in high medieval theology, above all that of Thomas Aquinas. Landgraf is not interested in the fact that many of the disagreements and uncertainties that characterize the history of fictive baptism remained unresolved by the Angelic Doctor. Nor was it Aquinas who settled those debates that were laid to rest. As we will see in the following, the teachings of no single master or group of masters proved definitive to their contemporaries and successors. Insofar as there are turning points, they are not found in the thought of Aquinas. There are also many historical contexts and literary genres in which fictive baptism was discussed which do not draw Landgraf's attention. This is certainly true of the type of fictive baptizand heading the list chronologically, the *Taufmime*.

The *Taufmime*

The *Taufmime* acquired this label because it was Germanophone scholars who first discovered and named him. "Him" is the operative term here, in fact as well as in English grammar, since the *Taufmime* is always masculine. He is a phenomenon of the Roman world of the third and fourth centuries, before the legitimation of the Christian church. His natural habitat is the late Roman theater. He is a pagan actor who converts while on stage, thus inspiring reprisals from his now-hostile pagan audience. He thus inhabits a particular subset of early Christian martyrs. He does have feminine counterparts, but the converted female actor is treated by hagiographers not as a *Taufmime* but as a species of the ascetic ex-harlot saint whose story accents the importance of her male mentor.[6]

5. Artur Michael Landgraf, "Die Wirking der Taufe im *fictus* und im *contritus*," in idem, *Dogmengeschichte der Frühscholastik*, 4 vols. in 8 (Regensburg: Friedrich Pustat, 1952–56), 3/2:87–131.

6. The single best treatment of this subject is Richard Lim, "Converting the Un-Christian-

The lives of several members of the *Taufmime* group are included in the *Acta Sanctorum* along with the dates of their feasts and the churches in which they are celebrated. These *vitae* were originally written in Greek and then translated into Latin. The editors of the *Acta Sanctorum* indicate neither the dates of their composition nor of their translation, so it is unknown how close in time these texts may be to the events they relate. Nor do we know how widely available the Latin versions, and the cult of their protagonists, may have been in the medieval west in churches without bilingual congregations. The only firmly dated *Taufmime* text is found in the Greek *Chronicon Paschale* (seventh century), which had no medieval Latin translation. It records the life and death of Gelasinus, converted and martyred in 296 during the reign of Diocletian. This *vita* contains many of the conventions of the genre although the hagiographer departs from them in two respects: He notes repeatedly that Gelasinus was second banana in his troupe and that he was lynched by an irate pagan mob, rather than being put to death on the orders of a duly constituted official.[7]

The histories of these figures have a great deal in common. The *Taufmime* always starts out as a pagan actor. With his troupe he enacts, and ridicules, the rites of Christian baptism before an appreciative pagan audience. These actors display an accurate grasp of the baptismal liturgy. The *Taufmime* plays the role of the baptizand. In the midst of the scenario, he is suddenly converted. Typically, there is an important magistrate in the audience. When the *Taufmime* announces that the dramatic fiction he has just enacted has become, for him, a religious fact, the magistrate has him arrested and put to death. The account of a particular *Taufmime* may add other circumstantial details, but in all cases his fictive baptism is regarded as sacramentally valid and he is received and venerated as a saint by the Christian community.

Martyred in 293 during the reign of Maximian and honored on April 14,

izable: The Baptism of Stage Performers in Late Antiquity," in *Conversion in Late Antiquity and the Early Middle Ages: Seeing and Believing*, ed. Kenneth Mills and Anthony Grafton (Rochester, NY: Rochester University Press, 2003), 84–126. See also William Tydeman, *The Theatre in the Middle Ages: Western European Stage Conditions, c. 800–1576* (Cambridge: Cambridge University Press, 1978), 24, for examples that diverge somewhat from those presented in Lim's study and in this book.

7. *Chronicon Paschale* 297, *PG* (Paris, 1865), 92:683–85. A good English version is provided in *Chronicon Paschale, 284–628 AD*, trans. Michael Whitby and Mary Whitby, Translated Texts for Historians 7 (Liverpool: University of Liverpool Press, 1989), 3–4. This text is noted by Everett Ferguson, *Baptism in the Early Church: History, Theology, and Liturgy in the First Five Centuries* (Grand Rapids, MI: William B. Eerdmans Publishing Company, 2009), 443. Ferguson's main interest is the point that the staged baptism of Gelasinus occurs by total immersion; he does not mention any of the members of the *Taufmime* cohort included in the *Acta Sanctorum*.

Ardalion's relatively brief *vita* sounds the genre's *Leitmotif*: "Making fun of the Christian religion," he and his troupe "acted out the rites of Christians." His hagiographer then prepares the ground for what follows, or, as we might say, gives away the punch line, with a generalization: "But God, who mocks the mockers, may turn a spectacle into a serious matter, fictions into oblations, and convert the actors."[8] This is indeed what happened to Ardalion: "For, while he was mocking the rites of Christians in the theater, he was suddenly changed, and confirmed it not only by his words but also by the testimony of his blood."[9] Having completed his fictive baptismal performance "before the tyrant," Ardalion proclaimed, in a loud voice, to him and the other spectators, "Don't think that what I just did was in jest, but accept it as the truth of the Christian religion. For I am indeed a Christian."[10] As expected, the prince puts him to death.

More detailed is the story of Porphyrius, venerated on September 15, whose conversion took place in 362: "Performing a farce before Julian the Apostate, he received baptism. Suddenly changed by God's power, he professed that he was a Christian ... and was crowned with martyrdom."[11] In this *vita*, we learn a good deal about the fictive rite itself as it was enacted on stage, complete with dialogue, props, and costumes. The actor playing the bishop, "having submerged him in water, proclaimed, 'Porphyrius is baptized in the name of the Father, Son, and Holy Spirit.' Emerging, he was clothed in white garments."[12] Then, denouncing paganism before the emperor, Porphyrius was condemned by the entire Senate and was elaborately tortured before being beheaded.[13]

Even more detailed, and telling, is the story of another Porphyrius, the first known *Taufmime*, venerated on November 14, a fictive baptizand during the reign of Aurelian (270–75). In his case, there was no senatorial deliberation and no emperor. The pagan authority figure involved was Alexander,

8. St. Ardalion, mimus, April 14, *AA SS*, 69 vols. (Brussels: Alphonsus Greuse, 1863–1940), 11/2:213: "In derisum Christianae religionis, ... acta Christianorum repraesentarent, sed Deum, qui irrisores irridet, jocus in rem seriam, fabulas in hostias, et mimos convertisse."

9. Ibid.: "qui cum sacris Christianorum in theatro illuderet, derepente mutatus, et non solum verbis, sed et testimonio sui sanguinis comprobavit."

10. Ibid.: "coram tyranno ... dixit: Nolite arbitrari me iam ludicra agere, sed in Christianae religionis veritate haec accipite. Ego autem Christianus sum."

11. St. Porphyrius, martyr, ex-mimus, September 15, *AA SS*, 45/4:37: "coram Juliano apostata per jocum baptisma suscipiens, Dei virtute derepente mutatus, Christianum se esse professus est ... martyrio coronatus."

12. Ibid.: "cum in aqua descendens immergeret, exclamavit: 'Baptizatur Porphyrius in nomine Patris et Filii et Spiritus Sancti'; sic emergens, albas vestes indutus."

13. Ibid.

the provincial governor of Caesarea in Cappadocia. Porphyrius was a native of Ephesus whose thespian repute ran before him, attracting the attention and patronage of Alexander, who brought him to Caesarea to perform. "After completing several other scenes," in what appears to have been a show consisting of a series of skits or turns, "the players proceeded to portray the venerated Christian rites of divine baptism. Some of them, mocking bishops, priests, deacons, and other clerics, brought forward Porphyrius, as if he were a catechumen receiving baptism."[14] The *vita* author stresses the fact that the pagan actors were thoroughly conversant with the liturgical details of the rite: "Then, in jest, they themselves carried out the rites of Christians according to the norms of the church."[15] But, the author adds, "little did these wretches know that Christ's power is not mocked." For, despite the farce, "God willed to confirm as valid the faith in Him enacted by the infidels, and performed a miracle."[16] *Quid ergo*? We should not be astonished, the author comments, since nothing is impossible with God.[17]

But more is to come in the tale of Porphyrius of Ephesus. At the precise moment when God accepted his fictive baptism as valid, a heavenly light shone forth and an angelic choir sang hymns of praise. These celestial manifestations made a deep impression on Porphyrius's fellow actors. They concluded that they, too, should become Christians. So, "coming down [from the stage], they went with Porphyrius to the Christian church, asking the bishop for true baptism."[18] We are given to understand that this prelate received the other members of the troupe as catechumens with an eye to their future instruction and ritual baptism. But, after questioning Porphyrius about his own recent experience, the bishop declared that his baptism was authentic. No further initiation on his part was needed.[19] And, testifying to his acceptance of Porphyrius's fictive baptism as valid, the bishop managed to visit him secretly in prison, bringing him the *viaticum* before his execution and translation to heavenly glory.[20]

14. St. Porphyrius of Ephesus, mimus, November 14, *AA SS* 66/2:230: "et variis ludis iam absolutis, processerunt actores Christianorum venerandos ritus divine baptismatis repraesentatur. Et quidem institutes episcopos et presbyteros, diaconosque cum ceteris ordinibus, produxerunt mimithemelae Porphyrium ut tamquam catechumenus baptismum susciperet."

15. Ibid.: "Tunc effingentes seipsos ad normam Ecclesiae, Christianorum mysteria per jocum absolverunt."

16. Ibid.: "ignorantes miseri quia non irridetur virtus Christi, … in infidelibus et fidem in seipsum valide confirmare volens, miraculum est operatus."

17. Ibid.: "Numquid istud apud Dei potentiam impossible."

18. Ibid.: "descendentes abierunt cum Porphyrio ad Christianorum ecclesiam, requirentes ab episcopo verum baptismum."

19. Ibid.

20. Ibid., 66/2:230–31.

These are only a few of the known *Taufmime* stories. A number of their features are striking, apart from what they tell us about theatrical practice in the later Roman Empire and the evident familiarity of pagans with the Christian baptismal liturgy. Those findings aside, and granted that, as in all saints' lives, God is the real protagonist in these *vitae*, they all involve His *ex machina* intervention. Especially when the *Taufmime*'s sudden conversion is attested by a celestial *son et lumière*, this *topos* seems conventional, even predictable, given ancient dramatic expectations. Equally of interest in the case of Porphyrius of Ephesus is the local bishop's willingness to accept as fact a hearsay report of the supernatural events betokening divine confirmation of the convert's new status. There is no indication in this *vita* that the bishop of Caesarea requested, or received, assurance of the neophyte's doctrinal or moral commitments. But it does appear that the actors' adherence to Christian ritual norms, punctiliously correct in word and gesture, is not entirely incidental in the turning of fictive into real baptisms in these *Taufmime* texts.

The Boys on the Beach

If a bishop of Caesarea could accept as valid the fictive baptism of a *Taufmime* in the age of the martyrs, so could a bishop of Alexandria accept as valid the baptismal play of children after the church was legitimized. And he could do so without the felt need for miraculous divine confirmation. The paradigmatic case is reported by Rufinus of Aquileia in his *Historia ecclesiastica* (395/410). This text is worth understanding in its own right, and quoting at some length, since it was destined to receive considerable use and abuse in later centuries. Our best guide to Rufinus's objectives in this work is Françoise Thelamon.[21] As she points out, on one level his goal is to update the ecclesiastical history of Eusebius for Latinophones, taking the story up to the end of the fourth century. On another level, he orchestrates a major theme—the triumph of orthodox Christianity over paganism and heresy. The diocese of Alexandria is central to his account. For it is here that the Arian heresy got off the ground. And it is here that the church had to battle not only the standard Greco-Roman gods but also the long-standing cults of the pagan Egyptians. The key hero in Rufinus's history is Athanasius,

21. Françoise Thelamon, *Païens et chrétiens au IVe siècle: L'apport de la "Histoire ecclésiastique" de Rufin d'Aquilée* (Paris: Études Augustiniennes, 1987); eadem, "Rufin historien de son temps," in *Rufino di Concordia e il suo tempo*, 2 vols., Antichità altoadriatiche 31 (Udine: Arti Grafiche Friuliane, 1987), 1:41–59.

bishop of Alexandria for much of the fourth century, a resolute defender of orthodoxy despite the sufferings caused by the machinations of his enemies. The courage and sanctity of Athanasius, and the divine miracles attesting to the correctness of his theology and that of the confrères who shared it, are central features of Rufinus's tale.

With this background and these considerations in mind, Rufinus relates the following episode when he first brings Athanasius on stage as bishop, following the death of his immediate predecessor, Alexander of Alexandria:

> Now I do not think it out of place to trace back briefly his early years and to explain how he was educated as a boy, as we have found out from those who lived with him. Once when Bishop Alexander was celebrating the day of Peter Martyr in Alexandria, he was waiting in a place by the sea after the ceremonies were over for his clergy to gather for a banquet. There he saw from a distance some boys on the seashore playing a game in which, as they often do, they were mimicking a bishop and the things customarily done in church. Now when he had gazed intently for a while at the boys, he saw that they were performing some of the more secret and sacramental things. He was disturbed and immediately ordered the clergy to be called to him and showed them what he was watching from a distance. Then he commanded them to go and get all the boys and bring them to him. When they arrived, he asked them what game they were playing and what they had done and how. At first they were afraid, as is usual at that age, and refused, but then they disclosed in due order what they had done, admitting that some catechumens had been baptized by them at the hands of Athanasius, who had played the part of bishop in their childish game. Then he carefully inquired of those who were said to have been baptized what they had been asked and what they had answered, and the same of him who had put the questions, and when he saw that everything was according to the manner of our religion, he conferred with a council of clerics and then ruled, so it is reported, that those on whom water had been poured after the questions had been asked and answered correctly need not repeat the baptism, but that those things should be completed which are customarily done by priests. As for Athanasius and those who had played the part of presbyters and ministers in the game, he called together their parents, and having put them under oath, handed them over to be reared for the church.[22]

22. Rufinus of Aquileia, *Historia ecclesiastica* 1.15, ed. and trans. Manlio Simonetti in Rufino di Concordia, *Scritti vari*, Corpus scriptorum ecclesiae Aquileiensis 5/2 (Aquileia: Città Nuova, 2000), 222–24: "Verum non mihi absque ordine pauca de huius viri origine supra repetere et cuius a puero institutionis fuerit, sicuti ab his, qui cum ipso vitam duxerant, accepimus, memorare. Tempore, quod apud Alexandriam Petri martyris diem Alexander episcopus agebat, cum post expleta sollemnia conventuros ad convivium suum clericos expectaret in loco mari vicino, videt eminus puerorum super oram maris ludum imitantium, ut fieri solet, episcopum atque ea, quae in eclesiis geri mos est. Sed cum intentus diutino pueros inspectaret, vi-

This anecdote accomplishes many things at once. It explains how Athanasius received his excellent education, being taken on as Alexander's protégé and groomed as his successor, "as Samuel was reared in the temple of the Lord."[23] Along with the other boy ministers, he was found preferment in the church, in his case succeeding Alexander as bishop of Alexandria. In this passage, Rufinus evokes a *topos* found in biblical and classical literature and reprised in hagiography, the great man's manifestation, in childhood, of his early calling and of the gifts he later displays in his adult role as a prophet, saint, or leader. This same trope had a specifically Egyptian resonance. As Thelamon notes, the pagan Egyptians held that some children were endowed with foresight, enabling them to act as oracles of the gods and mediums between the gods and the living. Rufinus Latinizes and Christianizes all of these traditions. The fact that the boys' baptismal play led by Athanasius includes rites that are secret as well as those that are manifest is another index of Athanasius's precocious insight into holy things, another sign of his divine election, and of Alexander's perceptiveness in recognizing and promoting it.[24]

Quite apart from what it is designed to convey about the prefiguration of Athanasius's career and holiness to come, this anecdote also sheds light on Alexander as a model bishop. In addition to his discernment of the early clerical calling of the boy ministers, Alexander grasps a central feature

det ab his geri quaedam etiam secretiora et mystica. Perturbatus ilico vocari ad se clericos iubet atque eis quid eminus ipse videret, ostendit. Tum abire eos et conprehensos ad se perducere omnes pueros imperat. Cumque adessent, quis eis ludus et quid egissent vel quomodo, percontatur. Illi, ut talis habere aetas, pavidi negare primo, dein rem gestam per ordinem pandunt et baptizatos a se esse quosdam catechumenos confitentur per Athanasium, qui ludi illius puerilis episcopus fuerat simulatus. Tum ille diligenter inquirens ab his, qui baptizati dicebantur, quid interrogati fuerint, quidve responderint, simul et ab eo, qui interrogaverat, ubi videt secundum religionis nostrae ritum cuncta constare, conlocutus cum concilio clericorum statuisse traditur illis, quibus integris interrogationibus et responsionibus aqua fuerat infusa, iterari baptismum non debere, sed adimpleri ea, quae a sacerdotibus mos est. Athanasium vero atque eos, quos ludus ille vel presbyteros habere visus fuerat vel ministros, convocatis parentibus sub dei obtestione tradit ecclesiae nutriendos." Translation: Rufinus of Aquileia, *The Church History, Books 10 and 11*, trans. Philip R. Amidon (New York: Oxford University Press, 1997), 26–27.

23. Rufinus, *Hist. eccl.* 1.15, 224: "ac velut Samuel in templo domini nutritur."

24. Thelamon, *Païens et chrétiens*, 17–18, 333–37; on pages 337–41 she cites other instances in early church history in which authors invoke the theme that the child has the eye of truth. Cf. Ferguson, *Baptism*, 457–58, who omits this aspect of Rufinus's text and who is concerned primarily with whether the pouring of water, rather than immersion, in this account reflects the boys' imitation of deathbed baptisms. On play as children's work, see Water J. Ong, intro. to Hugo Rahner, *Man at Play*, trans. Brian Battershaw and Edward Quinn (New York: Herder and Herder, 1972), xii–xiv.

of *homo ludens*: Children's games are not merely the idle amusements of youths as yet unburdened by adult responsibilities. Rather, they are serious work in which children test, rehearse, and develop the skills they will need in their mature professions and social roles. Alexander ascertains that the boys on the beach come from Christian families. They are conversant with baptismal ritual. They are catechumens, perhaps prime-signed, who in due course would present themselves at the font. He is concerned with their intentions, no less than with those of Athanasius and the other boy ministers. He recognizes that the boys' behavior is not unusual. They play at ecclesiastical ritual and imitate the clergy, as boys often do. Their game is undertaken not to mock or to ridicule, but to emulate his own episcopal practice. Their behavior is thus to be approved and their vocation nurtured.

Further, in validating the boys' fictive baptism and in guaranteeing their education and ecclesiastical promotion, Alexander displays foresight for the needs of the church and an exemplary executive style. He does nothing unilaterally or precipitously. On first sighting the boys' game, he does not rush to judgment. He waits; he observes; he inquires. After investigating what the boys have said and done, he makes his ruling in consultation with his clergy. In arranging for the boy ministers' preparation for their clerical future, he convenes their parents and gains their support for his plans. We may also note some omissions from Rufinus's account. There is no comparable conference with the parents of the boy baptizands. Yet, while the boys are evidently old enough to play on the beach without adult supervision, they are minors, legally under *patria potestas*. They lack the legal capacity to make an official baptismal commitment of their own without parental concurrence. Although some readers of Rufinus will flag this issue later, it is not one that Rufinus chooses to raise. Rather, he highlights the early indices of Athanasius's future prelacy and the excellence of the leadership of the bishop who promotes him and whom he so brilliantly succeeds.

Rufinus's history was well known in the Greek east. Two fifth-century Byzantine church historians, Socrates Scholasticus and Sozomen, make heavy use of it, including reference to the boys on the beach. Each gives his own emphasis to this tale, forecasting some of the reshapings that this passage will undergo in the Latin west. In his *Church History* (439/40), Socrates omits the meal which Alexander plans to host for his clergy following the liturgy celebrating the martyr Peter. He does not mention Alexander's clergy at all, or the convening of the boy ministers' parents. His Alexander performs a solo act. He observes the boys and makes his decision alone. What he discovers, according to Socrates, is that the boys have specifically chosen

Athanasius to act as their bishop; the other boys act only as priests and deacons, that is, as helpers but not as baptismal ministers themselves. Socrates also omits the point that the boys baptized were catechumens. Nor does he mention Alexander's ruling that, since their baptism was valid, they should not be rebaptized. What he emphasizes is that Alexander took Athanasius under his wing, secured his education, ordained him, and brought him to the Council of Nicaea as his adjutant and co-defender of orthodoxy. Socrates concludes by noting that the boys on the beach event related by Rufinus is far from unique and should not be questioned.[25]

As for Sozomen, his *Church History* (443/50) opens his discussion of the boys on the beach by noting that, on his deathbed, Alexander directs those voting to choose Athanasius as his successor. Far from being manipulative, Sozomen's Alexander is thereby expressing God's will. For his part, Athanasius at first resists election but later accepts it as God's will. Given his intelligence, his eloquence, and his skill at thwarting plots, he is definitely the man for the job. Rather than commenting on Alexander's role in mentoring the young Athanasius, Sozomen presents the latter as an autodidact from his earliest years. This is what explains Athanasius's accurate practice as a boy bishop. Sozomen includes the meal hosted by Alexander after the liturgy honoring the martyr Peter and shows Alexander observing the boys before his guests arrive. But, according to him, far from being disturbed at first by what he sees, Alexander is pleased, accepting the game as an innocent emulation of what bishops do. He grows concerned only when he notices the inclusion of secret matters, which, like Rufinus, Sozomen chooses not to identify. It is only then that Alexander is inspired to consult his clergy, or at least its leading members. It is not clear whether these constitute all the guests at his holiday meal, or some subset of them. On further investigation, Alexander and these clerics determine that the boys acting as catechumens had in fact never been initiated at all. Still and yet, finding that the boy ministers had followed the liturgical norms of the church, Alexander and his clergy rightly decide that their fictive baptism is valid and that they should not be rebaptized.

Sozomen agrees with Rufinus that all that was wanting were the unspecified offices performed only by priests. Following Rufinus more closely than Socrates, Sozomen includes Alexander's convening of the boy minis-

25. Socrates Scholasticus, *Historia ecclesiastica* 1.15.1–4, ed. Günther Christian Hansen, trans. Pierre Périchon and Pierre Maraval, 4 vols., SC 477 (Paris: Les Belles Lettres, 2004), 1:170–73. For the knowledge of Rufinus among Greek writers in the following centuries, see Thelamon, *Païens et chrétiens*, 15, 41–42.

ters' parents and his gaining of their support for their sons' education and clerical future. He closes by noting that Alexander took a personal interest in Athanasius's nurture, providing him with an excellent education, making him his secretary and aide, and ensuring that he was well prepared to rule the see of Alexandria in turn.[26] Sozomen omits the care with which Alexander questioned the boys about the interrogations made of the baptizands and their responses, and the fact that water had been poured, as fulfilling essentials of the rite. More important than the liturgical exactitude of what the boys on the beach did and underwent, in his account, is that the hand of God was at work in their fictive baptism, that Alexander recognized this fact, and that he and Athanasius were similarly inspired to provide well for the needs of the church.

As is well known, the histories of Socrates Scholasticus and Sozomen, along with that of their successor Theodorus, were the three sources which Cassiodorus had translated into Latin by Epiphanus and which he excerpted in his *Historia tripartita* (by ca. 562). That text, however, does not include the passages in which Socrates and Sozomen reprise Rufinus on the boys on the beach. It is likely that the Latin translations of their histories, along with the Greek texts, made their way into the papal libraries of Pelagius II (578–90) and of Gregory I (590–604). The popes disseminated manuscripts of the Latin versions, with copies turning up at Bobbio and Jarrow in the seventh century. They were put into wider circulation in the ninth century thanks to Hildebald of Cologne and Lupus of Ferrières, who were eager to obtain accurate archetypes of these translations from Rome.[27] Even in the absence of documented copies of the translations of these works in northern Europe, the contents of the histories of Socrates Scholasticus and Sozomen appear to have been transmitted in ways we cannot pinpoint; Averil Cameron has shown that the *History of the Franks* (576/94) of Gregory of

26. Sozomen, *Historia ecclesiastica* 2.17.6–10, ed. and trans. Günther Christian Hansen, 4 vols., Fontes Christiani 73/1–4 (Turnhout: Brepols, 2004), 1:260–63. According to Cornelia B. Horn, "Children at Play as Social Ritual," in *Late Ancient Christianity*, ed. Virginia Burrus (Minneapolis: Fortress Press, 2005), 95–116 on pages 113–14, what turned Alexander's pleasure into consternation, according to Sozomen, was that he saw the boys playing at the consecration and distribution of the Eucharist. There is no evidence in the text to support this reading.

27. Pierre Courcelle, *Late Latin Writers and Their Greek Sources*, trans. Harry E. Wedeck (Cambridge, MA: Harvard University Press, 1969), 338n38, 401–3. For more on the fortunes of Cassiodorus's library, see James J. O'Donnell, *Cassiodorus* (Berkeley: University of California Press, 1979), 240–41. Walter Berschin, *Greek Letters in the Latin Middle Ages from Jerome to Nicholas of Cusa*, trans. Jerrold C. Frakes (Washington, D.C.: The Catholic University of America Press, 1988), 78, 159–69, 302n23, also discusses Carolingian translations of Greek texts but without further information on the circulation of the works of Socrates and Sozomen.

Tours is surprisingly well informed on recent and current events discussed by Byzantine historians writing just before Gregory's own time, whose works are not known to have received Latin translations.[28]

Quite apart from the access which Latin translations of Socrates and Sozomen may have afforded, Rufinus himself was widely cited in patristic literature. He was known to Paulinus of Nola, Julianus of Eclanum, Augustine, Quodvultdeus, Victor of Vita, Orosius, and Gennadius of Marseille. As Rufinus's English translator puts it, his history was "an instant and lasting success ... [which] exerted great influence over both his contemporaries and later generations."[29] While patristic authors were familiar with Rufinus's history, none of them refers to the boys on the beach, although many of them devote attention to fictive baptism. Still, the availability of that passage, thanks to the translations of his Greek transmitters or the copying of Rufinus's own text, made possible its citation, and reinscription, when attention to it revived starting in the eleventh century.

The Age of the Church Fathers

Another one of Rufinus's contributions to the western Christian tradition was his zealous promotion of Jerome's Vulgate translation of the Bible, although Jerome joined other patristic authors in ignoring the boys on the beach and Alexander's ruling on their fictive baptism. Jerome offers a different perspective on that subject, in part derived from his predecessors and in part his own. His most influential treatment of fictive baptism occurs in a work frequently consulted by medieval exegetes in the effort to understand the most enigmatic of the Old Testament prophets, Ezekiel.

Jerome locates his discussion of fictive baptism in his comment on Ezekiel 16:4, one of the prophet's extended diatribes against the Israelites' faithlessness and immorality. Personifying Israel as Jerusalem, Ezekiel addresses that city as follows: "As for your birth, on the day you were born your navel string was not cut; you were neither washed with water to cleanse you, nor rubbed with salt, nor swathed with bands."[30] Jerome's

28. Averil Cameron, "The Byzantine Sources of Gregory of Tours," *Journal of Theological Studies*, n.s. 26 (1975): 421–26.

29. Amidon, intro. to his trans. of Rufinus, *Church History*, xiii. For further details on the knowledge of this text by Latin patristic writers, see Thelamon, *Païens et chrétiens*, 14–15; Simonetti, intro. to his ed. and trans. of Rufinus, *Hist. eccl.*, 177.

30. Vulgate: "Et quando nata est, in die ortus tui, non est praecisus umbilicus tuus, et aqua non est lota in salutem nec sale salita nec involuto pannis." Here and elsewhere, English translations of Bible passages are drawn from the RSV.

favorite stylistic device in this commentary is digression. From this text, he segues without missing a beat to Christ's advice to Nicodemus recorded in John 3:3–5: No one will be saved unless reborn of water and the Holy Spirit. This thought then leads Jerome to baptism and those who administer and receive it falsely and inefficaciously: "There are many ablutions," he observes, "by which the Gentiles and heretics are polluted in their rites, which may wash all, but not to salvation."[31] Even among orthodox Christians, alas, some people receive baptism hypocritically, with inadequate faith. As with heretics, in their case the rite is meaningless: "This applies not just to heretics but also to some in the church who want the salvific effects of baptism without a full faith. It can be said that they may receive the water but not the [Holy] Spirit. This was the case with Simon Magus, who sought to gain the grace of God for money. Such a one is baptized with water but is in no way baptized unto salvation."[32] We note here that Jerome uses conditional verbs when referring to these null ablutions. They may wash (*lavent*) their recipients, who may receive water (*acceperint aquam*). But Jerome is quite certain that unworthy baptizands are in no way (*nequaquam*) baptized unto salvation.

Before proceeding, it is important to recognize that, albeit his renown as a biblical scholar, Jerome's use of Simon Magus to illustrate the problem of fictive baptism is a significant departure from Simon's story as told in the Acts of the Apostles. A summary of the account in Acts follows.[33] The open-

31. Jerome, *Commentariorum in Hezechielem libri XIV* 4:16.4–5, ed. Franciscus Glorie, CCSL 75 (Turnhout: Brepols, 1964), 163: "multaque sunt lavacra quae ethnici, in mysteriis suis, et haeretici pollicentur, qui omnes lavent sed non lavent in salutem."

32. Ibid., 164: "quod quidem non solum de haereticis, sed de ecclesiasticis intelligi potest qui non plena fide accipiunt baptismum salutare, de quibus dicendum est quod acceperint aquam sed non acceperint Spiritum—sicut et Simon ille magus qui pecunia volebat redimere gratiam Dei, baptizatus quidem est in aqua sed nequaquam baptizatus in salutem." Jerome also cites Simon Magus expressly when referring to fictive baptism in *Tractatus in Psalmos* 80.8, although he gives the more usual description of Simon as seeking to traffic in holy things in *Tractatus in Marci Evangelium* 11:15–17, both in *Opera homiletica*, ed. D. Germanus Morin, CCSL 78 (Turnhout: Brepols, 1958), 79, 493. It should be noted that Alberto Ferreiro, *Simon Magus in Patristic, Medieval and Early Modern Traditions* (Leiden: Brill, 2005), does not mention Simon as a fictive baptizand but focuses on him as venal, a proponent of magic and witchcraft, of pseudo-apostolic traditions, and of Gnosticism or whatever is the arch-heresy of the day; Ferreiro looks mainly at apocryphal literature and does not consider either Jerome's exegetical texts as cited here or the treatments of Simon as fictive baptizand in later exegetes and theologians considered below.

33. Vulgate for texts in the passages following: Acts 1:8: "sed accipietis virtutem supervenientis Spiritus sancti in vos"; Acts 8:6–7: "Intendebant autem turbae his quae a Philippo dicebuntur unanimiter audientes et videntis signa quae faciebat. Multi eorum qui habebant

ing chapter of Acts itself sets the stage. In Christ's speech to his apostles just before his Ascension (Acts 1:8), He told them that the Holy Spirit that He was about to send them at Pentecost would grant them power: "But you shall receive power when the Holy Spirit has come upon you." Acts relates that this was indeed the case. In addition to enabling the apostles to speak in tongues, to preach effectively, and to maintain their resolve in the face of persecution, the gift of the Spirit empowered them to perform miracles, specifically miracles of healing (Acts 3:1–10, 3:12–16, 4:33, 5:16).

Some but not all of the powers accorded to the apostles characterized the mission of Philip in Samaria, the first mission to non-Jews which the text reports and the setting for the story of Simon Magus. As the text relates (Acts 8:6–7), "the multitudes with one accord gave heed to what was said by Philip, when they heard him and saw the signs which he did. For unclean spirits came out of many who were possessed, crying with a loud voice, and many who were paralyzed or lame were healed." Finding these miracles persuasive along with Philip's message of salvation, many citizens of Samaria of both sexes were baptized (Acts 8:12).

Simon is then introduced as a magician who, before Philip's arrival, had gained a following among the people of Samaria, dazzling them with his feats, feats which led them to believe that he had been empowered by God (Acts 8:9–10): "They all gave heed to him, from the least to the greatest, saying, 'This man is that power of God that is called Great.'" But, finding himself outclassed as a wonder-worker by Philip, Simon decided to concede, and to reinvent himself as a disciple of Philip (Acts 8:13): "Even Simon himself believed, and after being baptized he continued with Philip. And seeing signs and great miracles performed, he was amazed." The text suggests that it was not his message of salvation but the missionary's miraculous power that impressed Simon and inspired him to sign on with Philip.

---

spiritus immundos clamantes voce exhibant; multi autem paralytici et claudi curati sunt"; Acts 8:9–10: "cui ascultabant omnes, a minimo ad maximum, dicentes: Hic est virtus Dei, quo vocatur magna"; Acts 8:13: "Tunc Simon et ipse credidit et, cum baptizatus esset, adhaerebat Philippo; videns etiam signa et virtutes maximas fieri stupens admirabatur"; Acts 8:16–17: "ut acciperent Spiritum sanctum; nondum enim in quemquam illorum venerat, sed baptizati tantum erant in nomine Domini Iesu. Tunc imponebant manus super illos, et accipiebant Spiritum sanctum"; Acts 8:18–19: "cum vidisset autem Simon quia per impositionem manus apostolorum daretur Spiritus sanctus, obtulit eis pecuniam dicens: Date et mihi hanc potestatem, ut cuicumque imposuero manus accipiat Spiritum sanctum"; Acts 8:20–21: "Pecunia tua tecum in perditionem, quoniam donum Dei existimasti pecunia possideri. Non esto tibi pars neque sors in sermone isto; cor enim tuum non est rectum coram Deo"; Acts 8:23: "in felle enim amaritudinis et obligatione iniquitatis video te esse."

Simon's next move, as Acts specifies, occurred after his baptism. What he now sought as a personal advantage was the gift of the Holy Spirit. Acts presents this gift as given in a rite, the laying on of hands, subsequent to baptism, whether it be Simon's own baptism or the mass baptism of Philip's converts. It is a rite which Philip is presented as lacking the qualifications to administer. For, on learning of the success of Philip's mission, the apostles in Jerusalem took counsel among themselves and decided to send Peter and John to Samaria (Acts 8:14–17). The reason given for their arrival there (Acts 8:16) is so that the converts "might receive the Holy Spirit; for it had not yet fallen on any of them, but they had only been baptized in the name of the Lord Jesus." The converts may have been baptized with water and the Holy Spirit, but a distinct, post-baptismal rite was needed as the next step in the Christianization of Samaria. The Jerusalem apostles provided it (Acts 8:17): "Then they laid their hands on them and they received the Holy Spirit."

Was this rite transmitting the Holy Spirit imparted to all of Philip's neophytes, or only to some of them? The text of Acts does not answer this question, but it presents Simon as regarding it as a privilege from which he had somehow been excluded. For he now made a personal request for this rite and sought to buy it. Acts indicates what Simon thought this apostolic laying on of hands would impart (Acts 8:18–19): "Now when Simon saw that the Spirit was given through the laying on of the apostles' hands, he offered them money, saying, 'Give me also the power, that anyone on whom I lay my hands may receive the Holy Spirit.'"

Simon's wish to acquire the fullness of power possessed only by the apostles themselves gave understandable offense. Early on, Acts reports that the apostles' current procedure for adding to their number was the casting of lots among the candidates they deemed worthy (Acts 1:15–20). But Simon's request, in itself, revealed his profound unworthiness. Peter rejected it in no uncertain terms (Acts 8:20–21): "But Peter said to him, 'Your silver perish with you, because you thought you could obtain the gift of God with money! You have neither part nor lot in this matter, for your heart is not right before God.'" In his final words dismissing Simon, Peter adds (Acts 8:23), "for I see that you are in the gall of bitterness and in the bond of iniquity."

As the Acts of the Apostles presents him, Simon may be seen as having been at fault in acceding to baptism as a means of salvaging his lost fame as a wonder-worker, believing that he could do so by associating himself with Philip's miraculous power. But Philip raised no question about the intentions or the quality of the faith that Simon brought to the font. All involved appear to have regarded his baptism as valid. The author of Acts treats Simon as definitely at fault in his failed attempt to receive the laying on of hands, the post-baptismal rite seen as conveying gifts of the Holy Spirit beyond the charisms given in baptism, a rite available only from the apostles. He sought this latter rite in order to acquire their apostolic powers for himself. And it was this latter rite—not his baptism—that provoked Peter's denunciation and condemnation. In the case of both rites, the theme that Acts orchestrates is Simon's self-serving lust for power. But what sent him to perdition along with his money was not his baptism but his would-be purchase of the laying on of hands, which he could obtain only from the apostles whose ranks he sought so unsuccessfully to enter.

This is the Simon Magus of the Acts of the Apostles. In Jerome's hands, however, Simon has become a prototypical fictive baptizand. And this is Jerome's judgment not because of Simon's lust for power but because of his lack of faith. Other masters who treat fictive baptism may focus on other moral or intellectual sins. As we will see shortly, Augustine also treats Simon as a fraudulent baptizand and views Peter's rejection of him as a response to that sinfully received initiation rite, an assessment of Simon that likewise ignores his lust for power, charging him instead with a lack of charity. But such is Jerome's repute as a biblical exegete that it is Jerome who is cited as the authority of choice by the medieval thinkers who join him in opposing the efficacy of fictive baptism, some of whom also make Jerome's Simon Magus the touchstone of their arguments. For Jerome himself, leaving aside pagan rites which bespeak their own vacuity, it is incorrect faith or imperfect faith that he yokes to bad faith in his understanding of fictive baptisms, rites he sees as categorically devoid of salvific effect.

But Jerome was not a bishop faced with the administrative dilemmas surrounding insincere conversions. According to Peter Brown, fictive baptism emerged as a real issue for church leaders once Christianity became Rome's state religion and many people converted without true faith or moral commitment. In Brown's view, the fictive baptism problem was not solved until Augustine developed his mature ecclesiology and doctrine of predestination: In this life, the sheep and the goats will coexist in the church until the Day of Judgment, when God will recognize and reward the elect.[34] For all its elegance, this view is an oversimplification. While bishops in the late fourth and early fifth centuries were troubled by hypocritical conver-

34. Peter Brown, "St. Augustine's Attitude toward Religious Coercion," *Journal of Roman Studies* 54 (1964): 107–16; reprt. in idem, *Religion and Society in the Age of Saint Augustine* (London: Faber and Faber, 1972), 260–78.

sions, they urged catechumens not to defer their baptism but to proceed to the font when duly catechized.[35] And while they stressed the importance of catechetical instruction, clearly distinguishing it from the pedagogy required for initiation into Gnosticism and other mystery cults, they also considerably pruned the length of the catechumenate. Before the middle of the fourth century, church leaders typically required a catechumenate of three years. While local practice varied, after that point a catechumenate of forty days was more usual. Now labeled *competentes*, catechumens who intended to be baptized enrolled with their bishop on Epiphany Sunday, or at the beginning of Lent, for a preparation limited to the weeks just prior to their baptism at the end of the Easter vigil.[36]

In any case, fictive baptism as a problem demanding episcopal solution predates these pastoral and theological developments and, indeed, the period which Brown discusses. The prevalence of heresy and schism in the early church had already drawn notable attention by the time of Cyprian of Carthage. One of the issues he tackles is the attitude to be taken toward repentant *traditores*, Christians who had broken with the church as a result of persecution and who now sought readmission. There were others seeking to join the orthodox church who had been baptized by heretics or schismatics. In the mid-third century, Cyprian's North Africa was beset by serious problems in both of these respects. His response was decisive, controversial, and influential. If Christians had been baptized in the true church and had fallen away, but now repent and wish to be reconciled, he rules that they should not be rebaptized. But he applies a different and harsher standard to those baptized by heretics or schismatics, even if they had been martyred for their aberrant faith. In Cyprian's view, their baptisms are false baptisms and their martyrdoms are false martyrdoms. They have professed, lived by,

35. Éric Rebillard, "Le figure du catéchumène et le problème du baptême dans la pastorale d'Augustin," in *Augustine prédicateur (395–411)*, Actes du Colloque international de Chantilly, 5–7 septembre 1996, ed. Goulven Madec (Paris: Institut d'Études Augustiniennes, 1998), 285–92; reprt. as "Catechumens and the Delay of Baptism in the Preaching of Augustine," trans. Aaron Pelttari in idem, *Transformations of Religious Practices in Late Antiquity* (Farnham, UK: Ashgate, 2013), no. VII; Ferguson, *Baptism*, 618–24.

36. André Benoît, *Le baptême chrétien au second siècle: La théologie des pères* (Paris: PUF, 1953), 6–7, 17, 20–23, 117, 145–46, 169–70, 187, 215; André Benoît, Boris Bobrinsky, and François Coudreau, *Baptême: Sacrement d'unité* (Paris: Maison Marre, 1971), 28–37, 57–63, 74–78; Victor Saxer, *Les rites d'initiation chrétienne du IIe au VIe siècles: Esquisse historique et signification d'après leur principaux témoins* (Spoleto: Centro Italiano di Studi sull'Alto Medioevo, 1988), 66–106, 122–25, 129, 146–78, 192–214, 242–64, 294–95, 304–14, 324, 341–57, 372, 382–89, 423–26; Thomas M. Finn, *Early Christian Baptism and the Catechumenate: Italy, North Africa, and Egypt* (Collegeville, MN: Liturgical Press, 1992); idem, *From Death to Life: Ritual and Conversion in Antiquity* (New York: Paulist Press, 1997).

and died for a false faith. It gains them no merit: "If the baptism by public confession and blood can be unavailing for the heretic's salvation, since there is no salvation outside the church, how much more profitless is it for someone who feels the touch of adulterine waters, as if in secret and in the dens of thieves? Not only will his old sins not be removed, but will they not also be joined together with new and greater ones?"[37]

We should not be misled by the fact that Cyprian frames this judgment hypothetically and in the form of a rhetorical question. Nor is his choice of language and metaphor an idle one. Heterodox baptisms are ablutions in adulterine waters (*adulterae aquae*); they are illegal and immoral, luring souls away from their rightful home in the bosom of the true church. Their practitioners pollute what is holy. Cyprian describes their conventicles as dens of thieves (*spelunca latronum*), the term used by Christ in all three of the synoptic Gospels when He drives the money-changers out of the Temple (Matthew 21:13, Mark 11:17, Luke 19:26). These sectarian baptisms, for Cyprian, are empty shams. If someone has received such an illicit and unavailing rite and seeks to enter the true church, he should indeed be baptized. Baptized, Cyprian insists, not rebaptized, since the adulterine rite he underwent was no baptism at all.

The debates provoked by Cyprian's baptismal policy continued into the fourth and early fifth centuries. They were a particular conundrum in North Africa, where both Augustine and his Donatist opponents sought to annex Cyprian's legacy to their own causes. In Augustine's anti-Donatist *De baptismo* (400/10), he has to decide what is worth retaining in Cyprian's teaching and what he should jettison. He wants to have it both ways. In some passages in this work, he grants some merit to sectarian baptisms while in others he condemns them as ineffective fictive baptisms. In the

37. Cyprian of Carthage, *Epistulae* 73.22.2, ed. G. F. Diercks, CCSL 3C (Turnhout: Brepols, 1996), 555: "Quod si haeretico nec baptisma publicae confessionis et sanguinis proficere ad salutem potest, quia salus extra ecclesiam non est, quanto magis ei nihil proderit, si in latebra et in latronum spelunca adulterae aquae contigo tinctus nontantum peccata antiqua non exposuerit, sed ad huc potius nova et maiora cumulaverit?" On the North African circumstances encouraging Cyprian to take this harsh stance, see J. Patout Burns, "On Rebaptism: Social Organization in the Third Century," *Journal of Early Christian Studies* 1 (1993): 367–403; a less historically and socially contextualized and more strictly theological assessment is given by Abraham van den Beek, "Cyprian on Baptism," in *Cyprian of Carthage: Studies on His Life, Language, and Thought*, ed. Henk Bakker, Paul van Geest, and Hans van Loon (Leuven: Peeters, 2010), 143–64 on pages 148–55. On the controversy surrounding Cyprian's position, see Attilio Carpin, *Battezati nell'unica vera chiesa? Cipriano di Cartagine e la controversia battesimale* (Bologna: Edizioni Studio Domenicano, 2007); the same topic is treated primarily from the standpoint of conciliar history by Paolo Bernardini, *Un solo battesimo: Il concilio di Cartagine del settembre 256* (Bologna: Il Mulino, 2009).

first book of *De baptismo*, he is more generous toward these baptisms. But, in the seventh and last book, his deepening frustration with Donatism leads Augustine to change his mind. For in the conclusion to the entire work, his apparent final view, he aligns himself largely with Cyprian's harsh judgment of schismatic and heretical baptisms, attaching to them his own language and conditions.

Although it is not free from soft spots, Augustine's argument in *De baptismo* 7 is relatively straightforward. As is the case elsewhere in this work, his strategy here is to pose questions, or either/or possibilities, which he ascribes to his Donatist opponents and then addresses. His goal is to show that these Donatist positions cancel each other out or miss the point entirely. He opens the final chapters of this book with the following set of alternatives:

> It is asked whether a baptism should be accepted if it is received from someone who has not [himself] received it, if, out of curiosity, he happened to learn how it should be conferred; and whether it makes no difference whether the state of soul in the one who receives what is conferred is with deceit or without deceit. And, if with deceit, whether it occurs within the church, or in what is thought to be the church, or outside the church, or as a joke, as in a stage-play. And, which is worse, to receive it deceitfully within the church, or in heresy or schism without deceit, that is, without a simulated intention, or in heresy with deceit, or in a stage-play but with faith, if a performer should suddenly be moved by piety during the action.[38]

At once, Augustine drops the first possibility aired, the validity of baptisms administered by persons not already baptized. But he does refer to the *Taufmime*, using that example in his own chosen way. We should not be surprised, he says, that some people compare a staged baptism during which an actor is converted with a baptism received deceitfully within the Catholic church. Are these baptisms equally availing?

> When both the giver and the recipient are acting deceitfully within Catholic unity itself, should this be more acceptable as a baptism than one given in a stage-play, if any [in the cast] be found who, suddenly moved, receives it faithfully? With respect to men themselves, there is big difference between the one believing on stage and the one mocking in church. But there is no difference in the genuineness of

38. Augustine, *De baptismo libri VII* 7.53.101, ed. M. Petchenig, CSEL 51 (Vienna: F. Tempsky, 1908), 372–73: "Solet etiam quari, utrum adprobandum sit quod ab eo qui non accepit accipitur, si forte hoc curiositate aliqua didicit quemadmodum dandum sit, et utrum nihil intersit, quo animo accipiat ille cui datur, cum simulatione an sine simulatione, utrum fallens sicut in ecclesia vel in ea quae putatur ecclesia, an iocans sicut in mimo, et quid sit sceleratius, in ecclesia fallaciter accipere an in haeresi vel schismate sine fallacia, id est animo non simulato, et utrum in haeresi fallaciter an in mimo cum fide, si quasquam inter agendum repentina pietate moveatur...."

the sacrament. For if there is no difference in the genuineness of the sacrament in the Catholic church itself, whether some people celebrate it deceitfully or sincerely, so long as both celebrate the same thing, I do not see why it makes a difference outside [the church], in the event that the one who receives it does not do so cloaked in deceit but changed by religion.

Augustine adds that if a baptizand's deceit is later brought to light, he should not be rebaptized. He can rectify his situation by repentance. Or, if he chooses not to do so, he can be punished by excommunication.[39]

Having made this point, Augustine notes that no general or regional church council lays down a definite rule on how to evaluate a fictive baptism when it does not come to light. But he is willing to offer his own personal opinion: "So, I would say, on the basis of the sentiments I expressed above, that I would have no doubt whatsoever that those people possess baptism, however and by whomever administered, if they were consecrated with the words of the Gospel, and receive it without deceit and with some degree of faith, although it is unavailing to the salvation of their souls if they lack charity, by means of which they may be engrafted into the Catholic church."[40]

In addition to outlining the requirements for non-Christians entering the Catholic church, this statement appears to open the door to sectarian baptisms without really doing so. In effect, it also rules out the *Taufmime*. For, whatever his faith and charity, the actor converted on stage lacks baptism according to the church's liturgical norms, one of the stipulations attached to the policy Augustine lays down in the passage quoted. Augustine's evocation and then dismissal of the *Taufmime* is a calculated feature of his argument in *De baptismo* 7. The *Taufmime* functions as a loaded example,

39. Ibid., 273: "Cum et tradens et accipiens fallaciter agant in ipsa unitate catholica, utrum hoc magis baptisma sit acceptandum an illud quod mimo datur, si quis existat qui fideliter subito commotus accipiat, an, quantum ad ipsos quidem homines adtinet, plurimum distat inter credentem in mimo et inridentem in ecclesia, ad ipsius autem sacramenti integritatem nihil intersit. Si enim nihil interest ad integritatem sacramenti in ipsa catholica, utrum id aliqui fallaciter an veraciter agant, cum tamen hoc idem utrique agant, cur extra intersit non video, quando ille qui accepit non simulatione palliatus, sed religione mutatus est. An plus valent ad confirmandum sacramentum alii veraces inter quos agitur, quam ad frustrandum illi fallaces a quibus agitur et in quibus agitur? Et tamen, si postea prodatur, nemo repetit, sed aut excommunicando punitur illa simulatio aut paenitendo sanatur."

40. Ibid., 7.53.102, 373–74: "ut dicerem quid ipse sentirem, si eo modo adfectus essem quo eram cum ista dictarem, nequaquam dubitarem habere baptismum eos, qui ubicumque et a quibuscumque illud verbis evangelicis consecratum, sine sua simulatione et cum aliqua fide accepissent, quamquam eis ad salutem spiritalem non prodesset, si caritate caruissent, qua catholicae insererentur ecclesiae..."

signaling no departure from Augustine's ongoing hostility to the theater, an attitude which corrects the unregenerate youth he decries in his *Confessions* and on whose negative patristic associations he continues to capitalize. For the conditions which Augustine attaches to the validity of sectarian baptism are terms unacceptable to the Donatists. And failure to meet them renders schismatic and heretical baptisms "as fruitless as they are useless."[41] In his final judgment on this subject in *De baptismo* 7, Augustine's wording deliberately yokes these sectarian baptisms with stage plays and actors viewed in the most negative sense. Persons who have accepted baptism at the hands of heretics and schismatics have rejected communion with the true church and the true faith: "For neither was there any fellowship with this belief [i.e. that of the Catholic church] nor did the recipient believe it, but the whole event was performed as a farce, a play-act, as a joke." Anyone who doubts that such is the case should pray for divine guidance, a special revelation, advice which reads as ironic since Augustine's pejorative language appears to obviate the need for it.[42]

41. Ibid., 7.54.103, 375: "tam infructuose adque inutiliter tales talibus."

42. Ibid., 7.53.102, 374: "ubi autem neque societas ulla esset ita credentium neque ille qui ibi acceperet ita crederet, sed totum ludicre et mimice et iocullariter ageretur, utrum adprobandus esset baptismus qui sic daretur, divinum iudicium per alicuius revelationis oraculum concordi oratione et inpensis supplici devotione gemitibus inplorandum esse censerem...." See Augustine, *Confessiones* 3.2.2–4, ed. Lucas Verheijen, CCSL 27 (Turnhout: Brepols, 1981), 27–29, for his condemnation of his youthful attraction to the theater. In *De civitate dei* 1.31, 2.8–14, 4.27, ed. Bernardus Dombart and Alphonsus Kalb, 2 vols., CCSL 47–48 (Turnhout: Brepols, 1955), 47:31–33, 40–46, 121–22, Augustine invokes disesteem for the theater in the context of his critique of pagan religion. He turns to the theme of actors as hypocrites in *De sermone Domini in monte* 2.2–5, ed. Almut Mutzenbecher, CCSL 35 (Turnhout: Brepols, 1967), 95–96. Donnalee Dox, *The Idea of the Theater in Latin Christian Thought: Augustine to the Fourteenth Century* (Ann Arbor: University of Michigan Press, 2004), 11–29, 30, 38–40, gives an excellent account of Augustine's hostility to the theater but without mentioning *De baptismo*. Rosier-Catach, *La parole efficace*, 288, misses the dimensions of the *De baptismo* arguments noted here and assimilates that text to high medieval arguments pro and con Rufinus on Alexander of Alexandria. For the general criticism of actors and the theater in early Christian and patristic authors, reprising classical attitudes, see Amory, "Whited Sepulchers," 6, 12–17, 21, 22, 29–39, and Shadi Bartsch, *The Mirror of the Self: Sexuality, Self-Knowledge, and the Gaze in the Early Roman Empire* (Chicago: University of Chicago Press, 2006), 152–64. For a thorough conspectus of patristic texts on this subject, see Hartmut Jürgens, *Pompa diaboli: Die lateinischen Kirchenväter und das antike Theater*, Tübinger Beiträge zur Altertumswissenschaft 46 (Stuttgart: W. Kohlhammer, 1972). For the entry into modern historiography of the notion that this patristic hostility stamped out theater altogether once Rome became officially Christian, see Carol Symes, "The History of Medieval Theatre/Theatre of Medieval History," *History Compass* 7 (2009): 1–17, and Timothy Barnes, "Christians and the Theater," in *Beyond the Fifth Century: Interactions with Greek Tragedy from the Fourth Century BCE to the Middle Ages*, ed. Ingo Gildenbard and Martin Revermann (Berlin: Walter De Gruyter, 2010), 315–34.

At the same time, in *De baptismo* 1 Augustine departs from the view of Cyprian thus reformulated. Here, at some points he concedes that sectarian baptisms have a real, if imperfect, validity. He acknowledges that the Donatists he attacks profess the same Christology and Trinitarian theology as the Catholics and use the same liturgy in their baptismal rite. His general argument is that while Christian baptism can be conferred outside the Catholic church, it should not be so conferred since it is unavailing to the salvation of those who remain in schism. But if they renounce their schism and join the orthodox church, their sectarian baptism will become effective. On no account should they be rebaptized. For they, too, were baptized with water in the name of the Trinity. And it is God who acts in baptism, God who has the power to remit sins even without the sacraments, if He wills to do so. Moreover, conversion, while it begins at a particular point in time, is an ongoing process. The baptisms of heterodox Christians may thus serve as a starting point for the development of a full, and orthodox, faith. What Augustine wants to accent in *De baptismo* 1 is the availability of reconciliation and the welcome which the Catholic church will extend to ex-schismatics. This understanding extends beyond those with a defective faith to those with a defective moral attitude, continuing to harbor fraternal hatred in their hearts. Indeed, it is the lack of charity of fictive and sectarian baptizands that receives his primary attention. While he elides the physical and political hostilities currently involved in the Donatist-Catholic standoff, he presents the lack of charity reflected in their refusal of fellowship as the Donatists' chief failing. This brief inspires him to edit two of the biblical examples which he cites to buttress his case. They are Simon Magus, to whose story Augustine imparts a spin found neither in the Acts of the Apostles nor in Jerome on Ezekiel, and the wicked servant of the parable told in Matthew 18:23–34.

Augustine's argument in *De baptismo* 1 is extremely longwinded and repetitive. In what now follows, we will streamline it while citing more fully the passages which drew the attention of later thinkers. Early on, Augustine brings forward Simon Magus. While offering his own original interpretation of Simon's case, he argues that the Donatists misrepresent it. In his first reference to Simon, Augustine observes, following Acts, that he believed and was baptized. Then, adding an idea not mentioned in Acts, he states that Simon had no charity. If the Donatists imitate him, they, too, will be denied eternal salvation. St. Peter's rejection requited him for the lack of charity which Simon brought to his baptism, as Augustine sees it: "While she [i.e., the church] had given him birth, yet it was said that he had no part in the inheritance of Christ. Did he lack anything with respect to baptism, the Gospel, the sacraments? But, since he lacked charity, he was [re]born in vain. It might have been better for him had he never been born."[43]

Now it is the Donatists, he claims, who misread Acts. They argue that Simon's baptism was perfectly valid, as is the baptism which they provide. As with Simon's sins, so are the sins of Donatist baptizands remitted, proving that their own communion is the true church of Christ. How, then, Augustine asks, are we to understand Peter's rejection of Simon? "Was that Simon Magus fully imbued by the baptism of Christ? They [the Donatists] will say that he was: 'Yes,' they reply, as they are bound to do by the authority of Holy Scripture. I ask if they hold that his sins were remitted. They will profess that they were. When I then ask why Peter told him that he had no part in the lot of the saints, they will answer, 'Because afterwards he sinned by seeking to buy the gift of God, which he believed the apostles could sell.'"[44] Augustine firmly reroutes the issue back to Simon's baptism. He next asks: "What if he acceded fictively to baptism itself? Were his sins remitted or not?" There is no cogent Donatist answer to these questions, says Augustine. If they claim that Simon's baptism was valid, they are refuted by Wisdom 1:5: "The Holy Spirit of discipline flees from the fiction." If they claim that Simon's baptism was invalid, then why, "if he is later struck to the heart and confesses his fiction with true sorrow, should he be judged not to be baptized anew?"[45]

These disquisitions on Simon Magus usher in statements on fictive baptism itself, destined to play an important later role in medieval thought. Continuing the point just made, Augustine observes,

43. Augustine, *De baptismo* 1.9.12, 1.10.14, 157, 158–59; quotation at 1.10.14, 158–59: "Neque enim hi solum ad eam non pertinent qui separationis aperto sacrilegio manifesi sunt, sed etiam illi qui in eius unitate corporaliter mixti per vitam pessimam separantur. Etenim Simonem magum per baptisma ipsa pepererat, cui tamen dictum est quod non haberet partem in hereditate Christi numquid et baptismus, numquid evangelium, numquid sacramenta defuerunt? Sed quia ei caritas defuit, frustra natus est et ei expediebat fortasse non nasci."

44. Ibid., 1.11.15–1.11.17, 160–62; quotation at 1.11.17, 162: "Hanc eis quaestionem solvendam proponimus, magus ille Simon utrum vero Christi baptismate tinctus sit, respondebunt 'ita,' quia sanctae scripturae auctoritate coguntur. Quaero ergo utrum fateantur ei dimissa peccata. Profecto fatebuntur. Item quaero ergo utrum cur ei dixerit Petrus non eum habere partem in sorte sanctorum. 'Quia,' inquiunt, 'postea peccavit volens emere donum dei, cuius venditores apostolos credidit.'"

45. Ibid., 1.12.18, 162: "Quid, si ad ipsum baptismum fictus accessit, dimissa sunt ei peccata an non sunt dimissa? Eligant quod volunt; utrumlibet elegerint, sufficit nobis, si dimissa dixerint, quomodo ergo *sanctus spiritus disciplinae effugiet fictum*, si in isto fictio remissionem operatus est peccatorum? Si dixerint non esse dimissa, quaero, si postea fictionem suam corde concusso et vero dolore fateretur, denuo baptizando iudicaretur?"

And if it is thoroughly demented to say so, let them admit that a person can be baptized in the true baptism of Christ while his heart, persevering in malice and sacrilege, prevents the remission of his sins from occurring. From this let them know that, while people can be baptized in communions separated from the church, where the baptism of Christ is given and received in the same rite, it only begins to effect the remission of their sins when, reconciled in unity [with the Catholic church] they abandon the sacrilege of dissent, which had held them in their sins and impeded their remission. In the same way one who acceded fictively [to baptism] is not to be rebaptized, but cleansed by pious correction and true confession, which is not available without baptism, but which then enables what was earlier granted to begin to count toward salvation, since his fiction has departed thanks to his sincere confession.[46]

Augustine admits that the situation he has just outlined propounds a contradiction. But it is one, he argues, which he can resolve: "But if they say, with regard to the one who accedes fictively, that his sins are forgiven him at that very moment by the power of so great a sacrament, but that they return at once, since the Holy Spirit both came to his baptism so that his sins were remitted and also fled from his perseverance in fiction so that they returned, both statements are true." Each element in the aforementioned assertion can be proved from Holy Scripture. Augustine quotes Galatians 3:27: "For as many of you as were baptized have put on Christ," and then repeats his earlier citation of Wisdom 1:5 on the flight of the Holy Spirit from the fiction. Thus, for the sectarian as well as for the fictive candidate, "just as he puts on Christ because of the holiness of baptism, so also he is denuded of Christ because of the sinfulness of his fiction."[47] As an argument from

46. Ibid. 1.12.18, 162–63: "Quod si dementissimum est dicere, fateantur vero baptismo Christi baptizari posse hominem et tamen cor eius in malitia vel sacrilegio perseverans peccatorum abolitionem non sinere fieri, adque ita intellegant in communionibus ab ecclesia separatis posse homines baptizari, ubi Christi baptismus eadem sacramenti celebratione datur et sumitur, qui tamen tunc prosit ad remissionem peccatorum, cum quisque reconcilatus unitati sacrilegio dissensionis exuitur, quo eius peccata tenebantur et dimitti non sinebantur. Sicut enim in illo qui fictus accesserat fit ut non denuo baptizetur, sed ipsa pia correctione et veraci confessione purgetur, quod non posset sine baptismo, sed ut quod ante datum est tunc valere incipiat ad salutem, cum illa fictio veraci confessione recesserit. Sic etiam iste qui baptisma Christi, quod non amiserunt qui se separaverunt, inimicus caritatis et pacis Christi in aliqua haeresi aut schismate accepit, quo sacrilegio scelere peccata eius non dimittebantur, cum se correxerit et ad ecclesiae societatem unitatemque venerit, non iterum baptizandus est, quia ipsa reconcilatione ac pace iam prodesse incipiat sacramentum, quod acceptum in schismate prodesse non poterat."

47. Ibid., 1.12.19, 163: "Si autem dixerint in illo qui fictus accessit per sanctam vim tanti sacramenti dimissa quidem illi esse peccata in ipso temporis puncto, sed per fictionem ipsius redisse continuo, ut spiritus sanctus et adfuerit baptizato ut peccata recederent et perseverantiam fictionis fugerit ut redirent. Ut et illud verum sit: *Quotquot in Christo baptizati estis Chris-*

analogy, Augustine also adds that a person living in darkness can truly, if momentarily, see the light if it shines on him, even though he decides to return to the darkness.[48]

The second biblical citation which Augustine offers to support his argument is a truncated version of the parable of the wicked servant. This example is designed to illustrate two truths. The first is that "the sins remitted return, where there is no fraternal charity." In Augustine's retelling, the servant who cannot repay his debts to his master begs for and receives the master's forgiveness, although he refuses to forgive the debt which another servant owes to him. Augustine finds therein a second truth, this one relating to the master's response: "Nor did the fact that he had not yet forgiven his fellow-servant prevent his lord, when receiving his account, from forgiving him of all he owed at that time. But, given his retention of [fraternal] hatred, what did he benefit, since they [his sins] at once returned, redoubled on his head?"[49] Omitted here is what Matthew relates about both servant and master in the passages that precede and follow the segment of the parable which Augustine includes. It is from this example that Augustine segues to the conclusion for which he has so elaborately prepared the ground:

> Thus, the grace of baptism is not obstructed from giving remission of all sins, even if the one forgiven retains fraternal hatred in his soul. For the guilt of yesterday is remitted, and all guilt from before baptism and during baptism itself. But he [the fictive baptizand] thus becomes guilty again, not only for the days, hours, and minutes that follow [his baptism], but also for those of the past, since all [the sins] which had been remitted return. And this happens all too often in the church.[50]

---

tum induistis et illud: *Sanctus spiritus disciplinae effugiet fictum.* Id est ut et induat eum Christi sanctitas baptismi et exuat eum Christo pernicies fictionis...."

48. Ibid., 163–64.

49. Ibid., 1.12.20, 164–65: "Nam redire dimissa peccata, ubi fraterna caritas non est, apertissime dominus in evangelio docet de illo servo, quem cum invenisset debitorem decem milium talentorum deprecanti omnia dimisit, ille autem conservum suum qui ei debebat centum denarios cum miseratus non fuisset, iussit eum dominus reddere quae ei dimiserat. Tempus ergo quo accipitur indulgentia per baptismum tamquam tempus est reddendae rationis, ut omnia debita quae inventa fuerint dimittantur. Non tamen ille servus postea dedit conservo suo mutuam pecuniam, quam cum ille non posset reddere non eius miseratus est, sed iam ei debebat conservus eius, cum ipse rationem domino suo reddens tanti numeri debito solveretur, nec dimiserat conservo suo quod ei debebat ei sic accesserat, ut ei dominus dimitteret.... Nec tamen illud quod nondum conservo dimiserat impedivit domino eius, quominus illo tempore accipiendae rationis dimitteret ei omnia quae debebat. Sed quid profuit, quandoquidem in caput eius propter odiorum perseverantiam rursus omnia continuo replicata sunt?"

50. Ibid., 165: "Sic non impeditur baptismi gratia quominus omnia peccata dimittat, etiamsi odium fraternum in eius cui dimittuntur animo perseverat. Solvitur enim hesternus

Does this statement really resolve the contradictory points made previously, and the contradictory biblical passages presented in their defense? Does Augustine truly reconcile the fictive baptizand who, like Simon Magus, receives an invalid rite which does not remit his sins, with the fictive baptizand whose sins are remitted by a baptismal grace which they cannot impede, if just for a moment, only to return? It is not at all clear that Augustine finds a path out of the labyrinth he has constructed for himself, or that he seeks an Ariadne who might help him do so.

One potential solution, for instance, could be found in Ambrose of Milan's sermons on Luke. He offers this analysis: Some people are rich in intentions but impoverished in actions. Their actions being defective, their intentions prove to be in vain. Others abound in actions but are devoid of intentions. Ambrose includes in this latter group a cohort whose acts and intentions alike miss the mark. These are people who receive the rite of baptism, having agreed to reform their lives, but who fail to do so after they rise from the font. They refuse to inform themselves of what is required in order for them to live a Christian life. They thus fail to carry out their baptismal promises. Negligent in both the intention to reform and in the action needed to achieve it, they forego the grace received in baptism and fail to make profitable use of it.[51]

While Augustine was conversant with this work by Ambrose, he apparently regards the aforementioned case study as inapposite to the schismatics recast as fictive baptizands whose status he leaves so opaque in *De baptismo* 1. His attempts to explain it simply restate the conflicting claims he has already made: On the one hand, as with Augustine's Simon Magus, baptism does not remit the candidate's sins if he accedes to the rite fictively. He is morally worse off than if he had never entered the font. On the other hand, nothing obstructs the grace of baptism. All baptisms in Christian communities count as Christian baptisms. But, if a candidate accedes to the rite fictively, the grace of baptism is granted to him only momentarily. It remains unavailable, and unavailing to him, unless he repents. This fictive baptizand puts on Christ for an instant and is then denuded of Christ just

dies et quidquid supra est solvitur, etiam ipsa hora momentumque ante baptismum et in baptismo. Deinceps autem continuo reus esse incipit non solum consequentium sed etiam praeteritorum dierum horarum momentorum, redeuntibus omnibus quae dimissa sunt, et saepe ista contingunt in ecclesia."

51. Ambrose of Milan, *Expositionis Evangelii secundum Lucam* 1.9, ed. Marcus Andraien, trans. Giovanni Coppa, 2 vols., Sancti Ambrosii episcopi Mediolanensis opera 11–12 (Milan: Biblioteca Ambrosiana, 1978), 11:104.

as swiftly, given the retention of his fiction. The Holy Spirit is imparted to him and then immediately flees from him. Does God withdraw the grace which He gave to the *fictus* momentarily at the font, only to regrant it later on, if he repents? Or, does the *fictus* retain the grace momentarily given at the rite, in some kind of latent but unusable form, pending his repentance? Either way, how are we to understand the psychodynamics of that repentance? Leaving these questions unresolved, and providing multivalent arguments and carefully tailored proof-texts in *De baptismo* 1 for virtually all of them, Augustine moves on, determined to look at the bright side. If someone who accepted baptism fictively repents, replacing his malice with fraternal charity, then the grace of baptism will become effective in him, one way or another.

In sum, the conciliatory approach to sectarian baptisms seen as fictive baptisms that informs the first book of *De baptismo* is ill-assorted with Augustine's rejection of sectarian baptisms denounced as mere shams in its seventh book, albeit as shams whose status requires miraculous divine clarification. The main principle on which these two books of the *De baptismo* agree is that no Christian should ever be rebaptized. But contradictions exist, not only between the arguments made in these two books but also within the arguments in each of them. Augustine thus bequeathed to later medieval thinkers a legacy in *De baptismo* that is as perplexing as it is rich. It will be far from difficult for them to maintain divergent positions on fictive baptism documented by reference to this work, whether their goal is to support or to criticize him. And, given the involuted, redundant, and site-specific nature of his argument, it will be no surprise to find Augustine's *De baptismo* placed under the knife by his heirs, who will slice through its rhetoric to extract the meaty nuggets useful for their own treatments of fictive baptism.

That Augustine's contemporaries and immediate successors writing on fictive baptism may have seen his *De baptismo* as a hot potato best left untouched is suggested in the exegesis of Theodore of Mopsuestia. Theodore initiates a tradition, concurring with Jerome rather than with Augustine on Simon Magus, although without citing Jerome specifically. Comparing him with the good thief, Theodore raises the issue of Simon's fraudulent intentions in the context of discussing the qualities to be sought in a bishop, flowing from his exegesis of 1 Timothy. Prelates, he stresses, must make sure that those whom they receive at the font accede to it with the correct faith and moral attitude. Otherwise, these ministers will preside over rites that are vacuous. As for Simon, Theodore concludes, "he received no profit from the gift of baptism on account of his depraved intention; the Holy Spirit did not repose in him." While this message is a cautionary tale for would-be fictive baptizands, a term Theodore does not use, he offers it primarily a warning to prelates who err if they baptize people lacking "a perfect faith."[52]

Anglo-Saxon and Carolingian Exegetes

As with baptism by desire, the first thinker to revive discussion of fictive baptism after a hiatus of three centuries was Bede. He and the Carolingian masters of the ninth century all do so as biblical exegetes. While they have that interest in common, each of them gives his own emphasis to this theme. The Carolingian exegetes both comment on Ezekiel. Bede considers fictive baptism in commentaries on two books of the Bible, the Acts of the Apostles and Genesis. Both of these texts were long-term projects on which he worked simultaneously.

The first version of Bede's Acts commentary (702/09) was soon revised (708/16) and he continued to add corrections until close to his death in 735. He presents the Acts commentary as an addendum to the exegetical tradition, filling a gap on this part of the Bible left open by patristic writers. Acts is important for the historical information it supplies on the early church. It is also important for modeling the *vita apostolica*, which it is the duty of monks—Bede's primary audience—to embody. Bede indicates that he is aware of Augustine's language in *De baptismo* but aligns himself clearly with Jerome on Ezekiel. Both of these facts are noteworthy since his library at Jarrow/Wearmouth is not known to have contained copies of either of these texts.

Bede's commentary on the case of Simon Magus is fully germane to his exegesis of Acts. In presenting his *lemmata*, he sometimes folds in other biblical passages, or the views of patristic or classical authors on pertinent issues, and sometimes attaches his own reflections. He prefaces the story

52. Theodore of Mopsuestia, *In 1. Timotheum* 3:2, in *Theodori Episcopi Mopsuesteni in epistolas B. Pauli commentarii*, ed. and trans. Henry Barclay Swete, 2 vols. (Cambridge: Cambridge University Press, 1880–82), 2:107–8: "ex quibus discere poterant quoniam Simonem nihil adiuvavit baptismi donum propter propositi pravitatem, Spirito sancto in eo non requiescente; latrone vero ut in paradisi habitationem transiret nullum adtulit impedimentum, ob propositi eius virtutem, ea ratione qua non fuerat baptisma adsecutus. Dico autem haec non ad destructionem baptismis, sed propter eos qui sub occasionem baptismatis incuriam multam inducere adnituntur iudico iusti Dei; ... Nec aquae natura sed suscipientium fides perfectam Dei liberatatem in baptisma adtrahere solent." Noted by Ferguson, *Baptism*, 532.

of Simon by noting, in Acts 8:6, that Philip's successful mission in Samaria had a historical precedent, seen in the openness to conversion of its people when the Samaritan woman reported her encounter with Christ at the well to her fellow citizens, as related in John 4:7–39.[53] Moving then to Acts 8:13, Bede writes, "Then Simon also believed." As to whether he was drawn by Philip's words or deeds, Bede leaves no doubt that it was Philip's superiority as a miracle-worker that persuaded Simon. In the effort to associate himself with that power, he converted, "believing with respect to baptism that he could receive it while faking it, … as the story goes, so that he could learn from him [Philip] those arts by which he performed miracles."[54]

Bede makes it clear that he regards this baptism as fraudulent and damnable, as was Simon's post-baptismal attempt to purchase the gift of the Holy Spirit. He specifies that the latter rite was one which Philip was not authorized to confer. This is why the Jerusalem apostles sent Peter and John to Samaria. As Bede explains in Acts 8:14, the capacity to confer the Holy Spirit by the laying on of hands was confined to the apostles. At that time, Philip was distinguished from Peter and John as priests are now distinguished from bishops. Bede anchors this point with a quotation from Pope Innocent I (401–17), who rules that the grant of the Holy Spirit through the laying on of hands is a rite reserved to bishops alone.[55]

Jumping ahead to Peter's denial of this rite to Simon, in Acts 8:20 Bede quotes the apostle's condemnation, amplifying the *lemma* at some length with a passage from Gregory the Great's *Moralia in Iob* 4.1 on the conditions in which curses are appropriate. Simon certainly deserved Peter's repudiation, Bede concludes, with a crisp assertion of his own: "Thus this Simon, having received the curse of Peter, died in eternal damnation."[56] In

53. Bede, *Expositio Actuum Apostolorum* 8.6, ed. M. L. W. Laistner, CCSL 121 (Turnhout: Brepols, 1983), 39.

54. Ibid., 8:13, 39: "*Tunc Simon et ipse credidit.* Vel beati Philippi verbi et virtute devictus veraciter domino credidit vel, ut magis credibile est, credere se quoadusque baptisma susceperet simulavit, ut qui laudis erat avidissimus ita ut Christum se credi velit, sicut historiae narrant, artes ab eo quibus miracula faceret edisceret."

55. Ibid., 8:14, 39–40: "*Miserunt ad illos Petrum et Iohannem*.… Notandum autem quod Philippus qui Samariae evangelizabat unus de septem fuerit; si enim apostolus esset, ipse utique manum imponere potuisset ut acceperent spiritum sanctum. *Hoc enim solis pontificibus debetur. Nam presbyteres sive extra episcopum seu praesente episcopo cum baptizant chrismate baptizatos ungere licet; sed quod ab episcopo fuerit consecratum non tamen frontem ex eodem oleo signare, quod solis debetur episcopis cum tradunt spiritum paracletum baptizati.*" The reference to Innocent is given by the editor on page 39 *ad loc.*

56. Ibid., 8:20, 40: "*Pecunia tua tecum in perditione*, et cetera. *Sancti viri cum maledictionis sententiam proferunt non ad hanc ex voto ultionis sed ex iustitia examinis erumpunt; intus enim*

Bede's last words on Simon in this text, leaving aside the purely grammatical addendum he provides in his *Retractio* or final version of it, his *lemma* is Peter's rebuke in Acts 8:23: "For I see that you are in the gall of bitterness and in the bond of iniquity." After quoting that line, Bede offers this comment: "The Holy Spirit descends as a dove to teach those who want to receive Him how to be simple. Now someone who retains the gall of bitterness in his heart, however much he may appear to be baptized, is not freed from the bonds of iniquity. Appearing to be cleansed at the moment of baptism, he is at once oppressed seven times as much by the devil. Thus, he seeks in vain to buy the gift of the Spirit, since he makes no effort to rid himself of his raven-like mind."[57]

Bede accomplishes a number of things in that final passage. He agrees with Acts, and, we might add, with the Donatists rather than with Augustine, that Simon was damned for his unsuccessful attempt to purchase the gift of the Spirit after his baptism. In addition, and this can be seen as the reason why he made that attempt in the first place, he brought a sinful lust for power both into and out of his baptism. Bede's language reflects a famil-

---

subtile dei iudicium aspiciunt et mala foras exsurgentia, quia maledictio debeant ferire cognoscunt et in maledicto non peccant, ex quo et ab interno iudicio non discordant. Cum enim et maledicentis innocentia permanet, et tamen eum qui maledicitur usque ad interitum maledicto absorbet, ex utriusque partis fine colligitur quia ab uno et intimo iudice in reum sententia sumpta iaculatur. Unde et hic Simon qui a Petro maledictum accepit aeterna damnatione periit. . . ." The reference to Gregory is given by the editor on page 40 *ad loc.* In his *Retractio* at 8.20, ibid., 136, Bede's concern is only to note that the correct grammatical case should be *perditionem*, not *perditione*, and that perdition as a destination applies literally to Simon but metaphorically to his money.

57. Bede, *Expositio Actuum Apostolotum* 8:23, 40: "*In felle enim amaritudinis et obligatione iniquitatis* video te esse. Ideo spiritus sanctus in columba descendit, ut eos qui se accipere vellent simplices esse doceret. Nam qui fel amaratudinis in corde reservat, quamlibet baptizatus videtur, non est iniquitatis suae vinculis absolutus, sed quasi ad punctum hora baptizandi purgatur, mox acrior est daemone septempliciter oppressus. Frustra ergo gratiam spiritus emere temptat qui se mente corvina non curavit exuere." Landgraf, "Die Wirkung," 89, notes this passage but not Bede's position vis-à-vis Augustine and Jerome. For the dates and general characteristics of this work and the materials available to Bede, see George Hardin Brown, *A Companion to Bede* (Woodbridge, UK: Boydell Press, 2009), 5nn14–15, 14, 63–64, 155–56; see also idem, *Bede the Venerable* (Boston: Twayne Publishers, 1987), 42–61; Benedicta Ward, *The Venerable Bede*, Cistercian Studies Series 169 (Kalamazoo: Cistercian Publications, 1998), 58–60, 78–84. For Bede's library and the version of the biblical text he used, see M. L. W. Laistner, "The Library of the Venerable Bede," in *Bede: His Life, Times, and Writings*, ed. A. Hamilton Thompson (Oxford: Clarendon Press, 1935), 237–66, on pages 257–59 for his texts and on pages 263–66 for the titles in his library; idem, "The Latin Version of Acts Known to Bede," *Transactions of the Royal Historical Society*, n.s. 5/2 (1937): 37–50; both Laistner essays reprt. in idem, *The Intellectual Heritage of the Early Middle Ages*, ed. Chester G. Starr (New York: Octagon Books, 1983), 17–49 and 150–64.

iarity with Augustine's instant remission theory, which he rejects. Rather, he sides with Jerome in regarding Simon's baptism as fraudulent, a mere appearance. The sinful state in which he received it did obstruct the grace of baptism. The rite did not remit his sins, which, as the sequel shows, he had no intention of abandoning. In the end, Bede agrees with and reinforces Jerome's understanding of Simon Magus as a fictive baptizand and adds to his negative picture of Simon. Bede is certain that Simon acceded to baptism fictively. However much he may seem to have been baptized (*quamlibet baptizatus videtur*), he actually was not. His sins have prevented him from receiving the Holy Spirit, both as an aspect of baptismal grace and as the still richer gift given in the post-baptismal laying on of hands. His sins are multiplied sevenfold. Bede comes closest to Cyprian on this last point, although Cyprian's *Epistula* 73 is another patristic text not found in his library. Bede does not consider the idea that baptismal grace becomes operative for the *fictus* when he later repents. In any case, he does not present Simon Magus as repentant. Given that his baptism, for Bede, is apparent, not real, Simon would have been unable to activate a grace which he had never possessed. Bede acknowledges, as Augustine cannot bring himself to do, that the fictive baptizand can frustrate the grace of the sacrament. With Jerome, he regards fictive baptism as void. Simon Magus, and anyone else who seeks it, repels the dove of the Holy Spirit with the unconverted mind of the raven.

This allusion to doves and ravens comes into clearer focus when we consider the section on Noah in Bede's commentary on Genesis. This part of that text received an initial version (703/09) and a revised version (720 or 722/25). As Bede observes, when the great flood was over Noah first sent the raven from the ark, charged with discovering whether the waters had receded from the earth. The raven flew to and fro. But it did not return to the ark and report back to Noah. Suggesting the challenges faced by monastic missionaries and pastors in his own time and place, Bede compares the raven to people who have been catechized and admitted to the sacraments but who remain irresolute. They retain the blackness of their shifting attachment to secular delights. Their wanderings bespeak their spiritual instability. On the other hand, the dove that Noah then sends from the ark returns, on its second mission, with the olive branch signaling the return of vegetation to the earth. The dove, Bede explains, stands for the simplicity that is a gift of the Holy Spirit, the honesty and fidelity that characterize the elect. Beyond that general message, the raven stands for the perfidy and immorality of Simon Magus. In his Genesis commentary, Bede also notes that Simon was dismissed by Peter. Simon could not and did not receive the Holy Spirit: "He was rejected by him [Peter] since he was filled with the gall of bitterness and not with the innocent simplicity of the dove in a pious heart, maliciously retaining the blackness of the raven."[58] In this text, Bede does not state, as he does in his Acts commentary, that the rite which Peter withheld from Simon was not baptism itself but the post-baptismal laying on of hands. Here, he seems to conflate that latter event with the theme of fictive baptism.

The Simon of Bede's Acts commentary appears to undergo a nugatory baptismal rite, while the Simon of his Genesis commentary is denied an unspecified rite of initiation and is expelled from the church by Peter. Despite this difference in emphasis, in both works Bede ascribes to Simon the raven-like mind that stands for the retention of sin that marks any fictive baptizand and obstructs the grace of baptism. Even if he does receive the rite, it is far from being salvific in his case; rather, it compounds his iniquity.

If Bede acknowledges Augustine's momentary remission thesis, which he deftly sidesteps in favor of Jerome on Ezekiel, the Carolingian masters who treat fictive baptism ignore Augustine entirely and reprise Jerome more or less literally. Rabanus Maurus and Haimo of Auxerre are products, respectively, of the second and third generation of Carolingian exegesis. It used to be thought that the exegetes of their century could be lumped together and described as florilegists, concerned merely with compiling patristic readings of their preferred biblical texts. Recent scholarship has given us a more nuanced and less dismissive understanding of their work.[59]

58. Bede, *In Genesim* 8:7–11, ed. Charles W. Jones, CCSL 118A (Turnhout: Brepols, 1967), 123–24; quotation at 8:9–10, 124: "ab eo repulsus, eo quod *felle amaritudinis* plenus non innocentiam columbinae simplicitas, pio sed maligno potius in corde corvinam gestaret nigritudinem." We may note that Bede's identification of the raven with the perfidious and unconverted mind makes no reference or allusion to the passages in Leviticus 11:13–19 and Deuteronomy 14:12–18 which list ravens among the unclean and prohibited foods along with other birds that are raptors, eaters of carrion, or both.

59. For the older view, see M. L. W. Laistner, *Thought and Letters in Western Europe AD 500–900*, 2nd ed. (Ithaca, NY: Cornell University Press, 1957), 301–2, 305–6; Robert McNally, *The Bible in the Early Middle Ages* (Westminster, MD: Newman Press, 1959), 30, 48, as corrected by John J. Contreni, "Carolingian Biblical Studies," in *Carolingian Essays*, ed. Uta-Renate Blumenthal (Washington: The Catholic University of America Press, 1983), 71–98; idem, "Carolingian Biblical Culture," in *Johannes Scotus Eriugena: The Bible and Hermeneutics*, ed. Gerd Van Riel, Carlos Steel, and James McEvoy (Leuven: Leuven University Press, 1998), 1–23; the contributors to *The Study of the Bible in the Carolingian Era*, ed. Celia Chazelle and Burton Van Name Edwards (Turnhout: Brepols, 2003); and Ian Christopher Levy, ed. and trans., *The Bible in the Medieval Tradition: The Letter to the Galatians* (Grand Rapids, MI: William B. Eerdmans Publishing Company, 2011), 32–44.

Rabanus and Haimo are both relatively unusual in that they wrote commentaries on Ezekiel; most Carolingian exegetes were not attracted to the prophetic books of the Old Testament. Despite their common interest in this text, each master puts his own stamp on it.

The Ezekiel commentary of Rabanus Maurus was written prior to 842 while he was a master and abbot of the monastery of Fulda, before becoming archbishop of Mainz (847–56). His technique is to quote substantial passages from the authorities he finds valuable. He often cites them verbatim, although without always naming his sources. He combines them to substantiate his own readings. Rabanus certainly knows and makes use of Jerome on Ezekiel. He incorporates, virtually intact, the passage in Jerome's text that begins with the non-salvific ablutions of Gentiles and heretics and concludes with the case of Simon Magus. Rabanus makes two departures from Jerome. First, he puts the key verb in this passage into the present indicative. Where Jerome says that these non-Christian ablutions "may not wash" (*non lavent*), Rabanus says that they "do not wash" (*non lavant*) unto salvation.[60] Second, and focusing, as Jerome does not, on the obstetrical imagery in the prophet's address to Jerusalem, Rabanus accents the need for infant baptism; indeed, this is the topic within which he contextualizes Ezekiel's chastisement of Israel.

Haimo of Auxerre's commentary on Ezekiel is unpublished and survives in a single tenth-century manuscript, Paris Bibliothèque Nationale lat. 12302. A product of the monastic school of Saint-Germain of Auxerre, Haimo (d. ca. 875) became abbot of Cessy-les-Bois (Sasceium) in ca. 865. His writings as a whole date to ca. 840/60. His Ezekiel commentary was a late work, unfinished at the time of his death. Haimo is selective, not lemmatizing every line of his chosen text. He does not quote his sources but summarizes them in his own words. He sets himself two tasks as an exegete: He supplies his audience with lexical and grammatical explanations and he contrasts divergent readings, both patristic and more recent, often giving the reasons for his own preferences and opinions. Haimo's wider

60. Rabanus Maurus, *Commentaria in Ezechielem* 7, *PL* (Paris, 1864), 110:668A: "lavant, sed non lavant in salutem"; see ibid., 110:668A–B for the whole passage. On Rabanus as an exegete in himself and in his historical context, see Silvia Cantarelli Berarducci, *Hrabani Mauri Exegetica: Repertoria fontes*, 3 vols. (Turnhout: Brepols, 2006), 1:3–124, for a thorough review of previous scholarship and current interpretations and at 1:326–32 for her discussion of his Ezekiel commentary. Cantarelli Berarducci does not consider the particular *lemma* central to the present study. On the availability of Jerome's Ezekiel commentary in the Carolingian world, see McNally, *Bible*, 43; Rosamond McKitterick, *The Carolingians and the Written Word* (Cambridge: Cambridge University Press, 1989), 181.

message in this commentary is that Ezekiel's rebukes to the Israelites apply as well to the failings of his own contemporaries. Christians in various social registers are at fault. The fullest weight of his criticism falls on the misdeeds of the clergy, that is, the secular clergy. Haimo does not suggest that monks need correction.[61] While he complains that their worldliness and irresponsibility are pervasive, he does not accuse secular clerics of acceding to the font as fictive baptizands or of admitting *ficti* to the rite. To be sure, heresy and infidelity are current problems. Haimo refers specifically to Adoptionism, and to Charlemagne's policy initiatives against it, as an issue still echoing in the Carolingian church decades later.[62] And he does not fail to mention infidels. Haimo's infidels are the Northmen, the Slavs, and the Saracens. It is the latter group, he says, following Jerome, that is not washed unto salvation. Haimo singles out Saracens from the list of infidels as demanding particular comment. As he puts it, "we may see that there is water by which the bodies of [their] infants are washed, but not unto salvation. Baptism in the name of the Father, Son, and Holy Spirit is quite different from the 'baptism' of their children by the Saracens, lest they be attacked by demons. This water, indeed, does not save them; they are not cleansed [of sin] by it because they are not baptized in the [Christian] faith."[63]

To be sure, the Carolingian clergy could not attempt to preach to the

61. An outstanding study of Haimo on Ezekiel, and the transcriptions referred to in what follows, are provided by John J. Contreni, "'By Lions, Bishops Are Meant, by Wolves, Priests': History, Exegesis, and the Carolingian Church in Haimo of Auxerre's *Commentary on Ezechiel*," *Francia* 29 (2002): 29–56; reprt. in idem, *Learning and Culture in Carolingian Europe: Letters, Numbers, Exegesis, and Manuscripts* (Aldershot: Ashgate, 2011), no. V. Other recent scholarship on Haimo's exegesis focuses on his Pauline commentaries; see Kevin L. Hughes, "Haimo of Auxerre and the Fruition of Carolingian Hermeneutics," in *Second Thessalonians: Two Early Medieval Apocalypse Commentaries*, ed. and trans. Steven R. Cartwright and Kevin L. Hughes, TEAMS Commentary Series (Kalamazoo: Medieval Institute, 2001), 13–20; Ian Christopher Levy, "Trinity and Christology in Haimo of Auxerre's Pauline Commentaries," in *The Multiple Meanings of Scripture: The Role of Exegesis in Early-Christian and Medieval Culture*, ed. Ineke van t'Spijker (Leiden: Brill, 2008), 101–23.

62. Contreni, "'By Lions, Bishops,'" 33–34. On Adoptionism and the Carolingian response to it, see John Cavadini, *The Last Christology of the West: Adoptionism in Spain and Gaul, 785–820* (Philadelphia: University of Pennsylvania Press, 1993).

63. Haimo of Auxerre, *Commentaria in Ezechielem*, Paris BN lat. 12302, fol. 51r–51v, as quoted by Contreni, "'By Lions, Bishops,'" 33n20: "Videamus quae sit aqua qua abluuntur corpora infantum et non in salutem. Baptismus est utique quo baptizant Saraceni filios suos in nomine Patris, et Filii, et Spiritus Sancti, ne a demonibus invadantur. Haec enim aqua non est illis in salutem quia non mundantur in ea, quoniam non ex fide baptizantur." On Haimo's infidels as also including Northmen and Slavs, see Contreni, ibid., 33–34 and fol. 71v as quoted on page 33n18, commenting on Ezekiel 20:44.

Vikings during their hit-and-run raids. At the same time, the Carolingians sent missions to the Northmen who had settled in Denmark and Sweden, and to the Slavs and Avars in central and eastern Europe. As for the Saracens, Charlemagne had established cordial relations with the Caliphate in Baghdad. Closer to home, the Carolingians made no effort to do more than hold the line on their frontier with the Muslims in the Spanish March. For their part, Saracens under Carolingian rule showed no interest in approaching the font, whether sincerely or fictively. Although he singles out the Saracens and displays some familiarity with their ritual practice, Haimo is not really interested in his Ezekiel commentary in adult converts as fictive baptizands. Rather, he confines himself to contrasting Christian and Muslim ablution rites for infants. With Rabanus, Haimo rewrites the passage he takes from Jerome in the present indicative of the verb. The water used in Muslim ablutions "does not save them" (*non est illis in salutem*). Muslim practice "is quite different" (*est utique*) from Christian baptism. Haimo joins Bede and Rabanus in ignoring the Augustinian question of the subsequent moral state of candidates who bring erroneous, inadequate, or bad faith to the font. But this is because, Jerome and Simon Magus notwithstanding, none of these three exegetes really focuses on adults at all, whether as baptizands or as sponsors of the infants who now make up the majority of the baptized.

The Norman Ruse

As the Carolingian age gave way to the tenth century, European Christendom encountered a new version of fictive baptism, which arrived with the very Northmen whose paganism Haimo of Auxerre acknowledges in passing. In moving to this topic, we move from theology, exegesis, and homiletics to chronicles reporting the behavior of Northmen, whether as their chief topic or as a secondary theme. The latter is the case with the *Historiae* (989/90) of Richer of Reims. Richer's main goal is to support the legitimacy of the Robertians as kings of the western third of the former Carolingian Empire. He presents Odo (888–98), the founder of that line, as a valiant ruler defending his realm against the heathen Vikings in a stand-off between civilization and barbarism. In the episode which follows, another central figure is Ingo, a warrior in Odo's service. Given Richer's agenda it is no surprise that Odo and Ingo come off as heroes in their encounter with the Viking chief and fictive baptizand Catillus.

Battle with the Vikings rages and goes badly for the Franks at first, until Ingo, grasping the royal standard, moves to the vanguard and leads the Franks to victory. Catillus, the Vikings' "tyrant king," led in captivity to Limoges, is given the choice between life—that is, baptism—and death. He opts for baptism, making no objection. "But it is doubtful," says Richer, "that he had any faith whatever." The rite duly takes place at Pentecost. After fasting for three days, Catillus "was baptized, immersed three times in the name of the Father, Son, and Holy Spirit." As soon as the ceremony has been completed, however, Ingo takes up a sword and kills Catillus, his blood staining the water of the font.

Horrified, Odo has Ingo seized. But he allows Ingo to explain his shocking sacrilege. Reminding Odo of his loyalty and the many wounds and scars received in his service, Ingo says that he slew Catillus for Odo's protection. He knew that Catillus was faking it at the font, so that his Christian enemies would lower their guard and he could do them grievous harm. Odo's men are persuaded by Ingo that Catillus "received [baptism] fraudulently (*in dolo*)." Odo accepts this defense, "moved by the mercy of pity." The king forgives Ingo and rewards him with the fortress of Blois and the hand of the widow of its deceased former lord.[64]

While Richer's larger goal is to provide a foundation myth for Ingo's descendants as lords of Blois as well as for Robertian rule in Francia, this passage invites further comment. Richer first says that Catillus's possession of any faith is doubtful, but in the speech he gives to Ingo the Viking

64. Richer of Saint-Rémi, *Histories* 1.10–11, ed. and trans. Justin Lake, 2 vols., Dumbarton Oaks Medieval Library 10 (Cambridge, MA: Harvard University Press, 2011), 1:32–36; quotations at 1.10, 1:32–34: "rex tirannum captum secum Lemovicas ducit, ibique ei vitae ac mortis optionem dedit, si baptizaretur, vitam, sin minus mortem promittens. Tirannus mox absque contradictione baptismi petit, sed dubium an fidei quicquam habuerit. Quia ergo Pentecostes instabat sollempnitas, ac episcoporum conventus regi aderat, ab episcopis ei triduanum indicitur ieiunium. Die vero constituta cum in basilica sancti Marcialis post episcoporum peracta officia in sacrum fontem ab ipso rege excipiendus descenderet, iamque trina immersione in nomine patris et filii et spiritus sancti baptizatus esset, Ingo ante signifer, gladio educto, loetaliter eum transverberat ac fontem sacratum vulneris effusione immaniter cruentat"; and at 1:11, 1:36: "in dolo baptismum susciperat"; "pietatis clementiam suadent." The same readings of these passages with slightly different punctuation are given in Richer of Reims, *Historiae*, ed. Hartmut Hoffmann, MGH Scriptores 38 (Hannover: Hahn, 2000), 45–47. Excellent background on this topic is supplied by Margot E. Fassler, *The Virgin of Chartres: Making History through Liturgy and the Arts* (New Haven, CT: Yale University Press, 2010), 14–15; see also Hartmut Hoffmann, "Die Historien Richers von Saint-Remi," *Deutsches Archiv* 54/2 (2004): 445–532, and Jason Glenn, *Politics and History in the Tenth Century: The Work and World of Richer of Reims* (Cambridge: Cambridge University Press, 2004), 184n29, 190, 195–98. The latter two scholars accent the fantastic and implausible aspects of Richer's history and neither is interested in the issue of fictive baptism or the theme of the Norman ruse. Lake does not comment on this passage in his editor's introduction.

leader's dishonesty in accepting baptism is a sure thing. He is guilty not only of hypocrisy but of *dolus*, the term in Roman law for fraud. Ingo does not disclose how he arrived at this conclusion. In addition, while this fictive baptizand receives immediate as well as eternal requital, the event strikes a note which we will orchestrate in chapter 3 of this book, the baptism-or-death option presented to a pagan as a consequence of military defeat. Richer and his Franks are insensitive to the likelihood that constraint will occasion mental reservations, if not out and out guile, in those forced into the font. At the same time, this passage illustrates the awareness of the historian, his protagonists, and his audience of the theme of the Norman ruse, in this case divined and deactivated by Ingo.

Richer's wily Viking is undone before his deceit at the font can wreak destruction on his Christian enemies, but a less happy fate falls to the Christians at the hands of a fictive Viking baptizand in the *De moribus et actis primorum Normanniae ducum* (990/1015) of Dudo of St. Quentin. As the title of this work indicates, the Norman dukes—also Dudo's patrons—are its heroes. Dudo celebrates their settlement in Normandy and their achievements as major powers in northwestern France. By the time he writes, the Normans had been Christians for several generations. This fact is one of the contributions of Rollo, the duchy's founding father. The prehistory of the Normans as hostile pagans preying on Christian Europe, to which Rollo and his descendants put paid, is illustrated in Dudo's account of Rollo's binary opposite, the Viking leader Hastings, who may or may not have existed in the late ninth century.

The traducer of baptism and of other Christian rites, not to mention the good faith of his Christian victims, Hastings plots a ruse more elaborate and sophisticated than that of Catillus. And his ruse works. As Dudo recounts, having subjugated much of France, Hastings and his men turn greedy eyes toward Italy. They plan to conquer and sack Rome. Their assault starts at Luna, a city on whose location scholars disagree. With no lack of adjectives rehearsing the vices of Hastings, Dudo reports the Viking's opinion that, since Luna could not be taken by force, a subterfuge was in order—"a crafty plan, most infamously deceitful." Hastings sends an envoy to the city fathers, charged with relating that Hastings will spare them an attack on one condition. He is mortally ill and wants to be baptized and to be assured of a Christian funeral and burial in consecrated ground. The Lunans are completely taken in by this strategem. The envoy reports back "to his most infamous lord what fraudulent things he had said to them and what in his guile he had heard from them."

The "perfidious pagans" then activate their ruse. The bishop having prepared the font, Hastings is carried to it: "The betrayer enters the waters, which wash his body alone. The villain receives baptism, to the destruction of his soul." Anointed and wearing the white garment of the baptized, he returns to his ships. That same night, Hastings fakes his own death. Lamenting his demise, his men bring his "body" back to Luna for his obsequies. They have secreted weapons on their persons, which they bring into the church. What follows is the assassination of the clergy and notables assembled for the "funeral" and the plunder of the city, and then a rampage in which the Vikings ravage the entire region with fire and sword, returning to their ships with their spoils and captives.[65]

Scholars who have commented on this passage note the use of Hastings as a negative antitype of Rollo as well as the likely influence of Vergil's *Aeneid* on Dudo's text. Rollo's "good Normans" are heroes seeking a new homeland across the sea; Hastings's "bad Normans" are duplicitous aggressors, with his "corpse" serving as an update of the Trojan horse.[66] Whether or not one wants to go that far, it is clear that Hastings's ruse is a success. The Christians of Luna may have had the simplicity of the dove, but they are also remarkably credulous. If they win the crown of martyrdom, for Dudo, this is also because, in his own metaphor, they let themselves be led like sheep to the slaughter. Once the Normans themselves had adopted Christianity, fictive baptism was dropped from their repertoire of guile. But the faking of illness, or of death, remained recurrent themes in descriptions of the Normans' crafty maneuvers, cited with admiration by their own historians and with censure, at times combined with rueful if grudging respect, by anti-Norman writers.[67]

65. Dudo of St. Quentin, *De moribus et actis primorum Normanniae ducum* 1.5–7, ed. Jules Lair (Caen: F. Le Blanc-Hardel, 1865), 132–35; quotations at 1.5, 132: "dolosum reperit consilium nefandissimae fraudis"; at 1.5, 133: "Internuntius autem quaeque fraudulenter illis dixit, et quaecumque ab eis dolosus audivit, nefandissimo omnium seniori suo renuntiavit"; ibid.: "perfidi pagani"; at 1.6, 133: "Intrat perfidus fontes, corpus tantum diluentes, suscipit nefarius baptismum, ad animae suae interitam." Translation: Dudo of St. Quentin, *History of the Normans*, trans. Eric Christiansen (Woodbridge, UK: Boydell Press, 1998), 18–19. Good commentaries are provided by Leah Shopkow, *History and Community: Norman Historical Writing in the Eleventh and Twelfth Centuries* (Washington: The Catholic University of America Press, 1997), 69–71, 150, 182; Emily Albu, *The Normans and Their Histories: Propaganda, Myth, and Subversion* (Woodbridge, UK: Boydell Press, 2001), 2, 7–46.

66. Shopkow, *History and Community*, 150; Albu, *The Normans*, 5–6, 12–46; Fassler, *The Virgin of Chartres*, 15–16, 465n30.

67. On the ruse in later medieval treatments of the Normans, see Kenneth Baxter Wolf, *Making History: The Normans and Their Historians in Eleventh-Century Italy* (Philadelphia:

Publicists and Canonists

The historians describing the Norman ruse suggest agreement with the view that fictive baptism is invalid. These historians show no awareness of the *Taufmime* or the boys on the beach, or the complexities and contradictions of Augustine on fictive baptism. These approaches to the subject, and others, were revived initially by canonists and publicists deeply involved in the clerical reform movement of the eleventh century. Some of these writers cite Augustine, Jerome, and Bede verbatim. Several of them also cite Rufinus. Whether or not they are working from accurate versions of these texts, they tailor them to suit present needs. They show little interest in the issues that animate their authorities. While the authors in this group all support clerical reform and what they hold to be the appropriate spheres of spiritual and secular power, they also disagree among themselves on a number of points relating to fictive baptism.

The writer first known to have revisited the boys on the beach is Peter Damian. His *Liber gratissimus* (1052), written against Humbert of Silva Candida, another ardent reformer, quotes Rufinus more or less faithfully while annexing him to a question he does not raise, whether a priest ordained by a simoniac bishop should be reordained. Peter's argument tends to drift from the course of this announced topic, making landfall on a different shore. He cites Rufinus as the only authority who needs to be applied to the issue he addresses. Peter's reprise of Rufinus is fairly accurate. He reports the incident at the beach following Alexander's completion of the liturgy honoring the martyr Peter, as he awaits the arrival of the clerical guests invited to the holiday meal. He observes the "boys' game on the beach imitating the bishop and what is done in church, as is their wont, ... [including] even things secret and mystical." Peter's Alexander is alone when he observes the boys, calls them over, and questions them. Initially afraid, they are put at their ease by the bishop. They tell him that they are following the practice of the church and doing what the bishop himself does when he baptizes catechumens. Alexander is satisfied that the boy clerics have asked the candidates the right questions and that the candidates have made the right responses, and that "water has been poured." By

University of Pennsylvania Press, 1995), 132; Emily Albu, "Bohemond and the Rooster: Byzantines, Normans, and the Artful Ruse," in *Anna Komnena and Her Times*, ed. Thalia Gouma-Peterson (New York: Garland, 2000), 157–68; eadem, *The Normans*, 30, 65–68, 70, 72–73, 77–79, 85, 90–91, 105, 124–25, 134, 136, 143, 148, 156, 158, 160–62, 171–72, 184, 187–88, 195, 203–5, 209–10, 226, 227, 229, 237–38.

now, his clergy have arrived. Taking counsel with them, Alexander rules that the boys' baptism is valid and "should not be repeated." Without mentioning Athanasius, Peter notes that Alexander saw that the boys playing as ministers had an early vocation to the priesthood, and, "having assembled their parents, he enjoined them to swear under God that they would educate them for [service in] the church."[68]

Peter Damian thinks that Alexander got it right. The issue this passage illuminates, for him, is not the early intimations of Athanasius's future leadership or how he became Alexander's protégé. He wants to accent two other points. First, the assessment of both the status of the boy baptizands and the precocious calling of the boy ministers are strictly clerical judgments. They are made on the initiative and authority of Alexander in consultation with his clergy. It is only after he has made this determination that Alexander convenes the boy ministers' parents. He does not consult them about their sons' education and future careers. Rather, he informs them of what he has already decided and gives them their marching orders. Peter uses Rufinus to bolster the view that the proper role of the clergy is to make decisions for the laity and that the proper role of the laity is to accept those decisions without questioning either their substance or the sole right of the clergy to make them. Second, it follows, for Peter, that it is not the place of the laity to challenge the validity of the sacraments, read here the ordination of priests, even if simony was involved in their ordination. The personal failings of priests do not entitle the laity to criticize the validity of their ministry. It is up to the clerical authorities to judge, impose penalties on, or depose a priest found to be fraudulently ordained. Far from considering the concerns of Rufinus, or the topic which he himself announces at the head of this discussion, what Peter wants to underscore is the subservience of the laity to the clergy. While he thinks the baptism of the boys on the beach was valid and correctly judged by Alexander, the message Peter extracts from Rufinus is not really about fictive baptism. Rather, since rebaptism is forbidden,

68. Peter Damian, *Liber gratissimus*, ed. L. de Heinemann, MGH Libelli de lite imperatorum 1 (Hannover: Hahn, 1891), 66–67; quotations on page 66: "puerorum super ore maris ludum imitandum, ut fieri solet, episcopum atque ea quae in aeclesiis geri mos est"; "geri quosdam etiam secretiora et mystica"; "aqua fuerat infusa"; "collocatus cum concilio clericorum"; "iterari baptismi non defere"; on page 67: "convocatis parentibus, sub Dei obtestione tradidit aeclesiae nutriendos." For an excellent discussion of how Peter Damian applies this argument to the reformers' concern with limiting the roles of laypeople in the church, see Nicoangelo d'Acunto, *I laici nella chiesa e nella società secondo Pier Damiani: Ceti dominanti e riforma ecclesiastica nel secolo XI*, Istituto Storico Italiano per il Medio Evo, Nuovi studi storiche 50 (Rome: Nella Sede dell'Istituto, Palazzo Borromini, 1999), 68–71, 95–180, 382, 384–90.

the baptismal and other ministries of priests whose status is questionable should not be challenged.

If Peter Damian can cite Rufinus with a good deal of textual accuracy while applying him to simoniac or otherwise immoral priests and to the proper spheres of clergy and laity, of no interest to Rufinus, the continuator of a text ascribed to Anselm of Lucca performs an analogous maneuver in his handling of Augustine. Or at least he tries to do so. His success is highly debatable. Anselm wrote his *Collectio canonum* most likely during his time as titular bishop of Lucca (1073–86), titular because his attempt to force reform down the throats of the local clergy, not seen as needed either by them or by their fellow citizens, led to his acrimonious expulsion from his see and the Luccans' election of the anti-bishop Pietro (1080–90) to replace him. Anselm fled to the court of Countess Matilda of Tuscany and then to the abbey of St. Gilles in Provence, where he stayed despite Pope Gregory VII's repeated demands that he return to his see. Anselm claimed that he was doing penance for the fact that he had been invested as bishop of Lucca by Emperor Henry IV, shortly before Gregory had banned lay investiture. Although he then sought reinvestiture from that pontiff, Anselm's excuses cut no ice with Gregory. A later bishop of Lucca, Rangerio (1097–1112), wrote an adulatory metrical *vita* of Anselm, treating him as a saint. But Anselm was loathed in Lucca as an intransigent outsider disastrously out of step with local morés and as a shirker of his episcopal responsibilities. At best, aside from Rangerio, he was seen in Italy as having made a virtue of necessity; at worst, as a renegade who had betrayed his calling.[69]

Anselm's writings as a canonist and controversialist may have been an effort to redeem himself in papal eyes, since his theme song is papal primacy over the other bishops and clerical supremacy over lay rulers. With

69. A good brief biography is provided by Cinzio Violante, "Anselmo di Biaggo," in *Dizionario biografico degli italiani* (Rome: Enciclopedia Italiana, 1961), 3:397–404. For further details, see Hagen Keller, "Le origini sociali e famigliari del vescovo Anselmo"; Ameleto Spiccani, "L'episcopato Lucchese di Anselmo di Biaggo"; Mario Nobile, "Il 'Liber de anulo e baculo' del vescovo di Lucca Rangerio, Matilde, e la lotta per le investiture negli anni 1000–1111"; and Gabriella Severino, "La *vita metrica* di Anselmo di Lucca scritta da Rangerio: Ideologia e genere letterario," all in *Sant'Anselmo vescovo di Lucca (1073–1086) nel quadro delle trasformazioni sociali e della riforma ecclesiastica*, ed. Cinzio Violante (Rome: Istituto Storico Italiano per il Medio Evo, 1992), 27–50, 65–70, 185–94, 222–68; Kathleen G. Cushing, *Papacy and Law in the Gregorian Revolution: The Canonistic Work of Anselm of Lucca* (Oxford: Clarendon Press, 1998), 43–63; eadem, *Reform and Papacy in the Eleventh Century: Spirituality and Social Change* (Manchester: Manchester University Press, 2005), 96–97; Leidulf Melve, *Inventing the Public Sphere: The Public Debate during the Investiture Contest (1030–1122)*, 2 vols. (Leiden: Brill, 2007), 2:620–21.

other reformers, Anselm staunchly opposes simony and supports mandatory clerical celibacy. While he insists on the banning of lay investiture and of all lay usurpations of clerical rights and privileges, his strictures against clerical involvement in secular affairs are muted. The sacraments are not the prime focus of the continuator, occupying only three of the five books he added to the expanded *Collectio canonum*. He treats them largely from the standpoint of their ministers and the rules governing them which the clergy must enforce. There is but one allusion to Anselm's own ambiguous status in the part of the collection which he himself authored. He criticizes bishops who absent themselves from their sees for more than three successive weeks, "unless prevented by grave necessity," although he does not indicate how they should be sanctioned.[70]

In his treatment of the topics he includes, the continuator follows Anselm's practice of citing a single authority, excerpted from its original context, for each of the rules, principles, and desiderata he lays down. The vast majority of his sources are papal letters past and present. As with other authors of canonical collections of his era, he presents the sources he selects as establishing the law of the church, however widely accepted or contested they may be in comparison with the authorities he omits. In handling baptism, to which the continuator devotes half of Book 9, he departs from this usual practice by bringing Augustine back into play, drawing on passages from different parts of his *De baptismo* as well as from some of his other works. The continuator sometimes blends positions developed by Augustine in his anti-Donatist polemics, where the issue is sectarian baptisms, with his arguments against the Pelagians, where the issue is the necessity of infant baptism. As others in his cohort do with the sources they cite, he asks Augustine to answer questions which Augustine did not raise. He uses

70. Anselm of Lucca, *Collectio canonum* 6.168, ed. Friedrich Thaner, 2 vols. (Innsbruck: Universitätsverlag Wagner, 1906–15; reprt. Aalen: Scientia Verlag, 1965), 2:346. It is recognized that this edition is faulty; among other things it ends with Book 11 of the expanded work. But it is currently the only printed source for Book 9, where baptism is discussed. For the majority view which regards Anselm as the author of Books 1–7 only, see, for example, Gérard Fransen, "Anselme de Lucques canoniste?" in *Sant'Anselmo di Lucca* (as in note 69), 143–55 on pages 143–45; Christof Roelker, *Canon Law and the Letters of Ivo of Chartres* (Cambridge: Cambridge University Press, 2010), 65–66, 87–88. For a contrary view ascribing the entire work to Anselm, see Kathleen G. Cushing, "Polemic or Handbook? Recension Bb of Anselm of Lucca's *Collectio Canonum*," in *Bishops, Texts, and the Use of Canon Law around 1100: Essays in Honour of Martin Brett*, ed. Bruce C. Brasington and Kathleen G. Cushing (Aldershot: Ashgate, 2008), 69–77 on pages 70–72. It is generally agreed that support of the Gregorian reform movement informs this work, a point noted also by James A. Brundage, *Medieval Canon Law* (London: Longman, 1995), 37.

Augustine to support the validity of some fictive baptisms and to exclude others. He is less impressive for the accuracy and cogency of his handling of Augustine, whether access to his texts was direct or indirect, than for the applications he makes in his appeals to the bishop of Hippo for guidance in addressing his own contemporary concerns.[71]

The continuator begins with fictive baptism from the perspective of its ministers. In his initial citation, he maintains that the failings of ministers, including simony along with heresy and schism, do not impede the grace of the baptisms they perform, since these human agents merely mediate God's grace and cannot frustrate it. Next, moving to the recipients of baptism, he cites *De baptismo* 1 to support the view that those who accede to baptism perfidiously cannot thwart its efficacy either. Given the necessity of infant baptism derived from the anti-Pelagian Augustine, he adds that it is the perfidy of the adults presenting infants for baptism whose ability to obstruct grace he denies.[72] It would seem, then, that nothing can obstruct the grace of baptism on the part of its ministers or recipients alike. But the matter is not so simple. Perfidy is also what characterizes the adult *fictus*. There is a real question as to "whether a person who is baptized while remaining perfidious receives no remission of his sins, or does so at that very moment."[73] Anselm's continuator then restates and qualifies this alternative, avoiding an attempt to resolve it at this point: "The perfidious person, if he continues in his perfidy, does not receive remission of his sins by baptism whether inside or outside the church; or else, if he does so receive it at

71. Charles Munier, *Les sources patristiques du droit de l'église de VIIe au XIIIe siècle* (Mulhouse: Salvator, 1957), 59, 81n58, 127, 129, 139n8 sees Anselm of Lucca as the first to reintroduce Augustine's *De baptismo* on this topic and as having been the key source of this authority in the eyes of subsequent canonists from Deusdedit and Ivo of Chartres up through Gratian, although without noting the continuator's manhandling of Augustine. Peter Landau, "Gratian and the *Decretum Gratiani*," in *The History of Medieval Canon Law in the Classical Period, 1140–1234: From Gratian to the Decretals of Gregory IX*, ed. Kenneth Pennington and Wilfried Hartmann (Washington: The Catholic University of America Press, 2008), 22–54 on pages 32, 38, 39, notes that this work supplied Gratian with many of the texts he cites, without discussing how those authors treat these citations on baptism. Cushing, *Papacy and Law*, 94, notes Anselm's citation of Augustine without agreeing with the well-nigh exclusive role that Munier grants him in influencing later canonists to do likewise. Following her discussion of Anselm's sources on pages 64–102, she remarks, on page 102: "Anselm was not always entirely faithful to the intention, and perhaps ambition, of his original text or its formal source." Szaboles Anzelm Szuromi, *Anselm of Lucca as a Canonist* (Frankfurt: Peter Lang, 2006) does not address his treatment of baptism.

72. Anselm of Lucca, *Collectio canonum* 9.43–48, 2:475–79.

73. Ibid., 9.18, 2:464: "Qui in perfidia manens baptizetur aut nullam accepit remissionem aut ad temporis punctum."

that very moment thanks to the power of the sacrament, that same power is operative both inside and outside the church, just as the power of the name of Christ works to the expulsion of demons even outside the church."[74]

The aforementioned quotation elides the fact that Augustine was criticizing his Donatist opponents in the passage cited. There are other departures from his source in the way the continuator frames this point. In calling Augustine's *fictus* a *perfidus*, the author introduces the note of deliberate deceit, fraudulence with respect to the candidate's faith, in place of Augustine's concern with the harboring of hatred of his brother in his heart as the fictive baptizand's key vice. In his use of the language of *intra* and *extra ecclesiam*, *intus* and *foris*, the author does evoke Augustine's assertion in *De baptismo* 1 that baptisms in all Christian communions are Christian baptisms. Whatever the venue, this principle still leaves open whether baptism remits a fictive candidate's sins momentarily, or not at all, if he receives it retaining and continuing in his perfidy. But Anselm's continuator then adds an idea found nowhere in Augustine. He puts these baptismal rites, if deemed efficacious, on the same plane as exorcisms made in the name of Christ. Whether the latter are understood as ritual exorcisms, part of a candidate's pre-baptismal preparation, or as pious expressions that may be voiced at any time, they are scarcely commensurate with baptism. The invocation of the name of Christ is not a sacrament and does not remit sins.

On the heels of that inapposite comparison, the author returns to his chief interest—the minister of baptism. He gives detailed if confusing treatment to the validity of baptisms performed by priests who are heretics, schismatics, or guilty of simony and other sins. As he does in an earlier passage, here, too, he lumps these categories of malfeasance together. He has stated earlier that the sacraments administered by such priests are efficacious, since their power comes from God and not His fallible human agents. Unlike Augustine, the author now observes that some sectarians he has in mind use baptismal rites that differ liturgically from those of the orthodox church. "No one accepts" such rites, he avers; nor do they guarantee the reception of the Holy Spirit.[75] What about the baptisms of priests detached from communion when their liturgies do mirror those of the church? This problem is one certainly envisioned by Augustine in *De bap-*

74. Ibid.: "Perfidus si in perfidia permanenserit per baptismum nec intra ecclesiam nec extra ecclesiam remissionem accepit peccatorum, aut si propter vim sacramenti ad punctum temporis accipit et intus et foris ecclesiam vim operatur, sicut vis nominis Christi expulsionem daemonum etiam foris operabatur."

75. Ibid., 9.28, 2:468: "nemo accipit …."

tismo. For the author, these priests are not ministers initiated and ordained as sectarians but ministers who were originally members of the true church and were validly ordained within it. They are now dissociated from it but still claim authorization to perform its rites. He yokes Augustine to the situation of these priests as he envisions it. Regarding their ministry, he says, "We respond that such [a baptism] is not rightly held even when it is so given." In these passages, he rejects the acceptability of some baptisms conferred outside the church although elsewhere, more globally, he rules that extra-ecclesiastical baptisms are valid. So, despite his assertion that nothing obstructs the grace of baptism, it apparently can be obstructed by the defects of some priests and their liturgies, in circumstances not discussed or envisioned in his Augustinian citations.

Yet and still, with Augustine as his warrant, the continuator also maintains that those who receive baptism from these renegade priests, if they join the true church, should not be rebaptized, "since by their reconciliation there begins to be useful what was useless when it was given."[76] Useless because heretics, even those with a correct baptismal liturgy, baptize only "with respect to appearance, and not with respect to salvation."[77] Leaving that Augustinian contradiction standing, the author now returns to the fate of fictive recipients. After repeating the either/or position given earlier, he now makes a decision. Anselm's continuator supports Augustine's view of what can happen to a fictive baptizand later. There is hope for the repentant *fictus* who abandons the malice in his heart. The evidence for this happy outcome, however, is the parable of Matthew 18:23–34, a text which Augustine cites to prove a different set of conclusions. There, says Anselm's continuator, "as the Lord most plainly teaches," we encounter the wicked servant whose debts his king forgives. As the author presents this parable, its message is that the sins of the *fictus*, now described as having been remitted momentarily at the font but at once returning, are forgiven, since he later repents. So also the baptisms performed by heretics and schismatics are validated for their recipients, if they join the true church, despite their originally nugatory status.[78] Although it is Augustine's reference to this parable that alerts the author to it, he ignores the fact that Augustine

76. Ibid., 9.29, 2:468: "respondemus: sicut non recte foris habetur et tamen habetur, sic non recte foris datur et tamen datur.... Sic per eandem reconciliationem incipit utile esse, quod extra eam inutiliter datum est."

77. Ibid., 9.36, 2:471: "Heretici ... sacramenta et scripturas habent ad speciem non ad salutem."

78. Ibid., 9.23, 9.32, 9.38–40, 2:469–74; quotation at 9.40, 2:474: "apertissime Dominus docet...."

does not interpret it the same way he does. Augustine, as we have seen, presents the wicked servant not as having converted at any point but as remaining in his sins, despite the momentary forgiveness of his master. Nor has the continuator noticed how Matthew himself presents the parable. As the evangelist tells the tale, the master first condemns the servant for his failure to pay his debts, ordering that the servant and his family be sold into slavery to realize the sum he still owes. When the servant begs for mercy, the master relents and forgives him. But the servant does not forgive the fellow-servant indebted to him. When the master discovers that fact, he withdraws his forgiveness and condemns the wicked servant again, this time terminally. The wicked servant does not model the repentant *fictus* into whom the continuator tries to turn him.

In addition to his saddling his text with inapposite comparisons, citations of Augustine that miss the point as frequently as they report it correctly, and applications of Augustine's authority to topics he does not air, Anselm's continuator leaves hanging many of the questions which Augustine tries so manfully to answer. The overall effect of the author's treatment of fictive baptism is to complicate an already complex and inconsistent Augustinian legacy. Anselm's continuator interlards his Augustinian references with ideas not found in the texts cited. The bishop of Hippo might well have taken exception to some of them. Nonetheless, the *envoi* with which the author ends his discussion of fictive baptism does speak to the theme of reconciliation that frames Augustine's *De baptismo* 1. Before moving to the next sacrament on his list, he cites Augustine's appeal for unity in his *Epistola* 93 to the Donatist Vincentius Victor, since they share the same faith and baptism.[79]

While Book 9 of the canonical collection ascribed to Anselm of Lucca indeed reintroduces Augustine into the debates on fictive baptism, it can scarcely be said that the author of that book offers later thinkers much help in dealing with Augustine's contradictions, not to mention those which he adds in this often repetitive and unclearly organized text. His readers could find there that nothing obstructs baptismal grace and that the *fictus* does receive momentary remission of his sins at the font. The fiction of perfidious adults does not invalidate the rite for the infants they present for baptism. But it is an open question whether the perfidy of adult *ficti* frustrates their own reception of baptismal grace. Readers of this text could find that baptisms performed *extra ecclesiam* are both valid and useless, but, if useless, able to become useful if their recipients join the true church. While their

79. Ibid., 9.41, 2:474–75. Thaner, at ibid., 2:472n1, notes the author's conflation of competing Augustinian arguments and his citation of texts not pertinent to his own case.

validity is not compromised by heresy, schism, simony, and other priestly sins, they are invalid if performed by renegade ex-Catholic priests or in rites that differ from the Catholic liturgy. Unsurprisingly, the claim that, if they are valid, baptisms wherever performed are comparable to exorcisms made in the name of Christ is dropped without a backward look by readers of this text. Resurfacing in the sequel, and inviting criticism, is the author's use of the wicked servant parable to illustrate the forgiveness of the *fictus* who later repents. Even while drawing on the same sources, later authors are usually more adept at distinguishing what Augustine actually says on fictive baptism from what he does not say, and at using the genre of the canonical collection to express a distinctive viewpoint.

One canonist who has no trouble slicing through the contradictions on fictive baptism which Anselm's continuator leaves unresolved and which he compounds is Ivo of Chartres. While in some areas Ivo thinks that alternative rules should be left on the books so that the prelates who wield canonical authority can exercise prudence and discretion in applying them to concrete cases, fictive baptism is not one of them. Anselm's continuator may have suggested where to look in Augustine's works for pertinent material. But at Chartres, Ivo had access to one of the richest cathedral school libraries of the day. The presentation of his carefully edited citations suggests that the contradictions in the *De baptismo*, including those Augustine ascribes to his opponents, are all taken seriously by Augustine himself. Ivo adds ideas and solutions not found in Augustine. Far from merely anthologizing Augustine, Ivo's *Decretum* reflects an independent and critical mind at work. He lays out the problems in the Augustinian legacy on fictive baptism, as he sees them, in unequivocal terms:

> If a *fictus* accedes to baptism, are his sins remitted or not? ... If, as some say, they are remitted. ... how can this be since the Holy Spirit flees from the fiction? ... And if, as some say, they are not remitted, unless he is later struck to the heart with sorrow and confesses his fiction, I ask: Should he not be judged to be baptized anew? Now it is thoroughly demented to say that a person can be baptized, in what is accepted as true Christian baptism, with his sins canceled, although he retains malice and sacrilege in his heart. In the same way, they understand that people can be baptized in communities separated from the church, and that the same celebration of the sacrament is given and received and effects the remission of sins. But, with regard to anyone reconciled to unity [with the church] who abandons it for the sacrilege of dissension, they deem that his sins are retained and not remitted.[80]

80. Ivo of Chartres, *Decretum* 1.162, ed. Bruce Brasington and Martin Brett, 69: "Si ad baptismum fictus accessit, dimissa sunt ei peccata, an non dimissa? ... Si dimissa dixerint, quo-

Ivo offers his own take on the issues raised in this abridged Augustinian citation. Without mentioning the Donatists, he agrees that the either/or possibilities Augustine sets forth are thoroughly demented. The final case he mentions strikes a new note. It involves neither Augustine's lifelong sectarian nor the continuator of Anselm of Lucca's renegade ex-Catholic priest. Rather, Ivo conceives of someone who had once been a dissenter and was already reconciled to the true church but who then abandons it. While all the options listed are problematic, in Ivo's view the Augustinian instant remission thesis makes the heaviest weather, as well as being irrelevant to the problem of extra-ecclesial baptisms. He ridicules what he regards as false comparisons, whether or not he has the continuator of Anselm of Lucca in mind. As his own preferred handling of authorities affirms, if the *fictus* brings an unacceptable attitude to the font, the Holy Spirit will shun him. His sins are not remitted. It follows that his baptism is invalid. Since his sins are not remitted at the font, the rite fails to square with what is held to be true Christian baptism. If he retains his sins at the font and only receives remission of them later, when he sincerely repents, this would imply, or entail, rebaptism. Ivo raises this possibility simply to underscore its implausibility. As he presents it, the most ludicrous claim of all is that someone can lose his sins at the font and receive a valid baptism while retaining the same sins that were momentarily remitted. This Augustinian claim is basically self-defeating. It envisions a baptism that is at once both valid and invalid. It is a further folly to compare a fictive baptism, even if momentarily efficacious, with the invalid baptisms performed outside the church. People who want to hold such rites as valid, even though they also reject the forgiveness of those who engage in them since they have abandoned the true church, can be dismissed as arguing at cross purposes. This is a position which Ivo presents as equally rife with self-contradiction. Regardless of the liturgical similarities between the rites of the church and those of sects not in communion with it, the baptisms of the latter are not acceptable. And,

modo ergo Spiritus sanctus discipline effugiet fictum.... Si dixerint non esse dimissa, quero, si postea fictionem suam corde concusso et vere dolore fateretur, denuo baptizandus iudicaretur. Quod si dementissimum est dicere, fateantur vero baptismo Christi baptizari posse hominem, et tamen cor eius in malitia vel sacrilegio perseverans peccatorum abolitionem non sinere fieri, atque ita intelligant in communionibus ab ecclesia separatis posse homines baptizari, ubi Christi baptismus eadem sacramenti celebratione datur et sumitur, qui tamen tunc prosit ad remissionem peccatorum, cum quisque reconciliatus unitati sacrilegio dissentionis exuitur, quo eius peccata tenebantur, et dimitti non sinebantur." Accessible at http://project.knowledgeforge.net/ivo/decretum.html/, posted October 6, 2009.

with respect to them, Ivo draws some distinctions on topics ignored or blurred by the continuator of Anselm of Lucca's *Collectio canonum*.

We can agree, for instance, that nothing impedes the grace of baptism, but only with an important proviso. However awful an adult baptizand's sins may be, this principle holds if he truly admits and renounces them. If he does so, he receives forgiveness for his past and present sins. There are also provisions for dealing with the post-baptismal sins of the repentant convert and baptizand. The key, for Ivo, is that the person described by the sources he cites here is not a *fictus* but one who comes to the font with the right moral attitude and a true faith. Faith may be able to move mountains, but it is insufficient without charity, both at the font and in general. As for heretics and schismatics, Ivo grants that they may not dissent from Christian truth in all its particulars. We can certainly approve of them insofar as their doctrine accords with orthodoxy. But in some cases, they dissent deliberately, knowingly, and pertinaciously. Insofar as they separate themselves from Christian unity in these criminal ways, they remain bound in their sins. We should be exigent in preaching and exhorting them to embrace correct doctrine, reunion, and salvation, in charity and peace. But, to the extent that unity, charity, and peace are lacking in their attitude, so is salvation. There is no comparison here with the alleged momentary forgiveness of the fictive baptizand. The heretics and schismatics are comparable, rather, to the sinner who has not converted, whatever fictive rites he may appear to have undergone. The comparison between the power of baptismal grace and the power of exorcism is, quite plainly, irrelevant.[81]

What, then, about the baptisms performed by heretics and schismatics? Ivo is clear on this point. However similar these rites may be to those of the church, they are invalid. The only concession he is willing to make applies to those outside the church who are merely ignorant or confused. They can be classed with people inside the church who engage in baptismal rites without really understanding the Creed, whose sacramental acts can be regarded as neutral. But those who manifestly resist the Catholic faith, especially correct Trinitarian doctrine—Ivo's pointed example is Photius—do not benefit from this exception. Departing deliberately from the one faith associated with the Creed's one baptism, their baptismal rites are nugatory. Both groups of heretical and schismatic priests, the knowing and the ignorant or confused, must be contrasted with priests within the true church afflicted with various forms of moral turpitude. Unlike Anselm's continuator,

81. Ibid., 1.162–163, 68–69.

who treats simony as a form of heresy, Ivo classes simony with other sins which orthodox priests may commit. However serious their sins, Ivo stresses, their baptismal ministry remains valid. For it is the virtue of Christ, not the virtue of His ministers, in which the power of the sacrament resides.

Ivo's bottom line rests on the aforementioned distinctions. Some he finds in his sources while others are his own additions. In disallowing the validity of heretical and schismatic baptisms, he sides expressly with Cyprian, rejecting Augustine's departures from him.[82] As for immoral priests whose faith, intentions, and ritual practices are orthodox, nothing impedes the efficacy of their baptisms: "Baptism is always holy in the just and unjust alike. For even as no justice augments it, so no injustice diminishes it."[83] Although Ivo of Chartres does not exhaust what he has to say on fictive baptism in the foregoing discussion, it is evident that he makes great strides in clearing away the obfuscations propounded in the use and misuse of Augustine by Anselm of Lucca's continuator, and by Augustine himself.

The hard Cyprianic line against heretical and schismatic baptisms inspired a different reaction from a contemporary canonist, Alger of Liège. Alger speaks on behalf of priests like himself, caught willy-nilly in the crossfire of the investiture controversy still raging in his native Germany when he wrote his *De misericordia et iustitia* (ca. 1110). Alger was not a sitting bishop, like Ivo of Chartres, or one who had fled from his see, like Anselm of Lucca. He was a priest in the diocese of Liège, at that time part of the Holy Roman Empire. He protests what he sees as the unfair stigmatization of clerics, as trickle-down from the censure of their bishops. Indeed, Alger's own bishop had been declared schismatic owing to his support for Henry IV against Gregory VII. As a result, priests like Alger had been crushed between the hammer of the papacy and the anvil of the empire, on a guilt-by-association basis, even if they themselves had not been invested by lay rulers and were not guilty of simony, heresy, or schism. Alger pleads their case. Priests disadvantaged for any of these reasons who are truly at fault should undergo correction and do penance. But they should not be dismissed; nor should their baptismal ministry be called into question. In any event, he adds, local rules for enforcing clerical standards vary, and they should be respected.[84]

82. Ibid., 1.162, 1.164–167, 68, 70–72. On Photius: 1.165, 71; on Cyprian: 1.167, 72.

83. Ibid. 1.168, 72: "In homine iusto et in homine iniusto semper sanctum est baptisma, quod neque alicuius equitate augetur, neque iniquitate minuitur."

84. Excellent historical background on Alger is supplied by his editor in *Algers von Lüttichs Traktat "De misericordia et iustitia": Ein kanonistischer Konkordanz aus der Zeit des Investi-*

These situational concerns shed light on Alger's handling of fictive baptism, and, in particular, his interpretation of Rufinus's boys on the beach. Whether or not his source for this text was the same as Peter Damian's, his citation of it is more selective and adds a new, even a unique, gloss to it. The heading under which Alger does so is the unrepeatability of baptism, including emergency baptisms administered by pagans who do what the church intends. Since these baptisms are accepted as valid, so should we regard those administered by both sinful priests and those separated from communion with the church. Alger is well aware of the distinction drawn between these two types of priests. It is a distinction he rejects. For, as he sees it, those responsible for the ecclesiastical policy which he protests do not accept it either. But that policy, he argues, is undermined by the authority of Rufinus, as Alger reads him.

In Alger's account, both Alexander's initial observation of the boys and his judgment of them are solo acts. He omits the liturgy celebrating the martyr Peter, the scheduled repast on the beach, the bishop's consultation with his clergy, and his discussion with the boy ministers' parents concerning their education and later careers. The only people on the scene are Alexander and the boys themselves. And, according to Alger, the boys on the beach are pagans. This fact, he says, should not be seen as reducing Rufinus's credibility: "But the *Ecclesiastical History* is not to be held less authentic, although it is seen as less so [by some] because the baptism of these pagan boys by one of their number, in imitation of the bishop, was deemed fully efficacious (*ratum*) by the bishop of Alexandria."[85]

As to what Alexander saw, Alger makes no mention of ecclesiastical secrets and mysteries, or, for that matter, of ablution. Surprisingly, given the heading of this chapter, he does not report Alexander's ruling that the boy baptizands should not be rebaptized. Having cited Rufinus as a trustworthy source, Alger adds that he has also consulted Isidore of Seville as an intermediate authority on the same point. Isidore certainly agrees with the consensus view that an emergency baptism by a pagan is acceptable and should not be repeated. But neither on this topic nor elsewhere does Isidore cite Rufinus's boys on the beach. With or without Alger's reinscription of those boys as pagans, it is debatable whether the argument which he extrapolates

turstreits, ed. Robert Kretchmar, Quellen und Forschungen zum Recht im Mittelalter 2 (Sigmaringen: Jan Thorbecke, 1985), 27–57.

85. Alger of Liège, *De misericordia et iustitia* 1.51, 227–28: "Sed quia historia ecclesiastica minus iudicatur autentica, minus etiam autenticum videtur, ut huius pagani pueri, qui simulatus episcopus, baptisma ab Alexandrino episcopo ratum videatur esse concessum. . . ."

from this text supports either pagans who baptize *in extremis* or the routine ministries of sinful or sectarian priests. Nor is it evident that anyone responded to Alger's *cri du coeur* on behalf of the latter. Rather, his argument reflects the plasticity of Rufinus's account in the hands of medieval authors, whether they agree with Alexander's judgment or not.

An authority for later canonists who comment on fictive baptism, and also for some theologians, is Gratian's *Decretum*. The *De consecratione*, the part of the work credited to Gratian II, lays out a carefully edited version of the competing positions found in Augustine. While the *De baptismo* remains Gratian II's primary source, his selectivity differs in some respects from that of Anselm of Lucca's continuator and Ivo of Chartres. Gratian II introduces an Augustinian passage not cited by either of these predecessors. His inclusions and omissions pinpoint which of Augustine's views he takes seriously and which he finds not worth reporting. Gratian I, author of the first recension of the *Decretum*, also cites Rufinus on the boys on the beach, reflecting his assessment of that text as well.

As with earlier canonists, Gratian II discusses fictive baptism mainly from the standpoint of the minister. When he turns to the recipient, he presents the question in terms that initially evoke the citations of Anselm's continuator but that shepherd Augustine in a different direction. Gratian II condenses and combines in one passage the arguments Augustine gives at far greater length in *De bapismo* 1.12.19 and 1.12.20:

Concerning those who are baptized with fiction in their hearts, either their sins are in no way remitted since the Holy Spirit of discipline flees from the fiction, or they are remitted at that moment of time by the power of the sacrament but return because of the fiction, so that it is true that "As many of you as are baptized [have put on Christ]" and so is "The Holy Spirit of discipline flees from the fiction." That is, he [the fictive baptizand] puts on Christ thanks to the holiness of baptism and is denuded of Christ because of the sinfulness of his fiction. That the sins remitted return where there is no fraternal charity the Lord teaches most clearly in the Gospel about that servant who begged his lord to forgive his debt although he refused to forgive the debt owed him by his fellow-servant. Thus, the grace of baptism is not obstructed which remits all sin, even in the one whose fraternal hatred persists. For [the sin] of yesterday is remitted, and all that exists from before baptism and at the very hour and moment of baptism itself. But he begins to becomes guilty again, not only for [the sins of] the following time but also for those of the past days, hours, and minutes, with the return of all those that had been remitted.[86]

86. Gratian, *Decretum* D. 4. de cons. c. 41, ed. Aemilius Friedberg in *Corpus iuris canonici*, 2 vols. (Leipzig: Tauchnitz, 1879–80; reprt. Union City, NJ: Lawbook Exchange, 2000),

Gratian II's discussion of the parable of the wicked servant clearly rejects the interpretation of it given by the continuator of Anselm of Lucca in favor of Augustine's. He clearly supports the analysis and conclusions stated in the passage just quoted. He agrees with a selected number of findings from the range of possibilities that Augustine makes available: Nothing obstructs the grace of baptism, which remits all sins. The fictive baptizand's sins are forgiven, but only momentarily. For if the *fictus* remains unrepentant, they return at once. Gratian II does not advertise the existence of the passages in which Augustine, or earlier canonists, discuss the alternatives to these doctrines.

Gratian II also turns his attention to the later fortunes of the fictive baptizand. His citation from Augustine on that issue somewhat blurs the clarity of the passage just quoted. There, Gratian II presents the grace of baptism as given to the *fictus* momentarily, but as summarily withdrawn with the return of his unrepented sins. On that model, once he repents, that grace is regranted and, for the first time, becomes operational in his life. But in the next passage he cites, following the one just quoted, Gratian II advances another possibility: "When the fiction departs as a result of his true confession, baptism then starts to count toward his salvation. As for one who persists in malice and sacrilege, [baptismal] ablution has no effect on his sins."[87] This passage, Gratian II's final reference to fictive baptism as such, raises several questions: Is the model followed that of the grant, withdrawal, and regrant of baptismal grace or does the unrepentant fictive baptizand's momentary gift of baptismal grace stay with him, but in a mode he cannot use, so that it is not regranted but only needs to be activated when he repents? How does that

1:1379: "§. 6. His, qui fictio corde baptizantur, aut peccata nullatenus dimittuntur, quia Spiritus sanctus disciplinae effugiet fictum, aut in ipso tempore puncto per vim sacramenti dimissa iterum per fictionem replicantur, ut etiam illud verum sit: 'Quotquot in Christo baptizati estis,' et illud: 'Spiritus sanctus disciplinae effugiet fictum,' id est, induat eum Christum sanctitas baptismi, et exuat eum Christum pernicies fictionis. Nam redire dimissa peccata, ubi fraterna karitas non est, apertissime Dominus in evangelio docet in illo servo, a quo Domius dimissum debitum petivit, eo quod ille conservo suo debitum nollet dimittere. Sic non inpeditur baptismi gratia, quo minus omnia peccata dimittat, etiamsi fraternum odium in eius, cui dimittitur, animo perseverat. Solvitur hesternus dies, et quicquid superest, solvitur etiam ipsa hora momentumque ante baptismum, et in baptismo, dienceps autem continuo reus esse incipit non solum consequentium, sed etiam preteritorum dierum, horarum, momentorum, redeuntibus omnibus, que dimissa sunt."

87. Ibid., D. 4. de cons. c. 42, 1:1379: "Quando prosit baptismus ei, et qui ficte accedit [idem, i.e., Augustine, *De baptismo* 1]. X. Pars. Tunc valere incipit ad salutem baptismum, cum illa fictio veraci confessione recesserit, que corde in malicia vel sacrilegio perseverante, peccatorum ablutionem non sinebat fieri."

activation occur? And, if baptismal grace fails to count toward his salvation, is this because it was never granted, as Jerome or Bede would argue, or because it was granted but his fiction prevents it from affecting him? How are we to understand a grace that cannot be obstructed but that can be ineffectual in its recipients? These questions are not ones which Gratian II uses his citations to investigate. As we will see, a number of theologians of the high Middle Ages do wrestle with them. But for some of Gratian's glossators, such as Honorius of Kent in his *Summa de iure canonico tractaturus* (1185/91), what Gratian II proposes is the utter nullity of fictive baptism, a conclusion so evident that it is unnecessary to review even the abbreviated selection of conflicting positions which Gratian II offers on Augustine's authority.[88]

At the same time, and this oft-cited passage is one to which the author overtly attaches his opinion, Gratian I accepts the efficacy of the baptism of the boys on the beach in the first recension of the *Decretum*. With Alger of Liège, he places this text under the heading of the unrepeatability of baptism, whoever its minister may be. As with Alger, Gratian I omits the holiday meal, Alexander's consultation with his clergy, the convening of the parents, and the future education and careers of the boy ministers. He is also silent on the lack of a real parallel between this childish game and the emergency baptisms performed by well-intentioned pagans. But unlike Alger, Gratian I does mention Athanasius as the boy who acted as bishop, the liturgy celebrating the martyr Peter which he calls "sacraments of the Mass," the questioning of the boys regarding their interrogations and answers, and the pouring of water before the bishop decrees "that their baptism should not be repeated but completed by those things customarily done by priests."[89] Gratian I is as opaque as Rufinus and all previous authors who cite this part of the text as to what these priestly customs may be. Far from being pagans, as Alger would have it, the boy baptizands, in Gratian I's accurate report, were "some catechumens."[90] He implies that they were already incipient Christians. Whether, as minors, they had the

88. *Magistri Honorii Summa de iure canonico tractaturus* 1. d. 45. c. 3. C. 1. q. 1. c. 35, ed. Rudolf Weigand, Peter Landau, and Waltraud Kozur, Monumenta Iuris Canonici, Series A: Corpus Glossatorum 5/1 (Vatican City: Bibliotheca Apostolica Vaticana, 2004), 139, 287.

89. Gratian, *Decretum* C. 1. q. 1. d.p.c. 58, 1:380: "post expleta missarum sacramenta"; "iterari baptismum non debere, sed adimpleri ea, que sacerdotibus est mos."

90. Ibid.: "quosdam catechumenos." Rosier-Catach, *La parole efficace*, 288–89, discusses this passage in Gratian but does not mention his acceptance of the baptism of the boys on the beach. Gabriel Le Bras, "Alger de Liège et Gratien," *Revue des sciences philosophiques et théologiques* 20 (1931): 5–26, treats Alger as a formal source of Gratian but does not comment on baptism in general or on Rufinus in particular in either author.

legal capacity to make a real baptismal commitment is a question which he neither asks nor answers. But it is one that some of his commentators, and others, do raise, in judging Gratian's assessment of Alexander's ruling.

Reenter the *Taufmime*

Starting in the tenth century and widening their perspectives in the twelfth, some medieval authors dismiss patristic critiques of actors and stage plays and replace them with positive appraisals of drama. Their revaluations range from drama as good clean fun to drama as conducive to good health and good morals. This climate of opinion even made possible the reappearance of the *Taufmime*, to brief but enthusiastic acclaim. This appreciation of plays and players needs highlighting, given the prevailing historiography on the subject. Many scholars perpetuate the idea that the patristic view of plays as *pompa diaboli* continued unabated into the Middle Ages. Actors, so it is held, were universally condemned as reprobates. Their plays were seen as blasphemous attacks on Christian doctrine and values. The shows put on in ecclesiastical venues, despite repeated legislation against them, merely emboldened players to add to the fund of clerical foibles portrayed in their impious scenarios.

It is true that plays, like other genres of medieval satirical literature, lampooned clerical wolves in shepherds' clothing, along with quack doctors, pettifogging lawyers, nagging wives, and other stock characters. And medieval observers did recognize the intrinsically dramatic nature of the Christian liturgy and of rituals of all kinds. But, in the standard view, theatrics did not come into its own until the development of liturgical drama with its mystery, miracle, and morality plays, popularized in the later Middle Ages in dramatic cycles mounted in the vernacular by and for the laity, as well as by the learned appreciation of Aristotle's *Poetics* when it was translated into Latin. At the same time, critics continued to tax plays and players with impropriety, to ostracize actors from polite society, and even to advocate their exclusion from the Eucharist. There have been noteworthy efforts to correct this picture, but the evidence suggests that even more substantial revisions of it are needed.[91]

91. The best and most recent surveys of this past historiography and how it should be revised are provided by Symes, "The History of Medieval Theatre," 1–17; eadem, "The Tragedy of the Middle Ages," in *Beyond the Fifth Century: Interactions with Greek Tragedy from the Fourth Century BCE to the Middle Ages*, ed. Iugo Gildenbard and Martin Reverman (Berlin: Walter De Gruyter, 2010), 355–69; Barnes, "Christians and the Theater," ibid., 315–54; To the bibliog-

An early recognition that plays do not invariably lead Christians down the garden path to perdition is found in Ruotger of Cologne's *vita* of Bruno of Cologne (tenth century). As Ruotger relates, this sainted bishop, far from disparaging drama, loved "buffoonery and play-acting, which were brought forth in comedies and tragedies enacted in parts, sounded out and examined by the company with endless mirth, he himself reading these over and over in earnest."[92] The episcopal court in which these plays were so eagerly performed and studied was the same sort of environment that nurtured Roswita of Gandersheim (935–1001/2), who authored her well-known Latin plays, Christianizing Terence's comedies and feminizing the desert saints and early Christian martyrs, for the delectation of her monastic sisterhood.

In the early twelfth century, we find theologians and educators explaining the rationale for their positive appraisals of theatrical performances and performers. One of the followers of Anselm of Laon attacks head-on what he sees as unexcogitated hostility toward jongleurs and their art. He draws a careful distinction between two kinds of jongleurs, depending on the content of their songs and the reasons why they engage in their profession:

> This is what we should think about jongleurs. Some of them, who only ply their trade as buffoons, should be ejected from the church and no one should associate with them in any way. For they delude the minds of men with their nefarious art. In the guise of correcting others, they lead them astray. But there are others who are wont to sing in their songs of the deeds of kings, or of historical events, or of behavior which stirs up the minds of their hearers to defend the commonwealth or to the improvement of morals. Since they seek to gain no preferment by their craft but only to serve the common good, these are to be supported and in no way excommunicated.[93]

---

raphies of Symes and Barnes may be added Rahner, *Man at Play*, 53; Richard Axton, *European Drama of the Early Middle Ages* (Pittsburgh: University of Pittsburgh Press, 1974), 11, 17–19, 24–32, 61–74, 84–158, Jörg O. Fichte, *Expository Voices in Medieval Drama: Essays on the Mode and Function of Dramatic Exposition*, Erlanger Beiträge zur Sprach- und Kunstwissenschaft 35 (Nürnberg: Verlag Hans Carl, 1975), 1–3, 5–14, 127n16; Tydeman, *The Theatre in the Middle Age*, 16–20, 26–45; William Tydeman et al., ed., *The Medieval European Stage, 500–1500* (Cambridge University Press, 2000), 32–36, 43–46, 58–59, 82, 113–17; Ronald W. Vince, *A Companion to Medieval Theatre* (New York: Greenwood Press, 1989), 163, 239. On the revival of Aristotle, see Dox, *The Idea of the Theater*, 95; Alastair Minnis, "Acculturizing Aristotle: Matthew of Linköping's *translatio* of Poetic Representation," *Zeitschrift für deutsche Philologie*, Sonderheft 124 (2005): 238–51. On the dramatic character of public ritual more widely, see Carol Symes, *A Common Stage: Theatre and Public Life in Medieval Arras* (Ithaca, NY: Cornell University Press, 2007).

92. Ruotger of Cologne, *Vita Brunonis, PL* (Paris, 1884), 134:946–47, as quoted and translated by Symes, "Tragedy of the Middle Ages," 360–61.

93. Sentences of the School of Anselm of Laon 422, ed. Odon Lottin, *Psychologie et mo-*

While the Laon master clearly differentiates between performances that undermine moral values and those that inspire noble and unselfish acts of public service, he describes the bad jongleurs first. The distinction he draws is ignored by Hugh of St. Victor, whose appraisal of theater is wholly positive. In his *Didascalicon* (1120s), Hugh outlines an elaborate educational program, one whose values go well beyond what is useful to exegetes and preachers. Following his discussion of the liberal arts, he presents the mechanical arts. On the heels of athletics, approved for its recreational value, he lists the benefits of theater as even more worthwhile:

The science of plays is called theatrics from the theater, where people customarily gathered for performances. Not that this was the only setting where plays were produced, but theaters were more popular than other sites for this purpose. For some shows were put on in theaters, others in the forecourts of buildings, others in gymnasia, others in amphitheaters, others in arenas, others at feasts, still others at shrines. Deeds were portrayed in the theater, and songs were sung, and acted out with masks and puppets. There were choral processions and dances held on porches.... These entertainments were numbered among legitimate activities. For, natural heat is stimulated in the body through temperate activity, and pleasure refreshes the mind. And, since people need to get together at times for performances, it is most likely that locations were set aside for it, lest they frequent other meeting places where shameful and illicit things are done.[94]

---

rale aux XIIe et XIIIe siècle, 6 vols (Gembloux/Louvain: J. Duculot/Abbaye de Mont-César, 1948–60), 5:300–301: "De ioculatoribus hoc tenendum est quod si qui illorum sunt qui solo scurrili officio vivunt, de ecclesia eiciendi sunt, nec cum eis aliqua communio habenda, quamdiu tam nefanda arte mentes hominum deludunt. Sic et illi qui cum corrigenda alios decipiunt. Sunt autem alii qui quasdam cantilenas solent cantare de gestis regum vel de historiis vel etiam de moribus per quas excitant mentes audientium vel ad reipublice defensionem, vel ad moralem edificationem. Hi tales, quamdiu nichil officio adquirere intendunt, sed solum communi utilitati deserviunt, tolerandi sunt nec ullatenus excommunicandi." On this and related points, see Marcia L. Colish, "Another Look at the School of Laon," *AHDLMA* 53 (1986): 7–22; reprt. in eadem, *Studies in Scholasticism* (Aldershot: Ashgate, 2006), no. III.

94. Hugh of St. Victor, *Didascalicon: De studio legendi*, 2.27, ed. Charles Henry Buttimer (Washington: The Catholic University of America Press, 1939), 44: "Theatrica dicitur scientia ludorum a theatro ubi populus ad ludendum convenire solebat, non quia in theatro tantum ludus fieret, sed quia celebrior locus fuerat ceteris. Fiebant autem ludi, alii in theatris, alii in gabulis, alii in gymnasiis, alii in amphicircis, alii in arenis, alii in conviviis, alii in fanis. In theatro gesta recitabantur vel carminibus, vel personis, vel larvis, vel oscillis in gabulis choreas ducebant et saltabant.... Ludos vero idcirco inter legitimas actiones connumerabunt, quia temperato motu naturalis calor nutritur in corpore, et laetitia animus reparatur; vel, quod magis videtur, quia necesse fuit populum aliquando ad ludendum convenire, voluerunt determinata esse loca ludendi, ne in diversoriis conventicula facientes probosa aliqua aut facinorosa perpetrarent." Hugh also notes that theater is a mechanical art at 2.20, 3.1, 6.14, 38, 48, 131.

Hugh thus presents a variety of forms of theater as legitimate. Far from leading audiences into sin, they draw them away from it, and from unsavory venues and disgraceful and licentious activities. Beyond that, he sees plays as providing refreshment for mind and body. They speak to our natural needs, both individual and communal. The pleasure they afford is good for us, contributing to our physical and psychological health. Hugh does not specify who is responsible for establishing the theatrical institutions he mentions, or for erecting and maintaining the buildings where they are performed. Some of the locations on his list were features of the ancient Roman urban fabric built by governments and civic-minded plutocrats acting on the principle that *richesse oblige*, sites still visible in twelfth-century cities and, indeed, in some cases, still in theatrical use today. Unlike the Laon master, he does not comment on the plays' subject-matter, but, from his description, they embrace a wide range of genres.

Hugh uses verbs in the past tense in the passage quoted. He reflects his familiarity with Isidore of Seville, who does the same in the chapter on drama in his *Etymologies*. Hugh likewise opens this topic with the derivation of the word "theatrics." But his goal is not to present a backward look at a phenomenon now of mere historical interest. For his placement of drama in the *Didascalicon* indicates that it has a role to play in the curriculum which this work recommends to contemporaries.

That is certainly the way in which Hugh on drama was received later in the Middle Ages. Closest to him in time and spirit is the discussion of drama in the *Philosophia* of William of Conches (fl. 1120–54). William divides philosophy into speculative and practical sciences. He then divides practical sciences into the liberal and mechanical arts, with theater as the seventh and last in the latter group. Following Hugh, William leads off with the etymological derivation of "theatrics" and then notes the various locations in which plays were staged, some with masks and puppets. He adds his own touches in describing these settings. William does not include athletics as a separate topic among his mechanical arts but assimilates it to theater as spectator sport. In amphitheaters "they ran races" and in arenas "they conducted prize-fights." As for plays performed at shrines, he expands on them: "They sang songs in temples in praise of the gods." Having explained that the liberal arts are useful, William then asks in what sense this trait applies to theater. Here is its value, as he sees it:

> Two things are most greatly necessary to mankind, activity and pleasure: activity, lest the spirit languish, and, no less, pleasure, lest its exertions exhaust the body. Plays were instituted for this reason. For, as the body is fatigued by its labors all

week long, the spirit's outlook is revived by plays during holidays. These remedies for our ills are clearly necessary for us. We cannot live without what is necessary and suitable, even if we could live more blessedly without it.[95]

William thus agrees with Hugh of St. Victor that going to the show is good for our health. The pleasure afforded by theatrical performance provides refreshment which we need after our arduous work-week, although in his *envoi* he suggests that we would be better off if we lacked this need. Like Hugh, William writes about the venues where plays are staged in the past tense, although he presents their restorative merits in the present tense. He does not comment on the idea that legitimate plays draw audiences away from dens of iniquity. More abbreviated reprises of Hugh and William on drama are found later in the twelfth century in Richard of St. Victor; in the thirteenth century in Bonaventure, Vincent of Beauvais, John of Wales, Remigio de' Girolami, and Ralph of Longchamp; and in the early fourteenth century in John of San Giminiano. While the psychological benefits of attendance at plays do not include catharsis for any of these authors, the advocacy of drama launched by Hugh of St. Victor can be seen as promoting the attitude that was to make Aristotle welcome on that subject.[96]

Even more striking than the reappraisals of stage plays expressed by the Laon master and by Hugh of St. Victor and his followers is the analysis offered by Ivo of Chartres. For, in addition to his discussion of fictive baptism already noted, his *Decretum* makes specific reference to plays in which baptism is enacted, and the actor personifying the baptizand is converted on the stage. Ivo ushers the *Taufmime* back onto the platform for a remarkable star turn. His lead-in is a passage from Augustine's *De baptismo* 7. What Ivo omits and adds in treating this text is quite telling. We recall that Augustine rejects the validity of even a sincere actor's on-stage baptism given its

95. *Un brano inedito della "Philosophia" di Guglielmo di Conches*, ed. Carmelo Ottaviano, Collezione di testi filosofici inediti e rari 1 (Naples: Alberto Morano Editore, 1935), 34–35; quotations on page 34: "in amphicircis cursu currebant, in arenis pugilis exercebantur, … in templis laudes deorum cantebant; on pages 34–35: "Queritur quomodo theatrica pertinet ad intrinseca. Duo sunt hominibus maxime neccessaria, motus et gaudium: motus quidem ne animus tabescat, gaudium ne nimia exercitatione fatiscat corpus; idcirco ludi sunt constituti, ut cum per totam ebdomadam essent corporali exercitatione fatigati, in festis ludorum recrearentur visione animi: hec operationes contra infirmitatem nobis exhibentes necessarium. Necessitas vel commodum est id sine quo vivere non possumus: set felicius viveremus, si sine eo vivere possemus." Noted by Édouard Jeauneau, *Rethinking the School of Chartres*, trans. Claude Paul Desmarais (Toronto: University of Toronto Press, 2009), 93.

96. The seminal contribution on these figures is Glending Olson, "The Medieval Fortunes of 'Theatrics,'" *Traditio* 42 (1986): 265–86.

failure to meet his ritual and moral stipulations. This point is a rhetorical ploy en route to his dismissal of Donatist baptism as a mere farce, play-act, and joke. For his part, Ivo omits this manipulation of the *Taufmime* in aid of anti-Donatist polemic and takes the theme in a different direction. Some baptisms, he agrees, may be false when simulated "within the church, or in a venue thought to be the church, or play-acted, as on the stage." Of these three possibilities, "it is more abominable to accede [to baptism] deceitfully within the church than to do so heretically or schismatically, without deceit, that is, with a soul that does not dissimulate."[97] But Ivo then notes that, while some actors do dissimulate in enacting Christian rites, voicing on-stage convictions which they do not hold off-stage, we can also envision the on-stage portrayal of a baptism in which the protagonist moves from dissimulation to a sincerely held Christian faith. And such a one is to be praised, unlike dissembling baptizands of the other kinds: "How much more is baptism to be accepted in one who is given it on stage, if, suddenly moved, he accepts it faithfully." It is astonishing, Ivo continues, not that such an on-stage conversion may occur but that anyone should rate more highly the person deceitfully seeking baptism by traducing the Catholic liturgy. For "there is a great difference between the actor who comes to believe and the one who makes a travesty [of baptism] within the church."[98]

Ivo of Chartres has been hailed for his sensitivity to the importance of drama—as well as of music, dance, and the visual arts—as enhancing the celebration of the liturgy, and through it, teaching and inspiring the laity.[99] Beyond that, in the passages just cited, he also thinks that viewers will be edified by witnessing the theatrical performance of a baptism in which the protagonist is converted, turning his initially fictive baptism into a sacramental fact. Such a theatrical event benefits the audience and not just the baptizand. What Ivo suggests is not only the reappraisal of drama but also the revaluation of fiction itself in twelfth-century culture. Literary historians have pointed to that period's revival of philosophical poetry, to what

97. Ivo of Chartres, *Decretum* 1.162, 67: "Si cum simulatione, utrum fallens, sicut in ecclesia, vel in ea que putatur ecclesia, an iocans sicut in mimo. Et quid sit sceleratius in ecclesia fallaciter accipere, an in heresi vel schismate sine fallacia, id est animo non simulato."

98. Ibid.: "Quid enim prosit animus veraciter dantis fallaciter accipienti, non video. Sed arbitremur aliquem etiam fallaciter dantem, cum et tradens et accipiens, fallaciter agant in ipsa unitate catholica, utrum hoc magis baptisma sit acceptandum, an illud quod in mimo datur, si quis existat fideliter, subito commotus accipiens, an quantum ad ipsos quidem homines attinet plurimum distat inter credentem in mimo et in ecclesia irridentem, ad ipsius autem sacramenti integritatem nihil intersit."

99. Fassler, *The Virgin of Chartres*, 136–43, 166–67.

Barbara Newman calls "imaginative theology" and what Dennis H. Green sees as the recognition that make-believe could make believe.[100] Even within this literary and imaginative landscape, the sympathetic cameo role which Ivo assigns to the *Taufmime* is as puzzling as it is noteworthy. The fact that *De baptismo* 7 affords him an introduction to this figure does not in itself account for the decidedly anti-Augustinian lines that Ivo gives him to play. We would love to know how this character came to be one of his *dramatis personae*. We have no evidence of any medieval drama in which baptism was portrayed on stage, in Ivo's day or later. So far as is known, the one Christian rite that received such enactment was the Eucharist, in the fifteenth-century Croxton *Play of the Sacrament*. Here, the Eucharist is given an anti-Jewish twist. The play's theme is the inversion of a Jew's host desecration with his conversion by a host miracle.[101] As for the *Taufmime*, Ivo's appeal to him in the *Decretum* seems to have been his last medieval casting call. So, following the enthusiastic round of applause given to him by Ivo of Chartres, he makes his exit from the stage.

The Twelfth Century: Theology to Mid-Century

The theologians who participate in the debate on fictive baptism in the twelfth century turn their attention to a wider range of sources and problems than were raised earlier, and revive or develop some distinctive ways of framing the debate. The doctrinal discrepancies in Augustine's *De baptismo* inspire much discussion. Jerome on Ezekiel and Bede on Acts reenter the lists, although the citation of Simon Magus as a fictive baptizand does not always survive intact. Rufinus's boys on the beach also resurface. Many changes are rung on this text, with Alexander's ruling attracting substantial opposition as well as vigorous support on a variety of grounds. The contexts in which

100. Barbara Newman, *God and the Goddesses: Vision, Poetry, and Belief in the Middle Ages* (Philadelphia: University of Pennsylvania Press, 2003), 297–98, for this phrase and passim for its illustration; Dennis H. Green, *The Beginnings of Medieval Romance: Fact and Fiction, 1150–1220* (Cambridge: Cambridge University Press, 2002), chaps. 1–2. For more on this topic, see Marcia L. Colish, "Rethinking Lying in the Twelfth Century," in *Virtue and Ethics in the Twelfth Century*, ed. István P. Bejczy and Richard G. Newhauser (Leiden: Brill, 2005), 155–73 on pages 170–72; reprt. in eadem, *The Fathers and Beyond: Church Fathers between Ancient and Medieval Thought* (Aldershot: Ashgate, 2008), no. XV, 1–18 on pages 15–17.

101. For the text of this play, dated to 1461 or later, see *Medieval Drama: An Anthology*, ed. Greg Walker (Oxford: Blackwell, 2000), 215–33; for further discussion, see Axton, *European Drama*, 195–99; David Lawton, "Sacrilege and Theatricality: The Croxton *Play of the Sacrament*," *Journal of Medieval and Early Modern Studies* 33 (2003): 281–309.

these theologians treat fictive baptism differ, as do the arguments they invoke. The one overview of this stage of the story to date, that of Landgraf, dismisses twelfth-century theology as yielding "only a confused idea" of fictive baptism, one not dealt with to his satisfaction until the late thirteenth century.[102] Fits and starts there were, ideas that were left hanging, and no lack of disagreements. But a number of beachheads were won, and terminology and strategies of argument invoked, that reflect the astuteness of twelfth-century masters and that laid foundations built on by later thinkers. Some of the most influential of these contributions were made by theologians working in the first half of the twelfth century.

Looking at these thinkers from the standpoint of what came before, and not just what came after, we are impressed by their vigorous efforts to hack their way through the thickets found in the territory they inherited. They brought critical judgments and fresh conceptualizations to that endeavor. As with the Laon master who argues for an unprejudiced assessment of jongleurs, followers of Anselm of Laon embrace the task of exposing the failings of Augustine in areas where they think he makes no sense. Also significant is their application of the *sacramentum/res sacramenti* distinction to fictive baptism. The author of the Anselmian sentence collection entitled the *Liber Pancrisis* uses this distinction in agreeing with Jerome on Ezekiel and Bede on Acts: If a fictive baptizand such as Simon Magus accedes to the font, he receives the water of baptism only, the *sacramentum tantum*, not the *res*, the remission of sins. This master is well aware of the momentary remission thesis of Augustine's *De baptismo* 1 and does not hesitate to reject it. In his view, one much cited thereafter, the ex-*fictus* receives the baptismal *res* for the first time only when he repents. On no account should he be rebaptized. Anselm of Laon is thought to have been a key source for the treatise on penance in Gratian's *Decretum*.[103] It is also pos-

102. Landgraf, "Die Wirkung," 110: "nur eine konfuse Idee von *fictio* besass." His principle of selection is to flag those authors who contribute to the pre-history of the sacrament as efficacious *ex opere operato* in ibid., 114–28, 178–81.

103. *Liber Pancrisis* 52, ed. Odon Lottin, *Psychologie et morale* (as in note 93), 5:49. Cf. Cédric Giraud, *Per verba magistri: Anselme de Laon et son école au XIIe siècle* (Turnhout: Brepols, 2010), 275–76, who treats this handling of Augustine as more inconclusive than our reading of the text suggests. See Giraud, ibid., 193–211 for a general description of this work and its place in the Laon school texts. On the influence of the Laon masters on Gratian on penance, see John Wei, "Penitential Theology in Gratian's *Decretum*: Critique and Criticism of the Treatise *Baptizato homine*," *Zeitschrift der Savigny-Stiftung für Rechtsgeschichte*, kanonistische Abteilung 126 (2009): 78–100; Atria A. Larson, "The Influence of the School of Laon on Gratian: The Usage of the *Glossa ordinaria* and Anselmian *Sententiae* in the *De penitentia*," *Mediaeval Studies* 72 (2010): 197–244.

sible that Gratian II may have been responding to the teaching of the Laon masters on fictive baptism. While he does not indicate how a non-heretical *fictus* should be defined, another Laon master groups him with the heretic who receives the *res sacramenti* only when he accepts orthodoxy. One case which this master mentions, harking back to the continuator of Anselm of Lucca, is that of infants brought to the font by fictive sponsors, whose baptisms are not thereby compromised.[104]

The Laon master who gives the best sense of the state of play in the early decades of the twelfth century and who offers advice to those beleaguered by the contradictions in Augustine's *De baptismo* is the author of the *Expositio divinorum officiorum*. His solution deserves quotation at length:

> On baptism: Since the remission of sins is the *res* of this sacrament, it is asked what is remitted in baptism in one who accedes to it *ficte*. Now God does not remit the sins of the impenitent. And, if his sins are not remitted, the invocation of the Holy Trinity is clearly in vain. As we see it, it matters not how many [Trinitarian] names the invocation may have pronounced over the impenitent one. Augustine says that his sins are remitted but at once return. But other doctors of the church disagree with this opinion. They say that this person's baptism is not ratified at that point. What is conferred on him is a certain aptitude for salvation (*quedam aptitudo salvationis*), that is, the virtue of penitence, by which his sins may be remitted later, if he truly repents. So it is not appropriate to repeat the sacrament.[105]

The author adds that, for him, the *fictus* is not the heretic but the hypocrite, or someone unsure of the specifics of the Christian faith, or of his acceptance of it. On the one hand, he wants to challenge the patristic requirement that catechumens engage in penitential exercises, a view shared by other twelfth-century masters. On the other hand, he argues that correct liturgical formulae do not guarantee the *fictus*'s reception of the *res sacramenti*, not even momentarily. The most he receives, besides physical ablution, is the aptitude for his later repentance. The master does not describe or

104. Sentences of the School of Anselm of Laon 364, ed. Lottin (as in note 93), 5:273.

105. *Expositio divinorum officiorum*, ed. Heinrich Weisweiler in *Das Schrifttum des Schule Anselms von Laon und Wilhelms von Champeaux in deutschen Bibliotheken*, BGPTM 33/1-2 (Münster: Aschendorff, 1936), 87–88: "De baptismo: Cum remissio peccatorum sit res huius sacramenti, queritur, quid in baptismo remittatur ficte accedenti. Nulli enim remittit deus impenitenti. Si autem, non remittitur ei peccata, invocacio sancte trinitatis illis videbatur cassata. Ne igitur tanti nominis invocacio irrita habeatur, videamus, quid huic impenitenti conferatur. Augustinus dicit, quia remittuntur ei peccata; sed in momento redeunt. Ceteri autem ecclesie doctores huic sententie non consentiunt; non tamen irritum esse baptismus illius dicunt. Confertur igitur ei quedam aptitudo salvationis, virtus scilicet penitentie, per quam remittantur ei peccata postea, si vere peniteat, ut sacramentum iterare non opportet."

explain further this aptitude, but it is a suggestion that later theologians will adopt, reformulate, and develop.

The contradictions found in patristic theology and practice on fictive baptism are not resolved by Peter Abelard. His treatment of this question is limited to his *Sic et non*. While he quotes some passages not referred to by his predecessors, not all of them are truly apposite. At the same time, Abelard does not include some authorities who had already come to play an important role in the debate. Nor does he make use of the *sacramentum/res sacramenti* distinction.

Asking whether the sins of a *fictus* are remitted or not, *quaestio* 117 of the *Sic et non* leads off with Augustine, the prime authority who says that they are. Abelard presents Augustine's claim that nothing impedes the grace of baptism, including the hatred of his brother harbored by a *fictus*; his sins return at once but can be remitted later. But he next cites Augustine's remark that perfidious and blasphemous people who remain in that condition are held in their sins whether baptized inside or outside the church. Either unaware of it or choosing not to adopt Ivo of Chartres's careful distinction between the baptisms of heretics and schismatics and of *ficti* who accede to the Catholic font, Abelard then offers two final citations from Augustine's sermons. One emphasizes the importance of the adult convert's free will and the other refers to the point that the wheat and the tares will be mixed in the church in this life.[106] In addition to the fact that these last two citations are not really pertinent to fictive baptism, Abelard omits the issues associated with the later repentance of the momentarily graced *fictus*.

Moving on, Jerome is Abelard's major authority for the invalidity of fictive baptism. To Jerome on Ezekiel he adds Jerome on Galatians and Jerome on Matthew. The primary text he quotes is Jerome's citation of Simon Magus as the quintessential fictive baptizand, "who may be baptized in water but who is in no way [baptized] unto salvation." Simon's sin, for Abelard, is lack of a full faith, not the attempt to buy sacramental grace. His next two Jerome citations bring in morals as well. As the Galatians commentary says, to be baptized is to put on Christ. Now, one who receives only water at the font does not receive the Holy Spirit and does not put on Christ. Abelard presents a Jerome who is less certain of that conclusion here than he is elsewhere. For the Galatians commentary adds a disclaimer not found in the Ezekiel commentary. Jerome asks: What about "heretics

106. Peter Abelard, *Sic et non* q. 117, ed. Blanche Boyer and Richard McKeon (Chicago: University of Chicago Press, 1976), 363–64.

and hypocrites and those seen to accede to baptism for sordid reasons?" He responds, "I do not know whether they put on Christ or not; ... it is argued that they are not baptized in Christ." The *Sic et non* does not indicate how, or if, Abelard hopes to square this statement with Jerome's forthright nullification of the baptism of Simon Magus. Even more of a mystery is the use he plans to make of his final Jerome citation, the procedure laid down for Christ's apostles: "First they teach; then they immerse in water,"[107] a defense of pre-baptismal catechesis, not a position on fictive baptism. As with his final citations of Augustine on the other side of the debate, so also some of his references to Jerome look to be quite off the subject. A generous reading of this *quaestio* is that Abelard wants his students to detect these problems and to weed out the irrelevancies he has planted, as well as to address the larger pros and cons. In any case, here is where Abelard leaves fictive baptism, and here is where we must leave him as well. He plays no real role in moving this medieval debate in any particular direction.

If their grapplings with the legacy of conflicting patristic texts do not always yield solutions as clear as those of the school of Laon, there are other masters in the first half of the twelfth century who are more forthcoming than Abelard. On the basis of the unpublished Pauline commentaries of Gilbert of Poitiers (d. 1154), Heinrich Weisweiler reports that he takes an unusually harsh line on the efficacy of baptism: Only the elect receive its benefits.[108] This position would rule out the validity of fictive baptisms of any kind. The authors of two Porretan sentence collections dating to the 1140s present a more nuanced treatment of this topic, on which they also offer some ideas of their own. One of them expands on the *sacramentum/res sacramenti* distinction from the minister's viewpoint. The *sacramentum* includes the verbal formula used by the minister as well as the water of the font. In order for him to convey the *res sacramenti*, he also needs to have a correct baptismal intention. Absent that intention, the rite is invalid notwithstanding its conformity with liturgical norms.[109] In such a case, the

107. Ibid., 365–66; quotations of Jerome on page 365: "acciperint aquam sed non spiritum, sicut Simon Magus baptizatus quidem in aqua sed nequaquam in salutem"; on page 366: "Et haeretici et hypocritae et qui sordide victitant videntur quidem accipere baptismum, sed nescio an Christi habeant indumentum; ... arguatur non baptismus in Christo"; on page 366: "Primum docent, deinde intingunt in aqua."

108. Heinrich Weisweiler, intro. to his ed. of *Maître Simon et son groupe De sacramentis* (Louvain: Spicilegium Sacrum Lovaniense, 1937), xciii.

109. Nikolaus M. Häring, ed., "Die Sententie magistri Gisleberti magistri Pictavensis episcopi (I)," 7.1, 7.7, *AHDLMA* 45 (1978): 83–180 on pages 146–47, 148. Cf. Rosier-Catach, *La*

minister's action can be compared with the fictive baptisms of people who recite the Trinitarian formula as a game or when submerging or bathing someone else "playfully." Both Porretan authors back off from an across-the-board nullification of these events. Citing Augustine, they present the latter as doubtful cases on which divine guidance should be sought. They do not note that the context in which Augustine gives this advice is heretical and schismatic baptisms.[110] But one of them thinks that divine guidance is superfluous in the case of ministers with sub-sacramental intentions.[111]

Turning to the recipients of fictive baptism, the Porretan masters raise as many questions as they answer. They agree that if a fictively baptized person repents he should not be rebaptized. He is saved "without the baptismal rite or the shedding of blood."[112] Is this because his sins were remitted momentarily at the font or because he receives the *res sacramenti* only when he repents? One of our authors tries to deflect attention from this question by offering an ingenious if unresponsive distinction. The phrase "in baptism" (*in baptismo*) can be understood in two ways. It can mean "while he was being baptized" (*dum baptizatur*) or it can be understood causally, as "through baptism" (*per baptismum*). The latter sense could apply to a *fictus* who receives no immediate benefit at the font "because baptism is the cause through which his sins may be remitted later." Left unanswered is how this effect would work at a considerable temporal distance from its cause, and which of these alternatives these masters find the most acceptable.[113]

One thing they are sure of is that the *fictus* should not be subjected to penitential exercises before he accedes to the font. Since baptism remits all sin, why then did patristic authorities, such as Gregory the Great, make this demand of their catechumens? This question inspires our authors to display their penchant for historical criticism. In the age of the *ecclesia primitiva*, they observe, bishops were plausibly concerned with the many converts who sought the font for self-serving reasons. Methods had to be devised to screen them out. This is why Gregory required pre-baptismal penance,

parole efficace, 288–89, who sees Albert the Great as the first to include the verbal formula as part of the *sacramentum*.

110. "Die Sent. mag. Gisleberti (I)" 7.9, 148; Nikolaus M. Häring, ed., "Die Sententie magistri Gisleberti Pictavensis episcopi (II): Die Version der florentiner Handschrift" 7.8, *AHDLMA* 46 (1979): 48–105 on page 73.

111. "Die Sent. mag. Gisleberti (I)" 7.9, 148.

112. "Die Sent. mag. Gisleberti (II)" 7.25, 72: "Et hoc non fit in baptismo nec in effusione sanguinis." Cf. "Die Sent. mag. Gisleberti (I)" 7.25, 151.

113. "Die Sent. mag. Gisleberti (II)" 7.26, 72: "quia baptismus est causa quare tunc peccata ei remittantur."

"as a test, to ascertain if they were receiving baptism with a fictive soul or without fiction."[114]

Even back then, the masters assert, some authorities judged this policy to be unnecessary. Although others besides Gregory found it prudent, it is certainly redundant in the here and now. While the Porretan sentence collectors take a clear stand on this issue, they are less successful in dealing with the conflicting Augustinian positions with which they wrestle.

The author of the *Sententiae divinitatis*, also placed within the Porretan tradition, agrees with the historical relativizing of Gregory's practice but takes a firmer stand on fictive baptism itself. True, the Lenten preparation of catechumens in the patristic era involved penitential exercises. Tests were indeed needed "because there were mockers and people who acceded [to the font] fictively and for monetary gain; they were baptized frequently." Still, at that time, Augustine was surely right when he pointed out that the sacrament has such great power that "even if one receives it with fraternal hatred, the grace of baptism is not impeded." Anyway, should the fiction recede, so will the *fictus*'s sinful state. The author acknowledges that there are those who argue that "people who accede fictively receive no benefit" at the font. He cites this claim in order to disagree with it. This author clearly finds Augustine's position the most persuasive, while ignoring its problematic features.[115] He also presents Augustine as having written to refute Gregory's pastoral practice, as if it had not been characteristic of his own a century earlier. So we can see that, among disciples of Gilbert of Poitiers, opinions on fictive baptism are not unanimous, nor are their appeals to historical criticism equally on the mark.

The thinker in the first half of the twelfth century after Anselm of Laon and his followers who, more than anyone else, moves discussion on fictive baptism in a direction that proves decisive is Hugh of St. Victor. On this subject his theology is even more influential than his revaluation of drama. In his *De sacramentis*, Hugh places front and center the attitudes that determine what an adult convert receives at the font. In order to be baptized validly, he must have "true faith and charity unfeigned." He must

114. "Die Sent. mag. Gisleberti (I)" 7.29–30, 152: quotation at 7.30, on page 152: "ad experientium, ut sciretur, quo animo accederent vel fictio vel non fictio."

115. *Die Sententiae divinitatis: Ein Sentenzenbuch der gilbertischen Schule* 5.1, ed. Bernhard Geyer, BGPMA 7/2–3 (Münster: Aschendorff, 1909), 113*–15*; quotations on page 113*: "propter derisores et ficte accedentes et quod causa lucri frequenter baptizabantur"; on page 114*: "etiamsi quis fraterno odio accesserint, non impeditur gratia baptismi"; on pages 114*–15*: "qui ficte accedunt, quibus non prodest baptismus."

come to baptism knowingly and willingly. This requirement, for Hugh, is beyond dispute: "It has been proclaimed as a rule of the Christian faith that those who accept the faith voluntarily will be judged worthy of spiritual regeneration; those who reject the faith will be repulsed, judged unworthy of the reception of God's sacraments."[116] This lapidary judgment, presented as a consensus position, is sufficient to dispose of the Augustinian *fictus* who receives remission of his sins at the font, even momentarily. The Augustine whom Hugh presents as relevant to his case is, rather, the Augustine of *De baptismo* 7, who rules out heretical and schismatic baptism as a farce, as a play-act, as a joke. Hugh reprises this language, but he omits the point Augustine then makes about the need for divine guidance in such cases.

While Hugh, like the canonists, places this solution under the heading of the validity of heretical rites, he quickly moves on to another question: "It is asked whether those who are baptized as a play-act, that is, as a joke, receive the true and full sacrament of baptism." It is one thing, he says, to give or receive baptism "playfully or sportingly," not meaning it, and another to intend to give or receive it, even when acting playfully, in imitation of the rite. "It is ludicrous [to think] that, in the total absence of the intention to perform the act, that it is what is said to take place." If it manifests a baptismal intention, a baptism may be valid even if it occurs playfully, for Hugh. But he is more concerned with playful baptisms that are devoid of any baptismal intention. A *fictus* of any kind, be he the baptizand or the baptizer, can be compared with a priest who goes through the motions of celebrating the Eucharist without intending to do so. Such rites are null and void. Hugh also compares the playful baptism intended as a jest with the baptismal nullity of pronouncing the Trinitarian formula while bathing a baby by someone who has no intention of baptizing him. The use of the correct liturgical formulae in any of these cases is irrelevant. What is all-important, for ministers and recipients alike, is their intentions: "Nor can one make a prejudgment on the basis of form alone, where there is no [baptismal] intention."[117]

116. Hugh of St. Victor, *De sacramentis Christianae fidei* 2.6.7, 2.6.9, ed. Rainer Berndt, Corpus Victorinum 1 (Münster: Aschendorff, 2008), 388, 391; quotations at 2.6.7, 388: "fides vera et caritas non ficta"; at 2.6.9, 391: "Regula fidei christianae nuntiabatur ut vel sponte fidei adquiescentes digni regeneratione spiritali iudicarentur vel credere nolentes merito a perceptione sacramenti dei velut indigni, repellerentur." Cf. Larson, "The Influence of the School of Laon," 224–26, who faults Hugh for not framing his position on fictive baptism in terms of the *sacramentum/res sacramenti* distinction but without noting this passage. Rosier-Catach, *La parole efficace*, 290, rightly flags Hugh's importance on this point.

117. Hugh of St. Victor, *De sacramentis* 2.6.13, 394–95: "Queritur de his qui mimice id est

The twelfth century is famous for making intentionality central to its moral and sacramental theology. Hugh of St. Victor reinforces that principle and makes a signal advance in applying it to fictive baptism. In this respect, his *De sacramentis* is a real benchmark, laying down a fundamental rationale for nullifying fictive baptism, whatever the sub-sacramental intentions of the *ficti* may be. Later scholastics will pay careful attention to the parameters within which he frames this question, whether or not they add other authorities and arguments to those which Hugh advances or address aspects of the topic which he does not consider.

An initial witness to Hugh's influence is the largely Victorine *Summa sententiarum*, which amplifies his argument. The author attaches to it the *sacramentum/res sacramenti* distinction: "Those who accede fictively [to the font] without faith or with an impenitent heart [receive] the *sacramentum* and not the *res*." The author draws pointedly on a passage in which Augustine describes the deliberation, faith, and repentance that characterize the sincere baptizand.[118] He is well aware of Augustine's momentary remission thesis and applies it to a different issue. He agrees with the Porretans that Gregory the Great's policy of requiring pre-baptismal penance was misguided, if historically comprehensible as a means of eliminating those "who sought baptism faking it." As with the *Sententiae divinitatis*, the author ignores both Augustine's own catechetical requirements and the fact that he wrote a century earlier in presenting his claim that nothing impedes the grace of baptism as an express rejoinder to Gregory. But he also couples this point with his rejection of the momentary remission thesis. A *fictus* cannot put on Christ at the font, not even for an instant. For putting on Christ is an internal clothing, not like physical garb that can be put on and taken off at will.[119] So, for this author, Augustine's *De baptismo* supports the rejection of pre-baptismal penance even as it provides ballast for the rejection of Augustine's own momentary remission thesis, which the *Summa sententiarum* joins Hugh and the Laon masters in opposing.

A master writing in the first half of the twelfth century who applies his own blue pencil to the Augustinian legacy is Robert Pullen. Noting and

---

iocose baptizantur utrum plenum et verum sacramentum baptismi percipiant. Sed sciendum quia aliud est aliquid iocose vel lusorie dare sive accipere, et tamen velle dare aut accipere et hoc omnino intendere ut detur et accipiatur quod iocose vel datur et accipiatur.... Ridiculum autem omnino est ubi intentio agendi nulla constat opus esse dicatur.... Nec propter solam formam preiudicans, ubi intentio nulla est."

118. *Summa sententiarum* 5.5, *PL* (Paris, 1880), 176:130C: "Sacramentum et non rem illi qui ficte accedunt, vel sine fide et corde impoenitenti."

119. Ibid., *PL* 176:130C–131B.

dismissing ablutions that are intended to be nothing else, he considers a range of baptismal ablutions which he specifically deems fictive. His *Sentences* returns to the theme of playful or joking ablutions posing as baptisms. He includes baptisms administered according to the Catholic rite whose participants lack a baptismal intention. Reacting to the existence of antisacramental heresies in his day, Robert expands the list. Some baptisms are fictive because their participants reject the efficacy of the sacrament, or indeed, their very need for it. None of these baptisms are valid, in Robert's eyes. He takes a leaf from Hugh's book by comparing them with other rites invalidated by the absence of sacramental intention, such as marriage vows taken and confessions made by penitents in jest. These comparisons are not particularly useful. Conceivably, someone might later enter a valid marriage with the person to whom he had once pledged himself in jest. Or, he could contract a valid marriage with someone else. A fictive penitent could conceivably rectify his condition with a good future confession. But baptism is unrepeatable. While Robert wants to bring fictive baptism into line with his sacramental theology in general, he ignores these discrepancies. Still, he presents a firm position on fictive baptism itself: "Someone [fictively] baptized is not held to be cleansed [of his sins], ... since all these baptisms are the result of mockery. They effect nothing beyond the *sacramentum*." They do not convey the inner ablution of baptismal grace.[120]

Another modification of Hugh's position is Robert's conception of the *fictus* who is not playful or mocking but who brings to the font sins which he has no intention of abandoning. This individual is not Augustine's *fictus* harboring hatred of his brother in his heart. Nor is he Jerome's *fictus* seeking baptism for sordid and selfish reasons. Nor is he the *fictus* with a weak or heterodox faith. Robert's *fictus* suffers from sins of the flesh. Given their all-too-visible manifestations, these sins will be obvious to baptismal ministers. Robert thinks that ministers will also be able to ascertain that such *ficti* have no intention of giving them up. He thus enjoins ministers to reject these *ficti*: "Now if fornicators or drunkards or those given to any other kind of shameful behavior should seek it, they are unworthy of the font and should be denied it."[121] Robert does concede the rite to these *ficti* if their sins are venial. But, even so, they do not receive the *res sacramenti*: "For

120. Robert Pullen, *Sententiae in libri octo* 6.15, *PL* (Paris, 1854), 186:841D–842B; quotation at 842B: "Baptizatus ergo non mundatus videtur; ... sic ergo hinc inde tota baptismi actio irrisorie agitur, tantum sacramento nihil efficiunt...."

121. Ibid.: "Nam si aut fornicatores, aut ebriosi, aut alios quovis in flagitio perseverare malunt, indigni lavacro refutantur."

although they receive the *sacramentum* they do not receive its fruits."[122] While Robert Pullen widens the definition of fictive baptism to include those who scoff at the sacrament itself, he also extends it to apply to those beset by sins of the flesh. And he is unusually stern in excluding *ficti* whose sins are notorious, who should not be admitted to baptism at all.

A master writing in the same period who shares Hugh's outlook and who adds his own touches to a full-scale reprise of the Augustine versus Augustine program is Master Simon. Ignoring Ivo of Chartres's distinctions, he holds that the sectarian or moral defects of ministers do not prevent them from mediating sacramental grace to candidates who "accede [to the font] with a pure heart and not fictively."[123] If they accede fictively, the logic of the *sacramentum/res sacramenti* distinction obtains. Simon's *fictus* may be Augustine's, retaining hatred of his brother in his heart. Among his criminal vices, he may also retain the pride which leads him to scoff not just at baptism itself, as Robert Pullen notes, but also at the catechetical preparation that precedes it for adult converts: "If indeed he condemns the catechesis ordered to the sacrament of baptism which Holy Church prescribes, and accedes [to the font] scorning it, he sins, and the remission of sins does not result since he remains in his crimes, that is, his pride and contempt for the divine sacraments."[124]

Simon is thus willing to tackle head-on the claim that nothing impedes the grace of baptism, and to deny it. But while he rejects Augustine's momentary redemption of the *fictus*, he makes an effort to grasp how baptismal grace, inoperative at the font, becomes operative if the *fictus* repents. Simon offers a mild qualification of the view that the fictive baptizand receives only the *sacramentum* at the font and not the *res*. With the Laon master cited earlier, he thinks that more is granted to him than just external ablution. He also receives a gift that later facilitates his redemption: "The sins of those who accede [to the font] with fiction in their heart are not remitted. But the power of the sacrament is not lost to them although they cannot yet benefit from it on account of their sinfulness."[125] This power,

122. Ibid.: "Ergo percipiunt sacramentum nec percipiunt sacramenti fructum."

123. *Maître Simon et son groupe De sacramentis*, ed. Weisweiler (as in note 108), 11: "si corde puro non ficte accedant." On defects of the priest as no impediment, see ibid., 6–7.

124. Ibid., 12: "Si quis vero sacramento cathezizandi contempnens eo ordine ad baptismum, quem sancta observat Ecclesia, accedere spreverit, peccat et peccatorum remissionem non consequitur, cum in criminibus, id est superbia et contemptu divinorum sacramentorum, detineatur."

125. Ibid., 4: "Fictio corde accidentibus peccata non dimittuntur. Nec tamen baptismus vim suam amittit, quamvis isti pro nequitia sua non proficiat."

lodged in unrepentant *ficti*, enables the grace not activated at their baptism to remit their sins if they change their minds: "If they truly repent later, they are cleansed of both original and actual sin. And this occurs through the medium of baptismal grace, proposed to them in a sort of dormant state, which then begins to act in them."[126] As Simon sees it, grace is indeed offered to *ficti* at the font, although they are able to receive and retain it only in a kind of latent state (*quasi sospita*). It becomes operational when they repent.

At the same time, as we have noted in considering his treatment of baptism by desire, Simon introduces the theme of baptismal character. Although it is spiritual, he analogizes the character impressed on the baptizand's soul with a physical emblem of military office or political allegiance.[127] He is tantalizingly vague on how, or if, baptismal character differs from baptismal grace. He does not invoke the idea of character in explaining the turnaround of the ex-*fictus*. Still, his inclusion of that notion is a straw in the wind. The concept of baptismal character will prove important to later masters who deal with fictive baptism. Clearer, as an expansion of what it can involve, is Simon's inclusion of contempt for pre-baptismal catechesis as well as for the efficacy of the sacrament itself.

One master in this period whose *Sentences* reflects impatience with the pro- and anti-Augustinian analyses of his contemporaries is Roland of Bologna. He agrees with those who reject the instant remission thesis and offers his own simple and straightforward way to dispose of it. One and only one authority is needed to anchor what he presents as an irrefutable argument. It is a text quoted by Augustine himself and referred to indirectly and without ascription by many current and earlier thinkers, Wisdom 1:5. Roland cites it as a refutation of Augustine without further ado: "No sin of one who accedes fictively [to the font] is remitted. For 'the Holy Spirit of discipline' that dwells in the saints 'flees from the fiction.'" It is only if and when he abandons his fiction that "the baptism received fictively begins to take effect in him, resulting in the remission of sins of which he was earlier unworthy because of his mental fiction."[128] The Book of Wisdom thus cuts

126. Ibid., 4–5: "Si vero tamen peniterint postea, et ab originali et ab actualibus mundantur. Quod tamen baptismi gratia mediante consequuntur, quia tunc gratia in eis operari incipit, quem baptismo eis proposita quasi sospita fuit." Noted by Weisweiler's intro. on page lxxxv, although he wants to assimilate this notion to the anachronistic idea that the sacrament acts *ex opere operato*.

127. Simon, *De sacramentis*, 6: "In baptismo quippe caractere sui regis baptizatus insignitur...."

128. *Die Sentenzen Rolands nachmals Papstes Alexander III*, ed. Ambrosius M. Gietl

through the confusion inflicted on the Christian tradition by Augustine.

Beyond Augustine, there is another authority who needs to be routed, according to Roland: Rufinus on the boys on the beach. He regards Alexander's decision as thoroughly misguided. But another problem is that some people who have cited this passage have done so mistakenly. The issue which it addresses is neither the unrepeatability of baptism, nor the efficacy of the ministry of non-Christians, nor that of Christians not in communion with the church. The real context is the one in which Roland places it, "whether the intention of the baptized is necessary in baptism."[129] Roland agrees wholeheartedly with Hugh of St. Victor that an affirmative answer is the correct response to this question. He explains why he thinks Alexander got it wrong, in a rehearsal of the passage from Rufinus that does not match exactly the wording given in any of its previous citations.

"It is evident that the authority of Bishop Alexander should be opposed," he begins. Roland's account omits the beach picnic, the arrival of the clergy, Alexander's consultation with them and with the boy ministers' parents, the boys' future education and careers, and the unspecified priestly acts that remain to be performed. Beyond that, Alexander was not physically present on the beach when he first noticed the boys' game. Roland's Alexander "saw a group of boys playing on the beach while looking out the windows" of his cathedral, evidently located adjacent to the beach and not, as one would suppose, in the heart of downtown Alexandria. Having completed the celebration of the liturgy honoring the martyr Peter, Alexander observed that Athanasius "imitated what a bishop does, baptizing many catechumens in the sea." This immersion replaces the pouring of water, as Rufinus reports Alexander's findings. When he assembled the boys, he asked them "whether they were serious in doing what they did." Satisfied by their answers, "he approved their baptism and ruled that they should not be rebaptized, even if those who were baptized had only a minimal baptismal intention." It is on this decidedly shaky basis, Roland observes, that some commentators argue that baptismal intention is unnecessary. "To this, we say that it is necessary, if an adult or one at the age of discretion is to be validly baptized, whether the baptizer intends it or not, so long as the church's ritual is followed. But if it is a child who is baptized, his intention

(Freiburg: Herder, 1891), 200: "Fictio enim in corde accedenti nullum remittitur peccatum. 'Spiritus enim sanctae' habitans in sancti 'disciplinae effugiet fictum'; ... baptisma in fictione acceptam suum effectum in eo incipit haberat, et consequitur peccatorum remissionem, qua primo erat indignus, propter mentis fictioni."

129. Ibid., 205: "utrum intencio baptizati in baptismo sit necessaria."

is irrelevant and does not apply ... so long as it is done according to the church's norms."[130]

The critical point which Roland thinks has been overlooked both by Alexander initially and by those who later support his decision is that the boys on the beach, being children, suffered from defect of age. Thus, whether or not they intended to give and receive baptism is a *question mal posée.* They were minors. *Ipso facto*, they lacked the legal capacity to make a life-changing decision, such as baptism, by and for themselves. They were not adults who possess that legal capacity, for whom intention is indeed a basic requirement. The intentions behind the boys' childish play are thus a non-issue. As we will see, some theologians in the succeeding period agree with this legalistic point and other aspects of Roland's consideration of the boys on the beach.

The Later Twelfth Century: Peter Lombard and the Post-Lombardians

In chapter 1 of this book, we saw how the *Sentences* of Peter Lombard functions as a template for discussions of baptism by desire after his time. He is less of a seminal figure in the debates on fictive baptism, although commentaries or *quaestiones* based on his work are the genres of choice for many of his successors. Some of his opinions remain influential while others are amended or disputed even by his closest disciples. Peter's main contribution to the debates on fictive baptism is to streamline the arguments which oppose its validity, and to bring both Jerome and Rufinus into play along with a carefully edited version of Augustine. His largest single debt is to Hugh of St. Victor. While he was thoroughly familiar with Gratian,[131] his treatment

130. Ibid., 206: "Sed videtur contra auctoritas Alexandri episcopo, qui dum Petri martiris missarum sollempnia celebraret, proscipiens per cancellos vidit in littore maris chorum puerorum ludentem Athanasium puerum, quem sibi in vice episcopum prefecerat, sequentem, a quo quidem velut ab episcopo plerique catecumeni in mari sunt baptizati. Expletis missarum sollempniis Alexander episcopus pueros a se convocari iussit ac rei geste seriem ab eis inquirire cepit. Qui postquam est compertus, quod multi ab eo in forma ecclesie baptizati essent, baptisma approbavit, nec reiterandum iudicavit, licet qui baptizati sunt, baptizandi intencionem minime habuerint. Unde videtur, quod in baptismo intencio non es necessarium. Ad quod dicimus, si quis baptizaretur adultus atque discretus, necessarium est ratum, sive intencionem habeat qui baptizat sive non, dummodo illud in forma ecclesie tradatur. Si vero puer est qui baptizatur, eius intencio non exigitur, nec refert, utrum qui baptizat habet intencionem dandi vel non, dummodo id fiat in forma ecclesie."

131. For the Lombard's use of Gratian throughout his sacramental theology, see Marcia L. Colish, *Peter Lombard*, 2 vols. (Leiden: Brill, 1994), 2:516–697. On the copy of the *Decretum*

of the boys on the beach is closer to Roland of Bologna's. But he is usually not content to rest his case on single authorities. He feels the need to bolster the critique of positions he rejects with multiple countervailing witnesses, including those drawn from the *oeuvres* of the same thinkers he opposes.

The Lombard shunts consideration of the validity of priestly ministries to the subdivision of his treatise on the sacraments devoted to holy orders and treats fictive baptism primarily from the standpoint of the recipient. He uses the *sacramentum/res sacramenti* distinction to make his position unambiguous: "Those who accede [to the font] either without faith, or fictively, receive the *sacramentum* and not the *res*."[132] The Lombard anchors this point with Jerome on Ezekiel, minus Simon Magus. There are two broad categories of *ficti*. They may lack faith, not just a full faith but also a correct faith. Reflecting the usage of the Carolingian exegetes, Peter is not hypothetical as he rephrases Jerome: "There are Gentile and heretical ablutions, but they do not wash (*non lavant*) unto salvation. Even within the church, those who receive baptism without a full faith receive water but not the [Holy] Spirit."[133]

In addition to *ficti* with absent or problematic beliefs, some have moral inadequacies. Peter cites Augustine's *fictus* who harbors hatred of his brother. He does not mention other kinds of sin with which he may be afflicted. With the pro-Victorines, Ivo of Chartres, and Roland of Bologna, the Lombard rejects the momentary remission thesis. He does not speculate about latent grace or baptismal character. He agrees that the sins of the *fictus* begin to be remitted only if and when he repents. He finds Augustine's effort to explain this process both confused and uncertain. Augustine advanced his claims, he says, as a mere possibility, "not as an assertion but posing the question and canvassing the opinions of others." We can do better, by referring to what Augustine says elsewhere, and confirm that "the sins of one acceding fictively are not remitted [at the font]."[134]

---

of Gratian in his last will and testament, see Benjamin Edme Charles Guérard, ed., *Cartulaire de l'église Notre-Dame de Paris*, 4 vols., Collection des cartulaires de France 4–7 (Paris: Crapelet, 1850), 1:60.

132. Peter Lombard, *Sententiae in IV libros distinctae* 4. d. 4. c. 2.1, 3rd rev. ed., ed. Ignatius C. Brady, 2 vols. (Grottaferrata: Collegium S. Bonaventurae, 1971–81), 2:252: "Qui vero sine fide accedunt vel ficte sacramentum non rem suscipiant." Noted by Rosier-Catach, *La parole efficace*, 291–92.

133. Peter Lombard, *Sent.* 4. d. 4. c. 2.4, 2: 252: "Sunt lavacra gentilium, haereticorum, sed non lavant in salutem. In Ecclesia etiam, qui non plena fide baptismum accipiunt, non Spiritum sed aquam accipiunt." The point is repeated at ibid., 4. d. 4. c. 7.2, 2:262.

134. Ibid., 4. d. 4. c. 2.5, 2:254: "non asserendo, sed quaerendo et aliorum opinionum referando; ... Non igitur ficte accendentis peccata dimittuntur."

The Lombard also addresses the baptismal status of "one who is immersed as a game." As he sees it, there are three kinds of fictive baptisms of this sort. One is a baptismal rite portrayed on stage with accurate liturgical details by someone "who is mimicking it, like an actor." The actor in this statement is not Ivo of Chartres's *Taufmime* taking a delayed curtain call but the *Taufmime* of *De baptismo* 7.[135] Peter presents the Augustinian advice that we seek divine guidance as failing to supply "a definite rule." On this topic, Peter, like others before him, ignores the fact that Augustine is making a debater's point about heretical and schismatic baptisms which he denigrates by saying that they are conducted "as a farce, as a play-act, as a joke," tarring them with the brush of the late Roman stage. In any case, here, too, we can go Augustine one better. We have no grounds for hesitation and no need to wait for guidance from on high: "It is evident, to the wise, that this could not be baptism."[136]

The same principle applies to the other two groups of playful fictive baptizands. In the case of those who recite the Trinitarian formula when bathing a baby, as a prank, the baby is bathed, not baptized. Finally, the Lombard considers children playing at baptism. He removes them from Rufinus's seashore and places them at a riverside. But while he does not invoke the defect of age, he agrees with Roland of Bologna's judgment rather than Gratian's: "Just as when people are immersed in a bath or in a river in the name of the Trinity, this is not baptism, since it is done without a baptismal intention. For in this, as in the other sacraments, even as the correct form is to be observed, so also must the intention to celebrate them be present."[137] While Rufinus, as well as Roland's take on him, are clearly detectable here, and while, as we will see shortly, there is evidence that the Lombard referred to the boys on the beach in his oral teaching,[138] he prefers to buttress this conclusion with Augustine's

135. Ibid., 4. d. 6. c. 5.1, 2:272: "De illo qui pro ludo immergitur"; "qui iocans sicut mimus."

136. Ibid., 4. d. 6. c. 5.1, 2:273: "Hoc autem Augustinus non definit, ita inquiens: 'Si totum ludicre et mimice et iocülariter ageretur, utrum approbandus esset baptismus qui sic daretur, divinum iudicium, per alicuius revelationem miraculum, oratione implorandum esse censerem.' Videtur tamen sapientibus non fuisse baptismum."

137. Ibid.: "Ut cum aliqui in balneum, vel in flumen merguntur in nomine Trinitatis, non est tamen baptismus, quia non intentione baptizandi illud geritur. Nam in hoc et in aliis sacramentis, sicut forma est servanda, ita et intentio illud celebrandi est habenda."

138. Christopher P. Evans, in the notes to his ed. and trans. of Radulphus Ardens, *The Questions on the Sacraments: Speculum universale 8.31–92* (Toronto: Pontifical Institute of Mediaeval Studies, 2010), 63n110, states that, although not included in the text of the Lombard's *Sentences* by his editor, the Rufinus text is cited in two manuscripts of that work, Paris Mazarine 757 and Paris BN Ms. lat. 17464. Evans notes Gratian's citation and comments on Rufinus but not Roland of Bologna's. On the Lombard's oral teaching, see the discussion of Peter

Epistola 98, where he thinks the bishop of Hippo got it right. Where there is no appropriate intention, there is no regeneration at the font and no granting of the Holy Spirit, unless we are referring to infant baptism.[139] But, aside from the baby being bathed, none of the fictive baptizands whom the Lombard discusses, playful or otherwise, is an infant. For him, as for Hugh of St. Victor, the bottom line and the grounds for his sweeping rejection of all the forms of fictive baptism which he includes is their defective intentionality.

In the period immediately following that of the Lombard, a number of masters closely associated with his teaching take up fictive baptism, some adhering to his views quite faithfully and others adding their own insights. Gandulph of Bologna gives this topic only a brief mention. In his *Sentences*, he is content to ask whether baptismal grace, not received by an adult who accedes to baptism *ficto corde*, will take effect if his fiction departs. He agrees that it will, citing Augustine but ignoring the complexity of his teaching, to which the Lombard and earlier masters devote such careful attention.[140]

Peter Comestor is somewhat more forthcoming. In his *De sacramentis*, he refers to the Lombard's oral teaching while adding his own refinement to the *sacramentum/res sacramenti* distinction with which he precedes it. For Comestor, the *res sacramenti* of baptism is "internal justification and cleansing ... from all sins whether original or actual, and it releases us from all external satisfaction and punishment."[141] It is this more detailed *res sacramenti* which fictive baptizands fail to receive, according to the authorities as he reads them: "By these it is proved that the grace of remission is not conferred on adults in baptism who lack faith and repentance. They receive the *sacramentum* and not the *res*."[142] Comestor annexes both the Lombard's doctrine and that of Jerome and Augustine to his understanding of the baptismal *res*. He agrees that baptism counts for *ficti* who repent but without explaining how it happens.[143]

Comestor below. Rosier-Catach, *La parole efficace*, 288–90, also ignores Roland of Bologna and sees Gratian as the only source transmitting Rufinus's text between Rufinus himself and the scholastics who discuss the boys on the beach starting in the second half of the twelfth century.

139. Peter Lombard, *Sent.* 4. d. 6. c. 5.2, 2:273.

140. Gandulph of Bologna, *Sententiarum libri quatuor* 4.44–45, ed. Ioannes de Walter (Vienna: Aemilius Heim, 1924), 412–14.

141. Peter Comestor, *De sacramentis* 8, ed. Raymond-M. Martin as appendix to *Maître Simon et son groupe De sacramentis*, ed. Weisweiler (as in note 108), 17*: "interior mundicia et iustificatio ... et omni satisfactione exteriori et pena relaxamur."

142. Ibid., 18*: "Qui vero sine fide accedunt vel ficte, sacramentum quidem suscipiunt et non rem.... Hiis probatur adultis sine fide et vera penitudine non conferri gratiam remissionis in baptismo. Unde sacramentum, non rem, suscipiunt."

143. Ibid., 22, 28*: "Tunc enim valet baptismus, cum fictio recedit a mente."

With this foundation laid, Comestor takes up the issue of playful fictive baptisms. He omits the case of actors and focuses only on the baby in the bath and children's games. Tipping his hat to the canonists, and also reflecting the Lombard's relocation of the beach, he queries "whether those baptized as a joke should be rebaptized. It is asked whether, if someone is immersed jokingly or playfully in a bath or a river in the name of the Trinity, this is baptism." The two authorities who need to be considered, he says, are Augustine and Rufinus. Comestor finds that while Augustine raises this question in *De baptismo*, he does not resolve it, "claiming that its settlement requires divine assistance." Comestor follows the pattern of ignoring Augustine's context and rhetoric. Not all prelates are so unsure of what they observe. For, as Rufinus tells us, "Alexander bishop of Alexandria ... refused to rebaptize some catechumens baptized in the sea by the boy Athanasius, who acted as if he were their bishop. Master Peter says that this was not baptism, for the one did not intend to baptize, nor did the others intend to be baptized. For one must have the intention to celebrate this sacrament, and others, just as their form must be observed."[144] This passage reflects the teaching of both Roland of Bologna and the Lombard. As with Roland, Comestor represents the boys at the beach as baptized in the sea (*in mare*), although he initially asks about people immersed in the Lombard's river (*in flumine*). With both masters, he thinks that Alexander's judgment on the boys was wrong, although he could and did exercise his own authority without praying for divine aid. Comestor himself rejects the baptism of the boys on the beach along with the other forms of fictive baptism which he mentions; in no case do any of them merit a suspension of the rule against rebaptism.

Peter of Poitiers, Peter Comestor's successor in the chair of theology at Notre Dame in Paris, is another disciple of the Lombard who takes up fictive baptism under two headings, and who differs notably from both of these predecessors. Peter of Poitiers also cites Rufinus and gives this text

144. Ibid., 21, 27*: "Utrum baptizati debeant rebaptizati. Queritur, si iocose aliquis vel lusorie mergatur in balneo vel in flumine in nomine Trinitatis, utrum sit baptismus. Augustinus movet questionem hanc in libro *De baptismo* et non solvit, sed eam divino iudicio solvendum reliquid. Alexander episcopus Alexandrie, ut Ecclesiastica narrat hystoria, noluit baptizare quisdam catechumenis ita iocose in mare ab Athanasio puero, quem quasi episcopum suum instituerant. Magister autem Petrus non dicit esse baptismum, quia ne iste intendit baptizare, nec illi baptizari. Intencio namque et in hoc sacramento et in aliis celebrandi illud est habenda, sicut forma est observanda." Evans, intro. to his ed. and trans. of Radulphus Ardens (as in note 138), 232–33, notes the parallels with the Lombard's teaching, and Martin, intro. to his ed. of Peter Comestor on pages xxvi*–xxviii*, notes the parallels with that of Roland of Bologna.

a bizarre reading, one which reflects the interreligious tensions of his day. The context in which he refers to the boys on the beach in his *Sentences* is a standard one, whether the right to administer baptism should be denied to immoral priests. His initial response is also a standard one. This faculty should not be withdrawn "unless imminent necessity exists." Priests validly baptize, "both the good and the bad." He adds an unsurprising stipulation: "But the intention must be observed, just as the form, otherwise this is not baptism." Continuing, he notes that "when someone immerses someone else as a joke, reciting those words customarily said by those who baptize, he does not baptize."[145]

It is as a case study of how mistakes are made concerning these commonplace understandings of ministerial intention that Peter cites the Rufinus example. In addition to omitting a seaside or riverside location entirely, and much else, he garbles this text in two unique ways: "We read, concerning Bishop Athanasius, who, when he saw Jewish boys immersing each other and jokingly reciting the words used when adults accede to baptism, refused to baptize them or to have them rebaptized, deeming this first baptism efficacious, even though it was carried out as if it were a joke."[146] The first noteworthy thing in this passage is that, in the hands of Peter of Poitiers, Athanasius has morphed from the boy bishop of Rufinus into the bishop who observes and judges the fictive baptism on the beach. Next, he has turned the boys from catechumens, sons of Christian families, into Jews. Peter is concerned with their immersion of each other, that is, their farcical ministerial acts, not with their fictive reception. It is clear that he regards these actions, and the words spoken, as a desecration, not an emulation, of the Christian rite. The issue, for him, goes well beyond the defective intentions of these pint-sized mockers of the sacrament. It also embraces the reprehensible decision of the misnamed bishop who accepts this fictive baptism as valid. Rufinus, on this reading, presents a cautionary tale, an example of what those in authority in the church must avoid and condemn at all costs.

Much less idiosyncratic is Peter of Poitiers's explanation of who the other *ficti* are and why their baptisms should be disallowed. The second

145. Peter of Poitiers, *Sententiarum libri quinque* 5.8, *PL* (Paris, 1855), 211:1240D; "nisi immineat necessitas"; "tam bonis quam malis"; "Sed servanda est intentio sicut forma, aliter non enim esset baptismus. Unde ille qui ridiculose alterum immergit proferendo haec verba quae solent proferre baptizantes, non baptizat."

146. Ibid., 1240D–1241A: "Legitur tamen de Athanasio episcopo, qui pueros Judaeorum viderat se immergentes, et haec verba ridiculose proferentes quod adultis ad baptismum acesserant, eos noluit baptizare, ne in eis videtur iterare baptismus, aestimans primum baptismum, qui, quasi ridiculose factus fuerat, tunc habere efficaciam."

context in which he raises the question is headed by a more general issue, the efficacy of baptism in infants, in adults, in those cleansed of sin before baptism, and in *ficti*. The third group in this quartet received our attention in chapter 1 of this book. As for the *fictus*, Peter defines him narrowly as one who retains fraternal malice in his heart. He agrees with all the pro-Victorines that "ablution does not effect his interior cleansing insofar as he remains a *fictus*." It is only later, when he undergoes a change of heart, substituting charity for his former malice, that "he can merit eternal life, when his fiction recedes and his baptism begins to take full effect." This outcome can occur even though his baptism, when he underwent it, was unavailing. Were he to fail to repent, his fiction would remain a mortal sin that leads to his eternal damnation.[147]

This strong censure of fictive baptism does not exhaust what Peter of Poitiers has to say on the subject. He also offers his estimate of the current state of play. The *antiqui* accepted Augustine's position in *De baptismo* 1: "The ancients used to say that the sins of one who accedes [to the font] fictively are remitted while he is actually in the baptismal waters but they return at once as soon as he emerges from those waters." This view is now passé. The *moderni* hold a more up-to-date position, the one which Peter has just defended: "The moderns say that one fictively baptized receives no baptismal benefits." But if he abandons his evil ways and chooses good, "and the fiction recedes, the power of baptism begins to take effect; ... for he then receives the *res sacramenti*."[148] Peter's pointed use of verbs in the past and present tense to describe these ancient and modern views underscores his presentation of the modern position as articulating a new consensus that signals an advance in theological understanding.

While his observation holds for twelfth-century theologians who follow the Victorine and Lombardian tradition, it does not describe all of Peter of Poitiers's coevals. Odo of Ourscamp (d. 1171), also a former pupil of Peter Lombard, disagrees with him on many issues. The *Quaestiones* attributed to Odo suggest that some matters which Peter of Poitiers presents as settled remained in contention. Along with the *Sententiae divinitatis*, Odo

147. Ibid., 5.6, *PL* 211:1232D–1237B; quotations at 1235B–1236A: "Item, ablutio illa non efficit illam interiorem ablutionem, posito quod semper erit fictus"; "et postea eo merebitur vitam aeternam quando fictio recedet, et incipiet baptismum habere plenum efficaciam."

148. Ibid., 1236C–D: "Antiqui dixerunt quod ei ficte ad baptismum accedit, remittuntur peccata dum est in aquis baptismi, sed quam cito surgit de aquis baptismi redeunt peccata. Moderni tamen dicunt quod nihil prodest baptismus ei qui baptizatur fictus"; "et recedit fictio hanc incipit habens vim baptismus; ... tunc etiam suscipit rem sacramentum."

supports the instant remission thesis which Peter declares outmoded. He agrees with Augustine that the grace of baptism is not impeded by the sins of the *fictus*, whether instantly at the font or on an eventual basis if he repents. At the same time, Odo acknowledges that Augustine retracted many things he had earlier said and that his argument in *De baptismo* 1 is not the only feasible way of thinking about this question. He then qualifies the position just taken by arguing, with Gilbert of Poitiers, that the baptismal sign effects what it signifies only in the elect. What follows from this observation is another question which Odo does not address: Can a member of the elect be, at least initially, a fictive baptizand? The doctrine of election would seem to rule this out. But also ruled out, by Odo's formulation, is the possibility that a non-elect *fictus* can receive the effects of the sacrament, at the font or later.[149]

If Odo is irresolute or insensitive to the corollaries flowing from the position he takes on that issue, he is confident of his ability to pronounce on one aired by the Porretans and the author of the *Summa sententiarum*, Gregory the Great's requirement of pre-baptismal penance for his catechumens. Following the *Sententiae divinitatis* and the *Summa sententiarum*, Odo sees this policy as a departure from prevailing patristic practice invoked by Gregory, "so as to detect if anyone was acceding [to the font] fictively, since many did so."[150] With this semi-accurate historical datum, Odo concludes what he has to say on fictive baptism.

A much more independent contribution to the debate is made by Simon of Tournai. Simon was a pupil of Odo of Ourscamp who went on to become a lively and controversial master while serving as abbot of Ste. Geneviève in Paris from 1176 to 1192. We are indebted to Christopher Evans for printing the following passage from Simon's unedited *Institutiones in sacram paginam* (1170/75), which follows the organizational scheme of the Lombard's *Sentences* but which often departs from its teachings. In this work, Simon frames the now-standard question of what the *fictus* does or does not receive at the font in terms of semantic theory, more fully than Odo does: "The external sign is instituted to designate and to effect what it signifies. So the external ablution signifies and effects internal cleansing. For it always signifies, in and of itself; but it is not always efficacious in oth-

149. Odo of Ourscamp, *Quaestiones* c. 43, ed. Johannes Baptista Cardinalis Pitra in *Spicilegium Solmensis: Analecta novissima altera continuatio*, 2 vols. (Paris: Typus Tusculanis, 1885–88; reprt. Farnsborough, UK: Gregg Press, 1967), 2:46.

150. Ibid., c. 238, 2:81: "dispensatio erat, ad discernendum si quis ficte accederet, quia multi ficte accedebunt."

er respects.... It is indeed significant in *fictis*, but it is not efficacious with respect to them."[151] This analysis supports the idea that the sins of the *fictus* impede the grace of baptism at the font, although Simon is not interested in developing a critique of Augustine's *De baptismo* 1 in this work.

In his *Disputationes* (1165/70), however, Simon does just that, albeit he does not tackle the issue directly. He shares with Hugh of St. Victor and Robert Pullen the desire to integrate baptism into a broader sacramental theology and targets penance in this connection. Indeed, he brings up fictive baptism only in the context of discussing penance in his *disputatio* 33. What should we think about a hypocritical confession made by someone who completes the satisfaction assigned by his confessor? The performance of these external works of reparation does not help him, says Simon. Such a penitent remains mired in the sins which he failed to confess, and in the deceitful attitude which he brought to the sacrament. His works of satisfaction cannot cancel these moral defects. His spiritual condition can be improved only if he later acquires true contrition and cleans the slate in a later, honest confession. True, his confessor has pronounced the words of absolution. But they do not actually alter the false penitent's inner state. For one can call a man "Caesar" without making him Caesar. Simon then suggests that fictive and heretical baptisms provide a useful parallel. Like hypocritical confessions, they are invalid, granting the external *sacramentum* without the internal *res*. Another parallel he offers is that of a priest who goes through the motions of consecrating the Eucharist without intending to do so. These examples share the same disanalogies as those brought forward by Hugh and Robert. Still, Simon agrees with their conclusion, and that of the Lombard. Correct intention is required for any of these rites to be valid: "What is done with a bad intention is in no way a sacrament."[152]

A contemporary who shares Simon's selective approach to the wider

151. Simon of Tournai, *Institutiones in sacram paginam* as quoted in Evans, notes to his ed. and trans. of Radulphus Ardens (as in note 138), 237: "Signum exterius institutionum ob signatum interius signandum et efficiendum, ut ablutio exterior signaret et efficieret mundationem interiorem. Semper autem signet et, quantum in se, est semper efficit, sed non quanto in altero.... In fictis vero significat, non efficit quantum in ipsis est." Evans's manuscript sources are Paris BN Ms. lat. 144886 fol. 55rb, Paris Bibliothèque Arsenal 519 fol. 56 vb, London British Library Royal 9.E.XII fol. 37rb, and Oxford Merton College 132 fol. 149ra. For the dating of this work, see Richard Heinzmann, *Die "Institutiones in sacram paginam" des Simon von Tournai: Einleitung und Quästionenverzeichnis* (Munich: Schöningh, 1967), 10.

152. *Les Disputationes de Simon de Tournai* disp. 33, ed. Joseph Warichez (Louvain: Spicilegium Sacrum Lovaniense, 1932), 97–100; quotation on page 98: "quo fit mala intentione, nichilominus est sacramentum." For the dating of this work, which underwent several redactions during Simon's teaching career, see the editor's intro. at ibid., xxviii–xxxv.

debates and traditional discussions of fictive baptism is Peter the Chanter. In his *Summa de sacramentis et animae consiliis*, the Chanter, following the Lombard, if very tersely, agrees that fraudulent baptisms are invalid. He also agrees that, while fiction neutralizes baptismal grace at the font, the *fictus* can activate that grace if he repents. The Chanter does not explore further either of these ideas.[153]

In the same generation as the Chanter, a scholastic known only as Master Martinus left a *Conpilatio questionum theologie* (1190s) which restates Peter of Poitiers's contrast between the *antiqui* who adhered to Augustine's *De baptismo* 1 position and the *moderni*, including himself, who have abandoned it. Martinus adds a new wrinkle to Peter's assessment of the fate of those who die while remaining in their fiction: "The moderns say that the sins of one who receives [baptism] fictively are not remitted. On the contrary, baptism is the occasion of eternal death, for him, if not its cause, because of the evil use of something good."[154]

At the end of the twelfth century, a better-known master who left a richer legacy on fictive baptism is Prepositinus of Cremona. One of the headings under which he considers it in his *Summa theologiae* is a familiar one, the status of baptisms performed in jest, from the standpoint of those performing them. Prepositinus returns to Augustine and also to Rufinus, reflecting the ongoing disagreements about Alexander's judgment and, indeed, about what Rufinus's text actually says. Prepositinus plans to disagree with those who disallow the baptism of the boys on the beach and who criticize Alexander for ruling it valid. He thus sides with Gratian I while departing from Peter Lombard and Peter of Poitiers, although he does not comment expressly on the latter's Judaizing of the boys and misidentification of the bishop involved. Prepositinus also addresses Roland of Bologna's objection that their baptism is not acceptable because of the boys' defect of age.

Prepositinus begins by presenting the views he is going to attack: "Now the boy Athanasius, imitating a bishop, baptized some catechumens,

153. Peter the Chanter, *Summa de sacramentis et animae consiliis* 13, 17, 59, ed. Jean-Albert Dugauquier, 3 vols. in 5 (Louvain: Éditions Nauwelaerts, 1954–67), 1:46–50, 54–56, 58–60.

154. Master Martinus, *Conpilatio questionum theologie*, ed. Evans in his notes to his ed. and trans. of Radulphus Ardens (as in note 138), 237: "Hec opinio antiquata est. Et dicunt moderni quod ficte suscipienti baptismum non dimittuntur peccata, immo baptismus est ei occasio morte, non dico causa mortis eterne, quia bona non malo utitur...." The manuscripts on which Evans draws are Paris BN Ms. lat. 14526 fol. 130vb and Paris BN Ms. lat. 14556 fol. 252va. For the date of this work, see ibid., 20. An edition, which I have not consulted, is also provided by John Anderson Hall, "The Sacraments in the *Compilatio questionum theologie* of Magister Martinus: Critical Edition with Commentary," PhD diss., University of Notre Dame, 2010.

who were not [re]baptized later. It is held that he did not intend to baptize because he was a child and thus intention is unnecessary." Another position worthy of criticism is Augustine's claim, à propos of heretical and schismatic baptisms, a context which Prepositinus joins others in ignoring, that divine revelation is needed in assessing their merits: "Augustine says that if these things are done entirely as a play-act and a joke, divine aid should be sought. Even if baptisms are done as a play-act and a joke, without the intention to baptize, Augustine none the less doubts whether this is baptism; ... Why not doubt along with the doubting Augustine?"[155]

In preparing to answer this rhetorical question, Prepositinus observes that there are indeed playful baptisms that are clearly invalid. He cites the mother pronouncing the Trinitarian formula while bathing her baby: "He is bathed; and as I believe, no one says he is baptized, since there was no [baptismal] intention."[156] Prepositinus then returns to Athanasius's state of mind and to Alexander's judgment: "While objection is made concerning Athanasius, he intended to do what he saw done in church." As to the claim that "he was acting as a mocker, we say that someone can imitate while intending to do what the church does, and, if so, this is baptism. And, what was hidden from Augustine was manifest to Alexander bishop of Alexandria, who held that what was done in imitation by the boy Athanasius was ratified."[157] As Prepositinus sees it, Alexander got it right and needed no special divine revelation in order to do so. As to what Alexander got right, he recognized that there is a difference between imitation as mockery and imitation as emulation. As for the defect of age, since the boy Athanasius

155. *Praepositini Cancellarii de Sacramentis et de Novissimis (Summa Theologiae Pars Quarta)*, ed. Daniel Edward Pilarczyk, Collectio Urbaniana, ser. 3, Textus ac Documenta 7 (Rome: Editiones Urbanianae, 1964), 22: "Nam Athanasius puer simulatus episcopus quosdam catecumenos baptizavit, qui postea non sunt baptizati. Et videtur quod non intendebat baptizare quia puer erat, ergo intentio est non necessaria"; "Augustinus etiam dicit quod si totum mimice et ioculariter fieret, divinum esset implorandum auxilium. Sed si fuerat mimice et ioculariter non esset intentio baptizandi, et ita Augustinus dubitavit utrum esset baptisma si fieret absque intentione baptizantis. Cur non dubitas cum Augustinus dubitante?"

156. Ibid., 22–23: "Balneatus quidem est. Sed baptizatum, ut credo nemo dicit, et hoc propter intentio ibi non fuit."

157. Ibid. 23: "Et quod obicitur de Athanasio, ipse intendebat facere quod viderat fieri in eccleia; ... Quod ... obicit de mimice agente, dicimus quod potest mimice agere et tamen intendere facere quod facit ecclesia, et ita est baptisma. Et quod Augustino fuit occultum Alexandro episcopo Alexandrie fuit revelatum, qui mimice facta ab Athanasio puero rata habuit." Noted by Evans, notes to his ed. and trans. of Radulphus Ardens (as in note 138), 233, although his citation of Prepositinus, based on manuscript sources and not on Pilarczyk's edition, gives a slightly different wording.

could and did have a baptismal intention, that objection falls. Prepositinus comes closest to the pre-Gratian canonists and to Gratian I, not to mention Rufinus himself, cementing his assessment of the boys on the beach by using Alger of Liège's term "ratified" (*ratum*) in describing the baptismal efficacy of the event, to which he also attaches his pointed critique of Augustine.

Prepositinus also treats fictive baptism from the standpoint of the recipient. He joins most twelfth-century masters in rejecting Augustine's momentary remission thesis. He adds several refinements to what had emerged by his day as a largely consensus position. His weapon of choice against Augustine's *De baptismo* 1 is logic. Prepositinus frames his argument in syllogistic form: "Among the baptized, this one hates his brother. Thus, he has fraternal hatred. Thus, he does not have charity. Thus, none of his sin is removed; ... fiction inheres in him in baptism because he receives it fictively. Thus, baptism is of no value to him." This finding disproves Augustine's conclusion as well as his major premise. Moreover, it is no mere personal whim: "We say that it is valueless according to the common opinion held by everyone."[158] Prepositinus thus affirms what Peter of Poitiers in the previous generation and Master Martinus in his own day take to be the modern *status questionis* on Augustine's *De baptismo* 1 teaching.

This does not end the list of items that Prepositinus places on the bill of attainder against Augustine. With Roland of Bologna, he cites Wisdom 1:5 against Augustine: The Holy Spirit of discipline flees from the fiction. With the author of the *Summa sententiarum*, we can understand that baptizands put on Christ in two ways, externally, by the well-disposed and ill-disposed alike, and internally, by the well-disposed alone. An authority critical of Augustine whom Prepositinus is the first to cite since the Laon masters is Bede on Acts. Summing up his own position, Prepositinus affirms that it is to be held expressly because Bede too "strongly approves it." In any case, since "Augustine has been found to be self-contradictory," both reason and authority support the solution Prepositinus presents.[159]

Prepositinus, finally, considers how *ficti* can rectify their immoral state. Not all *ficti* are *ficti* to the same degree, he thinks. But however grievous

158. Prepositinus, *De sac.* 33: "Inter baptizandum odit ipse fratrem suum. Ergo tunc habet fraternum odium. Ergo non habet caritatem. Ergo nullum peccatum ei tollitur; ... in baptismo adest fictio quia ficte recepit. Ergo baptismus non valet ei"; "Dicimus quod non valet secundum communem omnium opinionem."

159. Ibid., 32–34; quotations on page 34: "hanc magis approbat"; "ipse Augustino contrarius inveniatur."

their sins, they can be removed by penance. What Prepositinus has in mind here is not merely the *fictus*'s inner conversion but the sacrament of penance, available as a post-baptismal remedy to all Christians: "With respect to the fiction itself, and any other [sins] he commits after [baptism], he needs to do penance, ... unless there is contrition of heart so powerful that it removes both guilt and punishment."[160] While Prepositinus concedes the possibility of perfect contrition, it is extremely rare. The level of repentance acceptable in the sacrament of penance is more attainable, and is what the *fictus* should aim for. Leaving to one side the unrepeatability of baptism, a non-issue as he sees it, Prepositinus reminds his readers that the repentant *fictus* does not have to despair of breathing the pure air of perfect contrition; he can be redeemed thanks to the readily available sacrament of penance.

It is not this argument but the willingness of Prepositinus to challenge the Lombardian criticism of Alexander of Alexandria that appears to have informed Radulphus Ardens, who offers valuable insight into the understanding of scholastic teachings on fictive baptism by a cleric not in the schools but a secular priest and royal chaplain. In his *Speculum universale*, Radulphus takes as read and reports without comment the idea that fictive baptisms are invalid although they may become valid if the fiction recedes.[161] He is much more interested in reprising the account of the boys on the beach, from which he draws conclusions not seen in this form in earlier theological literature.

Radulphus leads off with Augustine's *De baptismo* 7 attack on baptisms which he says are play-acts, mockeries, and travesties of the real thing, ignoring, as all his predecessors do, the anti-heretical and anti-schismatic context of this remark. What Radulphus focuses on is Augustine's doubts and his advice that we need special divine clarification. Where others may cite this passage as if it were a refutation of Rufinus's praise of Alexander, he joins Prepositinus in presenting Rufinus as a refutation of Augustine. Unlike Peter Lombard and Peter Comestor, he resituates the boys on the beach on the seashore, not on a riverbank: "On the other hand, we read in the *Ecclesiastical History* that Alexander bishop of Alexandria saw, on the seashore, the childish game imitating what is done in church." On his questioning, the boys admitted that "some catechumens were baptized by the boy Athanasius, acting as a bishop." Finding that the correct questions had

160. Ibid., 35: "De fictione autem de aliis qui postea commisit oportet agere poenitentiam ... nisi forte tanta fuerit cordis contritio que deleret culpam et poenam."

161. Radulphus Ardens, *Speculum universale* 8. q. 46, 8. q. 69, ed. Evans (as in note 138), 74, 138.

been asked and answered, the correct forms had been observed, and that water had been poured, Alexander "ruled ... that they should not be rebaptized, but that the things customarily done by priests should be added."[162]

Even more striking than this faithful reprise of Rufinus is the commentary which Radulphus appends to it. There are three conditions that determine the validity of a baptism, he says, depending on the intentions of the participants. If the person baptizing does not intend to baptize but the person being baptized intends to be baptized, the baptism is valid. If the person being baptized does not intend to be baptized but the person baptizing intends to baptize, then the baptism is also valid. A valid baptism fails to occur only if both participants lack a baptismal intention.[163] That said, what do these alternatives tell us about the boys on the beach, or about fictive baptism in general? Oddly, having taken the trouble to draw these distinctions, Radulphus does not apply them to the boys at the beach. Is what Alexander recognized the intention of Athanasius to baptize, or the intention of the boy catechumens to be baptized, or both? Any one of these options would justify Alexander's judgment, Radulphus's agreement with it, and his use of it to counteract Augustine's doubts. But he does not take this next step. Radulphus is content to give his three alternatives, which offer more latitude than some theologians would allow, and to leave Rufinus, and fictive baptism as a whole, at that.

As a nonprofessional theologian and chaplain in Poitou to Richard I of England, Radulphus Ardens may have felt more comfortable with loose ends than did colleagues in the schools. Stephen Langton, whose election as archbishop of Canterbury was later to run afoul of John, Richard's successor, was a renowned Paris master who treated fictive baptism across his teaching career. Langton deals with this topic repeatedly in the several versions of his *Quaestiones theologicae* (1195/1206 for the first redaction) that have come down to us.[164] They are unpublished as yet, and we owe a major

162. Ibid., 8. q. 43, 60–62; "Econtra in *Ecclesiastica Historia* legitur: Alexandrum, episcopum Alexandrie, vidisse super oram maris ludum puerorum ea, que in ecclesia geruntur, imitancium. Mox est quid egissent percunctatur. Illi quosdam catechumenos fuisse baptizatos confitentur per puerorum Astanasium [sic], que fuerat episcopus assimilatus. Ubi ex responsis eorum vidit secundum ritum omnia celebrata, statuit illos, quibus interrogacionibus et responsionibus integris aqua fuerat infusa, iterum baptizari non debere, sed adimplere ea, que sacerdotibus est mos."

163. Ibid., 62.

164. For the dating of the various recensions of Langton's *quaestiones* and the relationships among the manuscripts in which they have come down to us, see Riccardo Quinto, "La constitution du texte des *Quaestiones theologicae*," in *Étienne Langton: Prédicateur, bibliste, théologien*, ed. Louis-Jacques Bataillon, Gilbert Dahan, and Riccardo Quinto (Turnhout:

debt to their editor, Riccardo Quinto, for the transcriptions of the texts on which the following paragraphs are based. The aspect of the fictive baptism debate that interests Langton and to which he makes a signal contribution is the topic taken up by Prepositinus at the end of his account—the redemption of the *fictus* who repents. Without posing the alternatives of perfect contrition and the sacrament of penance, Langton is concerned with the *fictus*'s change of heart as a psychological process. In that process, which comes first: the conversion of the *fictus* arising from within or the grace of God? Is this change of heart a natural movement of his soul or does it occur because God chooses to infuse grace into him while he is still in his fictive state? While Langton agrees with the twelfth-century consensus on the interaction of free will and grace, which does he thinks first enables the *fictus* to profit from the baptismal grace initially impeded by his fiction at the font and reinforced by the sins since committed? Langton offers a clear and distinctive answer. The ability of the *fictus* to access baptismal grace depends on his reception of a prior infusion of grace, which triggers his contrition: "This proposition is true: the fiction recedes because of grace. And this proposition is false: grace is infused because the fiction recedes."[165]

For Langton the gift of grace involved in the *fictus*'s redemption occurs in two modes or stages. First comes what we may call advenient grace (a term suggested by Langton himself), which breaks the moral log-jam. It inspires the *fictus* and enables him to respond by acknowledging and renouncing his fiction. Since he is now repentant, he can receive and profit from the baptismal grace that is no longer obstructed by his fiction. He can now cooperate with baptismal grace as well in developing virtues. The sins which he brought to the font are forgiven and he can set forth afresh on the path to eternal life.

The activation of baptismal grace in the ex-*fictus*, for Langton, is also contingent on a still prior divine gift. It is one earlier encountered in Master Simon and some canonists but not heard from in theology since: "In baptism there is imprinted a character that remains. And thus, it is not to be marveled at that, if charity arrives, he [the *fictus*] revives."[166] In addition to proposing a

Brepols, 2010), 525–62. Our discussion is based on the passages on fictive baptism in the manuscripts which Quinto regards as giving Langton's fullest treatments of that topic.

165. Stephen Langton, *Quaestiones theologicae* q. 145, as transcribed by Riccardo Quinto from Cambridge St. John's College Library C7 fol. 309va–310ra: "Et hec propositio est vera: Quia huic gratia infunditur, recedit fictio. Et hec est falsa: Quia recedit fictio, infunditur gratia." See also ibid., fol. 141rb–142rb, 153vb–154rb, and 219vb–220ra for the same or similar wording.

166. Ibid. fol. 219vb: "In baptismo imprimatur caracter quod remanet, et ideo non est

synergy between grace and nature in the initial stage of the recession of the *fictus*'s sinful state, Langton sees the baptismal character, granted to each baptizand including a *fictus*, as an enabling condition that facilitates his ability to put on Christ in cooperation with baptismal grace. How that character can be understood, and how it works in relation to the other conditions operative in the redemption of the *fictus*, are questions to which Langton's medieval successors will devote much attention in the sequel.

The Thirteenth Century: Theology to Mid-Century

Scholastics writing in the thirteenth century continue the debates on fictive baptism largely in the terms set by their twelfth-century predecessors. Their innovations lie in two areas. They add new distinctions and arguments to defend or attack these inherited positions. And they add authorities not heard from earlier, whether they support the masters' positions or represent ideas that must be tested and discarded. Most of their authorities are familiar ones, and they are just as vulnerable to approval or criticism as they had been in the hands of twelfth-century masters. Augustine's instant remission thesis remains basically unpersuasive, and scholastics in this century find additional ways of disqualifying it. Rufinus's boys on the beach reappear in curtailed and rewritten form. While no one in this period agrees with Alger of Liège's paganizing of the boys, or Peter of Poitiers's Judaizing of them, some notable reworkings of this text occur. After the middle of the thirteenth century, scholastics lose interest in Rufinus, whether cited to support or oppose fictive baptism. One twelfth-century doctrine to resurface notably in the thirteenth century is baptismal character. Regarded by many masters as a theme they need to include in understanding the post-baptismal conversion of the *fictus*, this topic gains extensive if far from unanimous consideration. Masters disagree on whether *ficti*, or all *ficti*, receive it, on how to view its role in their moral turnaround, and, more fundamentally, on what it is. Thirteenth-century masters also vary on the headings under which they place fictive baptism and on the other issues with which they associate it. Those contributing to the

mirum si adveniente caritate reviviscat. Secus est de operibus. Vel melius: quedam dona sunt pura gratie Dei, ... et illa que Dei sunt reviviscunt gratia adveniente, sed opera que fiunt extra caritatem hominis sunt, et ideo non reviviscunt." The same point is made with the same or similar wording at ibid., fol. 141vb–153vb. Noted by Landgraf, "Die Wirkung," 146, 174. Cf. Rosier-Catach, *La parole efficace*, 292, who omits twelfth- and early-thirteenth-century references to baptismal character and who sees it as attributed to fictive baptizands only starting in the second half of the thirteenth century.

debates include secular masters as well as Franciscans and Dominicans. Mendicants in both orders freely borrow from, and criticize, the seculars and each other. Membership in one or another of these groups is not an index of how a given master handles this subject. So, our consideration of their teachings will follow a largely chronological order.

In his *Summa aurea*, William of Auxerre presents fictive baptism under two headings. One relates fictive baptism to the sacrament of penance. By William's day, it had become the practice for a scholastic to open with the positions he plans to criticize, and William follows suit. Some people say that when a *fictus* who has committed mortal sins since his baptism repents, the effect of baptism, of which he can now make use, "removes all the sins found in him, with respect to both guilt and punishment." Others think that "his repentance does not fully remove the mortal sins committed after his baptism." On this latter view, penance does not remit those post-baptismal sins for which he is not contrite and which he does not confess.[167]

Responding to these positions, William notes that the first relies on the momentary remission thesis. Rather than attacking Augustine directly, William adopts Peter Lombard's strategy for sidelining him. William proposes that his view was "an opinion which he withdrew." The correct answer, which demolishes both objections, is that "the one who accedes fictively to baptism receives baptism, but not its effect, so long as his fiction persists." When it recedes, he gains the effect of his earlier baptism, which "removes all the sins he had before baptism, but not those he committed after baptism, except with respect to guilt. For baptism was instituted not to remove future sins but only present and past ones."[168] In order to deal fully

167. William of Auxerre, *Summa aurea* 4. tract. 5. c. 2. q. 1, ed. Jean Ribaillier, 5 vols., Spicilegium Bonaventurianum 16–20 (Paris/Grottaferrata: CNRS/Collegium S. Bonaventurae, 1980–87), 4:80–81: "Item, aliquis ficte accedit ad baptismum et ficte suscipit, et post baptismum multa peccata mortalia facit; postea recedit fictio. Dicitur quod recedente fictione redit baptismi effectus. Aut igitur baptismi in isto delet omnia peccata que invenit et quantum ad culpam et quantum ad penam, aut non. Si sic, contra. Si non ficte suscipisset baptismum, penitentia in isto non deleret peccata mortalia totaliter facta post baptismum. Sed quod fictio permansit, non delet ei patrocinari, quia dolus nemini patrocinari. Si non delentur, contra. Nunc primo habet effectum suum baptismus in isto. Sed effectus baptismi est ut delet totaliter omnia peccata mortalia que invenit, ergo in isto delentur totaliter omnia peccata sua. Item, si non delentur totaliter, ergo, sicut in christiano qui penitet sed non conteritur, sufficienter, iniungitur ei penitentia exterior de omnibus peccatis suis. Et hoc falsum."

168. Ibid. 4:81: "Ad illud quo obicitur de ficto, dicimus aliquando Augustinus fuit in ista opinione, quod in ipso momento quod baptizatur fictus, dimittuntur ei omnia peccata, sed statim post baptismum redeunt. Sed hanc opinionem retractavit. Propter hoc dicendum quod fictus accedens ad baptismum suscepit baptismum sed non effectum baptismi, quamdiu durat

with his post-baptismal sins, the ex-*fictus* needs to receive the sacrament of penance. How that works depends on the nature and severity of his fiction.

There are two kinds of fiction. One involves incredulity. Here, William reprises a point made by Robert Pullen and Master Simon. His first *fictus* rejects the efficacy of the sacrament. Baptism does not remove his sin because he disbelieves in baptism itself. Penance is required in his case, if he repents. Another kind of *fictus* is one who accedes to the font without contrition. As William sees it, he is guilty of a sin of omission resulting from negligence. This fiction is removed entirely by his baptism. William's second *fictus* is not the Augustinian *fictus* actively harboring and retaining hatred of his brother in his heart. Rather, he is someone who is merely preoccupied, who did have contrition on his baptismal to-do list but who did not get around to accomplishing it before arriving at the font. Regarding this second *fictus*, William maintains that "baptism not only confers grace but also an increase of grace and also a character, illuminating his soul and enabling him to know what to do and what not to do to a far greater extent than he can know by natural means alone; and it weakens and remits the inclination to sin."[169] William thus casts the net of fictive disbelief quite narrowly. At the same time, he is unusually generous to the second kind of baptismal fiction which he envisions.

This last point leads to William's consideration of baptismal character as it applies to *ficti*. As we saw in chapter 1 of this book, William devotes considerable attention to that topic. He explains that baptismal character cannot be confused with the transitory physical medium of the sacrament since it is spiritual, imprinted indelibly on the baptizand's soul. And while he argues that it cannot be an Aristotelian *habitus*, disposition, or passion of the soul, he is less successful in distinguishing baptismal character from baptismal grace. As we also saw, he applies baptismal character differentially to the three modes of baptism. It is proper to baptism *fluminis* but is

fictio. Sed recedente fictione habet baptismus effectum suum, id est facit quod fecisse prius, nisi impedisset fictio. Unde delet omnia peccata que habebat iste ante baptismum, sed non delet illa que fecit post baptismum nisi quantum ad culpam. Baptismus enim non est institutus ad delendum futura, sed tantum pro presencia et preterita."

169. Ibid. 4:82: "Est enim duplex fictio: una secundum quod aliquis credit baptismum non prodesse, que est fictio incredulitas, et istam non delet baptismum, cum sit contraria baptismo. Unde de ista iniungenda est penitentia. Est alia fictio secundum quam aliquis non conteritur de peccatis, et sic non contritus suscepit baptismum. Et hec fictio est peccata omissionis vel negligencie. Ista deletur totaliter per baptismum. Baptismus enim non solum confert gratiam, sed etiam cumulum gratie. Est enim caracter illuminans animam ad sciendum quid faciendum, et quid non, magis quam sciat per solum naturalia, et debilitat fomitem et remittit."

granted in only a figurative sense to those baptized *sanguinis* or *flaminis*. In the passage just quoted, William adds new levels of complication to his understanding of baptismal character. He withholds it from his unbelieving *ficti* while granting it to his merely negligent *ficti*. And, he conflates the baptismal character of the latter with the effects of baptismal grace, including the weakening of the inclination to sin (*fomes peccati*). Moreover, he identifies their baptismal character, in effect, with *synderesis*, the faculty of the practical intellect that tells us what to do and what to avoid. While scholastics may see these moral principles as acquired, or innate, or both, they regard them as part of our natural mental endowment, not as modes of suprarational illumination. Altogether, William's treatment of fictive baptism under this first heading generates new problems even as it drifts from the mainland of its announced theme.

The second heading under which William treats fictive baptism deals with how to judge whether someone is validly baptized in doubtful cases. It is in order to resolve this question that he cites Rufinus. In his relation, a beach and an adjacent body of water of any kind vanish from the scene. So does Alexander's direct observation of the boys' game, with or without attendant clergy. So does the holiday repast. So do the details of the playful baptismal rite. So do the boys' parents, educations, and future careers. But another item, not found in Rufinus or in any previous citation of this text, is added. As William would have it, "Some people came to Alexander bishop of Alexandria asking whether some boys were to be baptized whom a certain boy Athanasius had baptized, in imitation of a bishop. Bishop Alexander called upon divine aid. And it was revealed to him that they were not to be baptized because that boy had the intention to baptize. For he intended to do what the church does."[170] In sharp contrast with predecessors, most recently Prepositinus, who argue that Alexander's decision on his own trumps Augustine's *De baptismo* 7 claim that we must pray for divine guidance, William sees Alexander as taking that advice in Rufinus's account. Ignoring the status and the presumed intentions of the boys whom Athanasius baptized, William thinks that Alexander got it right, even as he misapprehends, or misinterprets, what it took for Alexander to arrive at his ruling about what he describes as a hearsay event, one not witnessed by Al-

170. Ibid. 4. tract. 5. c. 3. q. 3, 4:103–4: quotation at 4:104: "Sicut cum venissent quidam ad Alexandrum, episcopum Alexandrie, querentes utrum quidam pueri baptizandi essent, quos quidam puer Athanasius factus simulatus episcopus baptizaverat. Alexander episcopus invocavit divinum auxilium, et revelatum ei, quod non erant baptizandi, quia puer ille habuit intentionem baptizandi. Intedabat enim facere quod facit ecclesia."

exander himself but merely reported to him. William does not even specify whether those who sought Alexander's opinion had themselves witnessed it. The most comprehensible reading we can offer of William's treatment of the boys on the beach is that, along with his policy toward the negligent *fictus*, it makes a generous, if problematic, effort to salvage at least some elements of the *De baptismo* arguments dismissed by other masters as illogical, erroneous, or inconclusive.

William of Auxerre's contemporary Alexander of Hales agrees that there can be more than one kind of fictive baptism. While in accord on this and other features of William's account, he also departs from William's handling of fictive baptism in notable ways. In his *Glossa* on the Lombard's *Sentences*, Alexander divides those who accede fictively to the font into several categories: "There are many modes of accession [to the font] by a *fictus*. One is an adult without contrition; another is one who does not believe that baptism remits sins; another is one who proclaims publicly that sins are not remitted in baptism; and another is one who disbelieves in [other] articles of the faith." These types of fiction can be further differentiated in terms of Aristotelian faculty psychology: "Fiction can be understood in three ways. One type, which involves belief or unbelief, is located in the rational [faculty]. Another, which involves lack of contrition, is located in the concupiscible [faculty]. And another, which involves contempt [for the sacrament], is located in the irascible [faculty]."[171]

Without indicating if he thinks these modes of fiction are equally reprehensible, Alexander moves at once to what occurs when these *ficti* repent. At this juncture, he indicates no need to retrace twelfth-century arguments about what happens at the font, simply agreeing that baptismal grace starts to become effective only when the fiction recedes. Alexander takes a traditional line on what that grace achieves. Reprising an objection cited by William of Auxerre, he notes that some people grant more than they should: "It is seen that when the fiction recedes, baptism takes effect. Now its effect is to remove the guilt and punishment which it finds. Thus it removes the sins of the interim with respect to guilt and punishment."[172] Alexander finds

171. Alexander of Hales, *Glossa in quatuor libros Sententiarum*, In *Sent.* 4. d. 4. a. 2–a. 4, ed. Collegium S. Bonaventurae, 4 vols. (Quaracchi: Collegium S. Bonaventurae, 1951–57), 4:73–75; quotation at a. 4, 4:74: "Est accessus fictus multis modis: unus modus, cum adultus sine contritione; qui non credit peccata in Baptismo dimitti; qui praedicat peccata non dimitti in Baptismi; qui discredit articulos fidei; ... intelligitur triplex fictio: una in rationali, quoad credere vel discredere; alia in concupiscibili, quoad non delere; alia in irascibili, quoad contemptum."

172. Ibid., a. 5, 4:74: "Quod videtur, quia recedente fictione habet baptismum effectum.

this reasoning faulty. It is only the pre-baptismal sins of the ex-*fictus* that are accorded this full remission. As for his post-baptismal sins, even with true repentance, guilt alone will be lifted, but not punishment; all ex-*ficti* need to receive penance. They will be given help in their conversion. Alexander factors into this process the baptismal character, which he holds all fictive as well as sincere baptizands receive and retain. Baptismal character facilitates the activation of baptismal grace. Alexander agrees with Stephen Langton that the work of character is itself stimulated by divine grace. But he does not differentiate between modes or stages of uncreated grace. It is one and the same grace throughout the *fictus*'s redemption.[173]

In a later passage, Alexander returns to the prior question of what happens to the *fictus* at the font. He supports the view that his fiction obstructs the grace of baptism, adding his own touch to this topic. Simon of Tournai had stated that the baptismal sign always signifies but it does not always effect what it signifies. Alexander proposes a different way to understand how baptismal grace can be impeded. True, it is one thing to be in a sign as its cause and another to be in a sign while not being its cause. But, as well as framing this point about the *sacramentum* and *res sacramenti* in terms of semantic theory, Alexander proposes the following analogy: The light from the sun, the heavenly body which is its source and cause, shines truly through the air. But a cloud can appear which obscures the sun's light and prevents it from reaching our eyes. No fault lies in the sun, which thereby suffers no loss of its causative power. So it is with fictive baptism. The baptismal *sacramentum* truly signifies the grace which is its cause. But the fictive intention of the baptizand obstructs this grace and prevents it from reaching and acting on his soul.[174] This analogy, to be sure, is imperfect since clouds, like the sun's rays, are natural phenomena not subject to human volition. But a number of later scholastics will find this comparison helpful, in itself and as a way of disposing of Augustine's claim that fictive baptizands cannot obstruct the grace of baptism and that they receive it, if momentarily, at the font.

Alexander of Hales also raises another question destined to receive much later attention, comparing fictive baptizands with other baptizands who lack internal consent. We will hear more about Alexander's sources

Sed effectus eius est tollere culpam et poenam quam invenit; ergo tollitur peccatum interim quoad culpam et poenam."

173. Ibid., 4:75: "Semper maneat character." Ibid for the whole passage flagged by this note.

174. Ibid., d. 4. a. 23, 4:92.

and influence in this area in chapter 3 of this book. Some people, he notes, do not give this consent because they cannot do so. In this class are the intellectually disabled (*amentes*) and the comatose (*dormientes*). There are also others who, like *ficti*, are mentally competent. But they are baptized against their will (*inviti*). Regarding the latter, Alexander offers a distinction:

There is a difference between unwillingness and unwillingness, compulsion and compulsion. One who is violently impelled and who imposes no objection to his salvation may undergo the sacrament of baptism. He consents, as it were, conditionally. As with one who accedes fictively, he receives the *sacramentum* and the character of Christianity and is bound to observe the Christian faith. But one who rejects [baptism] utterly and never truly consents receives neither the *res sacramenti* nor the character. For express contradiction is more consequential than minimal consent. Nor is it unknown for one who objects to relapse and to incur guilt by returning to the worship of idols.[175]

Alexander does not propose that these dissenters should not be baptized. As for the *amentes* and *dormientes*, they should receive baptism only if they expressly intended to do so before becoming disabled. If they are baptized anyway, unless they are in danger of death, they do not receive the baptismal character. For all of the above, Alexander concludes, "the performance of the sacrament impresses the character unless resistance is raised against it."[176] The basic question, for Alexander of Hales, is who receives the baptismal character and who does not. This will not be the heading under which many of his successors address the topic. Some of them will also associate fictive baptism with the baptism of the mentally challenged, or with forced baptism. As we will see in chapter 3 of this book, some masters will consider whether forced baptism is acceptable at all, and if so, under what conditions. Some, but by no means all, will recognize that it may lead to recidivism rather than to the conversion of the unwilling.

A master writing in the same period as Alexander of Hales is Guido of Orchellis. Guido, a secular priest, was an archdeacon of Théronne (1217–24), a canon of Meaux (1218), and a master of theology in Paris after 1224. The

175. Ibid., d. 5. a. 3, 4:98: "Ibi distinguunt inter invitum et invitum, coactum et coactum. Nam qui violenter attrahitur et, ne detrimentum incurrat salutis, Baptismi suscipit sacramentum, sicut is qui ficte accedit, characterem suscipit christianitas, et tamquam conditionaliter volens cogendus est ad observationem fidei christianae. Ille vero qui nunquam consenti sed penitus contradicit, nec rem nec characterem suscipit sacramenti, quia plus est expresse contradicere quam minime consentire; sicut nec ille notam alicuius reatus incurrit, qui contradicens et reclamans, idolis thurificare cogitur."

176. Ibid., 4:99: "Tunc ergo characterem imprimit sacramentalis operatio, cum obicem non invenit resistentem."

section of his *Summa de sacramentis et officiis ecclesiae* (1215/28) dealing with baptism returns to the boys on the beach, placed under the heading of intentionality. Guido studied with William of Auxerre and was familiar with the work of Prepositinus of Cremona and Stephen Langton. If his treatment of the Rufinus text is not entirely consonant with that of William or of Prepositinus, he reaches the same conclusion. Guido is concerned with the intentionality of baptismal ministers. One of the objections he plans to refute is the view that the minister's intention to baptize is not essential. This, he says, is why some say that valid baptisms can be performed by heretics, and also, a point brought up by Augustine, why valid baptisms within the church can be performed by drunkards who preside at the font. According to Guido, promoters of these objections cite Rufinus as an authority: "Item, the boy Anastasius [sic], imitating a bishop, baptized many [boys] who were not later rebaptized. But he did not have the intention of baptizing at that time." In his response, Guido affirms that, be he a non-believer or a heretic, a minister can have and must have the intention to baptize. Baptism differs from pre-Christian or non-Christian ablutions which may have purifying effects but which do not do what the church intends. As for the drunken minister, there are degrees of drunkenness. Some drunkards are able to act with ecclesial intentions. Turning to the objection regarding Athanasius, Guido points out that the objectors misread Rufinus. His text actually supports the opposite conclusion, which Guido also defends: "We say that he [Athanasius] did have the intention to do what the church does. And, this revelation was made to Alexander, bishop of Alexandria." Guido does not argue, as William of Auxerre does, that Alexander prayed for the divine assistance that enabled him to make this accurate judgment. But, noting the advice given in Augustine's *De baptismo* 7, Guido concludes, recycling Prepositinus, that some things are revealed to lesser minds that are concealed from greater ones; "therefore, the revelation was made to Alexander that was hidden from Augustine."[177]

Guido follows Stephen Langton closely on what happens when a fictive baptizand repents: "We say that, in the one who repents his fiction

177. Guido of Orchellis, *Tractatus de sacramentis et eius Summa de sacramentis et officiis ecclesiae* c. 3. a. 1.21, ed. Damien and Odulph Van den Eynde, Franciscan Instititute Publications, Text Series 4 (St. Bonaventure, NY: The Franciscan Institute, 1953), 25–26; quotations on page 25: "Item, Anastasius [*sic*] puer, simulatus episcopus, multos baptizavit qui non postea rebaptizati. Sed tunc intentionem non habebit"; on page 26: "dicimus quod habuit intentionem faciendi quod facit Ecclesia, et hoc revelatum fuit Alexandro, Alexandriae episcopo"; "Unde revelatum fuit Alexandro quid occultum fuerat Augustino."

after baptism, grace precedes the effect of baptism and chases the fiction from his soul." It is not the grace of baptism itself that initiates this conversion but a prior advenient grace, which enables the ex-*fictus* to respond to baptismal grace. Baptismal grace in turn accomplishes "the remission of punishment for all the sins committed before baptism, which is done by the power of baptism once he starts to repent of his fiction." The reason why events take place in this order is that "baptism vivifies [him] with the arrival of grace (*adveniente gratia*), by reason of the character which was impressed and which can remain thanks to grace." Guido confirms that "the impression of the character is the work of grace alone," although he also agrees with Langton that virtuous action requires the collaboration of the agent's free will.[178] Without placing this discussion in the context of the *sacramentum/res sacramenti* distinction, Guido nonetheless achieves a clarification of the nature and operation of baptismal character vis-à-vis baptismal grace, and vis-à-vis the notion of advenient grace, which he shares with Stephen Langton in his analysis of the conversion process.

The Mid-Thirteenth to the Early Fourteenth Century

As we move into the period from the mid-thirteenth to the early fourteenth century, debates on fictive baptism will be dominated by Franciscans and Dominicans. They do not always make use of the nuanced treatment of this subject available in the work of recent masters such as Stephen Langton and Guido of Orchellis. In the tractate on baptism in his *Quaestiones de sacramentis* (1245/49), the Franciscan William of Melitona discusses fictive baptism under two headings, character and playful baptism. His treatment of baptismal character harks back to that of William of Auxerre in some respects and displays similar problems. Noting that baptism has two aspects, the external sign and the internal effect which it signifies, he associates the latter with baptismal character. Baptismal character, he states, "is thus said to remain always, not with respect to the exterior deed but with respect to

178. Ibid., c. 3. a. 2.28, 30–32; quotations on page 31: "Ad hoc dicimus quod in illo qui de fictione sua paenitet post baptismum, gratia praecedit effectum baptismi et fugiat fictionem ab anima"; "dimissio poenae omnium peccatorum quae commissa sunt ante baptisma, quae fit ex virtute baptismi, cum incipit aliquis poenitere de fictione"; "Baptismus vivicatur adveniente gratia, rationis characteris qui imprimitur et qui potest manere cum gratia"; on page 32: "impressio charactere est opus solus gratiae." For details on Guido's life, the dates of his works, and his sources, see the editors' preface at ibid., xl.

the interior effect or *significatum*." This formula fails to explain if, or how, baptismal character differs from the *res sacramenti* of baptismal grace. In any case, William then comments that those who accede to the font fictively or unworthily do not have grace in their souls. Does this mean that *ficti* do not receive the baptismal character? William describes the effects of baptism without really answering this question. The two main effects of baptism, he says, are "vivification through grace and the impression of the character." Does this mean that these two gifts are always concomitant? Leaving that matter unresolved, William goes on to discuss the nature of character in its recipients: "There are three features of the character: it distinguishes, illuminates, and remains indelible. The function of distinguishing is called 'the seal'; the function of illuminating is called 'illuminating,' since *synderesis* sees more easily in the light of character; it is called 'custodian' by reason of its indelibility."[179] In addition to ignoring whether any but sincere baptizands receive baptismal character, this rather redundant account of it compounds a difficulty suggested by William of Auxerre in its express reference to *synderesis* as illuminated by character.

The second heading under which William of Melitona treats fictive baptism is that of playful baptisms, from the standpoint of those who administer them. Early in this *quaestio*, he affirms the Lombardian principle that God is not bound by His sacraments. Next, citing Augustine's *De baptismo* 7, he considers baptism conducted purely as a farce, as a play-act, as a joke. Contradicting Augustine and agreeing with some recent masters, he argues that, far from being dubious, such cases are crystal-clear. They do not require special divine guidance: "If it is done purely as a joke, there is no intention to baptize; thus, if intention is taken into account, it is certain that what is done entirely as a farce is not baptism."[180] Continuing, however, William does not rule out the possibility that a playful baptism may contain a baptismal intention: "If one baptizes playfully, and intends it, this is

179. William of Melitona, *Quaestiones de sacramentis* tract. 2. pars 2. q. 8.8b, q. 11.5, q. 12.2b, ed. Caelestinus Piana, 2 vols. (Quaracchi: Collegium S. Bonaventurae, 1961), 1:275, 283, 285; quotations at q. 8.8b, 1:275: "Dicitur igitur semper manere, non quantum ad opus sive signum exterius, sed quantum ad effectum interiorem sive significatum"; at q. 12.2b, 1:285: "Duo sunt effectus principales: vivicatio per gratiam et impressio characteris.... Tres sunt enim conditiones characteris: distinguit enim, illuminat et indelibiter inest. Ratio distinctionis dicitur 'sigillum'; ratione qua illuminat dicitur 'illuminatio,' facilius enim videt synderesis ex lumine characteris; 'custodia' dicit ratione indelibilitas."

180. Ibid., tract. 2. pars 9. q. 47.5a–6a, 1:423–24; quotation at 6a, 1:423–24: "Si igitur totum ludicre factum est, nulla est intentio baptizare; igitur, si requiritur intentio, certum est quod ubi totum ludicre est, non est baptismum."

a baptism. If one does not intend it, it is not a baptism whether performed in play or in any other way." Citing Gratian I, he refers to the boys on the beach in support of this point, although his abbreviated comment omits the beach setting and the details of what Alexander observed: "Bishop Alexander inquired, and certified what the boy Athanasius had done. And peradventure from his words [Alexander] could judge that he had the intention of baptizing. And a sign that such was the case was the fact that is was catechumens, not others, whom he baptized. Or else, it was firmly revealed to him by God that they were baptized."[181]

While Gratian I is his named authority, William of Melitona is more tentative than the Master of the *Decretum*. He shares with William of Auxerre the wish to fold Augustine's *De baptismo* 7 advice into Rufinus's account, although he has already rejected the Augustinian appeal for divine guidance in cases whose status is clear. William first presents the grounds on which Alexander made his ruling as conclusive. The evidence which Alexander has seen with his own eyes and which he has discovered by quizzing the boys provides solid grounds for it. This judgment is also confirmed, and warranted, by the status of the boys as catechumens. Together, these two facts yield certitude. Yet, at the same time, and confusingly so, William cites divine revelation as an alternative to the other two sources of Alexander's assurance. In effect, William washes his hands of the problem, leaving it up to the reader to decide which kind of certitude is more trustworthy.

If he waffles on how Alexander made his decision, William has still more to say on fictive baptism itself. At variance with Hugh of St. Victor, Robert Pullen, and Simon of Tournai, who compare fictive baptism with other forms of sacramental fraud, William contrasts it with marriage vows taken in jest. Unlike the verbal formula used by the baptismal minister, he notes, marriage vows are purely human words. And "insofar as they are human, they do not effect what they signify, as do divine words, that is, the words of the sacraments which God endows with divine power." In addition to eliding the role of the sacraments' physical media in transmitting

181. Ibid., tract. 2. pars 6. q. 33, 1:358: "Dicendum quod qui ludendo baptizat et hoc intendit, baptismum est; si non intendit, nisi ludere vel aliud aliquid, baptismum non est.... Alexander episcopus certius inquisivit de facto Athanasio pueri, et forsitan ex verbi suis conicere potuit quod intentionem habuit baptizandi, et signum fuit ad hoc quod baptizavit catechumenos, non alios; vel forte a Deo habuit revelationem quod fuerunt baptizati." For more on the same point, including the need to pour water and to follow the standard liturgical forms, see ibid., tract. 2. pars 9. q. 47.6b, 1:424. Cf. Rosier-Catach, *La parole efficace*, 289, 631–32, who cites William of Melitona on this issue as if the verbal baptismal formula was seen by him as being the key to baptismal efficacy.

grace, this observation flies in the face of the church's sacramentalization of marriage, and the understanding that marriage vows do signify the intentions of spouses and do establish their union as licit and sacramentally valid. Despite this problematic *envoi* to the topic of fictive baptism, William of Melitona signs off by naming Hugh of St. Victor as the chief authority bolstering the point that baptismal intentionality is of the essence.[182] This accolade to Hugh is well deserved, if it is one rarely found in thirteenth-century scholastics.

In the same decade in which William writes, the *Sentences* commentary of his Franciscan colleague Bonaventure moves the conception of fictive baptism in a new direction. Bonaventure also offers a concise restatement of the Lombard's conclusions, amplified by two comparisons drawn from Alexander of Hales. In his first *quaestio* on the topic, side by side with playful fictive rites, Bonaventure considers baptisms administered to adults who lack a baptismal intention because they lack a command of their rational faculties. Alexander of Hales had opened theological discussion of that topic, but Bonaventure extends his teaching, arguing that baptism may be entirely invalid if it is administered to the mentally disabled. In the ablution of the mentally disabled, as well as in the playful immersion of the rationally competent, "there is no sacrament because there is no [baptismal] intention, as with one who does consent, if he is immersed as a joke."[183] In none of these instances does the use of the correct liturgical formula alter Bonaventure's ruling.

In his next two *quaestiones*, Bonaventure treats what the *fictus* receives at the font, and later, if he repents. He notes Augustine's instant remission thesis and thinks it sufficiently refuted by the point that the *fictus* receives the *sacramentum* and not the *res sacramenti*. In explaining how his fiction impedes sacramental grace, Bonaventure turns to Alexander of Hales's analogy of the cloud blocking the sun's rays. In any event, even in sincere baptizands, faith and free will must interact with baptismal grace in order for recipients to profit from it. Bonaventure agrees with those who hold that a baptismal character is impressed on the soul of the *fictus*. He does not

182. William of Melitona, *Quaestiones de sacramentis* tract. 2. pars 9. q. 47.6b, 1:424: "quia verba humana, in quantum humana, non efficiunt sua significata, sicut verba divina, id est verba sacramentorum, quibus Deus intendit virtutem divina."

183. Bonaventure, *In IV Sententiarum*, In *Sent.* 4. pars 1. d. 4. q. 1. a. 1, in *Opera omnia*, ed. Collegium S. Bonaventurae, 10 vols. (Quaracchi: Collegium S. Bonaventurae, 1882–1902), 4:100: "quia non est intentio, non est sacramentum, cum nullus dicatur baptizatos esse, qui consentit, si immergi ad iocum...."

discriminate among types or degrees of fiction. Nor does he elaborate on the nature of this character or on the precise way in which it contributes to the repentance of the ex-*fictus*. He confines himself to observing that this conversion now enables him to profit from the baptismal grace which his fiction earlier obstructed, and that this grace, now operative, remits both the guilt (*culpa*) and the punishment (*poena*) of the sins he brought to the font. For sins committed post-baptismally he prescribes penance.[184]

Bonaventure's Dominican contemporary Albert the Great is even terser in the remarks he devotes to fictive baptism in his *Sentences* commentary. Yet he, too, adds a notable if unusual condition to the understanding of the repentant *fictus*. Albert is direct and to the point. If someone accedes to the font without believing, he does not receive the *res sacramenti*. If he repents and comes to believe, he will then receive, for the first time, not only baptismal grace but also the baptismal character. This last point is atypical. In addition to deferring the reception of baptismal character to the conversion of the *fictus*, Albert treats lack of belief as his key sin. Albert does not elaborate on how the fictive baptizand acquires the faith needed for his redemption. He does observe that, while a formed faith is the ideal, an unformed faith is sufficient to get the activation of character and baptismal grace going. The ex-*fictus* must also do his part: "He who created you without your own contribution does not justify you without it. As [John] Damascene says, God does not will evil. Nor does He compel virtue, since it would besmirch the praise of the good if it were given against our will."[185]

A decade later, Peter of Tarentaise disagrees with his fellow Dominican's timing of the grant of baptismal character. His treatment of fictive baptism in his own commentary on the *Sentences* is also, by comparison, quite diffuse. Peter finds it desirable to open with a discussion of why the ablutions of John the Baptist were not Christian baptisms. He agrees with Albert that this is because Christ did not institute ritual baptism until after His resurrection. At the same time, it would be wrong to classify John's baptizands as *ficti*. Peter's main point here is one made by the Porretans, the *Summa sententiarum*, and Odo of Ourscamp: While adult converts must resolve to abandon their sins, they are not required to undergo pre-baptismal

184. Ibid., pars 1. d. 4. q. 2–q. 3, 4:102–4.

185. Albert the Great, *In IV Sententiarum*, In *Sent*. 4. d. 4. a. 2 ad 3, a. 3 ad 1, a. 4, in *Opera omnia*, ed. Stephanus C. A. Borgnet, 38 vols. (Paris: Vivès, 1880–95), 29:83–86; quotation at a. 3 ad 1, 29:84: "quia creavit te sine te, non justificavit te sine te: non enim vult malitiam Deus, ut dicit Damascenus, nec compellit virtutem, quia jam sorderet laus boni, si etiam contra voluntatem daretur."

penance. Baptism itself must precede the reception of any other sacrament. It is not at all clear against whom Peter is making this argument. In any event, he ends this *quaestio* by observing that it is not baptismal grace alone that initiates converts into the Christian life but also that "baptismal character is the foundation of all the sacraments."[186]

Peter then reprises the debates on fictive baptism before returning to baptismal character, on which he has much more to say. He rehearses the Lombardian point that Augustine's instant remission thesis was a mere opinion, not a rule; it is also refuted by authorities such as Jerome on Ezekiel. Peter also expands on the parable of the wicked servant as discussed by Gratian II. He recognizes why this parable is irrelevant and actually opposed to the position which some thinkers have used it to defend. As the Gospel of Matthew relates, the master first condemns, then forgives, but finally recondemns the wicked servant. This sequence of events does not parallel God's forgiveness of the repentant *fictus*. The master reverses his forgiveness because he learns that the servant is not repentant; he has not forgiven the debt owed to him. But unlike the master, God is omniscient. He does not change His mind based on the acquisition of new information. What happens in the case at hand is a change not in God but in the fictive baptizand, who now repents and removes the obstruction which had impeded his reception of the *res sacramenti* at the font. This obstruction can inhere in any of the three Aristotelian mental faculties named by Alexander of Hales. If it is the unbelief that resides in the rational faculty, he may lack either a formed or an unformed faith. If he lacks the contrition located in the concupiscible faculty, the poster child for this defect is Jerome's Simon Magus. Or, he may have the contempt for the sacrament located in the irascible faculty. This last-mentioned obstruction is the one Peter finds the most deeply perverse.[187] But, however reprehensible his fiction, "he receives [baptismal] character but not grace" at the font. This character will enable him to dispose himself correctly in any and all of his mental faculties so as to receive grace when he repents. Peter specifies that the baptismal character does not infuse grace itself.[188]

Peter then launches into an extended discussion of baptismal character as such. The interior effect of baptism is twofold. With the *sacramentum*,

186. Peter of Tarentaise, *In Sententiarum*, In *Sent*. 4. d. 2. q. 2. a. 3 ad 3, ed. Joannes Baptista de Marinis, 4 vols. (Toulouse: Arnaldus Colomerius, 1648–52; reprt. Ridgewood, NJ: Gregg Press, 1968), 4:27: "Character baptismatis est fundamentum omnium sacramentorum...."

187. Ibid., d. 4. q. 1 praef., q. 1. a. 1–a. 2, 4:39–41, 47–48.

188. Ibid., d. 4. q. 1. a. 2 ad 2, 4:48: "ideo cum fictione character suscipitur non gratia."

the sincere baptizand receives both the *res sacramenti* and the character all at once. In normal cases, the character disposes the soul to the reception of grace, as the organization of the body of a fetus disposes it to the infusion of its soul. But, since the *fictus* has a contrary disposition, the character granted him at the font does not turn him toward grace. His fiction prevents his character from exercising its dispositive function. Thus, baptismal grace is obstructed in the *fictus*.[189] To this, Peter adds Alexander of Hales's example of the cloud that prevents the rays of the sun from reaching our eyes. If and when the cloud of fiction disperses, the *fictus* can receive the *res sacramenti* of baptism and with it the remission of guilt and punishment for his pre-baptismal sins. With William of Auxerre, Peter extends partial forgiveness of his post-baptismal sins to the ex-*fictus*, at least those that are venial, with respect to their *culpa* but not to their *poena*. For the remission of all his post-baptismal sins, Peter prescribes the traditional remedy—the sacrament of penance.[190]

Having circled the airport for some time, Peter now lands and devotes an entire *quaestio* to what the baptismal character actually is and how it works in the conversion of the *fictus*. It is not the physical and transitory *sacramentum*. Nor is it the *res sacramenti*. It is not an Aristotelian *habitus*, species, or power. Rather, he repeats, it is a disposition, an aptitude for grace. Like baptism itself, it was instituted not just for the benefit of individuals but for the community, "not only as a personal remedy but as a sign of distinction for the people of God." Peter claims that baptismal character can function as a sign although it is immaterial; "it signifies grace, insofar as it is somewhat like it, and acts as a cause, insofar as it is a sort of sanctifying power."[191] Baptismal character is a kind of power (*virtus*), although it is not an Aristotelian power. This claim is far from clear. Nor does Peter explain how this invisible sign makes a baptizand a distinguishable member of the church. Nor is its role in the redemption of a *fictus* all that comprehensible, given the qualifications with which Peter hedges baptismal character in the passage just quoted.

Nonetheless, soldiering on, Peter says that the baptismal character is lodged "principally in the cognitive faculty." He describes what happens

189. Ibid., d. 4. q. 1. a. 2, 4:48.

190. Ibid., d. 4. q. 1. a. 2 ad 1–2, ad 4, 4:48–49. See also ibid. d. 4. q. 2. a. 3, d. 4. q. 3. a. 1, 4:51–53.

191. Ibid., d. 5. q. 2. a. 1–a. 3, 4:60–64; quotations at a. 1, 4:61: "non solum in remedium personae sed in signum distinctionis populi Dei"; at a. 1 ad 3, 4:62: "scilicet gratiam significare, in quantum est eius similitudo quaedam: et causare, in quantum est virtus quaedam sanctificativa."

next as consistent with virtuous decision-making and moral action in general. Moral action first requires an intellectual *habitus* which inclines the subject to act appropriately, with self-recognition that he acts as a member of the church. This *habitus* then moves to the affective faculty, the will, which informs all the virtues and which translates the inclination into a moral act. So also, while the baptismal character is a gift of God that arrives at the font, it is lodged initially in the cognitive faculty. This idea is corroborated, for Peter, by the character's indelibility, since the intellect can grasp objects of knowledge that do not change. As with the transition from thought to moral action, the baptismal character imprinted on the baptizand's soul performs its causative and dispositive functions when activated by a subject's will: "The character by itself and in itself is a true sign. But in order to make something else happen, it depends on the subject, requiring the exercise of his will."[192]

Several problems in this account are readily evident. Peter has already established that the baptismal character is not an Aristotelian *habitus*. Yet he does not hesitate to compare it, point for point, with the intellectual *habitus* involved in moral action. Another difficulty is that what he has just described is the way he thinks baptismal character functions in the mind of a sincere baptizand. This activity, however, does not occur in the intellect and will of the *fictus*, owing to his contrary disposition. Without actually explaining how that disposition is turned around, enabling the *fictus*'s baptismal character to do the job just described, Peter ends his highly intellectualistic account of baptismal character with another unhelpful comparison, one which undercuts his earlier point that we should not view baptismal character as something physical and external, such as a brand that identifies livestock as the property of a particular owner. For he now says that the three sacraments that impart an indelible character make us three kinds of soldiers in the church militant, distinguishable by their different accoutrements and functions: The baptized are like recruits; the confirmed are like a special civic militia; the ordained are like the officers who lead the troops. So, sacramental character "is something that is impressed on the soul as a distinctive sign of the state of faith."[193]

Although one might expect Peter's treatment of playful baptism to

192. Ibid., d. 5. q. 2. a. 2, 4:63: "principaliter … in cognitione"; d. 5. q. 2. a. 1 ad 3, 4:62: "character per se est signum verum quantum est de se: sed quod aliter eveniat, contingit ex subiecti, quod voluntarium est. …"

193. Ibid., d. 5. q. 2. a. 3, 4:64: "sed illum quod animae imprimitur est signum distinctivum in statu fidei."

round out the discussion of fictive baptism which he provides before his lengthy consideration of baptismal character, he deals with it in a later *quaestio*, and in a manner both abrupt and conventional. As with some older and more recent masters, he is less concerned with its recipients than with those who administer it. He agrees that Augustine's *De baptismo* 7 is the authority to be refuted and makes short work of it, simply recycling Peter Lombard. No doubt should arise if a baptism is performed entirely as a farce, as a play-act, as a joke. It is easy enough to ascertain whether or not a minister seriously intends to do what the church intends by baptism. No divine guidance is needed. Peter rests his case with a lapidary quotation from the Lombard: "On this point the Master says that in this sacrament, as in others, just as the form is to be observed, so also the intention must be present, and is hence necessary."[194]

Peter of Tarentaise earns his highest marks for his analysis of the parable of the wicked servant, and why earlier uses to which it has been put are inapposite. Peter draws usefully on Alexander of Hales, both for his sun and clouds example and for his assignment of the ways in which a *fictus* can obstruct baptismal grace to Aristotle's three mental faculties. Along with Alexander and William of Auxerre, he thinks that some of the post-baptismal sins of the repentant *fictus* are remitted when his baptism takes effect, with respect at least to their guilt. On other matters pertinent to fictive baptism, he hews largely to a by now traditional Lombardian line. The one topic which he discusses in the greatest detail, baptismal character, falls flat, despite the attention he gives it. On this subject, Peter is disorganized, repetitive, and contradictory. Baptismal character is not an Aristotelian power or *habitus*, but it is a sort of power and is comparable to the mental *habitus* at work in ethical actions. In those actions, we exercise our natural capacities, but baptismal character derives from and is ordered to divine grace. Although it is not the same thing as grace, this character is sort of like grace. It is spiritual and signifies grace, another spiritual reality. It exists in *ficti* although they do not receive the grace which it is said to signify. It somehow distinguishes its possessors as members of the church, despite its invisibility. Since it is immaterial, it should not be compared with visible signs, but Peter so compares it. While he grants it to all *ficti*, in the end he never really comes to grips with how character works in their later conversion. In all, and on balance, Peter of Tarentaise's main achievement is to

194. Ibid., d. 6, 4:69–73; quotation at d. 6. a. 2, 4:69: "Dicit Magister hic, quod in hoc sacramento sicut in aliis sunt forma servanda est, ita intentio habenda, ergo est necessaria."

heighten the reader's frustration with his account of both baptismal character and fictive baptism alike.

We find ourselves in a far different atmosphere in the exactly contemporary *Sentences* commentary of Peter's fellow Dominican, Thomas Aquinas. His account of fictive baptism is both more focused and more clearly organized. Aquinas follows the layout of Peter Lombard's argument and makes his own additions to it. Aquinas opens by establishing that fictive baptism is invalid. Citing Jerome on Ezekiel, as the Lombard does, he omits Simon Magus and agrees that non-Christian ablutions do not wash (*non lavant*) unto salvation. He then cites passages from Augustine's *Sermo* 351 and his commentary on Psalm 77 to the effect that those approaching the font must be committed to abandoning their pre-Christian life. And so, "from these and other authorities it is clearly shown that the grace of remission is not conferred in baptism on adults who lack faith and true repentance; ... thus, if anyone accedes fictively, without having true contrition in his heart, he receives the *sacramentum* without the *res*."[195] Having laid this foundation, Aquinas makes short work of Augustine's instant remission thesis. Not only was he voicing a mere opinion in *De baptismo* 1, it is also one he contradicts elsewhere. The correct position is reinforced by Wisdom 1:5; the Holy Spirit of discipline flees from the fiction.[196]

Aquinas is well aware of the attention that many of his predecessors and contemporaries accord to baptismal character, a topic which post-dates the Lombard's teaching. Without sailing so far from the Lombardian itinerary that it falls off his radar screen, he presents his own views on this subject. Aquinas suggest that a clean-up operation is needed, eliminating issues he presents as no longer problematic and indicating those that he thinks still merit attention, before adding his own views. Positions he consigns to the scrap-heap include the claim that character is not a disposition toward grace, along with the idea that it can be understood as an Aristotelian *habitus*, power, or passion of the soul. All these options are readily disproved by John Damascene's teaching that character is a seal of some sort impressed on baptizands' souls at the font.[197] What Aquinas drops from this citation

195. Thomas Aquinas, *Scriptum super libros Sententiarum magistri Petri Lombardi episcopi Parisiensis*, In *Sent.* 4. d. 4. a. 2.–a. 2a, ed. Pierre Mandonnet and Maria Fabianus Moos, 4 vols. (Paris: Lethielleux, 1929–47), 4:140: "His aliisque testimoniis aperte ostenditur, adultis sine fide et poenitentia vera, in baptismo non conferri gratiam remissionis; ... si quis ergo ficte accedit, non habens veram cordis contritionem, sacramentum sine re accepit."

196. Ibid., d. 4. a. 2.3–4, 4:140–41.

197. Ibid., d. 4. q. 1. a. 1, 4:147–48.

of Damascene is as telling as what he includes. He omits reference to the illuminative function of baptismal character drawn from this text by William of Auxerre, William of Melitona, and Peter of Tarentaise. Aquinas has no wish to muddy the waters here with a discussion of epistemology, or of the psychogenesis of ethical acts. Nor, at this point, does he want to elaborate on what he thinks baptismal character is and does. Rather, his initial goal is to rule out positions with which he disagrees; he adds to the list Albert the Great's notion that fictive baptizands receive the baptismal character only when they repent.

Next, Aquinas turns to areas where concord has been reached on baptismal character, before proceeding to the disputed questions. The moderns agree that all unrepeatable sacraments impart a permanent character. They also agree that it is a sign in some sense, which distinguishes believers from infidels. Beyond that, however, disagreements proliferate. Rejecting the differentials posited by William of Auxerre, Aquinas holds that the same baptismal character is granted whether a person is baptized *fluminis*, *flaminis*, or *sanguinis*. Further, this character is granted to all *ficti* as well as to all sincere baptizands. Before offering further considerations on baptismal character, Aquinas finds it desirable to consider the larger question of who receives the *sacramentum* alone, the *res sacramenti* alone, and both.[198]

This brings Aquinas, like Alexander of Hales and Bonaventure, to adults who lack the use of reason. He lengthens their list of the mentally impaired. They may be insane (*furiosi*) as well as being of unsound mind for some other reason (*amentes*) or comatose (*dormientes*). Some say that we should not baptize persons rendered unconscious by illness or accident, since they cannot express their knowledge and consent. In his *sed contra*, Aquinas cites the account in Augustine's *Confessions* of his young friend, so ill that his life was despaired of, who was baptized in that state: "He was baptized without knowing it, and in his case this baptism was deemed efficacious.... Thus, even those lacking the use of reason can be baptized." But a distinction must be drawn with respect to *amentes* and *furiosi*. If their condition is congenital, they should be treated like infants and baptized. If they have lucid intervals, or were lucid before this mishap befell them, and expressed a desire for baptism at that time, they should be baptized even if they are not currently possessed of their wits. If, when lucid, they were opposed to being baptized, they should not be baptized. If, perchance,

198. Ibid., d. 4. q. 1. a. 4–a. 104, 4:148–64; his disagreement with the teaching of William of Auxerre is at a. 4.88, 4:162.

those in this latter situation are baptized anyway, they do not receive the *res sacramenti*. The point that Aquinas wants to make about the mentally impaired is that the effects of baptism are impeded in them if they consciously expressed their opposition to baptism when able to do so. But if they have not expressly rejected it, baptism is appropriate. For, their condition "is not a mental contradiction since they are informed, instead, by fantasies." And fantasies, unlike refusals based on real intellectual objections, do not impede the grace of baptism. For their part, neither should the *dormientes* be baptized if they expressed hostility to the rite before becoming comatose, unless they are in danger of death. In that case, the Augustinian exception holds.[199]

That said, should *ficti* be classed among these *amentes*, *furiosi*, and *dormientes*? On this question, Aquinas makes it plain that he is not really talking about *ficti* at the font, since he has already agreed that their fiction impedes baptismal grace. Rather, he addresses the *fictus* who repents. This *fictus*, he observes, has always been different from the mentally challenged people whose indisposition renders them incapable of the faith and repentance needed for valid baptism. The *fictus* was quite capable of presenting the correct disposition at the font but deliberately chose not to do so. But if he repents, and his fiction departs, baptismal grace will no longer be impeded: "Absent the cause, the effect is removed. But the cause obstructing the effect of baptism was the fiction. Thus, when the fiction is removed, baptism can have its effect."[200]

Aquinas now turns to the role of baptismal character in redeeming repentant fictive baptizands. The process is the same although types of fiction may vary. One kind of *fictus* is a liar who intends to deceive, doing or saying what he knows is untrue. Another kind of *fictus* is one who, unaware of the fact, does not know the truth, but acts anyway. The first *fictus* has no intention of renouncing his sinful way of life. The second lacks the faith needed for fruitful reception of the sacrament. Whether his fiction is moral or intellectual, he receives the baptismal character at the font. This character is the immediate cause disposing him toward grace when he repents. His

199. Ibid., d. 4. q. 3. a. 1, 4:181–84; *sed contra* at a. 1.196, 4:182: "baptizatus est nesciente, et tamen in ipso baptismus efficaciam habuit.... Ergo etiam carentibus rationis, baptismus dari potest"; and at a. 1 ad 3.215, 4:184: "Illi autem qui mentis usu non habent, non contradicunt mente, sed magis phantasia ducti. Et talis contradictio effectus baptismi non impedit...."

200. Ibid., d. 4. q. 3. a. 2.220–242, 4:185–89; quotation at a. 2.222, 4:186: "Remota causa removetur effectus. Sed causa impediens effectum baptismum erat fictio. Ergo remota fictione baptismus effectum suum habebit."

fiction at the font was doubly obstructive, as Aquinas sees it. It impeded the operation of his baptismal character as well as blocked his reception of baptismal grace. But, "with the recession of the fiction, which had impeded the effect of the character, the character which is present in his soul starts to have its effect." Once that happens, he is disposed toward baptismal grace, of which he can now make use. All his pre-baptismal sins are remitted, with respect to both guilt and punishment. Those sins he committed since baptism are remitted with respect to guilt, by virtue of the contrition which removed the fiction, but not with respect to punishment. Aquinas joins William of Auxerre, Alexander of Hales, and Peter of Tarentaise in granting immediate remission of guilt for the post-baptismal sins of the ex-*fictus*. What is a distinctive is that Aquinas sees this conversion as first activating the baptismal character, which then enables the ex-*fictus* to profit from baptismal grace, in a two-step process. He does not advert to Stephen Langton's notion of a prior advenient grace, needed to initiate the recession of the fiction which Aquinas sees as impeding both baptismal character and baptismal grace before the *fictus* repents.[201]

The final aspect of fictive baptism treated by Aquinas in his commentary on the *Sentences* is playful baptism. He first restates Peter Lombard's negative assessment. But, in an addendum to the text, he joins predecessors who challenge the Lombard on the boys on the beach. Aquinas dismisses the baptisms of those immersed as a joke or a play-act, although the Trinitarian formula is spoken, along with the doubts of Augustine's *De baptismo* 7: "It is understood by the wise that this is not baptism. As is the case when people are immersed in a bath or a river in the name of the Trinity, this is not baptism because it is done without a baptismal intention." Aquinas adds the Lombardian point that neither this nor any other sacrament is valid, even if the correct form is used, absent the intention to celebrate them as sacraments.[202] At the same time, along with Prepositinus and William of Melitona, he accepts Hugh of St. Victor's point that playful baptisms do not always lack baptismal intentions. Aquinas brings forward the boys on the beach as an illustration of the larger range of possibilities: "Games, it is

201. Ibid., a. 2 ad 1–ad 3.233–241, 4:188–89; quotation at a. 2 ad 3, 4:189: "Dicendum quod in baptismo imprimatur character qui est immediata causa disponens ad gratiam. Et ideo, cum fictio characterum non auferat, recedente fictione quae effectum characteris impediebat, character qui est praesens in anima incipit habere effectum suum."

202. Ibid., d. 6. q. 9–q. 9a, 4:226; quotation at q. 9a: "Videtur tamen sapientibus non fuisse baptismum: ut cum aliqui in balneum vel in flumine merguntur in nomine Trinitatis, non est tamen baptismus, quia non intentione baptizandi illud geritur."

said, sometimes exclude [baptismal] intentions, and sometimes do not. A game may be played without the intention of doing anything useful, just for fun." Even if this game includes the recitation of the Trinitarian formula, it lacks a baptismal intention. The people involved do not intend what the church intends by baptism. On the other hand, a game may well include a baptismal intention. Once again criticizing Augustine for his doubts and his appeal for divine guidance, Aquinas offers the counterexample of Alexander of Alexandria. Alexander was perfectly able to evaluate the game of Athanasius and his fellows without invoking divine aid: "It is said that the boy Athanasius, imitating a bishop, baptized several [playmates]. Having found that he did have the intention to baptize, Bishop Alexander judged that they should not be rebaptized. And this was evident since he baptized only catechumens."[203]

In this last-known thirteenth-century reference to the boys on the beach, Aquinas thus aligns himself with supporters of Alexander's decision, in itself and in the light of the boy baptizands' status as catechumens. Alexander's judgment was accurate, based as it was on the facts established by his observation and inquiry. This episode provides Aquinas with yet another occasion to chastise Augustine for failing to make a decision in an area where it lies within our power to do so. Beyond this particular case, Aquinas suggests, we should not prejudge the intentions motivating play. Baptismal play may be sacramentally neutral. It may also be an expression of baptismal intention. The one possibility which Aquinas does not canvass is that the players may intend to mock or traduce the rite. In any case, the relevant authorities have the capacity, and the duty, to investigate and to draw their own conclusions.

These debates continued between the last quarter of the thirteenth century and the first quarter of the fourteenth. Aquinas returns to fictive baptism in his *Summa theologiae*, where he treats it, more briefly, under the heading of whether deceit invalidates baptism. His *sed contra* states crisply that fiction impedes the effects of baptism. Whatever kind of fiction is involved, the action of the *fictus* fails to square with his inner intentions

203. Ibid., *expositio textus* 193, 4:258–59: "Et dicendum quod ludus aliquando excludit intentionem, et aliquando non. Cum enim ludo fieri dicantur quae praeter intentionem alicujus utilitas fiunt ad solum delectationem; ... Et ideo dicitur quod puer Athanasius ludendo simulans se episcopum baptizavit quosdam, ut judicium est Alexandro Episcopo non rebaptizarentur; quia inventum est quod ipse intentionem baptizandi habuit: quod etiam patet ex hoc quod non baptizabat nisi catechumenos."

and beliefs. The fiction may reflect lack of faith, lack of devotion, failure to receive the rite according to the norms of the church, or contempt for the sacrament itself. Aquinas does not hierarchize these failings. No *fictus* receives the *res sacramenti*. All *ficti*, however, receive the baptismal character, although it remains inert in them. Neither the correctness of the rite undergone nor the reception of the character turns a deceitful *fictus* into a sincere baptizand: "The sacrament is not ordered to changing the *fictus* into someone who is not a *fictus*."[204] In the following passage, giving Augustine's *De baptismo* 1 more credit here than he does earlier, Aquinas adds that a fictive baptism can become a true baptism if and when the *fictus* abandons the malice in his heart and replaces it with charity. The impediment to baptismal grace having been "removed by repentance, it follows that baptism at once has its effect."[205]

In his final words on this topic, Aquinas omits altogether his earlier consideration of baptismal character, fiction as impeding it, its role in the conversion of the *fictus*, and the notion of a two-step process that leads to the activation of his baptismal grace. Aquinas now maintains that baptismal grace takes effect immediately (*statim*) after the conversion of the ex-*fictus*. This conclusion suggests that he has become terminally impatient with the inconclusive discussions that surround baptismal character and registers them as a dead end by omitting the entire subject. Nor does Aquinas ruminate in the *Summa theologiae* on how the post-baptismal sins of the ex-*fictus* are to be remedied. The very concision of his treatment of the whole question in this work suggests a circumspect disengagement from battles from which he sees no clear exit strategy.

Much less is known about the shape of those battles in the immediate sequel. Neither the secular masters nor the Dominicans in the next decades who have interested modern editors and commentators appear to have added to the debates on fictive baptism. In most cases, they do not address it at all, so far as current research indicates. Baptism is remote from the aspects of their teaching that have drawn scholars to the Dominicans who taught in the two generations after Aquinas, be they Thomists or Albertists. There is one member of the Order of Preachers, Durandus of St. Pourçain, who

204. Thomas Aquinas, *Summa theologiae* IIIa. q. 68. a. 9, Blackfriars ed. and trans., 61 vols. (New York: McGraw-Hill, 1964–76), 57:148–50; quotation at a. 9 ad 2, 57:150: "Nec ad hoc sacramentum ordinatur, ut de ficto fiat aliquis non fictus...."

205. Ibid. q. 68. a. 10, 57:152: "Impeditur autem quandoque per fictionem. Unde oportet quod, ea remota per poenitentiam, baptismus statim consequatur suum effectum."

does make a signal contribution to the topic, and we will meet him in the following. But it is largely Franciscans in this period who take center stage, offering arguments both old and new.

Richard of Mediavilla reprises positions articulated by preceding mendicants in both orders, along with those of traditional authorities, in his *Sentences* commentary of the late 1290s. At the same time, he enjoys a special distinction. Richard is the only scholastic encountered thus far who pays attention to the historical context of Augustine's *De baptismo* 7, so frequently cited and criticized. This level of analysis is unique, as well, since Richard does not apply it to other sources he invokes.

Appearing to have Peter of Tarentaise in mind, one of Richard's initial goals is to lay to rest comparisons between fictive baptism and John the Baptist's ministry. He finds the notion of baptismal character useful in clarifying their difference: "God denied him [John the Baptist] the power either to confer grace or to impress the [baptismal] character." John's baptism was a mere preparation for the real thing. To be sure, we should not confuse baptismal character with baptismal grace itself.[206] Richard endorses the view that baptismal character is not an Aristotelian *habitus* or relation; it is, rather, a quality and a potentiality, disposing its recipients not just to the reception of baptismal grace but also to "grace acting efficaciously."[207] This distinction between grace merely given as a gift that does not act in its recipient and grace that is given and that does act efficaciously is a fresh, and influential, way of understanding what the *fictus* receives at the font.

Before presenting his own positive solutions, Richard reviews the larger debate, summing up positions which many of his predecessors dismiss as irrelevant or self-contradictory and which he plans to oppose in turn. He starts with the affirmation of Jerome on Ezekiel, and many others, that an adult baptizand lacking faith and repentance does not receive the *res sacra-*

206. Richard of Mediavilla, *In IV libros Sententiarum*, In *Sent.* 4. d. 2. a. 2. q. 3, ed. Ludovicus Silvestrius à Sancto (Brescia: De Consensu Superiorem, 1591; reprt. Frankfurt: Minerva GMBH, 1963), 29: "Deus autem noluit sibi dare virtutem gratiam conferendi, nec characterem imprimendi."

207. Ibid., d. 5. a. 2. q. 2, 63: "ad gratiam gratum facientem dispositiva." Corey L. Barnes, *Christ's Two Wills in Scholastic Theology: The Christology of Aquinas in Its Historical Contexts* (Toronto: Pontifical Institute of Mediaeval Studies, 2012), 210–12, notes that in *ST* IaIIae. q. 111. a. 4 and *ST* IIIa. q. 7. a. 7 Aquinas distinguishes between *gratia gratum faciens* and *gratia gratis data* in treating Christ the Teacher's mediation of grace; but he does not apply that distinction to the operation of grace in fictive baptism.

menti. True, Augustine says that his sins are remitted momentarily but at once return, since the grace of baptism is not impeded. Augustine is refuted by Wisdom 1:5: This grace is not granted since the Holy Spirit of discipline flees from the fiction. So, Augustine was merely expressing an opinion, and an unacceptable one at that. The *fictus* starts to receive baptismal grace only when he repents. Returning to Jerome, Richard concludes these introductory remarks by bringing forward Simon Magus, prudently omitted by Peter Lombard and Thomas Aquinas. Richard concurs with Jerome, viewing Simon as the prime fictive baptizand: "He did not profit from visible baptism because what was invisible was not present."[208]

If, in this passage, Simon's real history as related in the Acts of the Apostles is as occluded to Richard as it is to Jerome, Richard offers a telling explanation of why Augustine's *De baptismo* 7 is irrelevant both to its intended subject and to the current debate. As he points out, Augustine was writing a polemic against schismatics and heretics. If, indeed, their baptisms were merely a farce, a play-act, and a joke, if those they baptized were hypocrites, then the argument that they should not be rebaptized if they saw the light and joined the true church does not follow. Without invoking Cyprian, Richard argues that if Augustine was truly serious about the defects of these rites, if they really did involve the false intentions which he ascribes to them, then he should have judged them to be no baptisms at all. Thus, if their recipients joined the true church, their entrance rites would properly be baptisms, not rebaptisms. But by calling them rebaptisms, and by excluding them, Augustine contradicts himself.[209] Richard is scarcely the first thinker to censure Augustine for self-contradiction in the *De baptismo*. But he stands out for placing the aforementioned critique in the context of Augustine's actual agenda in the passage cited.

Richard has further negative things to say about the same Augustinian opinion. Picking up on fictive baptism as hypocrisy, Richard sees it as including both lack of faith, the intention not to abandon one's mortal sins, and contempt for the sacrament. Augustine is mistaken if he thinks that these conditions are doubtful and require special divine clarification. The counterauthority whom Richard cites here is not Rufinus but Gratian. And problematically so. For, in the text referred to (*Decretum* C. 1. q. 1 d.p.c 58), Gratian I is considering the absence of true baptismal intention in the min-

208. Richard of Mediavilla, In *Sent*. 4. d. 4. praef., 46–48; quotation on page 48: "visibilis baptismus non profuit, quia invisibiliter non adfuit...."

209. Ibid., d. 4. q. 2, 49.

ister, not the recipient.[210] So, Richard does not read Gratian with the same care which he applies to Augustine.

Returning to the rebaptism issue, Richard observes that another way of thinking about fictive baptism is to say that the repentant *fictus* should not be rebaptized because he received the baptismal character at the font. Once he repents, the character, latent until then, can begin to exercise its function of disposing him toward the reception of baptismal grace, which then remits his sins. Richard reprises Peter of Tarentaise's comparison of this aptitude with the organization of a fetus's body that disposes it to the infusion of its soul. He also invokes Alexander of Hales's image of the cloud which prevents the sun's rays from reaching our eyes. The latter comparison is less pertinent since it says nothing about baptismal character and its role in removing the impediment of fiction. In any case, Richard points out that the sin of a *fictus* is an actual sin, not an aspect of his original sin. Defending again in conclusion the unrepeatability of baptism, he ends his discussion of fictive baptism without being more specific about the *fictus*'s conversion process or about the remission of his post-baptismal sins.

The felt need among Franciscans in Richard's day to reaffirm opposition to rebaptism can also be seen in the *Ordinatio* of John Duns Scotus. In listing the objections he plans to refute, Scotus includes the rebaptism of the repentant *fictus* along with the claim that his fiction does not impede baptismal grace. His *sed contra* sets forth his opposition to these objections, stating forthrightly "that fiction prevented [interior] ablution from taking place in baptism, and hence impeded grace." There is no momentary remission of his sins, and he puts on Christ in name only.[211]

Continuing, Scotus acknowledges the widely held definition of fiction as pretense, the external display of a readiness to receive baptism without the internal disposition to do so. He includes the *fictus* who inwardly rejects what the church intends by baptism. Adding a perspective on the contemptuous *fictus* not heard from any theologian thus far, Scotus thinks that he is rightly forced to practice Christianity: "The church judges that he has consented to sacramental ablution and binds him to the observance of the Christian faith." This policy can be analogized to the church's acceptance of

210. Ibid., 50.

211. John Duns Scotus, *Ordinatio* 4. q. 4. pars 2. q. 2, ed. Josephus Rodríguez Carballo in *Opera omnia* (Vatican City: Typis Vaticanis, 2008), 11:250–60; for the objections, q. 2.87–89; *sed contra* at q. 2. a. 1, 11:250: "illa fictio impediebat ablutionem fieri in baptismo, et per consequens gratiam." On the point that the *fictus* puts on Christ only nominally and on the rejection of the instant remission thesis, see ibid., q. 2.117, q. 2.119, 11:260.

forced marriage, on the grounds that, over time, a false marriage vow may blossom into marital affection and true marital consent.[212] Scotus firmly rejects the disanalogy between baptism and marriage vows asserted by William of Melitona. He also departs from Robert Pullen's view that we can simply regard fictive baptisms and false marriage vows as null, and as having no institutional consequences. Scotus brings Wisdom 1:5 to bear on the point that fictive baptizands receive no grace at the font. He agrees with Albert the Great, citing Augustine's *Sermo* 149: "He who created you without your participation does not justify you without it," in observing that the converted *fictus* must repent and receive the sacrament of penance but that God will assist in his moral turnaround. Once that happens, he receives the baptismal grace that remits all the sins which he brought to the font.[213]

This leads to the question of whether fictive baptizands receive a baptismal character, what that character is, and how it operates in their conversion. Scotus devotes a lengthy discussion to this topic. He presents baptismal character as something of a newfangled idea, not found either in Augustine, Peter Lombard, or Gratian. Scotus is primarily concerned with telling his reader what baptismal character is not. In addition to the usual Aristotelian concepts which do not describe it, baptismal character is neither a substance nor an accident. It is not the same thing as grace. It is not the same thing as an infused virtue. If we want to regard it as a sign, on the authority of John Damascene and the Pseudo-Dionysius, it signifies in a purely metaphorical sense. The character is certainly not visible. Nor is it the only way to distinguish church members from infidels. All the activities that have been ascribed to baptismal character are acquired, and can take place without the need for it. Since the baptism of John the Baptist did not convey baptismal character, Christ never received it. Neither did the Virgin Mary. If that thought alone does not clinch the argument, Scotus states a principle for which William of Ockham is usually given credit: "multiplicity should not be posited without necessity." Baptismal character, quite simply, is not needed to convert the *fictus*. What does turn him around is his own contrition, and, more basically, the divine covenant which God has made with humankind, through which He empowers His sacramental signs and accepts our repentance: "Nor should we say that 'character operates in some way on the fiction.' For it is God alone who helps him later, that is, the one

212. Ibid., q. 2. a. 1.93–95, 11:251–52; quotation at a. 1.94, 11:251–52: "Ecclesia iudicaret eum consentire in ablutionem sacramentalem, et coget eum ad observantiam Christianae fidei...."

213. Ibid., a. 1.96–102, a. 1.104–116, 11:252–60; quotation at a. 1.96, 11:252: "Qui creavit te sine te, non justificavit te sine te."

whom He receives, because of this same covenant, thanks to which the obstruction is at once lifted."

Scotus, in short, grants as little as possible to baptismal character, and that grudgingly. The most he will say about character, in general, is that it is "a simple, indelible, spiritual form impressed on the soul of whoever receives an unrepeatable sacrament, which, by divine institution, signifies the grace of that sacrament and inclines [the recipient] toward Him." It reminds recipients of the sacraments received and of the obligation to conform themselves to Christ. "These items," he concludes, "exhaust the number of things that can be rationally said about character." Scotus finds it impossible to prove the host of other claims that have been made for it. And he comes closest to the Aquinas of the *Summa theologiae* in proposing that the grace of God acts directly in the conversion of the *fictus*, without the need for character as an intermediary. The notion that this grant is based on a prior divine-human covenant or pact is Scotus's distinctive addition to this topic.[214]

Scotus makes some alterations to his account of fictive baptism in his second commentary on the *Sentences*, the *Reportata Parisiensia* (1302/07). Here, he devotes two *quaestiones* to the subject. He gives the same general definition of the *fictus* as "someone who pretends one thing externally which he does not hold internally. Thus he accedes [to the font] pretending to be disposed toward the reception of grace but he is not so disposed, on account of his fiction, a mortal sin, which he does not repent; he receives the *sacramentum* and the character." And, it should be understood, not the *res sacramenti*. Attributing the next point to Richard, likely Richard of Mediavilla although many others have made it, Scotus adds that fiction obstructs the grace of baptism, not available to the *fictus* unless he abandons his fiction. Scotus also inserts the notion of covenant at this juncture: "Thanks to the same covenant by which He makes his sign efficacious in conferring grace [in a sincere baptizand], God confers the same grace once the fiction recedes, grace not infused in him earlier because of the fiction

214. Ibid., 4. d. 6. pars 4. a. 2. q. 1.189–q. 2.371, 11:353–410 for the extended discussion of character; quotations at q. 1.219, 11:363: "pluralitas non est ponenda sine necessitas"; at 4. q. 4. pars 2. q. 2. a. 1.103, 11:255: "Nec oportet dicere 'characterem in fictio aliquid operari,' sed solum quod Deus ex eadem pactione assistit etiam postea—ei qui suscipit—quam cito obex tollitur"; at d. 6. pars 4. a. 2. q. 2.334, 11:398: "forma simplex, spiritualis et impressa a Deo cuicumque suscipienti sacramentum non-iterabile; et quod ex institutione divina significet gratiam illius sacramenti, et quod disponat ad eum; ... et quod sit indelibilis.... Haec omnia, quae videntur rationabiliter concedenda de charactere."

which was its impediment." The *fictus* registers that he has undergone this change of heart by receiving the sacrament of penance.[215] Scotus continues to invoke the theme of a divine covenant or pact (*pactio*) which enables the sacramental sign to take effect in the formerly fictive baptizand.

In the *Reportata Parisiensia* he offers a somewhat different teaching from that in the *Ordinatio*. In the later work, he notes that an immoral *fictus* who lacks contrition may have attrition, or sorrow for his sins out of the fear of punishment. Attrition does not block baptismal grace as fully at the font. At the same time, the worst *fictus* he flags here is not the one with contempt for the sacrament but one "who seeks to profit from his sin," acceding to baptism for venal or self-serving reasons. This latter *fictus* gains no benefit at all from baptismal grace and can attain no merit whatsoever unless he undergoes sacramental penance.[216] While he thus grades *ficti*, Scotus maintains a clear distinction between all of them and sincere baptizands. Both sets of baptizands receive a baptismal character but they do so in different ways. Here, despite his reservations on the subject in the *Ordinatio*, he has recourse to visible imagery in explaining the difference he posits: "I say that, with respect to character, those fictively baptized put on Christ as a soldier puts on armor, not with respect to grace, as a son puts on a wedding garment."[217] Whatever the degree or mode of character received, it is indelible. And failure to activate it will lead to perdition. Even as he makes the aforementioned distinctions, Scotus advises caution in deciding who fits into which category. For *ficti* of all sorts are counted as members of God's household. The Father's house has

215. John Duns Scotus, *Reportata Parisiensia* 4. d. 4. q. 5 in *Opera omnia*, juxta ed. Waddingi a Patribus Franciscanis, 26 vols. (Paris: Vivès, 1891–95, reprt. Westmead, Farnsborough, UK: Gregg International, 1959), quotation at *responsio* 2, 23:608: "dicitur fictus qui praetendit aliquid exterius, quod non habet interius, et ideo talis accedens, praetendens se esse dispositum ad gratiam suscipiendam, et non est dispositus, propter peccatum mortale fictionis, de quo non conteritur, recepit sacramentum et characterem; … Sed Deus ex eadem pactione, qua assistit suo signo efficienti, ad conferendum gratiam, si fictio tunc tempore non infuisset, eadem confert gratiam, fictio recedente, quod fuit impedimentum quare gratia non infuit." On the need for sacramental penance, see ibid., q. 5.4, 23:609, 610. Noted by Nancy L. Turner, "Jewish Witness, Forced Conversion, and Island Living: John Duns Scotus and Judaism," in *Christian Attitudes toward the Jews in the Middle Ages*, ed. Michael Frassetto (New York: Routledge, 2007), 183–209 on page 196.

216. Duns Scotus, *Reportata* d. 4. q. 5. *responsio* 3, 23:609. For Duns Scotus and his predecessors on attrition with *loci* in his works and literature on his application of this idea to penance, see Heiko A. Oberman, *The Harvest of Medieval Theology: Gabriel Biel and Late Medieval Nominalism* (Cambridge, MA: Harvard University Press, 1963), 146–54.

217. Duns Scotus, *Reportata* d. 4. q. 5. *responsio* 4, 23:610: "dico quod ficti baptizati Christum induunt, quantum ad characterem, et quantum ad vestem armigeri, non autem quantum ad gratiam, vel vestem nuptialem, ut filius."

many mansions "in the estimation of the church, which does not judge hidden things but those that are clearly evident."[218] We should thus not prejudge other people's internal states. If we err, we should err on the side of leniency.

This appeal to leniency, however, is joined by Scotus to another issue in the second *quaestio* in which he treats fictive baptism in the *Reportata Parisiensia*, the baptism of the unwilling. His *ficti* as just described dissimulate their true intentions and, in some cases, their beliefs about the efficacy of baptism itself. But they present themselves willingly at the font. They can be contrasted with other people who inwardly reject baptism. The latter are those who are forced into the font whether or not they outwardly express their dissent. Scotus thus brings up in this *quaestio* the issue of forced baptism, raised before him by Alexander of Hales and others, to which he, and we, will return in more detail in chapter 3 of this book. Here, what is notable is the very fact that he yokes this topic with fictive baptism. We have moved beyond the mental incompetents discussed by Bonaventure and Aquinas. Scotus now extends to the forcibly baptized the comparison he makes in the *Ordinatio* between the fictively baptized and the forcibly married, whose initially fictive vows may develop into true marital consent. The forcibly baptized person who outwardly objects should not be baptized, and, if he is, he receives no baptismal grace. Sad to say, baptisms of this sort do occur. So do the forcible baptisms of dissenters who do not specifically refuse the font. Scotus imposes on such a forcibly baptized person the same requirements as he applies to the fictive baptizand who is rightly obliged to observe the Christian faith: "And thus he is bound by the practice of the church, so that he may no longer be a *fictus* but may become a true Christian."[219] So, although Scotus posits a clear difference between these two kinds of inwardly dissenting baptizands, he also argues that the fictive baptizand and the forced baptizand who offers no outward objection should both be constrained to Christian practice, which he presents as an agency for promoting their conversion.

The last topic which Scotus takes up is the baptizand "playfully im-

218. Ibid., *responsio* 5, 23:610: "ad judicium Ecclesiae, quae non judicat de occultis, sed de manifestis quae apparent."

219. Ibid., 4. d. 4. q. 4.7, 23:605–6: "nam simulans se recipere baptismum, et tamen dissentiens sacramento actu interiori simpliciter, dummodo non manifestetur signo exteriori, ut reclamando non contradicit, vel sic dissentiat, judicatur ab Ecclesia hoc sacramentum recipisse. Et ideo per censuram Ecclesiasticam compelli habet, ut de ficto fiat verus Christianus"; as versus the forced baptizand who does overtly object: "si autem sit ominino dissentiens et reclamans cum signo exteriori, nihil recipit...."

mersed in water." He acknowledges that not all immersions are baptisms. This observation can suggest, as it does to masters from Hugh of St. Victor to Aquinas, that playful baptisms can express baptismal intentions and, if so, they are sacramentally valid. Scotus looks on the other side of the ledger. His focus is on games not played just for fun but in order to mock the sacrament. In such cases, the baptizand receives neither the *res sacramenti* nor the baptismal character. Thus, if he later wants to enter the church, he should be baptized. This, Scotus insists, will constitute baptism in the first instance, not rebaptism.[220] Scotus ends this *quaestio* with a ringing defense not only of correct intentionality but also of free will as necessary in anyone who comes worthily to the font. At the same time, with the exceptions previously noted, the *fictus* who lacks belief but who changes his mind should not be rebaptized, "but constrained to abandon his fiction."[221]

In his most mature work, Duns Scotus thus gives fictive baptism rather ambiguous treatment. He now denies or in some sense limits the gift of baptismal character as well as baptismal grace to two sets of *ficti*, those who reject the very efficacy of the sacrament and those who mock it playfully. Also striking is his omission from the *Reportata Parisiensia* of a major topic which he treats earlier, the redemption of the *fictus*. He also ignores the many problems he sees with baptismal character, described at such great length in the *Ordinatio*. Scotus teaches in both works that God acts in baptism on the basis of His covenant with humankind. Insofar as Scotus sees any intermediary at work in the conversion of the *fictus*, that intermediary is ecclesiastical enforcement of his practice of Christianity. Scotus can couple this rather harsh prescription with comparative leniency toward the fictive baptizand who has attrition for his sins. These traits all endow Duns Scotus's doctrine of fictive baptism with its distinctive coloration.

A leading Franciscan master of the first quarter of the fourteenth century whose treatment of fictive baptism, if quite brief, also gives it a personal look is William of Ockham. His *Quaestiones* on the *Sentences* (1317/19) raise only a single issue, but it is one that reverberates well beyond this topic. Normally, a baptized Christian who commits sins voluntarily has

220. Ibid., d. 4. q. 4.8, 23:606: "Se jocose immergi in aqua, non omnino immersio in aqua est Baptismus, nec rem sacramenti recepit, quia respectu illius dissentit, et ita nihil recepit; ... et per consequens non recepit characterem, unde talis alius esset baptizandus ad salutem post fictionem."

221. Ibid.: "nec respectu istius potest cogi, non tamen recepit gratiam, quia non credit sacramentum et characterem, et ideo non est rebaptizatus, sed cogendus ad dimittendum fictionem."

recourse to the sacrament of penance. Without bothering to restate the point that the *fictus* receives no remission of sins at the font, Ockham notes that he retains his pre-baptismal sins until he repents, adding to them his post-baptismal sins. Once he does repent, two kinds of sins are remitted. These include his pre-baptismal actual sins, committed voluntarily, whose remission his fiction impeded. The *fictus* also brought original sin to the font. Now, since "original sin was contracted in him without his consent, it can be remitted without his consent by the power of the sacrament, even though he acceded to it fictively."[222] Once baptismal grace has been activated in the ex-*fictus*, a process which Ockham does not explore, he can proceed in the normal way to deal with his post-baptismal sins through penance, as other Christians do. The only other major point that Ockham makes in this context is that the remission of original sin occurs equally in baptism *fluminis*, *flaminis*, and *sanguinis*, although the latter two kinds of baptism are scarcely pertinent to the *fictus*. Recipients of none of these forms of baptism are to be rebaptized, a prohibition that also applies to the *fictus*. When he repents, "he receives the effects of baptism and is cleansed of original and of actual sin, and is in no way to be rebaptized."[223] This observation does not fully square with the idea that the fictive baptizand receives remission of his original sin without his consent, presumably at the font, albeit he accedes to it with mental reservations and without agreeing to reject his sins. Indeed, rather than addressing this possible contradiction, Ockham's main concern throughout this *quaestio* is to invalidate rebaptism under any circumstances. Of latent interest, however, is his observation that, since original sin is contracted without our consent, it can be removed by baptism without our consent, in virtue of the power of the sacrament.

The leading Dominican contemporary of William of Ockham who treats fictive baptism and related subjects is Durandus of St. Pourçain. He

222. William of Ockham, *Quaestiones in Librum Quartum Sententiarum* q. 5, in *Opera philosophica et theologica*, ed. Rega Wood, Gideon Gál, and Romuald Green, 10 vols. (St. Bonaventure, NY: St. Bonaventure University Press, 1967–86), 7:53: "Sed adultus ficte accedens ad Baptismum non consentit nec disponit se, qui commisit peccatum actuale, ponamus, tale peccatum actuale commissum cum consensu non sibi remittatur. Igitur cum peccatum originale sit in eo contractum sine consensu, videtur quid illud potest sibi remitti virtute sacramenti non obstante quod ficte accedat sine consensu."

223. Ibid., 7:53–55; quotation at 7:55: "Ad aliud dico quod nec ficte accedens ad Baptismum nec peccans actualiter quando baptizatur est rebaptizandus, quia tunc licet neuter recipiat effectum Baptismi, tamen post poenitere et acceptare Baptismum et tunc per poenitentiam [recepit] effectum Baptismi et mundatur tam ab originali quam ab actuali, et ideo nullo modo est rebaptizandus."

was a thorn in the flesh of his confrères once they had closed ranks in 1309 and in 1313, mandating the profession of Thomism within the order. Durandus's departures from Aquinas invited censure from the Dominicans. As is well known, he escaped their jurisdiction by becoming a bishop, first at Limoux (1317), then at Le Puy (1318), and finally at Meaux (1326–34). From the safe haven of prelacy, he continued to revise his *Sentences* commentary, the last version of which (1317/27) is the only one printed to date. There is nothing aggressively anti-Thomist in Durandus on fictive baptism, although he shows that he has profited as well from the work of the Franciscans. Durandus focuses mainly on baptismal fiction as perpetrated by its ministers. When he turns attention to its recipients, he appeals to ideas with a distinctly Scotist ring.

It is under the heading of baptismal character that Durandus presents his fullest account of the fictive minister. He repeats the now-standard view that this character cannot be identified with the material *sacramentum* of baptism and that none of the Aristotelian ways of conceiving of it apply. On the authority of an even more abbreviated citation of John Damascene than Aquinas gives, we can describe it as an indelible imprint on the soul, a divine gift. It is not a natural function of the intellectual faculty. In the case of ministers, it disposes them to perform the sacrament with the correct liturgy and intention. In this sense, what Durandus really describes here is the character imparted to priests by ordination. In any case, following Scotus, he sees this character as "a consequence of the divine covenant and institution," which deputizes priests to conduct their sacramental ministry. In summarizing this point, however, his account of baptismal character is far from unambiguous. He offers several alternatives: "It is called the baptismal seal or sign, whether of what is performed externally, or of the grace which it confers internally, or the deputation of the baptized by divine ordination to the undertaking of the sacraments." The reader is left to choose among these options.[224] The baptized person referred to in this passage is the priest. Durandus does not explain whether a fictive minister is fictive because of defects in his ordination, defects in his administration of bap-

224. Durandus of St. Pourçain, *In Petri Lombardi Sententias theologicas commentarium libri IIII*, In *Sent.* 4. d. 4. q. 5, 2 vols. (Venice: Ex Typographia Guerraea, 1571; reprt. Ridgewood, NJ: Gregg Press, 1964), 2:298r–299v; quotation at q. 5.11, 2:299r: "ex institutione vel pactione divina"; and at q. 5.14, 2:299r: "dicendum est quod sigillum vel signa baptismale, aut vocatur id quod exterius geritur, aut gratia interior quae confertur, aut deputatio baptizati ex ordinatione divina ad susceptionem sacramentorum." On the dating of Durandus's career and works, see Étienne Gilson, *History of Christian Philosophy in the Middle Ages* (New York: Random House, 1955), 473, whose account is accepted by later scholars.

tism, or both. Nor does he explain how something that is itself invisible can signify anything else, be it the physical medium of the sacrament or its invisible grace. But he clearly endorses Scotus's notion that the sacraments owe their efficacy to a divine covenant (*pactio*).

When Durandus turns to the recipient of fictive baptism, he finds it unnecessary to rehash debates on what the *fictus* receives at the font. He treats that issue as basically settled. Fiction impedes the grace of baptism, and we can move on to what happens when the *fictus* repents. Durandus knows what he thinks about positions that he finds problematic or unpersuasive. He is less decisive in reporting conclusions with which he agrees. He begins by noting that there are two kinds of *ficti*. One fakes his real commitment, presenting himself as willing to receive the sacrament although he has no intention of doing so internally. The other also presents himself as disposed to receive the sacrament although he has no intention of abandoning his sins. It has to be said that this distinction is elusive. But, either way, the *fictus* receives no benefit from the rite: "Since intention is deficient in the recipient, there is no sacrament"; that is, "he receives the *sacramentum* ... but not its effect, which is grace."[225]

That understood, Durandus largely agrees with both the Aquinas of the *Summa theologiae* and the Scotus of the *Reportata Parisiensia*. Some say that the ability of the repentant *fictus* to make use of baptismal grace involves the baptismal character he received at the font. This character disposes a baptizand's soul to the reception of grace, unless a supervenient impediment prevents it from doing so. His fiction is in fact such an impediment, preventing his baptismal character from exercising its function. When the fiction is removed, the character can do its work, and then baptismal grace can take effect. At least, that is what some people say. Durandus does not name anyone, but good candidates would be Peter of Tarentaise or the Aquinas of the *Sentences* commentary. Having presented this claim, Durandus explains why he opposes it. In the aforementioned position, we can understand the disposition to the reception of grace by baptismal character in two ways. Either this disposition preexists in the subject as a kind of form introduced into him, similar to "the clarity of the air which is the disposition needed for the reception of light," or the disposition can be compared with what necessarily follows the form, as with the disposition of a man's seed which results in the son he engenders. Now, neither understanding

225. Durandus, In *Sent.* 4. d. 4. q. 4.4–5, 2:299r–300r; quotation at q. 4.4, 2:299v: "deficiente intentione suscipientis nullum est sacramentum"; and at q. 4.5, 2:300r: "sacramentum ... sed non sacramenti effectum qui est gratia."

of disposition is an adequate description of baptismal character. Against the first view, there are people who never receive baptism, and who hence never receive a baptismal character, who are yet granted God's grace, "since grace can be received by the soul without a character." Against the second, it presupposes a metaphysical parity between cause and effect, like that of father and son, who are equally human. But between baptismal character and baptismal grace there is no such parity. So, Durandus concludes, the argument that fiction impedes the working of baptismal character, and that the activation of baptismal character necessarily precedes the activation of baptismal grace in the ex-*fictus*, falls on all counts.[226]

With that objection disposed of, Durandus turns to another claim which he finds problematic. This is the argument that the conversion of the ex-*fictus* is accomplished by his contrition. Durandus ascribes this teaching to the contemporary canonist Johannes Andreae. As he presents it, what produces the remission of his sins is the ex-*fictus*'s humble contrition of heart, not the power of the baptismal grace of which he can now make use. In rebutting this idea, Durandus stresses that it is not the inner attitude of the ex-*fictus* that is the cause here. In any case, the contrition which he brings to the auricular confession that remits his post-baptismal sins lifts his guilt but not all of his punishment. It is baptismal grace, as the church teaches, which remits both the *culpa* and the *poena* of the sins he brought to the font. Durandus accepts that perfect contrition can produce that wholesale effect. But he agrees with Prepositinus of Cremona that so rare a phenomenon does not provide a sound basis for a general rule.[227]

In the closest that he comes to stating an affirmative solution, Durandus cites the notion that baptism has no inherent efficacy but receives the power to remit all sins only because God so endows it by His covenant and ordinance. This divine covenant and ordinance make the sacrament efficacious when it is received by a normal baptizand. It is likely, Durandus observes, that it does the same in a repentant *fictus*: "There is another approach, and that is to say that no power inheres in the sacraments as such, but only the divine power present owing to the divine covenant and ordinance. It can be maintained, more probably, that when the fiction recedes, the baptism earlier undergone takes effect, because the divine covenant and ordinance make the sacrament efficacious." This outcome can occur if and

226. Ibid., q. 4.5–6, 2:300r; quotation at q. 4.6, 2:300r; "diaphaneitas quae est in aere est dispositio necessitatis ad recipiendum lumen"; "quia sine charactere potuit in anima recepti gratia."

227. Ibid., q. 4.7, q. 4.9, 2:300r.

when the earlier impediment of the baptizand's fiction is withdrawn.[228] The farthest that Durandus of St. Pourçain will go is to present this version of the redemption of the *fictus*, achieved thanks to the divine covenant empowering baptismal grace, as the opinion that can be most plausibly maintained (*potest probabiliter sustineri*). The overall effect of his account, in addition to emphasizing the covenant principle, is to soft-pedal the role of baptismal character to the point of eliminating it from the ex-*fictus*'s conversion. Nor is Durandus interested in replacing it with some other understanding of the psychodynamics of that event. God's pact with humankind serves to dissipate the obstruction of fiction, and to accomplish the saving work of baptism, and that is where he leaves the question.

The persistence of hesitation and uncertainty on major issues surrounding fictive baptism in the early fourteenth century can also be seen in the last scholastic we will consider, the Franciscan Walter of Chatton. In his *Sentences* commentary (1321/23), Walter, a regent master at Oxford in 1330, criticizes some masters of both mendicant orders as well as borrowing from them and from earlier authorities. His opening sally stresses the point that the ability of a sacrament to effect what it signifies is not universal or automatic. His *sed contra* states firmly that "a *fictus* can receive the *sacramentum*, and at the same time, not receive invisible grace."[229] He explains that there are two ways in which we can understand how baptismal grace is given. In one case, the grace given acts efficaciously. In the other case, grace is simply given as a gift that is not activated. In the baptism of a *fictus*, the latter situation obtains. He receives grace that does not act efficaciously in him: "'Grace' in this instance is understood simply as grace given as a gift, that is, faith and character. It can be a sign of grace acting efficaciously when he imposes no obstacle to it."[230] Here Walter develops the contrast between *gratia gratum faciens* and *gratia gratis data* applied to fictive baptism by Richard of Mediavilla and proposed, without this language, as early

228. Ibid., q. 4.8, 2:300r: 'Potest ergo alio modo dici, scilicet quod si in sacramentis non sit aliqua virtus inhaerere, sed solum divina virtus assistens per modum divinae pactione et ordinationis, tunc potest probabiliter sustineri, quod recedente fictione baptismus prius receptus habeat suum effectum, quia pactio et ordinatio divina potest esse de effectu sacramenti...."

229. Walter of Chatton, *Reportatio super librum IV Sententiarum* q. 2 *sed contra* in *Reportatio et lectura super Sententias*, ed. Joseph C. Wey and Girard J. Etzkorn, 5 vols. (Toronto: Pontifical Institute of Mediaeval Studies, 1989–2005), 4:253: "Fictus posset recipere sacramentum, et tamen non reciperet invisibilem gratiam."

230. Ibid., q. 2 ad 1, 4:253: "Debet intelligi quod virtute sacramenti imprimitur gratia gratum faciens. Sed 'gratia' ibi accipitur pro gratis data, scilicet fide et charactere, vel si sit signum gratiae gratum faciens, hoc erit quando non ponit obicem."

as Master Simon. It is designed to clarify how baptismal grace can be given to a *fictus* at the font, remaining in him but inactive so long as his fiction obstructs it, but activated once the fiction recedes. Less clear is the ability of Walter's formula to distinguish between baptismal character and baptismal grace. Walter does not venture an opinion on how the impediment of fiction is removed.

The *fictus* referred to in the above passage lacks contrition. For Walter there is also a kind of *fictus* who lacks faith. Two different outcomes occur at the font for these two *ficti*, as he sees it: "I say that there are two kinds of *fictus*. There is one kind who does not have contrition for all his mortal sins but still has faith. The other kind disbelieves but pretends to believe. The first receives the [baptismal] character, that is, infused faith. The second does not."[231] Walter agrees with William of Auxerre and the Duns Scotus of the *Ordinatio* that the baptismal character is withheld from some *ficti*. But he also rejects Scotus's assertion that baptismal character is not an infused virtue. The authority Walter cites on this point is an unusual one, the *Decretals* of Pope Gregory IX (X.3.42.3), not any of the scholastics who provide extensive discussions of baptismal character, however they define it and whether they assign it to all *ficti* or not.

As to other questionable recipients of baptismal character, and what it actually is and does, Walter takes an independent line. This character, he agrees, is indelible. It is granted to heretics, so long as they agree at least in part with orthodox doctrine. It remains in apostates, although they have utterly abandoned the faith, since it was granted to them at their baptism. They cannot lose it. But Walter's apostates do lose the infused faith which he sees as a feature of the indelible character given to them at the font. He holds that the baptismal character is not granted to infidels, among whom Walter includes *ficti* who pretend to have a faith which they lack. He does not say so, but it would appear that, since infidels and those who fake the faith do not receive a baptismal character, neither do they receive the infusion of faith *ipso facto*. Infused faith and indelibility are the main positive features which Walter feels comfortable attributing to baptismal character. But not all baptizands receive them, and apostates can retain the indelible character while abandoning the faith whose infusion is its attribute. Leaving this difficulty unresolved, Walter ends his discussion of baptismal character by casting doubt on the persuasiveness of other claims that have

231. Ibid., q. 2 ad 2, 4:258: "dico quod duplex est fictus. Unus qui non conteritur de omnibus mortalibus; credit tamen. Alius discredens sed simulans se credere. Primus recepit characterem, id est fidem infusam, secundum non."

been made for it. He opts for a minimal definition which now omits the infusion of faith: "I hold, therefore, with the determination of the church, that character is a kind of form impressed on the soul. But what it may be, I do not know."[232] Walter agrees with Scotus that baptismal character may be thought of as a form of some kind, in contrast with Durandus of St. Pourçain's argument dismissing it as a form which causes an effect or which provides a phenomenon's operative condition. It is not clear whether either Walter or Scotus understands baptismal character as form in the light of Aristotelian metaphysics. Despite this *envoi*, Walter of Chatton is in fact no witness to the existence of an ecclesiastical consensus on baptismal character, one which validates his own bare-bones teaching, or anyone else's. Rather, the reverse is the case. His terminal confession of ignorance is an adequate index of the inconclusiveness attaching not only to the theme of baptismal character but also to many aspects of fictive baptism as well, which remained in contention, as they had been since the age of the church fathers, up to Walter's own day.

Conclusion

A more thematic account may be in order in summarizing the history of the fictive baptism debates which we have just surveyed across the millennium covered. From its debut in the third century, this doctrine was, and remained, controversial. It presented an administrative no less than a theological problem to many of the church fathers who take opposing stands on it. Their medieval successors adapt the patristic legacy to their own situational needs and desiderata, with greater or lesser degrees of textual and contextual acumen. To that inheritance, they join new questions and new ways of conceptualizing fictive baptism. Relatively few principles achieve the status of consensus positions. Those that do are largely negative. What little the masters agree on by the end of our target period are primarily the positions they find untenable. They are far less likely to support the same positive conclusions. Disputes proliferate on what fictive baptism is, on whether it is always invalid or sometimes valid, on what fictive baptizands receive at the font, and on the conditions affecting their later redemption. The arguments adopted by the masters are as varied as their substantive solutions. Some masters counter-cite authorities against those they oppose. Some disqualify them as mere conjectures or as superseded opinions. Some

232. Ibid., 4:256–58; quotation at 4:256: "Teneo igitur con determinatione Ecclesiae quod character est aliqua forma impressa animae; sed quae sit illa nescio. . . ."

rest their case on logic, although on this subject they find Aristotle largely unhelpful. Some conceptual innovations attached to this debate in the twelfth and thirteenth centuries are widely adopted. Others attract support from a mere handful of masters whose successors bypass or reject them. Instead of resolving problems, new ways of framing the debate often add new complications and grounds for contention.

What masters exclude can be as telling as what they include. Masters sometimes elide topics as a way of saying that they regard the matter as settled, whether it actually is or not. Sometimes they delete a passage from a previously cited argument or authority, or ignore a position entirely, in order to dismiss its relevance. Sometimes their strategic omissions reflect irresolution; they may suppress or avoid questions to which they have no answers. Sometimes they express uncertainty by offering alternative solutions among which they decline to choose, or by advancing conclusions so hedged with qualifications that they leave the matter moot. While we can detect some shifting emphases along with the arrival of the few consensus positions that emerge, this history is not one of progressive doctrinal development. Rather, fictive baptism and the issues associated with it, no less than the tactics used to address them, remain widely and deeply contested.

Some patristic authors give warm support to the validity of fictive baptism while others have strong misgivings or reject it outright. The leading defenders of the doctrine are the authors of the *Taufmime vitae* and Rufinus of Aquileia. While the *Taufmime* is venerated as an early Christian martyr, he is invoked only to be dismissed by Augustine, as a surrogate for the sectarian baptisms he finds unacceptable. After the early fifth century, the *Taufmime* goes underground until Ivo of Chartres puts him back on stage, now playing a positive role. Even considering the twelfth century's revaluation of theater, Ivo's teaching is remarkable. He agrees that an actor performing the rite on stage can be converted and receive a valid baptism, to the edification of his audience as well as his own benefit. After this brief but impressive reception, however, the *Taufmime* exits from the medieval scene.

By contrast, the boys on the beach episode in Rufinus's *Ecclesiastical History* has an extensive reception history. This passage in Rufinus was subjected to more abridgement, misconstruction, and partisan manipulation than any other patristic text cited on fictive baptism. Frequently lost or abandoned in transmission are Rufinus's focus on the precocity of Athanasius and on the consultative style of Alexander, the bishop who validates the fictive baptism of the mini-prelate's playmates. Some medieval masters regard Alexander's ruling as a fundamental error. Roland of Bologna rejects it and the baptism on the beach as illegal, owing to the boys' defect of age. Peter Lombard, who relocates the event from the seashore to a riverbank, dismisses it by assimilating it to other forms of play, such as the non-sacramental bathing of a baby, which no one accepts as baptism. Peter Comestor and Peter of Poitiers agree. But, idiosyncratically, Peter of Poitiers misidentifies Athanasius as the bishop making the decision and redefines the boys as Jews. The mockery of baptism which he attributes to them suggests that he takes seriously the anti-Jewish canards in circulation in the Europe of his day.

Supporters of Alexander's judgment are equally inclined to reroute and rewrite this text. Peter Damian and Alger of Liège use it to bolster arguments on the status of the clergy which the eleventh-century reform movement unleashed, with Alger recasting the boys as pagans in far-fetched but hoped-for aid of his case. Alternatively, Gratian I, Prepositinus of Cremona, William of Melitona, and Thomas Aquinas in his *Sentences* commentary accent the status of the boys as catechumens, one reason why they think Alexander got it right. William of Auxerre and Guido of Orchellis agree, without mentioning this condition. While he does not advert to Rufinus, Hugh of St. Victor articulates a key principle cited by all masters who do, the critical importance of baptismal intention in validating or invalidating a playful baptism. William of Melitona is the only later master who specifically gives Hugh the credit he deserves on this point. But William of Melitona is also the only supporter of the boys on the beach who is inconclusive on the reasons for Alexander's judgment. It could have been based on the facts elicited by his own investigation, on the status of the boys as catechumens, or on special divine guidance. William of Auxerre also departs from Rufinus in asserting that Alexander received divine aid, and also that he did not observe the boys directly but ruled on the basis of hearsay evidence. More faithful to the text, Prepositinus and Aquinas reject the idea that Alexander received or needed divine aid. Rather, they present Rufinus's Alexander as an express refutation of Augustine's claim that divine guidance should be sought in evaluating fictive baptisms.

This brings us to the career of Augustine's *De baptismo*, easily the most heavily criticized text cited on fictive baptism. This work was reintroduced into medieval debates by the continuator of Anselm of Lucca, with desultory results. It was Ivo of Chartres who laid the foundation for the negative appraisal of this text that became an early and enduring consensus position. Two passages from the *De baptismo* earned this widespread condemnation. They disagree with each other, and each is internally inconsistent. In Book

1, defending the idea that nothing impedes the power of baptismal grace, Augustine argues that the sins of a *fictus* harboring fraternal malice in his heart are remitted, momentarily, at the font, but at once return; they can be remitted, again, if he later repents, although Augustine does not explain how. In Book 7, accepting, up to a point, Cyprian's view that there is no salvation outside the church and that extra-ecclesial baptisms are utterly void, he argues that heretical and schismatic baptisms are a farce, a play-act, and a joke. Yet, if their recipients join the true church, they should not be rebaptized. Ivo problematizes both arguments as self-contradictions. The masters after his time who follow his lead constitute a virtual roll call of those discussed in chapter 2 of this book. They may call on logic, on the dismissal of Augustine's arguments as mere opinions, on the countercitation of opposing authorities, or on all three of these tactics. But the late-twelfth-century assertion, by Peter of Poitiers and Master Martinus, that the instant remission thesis is a passé view now rejected by the *moderni* is substantially correct. The only medieval defenders of the instant remission thesis in our cohort are Gratian II, the author of the *Sententiae divinitatis*, and Odo of Ourscamp. They are exceptions who prove the rule. Some passages of the *De baptismo* that were ignored may have met that fate not because later masters deliberately omitted them but because they were consigned to the cutting-room floor in the transmission process. A likely candidate is Augustine's Simon Magus, cited in Book 7 as a fraudulent baptizand condemned for his lack of charity. He receives no mention in the sequel, even by thinkers who see Simon as a prototype of fictive baptism.

For those who dispose of Augustine by means of countercitation, the authority of choice is Jerome on Ezekiel 16:4, with occasional help from Wisdom 1:5. Essentially as a digression from his commentary on the prophet, Jerome categorically denies the efficacy of Gentile and heterodox ablutions and of those who seek the font fictively. Notwithstanding what the Acts of the Apostles says about his career, Simon Magus is Jerome's paradigmatic fictive baptizand. Bede, in his commentaries on Acts and Genesis, largely agrees. So do Rabanus Maurus and Haimo of Auxerre, the Carolingian exegetes of Ezekiel, although, for Haimo, the Saracens are the key Gentiles. Jerome on Ezekiel remains the most highly favored patristic opponent of fictive baptism in the Middle Ages, frequently and for the most part accurately cited, although Peter Lombard and Thomas Aquinas delete the example of Simon Magus in so doing.

Along with the critique of Augustine's inconsistencies launched by Ivo of Chartres and the followers of Anselm of Laon, and Hugh of St. Victor's stress on baptismal intention as the sacramental *sine qua non*, another early twelfth-century theme to win wide acceptance as a way to conceptualize fictive baptism is the distinction between the *sacramentum* and the *res sacramenti* promoted by the Laon masters. This distinction is welcomed as a handy and economical way to refute the instant remission thesis. For some masters, it also affords a way to integrate baptism with other sacraments. Hugh of St. Victor, Robert Pullen, and Simon of Tournai compare fictive baptism with penance, marriage, and the Eucharist, invalid when received or performed hypocritically. On the other hand, while agreeing that fictive baptizands do not receive the *res sacramenti*, John Duns Scotus aligns them with spouses forced into unwanted marriages. In time, he argues, their dissenting dispositions may change into true consent and yield sacramental effects. In neither case should the fraudulent recipient be excused from the obligations attached to these sacraments. An outlier here is William of Melitona, who objects to the comparison between fictive baptism and false marriage vows because he denies the status-changing efficacy of marriage vows themselves.

Given their rejection of the instant remission thesis and their acceptance of the *sacramentum/res sacramenti* distinction as a way to frame it, the masters still have to face three issues on which the church fathers offer scant guidance. How does fiction impede baptismal grace? Does it do so for all *ficti* or are different gifts given or denied in the light of different kinds of fiction? And, how can their redemption be understood? Innovative ideas are offered in all these areas in the twelfth and thirteenth centuries but without leading to more than sporadic and thinly populated agreements.

Some masters consider the obstruction of baptismal grace from the standpoint of the *fictus* while others do so from the perspective of the sacrament as such. Alexander of Hales offers an analogy which, despite its limits, is adopted by Bonaventure, Peter of Tarentaise, Richard of Mediavilla, and, to some extent, Durandus of St. Pourçain. A cloud can arise which prevents the sun's light from reaching our eyes; so, his fiction can prevent baptismal grace from reaching the *fictus*'s soul. The lack of parity between the natural laws governing clouds and the human volition involved in fiction is not acknowledged either by those who adopt this comparison or by those who do not. William of Auxerre is atypical in granting that some *ficti* do not obstruct baptismal grace entirely but receive mitigation of the inclination to sin, the *fomes peccati*, at the font. On the side of the sacrament itself, in normal cases the baptismal water signifies, and transmits, saving grace. Simon of Tournai proposes that signs, while they are significant in and of themselves, do not always impart what they signify. So it is in fictive baptisms. Gilbert of Poitiers and Odo of Ourscamp think that baptismal signs convey the grace they signify only to the elect; neither addresses the problematic features of this position. Moving beyond semiotic theory, Richard of Mediavilla and Walter of Chatton pick up on an alternative idea aired by Master Simon, who holds that the *fictus* does receive grace at the font but that it remains dormant or latent in him, pending his later repentance. Richard and Walter refine this notion into the distinction between grace given only as a gift and grace given efficaciously. It is the former that the fictive baptizand receives. There remains a fundamental gap between masters who think that the fictive baptizand receives grace at the font, although it is grace he cannot activate, and those who maintain that he is given no grace at the font but receives the *res sacramenti* for the first time only when he repents.

Masters from the twelfth century onward also go beyond the definitions of the *fictus* proposed by the church fathers as well as their understanding of what he receives at the font. In this connection, it is worth recalling that early church leaders had to deal with hypocritical pagan converts, with orthodox baptismal rites subject to local liturgical variations, and with heterodox or schismatic Christians whose rites might be identical to their own. The medieval masters who enlarge the concept of baptismal fiction had to deal with a Greek church whose theological and liturgical differences were established by a powerful Byzantine state to which the Crusades made Europeans increasingly hostile. They also faced a rash of anti-sacramental heresies in their own backyard, some of which looked less like misinterpretations of Christianity than like counter-religions. With respect to pagans, the depredations of Vikings on Christian Europe of the sort related by Richer of Reims and Dudo of St. Quentin gave way to the expansion of Christian Europe at the expense of resident pagans. Fictive baptism as a political ruse or as a consequence of military defeat took on new meanings. We can see these concerns reflected in the attention paid to pertinacious heresy and contempt for the sacrament in definitions of fictive baptism from Ivo of Chartres through Duns Scotus, side by side with venal motives, the lack of faith, and the lack of charity. Robert Pullen adds sins of the flesh. Master Simon adds contempt for the catechesis required of adult converts and Alexander of Hales adds the public preaching of contempt for baptism. Alexander also proposes an analysis seconded by Peter of Tarentaise. As these masters see it, contempt for the efficacy of baptism, a species of the primal sin of pride, is located in the irascible faculty, even as lack of faith is located in the cognitive faculty and lack of contrition is located in the concupiscible faculty. Other masters may agree on the seriousness of contempt for the sacrament without recasting the idea in terms of Aristotelian faculty psychology. William of Auxerre and Duns Scotus flag milder forms of fiction that do not rule out the font, negligence in William's case and attrition for sin in Scotus's. Neither idea is picked up by their immediate successors. Nor is Robert Pullen's repressive view that, since ministers can easily detect fictions based on sins of the flesh, they should deny those candidates the font altogether.

A new question that receives increasing attention in the thirteenth century is whether fictive baptizands should be classed with other people who are not internally disposed to receive baptism. For Alexander of Hales, Bonaventure, and Aquinas, the comparison is with the mentally incapacitated, whose disability makes it impossible for them to exercise free will or to give informed consent. All three masters contrast the mentally challenged with *ficti* who dissent internally but who present themselves willingly at the font, in full possession of their faculties. Returning to another note struck by Alexander, Duns Scotus shifts the comparison to *ficti* and baptizands who, like them, are mentally competent, and who, like them, reject baptism internally. They may or may not express that rejection overtly. If they are baptized anyway, they do not receive the *res sacramenti*. But also, like *ficti*, those who fail to express their dissent should be constrained to practice Christianity. As with his forced marriage analogy, Scotus thinks that this praxis may lead to their true consent.

However they define fictive baptizands, masters express other disagreements on what they receive at the font, and on the degree to which their post-baptismal sins are remitted once they repent, and, indeed, on how they envision that repentance itself. Folded into these aspects of the doctrine is the idea of baptismal character, destined to yield a rich crop of controversy. The Laon master who wrote the *Expositio divinorum officiorum* speaks of an aptitude for repentance granted to fictive baptizands, as distinct from the baptismal grace which they do not receive. An early, and vague, reference to baptismal character is offered by Master Simon. He sees it as a spiritual gift impressed on the soul but, confusingly, compares it to a physical emblem of office or allegiance. William of Auxerre and Alexander of Hales launch the elaborate discussions which baptismal character receives thereafter.

While Alexander of Hales and Peter of Tarentaise are alone in locating various forms of fiction in Aristotle's mental faculties, most masters agree that Aristotelian concepts such as *habitus*, relation, and passion of the soul are inapposite to it, some adding species, power, and disposition. Of these notions, disposition gains a fair amount of positive acceptance. A specific application of this term found only in Peter of Tarentaise and Richard of Mediavilla is that baptismal character disposes the soul of the repentant *fictus* to the reception of baptismal grace the way that the body of a fetus is disposed to receive the infusion of its soul. For Peter of Tarentaise, calling the description of baptismal character a power or a *habitus* is objectionable. But he invokes these terms in discussing it nonetheless. Duns Scotus staunchly opposes the description of character as an infused virtue, but Walter of Chatton thinks that baptismal character includes the infused virtue of faith. Walter does not explain how this character remains indelibly in one who abandons the faith. Both Scotus and Walter describe the character as a form without indicating how or if the Aristotelian sense of that term applies, although Durandus of St. Pourçain finds both the idea of form and that of disposition untenable. William of Auxerre, William of Melitona, and Peter of Tarentaise claim that baptismal character imparts a supernatural illumination to our moral sense—an idea conspicuously, and understandably, omitted by everyone else. Many masters say that baptismal character is a sign of baptismal grace. They are unable to explain how something immaterial can signify something else that is also immaterial. Nor can they explain how this works in fictive baptizands, who receive the indelible baptismal character but not the baptismal grace it signifies. Duns Scotus and Walter of Chatton stand alone in maintaining that some *ficti* do not receive a baptismal character at all, or receive it differentially. Albert the Great is unique in arguing that the baptismal character is not impressed at the font but is given to the fictive baptizand only when he repents.

That repentance itself is also fraught with disagreements. Stephen Langton, Peter of Tarentaise, and Aquinas in his *Sentences* commentary hold that fiction impedes the activity of the baptismal character as well as the activity of baptismal grace. Langton offers a distinctive account of the conversion scenario followed faithfully only by Guido of Orchellis. What initially moves the *fictus* to repent is advenient grace. This grace enables his baptismal character to dispose him toward baptismal grace, which then remits all his pre-baptismal sins. Alexander of Hales finds this idea somewhat appealing but insists that the grace involved is one and the same, without different modes or stages. After an exhaustive review of all the debates surrounding baptismal character and the *fictus*, Duns Scotus, invoking the principle of economy usually ascribed to William of Ockham, concludes that precious little that has been said about character can be rationally proved. He asserts that character is not needed when the fictive baptizand repents, a view he shares with the mature Aquinas, who omits baptismal character entirely from his account of fictive baptism in the *Summa theologiae*. Scotus goes on to replace baptismal character with another condition, with which Durandus of St. Pourçain agrees. The sacrament of baptism has no inherent power but has efficacy because God so endows it, thanks to a divine covenant or pact with humankind.

Masters also disagree on whether the activation of baptismal grace in the repentant *fictus* remits any of his post-baptismal sins. William of Auxerre, Alexander of Hales, Peter of Tarentaise, and the Aquinas of the *Sentences* commentary can envision an affirmative answer, at least for his venial sins and with respect to guilt if not punishment. All masters recognize that he must lament his sins. Both Prepositinus and Durandus acknowledge that perfect contrition can yield full remission of both the guilt and punishment due for his post-baptismal sins. But perfect contrition is so rare that it is unwise to make it the rule. The appropriate, and attainable, remedy is the sacrament of penance, the approach most masters prescribe. Although he promotes the priority of advenient grace, Stephen Langton insists that the free will of the repentant *fictus* must collaborate with grace. Albert the Great and Duns Scotus concur, observing that, while God creates us without our own participation, He does not justify us without it.

One of the last of the masters we have considered, William of Ockham, offers yet another perspective on fictive baptism which may be taken as a sign of the times. Ockham frames his entire discussion under the heading of the unrepeatability of baptism. This doctrine, settled for the scholastics, one might think, by the Nicene Creed, is one mentioned increasingly in connection with fictive baptism as the Middle Ages proceeds, along with the fiction of contempt for the sacrament. It may well reflect the problem of poorly catechized converts who do not understand Christian baptism as a unique, life-changing event. Ockham also makes an observation not hitherto aired in scholastic theology. The fictive baptizand brings to the font both original sin and the actual sins which he willed to commit. Both types of pre-baptismal sin are remitted when his repentance enables him to make use of baptismal grace. The sacrament of penance is the remedy for the sins he willed to commit after his baptism. But Ockham also observes that original sin is not a sin which we will to commit. We contract it against our will, and it is remitted against our will. Ockham does not clarify whether this unwilled remission of original sin always awaits a fictive baptizand's conversion, or whether it occurs at the font thanks to the power of the sacrament for all baptizands, including those not internally disposed to receive it. Coupled with the comparison Duns Scotus makes between fictive baptizands and people baptized under pressure, in contravention of their unwilling internal disposition, we can see a tendency in both masters to yoke fictive baptism conceptually with forced baptism. There are also many masters, early and late, who devote considerable attention to forced baptism as a topic in its own right. It is to their arguments, and to the historical conditions affecting debates on forced baptism, to which we now turn.

CHAPTER *Three*

FORCED BAPTISM

As we saw in chapter 2 of this book, some scholastics placed forced baptism under the same conceptual heading as fictive baptism, a practice which we will also encounter in chapter 3. At the same time, Christian attitudes toward these two baptismal issues have divergent medieval histories. Finding support for both forced baptism and opposition to it in the New Testament, Christian writers first addressed this topic in the age of the Latin apologists. Patristic theologians added contributions later cited as authoritative. In contrast with the other two baptismal debates treated it this book, there was virtually no time lag between the patristic and medieval chapters of the story. Some non-Christians were forcibly baptized in the Germanic kingdoms which succeeded the Roman Empire in the west, starting in the fifth century. Prelates and theologians condemned such events and explained why they regarded them as illicit and counterproductive. Nonetheless, conversion by compulsion gained momentum from the ninth century onward, fueled by the expansion of Christian Europe on the continent and in the Crusades movement. Voices were raised against this policy from the Carolingian era through the early fourteenth century. But commentators treated forced baptism as normal, and masters increasingly lent their skills to justifying it. Those in the ivory tower often mirrored the attitudes of colleagues in the missionary field. As we move into the later centuries of our target period, new distinctions and arguments emerged to rationalize the forced baptism of the unwilling. These doctrinal developments broadened the concept of infidels and refined the conditions deemed to make their forced baptism canonically and theologically acceptable. While a full consensus was not achieved, in this area of baptismal thought the high Middle Ages witnessed a notable movement in that direction.

Few scholars have risen to the task of surveying this subject. The two leading historians who have done so view it from contrasting perspectives. Karl Morrison offers an insightful and largely theoretical approach. He places forced baptism in the context of conversion as a moral and spiritual phenomenon. In Morrison's view, Christian thinkers from the early church through the twelfth century saw conversion as a process that required suffering. In their eyes,

> pain was necessary to break down the old, the deformed likeness, so that a new one could be formed in its place. Such healing, renewing pain could be voluntarily embraced, as it was by penitents and ascetics, or, because it was thought to be the due of brotherly love, it could be imposed by force on unbelievers or wrong-believers. Penance and persecution were twins, often linked to medical or surgical procedures that inflicted terrible pain in order to cure.[1]

On this account, forcing the unwilling into the font was the first incision of the healing knife, whose efficacy in curing non-belief was not questioned. But precisely there lies the limit of Morrison's analysis. Impressive as it is as an exercise of historical imagination taking us into the mindset of the persecutors, it does not do full justice to their opponents, or to the fact that debate ensued on this subject in the Middle Ages. Nor were the arguments in favor of forced baptism often informed by the claim of brotherly love.

Rather than trying to empathize with the persecutors, Hans Maier states that the basic Christian norm has always been the rejection of religious oppression and constraint of any kind. Early Christian writers recognized this principle. But, alas, not only were non-Christians forcibly baptized over the centuries but church leaders and theologians defended the practice. Maier surveys these defections from the Christian message from the third to the twentieth century, within Europe and in lands colonized by Europeans. All churches have been at fault. Their hypocrisy has

1. Karl F. Morrison, *Understanding Conversion* (Charlottesville: University of Virginia Press, 1992), xvi–xvii; see also 71, 79. On the rhetoric of harsh medical treatment as the cure for spiritual disease, see also Maijastina Kahlos, *Forbearance and Compulsion: The Rhetoric of Religious Tolerance and Intolerance in Late Antiquity* (London: Duckworth, 2009), 3, 70–71, with an excellent general bibliography.

provided grist for the mills of anti-Christian ideologies. Maier is happy to report, however, that this problem has now been consigned to the historical dustbin, although the churches must acknowledge their past sin and repent. Given the chronological sweep of his essay, it is perhaps unsurprising that Maier omits many stages of the medieval story. Thus, he leaps from Lactantius to Gratian and from Thomas Aquinas to the *Corpus iuris canonici* of 1983. And his *optique* is narrow. He focuses on interpretations of the parable (Luke 14:16–24) whose culminating *compelle intrare* provides his essay's title, as if the exegesis of that text had been the sole warrant advanced for forced baptism, and as if non-Christians were seen to be its only target. Maier does not distinguish between the forced baptism of infidels, the persecution of heterodox Christians, and religion as the grounds for a just war. Absent from the latter are the medieval campaigns against intra-European pagans. Given the religious hostilities reported in the daily news, the reader may judge that Maier's optimism is premature.[2] Aside from its truncated coverage of the Middle Ages, a more fundamental limitation of Maier's account is that it is less a historical overview than a penitential and homiletic exercise.

While the themes of conversion, religious persecution, and religious war will make appearances in the figures examined in the following, we will focus in chapter 3 on the historical circumstances in which the medieval theory and practice of forced baptism emerged and on the arguments presented for and against it. It is worth noting—a point which Maier flags—that the earliest Latin Christian writers to condemn religious coercion, Tertullian and Lactantius, do so in defense of Christianity. Against their Roman persecutors, they argue that Christians should be accorded religious liberty and not be punished for refusing to worship the pagan gods. In addition to making this case in principle, they offer practical reasons for it. Enforcing religious practices on unbelievers simply invites fakery and fraud. Tertullian adds, as a default position, that in any case the blood of martyrs is the seed of new Christians.[3]

2. Hans Maier, "*Compelle intrare*: Rechtfertigungsgründe für die Anwendung von Gewalt zum Schutz und zur Ausbreitung des Glaubens in der Theologie des abendländischen Christentums," in *Heilige Kriege: Religiöse Begründungen militärischer Gewaltanwendung. Judentum, Christentum und Islam im Vergleich*, ed. Klaus Schreiner with Elisabeth Müller-Luckner (Munich: R. Oldenbourg Verlag, 2008), 55–69.

3. Ibid., 55 for *loci* in these two apologists' writings; see also Kahlos, *Forbearance and Compulsion*, 20–55.

Late Antiquity

It is a striking fact that once Rome became officially Christian, neither secular nor religious leaders advocated the forced baptism of pagans. The chief targets of harassment and repression were heretics and schismatics. And the sanctions invoked against them did not involve forced baptism, even if the heterodox baptisms which they may have undergone were judged invalid. To be sure, the emperors legislated and enforced anti-pagan policies. Pagan temples and cult statues were seized and destroyed. The performance of pagan rites was prohibited and fiscal support was withdrawn from their officiants. Individual pagans suffered legal penalties, thwarted careers, the loss of economic prospects, the expropriation of their wealth, and occasional assaults on their persons. The early fifth-century Theodosian Code outlawed paganism as such. If anti-paganism at times led to outbreaks of violence which authorities condemned as breaches of law and order, there is little evidence that those responsible were punished. Some historians argue that Roman Christianity triumphed over paganism by a policy of systematic repression. Yet Ramsay MacMullen, the leading defender of this view, has found only one isolated case of a pagan forcibly baptized in Christian Rome.[4] Most historians disagree with MacMullen, whether they highlight theology, legislation, the gap between law on the books and law as enforced, local studies, or the self-understandings of Christians engaged in anti-pagan activity.[5] The one fig-

4. Ramsay MacMullen, *Christianity and Paganism in the Fourth to Eighth Centuries* (New Haven, CT: Yale University Press, 1997), 23. For his larger argument, see ibid., 1–73, 151, and works such as idem, *Christianity in the Roman Empire (AD 100–400)* (New Haven, CT: Yale University Press, 1984), 86–101; idem, "Cultural and Political Changes in the Fourth and Fifth Centuries," *Historia* 52 (2003): 465–95.

5. Peter Brown, "Religious Coercion in the Later Roman Empire: The Case of North Africa," *History* 47 (1963): 283–305; reprt. in idem, *Religion and Society in the Age of Saint Augustine* (London: Faber and Faber, 1972), 301–31; Kenneth Scott Latourette, *A History of the Expansion of Christianity*, 7 vols. (Grand Rapids, MI: Zondervan Publishing House, 1970), 1:174–91; David Hunt, "Christianizing the Roman Empire: The Evidence of the Code," in *The Theodosian Code: Studies in the Imperial Law of Late Antiquity*, ed. Jill Harries and Ian Wood (London: Duckworth, 1993), 143–58; the contributors to Pier Franco Beatrice, ed., *L'Intolleranza cristiana nei confronti dei pagani* (Bologna: Edizioni Dehoniane, 1993); John F. Matthews, *Laying down the Law: A Study of the Theodosian Code* (New Haven, CT: Yale University Press, 2000), 121, 147–52, 162; Michele Renee Salzman, "Rethinking Pagan-Christian Violence," in *Violence in Late Antiquity: Perceptions and Practices*, ed. H. A. Drake (Aldershot: Ashgate, 2006), 265–85; David Riggs, "Christianity and the Rural Communities of Late Roman Africa: A Process of Coercion or Persuasion?" in ibid., 297–308; Polymnia Athanassiadi, *Vers la pensée unique: La montée de l'intolérance dans l'Antiquité tardive* (Paris: Les Belles Lettres, 2010), 100–102; Alan Cameron, *The Last Pagans of Rome* (Oxford: Oxford University Press, 2011), 3–4, 6–13, 59–74,

ure who used to be cited as the emblematic pagan martyr is the Alexandrian philosopher Hypatia, who met her death at the hands of a Christian mob in 415. It is now recognized that what was at issue was not pagan-Christian hostilities in Alexandria, in which Hypatia took no part, but a stand-off between its two Christian leaders—the bishop Cyril and the military governor Orestes—of which she became the victim. No one in this troubled city, Hypatia included, was forcibly baptized.[6] Nor, except for the single case mentioned by MacMullen, was this the known fate of any other pagan in Christian Rome.

A less heavily populated non-Christian religion in Christian Rome was Judaism. Jews enjoyed legal protection authorizing the practice of their faith and their exemption from pagan rites. With some cut-backs in the late fourth century, these imperial enactments remained in force where Roman law prevailed. There was a substantial *Adversus Iudaeos* literature in the early church; it reflected intra-Christian polemics, not the effort to convert or oppress actual Jews.[7] It is certainly true that Jews in the Holy Land faced reprisals after their failed rebellion against Rome. But their religious liberties were not suspended elsewhere in the empire. Occasional attacks on synagogues and on the property and persons of Jews occurred in Christian Rome. A single case of forced baptism has come to light. Triggered in 418 by the discovery of what were thought to be the relics of the proto-martyr St. Stephen, put to death by the Jews (Acts 7:8–60), Christians in the Minorcan city of Magona seized its synagogue, assaulted the local Jews, and forcibly baptized one of them. The island's other Jews were expelled. This

---

797–98. Studies focusing on anti-pagan violence as a means of establishing a Christian identity include Michael Gaddis, *There Is No Crime for Those Who Have Christ: Religious Violence in the Christian Roman Empire* (Berkeley: University of California Press, 2005), 1, 5, 6, 10–16, 151–250; Thomas Sizgorich, *Violence and Belief in Late Antiquity: Militant Devotion in Christianity and Islam* (Philadelphia: University of Pennsylvania Press, 2009), 5–12, 21–143; for the rhetoric associated with this violence, see Maijastina Kahlos, *Debate and Dialogue: Christian and Pagan Cultures, c. 360–430* (Aldershot: Ashgate, 2007).

6. The single best account is Maria Dzielska, *Hypatia of Alexandria*, trans. F. Lyra (Cambridge, MA: Harvard University Press, 1995). See also Edward J. Watts, *City and School in Late Antique Athens and Alexandria* (Berkeley: University of California Press, 2006), 190–201; see idem, "The Murder of Hypatia: Acceptable or Unacceptable Violence?" in *Violence in Late Antiquity: Perceptions and Practices*, ed. H. A. Drake (Aldershot: Ashgate, 2006), 333–42, for an assessment of the attitudes of contemporary sources on these events. A brief comment on the account of Socrates Scholasticus is also provided by Szigorich, *Violence and Belief*, 222n59.

7. David Berger, "Mission to the Jews and Jewish-Christian Contacts in the Polemical Literature of the High Middle Ages," *American Historical Review* 91 (1986): 575–91; on pages 576–79 for late ancient and early medieval developments, with an excellent guide to the historiography on that subject.

incident was a clear violation of imperial law. But the perpetrators escaped prosecution owing to the confusion stemming from the sack of Rome in 410.[8] Along with the polemics against the Judaizing of fellow Christians, this episode stands on one side of a late ancient ledger whose other side was shaped by the theology of Augustine. He aims the famous *compelle intrare* argument of his *Epistola* 185 at Donatists, not Jews. In fact, he defends the protection of the Jews. As the original people of God whose revelation makes the Old Testament a sacred book for Christians, the Jews and their witness should be preserved until the Last Day, when they will be gathered in and converted. This Augustinian doctrine was to have a significant medieval impact.[9] But it was also a legacy freely abandoned in some quarters.

Medieval Jews

In the sixth and seventh centuries, there is evidence of the forced baptism of Jews in the Germanic successor states which replaced the Roman Empire in the west. Among early sources for it are the injunctions against it and the reasons for avoiding it in the letters sent to three bishops by Gregory the Great as Pope Gregory I in 591. Writing in June of that year to Virgil of Arles and Theodore of Marseille, Gregory states both the policy he requires and the rationale for it:

I will not remain silent on how errant souls should be saved. One after another, travelers in the Marseille region have brought to our attention that there are many men of the Jewish faith now living among you in that province. Many of these Jews are brought to the font by force rather than being led to it by preaching. Now, while I value the laudable goal of handing on the faith we profess out of love for our Lord, I am afraid that this intention is futile when it is inconsistent with Holy Scripture. Nor is the effort meritorious or without loss to any souls we seek to snatch in this way. Anyone brought to the font under constraint and not

8. Paula Fredrickson, *Augustine and the Jews: A Christian Defense of Jews and Judaism* (New York: Doubleday, 2008), 357–64, 416–17; Jean-Claude Schmitt, *The Conversion of Herman the Jew: Autobiography, History, and Fiction in the Twelfth Century*, trans. Alex J. Novikoff (Philadelphia: University of Pennsylvania Press, 2010), 146–47. More details about this event and about Severus, the bishop of Minorca who sent the news of it to Augustine, are supplied by David Abulafia, *The Great Sea: A History of the Mediterranean* (London: Allen Lane, 2011), 223–25, and in literature on pages 674–75nn24–36.

9. Peter Brown, "St. Augustine's Attitude toward Religious Coercion," *Journal of Roman Studies* 54 (1964): 107–16; reprt. in idem, *Religion and Society* (as in note 5), 260–78. Excellent treatments of the Augustinian legacy in the Middle Ages are provided by Fredrickson, *Augustine and the Jews*, and Robert E. Lerner, *The Feast of St. Abraham: Medieval Millenarians and the Jews* (Philadelphia: University of Pennsylvania Press, 2001).

by the sweetness of preaching will return to his original superstition. Where he is thought to have been reborn, he will die a worse death.... The prescription for people who deserve affliction with the scourge for their errors is preaching, so that those in darkness may be illuminated.[10]

In March 591 Gregory also writes to Peter of Terracina, where, as his intelligence network advises him, the issue is the illegal proscription of Jewish religious services. While forced baptism is not the topic, Gregory states here a policy requirement similar to that in his letter to Virgil and Theodore sometimes later applied to forced baptism. Using strong-arm tactics to force Jews to abandon their traditions is wrong and bound to fail:

As for those who disagree with the Christian religion, they must be encouraged and persuaded to join in unity with the faith through kindness and gentleness. It is only with the sweetness of preaching and warnings of the fearsome judgment to come that belief can be invited. They will be repelled by threats and intimidation. In order to make the word of God audible to them, you need to proceed with due kindness, rather than with an excessive harshness that only terrifies them.[11]

The fact that the gulf between theory and practice in post-Roman Europe to which these letters attest had opened, only to widen in later medieval centuries, has drawn much scholarly attention. Less focused on this period and on the forcible baptism of non-Christians than on hostility to a range of "Others" that includes but goes well beyond religious non-conformists, R. I. Moore sees anti-Judaism as just one facet of a wider persecutory attitude.[12]

10. Gregory the Great, *Registrum Epistolarum* 1.45, to Virgil of Arles and Theodore of Marseille, June 591, ed. Paul Ewald, MGH Epistolarum (Berlin: Weidemann, 1887), 1/1:75–76; quotation at 1/1:76: "quomodo errantium salvendae sint animae, non tacerem. Plurimi siquidem Iudiciae religionis viri in hoc provincia comanentes ac subinde in Massilae partibus pro diversis ambulentes ad nostram perduxere notitiam, multos consistentium in illis partibus Iudeorum vi magis ad fontem baptismatis quam praedicatione perductos. Nam intentionem quidem huiuscemodi et laude dignum censeo et de Domini nostri descendere dilectione profiteor. Sed hanc eadem intentionem, nisi competens scripturae sacrae comitetur effectus, timeo, ne aut mercedis opus exinde non proveniat, aut iuxta aliquid animarum quas eripi ad baptismatis fontem non praedicationis suavitate, sed necessitate pervenerit, ad pristinam superstitionem remeans inde deterius moritur, unde renatus esse videbatur.... Adhibendus ergo illis est sermo, qui et errorem in ipsos spinas urere debent et praedicando quod in his tenebrascit inluminant."

11. Ibid., 1.34, to Peter of Terracina, March 591, 1/1:47–48; quotation at 1/1:48: "Hos enim, qui a christiana religione discordant, mansuetudine, benignitate, admonendo, suadendo ad unitatem fide necesse est congregare, ne quos dulcedo praedicationis et praeventus futuri iudicis terror ad credendum invitare poterat, minis et terroribus repellantur. Oportet ergo magis, ut audiendum de vobis verbum Dei benigne conveniant, quam austeritate, quae supra modum extenditur, expavescant."

12. R. I. Moore, *The Formation of a Persecuting Society: Power and Deviance in Western Europe, 950–1250* (Oxford: Blackwell, 1987).

On the whole, this approach has not appealed to historians of medieval Judaism. Many of them stress the uniqueness of the relationship between *Synagoga* and *Ecclesia* and are not interested in placing Judaism in a comparative framework. Some approach the subject with the post-medieval elephants in the room as unavoidable reference points. Others seek to document Jewish life and medieval Christian attitudes toward Jews in a non-proleptic way.[13] But much of the discussion has been fiercely polemical. Here, we can but direct readers to a sampler of its most recent proponents. Indeed, the history of this historiography has itself become a matter for analysis.[14]

The debates largely revolve around two polar interpretations. One treats medieval Jewish history as a so-called "lachrymose chronicle." Historians in this camp see Christian hostility toward Judaism as an ideological given, deriving from the Jewish rejection of Christ as the Messiah and the role attributed to Jews in His death. Expressions of Christian tolerance of Jews are seen as mere blips on the screen which had no effect on basic anti-Jewish thought and action. According to this view, no Jew has ever voluntarily converted to another religion. All Jews who became Christians in the Middle Ages were forced into the font and did their best to remain crypto-Jews thereafter. This interpretation has attracted followers from the very beginning of the academic study of medieval Jewish history and continues to enlist authoritative exponents.[15] At the other pole stand the revisionists. They reject the idea that Jewish life in the Middle Ages was an unmitigated tale of woe. If medieval Christians were battling an abstraction that has been called the "hermeneutical Jew," so, too, they charge, have advocates of the lachry-

13. Two good recent examples of the straightforward approach are Benjamin Ravid, "The Forced Baptism of Jews in Christian Europe: An Introductory Overview," in *Christianizing Peoples and Converting Individuals*, ed. Guyda Armstrong and Ian N. Wood (Turnhout: Brepols, 2000), 157–67; Michael Frassetto, "Introduction," in *Christian Attitudes toward the Jews in the Middle Ages*, ed. Michael Frassetto (New York: Garland, 2007), xiii–xviii.

14. Helpful here is David Berger, "A Generation of Scholarship on Jewish-Christian Interaction in the Medieval World," and "From Crusades to Blood Libels to Expulsion: Some New Approaches to Medieval Anti-Semitism," in idem, *Persecution, Polemic, and Dialogue: Essays in Jewish-Christian Relations* (Boston: Academic Studies Press, 2010), 15–50; particularly useful in summarizing Hebrew-language scholarship is David Malkiel, *Reconstructing Ashkenaz: The Human Face of Franco-German Jewry, 1000–1250* (Stanford, CA: Stanford University Press, 2009).

15. See, for example, the contributions to standard reference works by Kenneth R. Stow, "The Church and the Jews," in *The New Cambridge Medieval History*, ed. David Abulafia (Cambridge: Cambridge University Press, 1999), 5:204–19; idem, "Jews in the Middle Ages," in *A Companion to the Medieval World*, ed. Carol Lansing and Edward D. English (Oxford: Wiley-Blackwell, 2009), 293–312.

mose chronicle invented essentialized abstract conceptions of both medieval Jews and medieval Christians. Documentable reality, for the revisionists, tells a different story. It tells of the support and protection that Jews received from Christian rulers, the amicable relations of Jews with their Christian neighbors, the existence of voluntary conversions to Christianity, and the Christian thinkers who reinforced the teachings of Augustine and Gregory the Great. Another revisionistic point calls on demography. If the destruction of medieval Jewry whether by massacre or by forced absorption into the church had been as extensive as is claimed by the lachrymose chronicle school, it would be impossible to account for the continued existence, and efflorescence, of Jewish communities in various parts of Europe where they continued to thrive.[16]

There is also a historiographical position located between these two poles. Scholars in this group accent two points. First, they argue that we should not generalize. The evidence for both anti-Judaism and friendly Christian-Jewish relations is basically local and circumstantial. It can best be understood in the light of the times, places, and situations involved. The factors accounting for particular outcomes in one situation may not be present elsewhere. Second, we should adopt a hermeneutic of suspicion toward the sources on all sides. They cannot be taken at face value. Accounts may have been rewritten or redacted well after the events described. They tell us not what the participants may have thought or experienced but rather what the authors attribute to them. Even when a report is close in time to the event it relates, we should be sensitive to the author's "rhetoric of the scene" and the place of the event in his larger story as well as the agenda underlying it. These historians maintain that the perspectives on Jewish-Christian relations found in the sources are multidirectional and ambiguous. We need to assess them critically and without preconceptions.[17]

16. See, for example, Robert Chazen, *Reassessing Jewish Life in Medieval Europe* (Cambridge: Cambridge University Press, 2010), with an exhaustive treatment of the historiography on this issue; for a synthesis of the revisionist perspective aimed as a less specialist, and purely Anglophone, audience, see Anna Sapir Abulafia, *Christian-Jewish Relations, 1000–1300* (London: Longman, 2011).

17. See, for example, Jeremy Cohen, *Living Letters of the Law: Ideas of the Jew in Medieval Christianity* (Berkeley: University of California Press, 1999): idem, "Christian Theology and Anti-Jewish Violence in the Middle Ages," in *Religious Violence between Christians and Jews: Medieval Roots, Modern Perspectives*, ed. Anna Sapir Abulafia (New York: Palgrave-Macmillan, 2002), 44–60; Jonathan Riley-Smith, "Christian Violence and the Crusades," in ibid., 3–20; Gavin I. Langmuir, "At the Frontiers of Faith," in ibid., 138–56; Schmitt, *The Conversion of Herman the Jew*, 146–57; on page 146 for "rhetoric of the scene"; on pages 146–47 for the fact that the

This brings us to cases of the forced baptism of Jews in the Germanic successor states as reported, and not merely as reflected in papal reactions. We will be alert to the circumstances so far as they are known and to the emphases given in the sources. Who, or what, occasions or initiates these events? Answers to this question found in the sources include secular rulers, local bishops, unlicensed Christian mobs, provocations ascribed to the Jews themselves, or some combination of these elements. Material is available from both Merovingian Gaul and Visigothic Spain.

Various kinds of sources report such episodes in Merovingian Gaul between 575 and 632/33, with actions of this type then abating until a new wave of anti-Jewish hostility was unleashed by the First Crusade in the late eleventh century. The fullest survey of the Merovingian chapter of the story is provided by Michel Rouche. His findings show that all of these forced baptisms occur in episcopal cities. Bishops are the central figures, although mobs are sometimes involved, and the bishops sometimes take their marching orders from the Frankish kings.[18]

In one of the first of these events, and the most richly attested, the forced baptism of the Jews of Clermont in 576, the key figure is the bishop, Avitus. This episode is reported in two distinct, but related, accounts, those of Venantius Fortunatus and Gregory of Tours.[19] Gregory had heard the

unique narrative account of the forced baptism of the Minorcan Jew in 418 dates to the sixth century. The seminal study of circumstantial persecution and toleration acknowledged by the aforementioned scholars is David Nirenberg, *Communities of Violence: Persecution of Minorities in the Middle Ages* (Princeton, NJ: Princeton University Press, 1996). Also valuable are the findings of Benjamin Z. Kedar, "Multidirectional Conversion in the Frankish Levant," in *Varieties of Religious Conversion in the Middle Ages*, ed. James Muldoon (Gainesville: University of Florida Press, 1997), 190–99, who notes that most of the conversions of Jews, Muslims, and Christians to each other's religions in the lands ruled by both western Europeans and Byzantines were voluntary. One group of voluntary converts were soldiers defeated in battle who were thus recruited into the victors' armies and given inducements to do so. Another group was comprised of non-Christian slaves whose baptism, far from being forced or encouraged by their Christian masters, was resisted as it would lead to their emancipation. While Wolfgang Giese, "In Iudaismus lapsus est: Jüdische Proselytenmacherei im frühen und hohen Mittelalter," *Historisches Jahrbuch* 88 (1968): 407–18, cites personal reasons for conversion such as inter-religious marriage, he is quite vague on the actual or likely circumstances of the cases he surveys.

18. Michel Rouche, "Les baptêmes forcés de Juifs en Gaule merovingienne et dans l'empire d'Orient," in *De l'antijudaïsme antique à l'antisémitisme contemporain*, ed. Valentin Nikiprowetsky (Lille: Presses Universitaires de Lille, 1979), 105–24; on page 108, Rouche criticizes the view that these forced baptisms occurred completely as a result of episcopal initiatives. For a more recent view of the importance of urban power relations, see Schmitt, *The Conversion of Herman the Jew*, 146–47.

19. Venantius Fortunatus, *Carmina* 5b, in *Opera*, ed. and trans. Stefano Di Biazzano,

news, most likely from a messenger. A former protégé of Avitus, he commissioned Venantius (ca. 540–600), a renowned man of letters, to write a poem celebrating Avitus's role. Venantius did so shortly after 576. When Gregory wrote his *History of the Franks*, he drew on, and edited, Venantius's poem.

Venantius opens his narrative on Ascension Day, May 14, 576. Underlying, but unspecified, hostility to the Jews of Clermont appears to exist. But he cites no precipitating incident to account for a Christian mob's destruction of the synagogue that day. The Jews then retreat to a fortified house, rightly fearing violence from the mob besieging it. On May 15 Avitus intervenes. His disinclination to forestall the razing of the synagogue, or his powerlessness to prevent it, receive no comment. Venantius gives Avitus a lengthy theological speech urging the Jews to convert. When they refuse, the angry mob demands baptism or death. Avitus intervenes again, with another option, baptism or exile. Those Jews who refuse baptism are expelled and sent to Marseille. Most of the others are forced into the font. After an elaborate description of the ensuing ceremony on Pentecost, May 24, 576, Venantius ends with praise for Avitus's pastoral zeal and reports the bishop's gratification at the addition of the new sheep to his flock.

Gregory abbreviates or omits Avitus's theological discourse, softens the mob's threats, and alters the timeline and the triggering of these events. The scene opens on April 3, 576, Good Friday, with Avitus praying for the conversion of the Jews. One of them requests baptism voluntarily. The ceremony is performed at a baptismal church outside the city gates. During the procession back into town, one of the convert's erstwhile co-religionists pours rancid oil on the neophyte's head. It is this mockery of baptismal chrism that incites the Christian mob, which destroys the synagogue on Ascension Day. Gregory's Jews do not barricade themselves against the death threats of a besieging mob. Rather, they hold a meeting in which Avitus makes a speech inviting them to convert. Gregory makes no men-

2 vols., Corpus Scriptorum Ecclesiae Aquileiensis 8/1–2 (Aquileia: Città Nuova, 2001), 1:296–302; Gregory of Tours, *Histoire des Francs* 5.11, ed. Henri Omont and Gaston Collon, rev. ed. René Poupardin (Paris: Alphonse Picard et Fils, 1913), 161–63. The best analysis, with comparison of these two versions, is by Marc Reydellet, "La conversion des Juifs de Clermont en 576," in *De Tertullien aux Mozarabes: Antiquité tardive et christianisme ancien (IIIe–VIe siècles). Mélanges offerts à Jacques Fontaine*, ed. Louis Holtz and Jean-Claude Fredouille, 2 vols. (Paris: Institut d'Études Augustiniennes, 1992), 1:371–79. Bernhard Blumenkranz, *Juifs et chrétiens dans le monde occidentale, 430–1096*, (Paris: Mouton et Cie., 1960), 140–41, conflates the two accounts. Rouche, "Les baptêmes," 105–6, and Schmitt, *The Conversion of Herman the Jew*, 146, give Gregory's account only.

tion of the baptism or death, or baptism or exile, alternatives. He presents the Jews' baptism, five hundred strong, which duly takes place on Pentecost, as spontaneous, or at least as motivated by the divine grace which Avitus mediates, the answer to his Good Friday prayer. Despite this shift in emphasis, with Avitus the peacemaker in Gregory's account saving the Jews from the consequences of their own act of desecration rather than from the murderous threats of the Christian mob, both authors make Avitus the hero of the story.

Fewer details are available for the forced baptism of Jews in 575, 581, and 582. In all three cases, the site is Uzès, whose bishop, Ferreolus, is admonished by two successive Frankish rulers and constrained to follow their orders. In the first two episodes, Childebert II of Austrasia objects to the fact that Ferreolus eats and drinks with local Jews. He exiles the bishop on that account. When Ferreolus returns, he is obliged to offer the Jews the choice of baptism or expulsion.[20] In 582 the same bishop is told by Chilperic of Neustria that he is canceling the baptism or expulsion option. Now, there is only one option for the Jews, forced baptism, with the death penalty for any baptized Jew who relapses.[21] One is left with the impression that, had the rulers not intervened, Ferreolus's relations with the Jews of Uzès would have remained friendly.

Although we lack local sources to reinforce the travelers' reports conveyed to Gregory the Great, the events for which he reproves the bishops of Arles and Marseille in 591 appear to have been the result of episcopal initiatives rather than actions the bishops took under the influence of secular rulers, the behavior of mobs, or provocations on the part of local Jews. Gregory does not reprise the particular circumstances which may have led these bishops to force their Jews into the font.[22]

The final reference to the forced baptism of Jews in Merovingian Gaul is related by the chronicler Pseudo-Fredegar. He states that, in 632/33, King Dagobert issued an edict ordering all the Jews in his realm to be baptized willy-nilly. Pseudo-Fredegar presents this item as an event in the *vita* of Sulpicius of Bourges, the bishop involved. He writes several decades after the alleged event. That it ever occurred has been greeted with suspicion and disbelief by modern historians, who have ample reason to question Pseudo-Fredegar's reliability, even though some ninth-century commentators take him seriously and treat the policy as a good idea.[23] Rouche, and others

20. Rouche, "Les baptêmes," 106.

21. Ibid., 106–7.

22. Ibid., 107.

23. Ibid., 107–8.

who have assessed this text, regard the royal order as entirely fictitious. The consensus of modern historians is that all these Merovingian cases were informed by politics, whether the issue was intra-urban tensions in episcopal cities, the relations between bishops and secular rulers, or the desires of both sets of leaders to replace the Roman law protection accorded to Jews with programs they regarded as more responsive to contemporary needs.

A proposal aired by Rouche at the end of his essay is that the Merovingians sought to emulate Byzantium, where a shift in Jewish policy took place in the sixth century.[24] This theory has won no support from historians of Byzantium and its dependencies. The situation in Byzantium was quite different from that in western Europe, and much more complex. Christological and Trinitarian heresies remained rife in the Greek church. There were many Jewish sects in Byzantium, with their own theologies and rites. Byzantium inherited ongoing wars with Persia and with the Slavs and Avars in the Balkans and soon faced the new threat of Islam. The first Byzantine anti-Jewish legislation dates to the reign of Justinian (527–65), who added the reconquest of formerly Byzantine lands in Europe to his crowded agenda. The claim made in the sixth century was that Byzantine Jews were traitors who collaborated with the Persians. Heraclius (610–41) took the unprecedented step of ordering the forced baptism of his Jewish subjects, many of whom then emigrated to Muslim-controlled areas where they received religious toleration. As Byzantinists have pointed out, the policy of Heraclius backfired, to the extent that it was ever enforced. The same applies when the precedent he set was invoked by Leo III (721–22), by Basil I (873–74), and again in the tenth and thirteenth centuries.[25] The one area of western Europe where we might expect to see the enforcement of imperial policy following Justinian's reconquest is southern Italy and Sicily. The existence, and toleration, of substantial Jewish communities there, under Byzantine, Muslim, and later Norman rule, indicate that imperial edicts on this subject remained a dead letter.[26]

24. Ibid., 114–24.

25. N. R. M. de Lange, "Jews and Christians in the Byzantine Empire: Problems and Prospects," in *Christianity and Judaism*, ed. Diana Wood, Studies in Church History 29 (Oxford: Blackwell, 1992), 15–32 on pages 22–23; Averil Cameron, *The Byzantines* (Oxford: Blackwell, 2006), 30, 114, 182–83.

26. Hubert Houben, "Gli ebrei nell'Italia meridionale tra la metà dell'XI e l'inizio del XIII secolo," in idem, *Mezzogiorno normanno-svevo: Monasteri e castelli, ebrei e musulmani* (Naples: Liguori, 1996), 193–211; idem, "Religious Toleration in the South Italian Peninsula during the Norman and Staufen Periods," in *The Society of Norman Italy*, ed. Graham A. Loud and Alex Metcalfe (Leiden: Brill, 2002), 319–39; Patricia Skinner, "Conflicting Accounts: Negotiating a

If the Merovingians were not imitating a largely notional Byzantine model, neither were the Visigoths in Spain, given that their own stance toward Byzantium was one of political hostility.[27] Both in their Arian days and after their acceptance of Catholicism, Visigothic Christians had their own local precedent, the events in Minorca of 418. The unique narrative account of that episode, written in the sixth century, presents a scenario different from the one known when it occurred. According to the anonymous sixth-century source, the *de facto* ruler of the city of Magona is a Jew named Theodore. He is clearly involved in a power struggle with the local bishop. Following the rising of the mob after the finding of the relics thought to be St. Stephen's, the bishop waits until the rioters have razed the synagogue—his timing much like that of Avitus of Clermont—before making his move. He receives one Jewish convert who comes to the font willingly. Theodore learns of this conversion in a dream, which he interprets as a prophesy of what is ordained to happen. This dream persuades Theodore to submit to baptism and to take his people with him.[28] Completely elided in this sixth-century account is the issue of forced baptism, or the option of baptism or expulsion. The anonymous turns the Jews' forced baptism into a fully voluntary act. The main point of the story, as he tells it, is that Theodore's political power is overcome. Jewish leadership is replaced by Christian leadership, whether at the hands of some other lay Christian or those of the bishop of Magona himself. The introduction of the dream which triggers the mass baptism of the Magonan Jews is an original, if conventional, literary touch.

If assisted by do-it-yourself oneiromancy on the part of Theodore, the

Jewish Space in Medieval Southern Italy, c. 800–1150 CE," in *Christian Attitudes toward the Jews in the Middle Ages*, ed. Michael Frassetto (New York: Garland, 2007), 1–13; Paul Oldfield, *City and Community in Norman Italy* (Cambridge: Cambridge University Press, 2009), 209–11, 227. The non-enforcement of Byzantine Jewish policy in Italy is also noted by Bernard Bachrach, *Early Medieval Jewish Policy in Western Europe* (Minneapolis: University of Minnesota Press, 1977), 39–40.

27. Bachrach, *Early Medieval Jewish Policy*, 12–26; for the argument for Byzantine influence, see Bat-Ševa Albert, "Un nouvel examen de la politique anti-juive wisigothique à propos d'un article recent," *Revue des études juives* 135 (1976): 3–29 on pages 22–24, 29; Norman Roth, *Jews, Visigoths, and Muslims in Medieval Spain: Cooperation and Conflict* (Leiden: Brill, 1994), 7–8, 37. Nor did the Arian Visigoths impose their faith on the Catholic subjects whom they had conquered in Spain, unlike the Arian Vandals, who did force the baptism, or rebaptism, of both Donatists and Catholics after their conquest of North Africa in the fifth century. On this issue, see Paul Fournier, "Rebaptism as a Ritual of Cultural Integration in Vandal Africa," in *Shifting Cultural Frontiers in Late Antiquity*, ed. David Brakke, Deborah Deliyannis, and Edward Watts (Farnham: Ashgate, 2012), 243–54.

28. Schmitt, *The Conversion of Herman the Jew*, 146–47.

sixth-century anonymous account gives an overtly political coloration to the Christianization of the Minorcan Jews. This fact, and local Iberian witness to it, has escaped the attention of historians of Spanish Jewry who begin their tale with the Visigoths, seen as planting the seeds that yielded the bitter harvest of later medieval and modern persecutions. A leading proponent of this approach is Bernhard Blumenkranz. He acknowledges that his reading of Visigothic history, the first act of the "Spanish drama," is proleptic. Unlike other medieval rulers, he maintains, the Visigoths did not employ Jewish subjects as administrators, counselors, diplomats, or personal physicians. Nor did they exploit them economically. The grounds for jealousy of the Jews that may have existed elsewhere were absent in Visigothic Spain. Yet, loyal and unthreatening subjects though they were, the Jews were the innocent victims of ever-increasing Visigothic oppression.[29] A more recent version of this interpretation casts the Catholic church as the villain of the piece. Its proponents see Visigothic Jewish policy as motivated essentially by *odium theologicum* and religious fanaticism. At most, politics informed the rulers' effort to create a Caesaropapism not envisioned in Catholic Europe until the age of Charlemagne.[30]

Historians of the early Middle Ages and specialists in Spanish history view this subject in a less monocular way. Jewish history, they urge, should not be studied in a vacuum. In the eyes of the rulers of Visigothic Spain, Jewish policy was a second-order concern. It was not merely an expression of religious prejudice, the drive for royal centralization, or political or economic rivalry. Basic to its comprehension is the fact that, throughout its history, the Visigothic monarchy was extremely weak. Many rulers were deposed or assassinated. Plots against royal authority itself, and not just the desire to unseat the current ruler, were frequent. The political scene was dominated by powerful aristocratic families who controlled offices in church and state and were prompt to revolt against royal efforts to limit their influence. After King Reccared's conversion to Catholicism in 589, many in these noble elites remained Arians. Catholic Christology was so offensive to them that Judaism could appear a viable alternative, at least in the eyes of royal propagandists. It was Arianism, not Judaism, that was the major religious and political threat to royal objectives. From this perspective, Visigothic anti-Judaism can best be grasped in the context of Visigothic anti-Arianism. Historians who

29. Blumenkranz, *Juifs et chrétiens*, 41–63, 97–134, 373–74.

30. Albert, "Un nouvel examen," 3–29; *odium theologicum* alone is stressed by Raúl González-Salinero, "Catholic Anti-Judaism in Visigothic Spain," in *The Visigoths: Studies in Culture and Society*, ed. Alberto Ferreiro (Leiden: Brill, 1999), 123–50.

offer this argument also note that Visigothic kings rarely had the power to enforce their own legislation, or earlier Roman law, or the decrees of church councils, whatever their content. So, while we can indeed document an increasingly harsh series of enactments against Jews, including their forced baptism, they look to be the campaign promises of a series of short-lived and unstable kings, ignored by them in practice and frequently overturned by their successors. The chronic weakness of the Visigothic state explains its extremely swift defeat by the Muslims in 711. And the new Muslim rulers found in Spain, and preserved, a large and vibrant Jewish community, one apparently unscathed by Visigothic legislation. In sum, Visigothic Spain may have been exceptional more for the would-be repression of Judaism than for the actual implementation of any such goal.[31]

While Visigothic rule was wiped off the map in 711, this realm left a legacy on the forced baptism of Jews which outlived it. This inheritance was, at the same time, authoritative and self-contradictory. Both features are found in the works of Isidore of Seville (d. 636), Visigothic Spain's most influential thinker. Isidore is important both for his own variegated opinions on this subject and for his presidency at Toledo IV (633), a key church council which also addressed it, ambiguously.

Isidore considers baptism, if not the baptism of Jews as such, in his *De ecclesiasticis officiis* (598/618). Here, he presents as actually in force patristic initiation practices already abandoned. Although most baptizands in his day were infants presented by Christian parents, he treats baptismal candidates as adult pagan converts. They have been instructed by Christian preaching. Thanks to divine grace, they have replaced their pagan idols with

31. An important initial stand against the lachrymose chronicle interpretation was taken by Bernard Bachrach, "A Reassessment of Visigothic Jewish Policy, 589–711," *American Historical Review* 78 (1973): 11–34; idem, *Early Medieval Jewish Policy*, viii–ix, 3–26; on page 138 he announces that "all the anti-Jewish policies launched during the early Middle Ages were failures." Historians of Spain have generally agreed and have amplified this analysis. See, for example, P. D. King, *Law and Society in the Visigothic Kingdom* (Cambridge: Cambridge University Press, 1972), 122–45; José Orlandis, "Le royaume wisigothique et son unité religieuse," in *L'Europe héritière de l'Espagne wisigothique*, ed. Jacques Fontaine (Madrid: Casa de Velázquez, 1992), 9–16; Roth, *Jews, Visigoths, and Muslims*, 1, 3, 7–40; Rachel L. Stocking, *Bishops, Councils, and Consensus in the Visigothic Kingdom, 589–633* (Ann Arbor: University of Michigan Press, 2000), 18, 25, 59–117, 145–73, 177–90; Roger Collins, *Visigothic Spain, 409–711* (Oxford: Blackwell, 2004), 113–16, 148–65; J. N. Hillgarth, *The Visigoths in History and Legend* (Toronto: Pontifical Institute of Mediaeval Studies, 2009), 48–49, 92. This position has been accepted as the standard view in the general survey of Chris Wickham, *The Inheritance of Rome: A History of Europe from 400 to 1000* (London: Allen Lane, 2009), 130–36, 138–40, 172–73, although he disagrees with the most acute diagnoses of the weakness of the Visigothic regime.

the worship of the one true God. They have agreed to reform their lives. Isidore cites the patristic distinction between catechumens who merely hear the Word and *competentes* who have requested baptism and are in the final stage of preparation for its reception. He gives fewer details on the rite itself than on this currently nonexistent process. As a sidebar, he notes that baptism can occur by water, by blood, and by desire, and that all three forms are valid. He restates many of these points in his *Etymologies*, which he was completing at the time of his death.[32]

Two works in which Isidore does treat Jews and their forced baptism expressly are his *History of the Goths, Vandals, and Suevi* (619, revised 624) and *Sententiae* (615). King Sisebut (612–21) did force Jews into the font, for which Isidore criticizes him: "Sisebut ... at the beginning of his reign drew Jews into the Christian faith out of his excess of zeal, but in a wrongheaded way. For he compelled by force those whom he should have persuaded by a reasoned faith, since it is written that Christ is to be preached according to the truth, when the time is ripe."[33] Isidore's *Sententiae* presents a much more equivocal set of prescriptions. Should those who fail to hold the true Christian faith be included in the church at all? He offers more than one answer. "Just as the holy Catholic church patiently tolerates those who live badly," he observes, "so also she casts out those who believe badly."[34]

32. Isidore of Seville, *De ecclesiasticis officiis* 20, 22, 25, ed. Christopher M. Lawson, CCSL 112 (Turnhout: Brepols, 1984), 94–95, 97, 102–3; cf. idem, *Etymologiae* 7.14, ed. W. M. Lindsay, 2 vols. (Oxford: Clarendon Press, 1911), 2:303. The fullest discussion is by Attilio Carpin, *Il battesimo in Isidoro di Siviglia*, Pontificia Universitas Gregoriana, Dissertatio ad doctorum facultate theologiae (Bologna: Grafiche S. Rufillo, 1984), 20–26, 31–53, 71; on pages 24–25 he notes the unlikelihood that the catechetical system described was still in effect in Isidore's day. That it had already been discontinued is a certainty according to Victor Saxer, *Les rites d'initiation chrétienne du IIe au VIe siècles: Esquisse historique et signification d'après leur principaux témoins* (Spoleto: Centro Italiano di Studi sull'Alto Medioevo, 1988), 452–58, 464, 532–57.

33. Isidore of Seville, *Las historias de los godos, vándalos y suevos de Isidoro de Sevilla* 60, ed. and trans. Cristobál Rodríguez Alonso (Léon: Centro de Estudios y Investigación "San Isidoro," 1975), 270–72: "Sisebutus ... initio regni Iudaeos ad fidem Christianam permovens aemulationem quidem habuit, sed non secundum scientiam: potestate enim conpulit, quos provocare fide ratione opportuit, sed per scriptum est, sive per occasionem sive per veritatem donec Christus adnuntiatur." On this point, see Pierre Cazier, "De la coercition à la persuasion: L'attitude d'Isidore de Séville face à la politique anti-juive des souverains visigothiques," in *De l'antijudaïsme antique à l'antisémitisme contemporain*, ed. Valentin Nikiprowetsky (Lille: Presses Universitaires de Lille, 1979), 125–46 on pages 126–27; idem, *Isidore de Séville et la naissance de l'Espagne catholique* (Paris: Beauchesne, 1994), 51–57; Jacques Fontaine, *Isidore de Séville: Genèse et originalité de la culture hispanique au temps des wisigoths* (Turnhout: Brepols, 2000), 132, 140, 229.

34. Isidore of Seville, *Sententiae* 1.16.3, ed. Pierre Cazier, CCSL 111 (Turnhout: Brepols, 1998), 55: "Sancta ecclesia catholica sicut male viventes in se patientes tolerat, ita mala creden-

Who are these people with bad beliefs? Isidore stigmatizes "those who have passed from idolatry into Judaism or heresy; ... they have moved from the error of infidelity to yet another error."[35] Here, he lumps Judaism and heresy together. But in another passage, he describes Jews as having two distinctions not shared by other infidels. They are sons of Abraham, on account of their descent. They are also sons of the devil, on account of their behavior.[36] While, in a way, any religious hypocrite can be called "Antichrist,"[37] in the age of the Antichrist to come, "the synagogue will fight against the church still more savagely than it persecuted her when the Savior Himself came."[38]

Isidore stresses the efficacy of baptism in removing original sin from all who receive it.[39] Faith is required for true felicity. And under no circumstances is faith to be coerced. Rather, it is to be induced by reason and example. For faith does not last in those violently constrained, on the analogy of "a young tree whose top, pushed over by force, springs back when the pressure is released."[40] For, "just as man, created with free will, turns away from God voluntarily, so also he returns to Him, believing because of his own conversion of mind. By his own voluntary choice he manifests his freedom of will. And so, having accepted the truth of the faith, he receives the benefit of grace."[41] In his final words on this subject in the *Sententiae*, Isidore observes that God scrutinizes men's hearts. He knows what they truly believe. Thus, "men cannot be excused who profess with their mouths a truth which they fake, retaining impious error in their hearts."[42] This as-

tes se repellit." There is also an edition of this text by Francesco Trisoglio (Brescia: Editiones Morcelliana, 2008) with readings slightly different from those of Cazier. We cite Cazier's edition here and in what follows.

35. Isidore, *Sent.* 1.16.5, ed. Cazier, 59: "Qui ab idolatria ad iudaismum vel heresem transeunt ... de infidelitas errore in errorem alium transierunt."

36. Ibid., 1.16.7, 59.

37. Ibid., 1.25.1, 79

38. Ibid., 1.25.6, 80: "contra ecclesiam desaeviet synagoga quam in ipso adventu salvatoris christianus est persecuta."

39. Ibid., 1.22.1–4, 73–74.

40. Ibid., 2.2.1–4, 94: quotation at 2.2.4: "Fides nequaquam vi extorquetur, sed ratione atque exemplis saudetur. Quibus autem exigitur violenter, perseverare in eis non potest: exemplo, ut ait quidam, novellae arboris cuius si quisque cacumen violenter inpresserit, denuo, dum laxatur, in id quod fuerat confestim revertitur."

41. Ibid., 2.2.5, 94: "Sicut homo libero arbitrio conditus, sua sponte divertit a Deo, ita ex propria mentis conversione credendo recurrit ad Deum, ut et libertas agnoscitur arbitrii per proprium voluntatem, et beneficium gratiae per acceptam fidei veritatem."

42. Ibid., 2.2.6, 95: "In corde respicit Deus fidem, ubi se non possunt homines excusare qui ore simulant veritatis professionem, et corde retentant erroris inpietatem."

sertion suggests that forced baptisms will yield fictive baptisms, but Isidore does not pursue that theme.

The dissonance among the aforementioned statements is enhanced by the fact that the *Sententiae* is a collection of individual opinions which Isidore supports rather than a treatise presenting a coherent argument. As a consequence, a number of conflicting positions can be and were supported with references to this work: the notion that faith cannot be compelled but requires intellectual conviction and the voluntary response of converts to God's grace; the efficacy of baptism, regardless of the condition of the person who receives it; the requirement that all baptizands be constrained to observe the faith; the expulsion from the church of those with an erroneous faith; the grouping together of heretics and Jews; the singling out of Jews for both praise and blame. There are echoes in the *Sententiae* of Gregory the Great's strictures against the forced baptism of Jews as wrong in itself and as likely to produce recidivism but no trace of Augustine's preservationist theology. Isidore's attitude toward the Jews in this work is and remains inconsistent—a point noted but not accounted for by commentators on it.[43]

This is the assortment of ideas on Jews and Judaism which Isidore brought to the presidency of Toledo IV. While historians agree that he dominated its proceedings and that its decrees reflect his priorities, they disagree on what those priorities were: reform of the Spanish clergy;[44] defense of the church against Arians and pagans;[45] opposition to all non-Catholics, especially Arians and recidivists;[46] equal-opportunity opposition to Arians and Jews;[47] a program of national unification in which the indigestibility of the Jews loomed larger than the problem of Arianism;[48] or implacable hostility toward Judaism, period.[49]

We can assess the chief concerns of the council fathers by turning to

43. Cazier, *Isidore de Séville*, 53–57, 253–57, 266.

44. Cazier, "De la coercition à la persuasion," 128–46.

45. Ibid.

46. Hans-Joachim Diesner, *Isidor von Sevilla und seine Zeit* (Stuttgart: Calwer Verlag, 1973), 37–39.

47. Cazier, *Isidore de Séville*, 257–62.

48. Jacques Fontaine, "Conversion et culture chez les wisigoths d'Espagne," in *Conversione al cristianesimo nell'Europa dell'alto medioevo*, Settimane di Studio del Centro Italiano di Studi sull'Alto Medioevo 14 (Spoleto: Centro Italiano de Studi sull'Alto Medioevo, 1967), 87–147; reprt. in idem, *Culture et spiritualité en Espagne du IVe au VIIe siècle* (London: Variorum Reprints, 1986), no. V.

49. Bat-Sheva Albert, "Isidore of Seville: His Attitude toward Judaism and His Impact on Early Medieval Canon Law," *Jewish Quarterly Review* 80 (1990): 207–20 on pages 208–12.

the decrees of Toledo IV themselves. After a prologue accenting clerical discipline, the observance of canon law, the purging of abuses, the enforcement of neglected customs, and the correct administration of the sacraments,[50] seventy-five canons follow. An early statement lays down the procedures to be observed at church councils.[51] Arianism is not named in this document and references to it are oblique, found in the council's affirmation of orthodox Trinitarian and Christological doctrine[52] and here and there in rules pertaining to the liturgy and the conduct of the clergy, topics found in the fifty-three canons that make up the bulk of the text.[53]

Canons 57 through 66 deal specifically with the Jews. One of these canons also contains a veiled reference to the Arians. Canon 57 spells out the Jewish policy to be followed from 633 onward: "Regarding the Jews, the holy council prescribes that none of them henceforth is to be forced to believe; ... for they will be saved willingly, not unwillingly, so that perfect justice is observed." For, the council fathers explain, "just as man perished through his own free will by obeying the serpent, so, called by the grace of God, he will be saved by believing through the conversion of his own mind. Thus, they are to be persuaded not by violence but voluntarily, by free will. They are not to be forced." Yet, as Canon 57 continues, the council fathers also rule that Jews who had been forcibly converted during the reign of Sisebut and had received baptism, chrism, and the body and blood of Christ should be constrained to observe the Christian faith: "They must be held to the faith even if they received it by force and necessity, lest the name of the Lord be blasphemed and the faith which they received be held vile and contemptible."[54]

The council fathers are aware that forced baptism is likely to lead to hypocrisy and recidivism. They seek to punish, and to forestall, these problems. Jews who have been baptized, forcibly or not, are to have nothing to

50. Toledo IV prologue, in *Concilios visigóticos e hispano-romanos*, ed. José Vives, España cristiana 1 (Barcelona/Madrid: Consejo Superior de Investigaciones Científicas, 1963), 186–87.

51. Ibid., can. 3–4, 188–90.

52. Ibid., can. 1, 187–88.

53. Ibid., can. 2, 5–56, 188, 190–210.

54. Ibid., can. 57, 210–11; quotations on page 210: "De iudaeis hoc praecipit sancta synodus nemini deinceps ad credendum vim inferre; ... non enim tales inviti salvandi sunt sed volentes, ut integra sit forma iustitiae"; and on page 211: "Sicut enim homo proprii arbitrii voluntati serpenti obediens periit, sic vocante gratia Dei propriae mentis conversione homo quisque credendo salvatur. Ergo non vi sed liberi arbitrii voluntati suadendi sunt non potius inpellendi"; "oportet ut fidem etiam quam vi vel necessitate susciperunt tenere cogantur, ne nomen Domini blasphemetur, et fidem quam susceperunt vilis ac contemptibilis habeatur."

do with recidivists or with the unconverted.[55] The testimony of recidivist Jews in secular cases is ruled unacceptable.[56] Severe penalties are to be imposed on converts who remain crypto-Jews. If they fail to abandon their old faith when exhorted by their bishops, their children are to be taken from them and reared as Christians in convents and monasteries. Although the recidivist parents are not to be deprived of most of their property, any slaves whom they had circumcised are to be freed.[57]

Toledo IV also imposes penalties on unconverted Jews. If a Jewish man marries a Christian woman, or a Christian man marries a Jewish woman, their children are to be raised in the faith of the Christian spouse.[58] Neither Jews nor their descendants are henceforth to hold public office or to buy, own, or receive Christian slaves. Any such slaves are to be freed.[59] There is one other canon pertaining to Jews which suggests the council fathers' belief that Judaism is serving as a proxy for Arian dissent. Canon 58 states that Spanish Christians, from bishops to priests to the laity, have gone over to Antichrist, as the document puts it, giving aid and comfort to the enemies of the church: "Many of these have rejected their [Christian] inheritance and have fallen into the pit of Jewish perfidy, lured by monetary gain."[60] Whether this claim is based on fact or fancy, Canon 58 appears early in the section of decrees on the Jews, offered as putative grounds for the punitive canons which follow. The restrictions which the council fathers place on the Jews may also be a backhanded attack on these presumptively Judaizing Christian apostates.

Although it is less extensive than the section of conciliar decrees dealing with the liturgy and clerical discipline, the next group of rulings, Canons 67 through 74, treats slavery in some detail and episcopal duties in that area.[61] Then follows a general, and lengthy, admonition. All are adjured to support and to implement the council's decrees. Canon 75 stresses the duty to avoid perjury on the part of the document's own subscribers. This final canon also underscores the duty to avoid *lèse majesté*. Under this heading, it lists the crimes of court intrigue, civil discord, and royal assassination. The council fathers do not hesitate to name the names of likely perpetrators of these delicts and to anathematize them prophylactically, and no doubt pro-

55. Ibid., can. 62, 212.

56. Ibid., can. 64, 213.

57. Ibid., can. 59–61, 211–12.

58. Ibid., can. 63, 213.

59. Ibid., can. 65–66, 213–14.

60. Ibid., can. 58, 211: "multi quippe huisque ... accipientes a iudeis munera perfidiam eorum patricinio suo foveant...."

61. Ibid., can. 67–74, 214–17.

phetically, before concluding with the signatures of the clerical participants of Toledo IV.[62]

That this council contains anti-Jewish legislation is incontestable. Also incontestable are the principled defense of free will and the proscription of future forced baptisms. At the same time, the forced baptisms already administered are ruled valid and binding. Their recipients are constrained to practice Christianity and to transmit it to their children. Recidivism bears with it harsh penalties. Given the relative amount of space devoted to Jews in this document, not to mention its inconsistencies in treating them, this subject seems to have been less compelling to the council fathers than the liturgy, clerical discipline, and, for that matter, slavery. It is also difficult to ignore the overtly political message with which Toledo IV ends. It contains a clear recognition that these conciliar decrees are likely to meet the political opposition which they in fact received in the sequel. In the event, the on-again off-again character of the enforcement of the policies of the Visigothic rulers of church and state alike renders moot in practice the efficacy of the anti-Jewish canons of Toledo IV. But, while this council may not have had a clear influence on later Visigothic history, its canons, like the ambiguous opinions of Isidore of Seville on the Jews, remained available for citation. Historians who have tracked their influence later in the Middle Ages have emphasized their anti-Jewish components. As they see it, the legacy of Visigothic Spain on forced baptism was limited to Jews and its impact was to perpetuate the policy of Sisebut.[63] We will be able to test this interpretation in the rest of chapter 3 of this study.

62. Ibid., can. 75, 217–25.

63. Paul Séjourné, *Saint Isidore de Séville, son rôle dans l'histoire du droit canonique* (Paris: Gabriel Beauchesne, 1929), 254–55; August Edward Anspach, "Das Fortleben Isidors im VII. bis IX. Jahrhundert," in *Miscellanea Isidoriana: Homenaje a S. Isidoro de Sevilla en el XIII centenario de su muerte*, ed. La Provincia de Andalusia S.J. (Rome: Typis Pontificae Gregorianae, 1936), 323–56; Bernhard Bischoff, "Die europäische Verbreitung des Werke Isidors von Sevilla," in *Isidoriana*, ed. Manuel Díaz y Díaz (Léon: Centro de Estudios "San Isidoro," 1961), 317–44; Albert, "Isidore of Seville," 216–20; Jacques Fontaine, "La figure d'Isidore de Séville dans le monde carolingien," in *L'Europe héritière de l'Espagne wisigothique*, ed. Jacques Fontaine (Madrid: Casa de Velázquez, 1992), 195–211. On the influence of Visigothic precedents in Carolingian thought, see also Mayke de Jong, "Adding Insult to Injury: Julian of Toledo and the *Historia Wambae*," in *The Visigoths from the Migration Period to the Seventh Century*, ed. Peter J. Heather (Woodbridge, UK: Boydell Press, 1999), 373–402; eadem, *The Penitential State: Authority and Atonement in the Age of Louis the Pious, 814–840* (Cambridge: Cambridge University Press, 2009), 144–45; Cullen J. Chandler, "A New View of a Catalonian *Gesta contra Iudaeos*: Ripoll 106 and the Jews of the Spanish March," in *Discovery and Distinction in the Early Middle Ages: Studies in Honor of John J. Contreni*, ed. Cullen J. Chandler and Steven A. Stofferahn (Kalamazoo: Medieval Institute Publications, 2013), 187–204.

For most scholars of European Jewry whose specialties take them beyond the early Middle Ages, the game-changer in the history of forced baptism was neither the influence of Toledo IV nor that of Isidore of Seville but the First Crusade. They emphasize the non-enforcement of the council's decrees, the sketchy incidence of actual forced baptisms of Jews in Spain or anywhere else in early medieval Europe, and the substantial evidence of the integration of Jews into Christian society before the late eleventh century. France and especially the Rhineland cities of Germany yield most of this documentation. Yet, as is well known, it was in precisely those areas that unlicensed preaching of the First and Second Crusades made Jews in these episcopal cities the targets of Christian hostility. They were subjected to forced baptism and faced with death or expulsion if they resisted. Some of the bishops of these cities denounced such actions as violations of canon law. In some cases, they, and the Jews' Christian neighbors, tried to protect them against the crusaders. Starting with Henry IV, German emperors issued edicts condemning the forced baptism of Jews and issued charters defending and reinstating them. It has to be said, however, that episcopal and imperial interventions were often ineffective or came too late. These leaders were embroiled in the politics of the investiture controversy and the papal-imperial feuds which consumed their energies. The debate now current among historians is whether the option of death or the font was imposed merely by hooligans, undisciplined hordes fueled by unofficial Crusade preachers, or whether the participants included professional soldiers and high-profile aristocrats. Wherever they come down on that issue, they agree that its net result was to intensify Christian hatred of the Jews. Jews came to be attacked not just out of jealousy and greed, not just for their actual theology and practice, but also for fantastic anti-Christian behaviors of which they were increasingly accused in the later Middle Ages.[64] Both the escalation of alleged Jewish malefaction and of

64. Good guides to the extensive historiography on this subject include Jonathan Riley-Smith, "The First Crusade and the Persecution of the Jews," in *Persecution and Toleration*, ed. W. J. Sheils (Oxford: Basil Blackwell, 1984), 51–72, who sees discontinuities with previous anti-Jewish activities and who accents the role of high-status participants; Friedrich Lotter, "'Tod oder Taufe': Das Problem der Zwangstaufen während des Ersten Kreutzzugs," in *Juden und Christen zur Zeit der Kreutzzüge*, ed. Alfred Haverkamp (Sigmaringen: Jan Thorbeke Verlag, 1999), 107–52, who notes that the continued existence and vitality of Jewish populations in the Rhineland suggests their limited effects; and Alfred Haverkamp, "Baptized Jews in Germany during the Twelfth Century," in *Jews and Christians in Twelfth-Century Europe*, ed. Michael Signer and John Van Engen (Notre Dame: University of Notre Dame Press, 2001), 255–310, with an excellent bibliography.

forced baptisms and other persecutions, on which a new chapter opened in Barcelona in 1391, are beyond the remit of this book. But, as we will see, whether they supported or dissented from these policies, Christian thinkers within our target period continued to discuss, and to disagree on, the forced baptism of Jews and of other non-Christians.

Preaching with an Iron Tongue: The Carolingians

Indeed, between the ninth and the early fourteenth centuries, the majority of non-Christians forced into the font were not Jews but Europe's indigenous pagans. Many of these groups did not adopt writing until after their Christianization. The reconstruction of their beliefs and attitudes depends on Christian accounts, amplified by the findings of archeology, numismatics, and in some cases the later redaction of oral traditions. While in some parts of Europe romantics later monumentalized pagan resistors as national heroes, their own local version of Vercingetorix, modern scholarship generally eschews a lachrymose chronicle approach to this history. As we have noted, pagans were not subjected to forced baptism in Christian Rome, or in the early Germanic successor states. A massive change in policy was initiated by Charlemagne. While he and his successors are renowned for their educational reforms, the Carolingian Renaissance did not make specific provisions for the catechizing of adults before their baptism. In this area, the Carolingians perpetuated Merovingian practice, or non-practice, the patristic catechumenate being long gone in Gaul by the sixth century. The well-known data found in penitentials and sermon literature testify to the superficiality of the faith imparted to the Franks' pagan converts.[65]

There is a vivid snapshot of the Merovingian approach to the induction of pagans inherited by the Carolingians in Gregory of Tours's famous account of the conversion of Clovis. As Gregory relates, the king repeatedly mocks the importunings of his Christian wife Clotild, castigating her and her God for the deaths of the couple's first two infant sons, on whose baptism she insists. Then, when his battle with the Alemanni goes badly and Clovis receives no help from his pagan gods, he decides to give Christ a try, and defeats his enemies. As Gregory observes, Clovis "was forced by necessity to accept what he had refused by his own free will."[66] When he returns

65. Saxer, *Les rites d'initiation chrétienne*, 526–29.

66. Gregory of Tours, *Hist.* 2.29–2.30, 60–61; quotation at 2.30 on page 61: "donec tandem aliquando bellum contra Alamannos commoveretur in quo conpulsus est confiteri necessitate,

home with this news, Clotild bids Remigius, bishop of Reims, "to impart the word of salvation to the king," in private. This theological instruction is as sketchy as it is brief. All it involves is the substitution of the Christian God, creator of heaven and earth, for Clovis's pagan gods. Clovis assents to this minimal norm, provided that his followers accept baptism as well. And so it was done. No sooner was Clovis received at the font, "like a new Constantine," in case readers have failed to get the point, than "more than three thousand of his army were baptized at the same time."[67]

Several features of this passage invite comment. Gregory presents Clovis as making a choice, although it is one impelled by military necessity. He assents to Christ as the lord of battles. Gregory editorializes neither on this fact nor on the exiguousness of the catechesis he receives from Remigius. The theology he mentions would not distinguish Christianity from any other form of monotheism, including heresies such as Arianism. And this, despite the fact that Gregory also reports the simultaneous reception of two sisters of Clovis who had earlier succumbed to Arianism.[68] No reference is made to any instruction of Clovis's troops. Whatever they may have believed, one thing they knew for certain was that it was perilous to gainsay their leader. The requital for insubordination was exemplary, brutal, and terminal. If Clovis was brought to the font by military necessity, the baptism *en masse* of his followers reflected military necessities of their own. Neither of these conditions problematizes these baptisms for Gregory of Tours.

The military necessities of the Saxons on whom Charlemagne made war starting in the 770s were of a different kind. Forced baptism was his weapon of choice whenever he defeated them, in a series of increasingly bloody campaigns which eventually involved mass slaughter and deportation. The Saxons, in turn, repudiated their forced baptism when circumstances allowed. As Kenneth Scott Latourette sums up the opening of this new chapter of church history, "So far as we know, never before had the adherence of any people to the Christian faith been brought about by quite so drastic a use of the mailed fist and with so much blood-letting among reluctant pagans.... We shall find the procedure repeated again and again

quod prius voluntate negavarit." Translation: Gregory of Tours, *History of the Franks*, trans. Lewis Thorpe (Harmondsworth: Penguin, 1974), 143.

67. Gregory, *Hist.* 2.31, 62–63; quotations on page 62: "Tunc regina arcessire clam sanctum Remigium Remensis urbis episcopum iubet ut regi verbum salutis insinuaret"; "procedit novus Constantinus ad lavacrum"; and on page 63: "De exercito vero eius baptizati sunt amplius tria mila." Translation: Thorpe, 143.

68. Gregory, *Hist.* 2.31, 63.

in the thousand years between the eighth and the nineteenth century."[69] While some historians have looked for links with Merovingian anti-heresy propaganda, or even to traditions harking back to the Old Testament,[70] most commentators second Latourette. Charlemagne's decisive substitution of coercion for the prescriptions of canon law placed Christian missionary activity on a new and violent path, one on which he was joined by the majority of Carolingian writers.[71]

It took Charlemagne over thirty years to make the forced baptisms of the Saxons permanent. One reason why this effort proved so intractable was that the Saxons were not politically united. No single leader could speak for the whole Saxon community, in contrast with other pagan groups whose kings could and did negotiate with the Carolingians and make binding decisions for their peoples. The latter option proved particularly useful in regions where the Roman and Greek churches competed for converts. Timely concession to Charlemagne could mean the swift rehabilitation of kings as quasi-independent dukes within his empire with little loss of their real power, bonds sweetened by Carolingian marriage alliances. No such opportunities existed for the Saxons. They were organized in small tribal subgroups whose leaders spoke only for them. In any case, defeat in a given fighting season, and the forced baptism it imposed, were seen as circumstantial, subject to reversal if victory replaced defeat, or of rebellion succeeded, in the following season. Whether or not there is sufficient evidence to characterize the Saxons as freedom fighters defending a "popular constitution," both they and the Carolingians saw the upshot of battle as

69. Latourette, *History of the Expansion of Christianity*, 2:105; on the Saxon mission more widely, ibid., 2:102–6.

70. Lawrence G. Duggan, "'For Force Is Not of God'? Compulsion and Conversion from Yahweh to Charlemagne," in *Varieties of Religious Conversion in the Middle Ages*, ed. James Muldoon (Gainesville: University of Florida Press, 1997), 49–62; Matthew Innes, "'Immune from Heresy': Defining the Boundaries of Carolingian Christianity," in *Frankland: The Franks and the World of the Early Middle Ages. Essays in Honour of Dame Jinty Nelson*, ed. Paul Fouracre and David Ganz (Manchester: Manchester University Press, 2008), 101–28. Cf. Yitzhak Hen, "Charlemagne's Jihad," *Viator* 37 (2006): 33–51 on pages 45–51, who sees this ideology as deriving from Visigothic Spain via Theodulph of Orléans.

71. Richard E. Sullivan, "Carolingian Missionary Theories," *Catholic Historical Review* 42 (1956): 273–95; Bernard Walter Scholz, intro. to his trans. of *Carolingian Chronicles* (Ann Arbor: University of Michigan Press, 1970), 1–11, 14; Ruth Mazo Karras, "Pagan Survivals and Syncretism in the Conversion of Saxony," *Catholic Historical Review* 72 (1986): 553–72 on pages 554–55; Carine van Rhijn, *Shepherds of the Lord: Priests and Episcopal Statutes in the Carolingian Period* (Turnhout: Brepols, 2007), 113; Rosamond McKitterick, *Charlemagne: The Formation of a European Identity* (Cambridge: Cambridge University Press, 2008), 251–56, 278, whose notes give full and up-to-date references to the relevant primary and secondary sources.

the acceptance, or rejection, of forced baptism as a feature of the victor's political arrangements.[72]

Also relevant to the understanding of this Carolingian policy, and the Saxons' acquiescence when constrained to undergo it, is the contemporary attitude toward public rituals of abasement. This phenomenon has been studied with respect to the public penance or enforced monastic profession of those bested politically. The person on the receiving end was conventionally represented as assenting voluntarily to the rite. Regardless of the real intentions of the participants, the correct performance of the ritual was a means of conflict resolution, saving face on all sides. This is not to say that the idea of hypocrisy was unknown. But a person's external actions were held to be an adequate index of his internal dispositions, and indeed, as helping to shape them. Further, ritual action could be undone, by a reverse ritual, if the situation changed. As Mayke de Jong puts the point, à propos of forced monastic profession, "While the notion of religious commitment being a matter of choice had not been relinquished, in Carolingian society, its definition of 'voluntary' entry into the cloister differed vastly from the original ideals of monasticism. If personal choice was not in evidence, it could be created by persuasion, or if need be, under duress."[73] The Carolingians may have regarded baptism as an irreversible, once-in-a-lifetime event, a ritual that could not be undone, unlike penance or monastic profession. This distinction was lost on the Saxons. But one thing both groups agreed on was that forced baptism did not necessarily involve religious conversion. What it did involve was a shift in political power relations. Conversion, if any, came after the fact. And, like baptism itself, it was occasioned

72. Robert Bartlett, "From Paganism to Christianity," in *Christianization and the Rise of Christian Monarchy: Scandinavia, Central Europe, and Rus' c. 900–1200*, ed. Nora Berend (Cambridge: Cambridge University Press, 2007), 47–72 on pages 66–67; quotation on page 66; Guy Halsall, *Barbarian Migrations and the Roman West, 376–568* (Cambridge: Cambridge University Press, 2007), 390; Wickham, *The Inheritance of Rome*, 378–80, with a useful comparison with the Carolingian incorporation of Bavaria. On the comparison with Bavaria, see also Warren C. Brown, *Unjust Seizure: Conflict, Interest, and Authority in an Early Medieval Society* (Ithaca, NY: Cornell University Press, 2001), who accents ways in which the Bavarians manipulated Carolingian agents and institutions in their own interest. An even stronger comparison exists in eastern European areas where the Carolingians competed with the Byzantines, on which see Nora Berend, Jósef Lazlovsky, and Béla Zsolt Szakács, "The Kingdom of Hungary," in *Christianization*, ed. Berend (as previously mentioned), 319–68.

73. Mayke de Jong, *In Samuel's Image: Child Oblation in the Early Medieval West* (Leiden: Brill, 1996), 256–66; quotation on pages 263–64; for an extended application of this idea to forced public penance and its reversal, see eadem, *The Penitential State*, passim and esp. 42–44, 52, 260–66.

by force. As the Paderborn anonymous remarks from his vantage point in the late ninth century, Charlemagne's missionary strategy "opened the gates of faith, preaching, as it were, with an iron tongue."[74]

The Paderborn anonymous is a Saxon cleric whose enthusiasm for this evangelical method receives support from other Carolingian observers. It is not Franks alone who share his opinion. In a poem on the Saxon wars (780s) attributed to Lul, the Anglo-Saxon bishop of Mainz, the author, denouncing the Saxons as "this obstinate nation" of devil-worshippers,[75] lauds Charlemagne for his bloodthirsty campaign. The emperor fought as the lieutenant in the field of Christ, ruler of the universe, conscripting new subjects into obeisance before His throne.[76] The author makes no reference to Christian doctrine or, for that matter, either to the Saxons' forced baptism or to their repudiation of it.

The author of this poem makes use of the *Frankish Royal Annals,* rewritten several times before the end of the ninth century. Unsurprisingly, they give a royalist account of the Saxon wars conducted between 775 and 804. From the beginning, as the annalists have it, the Saxons are treacherous treaty-breakers. This is what persuades Charlemagne to invade their territory, in requital. From the start, his goal is to Christianize or exterminate them. Forced baptism is a suitable penalty for Saxon perfidy. The Saxons are in the wrong and are themselves to blame for the punishment they receive.[77] This scenario repeats itself in 776, 777, 782, 785, and 794: The Saxons revolt. They are defeated. They are forced into the font, again. They pledge loyalty to Charlemagne, again. Then, they rebel, again. In 782 Charlemagne punishes the rebels by slaughtering four thousand of them at a blow. In 794

74. *Translatio S. Liborii* 5, ed. Georg Heinrich Pertz, MGH Scriptores 4 (Hannover: Hahn, 1891; reprt. Stuttgart: Anton Hieresmann, 1981), 151: "ut ianuam fidei aperiret, ferrea quodammodo lingua praedicavit." Noted by Karras, "Pagan Survivals," 555.

75. Lul (?), *Carmen de conversione Saxonum* 2.23–37, ed. Karl Hauck in *Karolingische Taufpfalzen im Spiegel hofnaher Dichtung: Überlieferung zur Ausmalung von Pfalzkirchen, Pfalzen und Reichsklöstern*, Nachrichten der Akademie der Wissenschaften in Göttingen 1: Philologisch-historische Klasse 1 (Göttingen: Vandenhoeck & Rupprecht, 1985), 62–64; quotation at 2.37, on page 63: "Hoc genus indocile." On pagans generally described as devil-worshippers, see Innes, "'Immune from Heresy,'" 110; this note tends to supersede the idea of pagans as "dogs" accented by Geneviève Bührer-Thierry, "Des païens comme chiens dans le monde germanique et slave du haut moyen âge," in *Impies et païens entre antiquité et moyen âge*, ed. Lionel Mary and Michael Sot (Paris: Picard, 2002), 176–87.

76. *Carmen de conversione Saxonum* 2.40–55, 63–64; see the commentary by Hauck in ibid., 43, 90–92, and that by Peter Godman, *Poets and Emperors: Frankish Politics and Carolingian Poetry* (Oxford: Clarendon Press, 1987), 41–90.

77. *Royal Annals*, in *Carolingian Chronicles*, trans. Scholz, 51.

Charlemagne realizes—belatedly, it would seem—that the forcibly baptized Saxons have no intention of observing Christianity, or any of their other promises. So, finally, in 804, after that year's defeat of the Saxons, Charlemagne depopulates the region by deporting those still standing to Francia and giving their lands to the Obdorites.[78]

While the royal annalists tell this story with no glimmer of reconciliation at its end, Einhard's *Life of Charlemagne* (817/30) takes a different approach. Einhard draws on the annalists and also presents the Saxons as fierce, obdurate, and untrustworthy devil-worshippers; "they did not judge it dishonorable to violate and traduce all law human and divine."[79] But he offers another reason why the Saxons were so hard to conquer: topography. Aside from a few forests and mountain ranges, Saxony is open country. No natural boundaries separate it from Frankish territory. Thus, there were many cross-border raids on both sides. This behavior was not unique to the Saxons.[80] Despite the fact that blame cannot be placed unilaterally on the Saxons, Einhard supports Charlemagne's decision to eliminate this unstable frontier.[81] The reason it took so long despite the emperor's resolve was the repeated perfidy of the Saxons. In response, Charlemagne exacted "a worthy penalty"—mass slaughter and deportation.[82] This punishment was merited, and it worked. It brought the protracted struggle to an end: "After such a longstanding war, the conflict was finally settled. Abandoning the worship of demons and their ancestral rites, they accepted the faith and sacraments of the Christian religion. And they were united with the Franks, making them a single people."[83]

78. Ibid., 55, 56, 61, 63, 73, 83. Latin text for the mass slaughter of 782: *Annales regni Francorum*, ed. Friedrich Kurtze, MGH Scriptores rerum germanicorum in usum scholarum 6 (Hannover; Hahn, 1895), 58–59. For the rewritings, revisions, and incorporation of material from other sources into these accounts, with editions and secondary literature on that topic, see Helmut Reimitz, "*Omnes Franci*: Identification and Identities of the Early Medieval Franks," in *Franks, Northmen, and Slavs: Identities and State Formation in Early Medieval Europe*, ed. Ildar H. Garipzanov, Patrick J. Geary, and Przemsyław Urbańczyk (Turnhout: Brepols, 2008), 51–68.

79. Einhard, *Vie de Charlemagne* 7, 2nd ed., ed. and trans. Louis Halphen (Paris: Les Belles Lettres, 1936), 22: "neque divina neque humana jura vel polluere vel transgredi inhonestum arbitrantur."

80. Ibid., 22.

81. Ibid., 24.

82. Ibid., 24–26; quotation on page 24: "misso exercitu perfidiam eorum ulcisceretur et dignam ab eis poenam exigeret...."

83. Ibid., 26: "per tot annos bellum constat esse finitum ut, abiecto daemonum cultu et relictis patriis caerimoniis, christianae fidei atque religionis sacramenta susciperent et Francis adnunati unus cum eis populus efficerentur."

It was only at the end of Einhard's career that the Carolingians made a visible effort to catechize the forcibly baptized Saxons. A case in point is the first version of the *De corpore et sanguine Domini* (831/33) of Paschasius Radbertus, abbot of Corbie. He wrote in response to a request from a former student, Warin, abbot of Corvey, Corbie's Saxon daughter house. Warin sought a work that would help him teach orthodox Eucharistic doctrine to his monks and to the Saxons more generally. Paschasius complied, phrasing his text in an untechnical style, so as to appeal to youths and the unlettered. Other uses were put to his later, revised, version of the same text.[84]

Did initiatives of this kind lead the preaching of Christianity with an iron tongue to give way to less violent modes of evangelization? We have two Saxon witnesses who offer their own answers to this question. One is the aforementioned Paderborn anonymous. He observes that the bishop of Paderborn installed by Charlemagne developed his own tactics for evoking piety in the Saxons, the veneration of relics. The author's main subject is the translation to Paderborn of the relics of Liborius, a fourth-century saint of LeMans, along with those of other saints. In his view, this was a prudent move on the bishop's part. The miracle-working properties of these relics, even while enroute to Paderborn, persuaded the neophyte Saxons of the power of the Christian God.[85] Indeed, much of his text is devoted to listing these miracles, and to describing the impression made by the pomp and ceremony with which they were received and venerated.[86] The author makes no reference to any other effort to instruct the Paderborn Saxons in Christian doctrine.

Our second witness, known only as the Poeta Saxo, was a monk of Corvey. His *Annalium de gestis Caroli magni imperatoris libri quinque* (888/91) is a eulogy of scant literary merit.[87] But this work is more than a mere rehash of earlier sources. True, the author agrees that the pagan Saxons were ob-

84. Timothy R. LeCroy, "Catechetical Context: Reading Paschasius Radbertus' *De corpore et sanguine domine* in Light of the Carolingian Mission to the Saxons," paper delivered at the 45th International Congress of Medieval Studies, Kalamazoo, May 2010. I thank the author for permission to cite the pre-publication copy. For further literature on the circumstances of the writing of this work and its place in the Christianization of the Saxons, see Celia Chazelle, "The Eucharist in the Early Middle Ages," in *A Companion to the Eucharist in the Middle Ages*, ed. Ian Christopher Levy, Gary Macy, and Kristin Van Ausdell (Leiden: Brill, 2012), 204–49 on pages 205–11; for its role in later Carolingian debates on the Eucharist, ibid., 235–49.

85. *Translatio S. Liborii* 2–9, 149–52.

86. Ibid., 10–31, 153–57.

87. For judgments on the poem, see Mary E. McKinney, intro. to her trans. of *The Saxon Poet's Life of Charlemagne* (New York: Pageant Press, 1956), vii, 1–7; Godman, *Poets and Emperors*, 182–83.

durate and perfidious devil-worshippers, reneging time and time again on their political oaths and baptismal promises. He agrees with Einhard that prior to the outbreak of the Saxon wars, both Saxons and Franks conducted cross-border raids, ravaging each other's lands with fire and sword. But the precipitating event, which led to Charlemagne's retaliation and the conflict which took thirty-three years to resolve, was a Saxon invasion in 774.[88] If the Saxons were duplicitous, on the poet's account they also possessed an excellent intelligence network, enabling them to stage their incursions and revolts when Carolingian armies were engaged elsewhere. Charlemagne had the advantage not only of superior generalship but also of numbers, the ability to draw on troops from the many peoples who made up his empire. Another advantage, as the poet sees it, was the disunity of the Saxons, permitting a divide-and-conquer strategy. Unlike modern historians, he does not see Saxon political fragmentation as an impediment explaining why it took the Carolingians so long to win.[89]

Forced, and, as the poet relates, fictive baptism of the Saxons occurred frequently, starting in 776. "Simulating a faith in Christ, he received baptism,"[90] the poet says of one of the defeated leaders. His forebears, he laments, did not take baptism seriously, treating it as a temporary expedient. At the same time, the poet holds that forced baptism was a punishment that fit the crime. The Saxons brought forced baptism and their mass execution and deportation on their own heads.[91] In his account, the year 795 marked a shift in Carolingian tactics, the use of the preemptive strike. Grasping at length that the Saxons were untrustworthy, Charlemagne was proactive. He attacked them without waiting for their next rebellion.[92] Even as the poet presents Charlemagne's military policy as justified, he sees him as fair-minded. The poet outlines the terms of the capitulation treaty of 803 which ended the wars. All things considered, it was lenient. The Saxons were to accept Christianity, once and for all. They were to obey the clergy placed over them. They were to pay tithes, but no tribute. They were to be loyal to

88. Poeta Saxo, *Annalium de gestis Caroli magni imperatoris libri quinque* 1, year 774, ed. Georg Heinrich Pertz, MGH Scriptores 1 (Hannover: Hahn, 1826; reprt. Stuttgart: Anton Hiersemann, 1976), 230. There is also another version edited by Paul von Winterfield, MGH Poetae latini aevi carolini 4/1 (Berlin: Weidemann, 1899). The Pertz edition will be cited here. The point that the Saxons chose to open hostilities while Charlemagne's troops were engaged elsewhere recurs in just about every annual entry between 774 and 778 presented in Bk. 1, 230–36.

89. Ibid., 1, year 774, ed. Pertz, 230, 232.

90. For example, ibid., 1, year 780, 236: "credere se Christo simulans baptismum recepit."

91. Ibid., 2, years 782–785, 238–41.

92. Ibid., 2, year 795, 251.

the Frankish kings. In return, Saxony was granted the status of a federated political entity within the Carolingian empire. These provisions suggest that there were enough Saxons surviving to make this outcome plausible. Not only does the poet end this portion of his work by channeling Einhard's celebratory claim that the Franks and Saxons are now united as a single people, he refers readers to Einhard's *Life of Charlemagne* for further details.[93]

This happy conclusion far from exhausts what the poet wants to convey. In his last two books, he shifts from the annalistic to the panegyric mode. Having devoted many lines to Charlemagne's other virtues, he devotes Book 5 to the way the emperor Christianized the subjugated Saxons. The poet accepts that this process was, and had to be, forcible, at least at first. But force was later supplemented by a milder and more lasting policy: "What he [Charlemagne] achieved could not have been accomplished otherwise. For he moved the stony hearts of the Saxons to submit to the Lord in two ways, now with the terror of war, and now with gifts. In the use of the former, he was magnanimous; in the use of the latter, munificent."[94]

What were these gifts? The poet specifies the sending of clergy who were learned men, who brought with them both books and literacy, and who taught by their appealing moral example as well as by precept. They won Saxon minds and hearts. Albeit this soft evangelization came only in the reigns of Charlemagne's successors, the poet presents Charlemagne himself as the one to be lauded for the education so purveyed. It is not only the Saxon people as a whole who owe the emperor a vote of thanks but each individual Saxon, a thought inspiring the poet to segue to his own personal case:

> What gratitude do we all now have, and what can each individual express according to his own measure? If any tiny spark of letters or any small knowledge or art illuminate my mind, shall I not justly give Charles a eulogy of praise, since it was thanks to him that I was privileged to acquire this boon? Our parents were unacquainted not only with the documents of the faith but were completely ignorant of all that is written. Recently, through Charles, what is upright in this life, and the hope of life eternal, have been given to us.[95]

93. Ibid., 3, year 803, 260–61.

94. Ibid., 5, 267: "Id quod tunc aliter non potuit fieri. / Usus enim gemina, Saxonum saxea corda, / Arte, suadebat subdere se Domino, / Nunc terrens bello, nunc donis allicendo, / Ille magnanimus, hic quoque munificus."

95. Ibid., 5, 267–68; quotation on page 267: "Quas igitur grates illi modo possumus omnes, / Vel quas quisque suo solvere pro modulo? / Si qua meam scripturarum scintillula mentem / Artis, et illustrat si qua scientola, / Nonne debit iuste Carolo praecona laudum. / Per quem nanscisi tale bonum merui? / Nostri, non solum fide documenta parentes, / Sed penitus cunctos nescierant apices; / Per Carolum nuper nobis est huius honestas,/ Ac pariter vita spes data perpetuae."

There is much to ponder here beyond the modest author *topos*. The Christianity in which the poet rejoices is not conversion without belief. It is not a piety based on external ritual or miraculous relics. As he sees it, war and the forced baptism of the Saxons had to happen. But at the war's end, and despite the brutal measures that settled it, Charlemagne was generous. He made provision for true Christian education in doctrine and morals through clerical teachers worthy of emulation and the book-culture which they brought. Literacy, learning, and the arts hitherto unknown to the Saxons are not the least of these benefits, benefits which the author himself is grateful for having been granted. The poet recognizes, and regrets, the subterfuges of his forefathers at the font. He presents himself, and the Saxons of his day, as now adhering to a faith unfeigned. Given that the late ninth century in which he writes was an age of political infighting among the descendants of Charlemagne, the poet may well be exaggerating his people's political and religious loyalty. By attributing the success of the Saxon mission to Charlemagne and not to any of the later rulers, he may also be hedging his bets on which of the current horses to back. Even if the impact of Christian education was limited to monks like himself, the Poeta Saxo makes the best case he can for the efforts of the Carolingians to impart Christian doctrine and ethics to the Saxons whose ancestors they had forcibly baptized.

While the Christianizing of the Saxons reported so differently by the Poeta Saxo and the Paderborn anonymous occurred only after the faith had been preached with an iron tongue, an initial process which neither author condemns, there were also Carolingians opposed to *ex post facto* catechesis. A trope found in the *vitae* of many Carolingian saints is that they strove mightily to persuade pagans by the Gregorian sweetness of their preaching, no less than by their miracles and personal holiness.[96] As early as 796, Alcuin criticized Charlemagne's forced baptism of the Saxons and implored him not to extend the same policy to the Avars, an appeal to Louis the Pious seconded by Rabanus Maurus in his *De institutione clericorum* (816/19). Remonstrances by both of these leading churchmen went unheeded.[97]

96. Richard E. Sullivan, "The Carolingian Missionary and the Pagans," *Speculum* 28 (1953): 705–40 on pages 712–27; idem, "Carolingian Missionary Theories," 291–93.

97. Alcuin, *Epistolae* 111, ed. Ernst Dümmler, MGH Epistolae karolini aevi 4 (Hannover: Hahn, 1895), 161–64; Rabanus Maurus, *De institutione clericorum* 25–26, ed. Aloisius Knoepfler, Veröffentlichen aus dem kirchlichen Seminar München 5 (Munich: J. J. Lentner'schen Buchhandlung, 1900), 44–45. The best discussion is Steven A. Stofferahn, "Staying the Royal Sword: Alcuin and the Conversion Dilemma in Early Medieval Europe," *The Historian* 71 (2009):

Some historians argue that the letter addressed by Charlemagne to his archbishops in 812 requesting information on baptism in their provinces was aimed not at enforcing liturgical uniformity but at implementing Alcuin's advice.[98] What all commentators agree on is that the responses were quite diverse—in several respects.[99] Some archbishops responded themselves. Others delegated the chore to their bishops, some of whom delegated it in turn to their clergy. Some responses report current diocesan practice. Some cite the norms on the books, whether or not they were locally observed. Many of the respondents simply ransacked the libraries available to them for any and all information on baptism. They assembled their findings helter-skelter, making no distinctions among theological treatises, polemics, sermons, papal letters, conciliar decrees, liturgical *ordines*, and commentaries on the liturgy. In many cases, authors simply recycled the responses of those who had been first out of the gate in answering the emperor's letter. The authorship and provincial provenance of many of these responses are unclear. One of their striking features is that their authors often describe the baptizands of whom they speak as adult pagans who seek the font of their own free will, and who receive elaborate pre-baptismal catechetical instruction. Quite a few of those who do so name Isidore of Seville's *De ecclesiasticis officiis* as their source.[100] Among

461–80; see also Sullivan, "Carolingian Missionary Theories," 277–95; Latourette, *History of the Expansion of Christianity*, 2:106, 111; Christine Veyrard-Cosme, "Le paganisme dans l'oeuvre d'Alcuin," in *Impies et païens entre antiquité et moyen âge*, ed. Lionel Mary and Michael Sot (Paris: Picard, 2002), 127–53 on pages 127–34; Susan A. Keefe, ed., *Water and the Word: Baptism and the Education of the Clergy in the Carolingian Empire*, 2 vols. (Notre Dame: University of Notre Dame Press, 2002), 1:3–6, 19; she cites the text of Alcuin's letter at 1:4n.9 and 1:6n.6; J. D. C. Fisher, *Christian Initiation: Baptism in the Middle Ages. A Study of the Disintegration of the Primitive Rite of Initiation* (London: SPCK, 1965; reprt. Chicago: Hillenbrand Books, 2004), 64–65; Hen, "Charlemagne's Jihad," 42–44; Douglas Dales, *Alcuin: His Life and Legacy* (Cambridge: James Clark and Co., 2012), 102–6. Arnold Angenendt, *Das Frühmittelalter: Die abendländische Christenheit von 400 bis 900* (Stuttgart: Kohlhammer, 1990), 412–53, accents the political dimension of baptism for Rabanus as well as his emphasis on instruction and free will, as specific to his dispute over predestinarianism with Gottschalk of Orbais.

98. Glenn C. J. Byer, *Charlemagne and Baptism: A Study of Responses to the Circular Letter of 811/812* (Lanham, MD: International Scholars Publications, 1999), 34–39; Keefe, *Water and the Word*, 1:5–6.

99. Byer, *Charlemagne and Baptism*, 92–101, 113–64; Keefe, *Water and the Word*, 1:6–8, 13–155; van Rhijn, *Shepherds of the Lord*, 112–23; McKitterick, *Charlemagne*, 310–23. Peter Cramer, *Baptism and Change in the Early Middle Ages, c. 200–c. 1100* (Cambridge: Cambridge University Press, 1993), 164–69, 186–97, 200–206, agrees but accents the respondents' interest in symbolic, mystical, and apocalyptic aspects of the sacrament.

100. Keefe, *Water and the Word*, texts 1–4, 15A, 16, 22, 26, 32, 34–38, 44, 46–47, 51, 58, 2:156, 171, 185, 187, 188, 200, 272, 284, 336, 385, 440, 468–69, 480, 490, 517, 530, 534–35, 558, 566. Those citing Isidore are texts 1, 2, 4, 22, 34, 36, 2:156, 171, 200, 336, 468–69, 517.

other things, this evidence shows that the post-Visigothic legacy of Isidore of Seville on baptism was scarcely confined to his anti-Jewish views. As with Isidore himself, far from describing how adult pagans were actually brought to the font in their own day, these Carolingian respondents were citing earlier practices which had fallen out of use centuries ago. After he collected this dossier, there is no indication that Charlemagne made any effort to revive these bygone patristic practices. As with the fruitless advice of Alcuin and Rabanus Maurus, these responses remained a dead letter.

Only the Saxons?

This is not to say that there were no other non-Christians in the expanding Carolingian empire who could have been catechized before baptism, as Alcuin proposed for the Avars, or forcibly baptized and catechized later, along the lines suggested by the Paderborn anonymous or the Poeta Saxo. The Muslims who came under Charlemagne's sway after his conquest of the Spanish March were, potentially, one such group. The Franks made no attempt to convert them. Charlemagne established cordial relations with the caliph Haroun al-Raschid in Baghdad, which may have stayed his hand vis-à-vis his new Muslim subjects. In any case, aside from the kings of Hungary, neither the Franks nor any other medieval Christian rulers with Muslim subjects forced them into the font, except in imaginative literature. For the *Song of Roland*, whose eleventh-century redactor celebrates Charlemagne's exploits in Spain, ascribes this practice to him. After his victory over the Muslims at Saragossa, the epic relates, Charlemagne offers them the choice of baptism or death:

> No sorcery of false cult will remain there.
> The king believes in God, he wishes to serve Him,
> His bishops bless the water,
> They lead the pagans to the baptistry.
> Now if there is anyone who opposes Charles,
> He orders him to be taken prisoner, burned, or put to death.
> Well over a hundred thousand are baptized
> True Christians.[101]

101. *La Chanson de Roland* laisse 3665–3672, ed. and trans. Gerald J. Brault (University Park: Penn State University Press, 1984), 222–23: "N'i remeindiat ne sorz ne falserie. / Li reis creit Deu, faire voelt sun servise, / E si evesque les eves beneïssent / Meiuent paìen entresqu'al baptisterie. / S'or ad cel qui Carle cuntredie, / Il le fait prendre o ardier ou ocive. / Baptizet sunt asez plus de .c. milie / Veir chrestïen..." Translation: Brault, ibid., 223–25. Gerald J. Brault,

Another neighboring people who offered largely unavailing opportunities for Carolingian evangelization, by the iron tongue or otherwise, were the pagan Danes. Ninth-century Denmark was an emerging elective monarchy whose king gave occasional aid to the Saxon rebels during Charlemagne's wars in that region. While King Gotfred reinforced his own southern border with fortresses to repel Carolingian invasion, he and his successors did not hesitate to attack the Carolingians and their allies by land and sea. These incursions were sometimes punctuated by treaties, seen as buying time. Gotfred was deposed and a lengthy conflict broke out among his sons and other contenders for the throne. The Carolingians had no real hope of using this situation to promote a Danish war of conquest and Christianization. They sent missionaries to Denmark starting in 820, who were repulsed. As evidenced by their burial practices and the iconography of their coinage, the ninth-century Danes remained resolutely pagan and hostile to Christianity. This attitude is reflected not only in the behavior of Viking raiders but also within the Danes' home territories. Diplomacy, when it was conducted with the Carolingians, could be as much an expression of enmity as of friendship, or a means of gaining protection from or support against domestic opponents.[102]

That such was the case, and that it was misinterpreted by the Franks, emerges in the alliance in 826 between Louis the Pious and Harald Klak of

ed., *The Song of Roland: An Analytical Edition*, 3 vols. (University Park: Penn State University Press, 1978), 1:132, observes that the redactor may have been influenced by the anti-Muslim attitudes of the Crusades era. But Riley-Smith, "The First Crusade," 65–66 indicates that only one crusader in the Holy Land, Raymond Pilet, is known to have imposed baptism on his Muslim subjects, in the area south of Antioch; he is the exception who proves the rule. As is noted by Suzanne Conklin Akbari, *Idols of the East: European Representations of Islam and the Orient, 1100–1450* (Ithaca, NY: Cornell University Press, 2009), 208–10, the *Song of Roland*, unlike some later European vernacular literature, does not present any Muslim as a hero or as a voluntary convert to Christianity. Her point, on page 210, that death by burning is Charlemagne's alternative to forced baptism because it represents a more complete "erasure" of the victim than other modes of death, is an extrapolation from the text. Nor does it say whether any of Charlemagne's captives accepted death rather than the font. On the forced baptism of Muslims in medieval Christian Hungary, see Nora Berend, *At the Gate of Christendom: Jews, Muslims and 'Pagans' in Medieval Hungary, c. 1000–c. 1300* (Cambridge: Cambridge University Press, 2001), 237–38, 243.

102. On the political and religious situation in ninth-century Denmark, the kinds of evidence available, and the debates of historians on its interpretation, including the author's view that a united Danish monarchy arose in reaction to Frankish expansion, see Ildar H. Garipzanov, "Frontier Identities: Carolingian Frontier and the *gens Danorum*," in *Franks, Northmen, and Slavs: Identities and State Formation in Early Medieval Europe*, ed. Ildar H. Garipzanov, Patrick J. Geary, and Przemysław Urbańczyk (Turnhout: Brepols, 2008), 113–42.

Denmark. This event was celebrated, although its Danish backstory was unknown or ignored, by Ermoldus Nigellus in his poem on the deeds of Louis the Pious (814/40). As Ermoldus tells the tale, the initiative came from Louis, who offered baptismal sponsorship as a diplomatic inducement. Harald, his wife, and his son duly arrived in Mainz to receive baptism. The importance of this alliance was signaled by the luxury and splendor of the ceremony laid on by the Carolingians. Louis, the empress Judith, and their son Lothar stood as godparents to the Danish guests. They, and the notables present, wore their richest clothes and accoutrements. The rite took place with elaborate pomp. Ermoldus makes no mention of religious faith or instruction. Rather, the idea was to bedazzle the baptizands with the lavish gifts and honors bestowed on them in an over-the-top extravaganza. In the event, this baptism proved to be a gamble which both Louis and Harald lost. As the Danes knew at the time, and as Saxo Grammaticus later reports in his *Gesta Danorum* (1208/18), Harald was not the king of the Danes but a pretender to the throne. Both his quest for foreign alliance and his baptism enraged his domestic rivals. He was deposed, and apostatized in 827, and Louis lost the ephemeral Christian ally gained at the font at such great expense.[103]

Outcomes of the sort illustrated by Harald's career were not unusual in Scandinavia, where Christianity was not generally adopted until around the turn of the millennium. The acceptance of Christianity by the vote of equals in the Icelandic Althing in 1000 was a one-off in medieval Scandinavian history.[104] The settlers of Iceland had moved there to escape monarchical consolidation in their native Norway. Elsewhere in Scandinavia, both the imposition of Christianity and the reinstatement of paganism occurred repeatedly during the ninth and tenth centuries, policy shifts that were a function of power politics in the hands of emergent kings and their rivals. Amidst the civil strife that characterizes much of this political history, the rulers in the saddle at any particular point imposed their own religious

103. *Ermold le Noir: Poème sur Louis le Pieux et Épîtres au roi Pépin*, 2nd ed., ed. Edmond Faral (Paris: F. Champion, 1964), 176. A good discussion is provided by de Jong, *The Penitential State*, 33–40, 90, 94, 150, 184. Cf. the account in Saxo Grammaticus, *Gesta Danorum* 9.4.36–37, ed. J. Olvik and H. Raeder, 2 vols. (Copenhagen: Levin and Munksgaard, 1931–37), 1:261–62. Saxo sees Harald as having taken the initiative and omits the details of the baptismal ceremony but elaborates Harald's defeat by Regner, his rival for the throne, and Harald's subsequent apostasy. On the political uses of royal and imperial godparenting, see Arnold Angenendt, *Kaiserherrschaft und Königstaufe: Kaiser, Könige und Papste als geistlichen Patrone in der abendländischen Missionsgeschichte* (Berlin: Walter De Gruyter, 1984).

104. *Njal's Saga*, chaps. 100–105, trans. Magnus Magnusson and Hermann Pálsson (Harmondsworth: Penguin, 1969), 216–26.

agendas. When they were pro-Christian, forced baptism was part of their repertoire. When they fell from power, their opponents enforced paganism with similar tactics. Few Scandinavian kings in this period possessed the resources—and the sheer implacability and ruthlessness—that enabled Charlemagne to impose Christianity on the Saxons. The Christianization of Scandinavia was a far more sporadic and protracted process.[105]

Preaching with an Iron Tongue: The Baltic Crusades

Such being the case, it is notable that Danish and Swedish Christians joined co-religionists from Poland and Germany in the Baltic Crusades. All involved put a religious gloss on expansionist policies which they were already conducting in this region. The wars which ensued between the twelfth and the fourteenth centuries were the most protracted effort to force infidels into the font in medieval history. There had certainly been a tradition of invasions and border raids among the Baltic pagans and between them and their Christian neighbors, as well as peaceful commercial relations. The twelfth-century shift to aggressive wars of conquest and Christianization east of the Elbe was fueled by two contemporary movements. One was the general expansion of Europe's eastern frontier between 1000 and 1350. The other was the Holy Land Crusades. While the First Crusade had won European outposts in the Near East, these establishments faced continuing Muslim attacks and growing Byzantine hostility. Their chronic manpower shortage led to the calling of new expeditions whose costs and hazards gained little or nothing. The material as well as spiritual rewards of crusading had already been extended to participants in the Spanish Reconquest. In the twelfth century, they were granted to participants in the Baltic wars as well. A reconceptualization of Crusade ideology was needed, and provided, to justify the invasion of regions which had never been in Christian hands and which were scarcely the locus of pilgrimage sites. The assorted kings, nobles, merchants, bishops, monks, friars, and members of military

105. Stéphane Coviaux, "Baptême et conversion des chefs scandinaves du IXe au XIe siècle," in *Les fondations scandinaves en Occident et les débuts du duché de Normandie*, ed. Pierre Bauduin (Caen: Publications du CRAHM, 2005), 67–80; Sverre Bagge and Saebjørg Walaker-Nordeide, "The Kingdom of Norway," in *Christianization and the Rise of Christian Monarchy: Scandinavia, Central Europe, and Rus' c. 900–1200*, ed. Nora Berend (Cambridge: Cambridge University Press, 2007), 121–66. Although it is not the focus of his book, Anders Winroth, *The Conversion of Scandinavia: Vikings, Merchants, and Missionaries in the Remaking of Northern Europe* (New Haven, CT: Yale University Press, 2012), 117–18, 150–52, confirms that both Christian and pagan rulers imposed their religious policies by force.

orders who were the direct participants in the Baltic Crusades did not wait for this *ex post facto* theorizing before turning Christian missions into wars of conquest, colonization, and forced conversion.

Nowadays, it is far easier to grasp these developments than used to be the case. Scholars from the countries of northeastern Europe have been eager of late to reappraise the history of this region and to publish their findings in widely read languages. Their work, and that of other specialists in Baltic studies, is no longer occluded by romantic nationalism, anti-German Soviet propaganda, or the need to view these histories as local instantiations of dialectical materialism. Placing the Baltic Crusades in a wider European perspective, recent historiography, while variegated in focus, has yielded a remarkable degree of consensus on the main narrative, enabling us to present the summary which follows.[106]

106. An excellent survey of the history of this historiography is provided by Linda Kaljundi and Kaspars Kļaviņš, "The Chronicler and the Modern World: Henry of Livonia and the Baltic Crusades in the Enlightenment and National Traditions," in *Crusading and Chronicle Writing: A Companion to Henry of Livonia*, ed. Marek Tamm, Linda Kaljundi, and Carsten Selch Jensen (Farnham: Ashgate, 2011), 409–56, which also considers visual arts, film, and other representations of this history in popular culture. An exception to the non-polemical approach is Latourette, *History of the Expansion of Christianity*, 2:211, who attacks the cruelties perpetrated by Germans on peoples of this region with an immediate post–World War II outlook. The single best concise narrative of the Baltic Crusades, with an excellent bibliographical guide, is Andres Kasekamp, *A History of the Baltic States* (New York: Palgrave-Macmillan, 2010), 20–36. Another useful brief account which puts this subject in the context of the Crusades movement as a whole is Christopher Tyerman, *God's War: A New History of the Crusades* (Cambridge, MA: Harvard University Press, 2006), 674–712. Other valuable treatments include Robert Bartlett, "The Conversion of a Pagan Society in the Middle Ages," *History* 70 (1985): 185–201 on Pomerania; William L. Urban, *The Baltic Crusade*, 2nd ed. (Chicago: Lithuanian Research and Studies Center, 1994); idem, *The Livonian Crusade*, 2nd ed. (Chicago: Lithuanian Research and Studies Center, 2004), both accenting military history; Marie-Louise Favreau-Lilie, "Mission to the Heathen in Prussia and Livonia: Attitudes of the Religious and Military Orders toward Christianity," in *Christianizing Peoples and Converting Individuals*, ed. Guyda Armstrong and Ian N. Wood (Turnhout: Brepols, 2000), 147–54, accenting the role of Cistercians, Franciscans, and Dominicans along with the military orders; Przemysław Urbańczyk, "The Politics of Conversion in North Central Europe," in *The Cross Goes North: Processes of Conversion in Northern Europe*, ed. Martin Carver (York: York Medieval Press, 2003), 15–27; Alan Palmer, *The Baltic: A New History of the Region and the People* (Woodstock, UK: Overlook Press, 2005), 30–64; Nora Berend, "Introduction," in *Christianization and the Rise of Christian Monarchy: Scandinavia, Central Europe, and Rus' c. 900–1200*, ed. Nora Berend (Cambridge: Cambridge University Press, 2007), 5–38; Eva Eihmane, "The Baltic Crusades: A Clash of Two Identities," in *The Clash of Cultures on the Medieval Baltic Frontier*, ed. Alan V. Murray (Farnham: Ashgate, 2009), 37–51, accenting the opportunistic use of alliances between Christian and pagan groups; Tiina Kala, "Rural Society and Religious Innovation: Acceptance and Rejection of Catholicism among the Native Inhabitants of Medieval Livonia," in ibid., 168–90. In eadem, "The Incorporation of the Northern Baltic

The first missions to the Baltic, to Pomerania in 1107–8 and 1124–25, already combined evangelization with conquest. Led by Otto I, bishop of Bamberg and Duke Boleslav III of Poland, their initial success forced the defeated into the font. But the baptized were regarded as traitors by other Pomeranians. Once Christian forces departed, they rebelled and repudiated Christianity. Another mission, sent in 1128, used the same tactics against the unbaptized and recidivists alike. It took two further generations before these methods brought Pomerania into the Christian fold on an ongoing basis.

The kings of Denmark launched the first of their repeated campaigns to colonize and Christianize the Baltic in 1136 and 1139. In 1167 the Danish royal mission to Estonia, whose architect was Eskil, archbishop of Lund, won the support of Pope Alexander III. Its goal was to establish ecclesiastical dependencies which would report back to Lund. The inroads made by these expeditions were no more durable than the failed Baltic Crusade preached by Bernard of Clairvaux in 1147, staffed mainly by German nobles.

The next major campaigns were engineered by Hartwig II, archbishop of Hamburg-Bremen, starting in 1186. He sent the Augustinian friar Meinhard to Livonia and consecrated him the first bishop of Üxküll (1187–96). Meinhard arrived with troops. After forcing baptism on the defeated Livonians, or inveigling them into the font, his heavy and unanticipated fiscal

Lands in the Western World," in *Crusade and Conversion on the Baltic Frontier, 1150–1500*, ed. Alan V. Murray (Aldershot: Ashgate, 2001), 13–20, the author accents the competition between bishops and other bishops, bishops and religious orders, and Germans and Danes; Kurt Villads Jensen, "Introduction," in ibid., xvii–xxv, surveys the full sweep of competing, and sometimes cooperating, Christian interests. Scholars focusing on Lithuania include Axel Ehlers, "The Crusade of the Teutonic Knights against Lithuania Reconsidered," in ibid., 21–44; Rosa Mažeika, "When Crusader and Pagan Agree: Conversion as a Point of Honor in the Baptism of King Mindaugas of Lithuania (c. 1240–63)," in ibid., 197–214; eadem, "Bargaining for Baptism: Lithuanian Negotiations for Conversion, 1250–1358," in *Varieties of Conversion in the Middle Ages*, ed. James Muldoon (Gainesville: University of Florida Press, 1997), 131–45. On the Danish role, see Ane Bysted, Carsten Selch Jensen, Kurt Villads Jensen, and John H. Lind, *Jerusalem in the North: Denmark and the Baltic Crusades, 1100–1522*, trans. Sarah and Frederick Pedersen (Turnhout: Brepols, 2012). Accenting papal policy are Iben Fonnesberg-Schmidt, *The Popes and the Baltic Crusades, 1147–1254* (Leiden: Brill, 2007); eadem, "Pope Honorius III and the Mission and Crusade in the Baltic Region," in *The Clash of Cultures*, ed. Murray (as mentioned previously), 103–22; and eadem, "Alexander III and the Crusades," in *Pope Alexander III (1159–81): The Art of Survival*, ed. Peter D. Clarke and Anne J. Duggan (Farnham: Ashgate, 2012), 341–63, all of whose studies track the shift from papal reaction to proaction; Barbara Bombi, *Novella plantatio fidei: Missione e crociata nel nord Europa tra la fine del XII e i primi decenni del XIII secolo*, Istituto Storico Italiano per il Medio Evo, Nuovi studi storici 74 (Rome: Nella Sede dell'Istituto, 2007), who focuses on the development of canonical norms; and eadem, "Celestine III and the Conversion of the Heathen on the Baltic Frontier," in *Pope Celestine III (1191–1198): Diplomat and Pastor*, ed. John Doran and Damian J. Smith (Aldershot: Ashgate, 2008), 145–58.

demands led to their revolt. The lesson that might have been learned from this series of events was not internalized by Meinhard or his successors, whose policies engendered the same result. The outcome was fatal in the case of Berthold, second bishop of Üxküll (1196–98), whose unpopularity led to his martyrdom.

Altogether more prepossessing, if no less harsh, was Albert of Buxhövden, nephew of Hartwig II and a canon of Bremen, who became the next bishop (1198–1228). He shifted his see to Riga, which was elevated to an archbishopric in 1225. Albert gained the support of Pope Innocent III, who no doubt welcomed an alternative to the scandalous Fourth Crusade. In 1202 Innocent chartered a new military order, the Sword Brethren, for service in the Baltic. Albert did what he could to coordinate their efforts with those of the German and Danish nobles, who put in a periodic appearance, and with those of the Teutonic Knights, who had relocated from the Holy Land to the Baltic in 1190. The remnants of the Sword Brethren, loathed for their rapacity and brutality and decimated by military losses, were absorbed by the Teutonic Knights in 1237. Albert invited Premonstratensians and Augustinians to serve as missionaries in Livonia. He divided the converted area into parishes and appointed parish priests, but without clarifying their responsibilities vis-à-vis those of the religious orders. Albert enforced the policy of baptism or death and exacted heavy tithes, which he used *inter alia* to finance the repression of rebels and recidivists. When the papal legate William of Modena (1225–27) chastised the Knights for their unbearable financial exactions, pointing out, correctly, that they were a recipe for recidivism and rebellion, he could well have been describing Albert's taxation as well. Neither Albert nor the Knights took his advice to heart.

In the reduction of one after another of the pagan groups in the Baltic to Christianity despite their frequent abjurations and revolts, the persistent, ongoing presence of the Teutonic Knights was a key factor. They remained on duty, in contrast with the intermittent participation of German and Scandinavian lay lords. The last Baltic group to yield, after more than a century of baptismal fits and starts, were the Lithuanians. Alone among these Baltic peoples, they had a monarchy. Occupation of its throne was frequently contested. In 1253 Mindaugas, who had triumphed by the slaughter or exile of his relatives and other rivals, accepted baptism in exchange for papal recognition of his royal title. He apostatized in 1263. But that move did not save Mindaugas from overthrow by his opponents. The event that brought the Lithuanian mission, and the Baltic Crusades, to a close is worth flagging, although it takes us beyond our target period. In

1386 the king of Catholic Poland died. His daughter Hedwig inherited the crown. Although betrothed to William of Habsburg, she offered her hand to Jagiello, king of Lithuania. This matrimonial prize, and with it the joint rule of the two adjacent realms, was too tempting to pass up. So Jagiello accepted Hedwig's proviso and was baptized. Krakow was well worth a Mass.

Far from being ecstatic at this development, the Teutonic Knights were chagrined. With the conversion of Lithuania, their Baltic mission lost its *raison d'être*. They sought a remedy at the papal court. But, given the Great Schism, which papal court? At length the Knights pressed their case at the Council of Constance in 1415. They argued that the Poles were basically anti-Christian. The council fathers had much more important items on their agenda and dismissed the case as a specious and despicable attack on a Catholic power, which they valued as a bulwark against Russian Orthodoxy in northeastern Europe.[107] So ends the narrative of the Baltic Crusades.

Moving from this agreed-upon sequence of events, historians have consulted several kinds of sources to access these developments from those closest to the scene. Leaving aside papal letters, which depend on indirect evidence and which tend to be reactive, not proactive, and often more in line with canonical tradition than with current events, we have *vitae* of bishops, and chronicles. The bishops are treated quasi-hagiographically. The *vita* authors portray them as edifying figures propagating the faith by their preaching and holy lives. If they failed, as was often the case, they are to be venerated as martyrs.[108] The chroniclers, who typically draw on these *vitae* and on previous accounts for the earliest portions of their histories, have their own chosen emphases and ways of rationalizing the forced baptism of defeated pagans.

The leading treatment of the twelfth-century stage of these Baltic wars is Helmold of Bosau's *Chronica Slavorum* (1167/72). Helmold begins his sto-

107. An excellent treatment of this effort on the part of the Teutonic Knights and its failure is given by Jürgen Miethke, "Heiliger Heidenkrieg? Theoretische Kontroversen zwischen Deutschem Orden und dem Königreich Polen vor und auf dem Konstanzer Konzil," in *Heilige Kriege: Religiöse Begründungen militärischer Gewaltanwendung. Judentum, Christentum und Islam im Vergleich*, ed. Klaus Schreiner with Elisabeth Müller-Luckner (Munich: R. Oldenbourg Verlag, 2009), 109–25. This case is not noted in the discussion of conversion policy in the new universities founded east of the Rhine in the later Middle Ages by Michael D. Bailey, "A Late-Medieval Crisis of Superstition?" *Speculum* 84 (2009): 635–61.

108. See Bartlett, "The Conversion of a Pagan Society," 187; Christopher Tyerman, "Henry of Livonia and the Ideology of Crusading," in *Crusading and Chronicle Writing: A Companion to Henry of Livonia*, ed. Marek Tamm, Linda Kaljundi, and Carsten Selch Jensen (Farnham, UK: Ashgate, 2011), 23–44; reprt. in idem, *Practices of Crusading: Image and Action from the Eleventh to the Sixteenth Century* (Farnham, UK: Ashgate, 2013), no. VII.

ry with Charlemagne's campaigns against the Saxons. For him, the Baltic mission is simply their continuation. Thanks to Charlemagne, the Saxons themselves are now leading the movement, with valued assistance from the Danes. Helmold rings a change on the theme of multilateral, cross-border raids prior to the full-scale Christian invasion. What they signify is that, at some point, at least, some of the lands conquered had been in Christian hands. Thus, it is just to make war to regain them. On the Carolingian model, preaching with an iron tongue is warranted. But Helmold also notes the role of Bernard of Clairvaux in the promotion of the Baltic Crusade. He reports the speech given by Bernard at Frankfurt in 1147. Preaching to the Germans, Bernard sensed that they were open to a crusade close to home. In his own words, he asserts that the pagans east of the Elbe, and not just the Muslims, are fitting targets. The Germans should take up the cross "to convert or utterly to destroy these peoples." Those who do so "are promised the same indulgence for their sins as those who take the road to Jerusalem."[109] Pope Eugenius III was present at Frankfurt to confirm this offer. Helmold reports how Bernard's audience responded: "They attached the sign of the cross to their clothes and armor. For it was understood by the leaders of the expedition that one part of the army was to go to the Orient, a second part to Spain, and a third part, indeed, to the Slavs, who live next to us."[110] For Helmold, this new inducement reinforces a policy already ratified by Carolingian precedent and rationalized as a recuperative just war.

There is another, later, group of chronicles written for, and sometimes by, the Teutonic Knights. Their rationales, and omissions, are of equal interest. They are quite capable of justifying their expeditions without mention-

109. Bernard of Clairvaux, *Epistola* 457, in *Opere di San Bernardo*, ed. Ferruccio Gastaldelli, trans. Ettore Paratore, 6 vols. (Milan: Scriptorium Claravalleno, 1989–2000), 6/2:122–26; quotation at 6:124: "ad delendas penitus, aut certe convertendas nationes illas, ... eamdem eis promittendes indulgentiam peccatorum quam et his versus Ierusolymam profecti." Text also available in *Sancti Bernardi opera*, ed. Jean Leclercq et al., 8 vol. in 9 (Rome: Editiones Cistercienses, 1955–77), 8:432–33. An account which accents the apocalyptic element in Bernard's address is Hans-Dietrich Kahl, "Crusade Eschatology as Seen by St. Bernard of Clairvaux," in *The Second Crusade and the Cistercians*, ed. Michael Gervers (New York: St. Martin's Press, 1992), 35–47; see also Yael Katzir, "The Second Crusade and the Redefinition of *Ecclesia*, *Christianitas*, and Papal Coercive Power," in ibid., 3–12; Tyerman, *God's War*, 27–28, 38–51, 253–57.

110. Helmold of Bosau, *Chronica Slavorum* 1.29, 3rd ed., ed. Johannes M. Lappenberg, rev. Bernhard Schmiedler, MGH Scriptores rerum germanicorum in usum scholarum (Hannover: Hahn, 1937), 114–15; quotation on page 115: "Fueruntque signati titulo crucis in vestibus et armatura. Visum autem fuit auctoribus expeditionis partem exercitus unam destinari in partes orientis, alteram in Hyspaniam, terciam vero ad Slavos, qui iuxta nos habitant." Tyerman, "Henry of Livonia," 23–44, underplays the Crusades ideology element in Helmold.

ing either Charlemagne or Bernard of Clairvaux. They begin their accounts with the arrival of the Knights in the Baltic in 1190, or the period just preceding it. Writing in Old High German verse that pays homage to the heroic romances of Wolfram von Eschenbach, Gottfried von Strassburg, and Hartmann von Aue, the anonymous author of the *Livonian Rhymed Chronicle* (late thirteenth century) begins in 1143 and is a primary source for the years 1267–1290.[111] The most striking feature of this chronicle is the absence of any mention of forced baptism. The author's treatment of the mission of Meinhard illustrates how he sanitizes this issue. Making no reference to Hartwig II of Hamburg-Bremen, he states that Meinhard was sent by the pope, who consecrated him as bishop and to whom he reported directly. His charge is to minister to Christian merchants already stationed in Livonia. Moved by his wisdom and virtue, some of the pagans seek him out and request baptism. True, some then complain and think twice of the rite when he demands their forced labor. But the real reason why war breaks out is that the baptized are attacked by those remaining pagan. It is necessary to protect these new converts. The author thus rewrites the Baltic Crusades as defensive wars, not as wars of justified aggression. Defeated pagans are required to pay tithes. But the author is silent on the baptisms inflicted on them, as a term of surrender, which make them liable to these exactions.[112] The only pagan baptizand he singles out by name is Mindaugas of Lithuania. The author acknowledges that he accepts baptism in exchange for papal recognition of his title and later relapses. In his view, however, this and other cases of pagan recidivism are best understood not as rejection of Christ, or of the sacrament, but as ingratitude to the Teutonic Knights for all the benefits they have brought to the region.[113]

More triumphal, more derivative, and more sensitive to legal issues and the culture of the pagans alike is the *Chronicle of Prussia* (1331/41) of Nicholas von Jeroschin. Based on a German translation of two Latin chronicles, it glorifies the deeds of the Teutonic Knights between 1190 and 1331.[114] As Nicholas presents them, the pagans are the aggressors. They invade and capture Christian lands and commit atrocities. The nobles of the region thus invite

111. *The Livonian Rhymed Chronicle*, trans. Jerry C. Smith and William Urban (Bloomington: Indiana University Press, 1977), xx–xxiv. As the translators note, their base text is the *Livänische Reimchronik*, ed. Leo Meyer (Paderborn: Ferdinand Schöningh, 1876), which we have not consulted.

112. *The Livonian Rhymed Chronicle*, 4–8, 20.

113. Ibid., 79–82.

114. Nicholas von Jeroschin, *The Chronicle of Prussia: A History of the Teutonic Knights of Prussia, 1190–1331*, trans. Mary Fisher (Aldershot: Highgate, 2010), 4–5.

the Knights to come and repel the pagans and to win back these lost lands. They grant the Knights dominion over the reconquered areas. Nicholas adds that the pope promises spiritual rewards. But his focus is clearly on the justice of these wars of reclamation and on the legal title of the Knights to the lands acquired.[115] As he presents it, the Christianization of the Baltic pagans is not on the original agenda. Still, the spread of the faith by the sword is not incidental. It is the price suitably paid by the defeated pagans. And God has reinforced the valor of the Knights with miracles. One is their heartening discovery of a major relic, the head of St. Barbara.[116] Making more of an impression on the pagans are the outnumbered Knights' miraculous victories in the field. The recantation of the pagans forcibly baptized following those victories continues to justify the Knights' ongoing campaigns.[117]

Nicholas mentions only one departure from the policy of forced baptism, an occasion when military action cedes to psychological warfare. The Knights know that the pagans place a high value on horses, in themselves and as acceptable sacrifices to their gods. They also know that pagan laws of hospitality forbid the refusal of any gift given. With these values in mind, Brother Dietrich gives a series of white horses to the pagan Droge. They are all found mysteriously strangled the next day. When he judges that Droge has been sufficiently spooked, Dietrich tells him that, unlike his pagan gods, the Christian God can and will protect gift horses, if he converts. Droge expresses his willingness. Dietrich then gives him another white horse which remains unscathed. Convinced of the superior power of the Christian God, Droge accepts baptism and draws other pagans to the font. Nicholas does not indicate that this event is accompanied by any other form of catechesis.[118] Nor does he intimate whether the horses have been strangled by a miracle or by a subterfuge on Dietrich's part. In any event, this is the sole baptism he reports that is not a penalty imposed on vanquished pagans.

Much more informative on both Christian and pagan attitudes toward baptism is the *Chronicon Livoniae* (1224/27) of Henry of Livonia. Henry was a Saxon cleric educated at the Augustinian house of Segeberg on the Baltic border, whose calling was the training of missionary priests. It is there that

115. Ibid., 2.1–7, 2.10–13, 3.36, 43–51, 62–65, 93–96.

116. Ibid., 3.5–6, 70–73.

117. Ibid., 3.3, 3.16–18, 3.31–40, 3.43–47, 3.49–67, 3.128, 3.186, 3.219, 69, 77–78, 88–100, 102–6, 106–19, 188–89, 204.

118. Ibid., 3.6, 72–73. For the pagan attitude toward horses in general, and pagan theology equated with non-religious folkways or dismissed as superstition, see ibid., 3.5, 70–72.

he acquired his knowledge of the languages and peoples of the region that made him of notable value to this mission. Henry arrived in Livonia in 1205 in the suite of Bishop Albert, who ordained him to the priesthood in 1208 and assigned him a parish. Henry served as interpreter to William of Modena during his papal legacy. His chronicle covers the years 1187 to 1227. For the period before his arrival, he drew on the testimony of eyewitnesses. Henry himself observed the events he relates between 1205 and 1227. He is regarded as the most accurate source for the period he treats.[119] Henry eschews miracles but does include some literary tropes and allusions, and makes his allegiances plain. By starting his chronicle when he does, he can avoid crediting missions prior to those masterminded by Hartwig II of Hamburg-Bremen and led by Albert of Riga. They are his heroes along with the Teutonic Knights. He criticizes, underestimates, or ignores the non-German participants in the Christianization of the Baltic and often glosses over the blind spots and misjudgments of the leaders he supports. While Henry has no sympathy for the pagans, he does recognize paganism as a real religion and not simply a mélange of uncivilized folkways. His chronicle offers priceless insights into the pagans' conception of baptism as merely one among the numerous odd customs brought by the Christian invaders.

Only one of these imports is accepted enthusiastically by the pagans: the stone fortress. They lack the technology for building in stone and at once grasp its value. So, when Meinhard offers to build them a stone fortress, asking for their baptism in return, they agree. But then Meinhard imposes heavy fiscal demands and forced labor for the upkeep of the fortress. The pagans protest that this was not part of the original bargain. They feel cheated and renounce their baptism. In Henry's eyes, it is the pagans who are duplicitous. This is the first of many such episodes in which he presents the pagans as accepting baptism mendaciously, only to reject it later, as they intended from the start.[120] It does not occur to him that Meinhard can be faulted for changing the ground rules unilaterally. Henry's presentation of this incident and its parallels later in his chronicle suggests that, while bad faith was bilateral in pagan-Christian relations, Henry perceives and condemns it only on the pagan side.

119. See Henry of Livonia, *Chronicon Livoniae*, ed. Piero Bugiani (Città del Castello: Books and Company, 2005), xiii–lxxx; James A. Brundage, "Introduction," in *Crusading and Chronicle Writing: A Companion to Henry of Livonia*, ed. Marek Tamm, Linda Kaljundi, and Carsten Selch Jensen (Farnham: Ashgate, 2011), 1–19, for the best accounts of Henry's life and work.

120. Henry of Livonia, *Chronicon* 1.5–6, 6, for the Meinhard episode. For other similar instances, see ibid., 1.7, 1.8, 2.5, 2.7, 4.3, 9.13, 10.13–15, 11.1–7, 14.11, 15.3, 15.7, 18.7, 19.3–4, 19.8, 21.5–6, 23.3, 23.6–9, 26.5, 6, 8, 11, 16, 18, 26, 58, 82, 100–102, 162, 174, 226, 238, 250, 270, 272, 292–94, 296.

Most typically, pagan baptisms follow their military defeats or are tactical maneuvers on their part. The pagans do not see these rites as annulling their own religion. It is traditional for them to cast lots to ascertain the will of their gods. Henry cites two occasions in which they do so to learn if the gods will find captured Christians acceptable sacrifices in place of oxen or horses. In deciding whether to accept baptism so as to gain a Christian ally against the Lithuanians, the Letts cast lots. The gods sanction baptism and tell them to choose the Catholic and not the Russian Orthodox rite. And so, "the lot fell to the Latins, and a great number joined the Livonians in the church of Riga."[121]

For the pagans, affiliations of this sort are a temporary expedient. They have ways of reversing them when the situation allows. Water rituals are a part of their own religion. Accompanied by a formula of renunciation, they achieve purification. Henry reports several rites of this type. After one pagan victory, "they thought that baptism, which they had received by water, could be washed off in the Dvina River, and sent back to Germany."[122] On another occasion, once the last German ship had set sail, "behold, the perfidious Livonians, emerging from their customary baths, sprinkled water from the Dvina River on themselves, saying, 'We wash off the faith which we received with tree branches, sending it away along with the departing Saxons.'" This time, the pagan reversal rite also includes the consumption of a ritual drink of hydromel, a mixture of beer and honey, and the ritual "drowning" of a Christian religious image in the Dvina, seen as analogous to one of their own cult statues.[123]

While baptism can thus be canceled, so, too, can Christian burial and

121. Ibid., 11.7, 102–4: "missis tamen prius sortibus et requisito consensu deorum suorum, an Ruthenorum ... an Latinos debeant subire baptismum.... Et cecidit sors ad Latinos et annumerati sunt cum Lyvonensi ecclesiae Rigensibus." On this practice, see Rosa Mažeika, "Granting Power to the Gods in Chronicles of the Baltic Crusades," in *Medieval Frontiers: Concepts and Practices*, ed. David Abulafia and Nora Berend (Aldershot: Ashgate, 2002), 153–71.

122. Henry of Livonia, *Chronicon* 1.8, 8: "baptismum, quem in aqua susceperant, in Dvina se lavando removere putant, remittendo in Theutoniam."

123. Ibid., 2.8, 20: "ecce perfidi Lyvones de balneis consuetis egressi, Dvine flumen aqua se perfundunt, dicentes, 'Hic iam baptismatis aquam cum ipsa christianitate removemus aqua fluminis et fidem susceptam exfestucantes post Saxones recedentes transmittimus.'" See also ibid., 9.8, 26.9, 58, 360, for other comparable episodes, in which, in addition to their own ablutions, the pagans use tree branches dipped in the water of the Dvina to de-Christianize their houses and fortresses. On the ritual importance of water in all forms of medieval religion, see Derek A. Rivard, *Blessing the World: Ritual and Lay Piety in Medieval Religion* (Washington: The Catholic University of America Press, 2009), 61–69, 79–86, 94–95, 97–98, 109, 166, 187–88, 210, 223, 224, 226, 269, 271.

Christian marriage. When they can, the pagans exhume their dead given Christian burial and commend them to the next life according to their own rites. Henry mentions cremation. Practices in this region also included inhumation, with the proper compass orientation of the corpse by gender and with status-appropriate grave goods. In addition to recovering and disposing properly of the dead, the pagans use these opportunities to regain their living loved ones, the multiple wives from whom the Christians had separated them. Henry does not indicate whether these surplus wives were sent back to their natal families or whether other provisions were made for them. But the wives, and their polygamous husbands, are quick to reconstitute their normal marital households when possible.[124]

There are some Christian customs which the pagans find so outlandish that they cannot be imposed. One pastoral strategy that misfires drastically is religious drama. As Henry relates, "they staged a play about the prophets, in the middle of Riga, in a most well-ordered way, so that the rudiments of the Christian faith could be seen by the pagan believers." The pagans were nonplused and fled. It had not occurred to the ecclesiastical authorities that the ability to be edified by a play depends on one's grasp of what a play is, a cultural mode entirely alien to the pagans. Another assessment targets the play's unusual subject, and the matter of language. The play was not performed in a local Baltic language and needed an interpreter to convey to the audience the action on stage. Adding to confusion on that score, the play portrayed Gideon and David fighting the Philistines and Herod's massacre of the innocents. Battle scenes were atypical in religious drama. The pagans may well have misinterpreted the stage props as real weapons that would be turned against them. Or, as Nils Holger Petersen suggests, the producers may have intended the play's unusual theme "both to to warn and to frighten the pagans who, as Henry's chronicle makes clear, were so highly resistant to conversion."[125] All they succeeded in doing, in the event, was alarming the pagans to the point of losing their audience altogether.

124. Henry of Livonia, *Chronicon* 12.6, 26.7–9, 123, 360, for mortuary rites and 26.7–9, 30.1, 360, 410, for wives. Henry's observations on the disposal of the dead have been borne out by archeology, on which see Marija Gimbutas, *The Balts* (New York: Frederick A. Praeger, 1963), 179, 188–91, 204; Kasekamp, *History of the Baltic States*, 7–8; see also Marek Tamm, "Martyrs and Miracles: Depicting Death in the Chronicle of Henry of Livonia," in *Crusading and Chronicle Writing: A Companion to Henry of Livonia*, ed. Marek Tamm, Linda Kaljundi, and Carsten Selch Jensen (Farnham: Ashgate, 2011), 135–57 on page 141; Marika Mägi, "Ösel and the Danish Kingdom: Revisiting Henry's Chronicle and the Archeological Evidence," in ibid., 317–41 on page 330.

125. Henry of Livonia, *Chronicon* 9.14, 60: "ludus prophetarum ordinatissimus in medio Riga, ut fidei christianae rudimenta gentilitos fide oculata." See Nils Holger Petersen, "The

Another genre which the missionaries hoped would make church attendance appealing was music. This notion also proved myopic. The pagans' own musical instruments were rudimentary recorders and reed flutes. They were aware of the drums and horns employed by Christian armies and took them in stride. They had no interest in manufacturing and using these instruments to guide their own troops. While the pagans were initially startled by church bells, they got used to them and prized them as booty.[126] On the other hand, religious music evoked their consternation. As Henry relates, at one point, when the Estonians were besieging a Christian fortress, a priest sat on the ramparts singing a hymn to God and accompanying himself on a musical instrument. Henry does not specify its identity. It was evidently portable and had a tonal range making it audible above the noise of battle. The sound of a stringed instrument would not have carried. The instrument was most likely the recently invented portative organ, a graduated series of pipes with a range of two octaves above Middle C, activated by a keyboard played with the right hand and a bellows with the left. "The barbarians," says Henry, "hearing the song and the high-pitched sound of the instrument (*sonitum instrumenti acutum*), never before heard in their land, suspended the battle." When told of the joyous burden of the song and invited to hear its like in church if they made peace and were baptized, they rejected the offer as derisory and offensive. If the priest's music was astonishing, it was also weird, and scarcely an inducement to accept baptism, given that the outcome of the current battle was far from clear.[127]

Despite the fact that religious drama and music are evangelical washouts, Henry suggests that the pagans are familiar with some elements of baptismal theology. When Innocent III learns of the prevalence of recid-

Notion of Missionary Theatre: The *ludus magnus* of Henry of Livonia's Chronicle," in *Crusading and Chronicle Writing: A Companion to Henry of Livonia*, ed. Marek Tamm, Linda Kajundi, and Carsten Selch Jensen (Farnham: Ashgate, 2011), 229–43; quotation on page 243.

126. Henry of Livonia, *Chronicon* 22.3, 280; on bells see Brundage, "Introduction," 9.

127. Henry of Livonia, *Chronicon* 12.6, 116–20; quotation on page 120: "Sed barbari audientes carmen et sonitum instrumenti acutum subsisterunt, quia in terra sua non audierant, et pausantes a bello causam tante leticie perquirebunt." The only study of the musical culture of Baltic paganism is Alan V. Murray, "Music and Cultural Conflict in the Christianization of Livonia," in *The Clash of Cultures on the Medieval Baltic Frontier*, ed. Alan V. Murray (Farnham: Ashgate, 2009), 293–305. Murray does not speculate on the identity of the instrument used by the priest. On the portative organ, see Curt Sachs, *The History of Musical Instruments* (New York: W. W. Norton, 1940), 286–87; Peter Williams, "Portative," in *The New Grove Dictionary of Musical Instruments*, ed. Stanley Sadie, 3 vols. (London: Macmillan, 1984), 3:140; Anthony Baines, "Portative Organ," in *The Oxford Companion to Musical Instruments*, ed. Anthony Baines (Oxford: Oxford University Press, 1992), 269.

ivism in the Baltic in 1195–96, he urges that punitive measures be taken against the abjurors. Before a pagan assembly, Bishop Berthold explains that this is why the Christians have renewed hostilities. Henry puts the following speech into the mouth of the pagan who responds: "You may compel those who have accepted the faith to observe it. But you should induce others to join it 'by words not by blows (*verbis, non verberibus*).'" Henry's editor traces this last phrase to Cicero's *Tusculan Disputations* 3.64. A more immediate source is likely to have been Gratian, whose *Decretum* enjoins bishops to exercise discipline "by words, not by the fear of blows."[128] Either way, this literary trope encapsulates the conundrum on the books since the seventh century: No one is to be forced into the font. But those so forced are required to practice the Christian faith. If the goal of the pagan spokesman was to hoist Berthold on the church's own petard, his tactics failed. Berthold's martyrdom in 1198 is attributable to his enforcement of only the punitive side of the canonical tradition.

The speech given by Henry to the speaker just noted raises the question of how the Baltic pagans were actually instructed. He cites only two examples. One involves the *ex post facto* catechizing of the forcibly baptized, starting with the most important men and then moving to less important men, women, and children.[129] Henry does not specify the doctrines deemed essential. The other is unique, a case in which a pagan is instructed prior to a baptism which he seeks voluntarily, without a military or political trade-off. In 1219, Henry tells us, the pagan businessman Kyriawanus approached the Christians with a tale of woe and a request. Up until now, his business had flourished, he says, thanks to the patronage of the pagan gods. But of late trade has fallen off, and the gods have not been helpful. Would the Christian God assist him? Henry associates himself with Kyriawanus's sponsors: "We promised him a propitious God, who would give him a sufficiency of temporal goods in this life, and life eternal in the future. And he believed us, and

128. Henry of Livonia, *Chronicon* 2.5, 16: "eos, qui fidem susceperunt, ad eam servandam compellas, alios suscipiendam eam *verbis non verberibus* allicias." The editor, at ibid., 17n15, and Carsten Selch Jensen, "'*Verbis non verberibus*': The Representation of Sermons in the Chronicle of Henry of Livonia," in *Crusading and Chronicle Writing: A Companion to Henry of Livonia*, ed. Marek Tamm, Linda Kaljundi, and Carsten Selch Jensen (Farnham: Ashgate, 2011), 177–206, on page 183, see Cicero as the source; the Gratian reference is missed by Brundage, "Introduction," ibid., 11: "Certainly I have never found a clear reference to Gratian's work in Henry's chronicle." Cf. Gratian, *Decretum* pars prima, q. 45. C. 1, ed Aemilius Friedberg in *Corpus iuris canonici*, 2 vols. (Leipzig: Tauchnitz, 1879–80; reprt. Union, NJ: Lawbook Exchange, 2000), 1:160: "verborum correctione, non verberibus timere debeant episcopi."

129. Henry of Livonia, *Chronicon* 30.5, 420.

we at once catechized him, and Rudolf, master of the [Teutonic] Knights, stood beside him as godfather." A pagan attack interrupts the baptism following this instant catechesis, but it is repelled and the rite duly takes place. And the promise of worldly prosperity is made good.[130] The deity who rewards Kyriawanus when he rises from the font is not the God of battles but the God of business. And Henry sees nothing inappropriate in the packaging of the gospel message in this way.

Being Germans, the Teutonic Knights in the aforementioned episode and throughout Henry's chronicle are heroes. While he shares the pro-German bias of Helmold of Bosau, Henry is far less even-handed in dealing with the mission's non-German participants. The Poles receive no mention whatsoever in his text. He expresses extremely mixed feelings toward the Danes. As recent additions to the Christian fold, their contribution is welcome. But, ignoring the fact that the Danish kings outrank the German participants, Henry demeans their expeditions as erratic, misinformed, and marginal. The Danes are upstarts with swelled heads. Instead of accepting their proper role as junior partners in a basically German enterprise, they have the effrontery to compete with the Germans for lands, souls, and ecclesiastical jurisdiction, which they seek to route back to Lund instead of to Riga where it belongs. Henry is deeply gratified when William of Modena's adjudication of the conflict between Danes and Germans over the division of Estonia in 1225 supports the Germans. In Henry's own judgment, the Danish mission should not seek to reap where it has not sown.[131]

As rivals in the Baltic, the Russians fare far worse. Henry criticizes them not as schismatics who depart from Catholic doctrine or practice but as predatory and perfidious competitors for the pagans' allegiance. Henry

130. Ibid. 23.7, 302: "Ad petitionem itaque ipsius importunatum ibidem Deum promisimus sibi propicium et temporalia sibi sufficienter eum in hac vita daturum et in futuro vitam eternam. Et credit nobis, et statim cathezizavimus eum, et astabat ei Rodolfus magister milicie patrinus."

131. Ibid., 23.2, 23.10, 25.1–26.5, 29.6, 290, 314–16, 334–56, 402–4; at 24.1–7, 318–19, Henry adds that the Danes actually put to death a convert because he had received baptism in the church of Riga, not that of Lund. Good discussions of Henry's attitude toward the Danes are provided by Kurt Villads Jensen, "Denmark and the Second Crusade: The Formation of a Crusader State?" in *The Second Crusade: Scope and Consequences*, ed. Jonathan Phillips and Martin Hoch (Manchester: Manchester University Press, 2001), 164–79, and Mägi, "Ösel and the Danish Kingdom," 317–41, who sees the contest for this strategic island as symptomatic of Henry's more general treatment of the Danes. See also Jensen, "'*Verbis non verberibus*,'" 199–201. A useful comparison can be made with Helmold, *Chronica Slavorum*, passim, who, despite his accent on Saxon leadership, gives the Danes equal time and who recognizes that both the Danish and the German efforts in the Baltic were intermittent and affected by problems in their homelands.

levels the following charges against the Russians: They ally freely with the pagans for their own selfish political ends. They force baptism on the pagans but do not really instruct or minister to them. Their goal is not to harvest souls but to exploit them economically. At his most vitriolic, Henry describes the Russians as the beast of the Apocalypse seeking to devour the infant of the woman who has just given birth (Rev. 12:1–6). This infant is the newborn church of Estonia. She was saved from the dragon by the church of Livonia, her true mother, "although many others sought to pose as her mother, to seduce her with many lies. One of these, Mother Russia, always sterile and barren, tried to conquer that land, not with the hope of its rebirth in the faith of Jesus Christ but rather for the sake of tribute and spoils."[132]

Irony is not an arrow in Henry's literary quiver, and in issuing this diatribe he ignores the fact that his German heroes engage in the self-same tactics for which he castigates the Danes and Russians. It is the Germans' extortionate and unreasonable demands which occasion the frequent rebellions and abjurations of baptism which he recounts. None of the German leaders appear to learn anything from the experience of their predecessors. Along with the heavy tithes, tributes, and the forced labor they impose on the pagans, they appropriate their lands and seize their beehives—honey, or possibly also beeswax, being a particularly important commodity in the local economy. Henry reports without comment William of Modena's criticism of the Knights in 1225 for their unbearable exactions, and the fact that they are counterproductive, as indeed they have been since the time of Meinhard and continue to be.[133] Henry's treatment of the German mission, in itself and in comparison with these rival missions, is thus an extended exercise in double-think.

Perhaps the most striking evidence that Henry's Germans do not breathe a purer air than their competitors occurs in the final episode he relates, the campaign against the Öselians. So obdurate are they in defending their island home that, in Henry's eyes, they do not merit even forced baptism: "On account of their depraved customs, which they refused to give up, and their continuing desire to drink Christian blood and to commit other

132. Henry of Livonia, *Chronicon* 28.4, 380–82; quotation on page 382: "licet plures sibi matres filiam hanc usurpantes, mentientes semper, attruxerint, quarum una mater Ruthenica sterilis semper et infecunda, que non spe regenerationis in fide Iesu Christi, sed spe tributorum et spoliarum terras sibi subiugare conatur." For other anti-Russian remarks, see ibid., 13.4, 14.2, 16.2, 20.3, 27.2–3, 134–36, 140, 192–93, 256, 368, 370–72. For Henry on the Russians, see Tyerman, "Henry of Livonia," 31–32; Jensen, "'*Verbis non verberibus*,'" 199–201.

133. Henry of Livonia, *Chronicon* 1.5–6, 15.5, 16.5, 28.7, 29.3, 6, 176–78, 202, 395, 398.

crimes owing to their evil-minded ways, they are not worthy of the gift of baptism. They deserve to be slain rather than baptized."[134] This is strong language indeed from a missionary priest. The drinking of Christian blood to which Henry refers may or may not be metaphorical. Helmold reports that the sacrifices offered to the pagan gods include captured Christians as well as oxen and sheep, and that the officiant ritually drinks the blood of the victims, which is thought to enhance his oracular powers.[135] This fate may have fallen to Christian victims not exempted by lot in Henry's Livonia. When the Teutonic Knights win the battle that inspires Henry's outburst, they do indeed slaughter the Öselians rather than baptize them.[136] Shortly thereafter, the last Öselian bastion falls, and the standard policy prevails: Hostages are taken, tribute is imposed, and the defeated are forcibly baptized. The event with which Henry ends his chronicle thus reinstates the normal rules of engagement. In his *envoi*, he proclaims the gratifying success of the Livonian mission by 1227: "Riga truly irrigates the Gentiles,"[137] thanks to the crusaders' remorseless hydraulic engineering.

The View from the Ivory Tower: Canonists in the Twelfth and Thirteenth Centuries

In Henry of Livonia's chronicle, as in other accounts of the Baltic Crusades, the forced baptism of defeated pagans is seen as standard practice by victors and vanquished alike, even if the pagans regard it as renegotiable and its efficacy is moot to missionaries who resubject abjurors to the font. As with early medieval reports that rewrite as voluntary the forced baptism of Jews, the chroniclers sometimes reinscribe compulsion as free will and highlight the rare baptisms not occasioned by political or military necessity. To that extent, even the most propaganda-driven accounts convey a whisper of doubt about the propriety of forced baptism. Authors not themselves on the scene had more occasion to consider the full resources of the Christian tradition on this subject. As teachers and as formulators of rules and principles, they had

134. Ibid., 30.4, 414: "qui consuetudines suas pravas derelinquere nolentes et sanguinem christianorum adhuc bibere sitientes et ceteras nequicias exercere cupientes donum sacri baptismi suis pessimis mentibus non meruerunt; … magis occidi quam baptizare meruerunt."

135. Helmold, *Chronica Slavorum* 1.52, 102: "hostias de bobus et ovibus, plerisque etiam de hominibus christianis, quorum sanguine deos suos oblectari iactitant. Post cesam hostiam sacerdos de cruore libat, ut sit efficacior oraculis capescendis."

136. Henry of Livonia, *Chronicon* 30.4, 418.

137. Ibid., 30.5–6, 420–24; quotation at 30.6, 424: "Riga vero irrigat gentes." Noted by Jensen, "'*Verbis non verberibus*,'" 200.

the duty to speak to it. Some popes directed letters to particular leaders of the campaigns against the pagans. These missives were *ad hoc* and usually *ex post facto*. Some of the same popes also addressed forced baptism in a broader and more theoretical vein. Their writings made their way into canonical collections. Indeed, until the early thirteenth century canon law took the lead in this area. Theologians had little or nothing to say on forced baptism in the twelfth century and remained heavily dependent on the canonists when they began to address it. Once they got their teeth into this topic, they amplified it, in some cases reinforcing their arguments with Aristotelian philosophy. But, in comparison with their treatments of baptism by desire and fictive baptism, they remained remarkably attentive to the canonists. Since the canonists exercised the influence they did in the ensuing debates on forced baptism, we will begin with them, and then turn attention to the scholastic theologians.

The early twelfth-century starting point was the *Panormia* attributed to Ivo of Chartres. This text reprises three patristic and early medieval statements pertaining to Jews. The first rules that Jews who seek baptism should undergo a catechumenate of eight months, "in order to test whether they are worthy of the grace of baptism." This timetable may be suspended if converts are in danger of death, lest they despair. While there is no evidence that mechanisms are in place for resuscitating the patristic catechumenate, the rationale given is the ancient one, the need for adequate instruction and scrutiny so as to screen out hypocrites and forestall recidivism.[138]

The *Panormia* then recycles Canon 57 of Toledo IV, largely in the council fathers' own words:

> Concerning the Jews this holy synod decrees that none of them henceforth are to be forced to believe.... For none of them will be saved unwillingly, but willingly, so that perfect justice may be observed. Just as man perished of his own free will by obeying the serpent, so he is saved by faith, called by the grace of God through the conversion of his own mind. For they are called in order to be converted by the faculty of free will. They are not to be compelled.

The *Panormia* follows this principled rejection of forced baptism with the endorsement of forced religious observance made later in the same decree:

138. *Panormia* 1.71, ed. Bruce Brasington and Martin Brett, 47: "si pura fide venire noscuntur, tunc demum baptismatis gratiam mereantur." Accessible at: http://wtfaculty.wtamu.edu/bbrasington/panorma.html, posted August 16, 2005. While in some jurisdictions Jews who did not want to convert were later forced to attend Christian sermons, evidence for the support of voluntary Jewish conversions suggests that where it occurred it was provided after, not before, their baptism. For one example in thirteenth-century England, see Joan Greatrex, "Monastic Charity for Jewish Converts: The Requisition of Corrodies by Henry III," in *Christianity and Judaism*, ed. Diana Wood, Studies in Church History 29 (Oxford: Blackwell, 1992), 133–43.

As for those already forced into Christianity, as was done in the time of the most pious prince Sisebut, since they have joined in the divine sacraments, have received the grace of baptism, have been anointed with chrism, and have partaken of the body and blood of the Lord, they are rightly constrained to observe the faith, even if they received it by force and necessity, lest the name of the Lord be blasphemed and the faith they have received be held vile and contemptible.[139]

In the third passage cited, the *Panormia* author seconds Toledo IV's ruling that the children of recidivist Jews be taken from their parents and raised as Christians by monks and nuns.[140] The tensions built into Toledo IV are thus left unreconciled in this text.

Toledo IV as found in the *Panormia* plays an important role in Gratian's *Decretum*, where it receives a more generalized and nuanced treatment. Gratian I places forced baptism in a context of his own. Distinction 45 of the first part of the work deals with the larger theme of how bishops should reprove their subordinates. With a nod to Gregory the Great, he advises mildness and fraternal charity rather than harshness: "Bishops should exercise correction by words, not by the fear of blows."[141] While most of this distinction treats the disciplining of the clergy, Gratian I also follows Gregory's advice on how bishops should evangelize non-believers: "Those who, with a sincere and upright intention, seek to draw into the faith those outside the Christian religion should proceed with blandishments, not with asperities." Non-believers are more likely to respond to plain and straightforward reasoning than to hostility.[142] Instruction should be aimed at all who need it, "whether delinquent believers or infidels."[143]

It is in this setting that Gratian I cites the *Panormia* reference to Can-

139. *Panormia* 1.72, 48: "De Iudeis autem hec precepit sancta sinodus, nemini dienceps ad credendum vim inferre. Cum enim vult Deus miseretur, et quem vult indurat. Non enim tales inviti salvandi sunt, sed volentes, ut integra sit forma iustitiae. Sicut homo propria arbitrii voluntate serpenti obediens periit, sic vocante se gratia Dei proprie mentis conversione homo quisque credendo salvatur. Ergo non vi sed libera arbitrii facultate ut convertantur vocandi sunt, non potius impellandi. Qui autem iam pridem ad Christianitatem coacti sunt, sicut factum est temporibus religiosissimi principis Sisemandi [*sic*], quia iam constat eos sacramentis divinis associatos et baptismi gratiam suscepisse, chrismate unctos esse, et corporis Domini et sanguinis exstitisse participes, oportet ut fidem etiam vi et necessitate susceperunt tenere cogantur, ne nomen Domini blasphemetur, fidesque quam susceperunt vilis ac contemptibilis habeatur."

140. Ibid., 1.73, 49.

141. Gratian, *Decretum* pars prima q. 45. C. 1, 1:160: "verborum correctione, non verberibus timere debent episcopi." See ibid., 1:160–67, for the entire distinction.

142. Ibid., C. 3, 1:160: "Qui sincera intentione extraneos a christiana religione ad fidem cupiunt rectam adducere, blandimentis debent, non asperititatibus studere, ne quorum mentem reddita a plano ratio poterat provocare, pellat procul adversitas."

143. Ibid., C. 7, 1:162: "fideles delinquentes aut infideles."

on 57 of Toledo IV, with a few changes in wording. Jews are not the only or the main issue. Even as Gratian I widens the application of the rule, he retains the council fathers' contradictions: "Just as Jews are not to be forced into the faith, so also converts are not to be allowed to abjure it." As he concludes his citation of the first part of Canon 57, Gratian I adds a thought not found either there or in the *Panormia*: "Thus, they are to be persuaded, converted not by force but through the faculty of free will." The grace of God must be supplemented by persuasion, conducted in a reasonable and courteous way, according to the program advanced earlier in distinction 45. Gratian I's other modification is to describe the Eucharist as "the body of the Lord," not His body and blood. But he ends by agreeing that, albeit forced into the font, the recipients of baptism, who have also received unction and the Eucharist, should rightly be constrained to Christian practice, lest the name of the Lord be blasphemed and the faith be held vile and contemptible.[144]

Gratian I thus achieves a number of things in distinction 45. He expands the focus of his sources to include infidels of all kinds. He urges that they should be invited into the fold with sympathy, not hostility. He rejects forced baptism. Rational persuasion must join the grace of God. Faith and salvation can be acquired only through the exercise of the believer's free will. At the same time, he supports the mandatory enforcement of Christian practice for all the baptized, even if they arrived at the font under the compulsion he impugns. Gratian has been regarded both as a staunch opponent of forced baptism and also as the point of departure for the canonical view that it is sacramentally valid.[145] His *Decretum*, indeed, is a source for both of these positions.

144. Ibid., C. 4–C. 5, 1:160–61, quotations at C. 5, 1:160: "Sicut non sunt Iudeis ad fidem cogendi, ita nec conversis ab ea recedens permittitur"; and, for the whole passage, at 1:160–61: "De Iudeis autem precipit sancta sinodus, nemini dienceps ad credendum inferre. Cui enim vult Deus miseretur, et quem vult indurat. Non enim tales inviti salvandi sunt, sed volentes, ut integra sit forma iustitiae. Sicut enim homo propria arbitrii voluntate serpenti obediens periit, sic vocante se gratia Dei propriae mentis conversione quisque credendo salvatur. Ergo non vi, sed libera arbitrii facultate ut convertantur suadendi sunt, non potius inpellandi. Qui autem (sicut factum est temporibus religiosissimi principis Sisebuti), quia iam constat eos sacramentis divinis associatos, et baptismi gratiam suscepisse, et crismate unctos esse, et corporis Domini exstitisse participes, oportet, ut fidem quam vi vel necessitate susceperint, tenere cogantur, ne nomen Domini blasphemetur, et fides, quam susceperunt, vilis ac contemptibilis habeatur."

145. On Gratian as opposing forced baptism, see, for example, Brundage, "Introduction," 12–14; on Gratian as enjoining punitive military action against pagans, see, for example, Frederick H. Russell, *The Just War in the Middle Ages* (Cambridge: Cambridge University Press, 1975), 55–85; on Gratian as a source for both sides of the question, see, for example, Mario Condorelli, *I fondamenti giuridici de la tolleranza religiosa nell'elaborazione canonistica del secolo XII–XIII: Contributo*

A significant amplification of Gratian's teaching occurs in the *Summa decretorum* (ca. 1164) of Rufinus of Bologna, one of his earliest commentators. As with Gratian, Rufinus locates forced baptism in the context of the mildness and fraternal charity to be used by bishops in correcting their subordinates. He refers to non-believers without distinction and not just to Jews in bringing Canon 57 of Toledo IV to bear on the question. He agrees that non-Christians should not be forced into the font. It is forbidden to use violence to bring them to it. But here Rufinus adds new notes not found in Gratian or earlier sources. On the words versus blows doctrine, he says, "Gratian states that one may apply blows of a sort, so long as one does not get carried away with harsh discipline, but preserves mercy therein."[146] Rufinus offers no clear guidance on where to draw this line. Also, agreeing that those baptized by force should be constrained to practice Christianity, he observes that more than one kind of force may be involved: "Now compulsion by force applied to one's body or goods is forbidden, and differs from the insistent pressure, be it on property or persons, required to effect it."[147] Outright physical compulsion is unacceptable. But baptism under threat is permitted. Since recipients of the latter also receive other sacraments, some degree of assent to baptism can be inferred in their case. Compulsory Christian observance will develop it into the full faith which they may initially lack. Rufinus thus goes well beyond Gratian in validating certain forms of battery and intimidation as exceptions to the ban on forced baptism and in offering an enhanced rationale for enforced religious praxis.

From Rufinus's day until the turn of the thirteenth century, other commentators on Gratian accept and amplify this reading of the *Decretum*. The author of the *Summa Parisiensis* (1160s) states that "it is illegal to scourge people in order to force them into the faith" but that it is licit to impose the faith on infidels if they are defeated in battle, or if they rebel. In the 1190s Bernard of Parma and Huguccio, teacher of the future Innocent III, reframe Rufinus's distinction as what they now call absolute and conditional

---

storico-dogmatico. Università di Catania, Pubblicazioni della facoltà di giurisprudenza 36 (Milan: A. Giuffrè, 1960), 32–34, 79–81; Benjamin Z. Kedar, *Crusade and Mission: European Approaches toward the Muslims* (Princeton, NJ: Princeton University Press, 1984), 73–74.

146. Rufinus of Bologna, *Summa decretorum* d. 45. C. 1, ed. Heinrich Singer (Paderborn: Ferdinand Schöningh, 1902; reprt. Aalen: Scientia Verlag, 1963), 104–5: "Gratianus ergo dicit inferre posse huiusmodi verbera, si cum disciplina non habetur amaritudinis elatio, sed in illa habetur misericordia."

147. Ibid., at d. 45. C. 5, 106: "Sed coactio alia est per corporalem vel propriarum rerum violentiam: quod hic interdicitur; alia per exactionis instantiam, utpote usurarum vel personis: quod ibi fieri mandatur." Noted by Brundage, "Introduction," 14.

coercion. They agree that a certain amount of harshness may be applied to bring infidels to the font and to enforce their subsequent religious practice. In ca. 1219 Alanus Anglicus argues that infidels who stubbornly resist conversion may be compelled to accept baptism by corporal constraints, "short of death (*citra mortem*)."[148]

Honorius of Kent strikes a note in his *Summa de iure canonico* that also reverberates in the sequel. Agreeing that baptism requires the consent of recipients at the age of discretion, he endorses Rufinus's view that Jews forcibly baptized who then receive other sacraments manifest baptismal consent in some sense. They cannot be regarded as rejecting the faith absolutely, and should be required to practice it. Honorius appears to be the first canonist to compare forced with fictive baptizands, and to bring to bear on them the theologians' discussions of *sacramentum*, *res sacramenti*, and baptismal character. He distinguishes between these two types of baptizands and then unites them. Neither group possesses a baptismal intention. Fictive baptizands pretend to have this intention and seek the font voluntarily. Forced baptizands do not seek baptism but may consent to it, at least to some extent. Both forced and fictive baptizands receive the external *sacramentum* and not the *res sacramenti*. But both receive the baptismal character which enjoins their practice of the faith, which practice, Honorius avers, will promote their true conversion and their eventual reception of baptismal grace.[149]

Such was the state of play when Innocent III entered the field. As with Gratian, he gives with one hand and takes with the other. Innocent incorporates and refines the expansions of and departures from Gratian on forced baptism found in the first half-century of commentary on his text. In his papal responses to specific reports and appeals, Innocent presents a far from homogeneous doctrine. Modern scholars have seen him as both an opponent and a defender of forced baptism.[150] The evidence is not one-

148. Kedar, *Crusade and Mission*, 72–74; quotation from the *Summa Parisiensis* on pages 72–73n88; quotation from Alanus and translation on page 72; texts of Huguccio and Bernard cited respectively on pages 73n90 and 74n91. For scholarship challenging the view that Innocent studied with Huguccio, see Kenneth Pennington, "The Legal Education of Innocent III," and "Further Thoughts on Pope Innocent III's Knowledge of Law," both in idem, *Popes, Canonists and Texts, 1150–1550* (Aldershot: Variorum Reprints, 1993), no. I and II.

149. *Magistri Honorii Summa de iure canonico tractaturus* d. 45. C. 5, ed. Rudolf Weigand, Peter Landau, and Waltraud Kozur, Monumenta Iuris Canonici, Series A: Corpus Glossatorum 5/1 (Vatican City: Biblioteca Apostolica Vaticana, 2004), 138–39. See also ibid., C. 1. q. 1. c. 35, 287. For other commentators who make this point, see Condorelli, *I fondamenti*, 38–67, 69–78, 88.

150. For example, Kedar, *Crusade and Mission*, 71, 73n85, and Morrison, *Understanding Conversion*, 81, see Innocent as supporting forced baptism, forced observance, and war against

sided. As already noted, his letter to Berthold of Üxküll urges that rebellious recidivists in the Baltic be reduced to Christian practice, by force of arms if need be.

Writing in 1209 to King Valdemar II, leader of the current Danish expedition, Innocent praises him for his valor in "the extirpation of pagan errors" and the destruction of pagan idols. He alludes to the *compelle intrare* text in commending the king for "drawing the barbarian nations into the feast of the orthodox faith." The pope underscores the legitimacy and commendability of Danish military action in thus expanding the boundaries of Christendom.[151] It was a well-known fact, in Rome and elsewhere, that Danish policy in the Baltic Crusades was the same as that of other participants. The Danes had forced baptism on the pagans they defeated since their earliest Baltic expeditions in the 1130s. Innocent's letter to Valdemar neither excludes nor condemns that practice. Its martial rhetoric strongly suggests that force of arms is an acceptable way to bring the pagans into the fold. Yet, in a letter dated October 5, 1199, to Albert of Riga, Innocent opposes the very same policy: "It is intolerable, according to the church's religious norms, to force [people] to believe against their will." He follows up this injunction in a letter to Albert on April 19, 1201. Citing Gregory the Great, Innocent maintains here that the sole justification for warfare in the Baltic is the defense of new converts.[152]

apostates; John A. Watt, "Jews and Christians in the Gregorian Decretals," in *Christianity and Judaism*, ed. Diana Wood, Studies in Church History 29 (Oxford: Blackwell, 1992), 93–105 on pages 99–100, 105, sees both sides of the picture but accents Innocent's contribution to the support of forced baptism; John C. Moore, *Pope Innocent III (1160–1216): To Root up and to Plant* (Leiden: Brill, 2003), 142, 273, also sees both sides of the picture but accents Innocent's rejection of forced baptism.

151. Innocent III, *Epistola* 103 to Valdemar II of Denmark, 1209, *PL* (Paris, 1855), 216: 117A–B: "tractisque barbaris nationibus in sagenum fidei orthodoxae; ... injungimus quatenus anime illius qui captivitatem nostram sua duxit virtute captivam, ad extirpandum paganitatis errorem et terminos Christianae fidei dilatandos viriliter te accingas ... in forti brachio et extento confundas cum suis idolis spurcitiam paganorum, ac tanquam strenuus miles Christi fortiter et potenter in hujus certaminis agone contendas, ... si legitime certaveris, coronandus." Noted by Kedar, *Crusade and Mission*, 71n85. Fonnesberg-Schmidt, *The Popes and the Baltic Crusades*, 93–94, 105–6, 110–11, sees this letter as a baffling and temporary departure from Innocent's basic policy toward the Baltic mission. As Bysted, Selch Jensen, Villads Jensen, and Lind, *Jerusalem in the North*, 50, 151–53, point out, this letter encouraged Valdemar II to expand his campaign in the Baltic to Finland; the pope's accent on violence reflects the general knowledge of the Danes' policy of forced baptism.

152. Cited by Iben Fonnesberg-Schmidt, "Riga and Rome: Henry of Livonia and the Papal Curia," in *Crusading and Chronicle Writing: A Companion to Henry of Livonia*, ed. Marek Tamm, Linda Kaljundi, and Carsten Selch Jensen (Farnham: Ashgate, 2011), 209–27 on pages

If the contrasts visible in these messages cannot be explained by differences in the Danish and German conduct of the Baltic mission, neither do they bespeak a development of doctrine on Innocent's part. For, in earlier, longer, and more reflective documents, he asserts both opposition to and support for forced baptism. On September 15, 1199, he drafted a letter whose addressee is Christian but unspecified. Internal evidence suggests that he is responding to an appeal made by Jews, also unspecified. Innocent acknowledges that the Jews have particular legal rights. Earlier popes have accorded them the protection which he confirms. Jews occupy a distinctive place among non-Christians. For, although they are perfidious and misinterpret their own prophets, they are not to be destroyed, "since through them the truth of our own faith is confirmed." Innocent enjoins the Christian recipient of this message to guarantee the Jews' legal rights without prejudice. Further, he prohibits their forced baptism: "We decree therefore that no Christian should force them into baptism by violence or against their will. But if any of them freely seeks refuge among Christians for the sake of the faith, let him be made a Christian without objection once his will is made manifest. For no one is deemed to have a true faith in Christianity who is known to come to Christian baptism unwillingly, not freely."[153] The aforementioned decrees, Innocent concludes, are enjoined on pain of excommunication, unless worthy satisfaction and amends are made.

When he is not responding to concerns specific to Jews, Innocent places forced baptism in a far broader perspective. In September or October 1201 he answered a letter from Imbert d'Argueres, archbishop of Arles, which goes

216–17, 219; quotation on page 217n28: "Sicut ecclesiastice religionis censura compelli non patitur ad credendum invitos...." For Innocent's letter to the same in 1201, see ibid., 219–20. In eadem, *The Popes and the Baltic Crusades*, 92–93, 128–30, she sees these letters as a principled repudiation of the policy of Celestine III and cites other scholars who agree with that assessment.

153. Innocent III, *Epistola* 276, September 15, 1199 in *Die Register Innocenz' III*, ed. Othmar Hageneder, Werner Maleczk, and Alfred A. Strnad (Rome/Vienna: Verlag der Österreichischen Akademie der Wissenschaften, 1979), 2:535–36: "Licet perfidem Iudeorum sit multipliciter improbanda, quia tamen per eos fidem nostra veraciter comprobatur, non sunt a fidelibus graviter opprimendi.... Sicut ergo Iudeis non debet esse licentia in sinagogis suis ultra quam permissum est lege presumere, ita in hiis, que sunt illis concessa, nulla debent preiudicium sustinere.... Nos autem, ... quia tamen nostre postulant defensionis auxilium, et christianae pietatis mansuetudine praedecessorum felicis memorie Calixti [II], Eugenii [II], Alexandri [III], Clementis [I], et Celestini [III], Romanorum pontificem, vestigiis inherentes, ipsorum petitionem admittimus eisque protectione nostre clippeum indulgemus. Statuimus enim, ut nullus Christianus invitos vel nolentes eos ad babtismum [sic] per violentiam venire compellat, sed si eorum quilibet sponte ad Christianos fidei cause confugerit, postquam voluntas eius faciat patefacta, sine qualibet efficiatur calumpnia christianus: verum quippe christianitatis fidem habere non creditur, qui ad christianorum baptisma non spontaneus sed invitus cognoscit pervenire."

well beyond his correspondent's query. The original text of Imbert's letter is not extant, nor is Innocent's response. Despite the care with which Innocent sought to preserve his own rulings and letters, the part of the papal register covering the year 1201 was lost. A number of compilations of his letters were made during his pontificate, some with his authorization, and others were made later. The canonists who put together these compilations sometimes change the wording of the documents they include. Via this route, what we have as Innocent's reply to Imbert made its way into the *Decretals* of Pope Gregory IX (1234), the major canonical text to which most succeeding medieval thinkers turn for access to Innocent's teaching—although, as we saw in chapter 2 of this book and will note again later, Alexander of Hales was able to quote from this letter of Innocent several years before its appearance in Gregory's compendium.

Imbert asks whether the baptismal character is granted if the comatose (*dormientes*) or mentally incapacitated (*amentes*) are baptized. After speaking to that question, Innocent moves on to fictive and forced baptism, presenting debated positions on those matters before giving his own. Some say that if *dormientes* and *amentes* are baptized in that condition they should be rebaptized if they awaken or regain their wits. Others reject that view on the grounds that the sacrament of baptism is efficacious in itself. The character it imprints on all recipients remains, although the mentally incompetent do not receive the *res sacramenti*. This second opinion has also been applied to the unwilling and to the *ficti* "who receive the rite dissenting in their hearts but not orally." Proponents of this latter view say that "those who are immersed unwillingly or reluctantly belong to the jurisdiction of the church on account of the rite; thus it is reasonable to force them to observe the rules of the Christian faith." That said, Innocent gives his own ruling:

> It is indeed against the Christian religion to force someone consistently unwilling and deeply opposed into the reception and practice of Christianity. But, without absurdity, some distinguish between unwillingness and unwillingness, compulsion and compulsion. One who is impelled to it violently, by intimidation and threats, and receives baptism to avoid suffering harm, is comparable to one who accedes to baptism fictively. He receives the imprint of the Christian character. Since he wills it, in a sense, conditionally, although he does not will it absolutely, he is bound to the observance of the Christian faith.

It is in connection with conditional compulsion, says Innocent, that the second part of Canon 57 of Toledo IV applies. He rehearses the text as Gratian I does, essentially verbatim. But he then adds a proviso not earlier attached to this position. In contrast with the person who is baptized with *coactio conditionaliter*, "someone who has never consented, and who deeply objects, receives neither the *res sacramenti* nor the baptismal character. For it is more consequential to contradict expressly than to consent minimally."[154] Drawing these distinctions with more precision than his predecessors, Innocent's formulation of this last point indicates that the baptism of non-Christians with *coactio absoluta* does in fact take place, although he regards it as sacramentally void. Despite that conclusion, Innocent does not forbid such

154. Innocent III to Imbert d'Agueres, archbishop of Arles, September/October 1201, as cited in Gregory IX, *Decretals* 10.3.42.3 in *Corpus iuris canonici*, ed. Aemilius Friedberg, 2 vols. (Leipzig: Tauchnitz, 1879–80; reprt. Union, NJ: Lawbook Exchange, 2000), 2:646: "Item, vero queritur, utrum hujusmodi dormientes et amentibus sacramenti saltem character in baptisme imprimatur, ut excitati ex somnium vel ab egritudine liberati non sint denuo baptizandi. Sunt autem nonnulli, qui dicunt quod sacramenta, que per se sortiuntur effectum, ut baptisma, et ordo, et ceterisque similia, non solum dormientibus et amentibus, sed invitus etiam et contradicentes, etsi non quantum ad rem, quantum tamen ad character conferuntur, ... sed et fecti [sic] qui quamvis non ore, corde tamen dissentiunt, recipiant sacramentum. Sed opponitur talibus, quod qui fuissent inviti et reluctantes immersi, saltem ratione sacramenti ad jurisdictionem ecclesiasticam pertinerent; unde ad servandam regulam fidei Chrsitianae fovent rationabiliter compellandi. Verum id est religioni Christianae contrarium, ut semper invitus et penitus contradicens ad recipiendam et servandam Christianitatem aliquis compellatur. Propter quod inter invitum et invitum, coactum et coactum, alii non absurde distinguunt, quod is qui terroribus atque suppliciis violenter attrahitur, et ne detrimentum incurrat, Baptismi suscipit sacramentum, talis (sicut et is qui ficte ad baptismum accedit) characterem suscipit Christianitas impressum, et ipse tanquam conditionaliter volens, licet absolute non velit, cogendus est ad observantiam fidei Christianae; in quo casu debet intelligi decretum Concilii Toletani, ubi dicitur quod qui jampridem ad Christianitatem coacti sunt, sicut factum est temporibus religiossimi Principis Sisebuti, quia jam constat eos sacramentis divinis associatos, et baptismi gratiam suscipisse, et crismate unctos esse, et corporis Domini extitisse participes; oportet etiam ut fidem, quam necessitate susciperunt, tenere cogantur, ne nomen Domini blasphemetur, et fides quam susceperunt vilis ac contemptibilis habeatur. Ille vero qui nunquam consentit, sed penitus contradicit, nec rem nec characterem suscipit sacramenti, quam plus est expresse contradicere quam minime consentire." In commenting on this passage, Watt, "Jews and Christians," 99, sees it as directed specifically against Jews although they are not mentioned as such in the text; he ignores the *dormientes*, *amentes*, and *ficti* with whom Innocent is also concerned. These other baptizands are likewise ignored by Kedar, *Crusade and Mission*, 73, but he offers a clear discussion of the two modes of compulsion and notes correctly that this analysis is aimed at infidels without specification. On the loss of the papal register for 1201 and the transmission of Innocent's letters in decretal collections prior to the *Decretales* of Gregory IX, see Condorelli, *I fondamenti*, 93–101; Kenneth Pennington, "The Making of a Decretal Collection: The Genesis of the *Compilatio tertia*," in idem, *Popes, Canonists and Texts* (as in note 148), no. VIII; idem, "The Decretalists: 1190 to 1234," and "Decretal Collections, 1190–1234," both in *The History of Medieval Canon Law in the Classical Period, 1140–1234: From Gratian to the Decretals of Gregory IX*, ed. Kenneth Pennington and Wilfried Hartmann (Washington: The Catholic University of America Press, 2008), 211–43, 292–317, on pages 226, 229–41, 293–309, 315, 316 for Innocent's letters in particular. For Alexander of Hales's quotation of Innocent's letter in the 1220s, see above, 186.

baptisms. We do not find in this text an express prohibition of baptisms effected with conditional compulsion, nor even of those inflicted with absolute compulsion, despite the perceived sacramental nullity of the latter. Innocent's letter to Imbert of Arles contains no ruling that parallels the ban on forced baptism, reinforced by the penalty of excommunication for those who violate it, spelled out specifically in his letter of 1199 on the Jews. Did Innocent have either set of considerations in mind in appearing to tolerate the forced baptisms of Valdemar's Baltic pagans while condemning those of Albert of Riga?

This is a question which, among others, Innocent does not answer. In comparison with preceding canonists, he considers a wider range of unwilling baptizands. He bans the baptism of unwilling Jews, clearly asserting, in their case, the necessity of free choice. But he does not exempt the mentally incompetent, the fictive, or the forced, although he holds that the rite is nugatory for those baptized with *coactio absoluta.* He omits Gratian's prescription of courtesy, mildness, and reasoned persuasion, and he does not comment on faith as a gift of divine grace. Innocent endorses the application of the punitive side of Canon 57 of Toledo IV made by recent canonists. He extends the obligation to practice Christianity to those who, faced with threats and intimidation, are baptized with *coactio conditionaliter*. They can be viewed, nonetheless, as offering minimal, but adequate, consent. Innocent leaves these inconsistencies for later thinkers to tackle. Some remain unresolved. Others are restated with added refinements.

The leading canonist of the next generation, the Dominican Raymond of Peñafort, finds Innocent's analysis too broad and argues a much more limited brief in his *Summa de paenitentia* (1225/27). This work is neither a systematic treatise on moral theology or canon law nor a handbook for the education of pastors along the lines of the contemporary *summa confessorum*. Rather, it is a collection of juristic rules whose contents and scheme of organization are Raymond's own. Book 1 treats simony, infidels, heretics, schismatics, apostates, vows, oaths, lying, sacrilege, ecclesiastical immunities, and Christian burial. The other two books treat various personal and economic crimes, holy orders, repeatable and unrepeatable sacraments, excommunication, penance, and the remission of sins. Forced baptism is located in the hodge-podge of Book 1 under the heading of infidels, whose slaves are of equal or greater interest. The only infidels in question are Jews and Saracens.

After helpfully defining both groups, Raymond invokes Gregory the Great by name and yokes him to a modification of Innocent's teaching as he turns to their Christianization:

Since, following Gregory, Jews and Saracens up until now are to be drawn to the Christian faith by authorities, reason, and blandishments, rather than by asperities, they are not to be compelled, since enforced service is unpleasing to God. But, if they are compelled conditionally, that is, they receive the sacrament of baptism in response to threats, the seizure of their property, or blows, or any similar kind of compulsion, and later abandon the faith, they are to be forced to return to it, lest the name of the Lord be blasphemed and the faith they received be held vile and contemptible. What I say here applies to conditional compulsion. For if absolute compulsion occurs, as when someone is dragged [to the font] with physical violence and water is poured on him, he does not receive the baptismal character.[155]

Raymond thus includes Jews and the Saracens not yet extant for Gregory in two incompatible categories: those who are not to be forced and those who may be baptized with *coactio conditionaliter*. He expands the range and intensity of the cruelties permitted under that condition and sharply restricts *coactio absoluta* to those dragged to the font by main force and held captive while the baptismal water is poured. After noting that willing converts should undergo a catechumenate of forty days, Raymond turns with more interest to the slaves of Jews and Saracens.[156] While in the passage quoted he rules that recividist converts should be forced back into the church, the apostates he considers in Book 1 are not converts but established Christians who are to be punished by excommunication.[157] One additional point made by Raymond concerns conditional baptism. In Book 3, he speaks not of the absolute/conditional distinction in forced baptism but of candidates whose past history is unknown or doubtful, and cites the liturgical formula to be used by the minister in that case.[158]

155. Raymond of Peñafort, *Summa de paenitentia* 1.4.2, ed. Xaviero Ochea and Aliosio Diez, Universa Biblioteca Iuris/B (Rome: Commentarium pro Religione, 1976), cols. 309–10: "Debent, sicut ait Gregorius, tam iudei quam saraceni auctoritatibus, rationibus et blandimentis, potius quam asperitatibus, ad fidem Christianam de novo suscipiendam provocari, non autem compelli, quia coactio servitia non placent Deo. Si tamen coacti conditionaliter, puta per minas, vel rerum suarum ablationem, vel verbera, vel alia similem coactionem susceperint aliqui sacramentum baptismi, et postea recesserunt a nostra fide, sunt compellendi redire, ne nomen Domini blasphemetur et fides, quam susceperunt, vilis et contemptibilis habeatur. Conditionaliter coacti ideo dico, quia si absolute coacti essent, puta quia corporaliter cum violentia traherentur et super infundaretur aqua, non conferretur character baptismi." Noted by Kedar, *Crusade and Mission*, 74; Brundage, "Introduction," 14. For the date, Raymond's sources, and general characteristics of the work, see the editors' intro. on pages lxxiv–lxxix.

156. Raymond of Peñafort, *Summa* 1.4.3–1.4.7, col. 311–16; 1.4.3, col. 311–12 for the forty-day catechumenate.

157. Ibid., 1.7.1-10, col. 330–38.

158. Ibid., 3.24.6, col. 661: "Non 'ego te baptizo,' sed 'si non est baptizatus, ego te baptizo

Raymond of Peñafort is known to have compiled the *Decretals* (1234) of Pope Gregory IX, which repeats this formula for conditional baptism along with a reprise of Innocent III's letter to Imbert of Arles. While this text quotes Innocent at length, and glides with him from the mentally incompetent to the forced, it also adds some items not found in Innocent, putting a fresh spin on forced baptism. Gregory begins by amplifying on the baptism of *dormientes* and *amentes*. He attaches a new condition to them. Their afflictions may be congenital, or supervenient. If the latter, the baptismal intentions they manifested beforehand are all-important: "When baptized, *amentes* and *dormientes* receive the baptismal character if, before the onset of their dementia or coma, they consented to being baptized. This is not the case with others. The forced receive it in a causative way."[159] Neither this condition as applied to the mentally incompetent nor this opaque comment attached to the forced appears in Innocent's letter. Nor does the next point made in the *Decretals*. The original sin of baptized *dormientes* and *amentes*, along with any actual sins which they acknowledged before their affliction, are remitted by the rite. For, "since original sin is contracted without our consent, it is remitted without our consent, by the power of the sacrament."[160]

That said, Gregory goes on to quote Innocent III on forced baptism. He notes that some say that the unwilling and the reluctant belong to the jurisdiction of the church, and it reasonable to force them to observe Christianity. He agrees with Innocent that "it is indeed against the Christian religion to force someone consistently unwilling and deeply opposed into the reception and practice of Christianity." He concurs with the distinction between unwillingness and unwillingness, compulsion and compulsion, and develops it in language almost identical to Innocent's. Baptism received under intimidation and threat, as a means of avoiding harm, conveys the *sacramentum* and the baptismal character also received by fictive baptizands. Gregory agrees that it is these conditionally forced baptizands to whom the

in nomine Patris et Filii et Spiritus Sancti.'" As is noted by Julien Bellamy, "Baptême dans l'église latine depuis le VIIIe siècle," in *DthC*, 2/1:250–96 at 2/1:273–74, this notion was known from the eighth century onward and confirmed in a decretal of Alexander III in 1159, but it did not take hold among theologians until its insertion into the *Decretals* of Gregory IX by Raymond.

159. *Decretales Gregorii IX* 3.42.3, 2:644: "Amentes et dormientes baptizati, si ante dementiam vel dormitionem baptizari volebant, characterem suscipiunt, alios secus; coacti vero causative suscipiunt." The formula for conditional baptism is given at 3.42. 2, 2:644.

160. Ibid., 3.42.3, 2:645: "Originale igitur, quod non consensu contrahitur, sine consensu per vim remittitur sacramenti..." As noted in chapter 2 of this book, this principle is applied by William of Ockham to fictive baptisms; see above, 211, and 225–26, 307n194.

second part of Canon 57 of Toledo IV refers. They are rightly constrained to practice the Christian faith, for the reasons given. Gregory adds Innocent's final stipulation. In contrast with one baptized with *coactio conditionaliter*, "someone who has never consented in any way, and who objects deeply, receives neither the *res sacramenti* nor the baptismal character. For it is more consequential to contradict expressly than to consent minimally." Then returning, as Innocent does not, to the *dormientes* and *amentes*, Gregory expands the rationale for baptizing them: "If they had earlier expressed the intention to be baptized and had enrolled as catechumens" and are now afflicted and in danger of death, the church counsels their baptism "since no voluntary objection imposes an impediment to it."[161] Gregory's juxtaposition of the mentally incompetent and the forced raises the question, which he does not answer, of whether the latter as well as the former receive remission of original sin at the font. His point about the absence of voluntary objection as imposing no impediment to baptism also drops a suggestion which some masters will pick up and apply to the forced, who are able to object, as well as to mental incompetents, who are not.

The View from the Ivory Tower: Scholastic Theologians to the Early Fourteenth Century

While later commentators on the *Decretals* or on Gratian may cite Gregory IX's rulings as definitive, the scholastic theologians, while taking them with great seriousness, do not regard the bidding as closed. Their discussions do not really get underway until the early thirteenth century. For all the attention which twelfth-century theologians devote to baptism by desire and to fictive baptism, and for all their insistence that a true baptismal intention is needed for the efficacious reception of the sacrament, they ignore forced baptism until the very end of the century. The first to address it is Peter the Chanter. Without citing Hugh of St. Victor, he takes for granted that master's ringing endorsement of intentionalism: "It has been proclaimed as a rule of the Christian faith that those who accept the faith voluntarily will be judged worthy of spiritual regeneration, and those who reject the faith

161. *Decretales* 3.42.3, 2:646: "Secus autem, si prius catechumeni exstitissent, et habuissent propositum baptizandi, unde tales in necessitatis articulo consuevit ecclesia baptizare. Tunc ergo characterem sacramentalis imprimi operatio, quum obicem voluntatis contrarie non invenit obsistentem." For some later thirteenth- and fourteenth-century canonists who repeat the amplifications of Innocent in the *Decretales*, see Kedar, *Crusade and Mission*, 169–70, 184–87, 223–24. Theologians who take up these themes are treated below.

will be repulsed, judged unworthy of the reception of God's sacraments."[162] As we recall, Hugh makes this sweeping assertion in connection with fictive baptism. The Chanter associates forced baptism with fictive baptisms that are purely jocular or fraudulent. The absence of true baptismal intention which invalidates such fictive rites also extends to "baptism violently administered." For the self-same reason, forced baptism is sacramentally null and void.[163]

Although Peter Lombard does not mention forced baptism, his commentators, starting in the early thirteenth century, do so, taking careful note of recent canonical opinions. Alexander of Hales reflects the period's burgeoning interest in the theme of baptismal character, placing forced baptism in that context in his *Glossa* on the *Sentences*. Alexander asks whether the unwilling, along with *dormientes* and *amentes*, receive the baptismal character. He draws largely on Innocent III and adds refinements similar to those of Gregory IX. Alexander sides with those who "distinguish between unwillingness and unwillingness, compulsion and compulsion." He agrees that "one who is drawn violently, who receives the sacrament of baptism to avoid danger to his health, wills it, in a sense, conditionally, and is bound to the observance of the Christian faith; as with one who accedes fictively, he receives the character of Christianity. One who never consents but deeply objects receives neither the character nor the *res sacramenti*. For it is more consequential to contradict expressly than to consent minimally."[164] To this Alexander adds that the comatose and mentally disabled, if immersed, do not receive the baptismal character if they had consistently rejected baptism before being afflicted. But if they had sought baptism earlier and had enrolled as catechumens, and are now in danger of death, they do receive the baptismal character, for the reasons Gregory IX gives.[165] That point apart, Alexander's

162. Hugh of St. Victor, *De sacramentis Christianae fidei* 2.6.9, ed. Rainer Berndt, Corpus Victorinum 1 (Münster: Aschendorff, 2008), 391: "Regula fidei christianae nuntiabatur ut vel sponte fidei adquiescentes digni regeneratione spiritali iudicarentur vel credere nolentes merito a perceptione sacramenti dei velut indigni repellentur."

163. Peter the Chanter, *Summa de sacramentis et animae consiliis* 20, ed. Jean-Albert Dugauquier, 3 vols in 5 (Louvain: Éditions Nauwelaerts, 1954–76), 1:58–60; quotation at 1:59: "de baptismo violenter collato."

164. Alexander of Hales, *Glossa in quattuor libros Sententiarum*, In *Sent.* 4. d. 5. a. 3, ed. Collegium S. Bonaventurae, 4 vols. (Quaracchi: Collegium S. Bonaventurae, 1951–57), 4:98: "Ibi distinguunt inter invitum et invitum, coactum et coactum. Nam qui violenter attrahitur et, ne detrimentum incurrat salutis, baptismi suscipit sacramentum, sicut is qui ficte accedit, characterem suscipit christianitas, et tanquam conditionaliter volens cogendus est ad observationem fidei christianae. Ille vero qui nunquam consentit sed penitus contradicit, nec rem nec characterem suscipit sacramenti, quia plus est expresse contradicere quam minime consentire."

165. Ibid., 4:98–99.

main contribution is to bring forced baptism, and the acceptability of conditional compulsion, into the mainstream of scholastic theology.

Theologians from the middle of the thirteenth century onward borrow freely from each other, as well as from the canonists, while adding fresh arguments and sources. Albert the Great takes up forced baptism briefly but in no uncertain terms in his *Sentences* commentary. He adds a qualification that has considerable later influence. As Albert frames the question, the issue is not merely that forced baptizands are unwilling and that they lack faith. Also critical is whether they openly and clearly protest being forced into the font: "There is, then, the unwilling person who does not believe but is subjected to the church's rites without voicing objection. There is also the unwilling person who does speak out against subjection to the church's rites. In the latter case, no result follows, even if he is immersed a thousand times."[166] Without using the language of absolute and conditional coercion, Albert clearly rejects the validity of forced baptism when the unwilling baptizand protests. The major leap he makes is to argue that it is the candidate's expression of his opposition, not his lack of faith or baptismal intention itself, which nullifies the rite he undergoes.

Bonaventure agrees that the efficacy of baptism depends on the intention of an adult recipient. But he rethinks the nature of the intentionality needed to validate a forced baptism. Bonaventure also substitutes *coactio sufficiens* and *coactio inducens* for Innocent's absolute and conditional coercion. *Coactio sufficiens* annuls the efficacy of baptism altogether. The recipient of such a rite is physically constrained, along the lines suggested by Raymond of Peñafort, held captive and thrust violently into the font: "Such a person is in no way baptized, since, in his case, there is no consent and free will at all, but, on the contrary, utter repugnance." Bonaventure's treatment of *coatio inducens* then raises the bar on that condition. The sufferings of a person baptized in this way do not merely intimidate him, or bring him just short of death, as Alanus Anglicus puts it. Rather, they bring him face to face with death itself: "He wills to be subjected to the church's sacrament rather than to suffer death." Bonaventure takes a hard line in estimating this individual's state of mind, and how he can be thought of as exercising a sacramentally viable free choice. If he seeks to avoid death by faking a baptismal intention which he in no way possesses, as with a *fictus*, then the

166. Albert the Great, *In IV Sententiarum*, In *Sent.* 4. d. 4E. a. 10 *solutio*, in *Opera omnia*, ed. Stephanus C. A. Borgnet, 38 vols. (Paris: Vivès, 1880–95), 29:139: "Est enim invitus non credens, tamen operationi Ecclesiae non reclamando se subjicens.... Est enim invitus aperte reclamans, et non subjicens se operationi Ecclesiae: et hic nihil consequitur, etiamsi millesies immergeretur."

rite is no sacrament. But Bonaventure envisions a situation in which, even though this baptizand lacks faith and the desire for grace, his motive is not primarily the wish to escape death but rather to accept what the church means by baptism: "Although lacking the desire for merit, there can still be consent and will, and this is not an involuntary act as such." For Bonaventure, the appeal of such a vaguely understood rite can be more persuasive than the fear of imminent death in one subjected to *coactio inducens*, to the point where his submission is judged as an act of free choice. This assent, or abandonment of resistance, is why, "according to the canons and doctors of theology, he is judged to be baptized."[167] After making a brief detour to explain that persons incapable of exercising free will, such as the insane, can be baptized *de facto* if not *de iure*,[168] Bonaventure concludes that, while *coactio sufficiens* invalidates the efficacy of baptism, *coactio inducens*, as he describes it, and to which he arrogates the alleged support of the Christian tradition, can result in the grant of baptismal character.[169]

Another mid-century commentator on the *Sentences*, Peter of Tarentaise, is less rigorous than Bonaventure, although he buys into the Franciscan master's language. Atypically concise in comparison with his treatment of fictive baptism, Peter brings his own insights to forced baptism. His context is the question of whether faith is mandatory in adult baptisms. He affirms that it is, if the rite is to grant the *res sacramenti*, which is grace. But in its absence it can still convey the *sacramentum*, which, he says, unhelpfully, is baptismal character.[170] Peter then moves on to three kinds of baptizands who

167. Bonaventure, *In IV Sententiarum*, In *Sent.* 4. pars 1. a. 2. q. 1, in *Opera omnia*, ed. Collegium S. Bonaventurae, 10 vols. (Quaracchi: Collegium S. Bonaventurae, 1882–1902), 4:100–101: "talis nullo modo baptizatus est, quia nullo modo fuit in eo consensus nec voluntas immo fuit omnino repugnans.... Coactio inducente, utpote minis vel flagellis, quod magis vult se subjicere sacramento Ecclesiae quam morte perire, dico, quod aut intendit alios illudere et mortem evadere, et tunc, quia non est intentio, non est sacramentum, cum nullus dicatur baptizatus esse, qui consentit, si immergi ad iocum; aut ipse vult, illud quod facit Ecclesia circa se fieri, magis, quam velit perire; et tunc, sive credat sive non, sive velit habere gratiam sive non, dicendum, quod recepit sacramentum, et quod, non sit ibi voluntas meritoria, est tamen ibi consensus et voluntas, nec est simpliciter involuntarium; ... et ideo secundum canones et doctores theologiae talis iudicandus est baptizatus."

168. Ibid., ad 4.1, 4:101.

169. Ibid., ad 4.3–4, 4:101. Cf. Irène Rosier-Catach, *La parole efficace: Signe, rituel, sacré* (Paris: Éditions de Seuil, 2004), 285, who sees Bonaventure as the first to distinguish levels of compulsion in forced baptism, who thinks that those subjected to his *coactio inducens* receive the *res sacramenti* and not merely the *sacramentum* and baptismal character, and who sees his doctrine as aimed at Jews exclusively, although they are not mentioned by Bonaventure in this passage.

170. Peter of Tarentaise, *In Sententiarum*, In *Sent.* 4. d. 6. q. 3. a. 2, ed. Johannnes Baptista Marinis, 4 vols. (Toulouse: Arnaldus Colomerus, 1649–52; reprt. Ridgewood, NJ: Gregg Press,

lack faith: the forced, the insane, and the mentally deficient. They also lack consent, equally necessary for the full reception of baptism. Peter draws a comparison with marriage: "Just as the consent of the woman with the man is required in marriage according to the flesh, so also consent is required in the spiritual marriage with God."[171] This condition is waived for people who are constitutionally unable to give consent, such as "infants, the permanently insane, and the naturally foolish; in them, will is not required." In the two latter groups, will is relevant only if their condition is not congenital and they expressed consent before becoming afflicted, or if they do so during lucid intervals. Otherwise, they receive only the *sacramentum* and baptismal character at the font.[172] Peter does not consider those now incapable of rendering consent who were once able to do so and who then rejected baptism.

Next, he takes up forced baptizands: "There is one sort of person seized in baptism, either compelled entirely by force since he is violently dragged, who receives neither the *sacramentum* nor the *res*, or conditionally, since he is impelled by fear; he receives the *sacramentum* but not the *res*." Main force, he agrees with Bonaventure and Raymond, invalidates the rite for the first forced baptizand. Intimidation, but not Bonaventure's prospect of imminent death, is what motivates the second forced baptizand. Peter then puts Bonaventure's terminology into the mouth of Innocent III: "It is said by him [Innocent] that the former is impelled into baptism *sufficiente*, that is, by force, not merely *inducente*, that is, by fear."[173] Aside from Peter's brevity, the previous passage reflects the blurring of the differences between the *sacramentum* and baptismal character, on which he and other masters of his time debated at such length, and so inconclusively.

Thomas Aquinas marks a departure from other mendicant masters in ignoring forced baptism in his *Sentences* commentary, reserving discussion of it to his *Summa theologiae*. In two *quaestiones* he treats the propriety of baptizing the children of non-believers against their parents' will. In one of these, he gives a straightforward negative answer, framed as a syllogism based on a general principle: "Injury should be done to no one. Now, injury

1964), 4:74–75; quotation at 4:74: "in adultis vero requiritur fides propria, non quidem ad susceptionem sacramenti, id est characteris, sed ad susceptionem rei sacramenti, id est gratiae."

171. Ibid. d. 6. q. 3. a. 3 *sed contra*, 4:75: "In desponsatione carnali mulieris ad virum consensus requiritur: ergo in desponsatione spirituale ad Deum."

172. Ibid.: "ut parvuli, et perpetuo furiosi, et naturaliter stulti; in his voluntas non requiritur."

173. Ibid.: "Cum ergo quis ad baptismum cogitur, aut est coactio omnimodo per vim, quia violenter attrahitur; est tunc non recepit sacramentum, nec rem; aut conditionata, quia per metum inducitur, et tunc recepit sacramentum, sed non rem.... Loquitur de eo [Innocent] qui cogitur ad baptisma, coactione sufficiente, scilicet per vim; non tamen inducente, scilicet per metum."

would be done to Jews if their children were baptized against their will, since they would lose their parental rights (*jus patriae potestatis*) over their children as soon as they became believers. Thus, they should not be baptized against their parents' will."[174]

Aquinas explains that this duty to do no injury rests on two foundations. The first is ecclesiastical tradition. This tradition is weighty and must be followed: "Now it has never been the practice of the church to baptize the children of Jews against their parents' will." True, some Christian princes have violated this rule. But their policy in no sense sets a precedent: "It thus seems perilous to assert, against ecclesiastical custom up to the present, that the children of Jews should be baptized against their parents' will." The hazard is also practical. It lies in "the danger to the faith," that is, the likelihood that parental pressure will persuade such forcibly baptized children to return to their ancestral creed once they come of age and can decide for themselves. The second foundation is a more universal tradition: "This practice would be repugnant to natural justice." It would contravene natural law to infringe on the rights of parents over their underage children. When the children come of age, it is acceptable to try to persuade them to become Christians. But interference with them before that point is illegitimate.[175]

Aquinas offers the self-same argument in another question applied not just to Jews but to the children of non-Christians in general. As he asserts, "It is not the custom of the church for the children of infidels to be baptized against their parents' will." Such a practice is likewise a contravention of the parents' natural legal rights. Here, Aquinas yokes this natural law position with the prohibition of forced baptism in the first part of Canon 57 of Toledo IV, cited in his *sed contra*, although natural law is not a principle invoked by the council fathers.[176] He concurs with their rule that faith can-

174. Thomas Aquinas, *Summa theologiae* IIaIIae. d. 10. a. 12 *sed contra*, Blackfriars ed. and trans., 61 vols. (New York: McGraw-Hill, 1964–76), 32:76: "Nemini facienda est injuriam. Fieret autem Judeis injuria si eorum filii baptizarentur eis invitis, quia amitterent jus patriae potestatis in filios iam fideles. Ergo invitis non sunt baptizati."

175. Ibid., *responsio*, 32:76–78; quotations at 32:76: "Dicendum quod maximam habet auctoritatem Ecclesiae consuetudo, quae semper est in omnibus aemulanda.... Hoc autem Ecclesiae usus nunquam habuit quod Judaeorum filiis invitis parentibus baptizarentur.... Et ideo periculosum videtur haec assertionem de novo inducere ut praeter consuetudinem in Ecclesia hactenus observandam, Judaeorum filii invitis parentibus baptizarentur"; "propter periculum fidei"; at 32:75: "quia repugnat justitiae naturali.... Unde contra justitiam naturalem esset, si puer antequam habet usum rationis, a cura parentum subtrahatur, vel eo aliquid ordinetur invitis parentibus."

176. Ibid., IIIa. q. 68. a. 10, 57:110–14; quotation in the *responsio* at 57:112: "Et ideo non habet hoc Ecclesiae consuetudo, quod filii infidelium, invitis parentibus, baptizentur." The point about natural law is given at ad 1 and ad 3, 57:112 and 57:114.

not be compelled since it requires the exercise of free will. He does not cite their decree that the children of recividists should be handed over to monks and nuns to be reared as Christians. But this is far from his last reference to Toledo IV.

Regarding adult baptizands able to know what they are doing and capable of exercising free will, Aquinas agrees that they must bring faith to the font if they are to receive baptism efficaciously. He accepts that their baptismal intentions may be generic and their faith imperfect, since no one possesses perfect faith in this life. If it is unclear to a baptismal minister whether a candidate meets these minimal requirements, Aquinas proposes the use of the formula for conditional baptism as given in the *Decretals* of Gregory IX.[177] The baptizands discussed in this question, however, are all assumed to have sought the font voluntarily.

But such is not really the case in the major question which Aquinas devotes to the forced baptism of adults. His entire presentation of this topic is of interest. Among the four objections which he plans to refute, he lists the statement opening Canon 57 of Toledo IV ruling that Jews henceforth are not to be forced to believe; "nor," he adds, "for the same reason, are any infidels to be forced into the faith." The other three objections come from works of Augustine. One states that we should not take punitive action against those lacking our beliefs, since God will sort out the wheat from the tares. The second states that, while we do some things unwillingly, we cannot believe unwillingly. The third notes that, since God does not seek the death of sinners, neither should we. Then comes the *sed contra*. Aquinas leads off with *compelle intrare* as his key authority. It supports the view that "some infidels are to be forced into the faith." In his response, Aquinas offers the following explanation:

> Infidels, that is to say, pagans and Jews who have never accepted the faith, should in no way be compelled to believe in the faith. For to believe is a voluntary matter. But, when feasible, they should be forced by the faithful not to impede the faith with blasphemies, evil persuasions, or open persecutions. And this is why those faithful to Christ often wage war against infidels, not so that they may be forced to believe, since even if they defeat them and take them captive they leave them free to believe as they will, but so that they may be forced not to obstruct the faith of Christ.

That said, Aquinas addresses the four objections with which he opens this question. The three drawn from Augustine, he notes, are irrelevant, since

177. Ibid., IIIa. q. 68. a. 7 *sed contra*, ad 1, ad 2, 57:102–6. For more on adults lacking the use of reason, and the semi-competent, amplifying on the discussion of *amentes*, *furiosi*, and *dormientes* in Aquinas' *Sentences* commentary, see IIIa. q. 68. a. 12, 57:118–20.

they deal with heretics, not with non-believers. As for the objection drawn from Canon 57 of Toledo IV, Aquinas opposes it with another passage from Canon 57, the rule requiring that all the baptized be forced to observe the Christian faith.[178]

In the light of the Baltic Crusades, Aquinas's claim that the wars waged against infidels are purely defensive and that, when defeated, infidels are left free to believe what they choose, is quixotic, not to say disingenuous. The citation of the second part of Canon 57 of Toledo IV against the objection based on its first part has no bearing unless there are, indeed, infidel forced baptizands whose observance of the faith is to be compelled. And, while Aquinas disqualifies the other three objections as applying to heretics, not infidels, he does not clarify whether his *compelle intrare* argument derives from Augustine's anti-Donatist *Epistola* 185 and is thus irrelevant for the very same reason.

Before leaving Aquinas, it is worth noting one further argument in his *Summa theologiae*, although he does not cite it in any of his discussions of baptism. It stems from Aristotle's *Nicomachean Ethics* 3.1, a work on which Aquinas produced a well-regarded commentary (1270/72) at the same point when he was completing the second part of the *Summa*. Aristotle distinguishes between compulsion and partly voluntary action. Compulsion occurs when a person is constrained to do something he does not want to do by forces beyond his control. In a partly voluntary action, the individual acts and is not merely acted upon. Forces beyond his control create the circumstances in which he chooses to do something he does not want to do. As examples, Aristotle cites two ship captains. The first captain's ship is blown off course by a storm, taking it, perforce, to an unintended and unwanted destination. The second captain, faced with a storm, jettisons cargo. Now, no one jettisons cargo voluntarily. But he chooses to do so for the safety of

178. Thomas Aquinas, *Summa theologiae* IIaIIae. q. 10. a. 8, 32:60–62, for the entire question; quotations at objection 2, 32:60: "Ergo pari ratione nec aliqui infideles sint ad fidem cogendi"; at *sed contra*, 32:60: "Ergo aliqui sunt compellendi ad fidem"; at *responsio*, 32:62: "Dicendum quod infidelium quidam sunt qui nunquam susceperunt fidem, sicut gentiles et Judaei, et tales nullo modo sunt ad fidem compellendi ut ipsi credant, quia credere voluntatis est. Sunt tamen compellendi a fidelibus, si adsit facultas, ut fidem non impediant vel blasphemiis, vel malis persuasionibus, vel etiam apertis persecutionibus. Et propter hoc fideles Christi frequenter contra infideles bellum movent non quidem ut eos ad credendum cogant, quia si etiam eos vicissent et captivos haberent in eorum libertate relinquirent an credere vellent; sed propter hoc ut eos compellant ne fidem Christi impediant." The citation of the second part of Canon 57 of Toledo IV is at ad 2, 32:62. Noted by Kedar, *Crusade and Mission*, 183, who sees this passage as aimed at legitimating the Holy Land Crusades, not as dealing with forced baptism as such.

those on board. In this analysis, as one Aristotle scholar has observed, "voluntariness is a property of actions, not of motivations."[179]

Now, motivations are of deep concern to Aquinas, who takes up this issue not only in his Aristotle commentary but also in the IaIIae of his *Summa theologiae*, where he develops a theory of action as background to the psychogenesis of moral acts. He cites Nemesius and the *Nicomachean Ethics* in his *sed contra*, but the ensuing analysis differs from Aristotle's. Aquinas agrees that what we do under compulsion is involuntary. But what we do when we are afraid we do of our own free will. The same exercise of the intellectual and affective faculties occurs as is operative in other acts of moral choice. We evaluate our options and decide using the calculus of greater and lesser goods and evils. Ignoring the fact that both of Aristotle's captains face storms at sea over which they have no control, Aquinas argues that compulsion alone is the consequence of external force, preventing someone from reaching the goal he judges to be good. Aquinas regards the decision of someone acting in response to fear as internal. This person wills to make a frightening choice, one judged to be deeply flawed, in order to avoid an outcome that he fears even more. The issue here, as Aquinas sees it, is the fearful agent's mastery of his own state of mind, his valorizing of one fear over another. It lies within his power to achieve his own attitude adjustment. Thus, the decision of the person moved by fear, as with the captain who jettisons cargo, "is quite simply voluntary."[180] Not even partly voluntary, as Aristotle has it. While this reinscription of *Nicomachean Ethics* 3.1 is not an argument which Aquinas applies to baptismal intention, his use of the terms force (*vis*) and fear (*metus*) recalls language invoked by predecessors and contemporaries in their distinctions between absolute and conditional compulsion.

In the next generation, a different appeal to Aristotle emerges in the *Sentences* commentary of Richard of Mediavilla. Under the heading of whether baptizands must possess the use of reason, he rejects the compari-

179. Aristotle, *Nicomachean Ethics* 3.1, ed. and trans. Roger Crisp (Cambridge: Cambridge University Press, 2000), 38; see Susan Sauvé Meyer, "Aristotle on the Voluntary," in *The Blackwell Guide to Aristotle's Nicomachean Ethics*, ed. Richard Kraut (Oxford: Blackwell, 2006), 137–57; quotation on page 150. As noted by Riccardo Saccenti, *Conservare la retta volontà: L'atto morale nelle dottrine di Filippo il Cancelliere e Ugo di Saint-Cher (1225–1235)* (Bologna: Il Mulinor, 2013), 155–56, Hugh of Saint-Cher was the first to cite this text but does not apply it either to the issue of moral culpability or to that of valid sacramental reception.

180. Thomas Aquinas, *Summa theologiae* IaIIae, q. 6. a, 6, 17:24: "Sic autem quod fit per metum est voluntaria, …unde manifestum est quod simpliciter voluntarium est." Cf. Thomas Aquinas, *Sententia libri Ethicorum* 3.1 in *Opera omnia*, iussu impensaque Leonis XIII P. M. edita, ed. Fratrum Praedicatorum, 48 vols. (Rome: Ex Typographia Polyglotta S. C. Propaganda Fide, 1882–1985), 47/1:117–20.

son with marriage made by Peter of Tarentaise, offering an alternative argument. An entity may receive its form without the cooperation of its matter. For matter, in this process, is passive. So, as with *dormientes*, *amentes*, and *furiosi*, adults can receive both the *sacramentum* and the *res sacramenti* passively, absent any moral or intellectual impediment. True, we can ascertain the current intentions of the mentally impaired only if they recover their wits or have lucid intervals. But if their afflictions are congenital, we should baptize them at once. Richard sees the baptism of these passive adults as having full sacramental validity. His argument puts an Aristotelian spin on Gregory IX's point about the aconsensual remission of original sin. This is why there is no parallel with marriage. For spouses must be "adults possessing the use of reason; their consent in act (*in actu*) or in habit (*in habitu*) is required."[181] Unspoken, but obvious, is Richard's recognition that validly married people must be able to grasp and carry out the duties of the wedded state. We can have no analogous expectations for the post-baptismal Christian life of the mentally disabled.

While Aristotelian terminology can thus clarify the situation of the intellectually challenged, it also assists Richard's analysis of forced baptism, as does another idea which he adds to the mix, divine omnipotence: "Since God is all-powerful, He can imprint the baptismal character [on an adult] by a special dispensation, even if there exists within him no intention to receive the sacrament, whether *in actu* or *in habitu*." If such a dispensation occurs, we should regard this individual as a member of the church and oblige him to practice Christianity. The same applies to a candidate who has a baptismal intention *in habitu* only. Both receive the *sacramentum* and the baptismal character. The practice of Christianity over time will enable the latter baptizand to translate his intention *in habitu* into one *in actu*, so that he receives the *res sacramenti* as well.[182] Richard is not forthcoming on how a baptismal intention *in habitu* or, *a fortiori*, a baptismal character received by divine dispensation, can be detected by church authorities.

Dropping that issue, he turns to the advice of Gregory the Great as reprised in Gregory IX's *Decretals*: "Those who, with a sincere intention, rightly seek to draw to the faith those outside the Christian religion should

181. Richard of Mediavilla, *In IV libros Sententiarum*, In *Sent.* 4. d. 6. a. 3. q. 2, ed. Ludovicus Silvestris à Sancto, 4 vols. (Brescia: De Consensu Superiorum, 1591; reprt. Frankfurt: Minerva GMBH, 1963), 4:76: "adultis habentibus usum rationis: in illis enim requiritur consensu actu, vel habitu."

182. Ibid., d. 6. a. 3. q. 3, 4:76–77; quotation at 4:77: "Posset Deus, cum sit omnipotens, imprimere charactere baptismalem ex speciali dispensatione, nulla existente in eis intentione, neque actu, neque habitu, ad suscipiendum sacramentum."

do so with blandishments, not with asperities." Richard agrees. He then reframes the distinction between modes of compulsion in Aristotelian terms. In one case, the person thrust into the font remains passive in the face of external constraints and says nothing to oppose his baptism. In another case, the person compelled protests, actively opposing his baptism. As with Albert the Great, Richard sees the validity of the rite as conditioned by what the forced baptizand says or does not say at the font, although he puts the idea in the language of action and passion. Richard is not particularly interested in spelling out the range and intensity of provocations that may be inflicted on these baptizands. In his first *quaestio* on this subject, he has two other points to make. First, the forced baptism of one who deeply objects is sacramentally void and "totally useless" to him. Second, it is also profitless to the church. It will simply produce crypto-infidels who, "in the guise of a simulated Christianity, may more easily seduce and pervert true Christians." Putting Aquinas' claim into the present indicative, he adds that, although the faithful "often fight just wars against the pagans, this is not in order to force them to believe." Then, capping his achievement as the only scholastic writing on fictive baptism to grasp that Augustine's *De baptismo* 7 is actually aimed at heretics and schismatics, Richard concludes, in a possible dig at Aquinas, that the *compelle intrare* argument of Augustine's *Epistola* 185 has no bearing on in the present question since it, too, refers to heterodox Christians and not to the forced baptism of infidels.[183]

Returning, in his next *quaestio*, to the assertion that a baptizand who never consents, who has no baptismal intention either *in habitu* or *in actu*, and who actively dissents, receives neither the *sacramentum* nor the *res sacramenti*, Richard makes his own the distinction between absolute and conditional coercion. While the absolutely coerced receive nothing at the font, he regards the conditionally coerced who fail to register their objection as expressing tacit consent. Richard pulls back from the extremely stark alternatives which Bonaventure posits for *coactio inducens*. His own conditionally coerced baptizand is not required to prize an amorphous idea of baptism over his own certain death. More in line with Innocent III and Gregory IX, he simply states that one conditionally coerced, although faced with intimidation and threats, receives the baptismal character and the obligation to

183. Ibid., d. 6. a. 3. q. 1, 4:77–78; quotations at 4:77: "Qui sincera intentio extraneos a Christiana religione ad fidem cupiunt rectum adducere blandimentes debent, non asperitatibus studere"; "coactio penitus inutilis esset"; and at 4:78; "infideles occulti quam manifesti, quia sub simulatione Christianitatis veros Christianos facilius seducunt et pervertent"; "contra infideles frequenter iusta bella movent, non quidem ut eos credendum cogent."

practice Christianity.[184] More or less as an afterthought, and without mentioning either *patria potestas* or natural law, Richard adds that the children of pagans and Jews should not be baptized against their parents' will.[185] But his chief concern is to mitigate Bonaventure's harshness and to impose the Aristotelian concepts of matter and form, action and passion, *actus* and *habitus*, on the distinction between absolute and conditional coercion, concurring with Albert the Great that, absent express dissent, tacit consent can be assumed in forced baptizands.

John Duns Scotus accepts much of the teaching of Richard of Mediavilla, while adding some arguments not hitherto applied to forced baptism. On balance, Scotus is primarily concerned with expanding the conditions in which forced baptizands can be deemed complaisant. This emphasis is not belied in the first *quaestio* in his *Ordinatio* dedicated to this theme, where he quotes Innocent III via Gregory IX in his *sed contra*: "One who is impelled to it violently, by intimidation and threats, and receives the sacrament of baptism to avoid suffering harm, is like one who accedes to baptism fictively. He receives the imprint of the character of Christianity. Since he wills it, in a sense conditionally, although he does not will it absolutely, he is bound to the observance of the Christian faith."[186] Before imparting his own distinctive interpretation to this passage, Scotus pauses to define the adult population to which it pertains. He makes the by-now-traditional exceptions, "the mentally deficient and the insane from birth" and the comatose. If they are congenitally afflicted and there is no prospect of their recovery, they should be baptized forthwith. If there is hope of their improvement, we should keep a watching brief, unless they are in danger of death. We should respect the positive, or negative, intentions which they expressed if they did so before the onset of their affliction. Scotus attaches an important addendum to this last point. If the mentally incompetent rejected baptism when they were able to do so, and they are baptized anyway, the rite is invalid. Scotus then takes the next logical step. Such nugatory baptisms should be forbidden.[187]

184. Ibid., d. 6. a. 3. q. 2, 4:78.

185. Ibid., d. 6. a. 3. q. 3, 4:78–79.

186. John Duns Scotus, *Ordinatio* 4. q. 4.5. pars 2. q. 1 *sed contra* 61, ed. Josephus Rodríguez Carballo in *Opera omnia* (Vatican City: Typus Vaticanis, 2008), 11:242: "Qui terroribus atque supliciis violenter attrahitur, et, ne detrimentum incurrat, baptismi suscepit sacramentum, talis, sicut is qui ficte ad baptismum accedit, characterem suscipit christianitatis impressum, et ipse, tamquam conditionaliter volens, licet absolute non velit, cogendus est ad observationem fidei christianae…"

187. Ibid., 1–2.62–67, 11:242–44; quotation at 63, 4:242: "fatuus et furiosus a nativitate."

Turning to adults with the use of reason, Scotus argues that the effects of their baptism and the consequences for their future lives depend on two factors. They may come to the font willingly or unwillingly. If unwilling, they may or may not express that unwillingness overtly. On this point, he agrees with both Albert the Great and Richard of Mediavilla. At the same time, he brings to bear on this issue the argument derived from *Nicomachean Ethics* 3.1 found in Aquinas but not applied by him to forced baptism. Scotus observes that our unwillingness to do something does not prevent us from doing it voluntarily. He cites the ship captain who jettisons cargo in the midst of a storm. With Aquinas, he sees this decision as motivated internally, an exercise of the captain's free will. With Aquinas, he elides the fact that the captain is confronted by a force of nature beyond his control. He omits Aquinas's consideration of our capacity to master our inner attitudes, and the psychogenesis of moral acts on which it rests. Instead, Scotus harnesses the Aristotelian analysis as he adapts it to the requirement that an unwilling baptizand must choose to speak out at the font. Since the church can judge only by what is manifest, the church takes silence for voluntary consent. The silent dissenter receives the baptismal character and is rightly compelled to practice Christianity. Praxis can promote a true conversion, turning tacit dissent into assent. Here, Scotus drops the comparison with forced marriage which he offers in arguing for the compulsory practice of the faith by fictive baptizands.[188] Scotus ends this question by agreeing that an unbaptized person who deeply and consistently rejects the rite ought not be baptized or required to practice Christianity. But he does not expressly prohibit baptisms of this sort, although he regards them as nugatory. Rather, he concludes, with Canon 57 of Toledo IV as cited by Gregory IX, that for those already forced into the font, the practice of Christianity is compulsory, lest the name of God be blasphemed. Since Scotus acknowledges that both absolute and conditional forced baptisms in fact occur, and since the fathers of Toledo IV make no distinction between them, the weight of his argument falls on narrowing the conditions that exempt the unwilling and on placing the burden of proving that state squarely on their own shoulders.[189]

A second context in which Scotus treats forced baptism in the *Ordinatio* is the propriety of baptizing the children of Jews and other infidels against their parents' will. He cites the second part of Canon 57 of Toledo IV here as well, extending the rule to non-believers in general but ignoring the fact that it is to recividists that the council fathers apply it. In sharp contrast

188. Ibid., 3.68–73, 11:244–46.

189. Ibid., 3.74–86, 11:244–49.

with Aquinas, Scotus thinks that these non-Christian children should be taken from their parents and baptized. For, "if they are given a good education," it is likely that their children and their children's children "unto the third and fourth generation will become true believers." The fact that this process can occur only if the parents' legal and natural rights are violated is an issue which Scotus omits. What he proposes is that this practice is less damaging to the church than allowing non-Christians to practice their religions with impunity.[190]

Easily the part of the aforementioned *quaestio* that has raised the most modern scholarly hackles is an argument applied by Scotus to the Jews alone. With the most minimal nod to Augustine, he concedes that the witness of the Jews should be preserved until they are gathered in and converted on the Last Day. For this purpose, however, only a handful of Jews need to survive: "It is not required that as many Jews as exist throughout the world should remain in existence, observing their law across the ages. It would suffice if a few of them were sequestered on some island and permitted to observe their law, and so to fulfill the prophesy of Isaiah."[191]

While this idiosyncratic recommendation and his support for the forced baptism of the children of non-Christians have drawn much notice, Scotus abandons both positions in his *Reportata Parisiensia*. While in his later work he recapitulates his earlier remarks on the baptism of the mentally disabled, he also adds some refinements to his teaching on the forced baptism of mentally competent adults. The effect of these refinements is to heighten the rigor of his *Ordinatio* teaching.

Asking whether the intention to receive baptism is always required, he responds that it is not, so long as baptism is not clearly and specifically rejected. Scotus now frames this stipulation as a double negative: "One who is not unwilling receives the effect of baptism.... For baptism is always received when no contrary objection of the will is found." Not to consent is not the

190. Ibid., 4. d. 4. pars 4. q. 3.2.166–170, 11:274–76; quotation at q. 3.2.170, 11:276: "si bene educarentur, in tertia et quarta progenie essent vere fideles." Noted by Kedar, *Crusade and Mission*, 187–88, who cites this view as seconded by Burchard of Strassburg (ca. 1311) and Robert Holcot (1333–34).

191. Duns Scotus *Ordinatio* 4. d. 4. pars 4. q. 3.2.172, 11:276: "non oportet tot Iudaeos, in tot partibus mundi, tantis temporibus sustinere in Lege sua persistare, sed sufficeret servare, aliquos paucos in aliqua insula sequestratos permitti Legem suam servare, de quibus tandem illa prophetia Isaiae impleretur." For modern commentators who flag this passage with opprobrium, see Lerner, *The Feast of St. Abraham*, 4; Nancy L. Turner, "Jewish Witness, Forced Conversion, and Island Living: John Duns Scotus on Jews and Judaism," in *Christian Attitudes toward the Jews in the Middle Ages*, ed. Michael Frassetto (New York: Routledge, 2007), 183–209.

same thing as expressly to dissent. The active expression of dissent is required to annul the reception of the *sacramentum* and *res sacramenti* of baptism. Scotus once again appeals to the *Nicomachean Ethics*. No external compulsion is involved when we act against our own interests voluntarily, as with the captain who jettisons cargo. Scotus continues to agree with Aquinas that the storm occasioning the captain's decision is not pertinent. And, with Aquinas, he treats Aristotle as here referring not to partly but to fully voluntary action. In the case of an adult with the use of reason, "if he simply dissents to the reception of baptism, if he simply refuses to have done to him what the church intends to do thereby, and is baptized anyway, it is simply against his will and he receives nothing.... He is in no way baptized." But in order to activate this proviso, he must give an unmistakable sign of his opposition. Failure to do so obviates this exemption. Further, this latter condition applies even if the forced baptizand is distracted or in a state of absence of mind, crushed by military defeat or the cocktail of physical and psychological travails imposed upon him, and is too traumatized to speak on his own behalf or even to grasp the need to do so. Scotus gives no quarter, as he systematically eliminates factors that would make a forced baptism a *coactio absoluta* that is null and void. The virtual lack of express dissent, whatever the circumstances, counts, for him, as fully voluntary consent, and the forced baptizand who is deemed to give it is rightly compelled to practice the Christian faith.[192]

William of Ockham does little to develop, or mitigate, the teachings of his Franciscan predecessors. Forced baptism is not a topic which he treats in any detail. He offers a general definition of baptism as "the ablution of man the *viator*, who dissents from it neither habitually nor actually." While Ockham uses Richard of Mediavilla's *actus/habitus* language, he does not expand on the theme. Ockham is less inflexible than Scotus on the baptizand's attitude: "For an adult to be truly baptized it is required that he consent, or at least that he not dissent, since no one can be baptized against his will." The authority on which Ockham bases this point is Gregory IX's *Decretals*, but he attributes the principle to the Christian tradition as such:

192. John Duns Scotus, *Reportata Parisiensia* d. 4. q. 4. a.1–8, in *Opera omnia*, iuxta ed. Lucae Waddingi a Patribus Franciscanis, 26 vols. (Paris: Vivès, 1891–95, reprt. Westmead, Farnsborough: Gregg International, 1959), 23:603–6; quotations at *sed contra*, 23:603: "non invitus recepit effectum Baptismi; ... quia Baptismus semper suscepitur, quando obex contrariae voluntatis non invenitur"; and at q. 4. a. 5, 23:605: "Ad quaestionem dico, adultus ratione utens, vel simpliciter dissentit susceptioni Sacramento, ita quod simpliciter nollet fieri aliquid circa ipsum, quod Ecclesia intendit facere, et ipsum baptizatum esse, est sibi simpliciter involuntarium, tunc dico quod nihil recipit; ... nullo modo baptizarentur." On the requirement to practice Christianity, see ibid., q. 4. a. 8, 23:606.

"I say that it is the intention of the Roman church, and of the minds of the saints, that, in an adult, consent, whether present or past, is required, as the decretal puts it, ... where it says that those who contradict and dissent do not receive either baptism or the [baptismal] character."[193] There Ockham leaves the matter. While, in discussing the fictive baptizand, his argument that original sin, contracted without his consent, is remitted by the sacrament without his consent[194] may have recycled and adapted Gregory IX's similar statement about the baptism of mental incompetents, Ockham offers no judgment on whether involuntary redemption is a feature of any mode of forced baptism.

The last early fourteenth-century scholastic we will consider is Durandus of St. Pourçain. The views on forced baptism in his *Sentences* commentary largely reiterate and amplify those of Aquinas, with one salient exception. On the forced baptism of adults, he espouses a highly personal position. Durandus shares Aquinas's disinclination to discuss baptismal character in this context. He concurs with Aquinas on the baptism of the mentally disabled. He agrees that an exception can be made for the comatose, although without citing Augustine's *Confessions* on that point. Durandus also supports the baptism of the intermittently insane who earlier rejected the rite, "even if they now say the opposite. For their contradiction derives not from their mind, since they lack the use of reason, but from their fantasy. And this sort of contradiction does not impede the effect of their baptism. They truly receive the *sacramentum* and the *res sacramenti*."[195]

Durandus then turns to the forced baptism of mentally competent

193. William of Ockham, *Quaestiones in Librum Quartum Sententiarum* 4. q. 2, in *Opera philosophica et theologica*, ed. Rega Wood, Gideon Gál, and Romuald Green, 10 vols. (St. Bonaventure, NY: St. Bonaventure University Press, 1967–86), 7:27, 7:29, 7:34–35; quotations at 7:27: "dico quod Baptismus est ablutio hominis viatoris, nec habitualiter nec actualiter dissentientis"; at 7:27: "Si vero baptizatus sit adultus, requiritur quod assentiat vel ad minus non dissentiat, quia nullus invitus baptizari potest, sicut patet Extra"; at 7:35: "dico de intentione Ecclesiae Romanae et de mente sanctorum est quod adulto requiritur consensus vel de presenti vel de praeterito, sicut patet in illa decretali ... ubi dicit quod contradicentes et dissentientes non recipiunt Baptismum nec characterem."

194. Ibid., q. 5, 7:53: "Igitur cum peccatum originale sit in eo contractum sine consensu, videtur quod illud potest sibi remitti virtute sacramenti non obstante quod ficte accedat sine consensu."

195. Durandus of St. Pourçain, *In Petri Lombardi Sententias theologicas commentarium libri IIII*, In *Sent.* 4. d. 4. q. 5, 2 vols. (Venice: Ex Typographia Guerraea, 1571; reprt. Ridgewood, NJ: Gregg Press Incorporated, 1964), 2:300r–300v; quotation at 300v: "etiam si tunc contradicant: quia contradictio eorum non est ex mente, cum non habeant usum rationis, sed ex sola phantasia. Et ideo talis contradictio non impedit effectum Baptismi, quin recipiant sacramentum et rem sacramenti."

adults. He leads off with the first part of Canon 57 of Toledo IV, the authority that counts for him, to which he adds the following observation:

It is acknowledged that, while to believe is an act of the intellect, matters of faith cannot be demonstrated or proved to be true on the basis of evidence, so that the intellect is constrained to assent [to them] of necessity.... No one can be forced, or required of necessity, to make an act of faith as such.... No man can reasonably or licitly be forced to accept matters that transcend reason, and which, by natural reason alone, are seen to be contrary to reason.... Thus, it is not reasonable or lawful for adult infidels to be compelled or impelled by temporal threats and punishments. And, if any of them should be so baptized, *de facto*, against his will, ... such a one receives neither the *sacramentum* nor the *res sacramenti*.[196]

This passage requires comment. What Durandus omits is as telling as what he includes, as is the way he frames this position. He makes no mention of revelation or divine grace as a means of access to the suprarational truths of faith. The standard he invokes for the persuasion of infidels, the demonstration of scientific truths that compels intellectual assent, is, deliberately, unattainable. It is one not compassed even by the most hyper-rationalistic of arch-Thomists. What Aquinas and his followers do support and what Durandus ignores are the prolegomena to belief in God's existence and basic attributes deemed accessible to natural reason, and its congruence with many revealed truths of faith. Some of these same truths, and their compatibility with reason, are also recognized in the learned traditions of Jews and Muslims, the non-Christians whom Durandus targets. Eliding these issues, Durandus argues, instead, that it is futile to try to persuade them, just as it is wrong to force them and nugatory to baptize them. How their minds and hearts may be turned around so that they seek the faith voluntarily is a question he neither asks nor answers. Durandus envisions no evangelical strategy that might convert them. The conclusion that follows, by implication, is that Christians should simply stop trying to preach the gospel to all nations. Non-Christians should be left in peace to practice their own religions. On this argument, Durandus offers the most sweeping rejection of forced baptism found in medieval theology.

196. Ibid., d. 4. q. 6, 2:300v–301r; quotation at 300v: "Sciendum est quod cum credere est actus intellectus, et ea quae sunt merè fidei non possunt demonstrari vel sic evidenter probari, ut eis necessarie assentiat intellectus, . . ideo nullus potest necessitari vel cogi simpliciter ad actum fidei.... Nullus homo potest rationabiliter et licitè compelli ad ea que sunt supra rationem, et utentibus sola ratione naturali, videretur esse contra rationalem.... Ergo infideles adultis non possunt rationabiliter et licitè ad talia compelli vel impelli minis et poenis temporabilibus. Et si de facto aliquis invitus baptizaretur, ... talis non reciperet aliquod sacramentum, nec rem sacramenti."

This discussion of the forced baptism of adults serves as a preface to Durandus's much more elaborate treatment opposing the baptism of infidel children against their parents' will. He supports Aquinas's reasons and amplifies them. Durandus agrees that this practice contravenes the divine and natural rights of parents over their underage children. But, sad to say, there are laws and laws. Civil law gives rulers the right to enslave captives, and masters have legal rights over their slaves. Ignoring the children of recividists, Durandus turns from the predicament of slaves to infidel parents who are free men. What of the minor children of free infidels whose parents die while traveling or engaging in trade in Christian lands? What of those who simply live in Christian lands? If it is a bad thing for rulers to seize and baptize the children of free subjects, "which was not the custom in the primitive church," it is still more reprehensible for those who are not rulers to do so, even if a child is in danger of eternal death: "One should not perpetrate evils so that goods may come of them." Worst of all is the forced baptism of a free non-believer's child by a private citizen. For private citizens have no rights over other private citizens: "They are equals, and one equal has no authority over another."[197]

Durandus rejects all these occasions for the baptism of infidel children against their parents' will, on principle as well as in order to forestall rebellions, even in cases allowed by civil law, and even if the parents express no outward objection. If such forced baptisms occur, they are invalid. But here Durandus offers an alternative to the evangelical dead end in which he leaves infidel adults. In the case of infidel children, there are opportunities for their conversion that infringe on no one's rights. He envisions such children as growing up alongside of Christian neighbors. The child will be positively impressed by the beliefs and good example of the Christians he knows. As he arrives at the age of discretion, he will live according to the natural law. Natural reason will show him that it is congruent with the law of Christ. At that point, we may hope, "but not before, God will inspire him concerning those things which are matters of faith and are above reason." While God is now involved, Durandus does not give Him the last word. The young convert has to ascertain, first, that this inspiration is truly God-given. Having done so, he then has to consider what is necessary for his salvation and to conclude that it requires baptism. Once these matters are resolved, he can come to the font of his own free will and receive bap-

197. Ibid., quotations at 2:301r: "quod in primitiva ecclesia non est usus"; "Non est eripendus ut liberetur à periculo mortis aeternae, non enim sunt facienda mala ut veniant bona"; "quia pares sunt, et par in parem non habet imperium."

tism efficaciously.[198] Durandus thus extends to the maturing children of infidels an aptitude for the informed, reasonable, and graced assent to baptism which he denies categorically to infidel adults. This is an inconsistency which he does nothing to reconcile.

It is a fact that the Middle Ages witnessed voluntary conversions from one religion to another, in all directions. Yet, for many scholastics, Durandus's scenario for evangelizing children of unwilling infidels looks to be too idealistic to take seriously, just as they might find his rejection of any possibility of proselytizing infidel adults an unrealistic and irresponsible abandonment of the missionary calling. In particular, Durandus's proposals pay no attention to the conditions on the Baltic frontier, where most of the forced baptisms of his day were taking place. In Durandus's one reference to events in the real world, he gets it wrong. Speaking of the licit capture, enslavement, and forced baptism of infidels in a just war, he refers to the actions of the Christian kings in Spain.[199] In so doing, he ignores the capitulation treaties they concluded, which permitted the free practice of Islam in most conquered regions. The Baltic Crusades receive a single scholastic mention, from Roger Bacon, two generations earlier. In his *Opus maius* (1266), Roger gets it partly right. He offers the following assessment:

> Christians, when they interact with pagans, such as the Prussians and other peoples, could persuade them easily. And, being convinced, they would recognize and give up their errors. In all likelihood, they would want to become Christians most gladly if the church would let them keep their liberty and enjoy their possessions in peace. But the Christian princes who labor for their conversion, especially the brethren of the Teutonic Order, want to reduce them to slavery, as the Dominicans and Franciscans and other good men throughout Germany and Poland are aware. Hence, they revolt. It is against violence that they resist, not against the rational argument of a superior religion.[200]

198. Ibid., d. 4. q. 7, 2:301r–302v; quotation at 302v: "Deus inspirat ea quae sunt fidei et super ratione, non prius."

199. Ibid., d. 4. q. 6, 2:300v.

200. Roger Bacon, *Opus maius* 7. pars 4. d. 2.1.21–22, in *Moralis philosophia*, ed. Eugenio Massa (Zurich: Thesaurus Mundi, 1953), 200: "Et Christiani, quando conferunt cum Paganis, sicut Pruseni et alie naciones, convincunt eas de facili; et convicte credunt et vident se erroribus detineri. Cuius probacio est quod libentissime volunt fieri christiani, si Ecclesia vellet dimittere eos cum libertate et gaudere bonis suis in pace. Set christiani principes, qui laborant ad eorum conversionem, et maxime fratres de domo teutonica, volunt eos reducere in servitutem, sicut certum est Praedicatoribus et Minoribus et aliis viris bonis per totam Alemanniam et Poloniam, et ideo repugnant; unde contra violenciam resistant, non ratione secte melioris." Noted by Kedar, *Crusade and Mission*, 177–80; Tyerman, "Henry of Livonia," 42. Amanda Power, *Roger Bacon and the Defence of Christendom* (Cambridge: Cambridge University Press, 2013), 238–39, cites this passage but omits the fact that Bacon gives the mendicants a pass.

If Durandus of St. Pourçain misconceives the history of the Spanish Reconquest, Roger Bacon hits the mark on only some features of the Baltic Crusades. While the Teutonic Knights are a religious order, it is not implausible to describe them as Christian princes, given their territorial ambitions and conquests. All those who engineered and prosecuted the Baltic mission, not excluding the mendicants whom Roger gives a pass, used the same tactics that he critiques and encountered the same recidivism and revolt. He is correct in noting that the missionaries in the Baltic do not engage in rational persuasion. Unlike the Jews and Muslims, the pagans of northern Europe have no authorities in common with Christianity and no traditions deemed learned enough to invite disputation. The chroniclers in that mission field rarely envision pagans as having a coherent theology and a religious praxis with any analogies to their own. The missionaries seek to attract them with a God whose kingdom is of this world, a God of battles, a God of business, a God whose dévotés perform miracles, even a God who monitors the strangulation of horses. Religious drama and music, when they are tried, fall flat. These appeals, however, are strategies marginal to the policy of baptism or death. Even the Poeta Saxo, who rejoices in the gift of literacy and the church's teachings on the meaning of life brought in the wake of Charlemagne's Saxon wars, agrees that preaching with an iron tongue was initially required, and that his forebears submitted to forced baptism with a feigned faith. Durandus and Roger notwithstanding, the norm of courteous rational persuasion, propounded by Gregory the Great, supported by Gratian I, retained by Raymond of Peñafort, and reiterated as late as the end of the thirteenth century by Richard of Mediavilla, lost the support of Innocent III and Gregory IX in the decretals cited as authoritative by most canonists and scholastic theologians. Whether they accept or reject forced baptism, the inhabitants of the ivory tower all treat it with inconsistencies and gaps in the fabric of their arguments. Most of the traffic runs in the direction of its support, as more and more masters envision more and more ways to make forced baptism acceptable. Despite the lip service they routinely pay to the principle of free will and baptismal intention, they find more and more ways to assign these dispositions to the forced, or to argue that they are less determinative than external dissent, or lack of it, at the font.

Conclusion

Across the centuries from late antiquity to the early fourteenth century, we can track both initial inconsistencies on the subject of forced baptism, the perpetuation of both poles of debate, and the introduction of new arguments on both sides of it, as masters redefine the groups to be exempted from this practice as well as those to whom it should be extended, and on what conditions. Those first subjected to forced baptism were the Jews, with a few Muslims and most notably Europe's indigenous pagans enlarging the ranks in the post-Roman period. The insistence of Augustine and Gregory the Great that Jews should retain the legal right to practice their religion unhindered, that their witness should be preserved, and that kindness and rational persuasion should be used to convert them are principles articulated in response to forced baptisms of Jews that did occur in late antiquity. As well, Gregory chastises individual bishops who tolerate, or promote, the persecution and forced baptism of Jews. There are reports of occasional outbreaks of this kind in Merovingian Gaul. They need to be assessed with caution given their authors' agendas and overall reliability. Some invent forced baptisms that never took place while others rewrite those that did occur as voluntary responses to charismatic bishops, divine inspiration, or prophetic dreams.

Visigothic Spain produced a crop of anti-Jewish literature, some of it associated with anti-Arianism after King Reccared embraced Catholicism. Isidore of Seville is both inconsistent and influential, both in his own writings and in his presidency over Toledo IV in 633, whose self-contradictory Canon 57 is later cited more frequently than any other medieval authority on both sides of the issue of forced baptism. The first part of this decree rules that Jews are not henceforth to be forced into the font, since faith requires free will and God's grace and cannot be compelled. But the second part of Canon 57 rules that those baptized, by whatever means, having received the sacraments, are to be forced to practice Christianity, lest God's name be blasphemed and the faith be held vile and contemptible. Important medieval authorities from the author of the *Panormia* to Gratian I to Innocent III to Thomas Aquinas cite both parts of Canon 57. The *Panormia*, Gratian I, and Innocent make no attempt to resolve the conundrum. At one point Aquinas upholds the first part of that decree, but at another argues that the second part annuls its first part. Most masters cite only the part of Canon 57 with which they agree. Some confine themselves to the forced baptism of Jews. Some extend the application of the decree to Muslims as well, or to infidels without specification, or to the children of unwilling infidels, without noting the council fathers' ruling later in Toledo IV that limits the forced baptism of children to those of recidivists. This selectivity is found both in masters who approve of forced baptism and in those who disapprove of it, for some or all of these groups.

While the church fathers described and carried out elaborate programs of catechetical instruction to prepare adult converts for baptism, the patristic catechumenate had evaporated by the sixth century. In its place were modes of Christian instruction, pre-baptismal or post-baptismal, that were sketchy indeed. Witness to this situation is the baptism of pagans such as Clovis and the new policy of preaching to the pagans with an iron tongue in the campaigns of Charlemagne against the Saxons and Avars. This practice yoked forced baptism to the conquest and subjugation of pagans on the borders of western Christendom. It set the precedent followed by the Baltic campaigns of the Danes, Poles, and Germans from the twelfth to the fourteenth century. Charlemagne provided the model well before these expeditions were redefined as just wars and their participants were granted the spiritual rewards accorded to those who took the cross. The bar was set low. External compliance with Christian ritual sufficed. The pagans regarded baptism as a circumstantial concession along with the predictable tribute, hostage taking, pillage, ravaging with fire and sword, and territorial conquest inflicted on the defeated. By the same token, all of these terms were subject to reversal if the vanquished became the victors in the next fighting season. In some cases, the pagans had their own religious rituals for undoing baptism. Those conducting the missions contributed to this impression by presenting forced baptism as part of the Christians' military and political package deal. Rebellions against Christian forces then justified renewed wars to enforce Christianity on the relapsed. If these recidivists traduced the sacrament of baptism, as the missionaries charged, their own profanation of it by forcing the defeated into the font was a parallel which they never acknowledged. These practices and attitudes, on both sides, are amply reported by the chroniclers of these campaigns from the Frankish royal annalists to the accounts lauding the Teutonic Knights.

While there are voices raised in opposition from Alcuin and Rabanus Maurus in the eighth and ninth centuries to Roger Bacon and Durandus of St. Pourçain in the thirteenth and early fourteenth, most of the canonists and theologians who write on this subject find ways to accommodate patristic injunctions, and the first part of Canon 57 of Toledo IV, to coercive action against infidels. While Aquinas can reject the baptism of infidel children against their parents' will as a violation of ecclesiastical tradition, *patria potestas*, and natural law, he can also characterize Christian wars against infidels as just wars aimed merely at preventing them from interfering with Christian faith and practice. These wars are not wars of aggression, he claims, and they are not fought to bring infidels forcibly to the font, but only to punish them for their own intolerance. Richard of Mediavilla takes the buttons off the foils and accepts that just wars against pagans are fought for their forced baptism, and rightly so. Despite his support of Aquinas on parental rights, Durandus is constrained to agree that the civil law does give victorious Christian princes, and masters of slaves, the authority forcibly to convert infidels in their power.

While rational persuasion, argument from authorities, and courtesy are prescribed for would-be missionaries by Gregory the Great, seconded by Gratian I, Raymond of Peñafort, and Richard of Mediavilla, and while the *Panormia* and Gratian I retain the need for divine grace found in Canon 57 of Toledo IV, these conditions increasingly go by the boards. They survive mainly in Durandus's idealistic scenario for the evangelization of the maturing children of infidels, although he rejects the same possibilities for the conversion of infidel adults. Despite his insistence elsewhere that Jews be exempted from forced baptism, Innocent III, in his letter of 1201 to Archbishop Imbert of Arles, drops rational persuasion and grace. Recycled in the *Decretals* of Gregory IX, that opinion carries great weight. Drawing on canonists of the preceding two generations, Innocent's teaching persuades thirteenth-century theologians to give increasingly perfunctory regard to the authorities opposing forced baptism and to widen the acceptability of this practice. While, in principle, they agree that the consent of a rationally competent adult is required for his valid baptism, they turn their ingenuity to the reconceptualization of consent itself.

Rufinus of Bologna makes a major breakthrough in this area. Some forced baptizands are truly overpowered by external constraints, he notes. But others offer consent of some sort at the font. This theme is developed by other commentators on Gratian in the second half of the twelfth century and receives a major boost from Innocent III. In his formula, we can distinguish between unwillingness and unwillingness, compulsion and compulsion. Those with *coactio absoluta* are dragged to the font, consistently and utterly unwilling. They have no baptismal intention whatsoever. Their baptism is null and void. Those with *coactio conditionaliter* are afflicted with intimidation and threats. If they knuckle under and accept baptism to escape harm, they are deemed to exercise sufficient free consent for the rite to impress on them the baptismal character that obliges them to practice Christianity. Their minimal consent eliminates the obstacle created by absolute unwillingness.

This key distinction, even before it is cited by Gregory IX, is adopted by Alexander of Hales and put on the agenda of the scholastic theologians, becoming their argument of choice. Indeed, in comparison with their discussions of baptism by desire and fictive baptism, their heavy reliance on canonical authority in their treatments of forced baptism is striking. Innocent's 1201 letter does not mention any particular subsets of infidels who may be subjected to the two modes of forced baptism he distinguishes. Some masters who cite him, such as Raymond of Peñafort, John Duns Scotus, and Durandus of St. Pourçain, refer to Jews, or Jews and Muslims, only. But most masters after Innocent speak of non-believers in general. Their exclusions are aimed not at those with particular belief systems but at reducing the number of forced baptizands to whom *coactio absoluta* applies.

Starting with Albert the Great, theologians stress the importance of the forced baptizand's outward indication of assent or dissent. For Albert, the issue is less the quality of the candidate's faith, or lack thereof, and less the type and level of the menace he faces than his express articulation of his acceptance or rejection of baptism. Bonaventure reframes Innocent's distinction as *coactio sufficiens* and *coactio inducens*. While he agrees that the first form of compulsion, with the candidate thrust into the font bound hand and foot and held captive while the baptismal water is poured on him, rules out a valid baptism, he elaborates the second condition in his own way. This second type of baptizand is not just intimidated. He is faced with imminent death. Bonaventure thinks that such an individual, although still an unbeliever, can valorize the appeal of a rite whose meaning he only vaguely grasps above the fear of certain death, to the point that he gives consent adequate to validate his baptism and his compulsory observance of Christianity.

Peter of Tarentaise and Richard of Mediavilla retain a more classically Innocentine analysis, although Peter puts the language of Bonaventure into Innocent's mouth and Richard applies to it the Aristotelian concepts of action and passion, matter and form, and *habitus* and *actus*. The most noteworthy application of Aristotelianism to forced baptism is made by Duns Scotus. It heightens the rigor of that doctrine. Scotus draws on an interpretation of *Nicomachean Ethics* 3.1 first made by Aquinas but not applied by him to baptism. Aristotle distinguishes between compulsion and partly voluntary action. He contrasts a captain whose ship is blown off course by a storm with a captain who jettisons cargo in the face of a storm. Following Aquinas, Scotus treats the second captain's action as fully, not partly, voluntary. Both masters elide the point that this captain acts in response to circumstances beyond his control. They both see him as making a freely willed choice as an internal moral decision. He illustrates the fact that we can choose voluntarily to do something we do not want to do. This analysis, for Scotus, explains the situation of the conditionally compelled forced baptizand. He consents to his baptism voluntarily. In his *Ordinatio*, Scotus also agrees with Albert the Great and Richard of Mediavilla that it is not the candidate's unwillingness as such, or his lack of a baptismal intention, but rather his declaration of his state of mind at the font that is determinative. In his later *Reportata Parisiensia*, Scotus stiffens this argument in two ways. He reframes it as a double negative: Not to consent is not the same thing as overtly to dissent. And, the unwilling baptizand is not exempted from this proviso even if the sufferings inflicted on him have so traumatized him that he is unable to speak for himself. The church judges by what is manifest. Silence at the font is taken not just for minimal consent, in Innocent's terms, but for fully voluntary consent.

In his *Ordinatio*, Scotus also offers two arguments which he later abandons in his *Reportata Parisiensia*. He drops the view, so obnoxious to Durandus of St. Pourçain, that the children of unwilling infidels should be taken from their parents, baptized, and reared as Christians. The second early argument which Scotus drops, that only a few Jews need to survive sequestered on some island to preserve their witness until the Last Day, can be classed with other oddities that fall off the scholastic radar screen. One is Bonaventure's description of the non-believing infidel impelled by *coactio inducens* who prioritizes a murkily grasped baptismal rite over certain death. Other scholastics understandably dismiss this psychological profile as unrealistic. Another one-off is Richard of Mediavilla's claim that baptismal character may be impressed on an unwilling unbeliever by a special divine dispensation. The inability of anyone to determine that such is the case consigns this notion, too, to the scrap-heap. No uncertainties of this kind are noted in the discussion of conditional baptism given by Raymond of Peñafort, Gregory IX, or Aquinas. Since Durandus is the last scholastic theologian we have considered, the fortunes of his argument on the non-convertibility of adult infidels remain a matter for future research. It has to be said that its prospects look to be slender.

The net effect of the doctrinal developments described is to posit a distinction without a difference, and then to narrow the gap between its poles. Over the course of the thirteenth and early fourteenth centuries, most forced baptisms are reclassified as conditionally compelled, that is, as minimally and then as fully voluntary. Absolute compulsion, with its nugatory sacramental effects, has become increasingly vestigial. The requirement to practice Christianity for the conditionally compelled—for Rufinus of Bologna, Honorius of Kent, Richard of Mediavilla, and Duns Scotus—has become an advantage, not a problem. Rather than embittering the forced baptizand and hardening his inner resistance, encouraging fraud, hypocrisy, recidivism, and revolt, the compulsory practice of Christianity, like forced baptism itself, has been reconfigured by these masters as a means of conversion, turning the recipient's internal dissent at the font into true assent. The existence of that dissent belies the claim that his forced baptism is voluntary. This is an inconsistency which proponents of this refinement on forced baptism do not acknowledge.

We can thus see among masters who rationalize forced baptism, as well as among those who oppose it, blind spots, gaps, contradictions, and the coexistence of countervailing arguments. And, while there is a distinct trend among the inhabitants of the ivory tower to accept and to justify the outlook of their colleagues in the missionary field, consensus is not total. There are noticeable differences in the way many of the same masters compare forced baptism with fictive baptism and the baptism of the mentally disabled, which they often discuss under the same heading. In the latter two cases, they are much more likely to view the candidate's baptismal intention as critical. They are much more likely to rule that, in cases where such baptisms are deemed inefficacious, they should be prohibited. While the category of the absolutely compelled forced baptizand grows increasingly microscopic in their teaching, they shrink from addressing the corollaries of its continued existence. They do not take the next logical step and forbid such baptisms outright. They do not advise on the ecclesiastical status of such persons if they are baptized nonetheless, nor do they offer guidance on whether they can be rebaptized—or, in effect—baptized for the first time, if they are later Christianized. The concern that some of them voice about rebaptism suggests that this practice may indeed be taking place. These are loose ends that remain, among others.

In this area, as is the case with baptism by desire and fictive baptism, all of the claims defended draw on a highly selective and manipulative treatment of the Christian tradition. The particular authorities who come in for the heaviest use and abuse differ in these three baptismal debates. In each instance, in addition to picking and choosing, and rewriting their sources at will, individual masters do not hesitate to state that the full weight of the church's tradition supports their own teachings, however commonplace, innovative, or eccentric they may be. Such claims are, and are recognized to be, debaters' points. All involved are fully aware that the tradition they have inherited is far from homogeneous and that the authorities they approve, reject, or manhandle are far from unanimous. In comparison with that technique as applied to baptism by desire and fictive baptism, the debates on forced baptism yield only one appeal to historical or literary criticism as a means of contextualizing, and dismissing, an earlier authority. The one master who gets high marks for his textual acumen is Richard of Mediavilla. He is unique in recognizing that Augustine's *compelle intrare* argument is about Donatists and is irrelevant to the forced baptism of infidels.

The most obvious trait that differentiates the debates on baptism by desire and fictive baptism from those on forced baptism is the willingness of many of the same masters who defend intentionalism in the first two areas to compromise it in support of forced baptism. Despite the disagreements that remain, there is more of an emerging consensus on forced baptism than there is on fictive baptism, if less concurrence than we find on baptism by desire. Still, the basic conundrum built into the notion of forced baptism, stated and restated since the patristic period, remains. Some masters simply report it. Others promote one of its principles at the expense of the other. All involved in these debates see themselves, and the other masters old and new with whom they strive, as fellow members of the orthodox Christian community. The assertion that the church has at all times professed only one position on any of the baptismal doctrines with which this study has been concerned, and the claims made to that effect in post-medieval catechisms or codes of canon law, would have struck these medieval masters as illusory, a category error, the confusion of rhetoric with historical reality. A judgment which they would regard as a more accurate assessment of the enterprise in which they were engaged is one recently offered by Robin M. Jensen. Jensen is an architectural historian. She examines how the form of baptistries reflects the ritual and theological diversities in late ancient North African Christianity. Her conclusions ring true for medieval debates on baptism and for much else as well:

> A ritual lives only so long as it can adapt to the exigencies of context. Just as the participants are transformed, reborn, or converted by the ritual, so too the ritual is transformed and renewed by succeeding generations who will claim its power and efficacy, perhaps without consciously recognizing that the flexibility to respond to change in the face of challenges that emerge in the course of history is ultimately essential. A community's long-term survival requires that it continually redefine its own identity as it resists, absorbs, or is rejected by others who have different perceptions of how and where the boundaries must be drawn.

Baptism, perhaps, more than any other rite, reveals these evolutionary changes.[201]

201. Robin M. Jensen, "Baptismal Rites and Architecture," in *Late Ancient Christianity*, ed. Virginia Burrus (Minneapolis: Fortress Press, 2005), 117–44; quotation on page 143.

AFTERWORD

This afterword will not attempt to write a full-scale, post-medieval history of the three baptismal questions treated in this book. But the early modern address to these debates is of no small interest, reflecting as it does how the history of Christian thought has continued to be reconceived, and rewritten, as these themes have been reassessed in the light of current concerns. The very fact that these debates have a history has sometimes been acknowledged, but more usually ignored. This sketch of the post-medieval story begins with the *Catechismus Romanus* written after the close of the Council of Trent in 1563 for the guidance of the Catholic clergy. Some of its precepts were implemented, and some were not, suggesting that the final arbiter of ecclesiastical authority lies not in its promulgation but in its acceptance by the faithful. The echoes of some of these debates still resonate to the present day.

The catechism of Trent which summed up sixteenth-century Catholic doctrine includes all three of the topics which inspired the medieval debates discussed in this book. Its authors in one case affirm what had become a largely consensus position by the early fourteenth century. In the other two cases, they take their own stand on issues that remained in sharp contention from the patristic period to the high Middle Ages. In one of those areas, they do not hesitate to attribute to the theological tradition a unanimity which it never in fact possessed.

They begin with baptism by desire. This is a doctrine, which, as we have seen, medieval masters had largely come to support by ca. 1300. The catechism authors preface their remarks by stressing the universal necessity of baptism, especially for infants.[1] The other baptizands whom they envision are those "of adult age who enjoy the perfect use of reason, persons, namely, born of infidel parents" to whom the faith has been presented, enabling them to be "persuaded and invited to embrace it." If unavoidable problems prevent their liturgical reception of the rite, their baptismal intention suffices: "Should any unforeseen accident make it impossible for adults to be washed in the salutary waters, their intention and determination to receive Baptism and their repentance of their past sins will avail them to grace and righteousness."[2] This formula reflects the desire of the authors to efface any lingering medieval objections to the doctrine, as well as to approach with caution the theology of their Protestant rivals. On the one hand, they agree with the magisterial Protestants, against the Anabaptists, that infant baptism is required. On the other hand, while they stress the key determinant of the baptizand's intentionality, they take issue with *sola fide* salvation and the *simul justus et peccator* status of neophytes, granting them righteousness as well as grace in baptism by desire, no less than at the font. Minus these sixteenth-century polemics, and likewise eliding the fact that baptism by desire had ever been controversial, this is the doctrine reaffirmed, along with the claim that the church has always taught it, in the post-Vatican II catechism quoted in the introduction to this book.

The Tridentine catechism takes an unequivocal stand against forced baptism. This position stands in stark opposition to the advocacy and sophisticated justifications given to forced baptism in the high medieval tradition, as masters in the ivory tower increasingly lent their support to actual practice in the missionary field. The authors of the catechism make no reference to the debates on this subject, aligning themselves with the handful of masters who categorically reject forced baptism. This document does not acknowledge either the conflicting advice found in Canon 57 of Toledo IV or the medieval distinction between *coactio absoluta* and *coactio conditionaliter* and its high medieval elaborations. Instead, the authors rewrite church history on this subject:

> The faithful are to be instructed in the necessary dispositions for Baptism. In the first place they must desire and intend to receive it; ... it is fit that it be admin-

1. *Catechism of the Council of Trent for Parish Priests*, trans. John A. McHugh and Charles J. Callan (New York: Joseph F. Wagner, 1923), 176–78. For the Latin text, see *Catechismus Romanus*, ed. Pedro Rodríguez et al. (Vatican City: Libreria Editrice Vaticana, 1989), 794–96.

2. *Catechism of the Council of Trent*, 178–79.

istered to those only who receive it of their own free will and accord; it is to be forced on none. Hence we learn from holy tradition that it has been the invariable practice to administer Baptism to no individual without previously asking him if he is willing to receive it.[3]

While, as we have seen, the theory and the practice of forced baptism tended to coalesce in the thirteenth and fourteenth centuries, in the early modern period practice moved in the opposite direction from Tridentine theory. Scholars have found evidence of the forced baptism of Jewish children in Italy, especially in papal Rome, between the sixteenth and the eighteenth centuries.[4] In some quarters, the forced baptism of Iberian Jews at the end of the fifteenth century has been seen as a curtain-raiser for the conquistadors' forced baptism of the natives of the New World, despite the differences between these two groups.[5] Proponents of that alleged policy transition do not note the contemporary objections to the baptism-or-expulsion of Iberian Jews,[6] or, for that matter, the debates surrounding the extension of the same policy a few years later to Iberian Muslims, a community previously exempted from this kind of victimization in most of Christian Europe.[7] Hispanic policy in the Americas certainly aroused debate. But its

3. Ibid., 180. Cf. Francesca Trivellato, *The Familiarity of Strangers: The Sephardic Diaspora, Livorno, and Cross-Cultural Trade in the Early Modern Period* (New Haven, CT: Yale University Press, 2009), 295n4, who thinks that forced baptism was seen as valid in early modern canon law and that "only during the Second Vatican Council of 1963 did the Roman church reject entirely the legitimacy of forced baptism," with the Venetian theologian Paolo Sarpi (1552–1623) as the only post-Tridentine dissenter.

4. Cecil Roth, "The Forced Baptisms of 1783 at Rome and the Community of London," *Jewish Quarterly Review*, n.s. 16/2 (1925): 105–12; reprt. Philadelphia: Dropsie College, 1925, with London entering Roth's story as the Roman Jews sought help from that community; David Ravid, "The Forced Baptism of Jewish Minors in Early-Modern Venice," *Italia* 13–15 (2001): 259–301, noting Venetian opposition to the practice; Lucia Frattarelli, "Sul battesimo dei bambini ebrei? Il caso di Livorno," in *Salvezza delle anime, disciplina dei corpi: Un seminario sulla storia del battesimo*, ed. Adriano Prosperi (Pisa: Scuola Normale Superiore, 2006), 449–82; Marina Caffiero, *Forced Baptism: Histories of Jews, Christians, and Converts in Papal Rome*, trans. Lydia Cochrane (Berkeley: University of California Press, 2011).

5. See, for example, Jonathan Boyarin, *The Unconverted Self: Jews, Indians, and the Identity of Christian Europe* (Chicago: University of Chicago Press, 2009), although with criticisms of other scholars who connect anti-Judaism with colonial attitudes toward natives of the Indies on pages 3–14, 17–18.

6. Giuseppe Marcocci, "'... per capillos adductos ad pillam': Il dibattito cinquecentesco sulla validità del battesimo forzato degli ebrei in Portogallo (1496–1497)," in *Salvezza delle anime, disciplina dei corpi: Un seminario sulla storia del battesimo*, ed. Adriano Prosperi (Pisa: Scuola Normale Superiore, 2006), 339–423.

7. See John Philip Lomax, "Frederick II, His Saracens, and the Papacy," in *Medieval Christian Perceptions of Islam: A Book of Essays*, ed. John Victor Tolan (New York: Garland, 1996),

proponents rarely take note of the ways that medieval masters frame this issue. Rather, they appeal to alternative versions of neo-Thomism. Franciso de Vitoria and Bartolomé de Las Casas, who oppose this policy, and Juan Ginés de Sepúlveda, who defends it, all invoke natural law theory as they understand it.[8] While many scholars regard the Las Casas/Sepúlveda

---

175–97, on Frederick's transfer of his Sicilian Muslim subjects to Lucera on the Italian mainland; Nora Berend, *At the Gate of Christendom: Jews, Muslims and 'Pagans' in Medieval Hungary, c. 1000–c. 1300* (Cambridge: Cambridge University Press, 2001), 210–23, 237–38, 243, for the forced baptism of Hungarian Muslims; on Iberian Muslims, see, for example, Ana Echeverría, *The Fortress of Faith: Attitudes toward Muslims in Fifteenth-Century Spain* (Leiden: Brill, 1999); contributors to *Christians, Muslims, and Jews in Medieval and Early Modern Spain*, ed. Mark D. Meyerson and Edward D. English (Notre Dame: University of Notre Dame Press, 2000); L. P. Harvey, *Muslims in Spain, 1500–1614* (Chicago: University of Chicago Press, 2005).

8. Francisco de Vitoria, *Relectio de Indis recenter inventis*, pars secunda 15–20, ed. and trans. Ada Lamacchia (Bari: Levante Editore, 1996), 61–67, which cites the first part of Canon 57 of Toledo IV; idem, *De iure belli* q. 3, trans. Carlo Galli (Rome: Editori Laterza, 2005), 26, citing Aquinas; Juan Ginés de Sepúlveda, *Demócrates segundo, o De las justas causas de la guerra contra los indios*, 2nd ed., ed. and trans. Ángel Losada (Madrid: Consejo Superior de Investigaciones Científicas, Instituto Francisco de Vitoria, 1984), 29, 44–47, 58–60, 65, 68, 80; *La controverse entre Las Casas et Sepúlveda*, trans. Nestor Capdevita (Paris: Vrin, 2007), with an excellent guide to bibliography on this subject. A sampler of notable views includes Bernice Hamilton, *Political Thought in Sixteenth-Century Spain: A Study of the Political Ideas of Vitoria, De Soto, Suárez, and Molina* (Oxford: Clarendon Press, 1963), 112–34; Ángel Losada, "The Controversy between Sepúlveda and Las Casas in the Junta of Valladolid," in *Bartolomé de Las Casas in History: Toward an Understanding of the Man and His Work*, ed. Juan Friede and Benjamin Keen (De Kalb: Northern Illinois University Press, 1971), 279–306, with the view that this debate is now relevant to aid to underdeveloped countries; Venancio D. Carro, "The Spanish Theological-Juridical Renaissance and the Ideology of Bartolomé de Las Casas," in ibid., 237–50, with the view that Vitoria and Las Casas were more up-to-date as neo-Thomists than Sepúlveda; Lewis Hanke, *All Mankind Is One: A Study of the Disputation between Bartolomé de Las Casas and Juan Ginés de Sepúlveda in 1550 on the Intellectual and Religious Capacity of the American Indian* (De Kalb: Northern Illinois University Press, 1974), 17–22, 97–99, 113–40, with emphasis on the subjugation and economic exploitation of the Indians; Conrado Castilla Rubio, "El debate indiano en la primera mitad del siglo XVI: Las Casas, Sepúlveda y Vitoria," in *Actas del Congreso internacional V centenario del nacimiento del Dr. Juan Ginés de Sepúlveda*, Pozoblanco, 13–16 febrero 1991 (Pozoblanco: Ayuntamiento de Pozoblanco, 1993), 211–20; José Joblin, "Significado histórico de la disputa de Sepúlveda con Las Casas," in ibid., 237–49; José Manuel Pérez-Prendes y Muñoz de Arracó, " Los criterios indianos de Juan Ginés de Sepúlveda," in ibid., 269–77, who see Sepúlveda, respectively, as a high papalist, a monarchist, and an orthodox Aristotelian; Anthony Padgen, *Lords of All the World: Ideologies of Empire in Spain, Britain, and France, c. 1500–c. 1800* (New Haven, CT: Yale University Press, 1995), 31, 42–43, 48, 50–52, 91–94, 99–101; Eduardo Andújar, "Bartolomé de Las Casas and Juan Ginés de Sepúlveda: Moral Theology versus Political Philosophy," in *Hispanic Philosophy in the Age of Discovery*, ed. Kevin White (Washington: The Catholic University of America Press, 1997), 69–87, accenting the use of basic positions and debater's points by both parties; Rafael Alvira and Alfredo Cruz, "The Controversy between Las Casas and Sepúlveda at Valladolid," in ibid., 88–110, accenting the fact that debate as such was

standoff as a draw, it did not halt the forced baptism of the conquered peoples of European colonialists of all confessions wherever they planted their imperial standards, until well into recent times. In the Catholic church, a repetition of the Tridentine catechism's prohibition of forced baptism was thus deemed necessary as late as the *Corpus iuris canonici* of 1983: "Men are not to be drawn by force to embrace the Catholic faith against their own conscience."[9] The authors of this canon, unlike their Tridentine forebears and unlike the authors of the post–Vatican II catechism on baptism by desire, are circumspect enough to drop the false claim that the church has always supported this principle.

The third baptismal issue contested from the age of the church fathers through the high Middle Ages and included in the Tridentine catechism is fictive baptism. As we have seen, fictive baptism wound its way into and out of medieval discussions of forced baptism, as well as the baptism of the mentally disabled. Of our three medieval debates, this one yielded the least consensus. To the extent that the masters agreed, they agreed primarily to reject Augustine's momentary remission thesis. Most other features of the doctrine remained controversial throughout the Middle Ages. Some observers on the scene and in the ivory tower recognize that fictive baptism easily leads to the recidivism of the *fictus* and the undermining of the faith of sincere Christians. After the patristic period, the effort to screen out *ficti* though an elaborate pre-baptismal catechesis goes by the boards. Most masters see fictive baptisms as inefficacious. But many support them, arguing that fictive baptizands receive the indelible baptismal character and

possible within the Spanish absolute monarchy; Diego Pirillo, "Il battesimo degli indios: Polemico del fine cinquecento," in *Salvezza delle anime, disciplina dei corpi: Un seminario sulla storia del battesimo*, ed. Adriano Prosperi (Pisa: Scuola Normale Superiore, 2006), 425–48, accenting the perpetuation of the debate despite Sepúlveda's *de facto* victory; Mercedes Junquera Gómez, "El impacto del padre Las Casas en la visión hispanoamérica," in *Responsabilidad histórica: Preguntas del nuevo al viejo mundo*, ed. Reyes Mate (Barcelona: Anthropos Editorial, 2007), 201–24; Mariano Delgado, "Los derechos de los pueblos y de las personas según el pensamiento de Bartolomé de Las Casas," in ibid., 285–310, who both, along with other contributors to this volume, focus on the eventual if not immediate influence of Las Casas on the development of ideas of modern human rights, arguing that he refutes the "Black Legend" of early modern Spain.

9. *Corpus iuris canonici* (1983) can. 748.2: "Homines ad amplectendam fidem catholicam contra ipsorum conscientiam per coactionem adducere nemini umquam fas est." Quoted by Hans Maier, "*Compelle intrare*: Rechtfertigungsgründe für die Anwendung von Gewalt zum Shutz und zur Ausbreitung der Glaubens in der Theologie des abendländischen Christentums," in *Heilige Kriege: Religiöse Begründungen militärischer Gewaltanwendung. Judentum, Christentum und Islam im Vergleich*, ed. Klaus Schreiner with Elisabeth Müller-Luckner (Munich: R. Oldenbourg, 2008), 55–69, on page 55n5.

that forcing them to observe the faith will convert their fictions into true baptismal intentions. How that turnaround might actually occur is also disputed. The conclusion that fictive baptisms should not be performed since they are null and void is a decidedly minority opinion.

The catechism of Trent does not acknowledge any of these debates. The authors ban fictive baptism outright. They make no attempt to compare or contrast fictive with forced baptism. They simply state their own position, taking the logical next step which so many medieval masters refuse to take. In the early modern period, the Catholic church made zealous efforts to improve Christian education and to promote the multimedia evangelization of its actual and hoped-for members. This concern is manifest in the catechism's address to fictive baptism: "The Church must take particular care that none approach this Sacrament through hypocrisy and dissimulation; the intentions of such as seek Baptism are [to be] better examined and ascertained," by means of a catechumenate that instructs the candidate "in the doctrine of the faith which he is to profess, and in the practice of the Christian life."[10] In addition to expressing his free will and true baptismal intention, the candidate must abandon his past sins and resolve to avoid them in the future. This proviso is a sine qua non: "Should anyone desire Baptism and be unwilling to correct the habit of sinning, he should be altogether rejected." For, if such a baptism is performed, it is null and void: "We well understand that, as far as regards sanctifying and saving grace, Baptism is received in vain by him who purposes to live according to the flesh, and not according to the Spirit."[11]

The catechism of Trent thus takes the hard line found so rarely in medieval discussions, forthrightly banning fictive baptism. Its authors accept, implicitly, that a *fictus* cannot later activate a baptismal grace which he never received at the font. His condition is not ameliorated by mandatory Christian praxis. It is worth noting that, while the catechism discusses baptismal character, it gives this topic a rather different treatment than it receives in the Middle Ages. For one thing, instead of viewing baptismal character in a punitive light, as imposing a distasteful obligation on a fictive or forced baptizand, the catechism presents baptismal character positively, as entitling its grantee to the reception of other sacraments. For another thing, the text pointedly declines to say whether or not fictive baptizands receive the baptismal character.[12]

10. *Catechism of the Council of Trent*, 179, 180.

11. Ibid., 181. Cf. Geoffrey Wainwright, *Christian Initiation* (London: Lutterworth Press, 1969), 59–60, who claims that the Tridentine doctrine held all baptisms valid if performed according to the correct liturgical form.

12. *Catechism of the Council of Trent*, 189.

The issue of whether to regard fictive candidates as true Christians, and whether to accept them in baptism or to deny them the font, has remained on the ecclesiastical agenda up to the present, but in a different context, the foreign missions. Despite modern advances in catechetical instruction, missionaries of all confessions continue to confront the problem of "rice Christians." Typically, these individuals are converts in Third World countries who accede to baptism for a range of sub-sacramental, and secular, reasons. They are drawn to the church because of the medical, educational, cultural, social, economic, and political services and advantages which membership affords. Churches in the mission field, of whatever confession, do not usually deny such *ficti* the font. Their leaders may deplore this phenomenon. Or, they may accept it, rationalizing that such converts create a target of opportunity through which true believers may be recruited. Or else, they simply retreat to the default position that the task of the missions is foreign aid.[13]

Closer to home, and while it may not be given this name, there is another aspect of fictive baptism that attracts multi-confessional concern. In an increasingly post-Christian world, as observers ruefully note, parents who have no real commitment to Christianity and no intention of raising children in the faith present their children for baptism nonetheless. They are comparable to people who want churches to preside over their weddings and funerals, although they do not subscribe to their teachings on Christian marriage or the afterlife. But churches do know how to lay on gratifying ceremonies to celebrate these important transitions in the life cycle. The leaders of many churches who accept both the importance of infant baptism and the validity of each other's baptisms find the baptism of the children of basically non-believing parents to be a troubling theological and pastoral issue. Yet, in the usual course of events, they baptize the infants anyway.

The medieval Christian tradition offers a solution to this problem, if one knows where to look. It will be recalled that the continuator of Anselm of Lucca and followers of Anselm of Laon, while they think that fiction nullifies adult baptisms, make a distinction for infants. Fiction on the part

13. See, for example, Kenneth Scott Latourette, *A History of the Expansion of Christianity*, 7 vols. (Grand Rapids, MI: Zondervan Publishing House, 1970), 6:437–38; Carl T. Smith, *Chinese Christians: Élites, Middlemen, and the Church in Hong Kong* (Hong Kong: Oxford University Press, 1985), 184; Siga Arles, "Christian Witness amidst Currents of Change in Today's India: The Local Church in the Cross-Currents of Evangelism," in *Preparing for Witness in Context*, ed. Jean S. Stoner (np: Presbyterian Church [USA], 1999), 250–63; Chung-Shin Park, *Protestantism and Politics in Korea* (Seattle: University of Washington Press, 2003), 107–8; Nan lai Cao, *Constructing China's Jerusalem: Christians, Power, and Peace in Contemporary Wenzkou* (Stanford, CA: Stanford University Press, 2011), 28–41.

of the parents or godparents who present the child for baptism is not a sacramental impediment, for the child. It does not prevent him from receiving a fully valid baptism.[14] We make this point in ending this afterword in proposing the advantages, no less than the chastening recognitions, to be gained by the study of the history of the Christian tradition, as contrasted with the ignorance of that history or the disingenuous history on which theologians and church officials have so often based their teachings from the Middle Ages to the present. The example given is merely one case in which medieval Christian thought might be invoked to resolve a perceived modern problem. Other current concerns might also be addressed constructively in the light of an accurate understanding of the Christian tradition and the often transitory circumstances and polemics that have conditioned its development. This tradition has always made room for principled disagreement within the orthodox consensus. Whatever its current elastic limits, that consensus has always possessed flexibility. The Christian tradition has repeatedly shown its ability to adapt, to select, to innovate, and to set aside doctrines and practices, as it incarnates its message anew across the centuries. The directions it has taken have not always been unilinear or irreversible. Its authority has always been provisional and functional, depending on the values which those who implement it actually accept. The three medieval baptismal debates whose history this book has presented map but one part of this variegated landscape. That larger terrain is one through which diverse trails have always been blazed, as Christian thinkers disregard or misread the lay of the land or make straight their paths to their common destinations.

14. Anselm of Lucca, *Collectio canonum* 9.43–48, ed. Friedrich Thaner, 2 vols. (Innsbruck: Universitätsverlag Wagner, 1906–15); reprt. Aalen: Scientia Verlag, 1965, 2:475–79; Sentences of the School of Anselm of Laon no. 364, ed. Odon Lottin, *Psychologie et morale aux XIIe et XIIIe siècle*, 6 vols. (Gembloux/Louvain: J. Duculot/Abbaye de Mont César, 1948–60), 5:273. For consideration of the theological and pastoral issues which churchmen do air on this matter in recent discussions, both in the Anglican Church—the author's main focus—and in the World Council of Churches, see Colin Buchanan, *Infant Baptism and the Gospel: The Church of England's Dilemma* (London: Darton, Longman and Todd, 1993).

BIBLIOGRAPHY

Primary Sources

Acta Sanctorum. 69 vols. Brussels: Alphonsus Greuse, 1893–1940.

Alain de Lille: Textes inédits, avec introduction sur sa vie et ses oeuvres. Edited by Marie-Thérèse d'Alverny. Paris: Vrin, 1965.

Alan of Lille. *De fide catholica contra haereticos libri quatuor*. In *Patrologia latina cursus completus*. Edited by J. P. Migne. Vol. 210:305D–430B. Paris, 1855.

Albert the Great. *In IV Sententiarum*. In *Opera omnia*. Edited by Stephanus C. A. Borgnet. 38 vols. Paris: Vivès, 1880–95.

Alcuin. *Epistolae*. Edited by Ernst Dümmler. Monumenta Germaniae Historica Epistolae karolingi aevi. Vol. 4. Hannover: Hahn, 1895.

Alexander of Hales. *Glossa in quattuor libros Sententiarum*. Edited by Collegium S. Bonaventurae. 4 vols. Quaracchi: Collegium S. Bonaventurae, 1951–57.

Alger of Liège. *Alger von Lüttichs Traktat "De misericordia et iustitia": Ein kanonistischer Konkordanz aus der Zeit des Investiturstreits*. Edited by Robert Kretchmar. Quellen und Forschungen zum Recht im Mittelalter 2. Sigmaringen: Jan Thorbecke Verlag, 1985.

Ambrose of Milan. *De consolatione Valentiniani*. Edited and translated by Thomas A. Kelly. Catholic University of America Patristic Studies 58. Washington: The Catholic University of America Press, 1940.

———. *Consolation on the Death of Valentinian*. Translated by Roy J. Deferrari. In *Funeral Orations by Saint Gregory Nazianzus and Saint Ambrose*. Fathers of the Church 22. New York: Fathers of the Church, Inc., 1953.

———. *Expositionis Evangelii secundum Lucam*. Edited by Marcus Andriaen. Translated by Giovanni Coppa. 2 vols. Sancti Ambrosii episcopi Mediolanensis opera 11–12. Milan: Biblioteca Ambrosiana, 1978.

———. *De obitu Valentiniani*. Edited and translated by Gabriele Banterle. In *Le orazioni funebri*. Sancti Ambrosii episcopi Mediolanensis opera 18. Milan: Biblioteca Ambrosiana, 1985.

———. *Political Speeches and Letters*. Translated by J. H. W. G. Liebeschuetz and Carole Hill. Translated Texts for Historians 42. Liverpool: Liverpool University Press, 2005.

A New Catechism: Catholic Faith for Adults. Translated by Kevin Smyth. New York: Seabury Press, 1993.

Annales regni Francorum. Edited by Friedrich Kurtze. Monumenta Germaniae Historica Scriptores rerum germanicorum in usum scholarum 6. Hannover: Hahn, 1895.

Anselm of Lucca. *Collectio canonum*. Edited by Friedrich Thaner. 2 vols. Innsbruck: Universitätsverlag Wagner, 1906–15. Reprint Aalen: Scientia Verlag, 1965.

Anselms von Laon systematische Sentenzen. Edited by Franz Bliemetzrieder. Beiträge zur Geschichte der Philosophie des Mittelalters 18/2–3. Münster: Aschendorff, 1919.

Aristotle. *Nicomachean Ethics*. Edited and translated by Roger Crisp. Cambridge: Cambridge University Press, 2000.

Augustine. *De baptismo libri VII*. Edited by M. Petchenig. Corpus scriptorum ecclesiasticorum latinorum 51. Vienna: F. Tempsky, 1908.

———. *De natura et origine animae*. Edited by Carolus F. Urba and Josephus Zycha. Corpus scriptorum ecclesiasticorum latinorum 40. Vienna: F. Tempsky, 1913.

———. *In Ioannis Evangelium tractatus libri CXXIV*. Edited by D. Radbodus Willems. Corpus christianorum series latina 36. Turnhout: Brepols, 1954.

———. *De civitate dei*. Edited by Bernardus Dombart and Alphonsus Kalb. 2 vols. Corpus christianorum series latina 47–48. Turnhout: Brepols, 1955.

———. *Quaestiones Levitici*. In *Quaestiones Heptateuchum libri VII*. Edited by Johannes Fraipont. Corpus christianorum series latina 33. Turnhout: Brepols, 1958.

———. *De sermone Domini in monte*. Edited by Almut Mutzenbecher. Corpus christianorum series latina 35. Turnhout: Brepols, 1967.

———. *De diversis quaestionibus octoginta tribus*. Edited by Almut Mutzenbecher. Corpus christianorum series latina 44A. Turnhout: Brepols, 1975.

———. *Confessiones*. Edited by Lucas Verheijen. Corpus christianorum series latina 27. Turnhout: Brepols, 1981.

———. *Retractationes*. Edited by Almut Mutzenbecher. Corpus christianorum series latina 57. Turnhout: Brepols, 1984.

Bandinus. *Sententiarum libri quatuor*. In *Patrologia latina cursus completus*. Edited by J. P. Migne. Vol. 192:965A–1112C. Paris, 1880.

Bede. *In Lucae Evangelium expositio*. Edited by David Hurst. Corpus christianorum series latina 120. Turnhout: Brepols, 1960.

———. *In Genesim*. Edited by Charles W. Jones. Corpus christianorum series latina 118A. Turnhout: Brepols, 1967.

———. *Expositio Actuum Apostolorum*. Edited by M. L. W. Laistner. Corpus christianorum series latina 121. Turnhout: Brepols, 1983.

———. *Commentary on the Acts of the Apostles*. Translated by Lawrence T. Martin. Cistercian Studies Series 17. Kalamazoo: Cistercian Publications, 1989.

———. *On Genesis*. Translated by Calvin B. Kendall. Translated Texts for Historians 48. Liverpool: Liverpool University Press, 2008.

Bernard of Clairvaux. *Sancti Bernardi opera*. Edited by Jean Leclercq et al. 8 vols in 9. Rome: Editiones Cistercienses, 1958–77.

———. *Opere di San Bernardo*. Edited by Ferruccio Gastaldelli. Translated by Ettore Paratore. 6 vols. Milan: Scriptorium Claravalleno, 1984–2000.

———. *On Baptism and the Office of Bishop*. Translated by Paulina Matarasso. Introduction by Emero Stiegman. Cistercian Fathers Series 67. Kalamazoo: Cistercian Publications, 2004.

Bibliorum Sacrorum iuxta Vulgatam Clementinam. New ed. Edited by Aloisius Gramatica. Vatican City: Typis Polyglottis Vaticanis, 1951.

Bonaventure. *In IV Sententiarum*. In *Opera omnia*. Edited by Collegium S. Bonaventurae. 10 vols. Quaracchi: Collegium S. Bonaventurae, 1882–1902.

Bonizo of Sutri. *Liber de vita christiana*. 2nd ed. Edited by Ernst Perels. Nachwort by Walter Berschin. Berlin: Weidemann, 1998.

Brault, Gerald J., ed. *The Song of Roland: An Analytical Edition*. 3 vols. University Park: Penn State University Press, 1978.

Carolingian Chronicles. Translated by Bernard Walter Scholz. Ann Arbor: University of Michigan Press, 1970.

Catechism of the Catholic Church. 2nd ed. Edited by Peter Cardinal Gasparri. Rome: Libreria Editrice Vaticana, 1994.

Catechism of the Council of Trent for Parish Priests. Translated by John A. McHugh and Charles J. Callan. New York: Joseph F. Wagner, 1923.

Catechismus Romanus. Edited by Pedro Rodríguez et al. Vatican City: Libreria Editrice Vaticana, 1989.

Chronicon Paschale. In *Patrologia graeca cursus completus*. Ed. J. P. Migne. Vol. 92:69A–1028C. Paris, 1865.

Chronicon Paschale, 284–628 AD. Translated by Michael Whitby and Mary Whitby. Translated Texts for Historians 7. Liverpool: University of Liverpool Press, 1989.

Concilios visigóticos e hispano-romanos. Edited by José Vives. España cristiana 1. Barcelona/Madrid: Consejo Superior de Investigaciones Científicas, 1963.

Cyprian of Carthage. *Epistulae*. Edited by G. F. Diercks. Corpus christianorum series latina 3C. Turnhout: Brepols, 1996.

———. *On the Church: Selected Letters*. Translated by Allen Brent. Crestwood, NY: St. Vladimir's Seminary Press, 2006.

Das Schrifftum der Schule Anselms von Laon und Wilhelms von Champeaux in deutschen Bibliotheken. Edited by Heinrich Weisweiler. Beiträge zur Geschichte der Philosophie und Theologie des Mittelalters 33/1–2. Münster: Aschendorff, 1936.

Decretales Gregorii IX. In *Corpus iuris canonici*. Edited by Aemilius Friedberg. 2 vols. Vol. 2:5–928. Leipzig: Tauchnitz, 1879–80. Reprint Union City, NJ: Lawbook Exchange, 2000.

Die Sententiae divinitatis: Ein Sentenzenbuch der gilbertischen Schule. Edited by Bernhard Geyer. Beiträge zur Geschichte der Philosophie des Mittelalters 7/2–3. Münster: Aschendorff, 1909.

Dudo of St. Quentin. *De moribus et actis primorum Normanniae ducum*. Edited by Jules Lair. Caen: F. LeBlanc-Hardel, 1865.

———. *History of the Normans*. Translated by Eric Christiansen. Woodbridge, UK: Boydell Press, 1998.

Durandus of St. Pourçain. *In Petri Lombardi Sententias theologicas commentarium libri IIII.* 2 vols. Venice: Ex Typographia Guerraea, 1571. Reprint Ridgewood, NJ: Gregg Publishing Incorporated, 1964.

Einhard. *Vie de Charlemagne.* 2nd ed. Edited and translated by Louis Halphen. Paris: Les Belles Lettres, 1936.

Ermoldus Nigellus. *Ermold le Noir: Poème sur Louis le Pieux et Épître au roi Pépin.* 2nd ed. Edited by Edmond Faral. Paris: F. Champion, 1964.

Gandulph of Bologna. *Sententiarum libri quatuor.* Edited by Johannes de Walter. Vienna: Aemilius Heim, 1924.

Gennadius of Marseille. *Liber de ecclesiasticis dogmatibus.* In *Patrologia latina cursus completus.* Edited by J. P. Migne. Vol. 58:979D–1000B. Paris, 1862.

Gratian. *Decretum.* In *Corpus iuris canonici.* Edited by Aemilius Friedberg. 2 vols. Vol. 1:1–1424. Leipzig: Tauchnitz, 1879–80. Reprint Union City, NJ: Lawbook Exchange, 2000.

Gregory Nazianzus. *Orationes.* Edited by Claudio Moreschini. Translated by Paul Gallay. Sources chrétiennes 358. Paris: Les Éditions du Cerf, 1991.

Gregory of Tours. *Histoire des francs.* New ed. Edited by Henri Omont and Gaston Collon. Revised by René Poupardin. Paris: Alphonse Picard et Fils, 1913.

———. *History of the Franks.* Translated by Lewis Thorpe. Harmondsworth: Penguin, 1974.

Gregory the Great. *Registrum Epistolarum.* Edited by Paul Ewald. Monumenta Germaniae Historica Epistolarum 1/1. Berlin: Weidemann, 1887.

Guérard, Benjamin Edme Charles, ed. *Cartulaire de l'église Notre-Dame de Paris.* 4 vols. Collection des cartulaires de France 4–7. Paris: Crapelet, 1850.

Guido of Orchellis. *Tractatus de sacramenti ex eius Summa de sacramentis et officiis Ecclesiae.* Edited by Damien and Odolph Van den Eynde. Franciscan Institute Publications, Text Series 4. St. Bonaventure, NY: The Franciscan Institute, 1953.

Häring, Nikolaus M., ed. "Die Sententie magistri Gisleberti Pictavensis episcopi (I)." *Archives d'histoire doctrinale et littéraire du moyen âge* 45 (1978): 83–180.

———, ed. "Die Sententie magistri Gisleberti Pictavensis episcopi (II): Die Version der florentiner Handschrift." *Archives d'histoire doctrinale et littéraire du moyen âge* 46 (1979): 45–105.

Helmold of Bosau. *Chronica Slavorum.* 3rd ed. Edited by Bernhard Schmiedler. Revised by Johannes M. Lappenberg. Monumenta Germaniae Historica Scriptores rerum germanicorum in usum scholarum. Hannover: Hahn, 1937.

Henry of Livonia. *Chronicle.* Translated by James A. Brundage. Madison: University of Wisconsin Press, 1961.

———. *Chronicon Livoniae.* Edited and translated by Piero Bugiani. Città del Castello: Books & Company, 2005.

Hugh of St. Victor. *Disascalicon: De studio legendi.* Edited by Charles Henry Buttimer. Washington: The Catholic University of America Press, 1939.

———. De *sacramentis Christianae fidei.* Edited by Rainer Berndt. Corpus Victorinum 1. Münster: Aschendorff, 2008.

Innocent III. *Registrum Epistolae* Anno XII. In *Patrologia latina cursus completus*. Edited by J. P. Migne. Vol. 216:9A–194B. Paris, 1891.

———. *Die Register Innocenz' III*. Edited by Othmar Hageneder, Werner Maleczek, and Alfred A. Strnad. Vol. 2. Rome/Vienna: Verlag der Österreichischen Akademie der Wissenschaften, 1979.

Isidore of Seville. *Etymologiae*. Edited by W. M. Lindsay. 2 vols. Oxford: Clarendon Press, 1911.

———. *Las historias de los godos, vándalos y suevos de Isidoro de Sevilla*. Edited and translated by Cristobál Rodríguez Alonso. Léon: Centro de Estudios y Investigación "San Isidoro," 1975.

———. *De ecclesiasticis officiis*. Edited by Christopher M. Lawson. Corpus christianorum series latina 113. Turnhout: Brepols, 1984.

———. *Sententiae*. Edited by Pierre Cazier. Corpus christianorum series latina 111. Turnhout: Brepols, 1998.

———. *Sentenze*. Edited and translated by Francesco Trisoglio. Brescia: Morcelliana, 2008.

Ivo of Chartres. *Decretum*. Edited by Bruce Brasington and Martin Brett. Available at: http://project.knowledgeforge.net/ivo/decretum.html/. Posted October 6, 2009.

———. *Panormia*. Edited by Bruce Brasington and Martin Brett. Available at: http://faculty.wtamu.edu/bbrasington/panormia.html/. Posted August 6, 2005.

Jerome. *In die domenica Pascha II*. 2nd ed. Edited by D. Germanus Morin. In *Tractatus sive homeliae*. Corpus christianum series latina 78. Turnhout: Brepols, 1958.

———. *Tractatus in Marci Evangelium*. In *Opera homiletica*. Edited by D. Germanus Morin. Corpus christianorum series latina 78. Turnhout: Brepols, 1958.

———. *Tractatus in Psalmos*. In *Opera homiletica*. Edited by D. Germanus Morin. Corpus christianorum series latina 78. Turnhout: Brepols, 1958.

———. *Commentarium in Hezechielem libri XIV*. Edited by Franciscus Glorie. Corpus christianorum series latina 75. Turnhout: Brepols, 1964.

———. *Commentarium in Mattheum libri IV*. Edited by David Hurst and Marcus Andriaen. Corpus christianorum series latina 77. Turnhout: Brepols, 1969.

John Duns Scotus. *Repertata Parisiensia*. In *Opera omnia*. Iuxta ed. Lucae Waddingi a Patribus Franciscanis. 26 vols. Paris: Vivès, 1891–95. Reprint Westmead, Farnsborough, UK: Gregg International, 1959.

———. *Ordinatio*. Book 4. Edited by Josephus Rodríguez Carballo. In *Opera omnia*. Vol. 11. Vatican City: Typis Vaticanis, 2008.

Keefe, Susan A., ed. *Water and the Word: Baptism and the Education of the Clergy in the Carolingian Empire*. 2 vols. Notre Dame: University of Notre Dame Press, 2002.

La Chanson de Roland. Edited and translated by Gerald J. Brault. University Park: Penn State University Press, 1984.

La controverse entre Las Casas et Sepúlveda. Translated by Nestor Capevita. Paris: Vrin, 2007.

Landgraf, Artur Michael, ed. *Écrits théologiques de l'école d'Abélard*. Louvain: Spicilegium Sacrum Lovaniense, 1934.

Lul (?). *Carmen de conversione Saxonum*. Edited by Karl Hauck. In *Karolingische Tauffalzen im Spiegel hofnaher Dichtung: Überlieferung zur Ausmalung von Pfalzkirchen, Pfalzen und Reichsklöstern*. Nachrichten der Akademie der Wissenschaften in Göttingen 1, Philologisch-historische Klasse. Göttingen: Vandenhoeck & Rupprecht, 1985.

Lumen gentium. In *The Documents of Vatican II (1963–1965)*. Edited and translated by Joseph Gallagher. New York: Guild Press, 1966.

Magistri Honorii Summa de iure canonico tractaturus. Edited by Rudolf Weigand, Peter Landau, and Waltraud Kozur. Monumenta Iuris Canonici, series A: Corpus Glossatorum 5/1. Vatican City: Biblioteca Apostolica Vaticana, 2004.

Maître Simon et son groupe De sacramentis. Edited by Heinrich Weisweiler. Louvain: Spicilegium Sacrum Lovaniense, 1937.

Medieval Literary Theory and Criticism, c. 1100–c. 1375. Edited and translated by A. B. Minnis and A. B. Scott with the assistance of David Wallace. Oxford: Clarendon Press, 1988.

Nicholas von Jeroschin. *The Chronicle of Prussia: A History of the Teutonic Knights of Prussia, 1190–1331*. Translated by Mary Fisher. Aldershot: Highgate, 2010.

Njal's Saga. Translated by Magnus Magnusson and Herman Pálsson. Harmondsworth: Penguin, 1969.

Odo of Ourscamp. *Quaestiones*. Edited by Johannes Baptista Cardinalis Pitra. In *Spicilegium Solmensis: Analecta novissima altera continuatio*. 2 vols. Paris: Typus Tusculanis, 1885–88. Reprint Farnsborough, UK: Gregg Press, 1967.

Otto of Freising. *Chronica sive historia de duabus civitatibus*. Edited by Adolfus Hofmeister. Monumenta Germaniae Historica Scriptores rerum germanicorum in usum scholarum 46. Hannover: Hahn, 1912.

———. *The Two Cities: A Chronicle of Universal History to the Year 1148 AD*. Edited by Austin P. Evans and Charles Knapp. Translated by Charles Christopher Mierow. Introduction by Karl F. Morrison. New York: Columbia University Press, 2002.

Peter Abelard. *Commentaria in Epistolam Pauli ad Romanos*. Edited by Eligius M. Buytaert. Corpus christianorum continuatio medievalis 11. Turnhout: Brepols, 1969.

———. *Theologia christiana*. Edited by Eligius M. Buytaert. Corpus christianorum continuatio medievalis 12. Turnhout: Brepols, 1969.

———. *Sic et non*. Edited by Blanche Boyer and Richard McKeon. Chicago: University of Chicago Press, 1976.

———. *Scito te ipsum*. Edited by Rainer M. Ilgner. Corpus christianorum continuatio medievalis 190. Turnhout: Brepols, 2001.

Peter Comestor. *De sacramentis*. Edited by Raymond-M. Martin as appendix to *Maître Simon et son groupe De sacramentis*. Edited by Heinrich Weisweiler. Louvain: Spicilegium Sacrum Lovaniense, 1937.

Peter Damian. *Liber gratissimus*. Edited by L. de Heinemann. Monumenta Germaniae Historica Libelli de lite imperatorum 1. Hannover: Hahn, 1896.

Peter Lombard. *Sententiae in IV libris distinctae*. 3rd rev. ed. Edited by Ignatius C. Brady. 2 vols. Grottaferrata: Collegium S. Bonaventurae, 1971–81.

Peter of Poitiers. *Sententiarum libri quinque*. In *Patrologia latina cursus completus*. Edited by J. P. Migne. Vol. 211:783D–1280D. Paris, 1855.

Peter of Tarentaise. *In Sententiarum*. Edited by Johannes Baptista de Marinis. 4 vols. Toulouse: Arnaldus Colomerius, 1649–52. Reprint Ridgewood, NJ: Gregg Press, 1964.

Peter the Chanter. *Summa de sacramentis et animae consiliis*. Edited by Jean-Albert Dugauquier. 3 vols. in 5. Louvain: Éditions Nauwelaerts, 1954–67.

Poeta Saxo. *Annalium de gestis Caroli magni imperatoris libri quinque*. Edited by Paul von Winterfield. Monumenta Germaniae Historica Poetae latini aevi carolini 4/1. Berlin: Weidemann, 1899.

———. *Annalium de gestis Caroli magni imperatoris libri quinque*. Edited by Georg Heinrich Pertz. Monumenta Germaniae Historica Scriptores 1. Hannover: Hahn, 1826. Reprint Stuttgart: Anton Hiersemann, 1976.

Praepositini Cancellarii de Sacramentis et de Novissimis (Summa Theologiae Pars Quarta). Edited by Daniel Edward Pilarczyk. Collectio Urbanianae, ser. 3, textus ac documenta 7. Rome: Editiones Urbanianae, 1964.

Rabanus Maurus. *Commentaria in Ezechielem*. In *Patrologia latina cursus completus*. Edited by J. P. Migne. Vol. 110:493D–1084B. Paris, 1864.

———. *De institutione clericorum*. Edited by Aloisius Knoepfler. Veröffentlichen aus den kirchlichen Seminar München 5. Munich: J. J. Lentner'schen Buchhandlung, 1900.

Radulphus Ardens. *The Questions on the Sacraments: Speculum Universale 8.31–92*. Edited and translated by Christopher P. Evans. Toronto: Pontifical Institute of Mediaeval Studies, 2010.

Raymond of Peñaforte. *Summa de paenitentia*. Edited by Xavierio Ochea and Aloisio Diez. Universa Biblioteca Iuris 1B. Rome: Commentarium pro Religione, 1976.

Richard of Mediavilla. *In IV libros Sententiarum*. Edited by Ludovicus Silvestris à Sancto. Brescia: De Consensu Superiorum, 1591. Reprint Frankfurt: Minerva GMBH, 1963.

Richer of Reims. *Historiae*. Edited by Hartmut Hoffmann. Monumenta Germaniae Historica Scriptores 38. Hannover: Hahn, 2000.

Richer of Saint-Rémi. *Histories*. Edited and translated by Justin Lake. 2 vols. Dumbarton Oaks Medieval Library 10. Cambridge, MA: Harvard University Press, 2011.

Robert of Melun. *Oeuvres de Robert de Melun*. Edited by Raymond-M. Martin. 3 vols. in 4. Louvain: Spicilegium Sacrum Lovaniense, 1932–52.

Robert Pullen. *Sententiarum libri octo*. In *Patrologia latina cursus completus*. Edited by J. P. Migne. Vol. 186:639D–1010B. Paris, 1859.

Robinson, J. Armitage, ed. *Passio S. Perpetuae*. Cambridge: Cambridge University Press, 1891.

Roger Bacon. *Opus maius*. Book 7. In *Moralis philosophia*. Edited by Eugenio Massa. Zurich: Thesaurus Mundi, 1953.

Roland of Bologna. *Die Sentenzen Rolands nachmals Papstes Alexander III*. Edited by Ambrosius M. Gietl. Freiburg: Herder, 1891.

Rufinus of Aquileia. *Orationum Gregorii Nazianzeni novem interpretatio*. Edited by Augustus Engelbrecht. Corpus scriptorum ecclesiasticorum latinorum 46. Vienna: F. Tempsky, 1910.

———. *The Church History, Books 10 and 11*. Translated by Philip R. Amidon. New York: Oxford University Press, 1997.

———. *Historia ecclesiastica*. Edited and translated by Manlio Simonetti. In Rufino di Concordia. *Scritti vari*. Corpus Scriptorum Ecclesiae Aquileiensis 5/2. Aquileia: Città Nuova, 2000.

Rufinus of Bologna. *Summa decretorum*. Edited by Heinrich Singer. Paderborn: Ferdinand Schöningh, 1902. Reprint Aalen: Scientia Verlag, 1963.

Ruotger of Cologne. *Vita Brunonis*. In *Patrologia latina cursus completus*. Edited by J. P. Migne. Vol. 134:940D–988B. Paris, 1884.

Saxo Grammaticus. *Gesta Danorum*. Edited by J. Olrik and H. Raeder. 2 vols. Copenhagen: Levin & Munksgaard, 1931–37.

Sepúlveda, Juan Ginés de. *Demócrates segundo, o De las justas causas de la guerra contra los indios*. 2nd ed. Edited and translated by Ángel Losada. Madrid: Consejo Superior de Investigaciones Científicas, Instituto Francisco de Vitoria, 1984.

Simon of Tournai. *Les Disputationes de Simon de Tournai*. Edited by Joseph Warichez. Louvain: Spicilegium Sacrum Lovaniense, 1932.

Socrates Scholasticus. *Historia ecclesiastica*. Edited by Günther Christian Hansen. Sources chrétiennes 477. Paris: Les Belles Lettres, 2004.

Sozomen. *Historia ecclesiastica*. Edited and translated by Günther Christian Hansen. 4 vols. Fontes Christiani 73/1–4. Turnhout: Brepols, 2004.

Stephen Langton. *Questiones theologicae*. Cambridge, St. John's College Library C7. [*Quaestio* 145 as transcribed by Riccardo Quinto].

Summa sententiarum. In *Patrologia latina cursus completus*. Edited by J. P. Migne. Vol. 176:42D–174A. Paris, 1880.

Tertullian. *Concerning Baptism*. Translated by Alexander Souter. London: SPCK, 1919.

———. *De baptismo*. Edited by J. G. P. Borleffs. Corpus christianorum series latina 1. Turnhout: Brepols, 1993.

The Bible in Medieval Tradition. Edited and translated by Ian Christopher Levy. Grand Rapids, MI: William B. Eerdmans Publishing Company, 2011.

The Livonian Rhymed Chronicle. Translated by Jerry C. Smith and William Urban. Bloomington: Indiana University Press, 1977.

Theodori Episcopi Mopsuesteni in epistolas B. Pauli commentarii. Edited and translated by Henry Barclay Swete. 2 vols. Cambridge: Cambridge University Press, 1880–82.

The Passion of Perpetua and Felicity. Edited and translated by Thomas J. Heffernan. Oxford: Oxford University Press, 2012.

The Saxon Poet's Life of Charlemagne. Translated by Mary E. McKinney. New York: Pageant Press, 1956.

Thomas Aquinas. *Sententia Libri Ethicorum*. In *Opera omnia*. Vol. 47/1. Iussu impensaque Leonis XIII P.M. edita. Edited by Fratrum Praedicatorum. 48 vols. Rome: Typographia Polyglotta S. C. De Propaganda Fidei, 1882–1985.

———. *Scriptum super libros Sententiarum magistri Petri Lombardi episcopi Parisiensis*. New ed. Edited by Pierre Mandonnet and Maria Fabianus Moos. 4 vols. Paris: Lethiellieux, 1929–47.

———. *Summa theologiae*. Edited and translated by Blackfriars. 61 vols. New York: McGraw-Hill, 1964–76.

Translatio S. Liborii. Edited by Georg Heinrich Pertz. Monumenta Germaniae Historica Scriptores 4. Hannover: Hahn, 1891. Reprint Stuttgart: Anton Hiersemann, 1981.

Venantius Fortunatus. *Opera*. Edited and translated by Stefano Di Brazzano. 2 vols. Corpus Scriptorum Ecclesiae Aquileiensis 8/1–2. Aquileia: Città Nuova, 2001.

Vitoria, Francisco de. *Relectio de Indis recenter inventis*. Edited and translated by Ada Lamacchia. Bari: Levante Editore, 1996.

———. *De iure belli*. Translated by Carlo Galli. Rome: Editori Laterza, 2005.

Walker, Greg, ed. *Medieval Drama: An Anthology*. Oxford: Blackwell, 2000.

Walter of Chatton. *Reportatio super librum IV Sententiarum*. Edited by Joseph C. Wey and Girard J. Etzkorn. 5 vols. Toronto: Pontifical Institute of Mediaeval Studies, 1989–2005.

William of Auxerre. *Summa aurea*. Edited by Jean Ribaillier. 5 vols. Spicilegium Bonaventurianum 16–20. Paris/Grottaferrata: CNRS/Collegium S. Bonaventurae, 1980–87.

William of Conches. *Un brano inedito della "Philosophia" di Guglielmo di Conches*. Edited by Carmelo Ottaviano. Collezione di testi filosofici inediti e rari 1. Naples: Alberto Morano Editore, 1935.

William of Melitona. *Quaestiones de sacramentis*. Edited by Caelestinus Piana. 2 vols. Quaracchi: Collegium S. Bonaventurae, 1966.

William of Ockham. *Quaestiones in Librum Quartum Sententiarum*. In *Opera philosophica et theologica*. Edited by Rega Wood, Gideon Gál, and Romuald Green. 10 vols. St. Bonaventure, NY: St. Bonaventure University Press, 1967–86.

Secondary Sources

Abulafia, Anna Sapir. *Christian-Jewish Relations, 1000–1300*. London: Longman, 2011.

———. "Continuity and Change in Twelfth-Century Christian-Jewish Relations." In *European Transformations: The Long Twelfth Century*. Edited by Thomas F. X. Noble and John Van Engen, pp. 314–37. Notre Dame: University of Notre Dame Press, 2012.

Abulafia, David. *The Great Sea: A History of the Mediterranean*. London: Allen Lane, 2011.

Akbari, Suzanne Conklin. *Idols in the East: European Representations of Islam and the Orient, 1100–1450*. Ithaca, NY: Cornell University Press, 2009.

Albert, Bat-Ševa. "Un nouvel examen de la politique anti-juive wisigothique à propos d'une article recent." *Revue des études juives* 135 (1976): 3–26.

———. "Isidore of Seville: His Attitude toward Judaism and His Impact on Early Medieval Canon Law." *Jewish Quarterly Review* 80 (1990): 207–20.

Albu, Emily. "Bohemond and the Rooster: Byzantines, Normans, and the Artful Ruse." In *Anna Komnena and Her Times*. Edited by Thalia Gouma-Peterson, pp. 157–68. New York: Garland, 2000.

———. *The Normans in Their Histories: Propaganda, Myth, and Subversion*. Woodbridge, UK: Boydell Press, 2001.

Alvira, Rafael and Alfredo Cruz. "The Controversy between Las Casas and Sepúlveda at Valladolid." In *Hispanic Philosophy in the Age of Discovery*. Edited by Kevin White, pp. 88–110. Washington: The Catholic University of America Press, 1997.

Amory, Fredric. "Whited Sepulchers: The Semantic History of Hypocrisy in the High Middle Ages." *Recherches de théologie ancienne et médiévale* 53 (1986): 5–39.

Andújar, Eduardo. "Bartolomé de Las Casas and Juan Ginés de Sepúlveda: Moral Theology versus Political Philosophy." In *Hispanic Philosophy in the Age of Discovery*. Edited by Kevin White, pp. 69–87. Washington: The Catholic University of America Press, 1997.

Angenendt, Arnold. *Kaiserherrschaft und Königstaufe: Kaiser, Könige und Papste als geistlichen Patrone in der abendländischen Missionsgeschichte*. Berlin: Walter De Gruyter, 1989.

———. *Das Frühmittelalter: Die abendländische Christenheit von 400 bis 900*. Stuttgart: Kohlhammer, 1990.

Angotti, Claire. "Sur les traces de la *lectio* des *Sentences* de Pierre le Mangeur." In *Pierre le Mangeur ou Pierre de Troyes: Maître du XIIe siècle*. Edited by Gilbert Dahan, pp. 149–89. Turnhout: Brepols, 2013.

Anspach, August Edward. "Das Fortleben Isidors im VII. bis IX. Jahrhundert." In *Miscellanea Isidoriana: Homenaje a S. Isidoro de Sevilla en el XIII centenario de su muerte*. Edited by La Provincia de Andalusia S.J., pp. 323–56. Rome: Typis Pontificiae Gregorianae, 1936.

Arles, Siga. "Christian Witness amidst Currents of Change in Today's India: The Local Church in the Cross-Currents of Evangelism." In *Preparing for Witness in Context*. Edited by Jean S. Stoner, pp. 250–63. Np: Presbyterian Church (USA), 1999.

Athanassiade, Polymnia. *Vers la pensée unique: La montée de l'intolérance dans l'Antiquité*. Paris: Les Belles Lettres, 2010.

Austin, Greta. *Shaping Church Law around the Year 1000: The Decretum of Burchard of Worms*. Aldershot: Ashgate, 2009.

Axton, Richard. *European Drama of the Early Middle Ages*. Pittsburgh: University of Pittsburgh Press, 1974.

Bachrach, Bernard. "A Reassessment of Visigothic Jewish Policy, 589–711." *American Historical Review* 78 (1973): 11–34.

———. *Early Medieval Jewish Policy*. Minneapolis: University of Minnesota Press, 1977.

Bagge, Sverre and Saebjørg Walaker-Nordeide. "The Kingdom of Norway." In *Christianization and the Rise of Christian Monarchy: Scandinavia, Central Europe, and Rus' c. 900–1200*. Edited by Nora Berend, pp. 121–66. Cambridge: Cambridge University Press, 2007.

Bailey, Michael B. "A Late-Medieval Crisis of Superstition?" *Speculum* 84 (2009): 635–61.

Baines, Anthony. "Portative Organ." In *The Oxford Companion to Musical Instruments*. Edited by Anthony Baines, p. 269. Oxford: Oxford University Press, 1992.

Barielle, G. "Baptême d'après les pères latins." *Dictionnaire de théologie catholique*. Vol. 2/1:208–11. Paris: Letouzey et Ané, 1932.

Barnes, Corey L. *Christ's Two Wills in Scholastic Thought: The Christology of Aquinas and Its Historical Contexts*. Toronto: Pontifical Institute of Mediaeval Studies, 2012.

Barnes Timothy. "Christians and the Theater." In *Beyond the Fifth Century: Interactions with Greek Tragedy from the Fourth Century BCE to the Middle Ages*. Edited by Iugo Gildenbard and Martin Reverman, pp. 315–34. Berlin: Walter De Gruyter, 2010.

Bartlett, Robert. "The Conversion of a Pagan Society in the Middle Ages." *History* 70 (1985): 185–201.

———. "From Paganism to Christianity." In *Christianization and the Rise of Christian Monarchy: Scandinavia, Central Europe, and Rus' c. 900–1200*. Edited by Nora Berend, pp. 42–72. Cambridge: Cambridge University Press, 2007.

Bartsch, Shadi. *The Mirror of the Self: Sexuality, Self-Knowledge, and the Gaze in the Early Roman Empire*. Chicago: University of Chicago Press, 2006.

Baumkirschner, Robert. "Bernhard von Clairvaux als Kirchenlehrer in dogmatischer Schau." *Cistercienser Chronik* 86, n.F. 145 (1979): 85–102.

Beatrice, Pier Franco, ed. *L'Intolleranza cristiana nei confronti dei pagani*. Bologna: Edizioni Dohoniane, 1993.

Beeley, Christopher A. *Gregory of Nazianzus on the Trinity and Knowledge of God: In Your Light We See Light*. Oxford: Oxford University Press, 2008.

Bellamy, Julien. "Baptême dans l'église latine depuis le VIII siècle." In *Dictionnaire de théologie catholique*. Vol. 2/1:250–96. Paris: Letouzey et Ané, 1932.

Benoît, André. *Le baptême chrétien au second siècle: La théologie des pères*. Paris: PUF, 1953.

Benoît, André, Boris Bobinsky, and François Coudreau. *Baptême: Sacrement d'unité*. Paris: Maison Marre, 1971.

Berend, Nora. *At the Gate of Christendom: Jews, Muslims and 'Pagans' in Medieval Hungary, c. 1000–c. 1300*. Cambridge: Cambridge University Press, 2001.

———. "Introduction." In *Christianization and the Rise of Christian Monarchy: Scandinavia, Central Europe, and Rus' c. 900–1200*. Edited by Nora Berend, pp. 5–38. Cambridge: Cambridge University Press, 2007.

Berend, Nora, Jósef Lazlovsky, and Béla Zsolt Szakács. "The Kingdom of Hungary." In *Christianization and the Rise of Christian Monarchy: Scandinavia, Central Europe, and Rus' c. 900–1200*. Edited by Nora Berend, pp. 319–68. Cambridge: Cambridge University Press, 2007.

Berger, David. "Mission to the Jews and Jewish-Christian Contacts in the Polemical Literature of the High Middle Ages." *American Historical Review* 91 (1986): 575–91.

———. *Persecution, Polemic, and Dialogue: Essays in Jewish-Christian Relations*. Boston: Academic Studies Press, 2010.

Bernardini, Paolo. *Un solo battesimo: Il concilio di Cartagine del settembre 256*. Bologna: Il Mulino, 2009.

Berschin, Walter. *Bonizo von Sutri*. Beiträge zur Geschichte und Quellenkunde des Mittelalters 2. Berlin: Walter De Gruyter, 1972.

———. *Greek Letters in the Latin Middle Ages from Jerome to Nicholas of Cusa*. Translated by Jerrold C. Frakes. Washington: The Catholic University of America Press, 1988.

Biermann, Martin. *Die Leichtenreden des Ambrosius von Mailand: Rhetorik, Predigt, Politik*. *Hermes* Einzelschriften 70. Edited by Jürgen Blänsdorf, Jochen Bleiken, and Wolfgang Kullmann. Stuttgart: Franz Steiner Verlag, 1995.

Bilby, Mark Glen. *As the Bandit Will I Confess You: Luke 23, 39–43 in Early Christian Interpretation*. Cahiers de Biblica Patristica 13. Strasbourg: Université de Strasbourg, 2013.

Bischoff, Bernhard. "Die europäische Verbreitung des Werke Isidors von Sevilla." In *Isidoriana*. Edited by Manuel Díaz y Díaz, pp. 317–44. Léon: Centro de Estudios "Isidoro de Sevilla," 1961.

Blumenkranz, Bernhard. *Juifs et chrétiens dans le monde occidentale, 430–1096*. Paris: Mouton et Cie., 1960.

Bombi, Barbara. *Novella plantatio fidei: Missione e crociata nel nord Europa tra la fine del XII e i primi decenni del XIII secolo*. Istituto Storico Italiano per il Medio Evo, Nuovi studi storici 74. Rome: Nella Sede dell'Istituto, 2007.

———. "Celestine III and the Conversion of the Heathen on the Baltic Frontier." In *Pope Celestine III (1191–1198): Diplomat and Pastor*. Edited by John Doran and Damian J. Smith, pp. 145–58. Aldershot: Ashgate, 2008.

Boyarin, Jonathan. *The Unconverted Self: Jews, Indians, and the Identity of Christian Europe*. Chicago: University of Chicago Press, 2009.

Brown, George Hardin. *Bede the Venerable*. Boston: Twayne Publishers, 1987.

———. *A Companion to Bede*. Woodbridge, UK: Boydell Press, 2009.

Brown, Peter. "Religious Coercion in the Later Roman Empire: The Case of North Africa." *History* 47 (1963): 283–305.

———. "St. Augustine's Attitude toward Religious Coercion." *Journal of Roman Studies* 54 (1964): 107–16.

———. *Religion and Society in the Age of Saint Augustine*. London: Faber and Faber, 1972.

Brown, Warren C. *Unjust Seizure: Conflict, Interest, and Authority in an Early Medieval Society*. Ithaca, NY: Cornell University Press, 2001.

Brundage, James A. *Medieval Canon Law*. London: Longman, 1995.

———. "Introduction." In *Crusading and Chronicle Writing: A Companion to Henry of Livonia*. Edited by Marek Tamm, Linda Kaljundi, and Carsten Selch Jensen, pp. 1–19. Farnham: Ashgate, 2011.

Buchanan, Colin. *Infant Baptism and the Gospels: The Church of England's Dilemma*. London: Darton, Longman and Todd, 1993.

Bührer-Thierry, Geneviève. "Des païens comme chiens dans le monde germanique et slave du haut moyen âge." In *Impies et païens entre antiquité et moyen âge*. Edited by Lionel Mary and Michael Sot, pp. 176–87. Paris: Picard, 2002.

Burns, J. Patout. "On Rebaptism: Social Organization in the Third Century Church." *Journal of Early Christian Studies* 1 (1993): 367–403.

———. "Appropriating Augustine, Appropriating Cyprian." *Augustinian Studies* 36 (2005): 113–40.

Byer, Glenn C. J. *Charlemagne and Baptism: A Study of Responses to the Circular Letter of 811/812*. Lanham, MD: International Scholars Publications, 1999.

Bysted, Ane, Carsten Selch Jensen, Kurt Villads Jensen, and John H. Lind. *Jerusalem in the North: Denmark and the Baltic Crusade, 1100–1522*. Translated by Sarah and Frederik Pedersen. Turnhout: Brepols, 2012.

Caffiero, Marina. *Forced Baptism: Histories of Jews, Christians, and Converts in Papal Rome*. Translated by Lydia Cochrane. Berkeley: University of California Press, 2011.

Cameron, Alan. *The Last Pagans of Rome*. Oxford: Oxford University Press, 2011.

Cameron, Averil. "The Byzantine Sources of Gregory of Tours." *Journal of Theological Studies*, n.s. 26 (1975): 421–26.

———. *The Byzantines*. Oxford: Blackwell, 2006.

Cantarelli Berarducci, Silvia. *Hrabani Mauri Exegetica: Repertoria Fontes*. 3 vols. Turnhout: Brepols, 2006.

Cao, Nan lai. *Constructing China's Jerusalem: Christians, Power, and Place in Contemporary Wenzkou*. Stanford, CA: Stanford University Press, 2011.

Carpin, Attilio. *Il battesimo in Isidoro di Siviglia*. Pontificia Universitas Gregoriana, Dissertatio ad doctorum facultate theologiae. Bologna: Grafiche S. Ruffillo, 1984.

———. *Battezati nell'unica vera chiesa? Cipriano di Cartagine e la controversia battesimale*. Bologna: Edizioni Studio Domenicano, 2007.

Carro, Venancio D. "The Spanish Theological-Juridical Renaissance and the Ideology of Bartolomé de Las Casas." In *Bartolomé de Las Casas in History: Toward an Understanding of the Man and His Work*. Edited by Juan Friede and Benjamin Keen, pp. 237–50. De Kalb: Northern Illinois University Press, 1971.

Castilla Rubio, Conrado. "El debate indiano en la primera mitad del siglo XVI: Las Casas, Sepúlveda y Vitoria." In *Actas del Congreso internacional V centenario del nacimiento del Dr. Juan Ginés de Sepúlveda*, Pozoblanco, 13–16 febrero 1991, pp. 211–20. Pozoblanco: Ayuntamiento de Pozoblanco, 1993.

Cavadini, John. *The Last Christology of the West: Adoptionism in Spain and Gaul, 785–820*. Philadelphia: University of Pennsylvania Press, 1993.

Cazier, Pierre. "De la coercition à la persuasion: L'attitude d'Isidore de Séville face à la politique anti-juive des souverains visigothiques." In *De l'antijudaïsme antique à l'antisémitisme contemporain*. Edited by Valentin Nikiprowetsky, pp. 125–46. Lille: Presses Universitaires de Lille, 1979.

———. *Isidore de Séville et la naissance de l'Espagne catholique*. Paris: Beauchesne, 1994.

Chandler, Cullen J. "A New View of a Catalonian *Gesta contra Iudaeos*: Ripoll 106 and the Jews of the Spanish March." In *Discovery and Distinction in the Early Middle Ages: Essays in Honor of John J. Contreni*. Edited by Cullen J. Chandler and Steven A. Stofferahn, pp. 187–204. Kalamazoo: Medieval Institute Publications, 2013.

Châtillon, Jean. "L'Influence de S. Bernard sur la pensée scolastique au XIIe et au XIIIe siècle." In *Saint Bernard théologien*. Actes du Congrès de Dijon, 15–19 septembre 1953, pp. 266–88. Analecta Sacri Ordinis Cisterciensis 9. Rome: Tipografia Pio X, 1953.

———. *D'Isidore de Séville à saint Thomas d'Aquin: Études d'histoire et de théologie*. London: Variorum Reprints, 1985.

Chazelle, Celia. "The Eucharist in Early Medieval Europe." In *A Companion to the Eucharist in the Middle Ages*. Edited by Ian Christopher Levy, Gary Macy, and Karen Van Ausdell, pp. 205–49. Leiden: Brill, 2012.

Chazelle, Celia and Burton Van Name Edwards, ed. *The Study of the Bible in the Carolingian Era*. Turnhout: Brepols, 2003.

Chazen, Robert. *Reassessing Jewish Life in Medieval Europe*. Cambridge: Cambridge University Press, 2010.

Chojnacki, P. Marek. *Il Battesimo e l'Eucharistia: Fonti rituali della vita cristiana secondo San Bernardo di Chiaravalle*. Rome: Pontificia Università Gregoriana, 2002.

Cohen, Jeremy. *Living Letters of the Law: Ideas of the Jew in Medieval Christianity*. Berkeley: University of California Press, 1999.

———. "Christian Theology and Anti-Jewish Violence in the Middle Ages." In

Religious Violence between Christians and Jews: Medieval Roots, Modern Perspectives. Edited by Anna Sapir Abulafia, pp. 44–60. New York: Palgrave-Macmillan, 2002.

Colish, Marcia L. "Another Look at the School of Laon." *Archives d'histoire doctrinale et littéraire du moyen âge* 53 (1985): 7–22.

———. "From the Sentence Collection to the *Sentence* Commentary to the *Summa*: Parisian Scholastic Theology, 1130–1215." In *Manuels, programmes de cours et techniques d'enseignement dans les universités médiévales.* Edited by Jacqueline Hamesse, pp. 9–29. Louvain-la-Neuve: Institut d'Études Médiévales, 1994.

———. *Peter Lombard.* 2 vols. Leiden: Brill, 1994.

———. "Why the Portiana? Reflections on the Milanese Basilica Crisis of 386." *Journal of Early Christian Studies* 10 (2002): 361–72.

———. "Authority and Interpretation in Scholastic Theology." In *Religious Identity and the Problem of Historical Foundation: The Foundational Character of Authoritative Sources in the History of Christianity and Judaism.* Edited by Judith Frishman et al., pp. 369–86. Leiden: Brill, 2004.

———. "Rethinking Lying in the Twelfth Century." In *Virtue and Ethics in the Twelfth Century.* Edited by István P. Bejczy and Richard G. Newhauser, pp. 155–73. Leiden: Brill, 2005.

———. *Studies in Scholasticism.* Aldershot: Ashgate, 2006.

———. *The Fathers and Beyond: Church Fathers between Ancient and Medieval Thought.* Aldershot: Ashgate, 2008.

———. "The Virtuous Pagan: Dante and the Christian Tradition." In *The Fathers and Beyond: Church Fathers between Ancient and Medieval Thought*, no. XVII. Aldershot: Ashgate, 2008.

———. "Fictive Baptism in the Early Middle Ages." *Archa Verbi* 6 (2009): 9–25.

———. "*De obitu Valentiniani*: Abelard, Bernard of Clairvaux, and the Canonization of Ambrose of Milan on Baptism by Desire." In *How the West Was Won: Essays in Literary Imagination, the Canon, and the Christian Middle Ages for Burcht Pranger.* Edited by Willemien Otten, Arjo Vanderjagt, and Hent de Vries, pp. 329–47. Brill's Studies in Intellectual History 188. Leiden: Brill, 2010.

———. "Otto of Lucca, Author of the *Summa sententiarum*?" In *Discovery and Distinction in the Early Middle Ages: Studies in Honor of John J. Contreni.* Edited by Cullen J. Chandler and Steven A. Stofferahn, pp. 57–72. Kalamazoo: Medieval Institute Publications, 2013.

Collins, Roger. *Visigothic Spain, 409–711.* Oxford: Blackwell, 2004.

Condorelli, Mario. *I fondamenti giuridici della tolleranza religiosa nell'elaborazione canonistica del secolo XII–XIII: Contributo storico-dogmatico.* Università di Catania, Pubblicazioni della facoltà di giurisprudenza 36. Milan: A. Giuffrè, 1960.

Consolino, Franca Ela. "L''optimus princeps' secondo S. Ambrogio: Virtù imperatorie e virtù cristiane nelle orazioni funebri per Valentiniano e Teodosio." *Rivista storica italiana* 96 (1984): 1025–45.

Contreni, John J. "Carolingian Biblical Studies." In *Carolingian Essays.* Edited by Uta-Renate Blumenthal, pp. 71–98. Washington: The Catholic University of America Press, 1983.

———. "Carolingian Biblical Culture." In *Johannes Scotus Eriugena: The Bible and Hermeneutics*. Edited by Gerd Van Riel, Carlos Steel, and James McEvoy, pp. 1–23. Leuven: Leuven University Press, 1998.

———. "'By Lions, Bishops Are Meant, by Wolves, Priests': History, Exegesis, and the Carolingian Church in Haimo of Auxerre's *Commentary on Ezechiel*." *Francia* 29 (2002): 29–56.

———. *Learning and Culture in Carolingian Europe: Letters, Numbers, Exegesis, and Manuscripts*. Aldershot: Ashgate, 2011.

Courcelle, Pierre. *Late Latin Writers and Their Greek Sources*. Translated by Harry E. Wedek. Cambridge, MA: Harvard University Press, 1969.

Courtenay, William J. "Sacrament, Symbol, and Causality in Bernard of Clairvaux." In *Bernard of Clairvaux: Studies Presented to Jean Leclercq*, pp. 111–22. Cistercian Studies Series 32. Kalamazoo: Cistercian Publications, 1973.

Courtray, Régis. "La figure des deux larrons chez Jérôme." In *Jerome of Stridon: His Life and Legacy*. Edited by Andrew Cara and Josef Lössl, pp. 105–16. Aldershot: Ashgate, 2009.

Coviaux, Stéphane. "Baptême et conversion des chefs scandinaves du IXe au XIe siècle." In *Les fondations scandinaves en Occident et les débuts du duché de Normandie*. Edited by Pierre Bauduin, pp. 67–80. Caen: Publications du CRAHM, 2005.

Cramer, Peter. *Baptism and Change in the Early Middle Ages, c. 200–c. 1150*. Cambridge: Cambridge University Press, 1993.

Cushing, Kathleen G. *Papacy and Law in the Gregorian Revolution: The Canonistic Works of Anselm of Lucca*. Oxford: Clarendon Press, 1998.

———. *Reform and Papacy in the Eleventh Century: Spirituality and Social Change*. Manchester: Manchester University Press, 2005.

———. "Polemic or Handbook? Recension Bb of Anselm of Lucca's *Collectio Canonum*." In *Bishops, Texts and the Use of Canon Law around 1100: Essays in Honour of Martin Brett*. Edited by Bruce C. Brasington and Kathleen G. Cushing, pp. 69–77. Aldershot: Ashgate, 2008.

D'Acunto, Nicoangelo. *I laici nella chiesa e nella società secondo Pier Damiani: Ceti dominanti e riforma ecclesiastica nel secolo XI*. Istituto Storico Italiano per il Medio Evo, Nuovi studi storici 50. Rome: Nella Sede dell'Istituto, Palazzo Borromini, 1999.

Dales, Douglas. *Alcuin: His Life and Legacy*. Cambridge: James Clark & Co., 2012.

Daley, Brian E. *Gregory of Nazianzus*. London: Routledge, 2006.

Dassmann, Ernst. *Ambrosius von Mailand: Leben und Werken*. Stuttgart: W. Kohlhammer, 2004.

De Jong, Mayke. *In Samuel's Image: Child Oblation in the Early Middle Ages*. Leiden: Brill, 1996.

———. "Adding Insult to Injury: Julian of Toledo and His *Historia Wambae*." In *The Visigoths from the Migration Period to the Seventh Century*. Edited by Peter Heather, pp. 373–402. Woodbridge, UK: Boydell Press, 1999.

———. *The Penitential State: Authority and Atonement in the Age of Louis the Pious, 814–840*. Cambridge: Cambridge University Press, 2009.

De Lange, N. R. M. "Jews and Christians in the Byzantine Empire: Problems and

Prospects." In *Christianity and Judaism*. Edited by Diana Wood, pp. 15–32. Studies in Church History 29. Oxford: Blackwell, 1992.

Delgado, Mariano. "Los derechos de los pueblos y de las personas según el pensamiento de Bartolomé de Las Casas." In *Responsabilidad historica: Preguntas del nuevo al viejo mundo*. Edited by Reyes Mate, pp. 285–310. Barcelona: Anthropos Editorial, 2007.

Diesner, Hans-Joachim. *Isidor von Sevilla und seine Zeit*. Stuttgart: Calwer Verlag, 1973.

Dölger, Franz Josef. "Tertullian über die Bluttaufe: *De baptismo* 16." In *Antike und Christentum: Kultur- und religionsgeschichtliche Studien*. 2nd ed. 2 vols. Vol. 2:117–41. Münster: Aschendorff, 1974.

Dox, Donnalee. *The Idea of the Theater in Latin Christian Thought: Augustine to the Fourteenth Century*. Ann Arbor: University of Michigan Press, 2004.

Doyle, Matthew A. *Bernard of Clairvaux and the Schools*. Spoleto: Centro Italiano di Studi sull'Alto Medioevo, 2005.

Duggan, Lawrence G. "'For Force Is Not of God': Compulsion and Conversion from Yahweh to Charlemagne." In *The Varieties of Religious Conversion in the Middle Ages*. Edited by James Muldoon, pp. 49–62. Gainesville: University of Florida Press, 1997.

Duval, Yves-Marie. "Formes profanes et formes biblique dans les oraisons funèbres de saint Ambroise." In *Christianisme et formes littéraires de l'antiquité en Occident*. Edited by Alan Cameron et al. Entretiens sur l'antiquité classique 23. Geneva: Fondation Hardt, 1997.

Dzielska, Maria. *Hypatia of Alexandria*. Translated by F. Lyra. Cambridge, MA: Harvard University Press, 1995.

Echeverría, Ana. *The Fortress of Faith: Attitudes toward Muslims in Fifteenth-Century Spain*. Leiden: Brill, 1999.

Ehlers, Axel. "The Crusade of the Teutonic Knights against Lithuania Reconsidered." In *Crusade and Conversion on the Baltic Frontier, 1150–1500*. Edited by Alan V. Murray, pp. 21–44. Aldershot: Ashgate, 2001.

Eihmane, Eva. "The Baltic Crusades: A Clash of Identities." In *The Clash of Cultures on the Medieval Baltic Frontier*. Edited by Alan V. Murray, pp. 37–51. Farnham, UK: Ashgate, 2009.

Elm, Susanna. "Inscriptions and Conversions: Gregory of Nazianzus on Baptism (*Or.* 38–40)." In *Conversion in Late Antiquity and the Early Middle Ages: Seeing and Believing*. Edited by Kenneth Mills and Anthony Grafton, pp. 1–35. Rochester, NY: University of Rochester Press, 2003.

Fassler, Margot E. *The Virgin of Chartres: Making History through Liturgy and the Arts*. New Haven, CT: Yale University Press, 2010.

Favreau-Lilie, Marie-Louise. "Mission to the Heathen in Prussia and Livonia: Attitudes of the Religious and Military Orders toward Christianity." In *Christianizing Peoples and Converting Individuals*. Edited by Guyda Armstrong and Ian N. Wood, pp. 147–54. Turnhout: Brepols, 2000.

Feiss, Hugh. "*Bernardus Scholasticus*: The Correspondence of Bernard of Clairvaux and Hugh of St. Victor on Baptism." In *Bernardus Magister*. Edited by John R. Sommerfeldt, pp. 349–78. Kalamazoo: Cistercian Publications, 1992.

Ferguson, Everett. *Baptism in the Early Church: History, Theology, and Liturgy in the First*

Five Centuries. Grand Rapids, MI: William B. Eerdmans Publishing Company, 2009.

Ferreiro, Alberto. *Simon Magus in Patristic, Medieval, and Early Modern Traditions*. Leiden: Brill, 2005.

Fichte, Jörg O. *Expository Voices in Medieval Drama: Essays on the Mode and Function of Dramatic Exposition*. Erlanger Beiträge zur Sprach- und Kunstwissenschaft 35. Nürnberg: Verlag Hans Carl, 1975.

Finn, Thomas M. *Early Christian Baptism and the Catechumenate: Italy, North Africa, and Egypt*. Collegeville, MN: Liturgical Press, 1992.

———. *From Death to Life: Ritual and Conversion in Antiquity*. New York: Paulist Press, 1997.

Fisher, J. D. C. *Christian Initiation: Baptism in the Middle Ages. A Study of the Disintegration of the Primitive Rite*. London: SPCK, 1965. Reprint Chicago: Hillenbrand Books, 2004.

Fonnesberg-Schmidt, Iben. *The Popes and the Baltic Crusades, 1147–1254*. Leiden: Brill, 2007.

———. "Pope Honorius III and the Mission and Crusade in the Baltic Region." In *The Clash of Cultures on the Medieval Baltic Frontier*. Edited by Alan V. Murray, pp. 103–22. Farnham, UK: Ashgate, 2009.

———. "Riga and Rome: Henry of Livonia and the Papal Curia." In *Crusading and Chronicle Writing: A Companion to Henry of Livonia*. Edited by Marek Tamm, Linda Kaljundi, and Carsten Selch Jensen, pp. 209–27. Farnham, UK: Ashgate, 2011.

———. "Alexander III and the Crusade." In *Pope Alexander III (1159–81): The Art of Survival*. Edited by Peter D. Clarke and Anne J. Duggan, pp. 341–63. Farnham, UK: Ashgate, 2012.

Fontaine, Jacques. "Conversion et culture chez les wisigoths d'Espagne." In *Conversione al cristianesimo nell'Europa dell'alto medioevo*. Settimane di Studi del Centro Italiano di Studi sull'Alto Medioevo 14, pp. 87–147. Spoleto: Centro Italiano di Studi sull'Alto Medioevo, 1967.

———. *Culture et spiritualité en Espagne du IVe au VIIe siècle*. London: Variorum Reprints, 1986.

———. "La figure d'Isidore de Séville dans le monde carolingien." In *L'Europe héritière de l'Espagne wisigothique*. Edited by Jacques Fontaine, pp. 195–211. Madrid: Casa de Velázquez, 1992.

———. *Isidore de Séville: Genèse et originalité de la culture hispanique*. Turnhout: Brepols, 2000.

Fournier, Paul. "Rebaptism as a Ritual of Cultural Integration." In *Shifting Cultural Frontiers in Late Antiquity*. Edited by David Brakke, Deborah Deliyannis, and Edward Watts, pp. 243–54. Farnham, UK: Ashgate, 2012.

Fransen, Gérard. "Anselme de Lucques, canoniste?" In *Sant'Anselmo vescovo di Lucca (1073–1086) nel quadro delle trasformazioni sociali e della riforma ecclesiastica*. Edited by Cinzio Violante, pp. 143–55. Rome: Istituto Storico Italiano per il Medio Evo, 1992.

Frassetto, Michael, ed. *Christian Attitudes toward the Jews in the Middle Ages*. New York: Garland, 2007.

Frattarelli, Lucia. "Sul battesimo dei bambini ebrei? Il caso di Livorno." In *Salvezza delle anime, disciplina dei corpi: Un seminario sulla storia del battesimo*. Edited by Adriano Prosperi, pp. 449–82. Pisa: Scuola Normale Superiore, 2006.

Fredrickson, Paula. *Augustine and the Jews: A Christian Defense of Jews and Judaism*. New York: Doubleday, 2008.

Gaddis, Michael. *There Is No Crime for Those Who Have Christ: Religious Violence in the Christian Roman Empire*. Berkeley: University of California Press, 2005.

Garipzanov, Ildar H. "Frontier Identities: Carolingian Frontier and the *gens Danorum*." In *Franks, Northmen, and Slavs: Identities and State Formation in the Early Middle Ages*. Edited by Ildar H. Garipzanov, Patrick J. Geary, and Przemysław Urbańczyk, pp. 113–42. Turnhout: Brepols, 2008.

Gatto, Ludovico. *Bonizone di Sutri e il suo Libro ad Amicum: Ricerche sull'età gregoriana*. Pescara: Editrice Trimestre, 1968.

Giese, Wolfgang. "In Iudiasmus lapsus est: Jüdische Proselytenmacherei im frühen und hohen Mittelalter." *Historisches Jahrbuch* 88 (1968): 407–18.

Gillmann, F. "Der 'sakramentale Character' bei den Glossatoren Rufinus, Johannes Faventinus, Sicard von Cremona, Huguccio und in der *Glossa ordinaria* des Dekrets." *Der Katholik* 90, ser. 4/5 (1910): 300–13.

———. "Zur Lehre vom 'sakramentalen Character'." *Der Katholik* 90, ser. 4/6 (1910): 215–18.

Gilson, Étienne. *History of Christian Philosophy in the Middle Ages*. New York: Random House, 1955.

Gimbutas, Marija. *The Balts*. New York: Frederick A. Praeger, 1963.

Giraud, Cédric. *Per verba magistri: Anselme de Laon et son école au XIIe siècle*. Turnhout: Brepols, 2010.

Glenn, Jason. *Politics and History in the Tenth Century: The Work and World of Richer of Reims*. Cambridge: Cambridge University Press, 2004.

Godman, Peter. *Poets and Emperors: Frankish Politics and Carolingian Poetry*. Oxford: Clarendon Press, 1987.

———. *Paradoxes of Conscience in the High Middle Ages: Abelard, Heloise, and the Archpoet*. Cambridge: Cambridge University Press, 2009.

González-Salinero, Raúl. "Catholic Anti-Judaism in Visigothic Spain." In *The Visigoths: Studies in Culture and Society*. Edited by Alberto Ferreiro, pp. 123–50. Leiden: Brill, 1999.

Grayzel, Solomon. *The Church and the Jews in the XIIIth Century: A Study in Their Relations during the Years 1199–1254 Based on the Papal Letters and the Conciliar Decrees of the Period*. Rev. ed. 2 vols. New York: Hermon Press, 1966.

Greatrex, Joan. "Monastic Charity for Jewish Converts: The Requisition of Corrodies by Henry III." In *Christianity and Judaism*. Edited by Diana Wood, pp. 133–43. Studies in Church History 29. Oxford: Blackwell, 1992.

Green, Dennis H. *The Beginnings of Medieval Romance: Fact and Fiction, 1150–1220*. Cambridge: Cambridge University Press, 2002.

Halsall, Guy. *Barbarian Migrations and the Roman West, 376–568*. Cambridge: Cambridge University Press, 2007.

Hamilton, Bernice. *Political Thought in Sixteenth-Century Spain: A Study of the Political Ideas of Vitoria, De Soto, Suárez, and Molina*. Oxford: Clarendon Press, 1963.

Hanke, Lewis. *All Mankind Is One: A Study of the Disputation between Bartolomé de Las Casas and Juan Ginés de Sepúlveda in 1550 on the Intellectual and Religious Capacity of the American Indians*. De Kalb: Northern Illinois University Press, 1974.

Häring, Nikolaus M. "St. Augustine's Use of the Word *Character*." *Mediaeval Studies* 14 (1952): 79–97.

———. "Character, Signum, und Signaculum: Die Einführung in die Sakramententheologie des 12. Jahrhunderts." *Scholastik* 31 (1956): 182–212.

Harvey, L. P. *Muslims in Spain, 1500–1614*. Chicago: University of Chicago Press, 2005.

Haverkamp, Alfred. "Baptized Jews in German Lands during the Twelfth Century." In *Jews and Christians in Twelfth-Century Europe*. Edited by Michael Signer and John Van Engen, pp. 255–310. Notre Dame: University of Notre Dame Press, 2001.

Heinzemann, Richard. *Die "Institutiones in sacram paginam" des Simon von Tournai: Einleitung und Quästionenverzeichnis*. Munich: Schöningh, 1967.

Hen, Yitzhak. "Charlemagne's Jihad." *Viator* 37 (2006): 33–51.

Hillgarth, J. N. *The Visigoths in History and Legend*. Toronto: Pontifical Institute of Mediaeval Studies, 2009.

Hoffmann, Hartmut. "Die Historien Richers von Saint-Remi." *Deutsches Archiv* 54/2 (1998): 445–532.

Horn, Cornelia B. "Children's Play as Social Ritual." In *Late Ancient Christianity*. Edited by Virginia Burrus, pp. 95–116. Minneapolis: Fortress Press, 2005.

Houben, Hubert. "Gli ebrei nell'Italia meridionale tra la metà dell'XI e l'inizio del XIII secolo," pp. 193–211. In *Mezzogiorno normanno-svevo: Monasteri e castelli, ebrei e musulmani*. Naples: Liguori, 1996.

———. "Religious Toleration in the South Italian Peninsula during the Norman and Staufen Periods." In *The Society of Norman Sicily*. Edited by Graham A. Loud and Alex Metcalfe, pp. 319–39. Leiden: Brill, 2002.

Hughes, Kevin L. "Haimo of Auxerre and the Fruition of Carolingian Hermeneutics." In *Second Thessalonians: Two Early Medieval Apocalypse Commentaries*. Edited and translated by Steven R. Cartwright and Kevin L. Hughes, pp. 13–20. TEAMS Commentary Series. Kalamazoo: The Medieval Institute, 2001.

Hunt, David. "Christianizing the Roman Empire: The Evidence from the Code." In *The Theodosian Code: Studies in the Imperial Law of Late Antiquity*. Edited by Jill Harries and Ian Wood, pp. 143–58. London: Duckworth, 1993.

Innes, Matthew. "'Immune from Heresy': Defining the Boundaries of Carolingian Christianity." In *Frankland: The Franks and the World of the Early Middle Ages. Essays in Honour of Dame Jinty Nelson*. Edited by Paul Fouracre and David Ganz, pp. 101–25. Manchester: Manchester University Press, 2008.

Jeauneau, Édouard. *Rethinking the School of Chartres*. Translated by Charles Paul Desmarais. Toronto: University of Toronto Press, 2009.

Jensen, Carsten Selch. "'*Verbis non verberibus*': The Representation of Sermons in the Chronicle of Henry of Livonia." In *Crusading and Chronicle Writing: A Companion to Henry of Livonia*. Edited by Marek Tamm, Linda Kaljundi, and Carsten Selch Jensen, pp. 177–204. Farnham, UK: Ashgate, 2011.

Jensen, Kurt Villads. "Denmark and the Second Crusade: The Formation of a Crusader State." In *The Second Crusade*. Edited by Jonathan Phillips and Martin Hoch, pp. 164–79. Manchester: Manchester University Press, 2001.

———. "Introduction." In *Crusade and Conversion on the Baltic Frontier, 1150–1500*. Edited by Alan V. Murray, pp. xvii–xxv. Aldershot: Ashgate, 2001.

Jensen, Robin M. "Baptismal Rites and Architecture." In *Late Ancient Christianity*. Edited by Virginia Burrus, pp. 117–44. Minneapolis: Fortress Press, 2005.

Joblin, José. "Significado histórico de la disputa de Sepúlveda con Las Casas." In *Actas del Congreso internacional V centenario del nacimiento del Dr. Juan Ginés de Sepúlveda*, Pozoblanco, 13–16 febrero 1991, pp. 237–49. Pozoblanco: Ayuntamiento de Pozoblanco, 1993.

Junquera Gómez, Mercedes. "El impacto del padre Las Casas en la visión hispanoamérica." In *Responsabilidad historica: Preguntas del nuevo al viejo mundo*. Edited by Reyes Mate, pp. 201–24. Barcelona: Anthropos Editorial, 2007.

Jürgens, Hartmut. *Pompa diaboli: Die lateinischen Kirchenväter und das antike Theater*. Tübinger Beiträge zur Altertumswissenschaft 46. Stuttgart: W. Kohlhammer, 1972.

Kahl, Hans-Dietrich. "Crusade Eschatology as Seen by St. Bernard of Clairvaux." In *The Second Crusade and the Cistercians*. Edited by Michael Gervers, pp. 35–47. New York: St. Martin's Press, 1992.

Kahlos, Maijastina. *Debate and Dialogue: Christian and Pagan Cultures, c. 360–430*. Aldershot: Ashgate, 2007.

———. *Forbearance and Compulsion: The Rhetoric of Religious Tolerance and Intolerance in Late Antiquity*. London: Duckworth, 2009.

Kata, Tiina. "The Incorporation of the Northern Baltic Lands into the Western World." In *Crusade and Conversion on the Baltic Frontier, 1150–1500*. Edited by Alan V. Murray, pp. 3–20. Aldershot: Ashgate, 2001.

———. "Rural Society and Religious Innovation: Acceptance and Rejection of Catholicism among the Native Inhabitants of Medieval Livonia." In *The Clash of Cultures on the Medieval Baltic Frontier*. Edited by Alan V. Murray, pp. 168–90. Farnham, UK: Ashgate, 2009.

Kaljundi, Linda and Kaspars Kļaviņš. "The Chronicler and the Modern World: Henry of Livonia and the Baltic Crusades in the Enlightenment and National Traditions." In *Crusading and Chronicle Writing: A Companion to Henry of Livonia*. Edited by Marek Tamm, Linda Kaljundi, and Carsten Selch Jensen, pp. 409–56. Farnham, UK: Ashgate, 2011.

Kantorowicz, Ernst. "The Baptism of the Apostles." *Dumbarton Oaks Papers* 9/10 (1956): 203–51.

Karras, Ruth Mazo. "Pagan Survivals and Syncretism in the Conversion of Saxony." *Catholic Historical Review* 72 (1986): 553–72.

Kasekamp. Andres. *A History of the Baltic States*. New York: Palgrave Macmillan, 2010.

Katzir, Yael. "The Second Crusade and the Redefinition of *Ecclesia*, *Christianitas*, and Papal Coercive Power." In *The Second Crusade and the Cistercians*. Edited by Michael Gervers, pp. 3–12. New York: St. Martin's Press, 1992.

Kedar, Benjamin Z. *Crusade and Mission: European Approaches toward the Muslims.* Princeton, NJ: Princeton University Press, 1984.

———. "Multidirectional Conversion in the Frankish Levant." In *Varieties of Conversion in the Middle Ages*. Edited by James Muldoon, pp. 190–99. Gainesville: University of Florida Press, 1997.

Keller, Hagen. "Le origini sociali e famigliari del vescovo Anselmo." In *Sant'Anselmo di Lucca (1073–1086) nel quadro delle trasformazioni sociali e della riforma ecclesiastica.* Edited by Cinzio Violante, pp. 27–50. Rome: Istituto Storico Italiano per il Medio Evo, 1992.

King, P. D. *Law and Society in the Visigothic Kingdom.* Cambridge: Cambridge University Press, 1972.

King, Ronald F. "The Origin and Evolution of a Sacramental Formula: *Sacramentum tantum, res et sacramentum, res tantum.*" *The Thomist* 31 (1987): 21–82.

Knoch, Wendelin. *Die Einsetzung der Sakramente durch Christus: Eine Untersuchung zur Sakramentalentheologie der Frühscholastik von Anselm von Laon bis zu Wilhelm von Auxerre.* Beiträge zur Geschichte der Philosophie und Theologie des Mittelalters, n.F. 24. Münster: Achendorff, 1963.

Laistner, M. L. W. "The Library of the Venerable Bede." In *Bede: His Life, Times, and Writings.* Edited by A. Hamilton Thompson, pp. 237–66. Oxford: Clarendon Press, 1935.

———. "The Latin Version of Acts Known to Bede." *Transactions of the Royal Historical Society*, n.s. 5/2 (1937): 37–50.

———. *Thought and Letters in Western Europe AD 500–900.* 2nd ed. Ithaca, NY: Cornell University Press, 1957.

———. *The Intellectual Heritage of the Early Middle Ages.* Edited by Chester G. Starr. New York: Octagon Books, 1983.

Lampen, Willibrord. *De causalitate sacramentorum iuxta scholam Franciscanam.* Bonn: Petrus Hanstein, 1931.

Landau, Peter. "Gratian and the *Decretum Gratiani.*" In *The History of Medieval Canon Law in the Classical Period, 1140–1234: From Gratian to the Decretals of Gregory IX.* Edited by Kenneth Pennington and Wilfried Hartmann, pp. 22–54. Washington: The Catholic University of America Press, 2008.

Landgraf, Artur Michael. "Das *sacramentum in voto.*" In *Dogmengeschichte der Frühscholastik.* 4 vols. in 8. Vol. 3/1:210–53. Regensburg: Friedrich Pustat, 1952–56.

———. "Die Wirkung der Taufe im *fictus* und im *contritus.*" In *Dogmengeschichte der Frühscholastik.* 4 vols. in 8. Vol. 3/2:87–181. Regensburg: Friedrich Pustat, 1952–56.

———. "Der hl. Bernhard in seinem Verhältnis zur Theologie des 12. Jahrhundert." In *Bernhard von Clairvaux: Mönch und Mystiker.* Edited by Joseph Lortz, pp. 44–62. Wiesbaden: Franz Steiner Verlag, 1955.

Langmuir, Gavin I. "At the Frontiers of Faith." In *Religious Violence between Christians and Jews: Medieval Roots, Modern Perspectives.* Edited by Anna Sapir Abulafia, pp. 138–56. New York: Palgrave-Macmillan, 2002.

Larson, Atria A. "Early Stages of Gratian's *Decretum* and the Second Lateran Council." *Bulletin of Medieval Canon Law*, n.s. 27 (2007): 21–56.

———. "The Influence of the School of Laon on Gratian: The Usage of the *Glossa ordinaria* and the Anselmian *Sententiae* in the *De penitentia*." *Mediaeval Studies* 72 (2010): 147–244.

Latourette, Kenneth Scott. *A History of the Expansion of Christianity*. 7 vols. Grand Rapids, MI: Zondervan Publishing House, 1970.

Lawton, David. "Sacrilege and Theatricality in the Caxton *Play of the Sacrament*." *Journal of Medieval and Early Modern Studies* 33 (2003): 281–309.

Le Bras, Gabriel. "Alger of Liège et Gratien." *Revue des sciences philosophiques et théologiques* 20 (1931): 5–26.

Le Croy, Timothy R. "Catechetical Context: Reading Paschasius Radbertus' *De corpore et sanguine domini* in Light of the Carolingian Mission to the Saxons." Unpublished.

Lerner, Robert E. *The Feast of St. Abraham: Medieval Millenarians and the Jews*. Philadelphia: University of Pennsylvania Press, 2001.

Levy, Ian Christopher. "Trinity and Christology in Haimo of Auxerre's Pauline Commentaries." In *The Multiple Meanings of Scripture: The Role of Exegesis in Early-Christian and Medieval Europe*. Edited by Ineke van t'Spijker, pp. 101–23. Leiden: Brill, 2008.

Lim, Richard. "Converting the Un-Christianizable: The Baptism of Stage Performers in Late Antiquity." In *Conversion in Late Antiquity and the Early Middle Ages: Seeing and Believing*. Edited by Kenneth Mills and Anthony Grafton, pp. 84–126. Rochester, NY: University of Rochester Press, 2003.

Löhr, Winrich. "Religious Truth, Dissimulation, and Deception in Late Antique Christianity." In *Double Standards in the Ancient and Medieval World*. Edited by Karla Pollmann, pp. 287–304. Göttingen: Duehrkohp & Radicke, 2000.

Lomax, John Philip. "Frederick II, His Saracens, and the Papacy." In *Medieval Christian Perceptions of Islam: A Book of Essays*. Edited by John Victor Tolan, pp. 175–97. New York: Garland, 1996.

Losada, Ángel. "The Controversy between Sepúlveda and Las Casas in the Junta of Valladolid." In *Bartolomé de Las Casas in History: Toward an Understanding of the Man and His Work*. Edited by Juan Friede and Benjamin Keen, pp. 279–306. De Kalb: Northern Illinois University Press, 1971.

Lotter, Friedrich. "'Tod oder Taufe': Das Problem der Zwangstaufen während des Ersten Kreutzzugs." In *Juden und Christen zur Zeit der Kreutzzüge*. Edited by Alfred Haverkamp, pp. 107–52. Sigmaringen: Jan Thorbecke Verlag, 1999.

Lottin, Odon. *Psychologie et morale aux XIIe et XIIIe siècle*. 6 vols. Gembloux/Louvain: J. Duculot/Abbaye de Mont César, 1948–60.

Luscombe, David E. *The School of Peter Abelard: The Influence of Abelard's Thought in the Early Scholastic Period*. Cambridge: Cambridge University Press, 1970.

MacMullen, Ramsay. *Christianity in the Roman Empire (AD 100–400)*. New Haven, CT: Yale University Press, 1984.

———. *Christianity and Paganism in the Fourth to Eighth Century*. New Haven, CT: Yale University Press, 1997.

———. "Cultural and Political Changes in the Fourth and Fifth Centuries." *Historia* 52 (2003): 465–95.

Mägi, Marika. "Ösel and the Danish Kingdom: Revisiting Henry's Chronicle and the Archeological Evidence." In *Crusading and Chronicle Writing: A Companion to Henry of Livonia*. Edited by Marek Tamm, Linda Kaljundi, and Carsten Selch Jensen, pp. 317–41. Farnham, UK: Ashgate, 2011.

Maier, Christoph T. *Preaching the Crusades: Mendicant Friars and the Cross in the Thirteenth Century*. Cambridge: Cambridge University Press, 1994.

Maier, Hans. "*Compelle intrare*: Rechtfertigungsgründe für die Anwendung von Gewalt zum Schutz und zur Ausbreitung des Glaubens in der abendländischen Christentums." In *Heilige Kriege: Religiöse Begründungen militärischer Gewaltanwendung. Judentum, Christentum und Islam im Vergleich*. Edited by Klaus Schreiner with Elisabeth Müller-Luckner, pp. 55–69. Munich: R. Oldenbourg Verlag, 2008.

Malkiel, David. *Reconstructing Ashkenaz: The Human Face of Franco-German Jewry, 1000–1250*. Stanford, CA: Stanford University Press, 2009.

Marcocci, Giuseppe. "'. . . per capillos adductos ad pillum': Il dibattito cinquecentesco sulla validità del battesimo forzato degli ebrei in Portogallo (1496–1497)." In *Salvezza delle anime, disciplina dei corpi: Un seminario sulla storia del battesimo*. Edited by Adriano Prosperi, pp. 339–423. Pisa: Scuola Normale Superiore, 2006.

Martin, Raymond-M. "Les idées de Robert de Melun sur la péché originel." *Revue des sciences philosophiques et théologiques* 11 (1922): 390–415.

Matthews, John F. *Laying down the Law: A Study of the Theodosian Code*. New Haven, CT: Yale University Press, 2000.

Mažieka, Rosa. "Bargaining for Baptism: Lithuanian Negotiations for Conversion, 1250–1358." In *Varieties of Religious Conversion in the Middle Ages*. Edited by James Muldoon, pp. 131–45. Gainesville: University of Florida Press, 1997.

———. "When Crusaders and Pagans Agree: Conversion as a Point of Honor in the Baptism of King Mindaugas of Lithuania (c. 1240–63)." In *Crusade and Conversion on the Baltic Frontier*. Edited by Alan V. Murray, pp. 197–214. Aldershot: Ashgate, 2001.

———. "Granting Power to Enemy Gods in the Chronicles of the Baltic Crusades." In *Medieval Frontiers: Concepts and Practices*. Edited by David Abulafia and Nora Berend, pp. 153–71. Aldershot: Ashgate, 2002.

Melve, Leidulf. *Inventing the Public Sphere: The Debate during the Investiture Contest (1030–1122)*. 2 vols. Leiden: Brill, 2007.

Mews, Constant J. "On Dating the Works of Peter Abelard." *Archives d'histoire doctrinale et littéraire du moyen âge* 52 (1984): 73–134.

———. *Abelard and His Legacy*. Aldershot: Ashgate, 2001.

———. *Abelard and Heloise*. Oxford: Oxford University Press, 2005.

———. "Between the Schools of Abelard and Saint-Victor in the Mid-Twelfth Century: The Witness of Robert of Melun." In *L'École de Saint-Victor de Paris: Influence et rayonnement du moyen âge à l'époque moderne*. Edited by Dominique Poirel, pp. 121–38. Bibliotheca Victoriana 22. Turnhout: Brepols, 2010.

Meyer, Susan Sauvé. "Aristotle on the Voluntary." In *The Blackwell Guide to Aristotle's Nicomachean Ethics*. Edited by Richard Kraut, pp. 137–57. Oxford: Blackwell, 2006.

Meyerson, Mark D. and Edward D. English, ed. *Christians, Muslims, and Jews in Medi-*

eval and Early Modern Spain. Notre Dame: University of Notre Dame Press, 2000.

Miethke, Jürgen. "Heiliger Heidenkrieg? Theoretische Kontroversen zwischen Deutchem Orden und dem Königreich Polen vor und auf dem Konstanzer Konzil." In *Heilige Kriege: Religiöse Begründungen militärischer Gewaltanwendung. Judentum, Christentum und Islam im Vergleich*. Edited by Klaus Schreiner with Elisabeth Müller-Luckner, pp. 109–25. Munich: R. Oldenbourg Verlag, 2008.

Minnis, Alistair. "Acculturizing Aristotle: Matthew of Linkölping's *translatio* of Poetic Representation." *Zeitschrift für deutsche Philologie*. Sonderhaft 124 (2005): 238–51.

Moore, John C. *Pope Innocent III (1160/61–1216): To Root up and to Plant*. Leiden: Brill, 2003.

Moore, R. I. *The Formation of a Persecuting Society: Power and Deviance in Western Europe, 950–1250*. Oxford: Blackwell, 1987.

Moreschini, Claudio. "Rufino traduttore di Gregorio Nazianzeno." In *Rufino di Concordia e il suo tempo*. 2 vols. Vol. 1:227–85. Antichità altoadriatiche 31. Udine: Arti Grafiche Friulane, 1987.

———. "Il battesimo come fondamento dell'istruzione del cristiano in Gregorio Nazianzeno." In *Sacerdozio battesimale e formazione teologica nella catechesi e nella testimonianza dei Padri*. Edited by Sergio Felice, pp. 73–82. Rome: Libreria Ateneo Salesiano, 1992.

———. *Introduzione a Gregorio Nazianzeno*. Brescia: Morcelliana, 2006.

Morrison, Karl F. *Understanding Conversion*. Charlottesville: University Press of Virginia, 1992.

Munier, Charles. *Les sources patristiques du droit de l'église de VIIe au XIIIe siècle*. Mulhouse: Salvator, 1957.

Murray, Alan V. "Music and Cultural Conflict in the Christianization of Livonia, 1190–1290." In *The Clash of Cultures on the Medieval Baltic Frontier*. Edited by Alan V. Murray, pp. 293–305. Farnham, UK: Ashgate, 2009.

McGuckin, John A. *St. Gregory Nazianzus: An Intellectual Biography*. Crestwood, NY: St. Vladimir's Seminary Press, 2001.

McKitterick, Rosamond. *The Carolingians and the Written Word*. Cambridge: Cambridge University Press, 1989.

———. *Charlemagne: The Formation of a European Identity*. Cambridge: Cambridge University Press, 2008.

McLynn, Neil B. *Ambrose of Milan: Church and Court in a Christian Capital*. Berkeley: University of California Press, 1994.

McNally, Robert E. *The Bible in the Early Middle Ages*. Westminster, MD: Newman Press, 1959.

Newman, Barbara. *God and the Goddesses: Vision, Poetry, and Belief in the Middle Ages*. Philadelphia: University of Pennsylvania Press, 2003.

Nirenberg, David. *Communities of Violence: Persecution of Minorities in the Middle Ages*. Princeton, NJ: Princeton University Press, 1996.

Nobile, Mario. "Il 'Libro de anulo et baculo' del vescovo di Lucca Rangerio, Matilde, e la lotta per le investiture negli anni 1000–1111." In *Sant'Anselmo vescovo di Lucca (1073–1086) nel quadro delle trasformazioni sociali e della riforma ecclesiastica*. Edited by

Cinzio Violante, pp. 185–94. Rome: Istituto Storico Italiano per il Medio Evo, 1992.

Oberman, Heiko A. *The Harvest of Medieval Theology: Gabriel Biel and Late Medieval Nominalism.* Cambridge, MA: Harvard University Press, 1963.

O'Donnell, James J. *Cassiodorus.* Berkeley: University of California Press, 1979.

Oldfield, Paul. *City and Community in Norman Italy.* Cambridge: Cambridge University Press, 2009.

Olson, Glending. "The Medieval Fortunes of 'Theatrica'." *Traditio* 42 (1986): 265–86.

Orlandis, José. "Le royaume wisigothique et son unité religieuse." In *L'Europe héritière de l'Espagne wisigothique.* Edited by Jacques Fontaine, pp. 9–16. Madrid: Casa de Velázquez, 1992.

Ott, Ludwig. *Untersuchung zur theologischen Briefliteratur der Frühscholastik unter besonderer Berüchsichtigung des Viktorinerkreises.* Beiträge zur Geschichte der Philosophie und Theologie des Mittelalters 34. Münster: Aschendorff, 1937.

Padgen, Anthony. *Lords of All the World: Ideologies of Empire in Spain, Britain, and France, c. 1500–c. 1800.* New Haven, CT: Yale University Press, 1995.

Palmer, Alan. *The Baltic: A New History of the Region and the People.* Woodstock, UK: Overlook Press, 2005.

Park, Chung-Shin. *Protestantism and Politics in Korea.* Seattle: University of Washington Press, 2003.

Pearson, Joseph H. "The Anti-Jewish Polemic of Alan of Lille." In *Alain de Lille, le docteur universel: Philosophie, théologie, et littérature au XIIe siècle.* Edited by Jean-Luc Solère et al., pp. 83–106. Turnhout: Brepols, 2005.

Pennington, Kenneth. "Further Thoughts on Innocent III's Knowledge of Law." In *Popes, Canonists and Texts, 1150–1550,* no. II. Aldershot: Variorum Reprints, 1993.

———. "The Legal Education of Innocent III." In *Popes, Canonists and Texts, 1150–1550,* no. I. Aldershot: Variorum Reprints, 1993.

———. "The Making of a Decretal Collection: The Genesis of *Compilatio tertia.*" In *Popes, Canonists and Texts, 1150–1550,* no. VIII. Aldershot: Variorum Reprints, 1993.

———. "Decretal Collections, 1190–1234." In *The History of Medieval Canon Law in the Classical Period, 1140–1234: From Gratian to the Decretals of Gregory IX.* Edited by Kenneth Pennington and Wilfried Hartmann, pp. 293–317. Washington: The Catholic University of America Press, 2008.

———. "The Decretalists, 1190–1234." In *The History of Medieval Canon Law in the Classical Period, 1140–1234: From Gratian to the Decretals of Gregory IX.* Edited by Kenneth Pennington and Wilfried Hartmann, pp. 211–43. Washington: The Catholic University of America Press, 2008.

Pennington, Kenneth and Wolfgang P. Müller, "The Decretists: The Italian School." In *The History of Medieval Canon Law in the Classical Period, 1140–1234: From Gratian to the Decretals of Gregory IX.* Edited by Kenneth Pennington and Wilfried Hartmann, pp. 121–73. Washington: The Catholic University of America Press, 2008.

Pérez-Prendes y Muñoz de Arracó, José Manuel. "Los criterios indianos de Juan Ginés de Sepúlveda." In *Actas del Congreso internacional V centenario del nacimiento del Dr. Juan Ginés de Sepúlveda,* Pozoblanco, 13–16 febrero 1991, pp. 269–77. Pozoblanco: Ayuntamiento de Pozoblanco, 1993.

Petersen, Nils Holger. "The Notion of a Missionary Theatre: The *ludus magnus* of Henry of Livonia's Chronicle." In *Crusading and Chronicle Writing: A Companion to Henry of Livonia*. Edited by Marek Tamm, Linda Kaljundi, and Carsten Selch Jensen, pp. 229–43. Farnham, UK: Ashgate, 2011.

Pioppi, Carlo. "Teologia e politica in un cardinale del tempo d'Innocenzo III: L'opera di Pietro Capuano." *Annales theologici* 29 (2006): 127–47.

Pirillo, Diego. "Il battesimo degli indios: Polemiche del fine cinquecento." In *Salvezza delle anime, disciplina dei corpi: Un seminario sulla storia del battesimo*. Edited by Adriano Prosperi, pp. 425–48. Pisa: Scuola Normale Superiore, 2006.

Pollmann, Karla. "The Splitting of Morality in Matthew 23 and Its Exegetical Consequences." In *Double Standards in the Ancient and Medieval World*. Edited by Karla Pollmann, pp. 263–86. Göttingen: Duehrkohp & Radicke, 2000.

———. "Hypocrisy and the History of Salvation: Medieval Interpretations of Matthew 23." *Wiener Studien* 114 (2001): 469–82.

Power, Amanda. *Roger Bacon and the Defence of Christendom*. Cambridge: Cambridge University Press, 2013.

Quinto, Riccardo. "La constitution du texte des *Quaestiones theologicae*." In *Étienne Langton: Prédicateur, bibliste, théologien*. Edited by Louis-Jean Bataillon, Gilbert Dahan, and Riccardo Quinto, pp. 525–62. Turnhout: Brepols, 2010.

Rahner, Hugo. *Man at Play*. Translated by Brian Battershaw and Edward Quinn. Introduction by Walter J. Ong. New York: Herder and Herder, 1972.

Ravid, Benjamin. "The Forced Baptism of Jews in Christian Europe: An Introductory Overview." In *Christianizing Peoples and Converting Individuals*. Edited by Guyda Armstrong and Ian N. Wood, pp. 157–67. Turnhout: Brepols, 2000.

———. "The Forced Baptism of Jewish Minors in Early-Modern Venice." *Italica* 13/15 (2001): 259–301.

Rebillard, Éric. "La figure du catéchumène et le problème du delai du baptême dans la pastorale d'Augustin." In *Augustine prédicateur (395–411)*. Actes du Colloque international de Chantilly, 5–7 septembre 1996. Edited by Goulven Madec, pp. 285–92. Paris: Institut d'Études Augustiniennes, 1998.

———. "Catechumens and the Delay of Baptism in the Preaching of Augustine." Translated by Aaron Pelttari, no. IV. In *Transformations of Religious Practices in Late Antiquity*. Farnham, UK: Ashgate 2013.

Reimitz, Helmut. "*Omnes Franci*: Identifications and Identities of the Early Medieval Franks." In *Franks, Northmen, and Slavs: Identities and State Formation in Early Medieval Europe*. Edited by Ildar H. Garipzanov, Patrick J. Geary, and Przemysław Urbańczyk, pp. 51–68. Turnhout: Brepols, 2008.

Reydellet, Marc. "Le conversion des Juifs de Clermont en 576." In *De Tertullien aux Mozarabes: Antiquité tardive et christianisme ancien (IIIe–VIe siècles). Mélanges offert à Jacques Fontaine*. Edited by Louis Holtz and Jean-Claude Fredouille. 2 vols. Vol. 1:371–79. Paris: Institut d'Études Augustiniennnes, 1992.

Riggs, David. "Christianizing the Rural Community of Late Roman Africa: A Process of Coercion or Persuasion?" In *Violence in Late Antiquity: Perceptions and Practices*. Edited by H. A. Drake, pp. 297–308. Aldershot: Ashgate, 2006.

Riley-Smith, Jonathan. "The First Crusade and the Persecution of the Jews." In *Persecution and Toleration*. Edited by W. J. Sheils, pp. 51–72. Oxford: Basil Blackwell, 1984.

———. "Christian Violence and the Crusades." In *Religious Violence between Christians and Jews: Medieval Roots, Modern Perspectives*. Edited by Anna Sapir Abulafia, pp. 3–20. New York: Palgrave-Macmillan, 2002.

Rivard, Derek A. *Blessing the World: Ritual and Lay Piety in Medieval Religion*. Washington: The Catholic University of America Press, 2009.

Rolker, Christof. "Ivo of Chartres and the *Panormia*: The Question of Authorship Revisited." *Bulletin of Medieval Canon Law*, n.s. 28 (2008): 39–53.

———. *Canon Law and the Letters of Ivo of Chartres*. Cambridge: Cambridge University Press, 2010.

Rosemann, Philipp W. *Peter Lombard*. Oxford: Oxford University Press, 2004.

Rosier-Catach, Irène. *La parole efficace: Signe, rituel, sacré*. Paris: Éditions du Seuil, 2004.

———. "Speech Act and Intentional Meaning in the Medieval Philosophy of Language." *Bulletin de philosophie médiévale* 52 (2010): 55–80.

Roth, Cecil. "The Forced Baptism of 1783 at Rome and in the Community of London." *Jewish Quarterly Review*, n.s. 16/2 (1925): 105–15. Reprint Philadelphia: Dropsie College, 1925.

Roth, Norman. *Jews, Visigoths, and Muslims in Medieval Spain: Cooperation and Conflict*. Leiden: Brill, 1994.

Rouche, Michel. "Les baptêmes forcés des Juifs en Gaule merovingienne et dans l'empire d'Orient." In *De l'antijudaïsme antique à l'antisémitisme contemporain*. Edited by Valentin Nikiprowetsky, pp. 105–24. Lille: Presses Universitaires de Lille, 1979.

Rozynski, Franz. *Die Leichtenreden des hl. Ambrosius inbesonderere auf ihr Verhältnis zu der antike Redekunst und den antiken Trostschriften untersucht*. Breslau: Buchdruckerei der Schlesischen Volkszeitung, 1910.

Russell, Frederick H. *The Just War in the Middle Ages*. Cambridge: Cambridge University Press, 1975.

Saccenti, Riccardo. *Conservare la retta volontà: L'atto morale nelle dottrine di Filippo il Cancelliere e Ugo di Saint-Cher (1225–1235)*. Bologna: Il Mulino, 2013.

Sachs, Curt. *The History of Musical Instruments*. New York: W. W. Norton, 1940.

Salzman, Michele Renee. "Rethinking Pagan-Christian Violence." In *Violence in Late Antiquity: Perceptions and Practices*. Edited by H. A. Drake, pp. 265–85. Aldershot: Ashgate, 2006.

Sattler, Dorothea. "Begierdetaufe." In *Lexikon für Theologie und Kirche*. Vol. 2:143. Freiburg: Herder, 1994.

Saxer, Victor. *Les rites d'initiation chrétienne du IIe au VIe siècles: Esquisse historique et signification d'après leur principaux témoins*. Spoleto: Centro Italiano di Studi sull'Alto Medio Evo, 1988.

Schmitt, Jean-Claude. *The Conversion of Herman the Jew: Autobiography, History, and Fiction*. Translated by Alex J. Novikoff. Philadelphia: University of Pennsylvania Press, 2010.

Séjourné, Paul. *Saint Isidore de Séville, son rôle dans l'histoire du droit canonique*. Paris: Gabriel Beauchesne, 1929.

Severino, Gabriella. "La *vita metrica* di Anselmo di Lucca scritta da Rangerio: Ideologia e genere letterario." In *Sant'Anselmo vescovo di Lucca (1073–1086) nel quadro delle trasformazioni sociali e della riforma ecclesiastica*. Edited by Cinzio Violante, pp. 222–68. Rome: Istituto Storico Italiano per il Medio Evo, 1992.

Shopkow, Leah. *History and Community: Norman Historical Writing in the Eleventh and Twelfth Centuries*. Washington: The Catholic University of America Press, 1997.

Sizgorich, Thomas. *Violence and Belief in Late Antiquity: Militant Devotion in Christianity and Islam*. Philadelphia: University of Pennsylvania Press, 2009.

Skinner, Patricia. "Conflicting Accounts: Negotiating a Jewish Space in Medieval Southern Italy, c. 800–1150 CE." In *Christian Atitudes toward the Jews in the Middle Ages*. Edited by Michael Frassetto, pp. 1–13. New York: Garland, 2007.

Smith, Carl T. *Chinese Christians: Élites, Middlemen, and the Church in Hong Kong*. Hong Kong: Oxford University Press, 1985.

Sommerfeldt, John R. "Bernard of Clairvaux and Scholasticism." *Papers of the Michigan Academy of Sciences, Arts, and Letters* 48 (1963): 265–77.

Spiccani, Amleto. "L'episcopato Lucchese di Anselmo di Biaggo." In *Sant'Anselmo vescovo di Lucca (1073–86) nel quadro delle trasformazioni sociali e della riforma ecclesiastica*. Edited by Cinzio Violante, pp. 65–70. Rome: Istituto Storico per il Medio Evo, 1992.

Stocking, Rachel L. *Bishops, Councils, and Consensus in the Visigothic Kingdom, 589–633*. Ann Arbor: University of Michigan Press, 2000.

Stofferahn, Steven A. "Staying the Royal Sword: Alcuin and the Conversion Dilemma in Early Medieval Europe." *The Historian* 71 (2009): 461–88.

Stow, Kenneth R. "The Church and the Jews." In *The New Cambridge Medieval History*. Edited by David Abulafia. Vol. 5:204–19. Cambridge: Cambridge University Press, 1999.

———. "Jews in the Middle Ages." In *A Companion to the Medieval World*. Edited by Carol Lansing and Edward D. English, pp. 293–312. Oxford: Wiley-Blackwell, 2009.

Sullivan, Richard E. "The Carolingian Missionary and the Pagans." *Speculum* 28 (1953): 705–40.

———. "Carolingian Missionary Theories." *Catholic Historical Review* 42 (1956): 273–95.

Symes, Carol. *A Common Stage: Theatre and Public Life in Medieval Arras*. Ithaca, NY: Cornell University Press, 2007.

———. "The History of Medieval Theatre/Theatre of Medieval History: Dramatic Documents and the Performance of the Past." *History Compass* 7 (2009): 1–17.

———. "The Tragedy of the Middle Ages." In *Beyond the Fifth Century: Interactions with Greek Tragedy from the Fourth Century BCE to the Middle Ages*. Edited by Iugo Gildenbard and Martin Reverman, pp. 335–69. Berlin: Walter De Gruyter, 2010.

Szuromi, Szaboles Anzelm. *Anselm of Lucca as a Canonist*. Frankfurt: Peter Lang, 2006.

Tamm, Marek. "Martyrs and Miracles: Depicting Death in the Chronicle of Henry of Livonia." In *Crusading and Chronicle Writing: A Companion to Henry of Livonia*. Edited by Marek Tamm, Linda Kaljundi, and Carsten Selch Jensen, pp. 135–57. Farnham, UK: Ashgate, 2011.

Thelamon, Françoise. *Païens et chrétiens au IVe siècle: L'apport de la "Histoire ecclésiastique" de Rufin d'Aquilée*. Paris: Études Augustiniennes, 1981.

———. "Rufin historien de son temps." In *Rufino di Concordia e il suo tempo*. 2 vols. Vol. 1:41–59. Antichità altoadriatiche 31. Udine: Arti Grafiche Friuliane, 1987.

Trivellato, Francesca. *The Familiarity of Strangers: The Sephardic Diaspora, Livorno, and Cross-Cultural Trade in the Early Modern Period*. New Haven, CT: Yale University Press, 2009.

Trumbower, Jeffrey A. *Rescue from the Dead: The Posthumous Salvation of Non-Christians in Early Christianity*. New York: Oxford University Press, 2004.

Turner, Nancy L. "Jewish Witness, Jewish Conversion, and Island Living: John Duns Scotus on Jews and Judaism." In *Christian Attitudes toward the Jews in the Middle Ages*. Edited by Michael Frassetto, pp. 183–209. New York: Garland, 2007.

Tydeman, William. *The Theatre in the Middle Ages: Western European Stage Conditions, c. 800–1576*. Cambridge: Cambridge University Press, 1978.

Tydeman, William, et al., ed. *The Medieval European Stage, 500–1500*. Cambridge: Cambridge University Press, 2000.

Tyerman, Christopher. *God's War: A New History of the Crusades*. Cambridge, MA: Harvard University Press, 2006.

———. "Henry of Livonia and the Ideology of Crusading." In *Crusading and Chronicle Writing: A Companion to Henry of Livonia*. Edited by Marek Tamm, Linda Kaljundi, and Carsten Selch Jensen, pp. 23–44. Farnham, UK: Ashgate, 2011.

———. *The Practices of Crusading: Image and Action from the Eleventh to the Sixteenth Century*. Farnham, UK: Ashgate, 2013.

Urban William. *The Baltic Crusade*. 2nd ed. Chicago: Lithuanian Research and Study Center, 1994.

———. *The Livonian Crusade*. 2nd ed. Chicago: Lithuanian Research and Study Center, 2004.

Urbańczyk, Przemysław. "The Politics of Conversion in North Central Europe." In *The Cross Goes North: Processes of Conversion in Northern Europe*. Edited by Martin Carver, pp. 15–27. York: York Medieval Press, 2003.

Van den Beek, Abraham. "Cyprian on Baptism." In *Cyprian of Carthage: Studies on His Life, Language, and Thought*. Edited by Henk Bakker, Paul van Geest, and Hans van Loon, pp. 143–64. Leuven: Peeters, 2010.

Van Rhijn, Carine. *Shepherds of the Lord: Priests and Episcopal Statutes in the Carolingian Period*. Turnhout: Brepols, 2007.

Veyrard-Cosme, Christiane. "Le paganisme dans l'oeuvre d'Alcuin." In *Impies et païens entre antiquité et moyen âge*. Edited by Lionel Mary and Michael Sot, pp. 127–53. Paris: Picard, 2002.

Vince, Ronald W., ed. *A Companion to the Medieval Theatre*. New York: Greenwood Press, 1989.

Violante, Cinzio. "Anselmo di Biaggo." In *Dizionario biografico degli italiani*. Vol. 3:397–404. Rome: Enciclopedia Italiana, 1961.

Wainwright, Geoffrey. *Christian Initiation*. London: Lutterworth Press, 1969.

Ward, Benedicta. *The Venerable Bede*. Cistercian Studies Series 169. Kalamazoo: Cistercian Publications, 1998.

Watt, John A. "Jews and Christians in the Gregorian Decretals." In *Christianity and*

Judaism. Edited by Diana Wood, pp. 93–105. Studies in Church History 29. Oxford: Blackwell, 1992.

Watts, Edward J. *City and School in Late Antique Athens and Alexandria*. Berkeley: University of California Press, 2006.

———. "The Murder of Hypatia: Acceptable or Unacceptable Violence?" In *Violence in Late Antiquity: Perceptions and Practices*. Edited by H. A. Drake, pp. 333–43. Aldershot: Ashgate, 2006.

Weber, Hubert Philipp. "The *Glossa in IV Sententiarum* by Alexander of Hales." In *Mediaeval Commentaries on the Sentences of Peter Lombard*. Edited by Philipp W. Rosemann. Vol. 2:79–109. Leiden: Brill, 2010.

Wei, John. "Penitential Theology in Gratian's *Decretum*: Critique and Criticism of the Treatise *Baptizato homine*." *Zeitschrift der Savigny-Stiftung für Rechtsgeschichte*, kanonistische Abteilung 126 (2009): 78–100.

Weingart, Richard E. "Peter Abailard's Contribution to Medieval Sacramentology." *Recherches de théologie ancienne et médiévale* 34 (1967): 159–78.

———. *The Logic of Divine Love: A Critical Analysis of the Soteriology of Peter Abailard*. Oxford: Clarendon Press, 1970.

Wickham, Chris. *The Inheritance of Rome: A History of Europe from 400 to 1000*. London: Allen Lane, 2009.

Williams, Peter. "Portative." In *The New Grove Dictionary of Musical Instruments*. Edited by Stanley Sadie. Vol. 3:140. London: Macmillan, 1984.

Winroth, Anders. *The Making of Gratian's Decretum*. Cambridge: Cambridge University Press, 2000.

———. "The Making of Gratian's *Decretum*." *Bulletin of Medieval Canon Law*, n.s. 26 (2004–06): 1–29.

———. "Marital Consent in Gratian's *Decretum*." In *Readers, Texts and Compilers in the Earlier Middle Ages: Studies in Medieval Canon Law in Honour of Linda Fowler-Magerl*. Edited by Martin Brett and Kathleen G. Cushing, pp. 111–21. Aldershot: Ashgate, 2009.

———. *The Conversion of Scandinavia: Vikings, Merchants, and Missionaries in the Remaking of Northern Europe*. New Haven, CT: Yale University Press, 2012.

Witt, Ronald G. *The Two Latin Cultures and the Foundation of Renaissance Humanism in Italy*. Cambridge: Cambridge University Press, 2012.

Wolf, Kenneth Baxter. *Making Histories: The Normans and Their Historians in Eleventh-Century Italy*. Philadelphia: University of Pennsylvania Press, 1995.

Zelzer, Michaela. "Zur Überlieferung und Rezeption der Kaiserreden des Ambrosius in mailänder Raum." In *"Chartae caritatis": Études de patristique et d'antiquité tardive en hommage à Yves-Marie Duval*. Edited by Benoît Gain, Pierre Jay, and Gérard Nauroy, pp. 113–25. Paris: Institut d'Études Augustiniennes, 2004.

———. "Quelques remarques sur la tradition des oeuvres d'Ambroise et sur leurs titres originaux." In *Lire et éditer aujourd'hui Ambroise de Milan*. Edited by Gérard Nauroy, pp. 21–35. Bern: Peter Lang, 2007.

INDEX

Abraham, 46, 56, 244
Acta Sanctorum, 94. *See also* Hagiography
Actors, 4, 6, 93–95, 110, 111, 112, 146, 147, 150, 151, 153, 167, 218; female, as converts, 93; *jongleurs*, 6, 147–48, 153; *Taufmime*, 4, 93–97, 110, 111, 112, 130, 146, 150–51
Acts of the Apostles, 18, 22, 32, 34, 104–7, 113, 114, 119–22, 123, 152, 153, 176, 204, 220
Adoptionism, 125
Adrianople, battle of, 15
Afterlife, Christian, 325
Alan of Lille, *De fide catholica contra haereticos libri quatuor*, 70–71, 73, 89
Alanus Anglicus, 284, 294
Albert of Buxhövden, bishop of Üxküll, archbishop of Riga, 267, 272, 285, 289
Albert the Great, comm. on *Sentences*, 80–82, 89, 92n4, 157n109, 192, 198, 206, 224, 225, 294, 302, 303, 304, 315, 316
Alcuin, 259, 260, 261, 313; *Epistola* 111, 259
Alemanni, 250
Alexander III, pope, 266, 286n153, 291n158
Alexander, bishop of Alexandria, 4, 98–102, 103, 112n42, 130–31, 142, 143, 145, 146, 152, 164, 169, 174, 175, 177–78, 183–84, 187, 190, 201, 218–19
Alexander, governor of Caesarea, 95–96
Alexander of Hales, *Glossa* on *Sentences*, 75–77, 78, 82, 88, 184–86, 191, 193, 194, 196, 198, 200, 205, 209, 221, 222, 223, 224, 225, 287, 293–94, 314
Alexandria, 97, 98, 99, 102, 112n42, 142, 164, 169, 175, 177, 183, 187, 201, 231
Alger of Liège, *De misericordia et iustitia*, 141–43, 145, 176, 180, 219
Ambrose of Milan, ix, 3, 11, 13, 14–18, 19, 20, 25, 35–38, 39, 40–41, 42, 44–45, 46, 47, 48, 49, 53, 54, 55, 57, 59, 60, 65, 68, 76, 78, 81, 84, 85, 86, 87, 88, 89–90, 117; *De obitu Valentiniani*, ix, 14–18, 25, 35, 36–38, 40–41, 42, 44, 46, 47, 53, 54, 55, 57, 59, 60, 65, 68, 76, 78, 81, 84, 85, 86, 87, 88, 89–90; on Luke, 19, 20, 117
Amory, Fredric, 92
Anabaptists, 320
Anglo-Saxons, 5, 119, 254
Anonymous, Carolingian, 26–27, 28
Anonymous, Paderborn, *Translatio S. Liborii*, 254, 256, 259, 261
Anselm, bishop of Lucca, *Collectio canonum*, 43n78, 132–38, 139, 140, 141, 143, 144, 154, 219, 325–26; continuator of, 133–38, 139, 140, 141, 43, 144, 154, 219, 325–26
Anselm of Canterbury, 43n78
Anselm of Laon, 33–35, 40, 41, 42, 58, 147, 153, 158, 220, 221, 223, 325–26; followers of, 33–35, 40, 41, 42, 58, 147–48, 149, 153–55, 156, 158, 160, 162, 176, 220, 221, 223, 325–26
Antichrist, apostates as, 247; religious hypocrites as, 244
Apiculture, Baltic, 278
Apocalypse, 7, 277
Apostates, 23, 216, 224, 247, 263, 267, 289, 290

Arbogast, *magister militum*, 15, 54
Arcadius, son of Theodosius I, 15
Ardalion, *Taufmime*, 95
Ariadne, 117
Arianism, 97, 240, 241–42, 245, 246, 247, 251, 312
Aristotelianism, 62, 72, 82, 84, 146, 150, 182, 184, 193, 194, 195, 196, 197, 203, 206, 212, 217, 218, 222–23, 223–24, 280, 299–301, 302, 303, 304, 306, 315, 322n8; faculty psychology, 184, 193, 194–95, 196, 222–23; *Nicomachean Ethics*, 299–300, 304, 306, 315; *Poetics*, 146, 147n91, 150
Aristotle. *See* Aristotelianism
Arles, 232, 238
Ascension, Christ's, 105; Ascension Day, 237
Athanasius, bishop of Alexandria, 4, 97–100, 101, 102, 131, 145, 164, 169, 170, 174, 175, 177, 178, 183, 190, 201, 218, 219
Augustine, 3, 5, 6, 11, 18–19, 20–24, 26, 28, 29, 30, 31, 32, 33, 35, 36, 38, 40, 41, 42, 44, 45, 46, 47, 48, 49, 50, 51n109, 53, 56, 57, 58, 59, 60, 62, 64, 68, 76, 78, 81, 82, 84, 85, 87–88, 92n1, 103, 107, 109–17, 118, 119, 121, 122, 123, 130, 132, 133, 134, 135, 136, 137, 138, 139, 141, 143, 144, 145, 150–51, 152, 153, 154, 155, 156, 157, 158, 159, 160, 162, 163, 164, 165, 166, 167–68, 169, 171, 172, 173, 174, 175, 176, 177, 178, 180, 181, 182, 183, 185, 187, 189, 190, 196, 197, 198, 200, 201, 202, 203, 204, 205, 206, 218, 219–20, 230, 235, 245, 298, 299, 302, 305, 307, 312, 323; *Ad Fortunatum*, 33; *Confessions*, 112, 198, 307; *De baptismo*, 18–19, 20–21, 23, 28, 30, 31, 32, 34, 36, 38, 40, 41, 42, 45, 46, 47, 56, 57, 59, 60, 64, 68, 76, 78, 81, 85, 109–17, 118, 119, 133, 134, 135–36, 137, 138, 143, 150–51, 152, 153, 159, 160, 167, 169, 171, 172, 173, 174, 176, 177, 183, 184, 187, 189, 190, 196, 197, 200, 202, 203, 204, 219–20, 302, 318; *De civitate dei*, 53, 112n42; *De diversis quaestionibus octoginta tribus*, 18, 23; *De natura et origine animae*, 21; *De sermone Domini in monte*, 112n42; *De trinitate*, 81, 88; *Epistola* 93, 137; *Epistola* 98, 168; *Epistola* 185, 232, 299, 302, 318; on Jews, 232, 235, 245, 305, 312; on John, 22–23, 53n111; on Leviticus, 22, 47, 58, 78, 84, 88; on Psalm 57, 84; on Psalm 77, 197; *Retractationes*, 23–24, 34, 36, 40, 42, 47, 57, 60, 78, 81, 88; *Sermo*, 149, 206; *Sermo*, 351, 197
Augustinian friars, 266, 267, 271
Aurelian, emperor, 95
Avars, 126, 239, 259, 261, 313
Avitus, bishop of Clermont, 236, 237–38, 240

Baghdad, 126, 261
Balkans, 239
Bandinus, *Sententiarum libri quatuor*, 58–59
Baptism by blood, 4, 11, 12, 14, 17, 20, 21, 24–25, 26–27, 29, 30, 31, 37, 40, 41, 41–42, 43, 45, 46, 52, 54, 56, 57, 58, 59, 61, 63, 68, 71, 73, 74, 75–76, 77, 78, 79, 80, 81, 82–83, 84, 85, 87, 88, 89, 93, 108, 147, 157, 229, 243
Baptism by desire, ix, x, 1–2, 3, 5, 6, 9, 10, 11–90, 93, 165, 171, 227, 243, 280, 292, 315, 317, 318, 319, 320, 326
Baptism, conditional, 49n102, 290, 298, 316
Baptism, date of institution by Christ, 14, 26, 43–44, 46, 47, 48, 49, 56, 57, 59, 60, 62, 67, 68, 79, 80–81, 82, 89, 192
Baptism, date received by Christ's apostles, 22, 29, 80
Baptism, fictive, x, 2, 3, 4–6, 9, 10, 32, 52, 90, 91–226, 227, 245, 257, 280, 284, 289, 291, 292, 293, 294, 295, 303, 304, 307, 315, 317, 318, 323–36; acted on stage, 4, 5, 93–97, 110–12, 150–51, 159, 167, 177, 189, 196, 204, 218; playful, 4, 97–103, 110, 112, 118, 130, 142, 151, 157, 159, 160, 161, 164–65, 167–68, 169, 170, 174, 175, 177, 180, 183, 187, 188, 189–90, 191, 195, 196, 200–201, 204, 209–10, 218, 219, 220, 293
Baptism, forced, x, 1, 2, 3, 6, 7–10, 52, 128, 186, 209, 223, 226, 227–318, 320–23, 324, 326
Baptism, infant, 21, 30, 34, 63, 65, 69, 77, 124, 126, 133, 134, 137, 154, 168, 171, 198, 242, 296, 303, 304–5, 309–10, 312, 313, 316, 320, 325–26; against parental will of Jews and/or infidels, in Durandus of St. Pourçain, 309–10; in John Duns Scotus, 304–5, 316; in Peter of Tarentaise, 303; in Thomas Aquinas, 296–98, 313; with unbelieving parents/godparents, in continuator of Anselm of Lucca, 134, 325–26, in follower of Anselm of Laon, 154, 325–26, in World Council of Churches, 326n14

Baptism, ritual, 1, 3, 4, 6, 7, 9, 11, 12, 14, 16, 17, 18, 20, 21, 22–23, 24–25, 26–27, 28, 30, 31, 32, 35, 36, 37, 39, 41, 42, 43–44, 45, 46, 47, 48, 49, 50, 52, 56, 57, 58, 59, 60, 61, 63, 64, 66, 68, 70, 71, 72, 73, 75, 76, 77, 78, 80, 81, 82, 83, 84, 85, 86, 88, 92, 93, 94–97, 100, 101, 102, 105, 106, 107, 111, 113, 114, 121, 123, 125, 126, 127, 129, 135, 139, 154, 156, 157, 159, 161, 164, 170, 202, 212, 243, 260, 263, 270, 273, 289, 302, 304, 307, 313, 314, 315, 316, 318, 320
Barbara, St., 271
Barcelona, 250
Basil I, emperor, 239
Bavaria, 253n72
Bede, 5, 25–26, 27, 34, 76, 88, 119–23, 126, 130, 145, 152, 153, 176, 220; on Acts, 119–22, 123, 152, 153, 176, 220; on Genesis, 119, 122–23, 220; on Luke, 25–26
Berengar of Tours, 33
Bernard of Clairvaux, ix, 3, 35, 38–41, 45, 56, 57, 75, 76, 78, 81, 88, 89, 266, 269, 270; *Epistola*, 77, 38–41, 76; *Epistola* 457, 269
Bernard of Parma, 283, 284n148
Berthold, bishop of Üxküll, 267, 276, 285
Blois, 127
Blumenkranz, Bernhard, 241
Bobbio, abbey of, 102
Boleslav III of Poland, duke, 266
Bonaventure, comm. on *Sentences*, 77–78, 150, 191–92, 198, 209, 221, 223, 294–95, 296, 302, 303, 315, 316
Bonizo of Sutri, *Liber de vita christiana*, 27–29, 31, 33, 43n78
Brown Peter, 107, 108
Bruno of Cologne, 147
Burchard of Strassburg, 305n190
Burial practices, of Baltic pagans, 262, 274
Byzantines. *See* Byzantium
Byzantium, 100, 103, 222, 236n17, 239, 240, 253n72, 264

Caesarea, 96, 97
Caesaropapism, 241
Calixtus II, pope, 286n153
Cameron, Averil, 102
Canonists, 2, 5, 7, 9, 27–33, 44, 51, 59, 88, 89, 130–46, 150–52, 159, 169, 176, 179, 190, 204, 214, 216, 227, 279–92, 294, 295, 311, 313, 315, 317–18. *See also* Law, canon
Canterbury, 178
Carolingians, 5, 119, 123–26, 166, 227, 250, 251–64, 269, 311, 313; as biblical exegetes, 5, 119, 123–26, 166, 220; Carolingian Renaissance, 250; military missions of, 250, 251–61, 262–64, 269, 311, 313; writers opposing, 259–60, 261, 313; writers supporting, 252, 253–55, 256–59. *See also* Alcuin; Anonymous, Carolingian; Anonymous, Paderborn; Charlemagne; Einhard; *Frankish Royal Annals*; Franks; Haimo of Auxerre; Louis the Pious; Lul; Poeta Saxo; Rabanus Maurus
Cassiodorus, *Historia tripartita*, 102
Catechesis, 10, 16, 37, 108, 122, 156, 158, 160, 162, 163, 225, 242, 243n32, 250, 251, 256, 258, 259, 260, 261, 263, 271, 276–77, 278, 313, 323, 324
Catechism, Catholic, 1, 2, 318, 319–25; post–Tridentine, 319–25; post–Vatican II, 1, 2, 320, 323
Catechumens, 1–2, 12, 13, 16, 17, 23, 25, 29, 30, 32, 48, 59, 96, 100, 101, 108, 130, 135, 145, 154, 157, 164, 170, 174 177, 178, 190, 201, 219, 243, 250, 280, 290, 292, 293, 313, 324
Cathars, 70
Catillus, Viking leader, 126, 127, 128
Celestine III, pope, 153, 266n106, 286n153
Celibacy, clerical, 133
Cessy-les-Bois, abbey of, 124
Character, baptismal, 6, 50–52, 56, 72–73, 74–75, 76, 77, 82, 85, 87, 89, 163, 179, 180, 182–83, 185, 186, 188–89, 191, 192, 193–95, 196, 197–98, 199–200, 202, 203, 205, 206–7, 208, 210, 212, 213–14, 215, 216–17, 223, 224–25, 284, 287, 288, 291, 292, 293, 295, 296, 301, 302, 303, 307, 316, 323, 324; in other sacraments, 50–51, 195, 212
Charlemagne, 8, 26, 125, 126, 241, 250, 251–55, 256–61, 262, 264, 269, 270, 311, 313
Childebert II, king of Austrasia, 238
Chilperic, king of Neustria, 238
Christology, 113, 234, 239, 241, 246
Chronicles, 5, 91, 94, 100–103, 126–30, 169n144, 177, 178n162, 218, 238–39, 243,

Chronicles *(cont.)*
254–56, 257, 258, 263, 268–79, 313. *See also* Cassiodorus; *Chronicon Paschale*; Dudo of St. Quentin; Einhard; Eusebius; *Frankish Royal Annals*; Gregory of Tours; Helmold of Bosau; Henry of Livonia; *Livonian Rhymed Chronicle*; Nicholas of Jeroschin; Otto of Freising; Pseudo-Fredegar; Richer of Reims; Rufinus of Aquileia; Saxo Grammaticus; Socrates; Scholasticus; Sozomen; Theodorus
Chronicon Paschale, 94
Cicero, *Tusculan Disputations*, 276
Circumcision, 72, 247
Cistercians, 265n106
Clement I, pope, 286n153
Clermont, 236–38
Clotild, wife of Clovis, 250, 251
Clovis, king of Franks, 250–51, 313
Colonialism, European, 228, 265, 323
Compelle intrare, 229, 232, 285, 298, 318. *See also* Augustine, *Epistola* 185; Innocent III
Confirmation, sacrament of, 65–66, 67, 69, 195
Constance, council of, 268
Constantine, emperor, 251
Conversion, religious, 4, 13, 24, 30, 31, 32, 34, 36, 37, 40, 41, 42, 45, 46, 58, 59, 60, 61, 62, 63, 64, 65, 69, 71, 74, 76, 81, 89, 94–97, 105–6, 107–8, 110–11, 113, 120, 137, 140, 150, 151, 157, 188, 192, 193, 194, 196, 202, 205, 214, 225, 228, 229, 231, 232, 234, 235, 236n17, 237, 240, 242, 244, 245, 246, 247, 250, 253, 259, 268n107, 270, 271, 276, 280, 282, 284, 285, 290, 304, 308, 309–10, 312, 313, 314, 316, 317, 318, 324, 325. *See also* Repentance
Corbie, abbey of, 256
Cornelius (in Acts 10:1–44), 18, 20, 21, 22, 28, 30, 32, 34–35, 37, 46, 47, 48, 49, 58, 62, 69–70, 78, 81, 86; in Albert the Great, 81; in Augustine, 18, 20, 21, 22, 32, 34, 37, 78; in Bonaventure, 78; in Bonizo of Sutri, 28; in followers of Anselm of Laon, 34–35; in Gratian II, 32; in Master Simon, 49; in Peter Abelard, 37; in Peter Lombard, 58; in Peter of Tarentaise, 86; in Porretans, 48; in Radulphus Ardens, 69–70, in Robert Pullen, 46, 47
Corpus iuris canonici (1983), 229, 318, 323
Corvey, abbey of, 256
1 Corinthians, 36
Covenant, God's, with humankind, in John Duns Scotus, 206–7, 208, 210, 225; in Durandus of St. Pourçain, 212, 213, 214, 215, 225
Creed, Nicene, 9, 15, 16, 81, 140, 225
Crusades, 8–9, 222, 227, 236, 249 262n101, 264–79, 299, 310, 311, 313; Baltic, 8–9, 264–79, 299, 310, 311, 313; First, 236, 249, 264; Fourth, 267; Second, 249, 269
Cyprian, bishop of Carthage, 12–13, 20, 26, 28, 31, 42, 48, 49, 56, 60, 64, 75, 76, 78, 82, 85, 108–10, 113, 122, 141, 204, 220; *Epistula* 73, 108–10, 122
Cyril, bishop of Alexandria, 231

Dagobert, king of Franks, 238, 239
Danes, 262, 264, 266, 267, 269, 277, 278, 285, 286, 313; in Baltic Crusades, 264, 266, 267, 277, 278, 285, 286, 313
David, king, 274
De Jong, Mayke, 253
Denmark, 126, 262–63, 266
Deusdedit, 134n71
Deuteronomy, Book of, 123n58
Dietrich, Teutonic Knight, 271
Dinocrates, brother of Perpetua, 21, 36, 88
Diocletian, emperor, 94
Disability, mental, as baptismal impediment, 186, 191, 198–99, 209, 223, 287, 289, 291, 292, 293, 296, 301, 303, 305, 307, 317, 323
Dominicans, 80, 82, 85, 89, 181, 188, 192, 197, 202–3, 211–12, 265n106, 310
Donatism, 18, 19, 20, 21, 29, 30, 31, 32, 88, 109, 110, 112, 113, 114, 121, 133, 135, 137, 139, 150, 232, 240n27, 299, 318
Drama, as misunderstood by Baltic pagans, 274, 311; as vehicle for fictive baptism that may or may not become fact, 4, 5, 93–97, 110–12, 150–51, 159, 167, 177, 189, 196, 204, 218; liturgical, 6, 146, 274; patristic hostility to, 6, 112, 146, 167; positive medieval attitudes to, 6, 146–52, 158, 311
Droge, Baltic pagan convert, 271
Drunkenness, as affecting validity of baptism, 187

Dudo of St. Quentin, *De moribus et actis primorum Normanniae ducum*, 128–29, 222
Durandus of St. Pourçain, comm. on *Sentences*, 85, 203, 211–15, 217, 221, 224, 225, 307–11, 313, 314, 315, 316
Dvina, river, use in Baltic pagan ritual, 273

Easter Vigil, as date for baptizing catechumens, 13n3, 23, 108
Ecclesia primitiva, 52, 67, 119, 309
Ecclesiology, 107, 109, 113, 155, 298
Egyptians, pagan religion of, 97, 99
Einhard, *Life of Charlemagne*, 255–56, 257, 258
Elbe, river, 264, 269
England, 46, 66, 178, 280n138
Ephesians, Epistle to the, 83
Epiphanus, 102
Epiphany Sunday, as date for enrolling *competentes*, 13, 22, 105
Ermoldus Nigellus, 263
Eskil, archbishop of Lund, 266
Estonia, 266, 277, 278
Estonians, 275
Eucharist, 24, 87, 92, 96, 146, 152, 159, 173, 221, 246, 256, 282; as *viaticum*, 96
Eugenius III, pope, 269
Eugenius, would-be emperor, 15
Eusebius, *Ecclesiastical History*, 4, 97
Evans, Christopher P., 172
Excommunication, 5, 27, 111, 142, 147, 243, 245, 286, 289, 290
Exegesis, biblical, 3, 5, 8, 11, 13–14, 18–20, 22–23, 25–26, 27, 28, 42, 45–46, 47, 53n111, 57, 58, 59, 60, 71, 78, 80, 84, 88, 89, 91, 103–7, 113–14, 116, 118, 119–26, 148, 155, 156, 166, 176, 193, 197, 204, 220, 229. *See also* Acts of the Apostles; Ambrose; Augustine; Bede; Ezekiel; Galatians; Genesis; Gilbert of Poitiers; *Glossa* ordinaria, Haimo of Auxerre; Hebrews; Jerome; John; Luke; Matthew; Peter Lombard; Psalms; Rabanus Maurus; Robert of Melun; Romans; Theodore of Mopsuestia; 1 Timothy
Expositio divinorum officiorum. *See* Anselm of Laon, followers of
Ezekiel, prophet, 5, 47, 88, 103–7, 113, 119, 123, 124, 125, 126, 152, 153, 155, 166, 193, 197, 203
Faventius, 51n109
Feiss, Hugh, 39
Ferreolus, bishop of Uzès, 238
Fomes peccati, 69, 182, 183, 221
France, 29, 127, 128, 249, 255
Franciscans, 77, 78, 79, 80, 81, 181, 188, 203, 205, 210, 212, 215, 265n106, 295, 306, 310
Frankfurt, 269
Frankish Royal Annals, 254–55, 313
Franks, 126, 127, 236–40, 250, 255, 257, 258, 261, 262. *See also* Carolingians; Merovingians
Fraud, 5, 6, 118, 120, 121, 127, 128, 131, 135, 174, 190, 221, 229, 293
Fulda, abbey of, 124
Fulgentius, 58n123

Galatians, Epistle to the, 115, 143, 155–56
Galla, sister of Valentinian II, second wife of Theodosius I, 16
Gandulph of Bologna, *Sententiarum libri quatuor*, 59–60, 168
Gaul, 7, 15, 16, 54, 236–40, 250, 312; Merovingian, 7, 236–40, 250, 312
Gelasinus, *Taufmime*, 94
Genesis, Book of, 119, 122–23, 220
Gennadius of Marsielle, 24–25, 28–29, 32, 36, 40, 48, 58, 68, 69, 83, 88, 103
Gentiles, 5, 20, 25, 54, 72, 104, 105, 111, 124, 166, 220. *See also* Infidels; Pagans
Germans, in Baltic Crusades, 264, 266, 267, 269, 272, 277, 278–79, 286, 313
Germany, 141, 249, 264, 265, 273, 310
Gideon, 274
Gilbert of Poitiers, 47, 48, 156, 158, 172, 222
Glossa ordinaria, biblical, 57, 83, 85, 88, 153n103
Gnosticism, 104n32, 108
Godman, Peter, 92
Good Friday, 237
Gotfred, king of Danes, 262
Gottfried von Strassburg, 270
Gottschalk of Orbais, 260n97
Grace, 6, 17, 21, 25, 26n32, 30, 32, 33, 34, 37, 38n63, 40, 43, 44, 46, 47, 50, 54, 57, 58, 61, 62, 65, 69, 72, 73, 75, 79, 82, 84, 87, 89, 116, 117, 118, 121, 122, 123, 134, 136, 140, 143, 144, 145, 155, 160, 161, 162, 163, 168, 172, 173, 174, 179, 180, 182, 183, 184, 185, 188, 189, 191, 192, 193,

Grace *(cont.)*
194, 196, 197, 199, 200, 202, 203, 204, 205, 206, 207, 208, 209, 210, 211, 212, 213, 214, 215–16, 220, 221, 222, 223, 224, 225, 244, 245, 246, 280, 284, 288n154, 289, 295, 308, 310, 312, 314, 320, 324; advenient, 179, 188, 200, 224, 225; *gratia gratis data/gratia gratum faciens* distinction, 203, 215–16, 222
Gratia, sister of Valentinian II, 16, 17
Gratian, *Decretum*, 31–33, 44, 134n71, 143–46, 153–54, 165, 166n131, 167, 168n138, 174, 175, 189, 193, 204–5, 206, 219, 220, 229, 276, 281–83, 284, 287, 289, 292, 311, 312, 314; Gratian I, 31, 143, 145–46, 174, 175, 189, 204–5, 219, 276, 281–83, 284, 287, 289, 311, 312, 314; Gratian II, 31–33, 143–45, 153–54, 193, 220
Gratian, emperor, 15, 16, 17
Great Schism, 268
Green, Dennis H., 152
Gregory I, pope, 102, 232–33, 235, 236, 238, 245, 259. *See also* Gregory the Great
Gregory VII, pope, 132, 141
Gregory IX, pope, *Decretals*, 216, 287, 288n154, 291–92, 293, 298, 301–2, 303, 304, 306–7, 311, 314, 316
Gregory Nazianzus, 13–14, 22, 26, 28, 88
Gregory the Great, 36, 37, 120, 157–58, 160, 232–33, 235, 236, 238, 245, 259, 281, 285, 289–90, 301–2, 311, 312, 314; *Moralia in Iob*, 120; on Jews, 232–33, 235, 236, 245
Gregory of Tours, *History of the Franks*, 102–3, 236–38, 250–51
Guido of Orchellis, *Summa de sacramentis et officiis ecclesiae*, 186–88, 219, 224

Hagiography, 4, 6, 21, 36, 37, 91, 93–97, 132, 147, 259, 268. *See also Acta Sanctorum*; *Chronicon Paschale;* John the Deacon; Perpetua; *Taufmime*
Haimo of Auxerre, on Ezekiel, 123, 124–26, 166, 220
Harald Klak, pretender to Danish throne, 262–63
Haroun al-Raschid, caliph, 126, 261
Hartmann von Aue, 270
Hartwig II, archbishop of Hamburg-Bremen, 266, 267, 270, 272
Hastings, actual or fictitious Viking leader, 128, 129
Heathens. *See* Gentiles; Infidels; Pagans
Hebrews, Epistle to the, 57, 58, 59, 60, 68, 71, 83, 84, 85
Hedwig, queen of Poland, 268
Helmold of Bosau, *Chronica Slavorum*, 268–69, 277, 279
Heresy, 4, 7, 11, 12, 13, 14, 20, 21, 27, 32, 55, 63, 70, 73, 97, 104, 108, 109, 110, 112, 113, 115, 124, 125, 133, 134, 135, 136, 138, 140, 141, 145, 151, 154, 155, 156, 157, 159, 161, 162, 166, 167, 173, 175, 177, 187, 204, 216, 220, 222, 228, 229, 230, 239, 240, 241–42, 244, 245, 246, 247, 251, 289, 299, 302, 312. *See also* Adoptionism; Arianism; Cathars; Montanism; Pelagianism
Henry III, king of England, 280n138
Henry IV, Holy Roman Emperor, 132, 141, 249
Henry of Livonia, *Chronicon Livoniae*, 265n106, 268n108, 271–79, 311; on education and role in Baltic Crusades, 271–72; on catechesis of pagans, 275, 276–77; on pagans' religion and culture, 272–74, 275, 278–79; on problematic missionary strategies, 274–75, 311; on Danes, Poles, Russians as missionaries, 277–78
Heraclius, emperor, 239
Hereseology, 92
Herod, king, 274
Heterodoxy. *See* Heresy; Schism
Hildebald of Cologne, 102
Histories. *See* Chronicles
Holy Innocents, 59, 63, 274; massacre of, in play misunderstood by Baltic pagans, 274
Holy Land, 231, 264, 267, 299n178
Holy Orders, sacrament of, 66, 130, 131, 132, 136, 166, 195, 212, 289
Holy Roman Empire, 53, 141. *See also* Germany
Honorius III, pope, 266n106
Honorius of Kent, *Summa de iure canonico*, 145, 284, 316
Honorius, son of Theodosius I, 15
Hospitality, laws of, among Baltic pagans, 271
Hugh of Saint-Cher, 300n179

Hugh of St. Victor, *De sacramentis*, 3, 38–39, 41–42, 44, 45, 55, 67n147, 76, 88, 89, 158–60, 161, 164, 165, 166, 168, 171, 173, 190, 191, 200, 210, 219, 220, 221, 292, 293; *Didascalicon*, 6, 148–50, 158
Huguccio, 51, 283, 284n148
Humbert of Silva Candida, 130
Hungary, 253n72, 261, 262n101, 322n7
Hydromel, Baltic pagan ritual drink, 273
Hypatia of Alexandria, 231
Hypocrisy, 4, 5, 6, 32, 92, 104, 107–8, 110, 111, 129, 134, 137, 151, 154, 173, 199, 204, 205, 209, 213, 216, 221, 222, 228, 244, 246, 253, 257, 259, 272, 324

Iberia. *See* Spain
Iceland, adoption of Christianity in, 263
Idolatry, 186, 229, 242, 273, 285
Illyrium, 15
Imbert d'Argueres, archbishop of Arles, 286–87, 288n154, 289, 291, 314
Indulgences, for crusading, 269
Infidels, 96, 125, 198, 206, 216, 228, 229, 244, 264, 281, 282, 283, 284, 288n154, 289, 296–98, 299, 302, 308, 309–10, 313, 314, 315, 316, 320. *See also* Gentiles; Muslims; Pagans; Saracens
Ingo, follower of Frankish leader Odo, 126–27, 128
Innocent I, pope, 120
Innocent III, pope, 267, 275, 283, 284–89, 291, 292, 293, 294, 296, 302, 303, 311, 312, 314, 315, 316
Innocent V, pope. *See* Peter of Tarentaise
Investiture controversy, 27, 29, 132, 133, 141, 249. *See also* Gregory VII; Henry IV; Reform movement, Gregorian
Isaiah, prophet, 305
Isidore of Seville, 7, 142, 149, 242–45, 248, 249, 260–61, 312; *De ecclesiasticis officiis*, 242–43, 260; *Etymologies*, 149, 243; *History of the Goths, Vandals, and Suevi*, 243; *Sententiae*, 243–45; presidency of Toledo IV, 242, 245, 312
Islam, 239, 310. *See also* Muslims; Saracens
Israelites, 14, 22, 26, 49, 103, 125
Italy, 27, 128, 239, 240n26, 321
Ivo of Chartres, 5, 6, 29–31, 88, 134n71, 138–41, 143, 150–52, 155, 162, 166, 218, 219, 220, 222, 280–81, 282, 312, 314; *Decretum*, 138–41, 150–52, 218, 222; *Panormia* ascribed to him, 29–31, 88, 280–81, 282, 312, 314

Jagiello, king of Lithuania, 268
Jarrow, abbey of, 102, 119
Jensen, Robin M., 318
Jeremiah, prophet, 12, 88
Jerome, 5, 19–20, 21, 25, 60, 103–7, 113, 118, 119, 121n57, 122, 123, 124, 126, 130, 145, 152, 153, 155–56, 161, 165, 166, 168, 193, 197, 203, 204, 220; *In die domenica Pascha*, 20n19; on Ezekiel, 5, 103–7, 113, 119, 123, 124, 125, 126, 152, 153, 155–56, 161, 165, 166, 168, 193, 197, 203, 220; on Galatians, 155–56; on Mark, 104n32; on Matthew, 19, 21, 155, 156; on Psalms, 104n32, Vulgate Bible of, 103, 104–5n33
Jerusalem, 103, 106, 120, 124, 269
Jews, 7–8, 20, 25, 54, 72, 152, 170, 174, 180, 208n215, 218, 231–50, 261, 279, 280, 281, 282, 284, 286, 288n154, 289, 290, 295n169, 296–98, 303, 304–5, 308, 311, 312, 315, 316, 321
Johannes Andreae, 214
John the Baptist, 14, 26, 62, 88, 192, 203, 206
John Damascene, 72, 83, 84, 88, 192, 197–98, 206, 212
John the Deacon, 36, 37
John Duns Scotus, 79–80, 85, 87, 88, 92n4, 205–10, 212, 213, 216, 217, 221, 222, 223, 224, 225, 226, 303–6, 315–16; *Ordinatio*, 79–80, 205–7, 208, 209, 210, 216, 303–5, 315–16; *Reportata Parisiensia*, 207–10, 213, 305–6, 316
John, Gospel of, 22–23, 29, 32, 37, 42–43, 45, 46, 47, 50, 53n111, 54, 55, 56, 57, 59, 60, 62, 65, 68, 69, 70, 74, 78, 79, 80, 88, 104, 120
John, king of England, 178
John of San Giminiano, 150
John, St., 23, 79, 106, 120
John of Wales, 150
Jordan, river, 14, 43, 56, 59, 89
Judea, 42, 43
Judges, Book of, 83, 88
Judgment, Day of, 107. *See also* Last Day
Judith, wife of Louis the Pious, 263

Julian the Apostate, emperor, 95
Julianus of Eclanum, 103
Just war, 229, 264, 269, 271, 285, 298, 299, 302, 310, 313–14
Justa, sister of Valentinian II, 16, 17
Justina, mother of Valentinian II, 15, 16
Justinian, emperor, 239

Koch, Wendelin, 62
Krakow, 268
Kyriawanus, Baltic pagan convert, 276–77

Lactantius, 229
Lampen, Willibrord, 79
Landgraf, Artur Michael, 93, 153
Las Casas, Bartolomé de, 322–23
Last Day, 232, 305, 316
Last Supper, 29, 80
Latourette, Kenneth Scott, 251, 252
Law, canon, 7, 27, 28, 29, 33, 50, 55, 91, 111, 133, 141, 146, 228, 242, 246, 248, 249, 252, 266n106, 276, 280, 285, 286, 289, 295, 297, 307, 314, 315. *See also* Canonists; *Corpus iuris canonici*
Law, civil, 7, 100, 109, 128, 145–46, 165, 174, 175–76, 219, 230–32, 233, 239, 242, 247, 248, 249, 252, 255, 270–71, 276, 280, 286, 295, 297, 303, 305, 308, 309, 310, 312, 313, 314. *See also* Jews; *Patria potestas*; Slavery; Theodosian Code
Law, natural, 297, 303, 305, 313, 323
LeMans, 256
Lent, 108, 158
Leo III, emperor, 239
Letters, papal, 133, 232–33, 235, 236, 245, 268, 275–76, 280, 284, 285–89, 291, 292, 293, 314, 315. *See also* Gregory I; Innocent III
Letts, 273
Leviticus, Book of, 22, 47, 58, 78, 84, 123n58
Liber Pancrisis. *See* Anselm of Laon, followers of
Liborius, relics of, 256
Limoges, 127
Lithuania, 266n106, 268, 270
Lithuanians, 267, 273
Liturgy, 4, 6, 26, 28, 29, 79, 82, 87, 92, 94–97, 100, 101, 102, 111, 113, 135, 136, 138, 139, 142, 145, 146, 151, 154, 156, 159, 164, 167, 191, 212, 222, 246, 248, 260, 290. *See also* Baptism, ritual; Ritual
Livonia, 266, 267, 270, 272, 277, 278, 279
Livonian Rhymed Chronicle, 276
Livonians, 266, 273
Löhr, Winrich, 92
Lothar, son of Louis the Pious, 263
Louis the Pious, 259, 262, 263
Lucca, 43n78, 132
Luke, Gospel of, 18, 19, 21, 22, 25, 109, 229
Lul, bishop Mainz, putative author of *Carmen de conversion Saxonum*, 254
Lumen gentium, 1, 2
Luna, 128–29
Lund, 266, 277
Lupus of Ferrières, 102

MacMullen, Ramsay, 230, 231
Magona, 231, 232n8, 240, 246
Maier, Hans, 228–29
Mainz, 124, 263
Mark, Gospel of, 109
Marriage, sacrament of, 66, 161, 190–91, 206, 209, 221, 223, 274, 296, 301, 304, 325
Marsielle, 232, 236, 238
Martin, Master, *Conpilatio questionum theologie*, 174, 176
Martyrdom, Christian. *See* Baptism by blood
Matilda, countess of Tuscany, 27, 132
Matthew, Gospel of, 19, 21, 25, 32, 43, 56, 80, 88, 92n2, 109, 113, 116, 136, 137, 155, 156, 193
Matthew, St., 137
Maximian, emperor, 94
Meinhard, bishop of Üxküll, 266, 267, 270, 272
Merovingians, 7, 236–40, 250, 252
Milan, 15, 16, 17
Mindaugas, king of Lithuania, 266n106, 267, 270
Minorca, 231, 236n17, 240–41
Montanism, 12
Moore, R. I., 233
Morrison, Karl F., 228
Music, in Baltic Crusades, 275, 311
Muslims, 8, 126, 239, 242, 261, 264, 269, 308, 311, 312, 315, 321. *See also* Infidels; Saracens

Nemesius, 300
Newman, Barbara, 152
New World, 321, 323
Nicaea, council of, 101
Nicholas von Jeroschin, *The Chronicle of Prussia*, 270–71
Nicodemus (in John 3:3–5), in Albert the Great, 80; in Augustine, 22, 23; in Gandulph of Bologna, 60; in Jerome, 104; in Master Simon, 49; in Peter Lombard, 56; in Peter of Poitiers, 62; in Radulphus Ardens, 68, 69; in Robert Pullen, 47; in Roland of Bologna, 44; in *Summa sententiarum*, 42; in William of Ware, 79
Noah, 122
Nonbelievers, 7, 16, 187, 228, 229, 231, 233, 250, 281, 283, 288, 299, 304, 305, 308, 309, 315, 316. *See also* Gentiles; Infidels; Jews; Muslims; Pagans; Saracens
Normandy, 128
Normans, 5, 126–29, 130, 222, 239; rule in southern Italy and Sicily, 239; the Norman ruse, 5, 126–29, 130, 222
North Africa, 108, 109, 240n27, 318
Northmen, 125, 126–29. *See also* Vikings
Norway, 263
Notre Dame, Paris, school of, 60, 61, 169
Notule super IIII librum Sententiarum, 62–63

Obdorites, 255
Odo, founder of Robertian dynasty, 127
Odo of Ourscamp, *Quaestiones*, 171–72, 192, 220, 222
Old Testament, continuities/discontinuities with New Testament beliefs, values, rites, 11, 13–14, 20, 22, 26, 27, 28, 46, 47, 56, 61, 62, 68, 72, 84, 88, 232. *See also* Baptism by desire; Circumcision; Israelites; Jews; Ritual, pre-Christian
Orestes, governor of Alexandria, 231
Orosius, 103
Orthodox Church, Greek, 222, 239, 252, 253n72; Russian, 268, 273, 277
Öselians, 278–79
Otto I, bishop of Bamberg, 266
Otto, bishop of Lucca, 43n78
Otto of Freising, *The Two Cities*, 53–55, 79, 86, 79
Oxford, university of, 79, 215

Paderborn, 256
Pagans, 4, 5, 7, 8–9, 36, 37, 38, 93–97, 108, 126, 128, 129, 142, 143, 145, 219, 222, 229, 230, 231, 242, 245, 250–59, 260, 261, 262, 263, 264–79, 285, 298, 302, 303, 311, 312, 313, 314. *See also* Crusades, Baltic; Egyptians; Gentiles; Infidels
Palm Sunday, 23
Panormia. *See* Ivo of Chartres
Papal-imperial feud, 5, 141, 249. *See also* Investiture controversy
Paris, schools of, 53, 60, 61, 64, 65, 66, 70, 79, 169, 172, 178; university of, 79, 186. *See also* Notre Dame, Ste. Geneviève
Paschasius Radbertus, *De corpore et sanguine Domini*, 256
Patria potestas, 100, 297, 303, 313
Paul, St., 45, 56, 57, 59, 78, 83, 125n61, 156
Paulinus of Nola, 103
Pelagianism, 21, 22, 24, 30, 33, 34, 40, 42, 48, 57, 59, 60, 85, 87–88, 133, 134
Pelagius II, pope, 102
Penance, sacrament of, 14, 46, 53n14, 66, 69–70, 88, 92, 141, 161, 173, 177, 179, 181, 182, 185, 192, 194, 206, 208, 211, 214, 221, 225, 228, 253, 289. *See also* Repentance
Penitentials, 250
Pentecost, 71, 105, 127, 237, 238
Perpetua, 21, 36
Persecution, religious, 7, 8, 52, 108, 228, 229, 230, 231, 233, 236n17, 237–42, 244, 246–47, 249–50, 286, 298, 308, 312
Persia, 239
Peter Abelard, ix, 3, 35–38, 39, 40, 41, 45, 88, 89, 155–56; on Romans, 37; *Scito teipsum*, 37; *Sic et non*, 36–37, 155, 156; *Theologia christiana*, 36, 37–38
Peter, bishop of Terracina, 233
Peter of Capua, *Summa theologiae*, 65–66, 67
Peter the Chanter, *Summa de sacramentis et animae consiliis*, 63–64, 173–74, 292–93
Peter Comestor, *De sacramentis*, 60–61, 63, 167–68n138, 168–69, 177, 219

Peter Damian, *Liber gratissimus*, 130–32, 142, 219
Peter Lombard, on Hebrews, 57, 58, 58, 59, 60, 68, 71, 83, 84, 85; *Sentences*, 35, 51n109, 55–58, 59, 60, 61, 62, 65, 66, 67, 68, 69, 70, 71, 75, 76, 77, 78 79, 80, 81, 83, 85, 87, 89, 165–68, 169, 171, 172, 173, 174, 177, 181, 184, 189, 191, 192, 193, 196, 197, 200, 203, 206, 207, 210, 212, 215, 219, 220, 293, 295, 296
Peter, martyr, 98, 100, 101, 130, 142, 145, 164
Peter of Poitiers, *Sententiarum libri quinque*, 61–62, 63, 88, 169–71, 174, 176, 180, 219
Peter of Tarentaise, comm. on *Sentences*, 85–87, 192–97, 198, 200, 203, 205, 213, 221, 222, 223, 224, 225, 295–96, 301, 315
Peter, St. 18, 22, 28, 29, 34, 70, 106, 107, 113, 114, 120, 121, 123
Petersen, Nils Holger, 274
Philip, apostle, 105–6, 120
Philip the Chancellor, 300n179
Philistines, 42, 43, 274
Photius, patriarch of Constantinople, 140
Pietro, anti-bishop of Lucca, 132
Play of the Sacrament, Croxton, 152
Poeta Saxo, *Annalium de gestis Caroli magni imperatoris*, 256–59, 261, 311
Poitou, 66, 178
Poland, 258, 310
Poles, in Baltic Crusades, 264, 266, 268, 277, 313
Pollmann, Karla, 92
Pomerania, 266
Porphyrius, *Taufmime*, 95
Porphyrius of Ephesus, *Taufmime*, 95–96, 97
Porretan sentence collectors, 47–49, 52, 156–58, 160, 172, 192; on single vs. triple immersion in baptism, 48
Portative organ, 275
Predestination, 21, 37, 38, 52, 53n111, 107, 122, 156, 172, 222
Premonstratensians, 267
Prepositinus of Cremona, *Summa theologiae*, 64–65, 174–77, 179, 183, 187, 200, 214, 219, 225
Protestants, 320
Prussians, 310
Psalms, Book of, 26, 57, 84, 197
Pseudo-Dionysius, 206
Pseudo-Fredegar, 238–39
Pseudo-Peter of Poitiers gloss on *Sentences*, 51n109

Quinto, Riccardo, 179
Quodvultdeus, 103

Rabanus Maurus, *De institutione clericorum*, 259, 260n97, 261, 313; on Ezekiel, 123, 124, 126, 166, 220
Radulphus Ardens, *Speculum universale*, 66–70, 74, 87, 89, 169n144, 173n151, 174n154, 175n157, 177–78
Ralph of Longchamp, 150
Rangerio, bishop of Lucca, *Vita Anselmi*, 132
Raymond of Peñafort, as compiler of *Decretals* of Gregory IX, 291; *Summa de poenitentia*, 289–90, 294, 296, 311, 314, 315, 316
Rebaptism, 4, 9, 98, 101, 108, 109, 111, 113, 114, 118, 131, 136, 138, 139, 142, 145, 153, 154, 157, 161, 164, 169, 170, 175, 177, 178, 187, 201, 204, 205, 210, 211, 220, 225, 240n27, 253, 279, 287, 317
Reccared, king of Visigoths, 241, 312
Recidivism, 9, 186, 233, 238, 244, 245, 246, 247, 248, 251, 252, 254, 257, 266, 267, 270, 271, 272, 273, 275–76, 278, 279, 280, 281, 285, 290, 297, 298, 304, 309, 311, 312, 313, 316, 323
Red Sea, 14, 22, 26, 27, 56
Reform movement, Gregorian, 5, 27, 130, 133, 219
Regner, would-be king of Danes, 263n103
Remigio de' Girolami, 150
Remigius, bishop of Reims, 251
Repentance, 1, 6, 14, 20, 21, 26, 28, 30, 40, 41, 42, 47, 56, 57, 59, 61, 63, 64, 66, 68, 69, 71, 75, 76, 78, 81, 83, 84, 85, 88, 108, 111, 114, 117, 118, 122, 132, 136, 138, 139, 140, 141, 144, 154, 155, 157–58, 160, 162, 163, 168, 171, 172, 173, 174, 177, 179, 181, 182, 184, 185, 187, 188, 191, 192, 193, 197, 199, 200, 202, 203, 204, 205, 206, 207, 208, 211, 213, 214, 216, 223, 224, 225, 228, 229, 320; attrition for sin in, 208, 210, 223; contrition for sin in, 40, 47, 56, 59, 60, 61, 63, 68, 69, 78, 81, 83, 85, 173, 177, 179, 181, 182, 184, 193, 197, 200, 206, 208, 214, 216, 225
Revelation, Book of, 278

Rhineland, 249
"Rice Christians," 325
Richard I, king of England, 66, 178
Richard of Mediavilla, comm. on *Sentences*, 78–79, 92n4, 203–5, 207, 215, 221, 222, 224, 300–303, 304, 306, 311, 314, 315, 316, 317–18
Richard of St. Victor, 150
Richer of Reims, *Historiae*, 5, 126–28, 222
Riga, 267, 273, 274, 277, 279
Ritual, Christian, 1, 3, 4, 5, 16, 43, 56, 58, 61, 72, 92, 100, 102, 104, 106–7, 108, 109, 113, 115, 121, 123, 124, 125, 126, 127, 130, 135, 136, 138, 139, 140, 141, 146, 150, 159, 164, 170, 173, 187, 197, 202, 204, 220, 222, 230, 231, 243, 253, 259, 273, 293, 294–95, 302, 318; denoting reversible defeat or abasement, 253; exorcism in, 135, 138, 140; non-Christian, 5, 104, 107, 108, 124, 125, 126, 166, 187, 197, 220, 230, 231; pre-Christian, 56, 61, 72, 187. *See also* Baptism, ritual; Gentiles; Israelites; Liturgy; Pagans; Saracens
Robert Holcot, comm. on *Sentences*, 305n190
Robert of Melun, *Quaestiones de divina pagina*, 45; *Quaestiones de Epistolas Pauli*, 45–46; *Sentences*, 46
Robertians, 126, 127
Robert Pullen, *Sententiarium libri octo*, 46–47, 62, 160–62, 173, 182, 190, 206, 221, 222, 223
Roger Bacon, *Opus maius*, 310, 311, 313
Roland of Bologna, *Sentences*, 43–45, 47, 53, 62, 81, 86, 163–65, 166, 167, 168n138, 169, 174, 176, 219
Rollo, founder of duchy of Normandy, 128, 129
Romans, Epistle to the, 45, 56, 68, 78
Rome, 4, 7 15, 52, 53, 93, 102, 107, 112n42, 128, 149, 227, 230–32, 250, 285, 321; Christian, 4, 7, 107, 112n42, 230–32, 250; policy toward Jews, 7, 231–32, 239, 321; pre-Christian, 4, 52, 93
Rosier-Catach, Irène, 92–93
Roswita of Gandersheim, 147
Rouche, Michel, 236, 238
Rudolf, master of Teutonic Knights, 277
Rufinus of Aquileia, *Ecclesiastical History*, 4, 13, 97–103, 112n42, 130–32, 142–43, 145–46, 152, 164–65, 167, 169–70, 174–76, 177–78, 180, 183–84, 187, 190, 193, 200–201, 204, 218–19; as translator of Gregory Nazianzus, 13
Rufinus of Bologna, *Summa decretorum*, 51n109, 283, 284
Ruotger of Cologne, *Vita Brunonis*, 147
Russians, 277–78

Sacraments, 2, 4, 5, 6, 9, 14, 20, 27, 28, 36, 46, 50–52, 53n111, 54, 58, 61, 65–66, 67, 69, 70, 78, 79, 81, 84, 85, 87, 89, 92, 114, 122, 131, 132, 133, 135, 141, 146, 152, 159, 161, 166, 167, 169, 173, 177, 179, 181, 182, 185, 189, 190–91, 192, 193, 194, 195, 198, 200, 206, 207, 208, 209, 211, 212, 214, 221, 223, 225, 228, 246, 253, 255, 256, 274, 282, 283, 284, 289, 293, 296, 301, 304. *See also* Baptism by blood; Baptism by desire; Baptism, conditional; Baptism, fictive; Baptism, forced; Baptism, infant; Baptism, ritual; Character, baptismal; Confirmation; Eucharist; Holy Orders; Marriage; Penance; *Sacramentum/res sacramenti* distinction; Unction
Sacramentum/res sacramenti distinction, 6, 33, 34–35, 42, 48, 52, 56, 58, 59, 60, 61, 68, 70, 72, 73, 75, 77–78, 79, 81, 82, 83, 85, 87, 89, 153, 154, 156, 159n116, 160, 161–62, 166, 168, 171, 173, 185, 186, 188, 189, 191, 192, 193–94, 197, 198, 199, 202, 203–4, 207, 210, 212, 213, 221, 222, 223, 284, 287, 288, 291, 292, 293, 295, 296, 301, 302, 306, 307, 308
Sacrifice, among Baltic pagans, animal, 271, 273, 278–79; human, 273, 278–79
Saint-Germain of Auxerre, school of, 124
Samaria, 43, 105–6, 120; Samaritan woman (in John 4:7–30), 43, 120
Samuel, prophet, 99
Saracens, 125, 220, 289, 290. *See also* Infidels; Muslims
Saragossa, 261
Sarpi, Paolo, 321n3
Saxo Grammaticus, *Gesta Danorum*, 263
Saxons, 8, 251–59, 261, 262, 264, 269, 271, 311, 313
Scandinavia, 263–64, 267. *See also* Danes; Denmark; Iceland; Norway; Sweden
Schism, 4, 7, 11, 12, 13, 20, 27, 32, 108, 109, 110, 111, 112, 113, 115, 117, 118, 133, 134, 135, 136, 138,

Schism *(cont.)*
140, 141, 151, 155, 157, 159, 162, 167, 175, 177, 204, 220, 222, 228, 229, 230, 277, 289, 299, 302, 318. *See also* Donatism; Papal-imperial feud; Reform movement, Gregorian; Russians
Scholastics, 2, 3, 6, 9, 11, 25, 26, 33–53, 55–90, 93, 145, 152–217, 227, 280, 292–311, 313, 314, 316, 317–18
Sectarianism. *See* Heresy; Schism
Segeberg, Augustinian friary of, 271
Senate, Roman, 95
Sententiae divinitatis, 52–53, 55, 86, 158, 160, 171, 172
Sententie Hermannus, 38n64
Servant, wicked (in Matthew 8:23–35), in Augustine, 113, 116, 136–37, 144; in continuator of Anselm of Lucca, 136–37, 138, 144; in Gratian II, 143–44, 193; in Peter of Tarentaise, 193, 196
Sepúlveda, Juan Ginés de, 322–23
Severus, bishop of Minorca, 232n8
Sicard of Cremona, 51n109
Sicily, 239, 322n7
Simon Magus (in Acts 8:9–23), in Acts of the Apostles, 104–7, 152, 166; in Augustine, 107, 113–14, 117, 121, 220; in Bede, 119–23; in Gratian II, 32; in Jerome, 5, 104, 118, 122, 126, 155–56, 193, 197; in *Liber Pancrisis*, 153; in Peter Abelard, 155; in Rabanus Maurus, 124; in Richard of Mediavilla, 204; in Theodore of Mopsuestia, 118–19
Simon, Master, *De sacramentis*, 49–52, 53, 55, 79, 86–87, 162–63, 179, 182, 215, 222, 223
Simon of Tournai, *Disputationes*, 173, 185, 190, 221; *Institutiones*, 172
Simony, 5, 130, 131, 132, 133, 134, 135, 138, 141, 289
Sin, 6, 14, 23, 25, 26, 28, 43, 53n111, 60, 61, 63, 66, 69, 70, 73, 74, 75, 78, 79, 83, 84, 106, 107, 109, 114, 115, 116, 117, 121–22, 123, 125, 134, 135, 136, 137, 138, 139, 140, 143, 144, 153, 154, 155, 157, 159, 160, 161, 162, 163, 166, 168, 171, 172, 173, 174, 176, 177, 179, 180, 181–82, 184, 185, 188, 191, 192, 193, 194, 196, 197, 200, 204, 205, 206, 208, 211, 214, 220, 221, 223, 224, 225, 244, 269, 289, 291, 292, 301, 307, 320, 323, 324; actual, 60, 63, 168, 205, 211, 225; original, 60, 63, 163, 168, 205, 211, 225, 244, 291, 292, 301, 307; theory of momentary remission of, in Augustine, 6, 115, 116, 117, 118, 121–22, 123, 134–35, 137, 139, 140, 144, 153, 154, 155, 157, 159, 160, 180, 181, 185, 188, 193, 197, 204, 220, 221, 224, 323; in Bede, 121–22; in Bonaventure, 191; in continuator of Anselm of Lucca, 134–35, 136, 137; in *Expositio in divinum officiorum*, 154; in Gratian II, 143, 144, 220; in Hugh of St. Victor, 159, 166; in Ivo of Chartres, 139, 140, 166; in John Duns Scotus, 205; in *Liber Pancrisis*, 153, 221; in Master Simon, 162; in Odo of Ourscamp, 172, 220; in Peter Lombard, 166, 193; in Peter of Tarentaise, 193; in Porretans, 157; in Prepositinus of Cremona, 176; in Richard of Mediavilla, 204; in Roland of Bologna, 163, 166; in *Sententiae divinitatis*, 160, 172; in *Summa sententiarum*, 160, 166, 171; in Thomas Aquinas, 197; in William of Auxerre, 181. *See also* Penance; Repentance
Sisebut, king of Visigoths, 243, 246, 248, 281, 282n144, 288n154
Slavery, 236n17, 247, 248, 289, 290, 309, 310, 314
Slavs, 125, 126, 239, 269
Socrates Scholasticus, *Historia Ecclesiastica*, 100–101, 102, 103
Song of Roland, 261, 262n101
Sozomen, *Historia Ecclesiastica*, 100, 101–2, 103
Spain, 7, 8, 126, 236, 240–48, 249, 250, 260, 261, 264, 269, 310, 311, 312, 321; Reconquest of, 8, 264, 269, 310, 311; Spanish March in, 126, 261; Visigothic, 7, 236, 240–48, 252n70, 260, 312. *See also* Successor states, Germanic; Visigoths
Ste. Geneviève, abbey and school of, 172
Stephen Langton, *Quaestiones theologicae*, 51n109, 178–80, 185, 187, 188, 200, 224, 225
Stephen, St., 231, 240
St. Gilles, abbey of, 132
Successor states, Germanic: Merovingian Gaul, 7, 236–40, 250, 252, 312; Vandal North Africa, 240n27; Visigothic Spain, 7, 236, 240–48, 252n70, 260, 261, 312
Sulpicius, bishop of Bourges, 238

Summa confessorum, 289
Summa Parisiensis, 283
Summa sententiarum, 42–43, 55, 160, 172, 176, 192
Sweden, 126
Swedes, in Baltic Crusades, 264
Sword Brethren, 267
Synderesis, 183, 189, 224

Taufmime, 4, 93–97, 110, 111, 130, 146, 150–51, 152, 167, 218; in Augustine, 110, 111, 112, 150, 167, 218; in Ivo of Chartres, 146, 150–52, 167, 218
Terence, 147
Tertullian, 12, 21, 82, 229
Teutonic Knights, 266n106, 267, 268, 269, 270, 271, 272, 277, 278, 279, 310, 311, 313
Theater, Theatrics. *See* Drama
Thelamon, Françoise, 97, 99
Theodore, bishop of Marseille, 232, 233
Theodore, Jew of Magona, 240
Theodore of Mopsuestia, on 1 Timothy, 24, 118–19
Theodorus, Byzantine church historian, 102
Theodosian Code, 230
Theodosius I, emperor, 15, 16
Theodulph of Orléans, 252n70
Theory, semantic, 92, 172–73, 185, 221–22
Thief, good, on the cross (in Luke 23:40–43), in Alexander of Hales, 75–76, 77; in Ambrose, 19; in Augustine, 18, 20–24, 26, 28, 31, 34, 40, 42, 47, 48, 56, 57, 78, 85; in Bede, 25–26, 76; in Bernard of Clairvaux, 40, 41; in Bonaventure, 78; in Bonizo of Sutri, 28; in Cyprian, 20, 26, 28, 30, 31, 42, 56, 85; in followers of Anselm of Laon, 34; in Gratian II, 31–32, 33; in Jerome, 19–20; in Master Simon 49; in Peter Comestor, 60; in Peter Lombard, 57; in Peter of Tarentaise, 85; in Porretans, 48; in Prepositinus of Cremona, 64; in Robert Pullen, 47; in *Sententiae divinitatis*, 52; in *Summa sententiarum*, 42; in Theodore of Mopsuestia, 24, 118
Thomas Aquinas, comm. on *Sentences*, 82–83, 84, 89, 197–201, 209, 210, 212, 213, 219, 220, 223, 224, 225, 298n177, 307, 316; on *Nicomachean Ethics*, 299–300, 304, 306, 315; *Summa theologiae*, 83–85, 92n4, 93, 201–2, 203n207, 207, 212, 213, 225, 229, 296–300, 302, 304, 306, 308, 309, 312, 313–14, 322n7
Thomism. *See* Thomas Aquinas
1 Timothy, Epistle of, 24, 118
Toledo IV, council of, 7, 242, 245–48, 280–81, 281–82, 283, 287, 288n154, 289, 292, 297–98, 299, 304, 308, 312, 313, 314, 320, 322n7
Trajan, emperor, 36, 37, 38
Trent, council of, 319
Trinity doctrine of, 113, 140, 239, 246
Trojan horse, 129

Unction, sacrament of, 50–52
Unrepeatability of baptism. *See* Rebaptism
Uzès, 238

Valdemar II, king of Denmark, 285, 289
Valentinian II, emperor, ix, 14–18, 37–38, 41, 41–42, 44, 53, 54, 55, 84, 86
Vandals, 240n27
Vatican II, council of, 1, 321n3
Venantius Fortunatus, 236, 237
Vercingetorix, 250
Vergil, *Aeneid*, 129
Victor of Vita, 103
Vikings, 5, 126, 127, 128, 129, 222, 262
Vincent of Beauvais, 150
Vincentius Victor, 32, 137
Virgil, bishop of Arles, 232, 233
Virgin Mary, 62, 80, 88, 206
Visigoths, 7, 240–48, 260
Vitoria, Francisco de, 322

Walter of Chatton, comm on *Sentences*, 215, 222, 224
Warin, abbot of Corvey, 256
Wearmouth, abbey of, 119
Weisweiler, Heinrich, 156
Will, free, 9, 21, 30, 44, 46, 47, 56, 64, 65, 76, 79, 89, 155, 159, 179, 186, 188, 191, 192, 194, 209, 210, 211, 223, 225, 226, 228, 235, 236n17, 237, 238, 240, 244, 245, 246, 248, 250, 253, 260, 276, 279, 280, 282, 284, 285, 286, 287, 289, 290, 291, 292, 293, 294, 295, 296–98, 299–300, 303–4, 305, 306, 308, 309–10, 311, 312, 313, 314, 315–16, 317, 321, 324

William of Auxerre, *Summa aurea*, 71–75, 76, 77, 82, 87, 181–84, 187, 188, 189, 190, 194, 196, 198, 200, 216, 219, 221, 223, 224, 225
William of Conches, *Philosophia*, 149–50
William of Habsburg, 268
William of Melitona, *Quaestiones de sacramentis*, 188–91, 198, 200, 206, 219, 221, 224
William of Modena, papal legate, 267, 272, 277, 278
William of Ockham, comm. on *Sentences*, 206, 210–11, 224, 225, 306–7
William of Ware, comm. on *Sentences*, 79
Wisdom, Book of, 114, 115, 138, 143, 163–64, 176, 197, 204, 206, 220
Wolfram von Eschenbach, 270
World Council of Churches, 326n14

Ysagoge in theologiam, 38, 40

Faith, Fiction, and Force in Medieval Baptismal Debates was designed in Caslon with Garda Titling display type and composed by Kachergis Book Design of Pittsboro, North Carolina. It was printed on 60-pound Sebago Cream and bound by Maple Press of York, Pennsylvania.